studies in jazz

Institute of Jazz Studies
Rutgers—The State University of New Jersey
General Editors: Dan Morgenstern and Edward Berger

1. BENNY CARTER: A Life in American Music, *by Morroe Berger, Edward Berger, and James Patrick, 2 vols., 1982*
2. ART TATUM: A Guide to His Recorded Music, *by Arnold Laubich and Ray Spencer, 1982*
3. ERROLL GARNER: The Most Happy Piano, *by James M. Doran, 1995*
4. JAMES P. JOHNSON: A Case of Mistaken Identity, *by Scott E. Brown;* Discography 1917–1950, *by Robert Hilbert, 1986*
5. PEE WEE ERWIN: This Horn for Hire, *as told to Warren W. Vaché, Sr., 1987*
6. BENNY GOODMAN: Listen to His Legacy, *by D. Russell Connor, 1988*
7. ELLINGTONIA: The Recorded Music of Duke Ellington and His Sidemen, *by W. E. Timner, 1988; 4th ed., 1996*
8. THE GLENN MILLER ARMY AIR FORCE BAND: Sustineo Alas / I Sustain the Wings, *by Edward F. Polic;* Foreword *by George T. Simon, 1989*
9. SWING LEGACY, *by Chip Deffaa, 1989*
10. REMINISCING IN TEMPO: The Life and Times of a Jazz Hustler, *by Teddy Reig, with Edward Berger, 1990*
11. IN THE MAINSTREAM: 18 Portraits in Jazz, *by Chip Deffaa, 1992*
12. BUDDY DeFRANCO: A Biographical Portrait and Discography, *by John Kuehn and Arne Astrup, 1993*
13. PEE WEE SPEAKS: A Discography of Pee Wee Russell, *by Robert Hilbert, with David Niven, 1992*
14. SYLVESTER AHOLA: The Gloucester Gabriel, *by Dick Hill, 1993*
15. THE POLICE CARD DISCORD, *by Maxwell T. Cohen, 1993*
16. TRADITIONALISTS AND REVIVALISTS IN JAZZ, *by Chip Deffaa, 1993*
17. BASSICALLY SPEAKING: An Oral History of George Duvivier, *by Edward Berger;* Musical Analysis *by David Chevan, 1993*
18. TRAM: The Frank Trumbauer Story, *by Philip R. Evans and Larry F. Kiner, with William Trumbauer, 1994*
19. TOMMY DORSEY: On the Side, *by Robert L. Stockdale, 1995*
20. JOHN COLTRANE: A Discography and Musical Biography, *by Yasuhiro Fujioka, with Lewis Porter and Yoh-ichi Hamada, 1995*
21. RED HEAD: A Chronological Survey of "Red" Nichols and His Five Pennies, *by Stephen M. Stroff, 1996*

22. THE RED NICHOLS STORY: After Intermission 1942–1965, *by Philip R. Evans, Stanley Hester, Stephen Hester, and Linda Evans, 1997*
23. BENNY GOODMAN: Wrappin' It Up, *by D. Russell Connor, 1996*
24. CHARLIE PARKER AND THEMATIC IMPROVISATION, *by Henry Martin, 1996*
25. BACK BEATS AND RIM SHOTS: The Johnny Blowers Story, *by Warren W. Vaché, 1997*
26. DUKE ELLINGTON, A Listener's Guide *by Eddie Lambert, 1998*
27. SERGE CHALOFF: A Musical Biography and Discography, *by Vladimir Simosko, 1998*
28. HOT JAZZ: From Harlem to Storyville, *by David Griffiths, 1998*
29. ARTIE SHAW: A Musical Biography and Discography, *by Vladimir Simosko, 1999*
30. JIMMY DORSEY: A Study in Contrasts, *by Robert L. Stockdale, 1998*
31. STRIDE!: Fats, Jimmy, Lion, Lamb and All the Other Ticklers, *by John L. Fell and Terkild Vinding, 1999*
32. GIANT STRIDES: The Legacy of Dick Wellstood, *by Edward N. Meyer, 1999*
33. JAZZ GENTRY: Aristocrats of the Music World, *by Warren W. Vaché, Sr., 1999*
34. THE UNSUNG SONGWRITERS: America's Masters of Melody, *by Warren W. Vaché, Sr., 2000*
35. THE MUSICAL WORLD OF J. J. JOHNSON, *by Joshua Berrett and Louis G. Bourgois, III, 1999*
36. THE LADIES WHO SING WITH THE BAND, *by Betty Bennett, 2000*
37. AN UNSUNG CAT: The Life and Music of Warne Marsh, *by Safford Chamberlain, 2000*

The Unsung Songwriters

America's Masters of Melody

Warren W. Vaché

Studies in Jazz, No. 34

The Scarecrow Press, Inc.
Lanham, Maryland, and London
2000

SCARECROW PRESS, INC.

Published in the United States of America
by Scarecrow Press, Inc.
4720 Boston Way
Lanham, Maryland 20706

4 Pleydell Gardens, Folkestone
Kent CT 20 2DN, England

British Library Cataloguing in Publication Information Available

Library of Congress Cataloging-in-Publication Data

Vaché, Warren W., 1914–
The unsung songwriters : America's masters of melody / Warren W. Vaché.
p. cm.—(Studies in jazz : #34)
Includes bibliographical references and index.
ISBN 0-8108-3570-3 (cloth : alk. paper)
1. Composers—United States—Biography. 2. Lyricists—United States—Biography. 3. Popular music—United States—History and criticism. I. Title. II. Series : Studies in jazz : no. 34.

ML390.V114 2000
782.42164′092′273—dc21
[B] 98–49551

∞ ™The paper used in this publication meets the minimum requirements of American National Standard for Information Services—Permanence of Paper for Printed Library Materials, ANSI/NISO Z39.48-1992.
Manufactured in the United States of America.

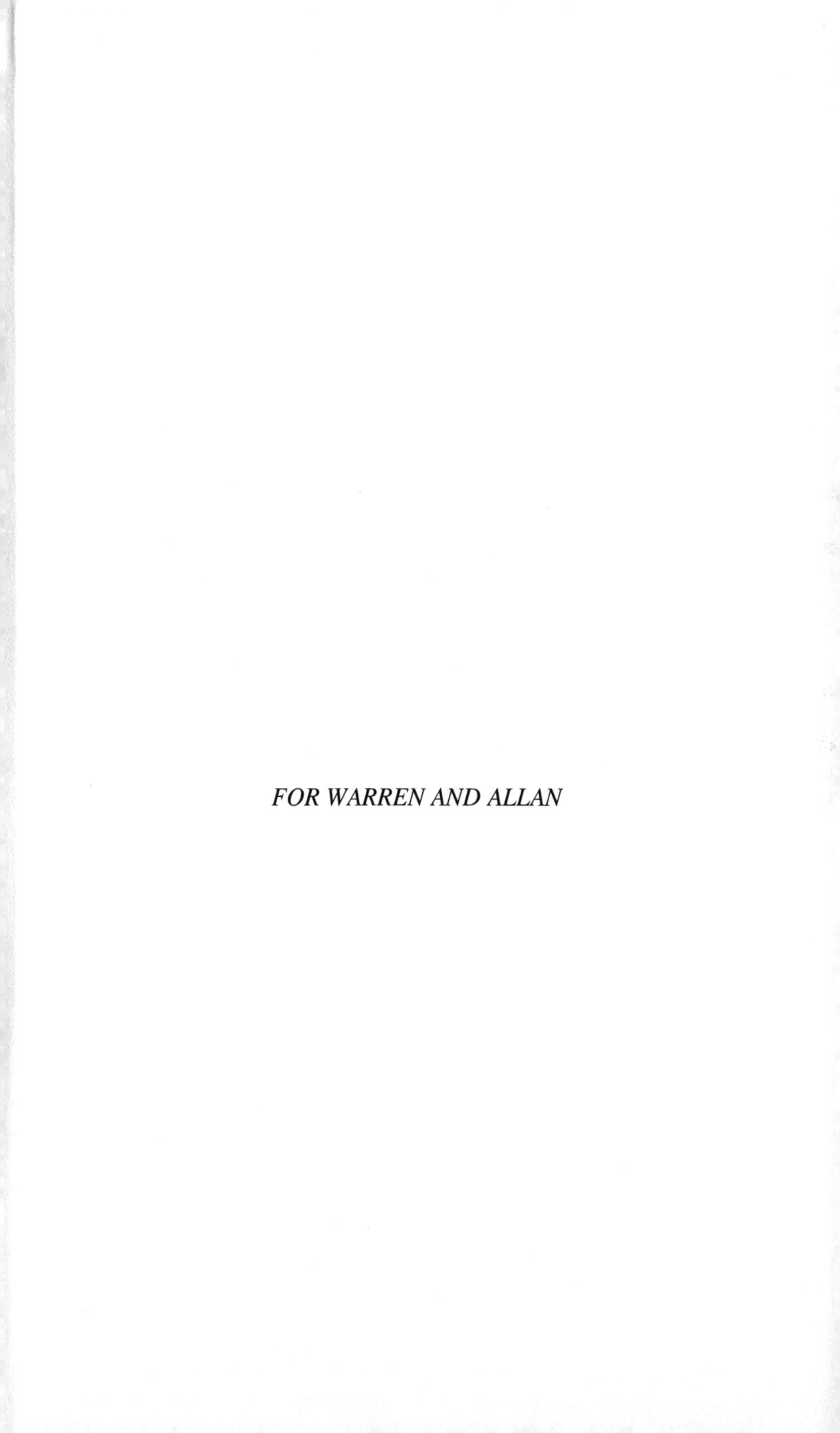

FOR WARREN AND ALLAN

Contents

Foreword *by Jack D. Stine* xxi
Preface xxv
Why Some Songwriters Are Not Included in This Book xxix
Acknowledgments xxxi

ABRAMS, MAURIE 1
ADAIR, TOM 1
ADAMS, STANLEY 2
ADAMSON, HAROLD 3
ADLAM, BASIL G. (BUZZ) 3
AGER, MILTON 4
AHLERT, FRED E. 6
AKST, HARRY 8
ALLEN, STEVE 9
ALTER, LOUIS 10
ALTMAN, ARTHUR 11
ARCHER, HARRY 12
ARLEN, HAROLD 13
ARMSTRONG, LIL HARDIN 15
ARNHEIM, GUS 15
ARSHAWSKY, ARTHUR (*See* Artie Shaw)
AUSTIN, GENE 16

BAER, ABEL 19
BARBOUR, DAVE 20
BARRIS, HARRY 20
BASIE, WILLIAM (COUNT) 23
BASKETTE, BILLY 24
BAUDUC, RAY 24
BAXTER, PHIL 25
BEIDERBECKE, LEON BIX 25

BENJAMIN, BENNIE 27
BERNARD, FELIX 27
BERNIE, BEN 28
BERNIER, BUDDY 29
BIBO, IRVING 30
BLAKE, EUBIE 31
BLANE, RALPH 31
BLOOM, RUBE 32
BOLAND, CLAY 33
BOWMAN, BROOKS 35
BROCKMAN, JAMES 35
BROOKS, HARRY 36
BROOKS, SHELTON 37
BROWN, LEW 38
BROWN, NACIO HERB 40
BRYAN, ALFRED 41
BUCK, GENE 42
BULLOCK, WALTER 43
BURKE, JOE 43
BURKE, JOHNNY 44
BURTNETT, EARL 46
BURTON, NAT 47
BURTON, VAL 47
BUSSE, HENRY 48

CAESAR, IRVING 49
CAHN, SAMMY 50
CAREY, WILLIAM D. 51
CARLE, FRANKIE 51
CARLETON, ROBERT L. (BOB) 52
CARMICHAEL, HOAGY 53
CARROLL, HARRY 56
CARTER, BENNY 56
CAVANAUGH, JAMES 58
CHAPLIN, SAUL 59
CHASE, NEWELL 61
CLARE, SIDNEY 61
CLARKE, GRANT 61
CLEARY, MICHAEL H. 62
CLIFFORD, GORDON 63

CLINTON, LARRY 63
COBB, GEORGE L. 64
COBB, WILL D. 64
COBURN, RICHARD 65
COHAN, GEORGE M. 65
COLUMBO, RUSS 66
COMDEN, BETTY 67
CONFREY, EDWARD E. (*ZEZ*) 67
CONLEY, LARRY 68
CONNOR, JOSEPH P. (*PIERRE NORMAN*) 69
CONRAD, CON (*CONRAD K. DOBER*) 70
COOTS, J. FRED 71
COSLOW, SAM 72
COWARD, NOËL 73
CREAMER, HENRY 75
CURTIS, MANN (*See* Manny Kurtz)

DANIELS, CHARLES NEIL (NEIL MORET) 77
DAVID, HAL 78
DAVID, MACK 79
DAVIS, BENNY 80
DELANGE, EDDIE 83
DELUGG, MILTON 84
DENNIKER, PAUL 86
DENNIS, MATT 86
DEPAUL, GENE 87
DEROSE, PETER 88
DESYLVA, BUDDY 89
DEUTSCH, EMERY 93
DICK, DOROTHY (*See* Dorothy Dick Link)
DIETZ, HOWARD 93
DIXON, MORT 94
DOBER, CONRAD K. (*See* Con Conrad)
DOLAN, ROBERT EMMETT 95
DONALDSON, WALTER 95
DORSEY, JIMMY 98
DORSEY, TOMMY 99
DOUGHERTY, DAN 100
DOWELL, HORACE KIRBY (SAXIE) 101
DOYLE, WALTER 102

DRAKE, MILTON 103
DRESSER, PAUL 104
DREYER, DAVE 104
DUBIN, AL 106
DUKE, VERNON 107

EDWARDS, GUS 111
EGAN, RAYMOND B. 112
ELISCU, EDWARD 114
ELLINGTON, DUKE 115
ELLINGTON, MERCER 116
ELLIOTT, JOHN M. (JACK) 117
ELLIS, VIVIAN 117
EMMERICH, BOB 119
ERDMAN, ERNIE 120
EVANS, RAY 121
EVANS, REDD 121

FAIN, SAMMY 123
FIELDS, ARTHUR 124
FIELDS, ARTHUR B. (BUDDY) 125
FIELDS, DOROTHY 126
FISCHER, CARL THEODORE 128
FISHER, DORIS 129
FISHER, FRED 130
FISHER, MARK 132
FRANKLIN, DAVE 133
FREED, ARTHUR 134
FREED, RALPH 135
FRIEND, CLIFF 136
FRIML, RUDOLF 137
FULTON, JOHN COLLINS (JACK) 139

GALLOP, SAMMY 141
GANNON, JAMES KIMBALL (KIM) 141
GASKILL, CLARENCE 143
GENSLER, LEWIS E. 144
GEORGE, DON 144
GIFFORD, GENE 145
GILBERT, L. WOLFE 146

GILLESPIE, HAVEN 147
GOERING, AL (*See* Jack Pettis & Al Goering)
GOLDEN, JOHN 148
GOODHART, AL 148
GOODMAN, BENNY 150
GOODWIN, JOE 151
GORDON, IRVING 152
GORDON, MACK 153
GORNEY, JAY 156
GOTTLER, ARCHIE 157
GRAY, CHAUNCEY 158
GRAY, JERRY 159
GREEN, BUD 160
GREEN, JOHNNY 161
GREENE, MORT 163
GREER, JESSE 163
GREY, CLIFFORD 164
GRIER, JIMMIE 165
GROFÉ, FERDE 167
GROSS, WALTER 168
GROSZ, WILHELM (HUGH WILLIAMS) 168
GROUYA, THEODORE (*TED*) 170
GUMM, ALBERT (*See* Albert Von Tilzer)
GUMM, HAROLD (*See* Harry Von Tilzer)

HAGGART, BOB 171
HAMILTON, GEORGE (*SPIKE*) 172
HAMMERSTEIN II, OSCAR 173
HANDMAN, LOU 174
HANDY, WILLIAM CHRISTOPHER (W.C.) 175
HANIGHEN, BERNIE 177
HANLEY, JAMES F. 178
HARBACH, OTTO 179
HARBURG, E. Y. (*YIP*) 180
HARLING, FRANK W. 181
HARRIS, CHARLES K. 182
HAYES, CLARENCE LEONARD (*CLANCY*) 183
HEFTI, NEAL 184
HEINDORF, RAY 185
HENDERSON, CHARLES 186

HENDERSON, FLETCHER 186
HENDERSON, RAY 187
HERBERT, VICTOR 189
HERMAN, WOODROW (WOODY) 190
HEYMAN, EDWARD 191
HEYWARD, DUBOSE 193
HEYWOOD, EDDIE, JR. 193
HICKMAN, ART 194
HILL, ALEX 195
HILL, BILLY 196
HILLIARD, BOB 198
HIMBER, RICHARD 199
HINES, EARL 200
HIRSCH, LOUIS A. 202
HIRSCH, WALTER 203
HODGES, JOHNNY 203
HOFFMAN, AL 204
HOLINER, MANN 207
HOLLANDER, FRED 208
HOPKINS, CLAUDE 209
HOSCHNA, KARL 210
HOWARD, EDDY 210
HOWARD, JOE 211
HUBBELL, RAYMOND 212
HUDSON, WILL 213
HUPFELD, HERMAN 214

INGRAHAM, ROY 217

JAFFE, MOE 219
JASON, WILL 220
JENKINS, GORDON 220
JEROME, M. K. 221
JEROME, WILLIAM 222
JOHNSON, HOWARD E. 223
JOHNSON, J. C. (JIMMY) 223
JOHNSON, JAMES P. 225
JOHNSTON, ARTHUR 226
JOLSON, AL 227
JONES, ISHAM 228
JURGENS, DICK 230

KAHAL, IRVING 233
KAHN, GUS 233
KALMAR AND RUBY (See Bert Kalmar)
KALMAR, BERT 236
KAPER, BRONISLAW 237
KASSEL, ART 238
KENDIS, JAMES 239
KENNY, CHARLES 240
KENNY, NICK 240
KENT, WALTER 241
KING, JACK 242
KING, WAYNE 243
KLAGES, RAYMOND 244
KLENNER, JOHN 246
KLUCZKO, JOHNNY (JOHNNY WATSON) 247
KOEHLER, TED 247
KRAMER, ALEX CHARLES 250
KRAMER, ZOE PARENTEAU (JOAN WHITNEY) 251
KURTZ, EMANUEL (MANNY) (MANN CURTIS) 252

LANE, BURTON 253
LATOUCHE, JOHN 254
LAWNHURST, VEE 255
LAWRENCE, JACK 256
LAYTON, TURNER 257
LEE, PEGGY 257
LEIGH, CAROLYN PAULA 258
LERNER, ALAN JAY 259
LERNER, SAMUEL MANUEL (SAMMY) 259
LESLIE, EDGAR 261
LEVANT, OSCAR 262
LEVINSON, JERRY (See Jerry Livingston)
LEWIS, AL 263
LEWIS, SAM M. 265
LINK, DOROTHY (DOROTHY DICK) 266
LINK, HARRY 267
LITTLE, JACK (LITTLE JACK) 268
LIVINGSTON, FUD 269
LIVINGSTON, JAY 270
LIVINGSTON, JERRY 272
LOEB, JOHN JACOB 274

LOESSER, FRANK 275
LOEWE, FREDERICK 279
LOMBARDO, CARMEN 280
LOWE, RUTH 281
LOWN, BERT 281
LYMAN, ABE 282

MACDONALD, BALLARD 285
MACK, CECIL 286
MADDEN, EDWARD 287
MAGIDSON, HERB 288
MALNECK, MATTY 290
MALTIN, BERNARD 293
MANCINI, HENRY 294
MANDEL, JOHNNY 294
MANN, DAVID 295
MANN, PAUL 296
MARCUS, SOL 297
MARES, PAUL 299
MARION, GEORGE, JR. 300
MARKS, GERALD 301
MARKS, JOHNNY 303
MARTIN, HUGH 303
MCCARTHY, JOSEPH 304
MCHUGH, JIMMY 306
MCRAE, THEODORE (TEDDY) 308
MELROSE, WALTER 309
MENCHER, MURRAY (TED MURRAY) 309
MENDOZA, PETER HYGHAM (PETER VENNING) 310
MERCER, JOHNNY 315
MERTZ, PAUL MADEIRA 317
MESKILL, JACK 317
MEYER, GEORGE W. 319
MEYER, JOSEPH 322
MILLS, IRVING 325
MITCHELL, SIDNEY D. 326
MIZZY, VIC 328
MOLL, BILLY 328
MONACO, JAMES V. 329
MORET, NEIL (See Charles Neil Daniels)

MORGAN, RUSS 332
MORTON, FERDINAND (JELLY ROLL) 333
MUNDY, JAMES (JIMMY) 334
MURRAY, JACK (JOHN) 335
MURRAY, TED (See Murray Mencher)
MYERS, RICHARD 336
MYROW, JOSEF 336
MYSELS, SAMMY 338

NASET, CLAYTON E. 341
NASH, OGDEN 341
NEIBURG, AL J. (ALLEN) 342
NELSON, ED G. 343
NEMO, HENRY 344
NEWMAN, CHARLES 345
NICHOLS, ALBERTA 348
NOBLE, JOHNNY (JOHN AVERY) 349
NOBLE, RAY 349
NORMAN, PIERRE (See Joseph P. Connor)
NORTON, GEORGE A. 353

OAKLAND, BEN 355
O'FLYNN, CHARLES 356
OLIVER, JOSEPH (KING) 357
OPPENHEIM, DAVE 358
ORIGINAL DIXIELAND JAZZ BAND 359
OSBORNE, WILL 360
OWEN, HARRY (ROBERT) 361

PALMER, JACK 363
PARISH, MITCHELL 365
PERKINS, FRANK 366
PERKINS, RAY 367
PETKERE, BERNICE 368
PETTIS, JACK, & GOERING, AL 369
PHILLIPS, SID 374
PIANTADOSI, AL 375
PINKARD, MACEO 375
POLLACK, LEW 377
POSFORD, GEORGE 379
POWELL, TEDDY 380

QUADLING, LEW 383

RAINGER, RALPH 385
RAYE, DON (DONALD McCRAE WILHOITE) 387
RAZAF, ANDY 389
REDMAN, DON 391
REICHNER, BICKLEY (BIX) 393
RENE, LEON T., & RENE, OTIS J., JR. 394
REVEL, HARRY 395
RICH, MAX 397
RICHMAN, HARRY 399
RINGLE, DAVE 400
ROBERTS, ALLAN 401
ROBERTS, LUCKEYTH (LUCKY) 402
ROBERTSON, DICK 402
ROBIN, LEO 403
ROBINSON, J. RUSSEL 407
ROBISON, WILLARD 409
ROGERS, DICK 414
ROMBERG, SIGMUND 415
ROSE, BILLY 416
ROSE, FRED 418
ROSE, VINCENT 419
RUBY, HARRY 420
RUBY, HERMAN 422
RUSSELL, CHARLES ELLSWORTH (PEE WEE) 423
RUSSELL, LUIS 424
RUSSELL, SIDNEY KEITH (BOB) 425

SAMPSON, EDGAR 429
SAMUELS, WALTER 430
SANDERS, JOE 431
SANTLY BROTHERS (HENRY, JOSEPH H., LESTER) 432
SAVITT, JAN 433
SCHERTZINGER, VICTOR 434
SCHOEBEL, ELMER 435
SCHUSTER, IRA 436
SCHWARTZ, ARTHUR 437
SCHWARTZ, JEAN 440
SCOTT, JOHNNIE NEWHALL 442

SCOTT, RAYMOND (*HARRY WARNOW*) 442
SEILER, EDDIE 443
SEYMOUR, TOT 444
SHAFER, BOB 446
SHAND, TERRY 446
SHANNON, JAMES ROYCE 447
SHAPIRO, TED 448
SHAW, ARTIE (*ARTHUR ARSHAWSKY*) 449
SHAY, LARRY 450
SHERMAN, AL 451
SHERWIN, MANNING 453
SHIELDS, REN 454
SHILKRET, NAT 455
SIGLER, MAURICE 456
SIGMAN, CARL (*JESSIE BARNES, CRAIG LEE, LEE BURKE*) 457
SIGNORELLI, FRANK 459
SILVER, ABNER 461
SIMON, NAT 461
SIMONS, SEYMOUR R. 462
SINGER, LOUIS C. 463
SISSLE, NOBLE 464
SKYLAR, SUNNY (*SELIG, SIDNEY, SHAFTEL*) 465
SMITH, CHRIS 466
SMITH, EZEKIAL L. G. (*See* Stuff Smith)
SMITH, HARRY BACHE 466
SMITH, RICHARD B. (*DICK*) 468
SMITH, STUFF (*EZEKIAL LEROY GORDON SMITH*) 468
SNYDER, TED 469
SPINA, HAROLD 470
STAMPER, DAVID 472
STEPT, SAM H. 472
STERLING, ANDREW B. 473
STERN, JACK 475
STITZEL, MEL 475
STOCK, LARRY 476
STORDAHL, AXEL 477
STOTHART, HERBERT 478
STRAYHORN, BILLY 480
STRIDE, HARRY 481
STYNE, JULE 481

SUESSE, DANA 485
SWAN, EINAR AARON 486
SWANSTROM, ARTHUR 487
SWIFT, KAY 488
SYMES, MARTY 489

TAUBER, DORIS 491
THOMPSON, HARLAN 491
TIERNEY, HARRY AUSTIN 492
TINTURIN, PETER 493
TIZOL, JUAN 495
TOBIAS, CHARLES 495
TOBIAS, HARRY 497
TOBIAS, HENRY 499
TODD, CLARENCE E. 499
TOMLIN, TRUMAN (PINKY) 500
TORMÉ, MEL 501
TRACEY, WILLIAM G. 502
TRENT, JO 502
TURK, ROY 503

VALLEE, RUDY 507
VAN ALSTYNE, EGBERT 508
VAN HEUSEN, JIMMY 509
VENNING, PETER (See Peter Hygham Mendoza)
VENUTI, JOE 511
VERGES, JOE 511
VINCENT, NAT 512
VON TILZER, ALBERT (ALBERT GUMM) 513
VON TILZER, HARRY (HAROLD GUMM) 515

WAGNER, LARRY 517
WALLACE, OLIVER 517
WALLER, THOMAS (FATS) 518
WARD, CHARLES B. 521
WARNOW, HARRY (See Raymond Scott)
WARREN, HARRY 521
WASHBURNE, JOE (COUNTRY) 523
WASHINGTON, NED 524
WATSON, JOHNNY (See Johnny Kluczko)

WATTS, GRADY 526
WAYNE, MABEL 527
WEBSTER, PAUL FRANCIS 529
WEILL, KURT 531
WELDON, FRANK 533
WENDLING, PETE 534
WENRICH, PERCY 535
WEST, EUGENE 536
WESTON, PAUL (PAUL WETSTEIN) 537
WETSTEIN, PAUL (See Paul Weston)
WEVER, NED 538
WHITCUP, LEONARD 539
WHITING, GEORGE 540
WHITING, RICHARD 541
WHITNEY, JOAN (See Zoe Parenteau Kramer)
WILDER, ALEC 543
WILHOITE, DONALD MCCRAE (See Don Raye)
WILLIAMS, CLARENCE 544
WILLIAMS, HARRY 545
WILLIAMS, HUGH (See Wilhelm Grosz)
WILLIAMS, MARY LOU 547
WILLIAMS, SPENCER 548
WILLSON, MEREDITH 549
WODEHOUSE, P. G. (PELHAM GRENVILLE WODEHOUSE) 550
WOODS, HARRY 551
WRUBEL, ALLIE 559

YELLEN, JACK 561
YOUMANS, VINCENT 563
YOUNG, JOE 565
YOUNG, VICTOR 569

ZARET, HY 573

Bibliography 575
Appendix 577
Song Title Index 651
About the Author 737

Foreword

This is a book about the legions of unsung writers of the songs that have contributed so much to this century's treasury of popular music. One is almost bound to qualify this volume as being this century's treasury of *American* popular music because a good 90 percent of the songs you will encounter within these pages have a peculiarly American spin to them. Here is music of a nation with an appetite for uncluttered songs of unembarrassed innocence and easygoing charm, a sleeping giant of a nation that could win wars or sing songs of love with equal intensity. More of this later.

There have been other books about the writers of popular music but very few delved below the ranks of the big hitters in the trade, leaving the vast field of lesser known writers—the unsung ones of the book's title—still consigned to the state of relative obscurity. With the publication of this book such writers as Al Neiburg (*It's the Talk of the Town*), Frank Perkins (*Emaline* and *Stars Fell on Alabama*), Maceo Pinkard (*Sweet Georgia Brown* and *Sugar*), and Ralph Rainger (*When a Woman Loves a Man*) will at long last get their day in court. I could name a couple hundred others just as worthy who have escaped the fame they deserved. So could you after you read this book.

The points this long overdue compilation makes bring to mind an old story that made the rounds in the trade a long time ago. You may have heard it. If so, you can just skip right ahead to the funnies or you can hang around for one or more retelling. I want to get it in here because it says a little something about the varying degrees of fame that exist in the music business, fame that did not always smile on many whose efforts fed the fire, about how appropriate the word "unsung" is as applied to too many of them. And, like any good old tune, this little anecdote can stand one more "one more time."

All right then ...

One morning a musician is walking past a pet store, and he can't believe his ears. There, just outside the store's entrance, is a gorgeous golden canary in a splendid gilded cage singing *Tea for Two*. After taking a few more steps the musician is forced to return, for now the bird has broken in to *Roses of Piccardy*. The store owner is standing in the doorway cooling it.

"Gotcha," says the musician. "A ventriloquist."

"Ventriloquilist shmentriloquist," says the man. "You got it wrong, Jack. This bird's for real, a major talent, another Dolly Dawn. Listen."

Now the bird is singing *Take Me Out to the Ballgame*, and it's too much for the musician. He's got to have it. "So how much for the bird?"

"Twenty dollars."

"I'll take it."

"Not so fast. If you take this bird, you have to take this one also." The storekeeper takes the musician into a dark back room where there's another canary, but this one is different. It is scrawny, has the shakes, is losing its feathers, has runny eyes, and seems to have trouble standing.

"Okay, throw it in," says the musician, thinking of the cat back home. "How much you want?"

"Five twenty," says the storekeeper. "Five hundred for this one, twenty for the thrush. They go together. I couldn't break up the set so don't ask me to."

"Five yards for this one, twenty for the one out front? I don't get it."

"Simple," says the storekeeper. "This one does the arrangements."

This it seems to me underlines in its own way the great imbalance in the world of music between fame and obscurity, between the star and the person or persons who make stardom possible. Much of this disparity is often expressed in terms of money and that's okay because among the players you never hear complaints about the kind of bread stars like Clooney, Sinatra, or Bennett can command for a gig. Their names on any marquee will put customers in the seats. That's star power for you, and in a business where popular songs are part of the equation, it's the star that keeps the industry in the black. Still, show business also depends on the writers and arrangers of songs to keep the supply of material coming, and that's the other half of the equation. The rub is that the songwriter's credit is often limited to a small-print mention on a record label or in a liner note, and the financial reward is more often than not limited to whatever the royalties bring in.

That's why this book is important, not only for its reference value but also as a kind of redress to all those men and women of music, the horde of the unsung, for having been glossed over for so many years.

In reading the various biographies here you will be impressed with how American the whole popular music business is. Among the songwriters you will meet here the overwhelming majority are bona fide native borners. Many of those not actually born in America are invariably first-generation offspring of parents who immigrated here from a dozen or so other countries, looking for something better. Then, too, some left their native countries as songwriters and continued with their trade once they arrived here. They all had Tin Pan Alley in mind.

What they all have is the prescient ability to capture in song the rhythm of the land of Lucky Lindy, the Tin Lizzie, the Twentieth-Century Limited, the Times Square traffic jam, and the nation itself that is not at all embarrassed to wear its heart on its sleeve while singing of romance, of love lost, of good humor, of faith and loyalty, and of confession and silliness. In short, listen to their songs and you'll hear America singing. Kurt Weill could write *September Song* or *Speak Low* in America, but probably not in Germany. Had Vernon Duke stayed in Russia, we almost certainly would never have had *I Can't Get Started With You.* This is a game we could play till next week, but you get the idea. And by the way, is there a writer on any other continent who could have conceived, for better or worse, *Mairzy Doats?*

And now I see that my time is about up, but there remains one last point to make and that is to offer a salute to the songwriters' partners, the wonderful lyricists who provided the message to go with the tunes. They are all here in this book, and it's about time you met them.

Jack D. Stine

Preface

It will probably be difficult at this late stage for anyone who wasn't around during the first couple of decades of the twentieth century to understand the prevailing attitude toward popular music at that time. To put it mildly, while it was popular, it received no respect. A popular song—along with those who composed it and played it—was considered "bad," with no lasting merit. The hit tune of today was forgotten tomorrow, and the recordings and piano rolls were hidden away in a cabinet, or discarded in the rubbish, never to be played again.

I could never understand this idea, even as a kid, and I certainly have no sympathy with it today. I distinctly remember bumping into it head-on in the "music appreciation class" in school. The teacher asked members of the class to bring in phonograph records for her to play, and they did. I brought in half a dozen myself—mostly Paul Whiteman Victors. The teacher sorted through the contributions, and we heard string quartets, symphonies, piano concertos, and other "long hair" varieties of European classical music, but no Whiteman. After being shut out of the program several times, I finally got up enough nerve to ask the teacher why. She was polite about it, and smilingly explained that the class was designed for the appreciation of "good" music, and dance music didn't qualify. I didn't follow her logic, but I recognized defeat, and never brought in any more records.

The teacher wasn't alone in her opinion. Any youngster lucky enough to take music lessons was automatically subjected to the propaganda that popular music—especially American jazz and its derivations—was "bad" music, and playing it could lead to the ruination of a potentially good musician. It followed that jazz and dance band musicians were woefully inferior in talent and execution to those who studied and played the classics, and the only reason composers wrote popular music was to make money, usually stealing their ideas from the classics. Although the American public—the great "unwashed" and musically ignorant—continued to buy and enjoy the popular tunes of the day, there was a definite tendency on all sides to accept the judgment of the musicians and conductors with the long, unpronounceable names. The premise was very basic—if the music didn't come from Europe, or wasn't based on European sources, it had no merit.

Paul Whiteman, a classically trained musician, was among the first to recognize this lack of respect for contemporary developments in American music and made an effort to make it more "respectable" by promoting the works of composers like Ferde Grofé and George Gershwin in ponderous arrangements called "symphonic jazz." He succeeded to some extent in elevating the status of the dance band musician, and in reaching the segment of the public with no understanding or appreciation of the essential character of American music, but he failed to convince most of the musicians who played the music, and a good many of those who wrote it.

So the music continued to evolve, and as time went on jazz musicians and dance band musicians perfected techniques and musical formulas of their own, attaining a degree of efficiency that has become the envy of the world. The composers of our popular songs learned how to blend the earthy influences of jazz and the blues with sophisticated chord patterns and harmonies and matured a musical product unique to a distinctly American tradition. The more so, because it is the creation of a typically American mélange of races and nationalities.

Record collectors deserve a great vote of appreciation for the respect that American popular music now enjoys. When most people were discarding their records as not worth preserving, along with the music on them, the much-maligned collector was doing his best to preserve both for the future; his dedication has paid off for everybody concerned—the musicians, the composers, and all those who love good music. Now our popular music is recognized as "good" music. Ironically, it is probably more greatly appreciated abroad than at home, but there is no longer any question that it is a major contribution to the music of the world.

One of the nicer chores during my long tenure as editor of *Jersey Jazz*, the monthly publication of the New Jersey Jazz Society, was researching and writing for each issue the column that I called "The Unsung Songwriters." I enjoyed it because it gave me a sense of satisfaction in awarding credit where, in most instances, credit is long overdue. Then, too, in a quiet way there were other compensations. For instance, a recent phone call from a very nice lady who informed me her sister is Mrs. Arthur Johnston, widow of the fine songwriter who, among other great tunes, wrote *Pennies from Heaven*. The lady was relaying a word of thanks from Mrs. Johnston in appreciation of a column written a number of years ago on Arthur Johnston, which I was told has been well circulated in the family.

The American heritage of popular songs is unique in musical history. It can perhaps be traced back to the ditties composed by Stephen Collins Foster, and there were primitive songs that caught the public's fancy, such as *Yankee Doodle*, but the period I refer to as the "Golden Age" of songwriting is a twentieth-century phenomenon that began during or right after the First World War. It has to be admitted that the starting point is indefinite, but it takes only a brief glance at the number of songs published year after year from that point forward to establish the fact that many of the songwriting giants got their start in the twenties. The craft reached its peak of perfection in the thirties. Thus, I contend that while a number of quality songs appeared earlier, and some later, the Golden Age can be roughly established from 1917 to 1950. The composers and lyricists in this book either worked and published during this period, or their material complies with the format and traditions established at that time.

There have never been any rules or regulations governing the art of songwriting. Anybody and everybody so inclined have been welcome to participate, and as a result there are hundreds of people who have written one or two songs—or for some reason or another managed to have their names listed in the credits—but unless the result was an exceptionally fine composition, you won't find them in this book. Nor will you find the writers of country and western or rock. These are categories I consider outside the loose guidelines I have established for this work. No doubt they will be adequately covered by writers more expert with the material.

My main purpose is to bring greater recognition to the men and women I consider the originators and developers who brought the craft to a level of artistry in the Golden Era. Although this means not every songwriter who ever penned a ditty will be included, I think the field will be well covered.

Why Some Songwriters Are Not Included in This Book

The title of this book is "The Unsung Songwriters," and in planning it my intention was to give overdue credit to the vast army of lyricists and composers who, for the most part, are unfamiliar names to the general public. With this idea in mind, the next step was to determine—at least to my own satisfaction—what qualified a songwriter as "unsung." Since the majority of them seem to fall into this class, it was easier to work in reverse and eliminate those who are so famous that their names have become synonymous with the trade; those who are well known to the man in the street; those who, in the minds of most people, composed our greatest popular songs.

The first name on this list is Irving Berlin. His long and prolific career has been well documented, and anything I would be able to write about him would be mere repetition. The next name is George Gershwin. The reasoning applied to Berlin is also valid here. Both George and brother Ira have been thoroughly covered in articles and books. Biographies of George Gershwin include *A Journey to Greatness*, by David Ewen; *Gershwin*, by Isaac Goldberg; *The Gershwin Years*, by Edward Jablonski and Lawrence Stewart; *George Gershwin*, by Robert Payne; and *The Gershwins*, by Robert Kimball and Alfred Simon. The 1945 movie *Rhapsody In Blue* depicted Gershwin's life and career, and Robert Alda starred as Gershwin. By no means of lesser stature, Jerome Kern also doesn't qualify among the unsung. His career has been celebrated like those of the foregoing in a biographical movie, *Till the Clouds Roll By*, with Robert Walker portraying Kern, and again in books like the biography *The World of Jerome Kern*, by David Ewen. Which brings us to Cole Porter, subject of several books: *Cole*, edited by Robert Kimball, with a biographical essay by Brendan Gill; *The Cole Porter Story*, by Richard Hubler; *Cole Porter, the Life That Late He Led*, by George Eells. In 1946 Cary Grant portrayed Cole Porter in the film *Night and Day*. Clearly, Mr. Porter hasn't been "unsung." Richard Rodgers completes our list of the unqualified. Again, there are several biographies: *Some*

Enchanted Evenings, by Deems Taylor; *Richard Rodgers*, by David Ewen; and *The Rodgers and Hammerstein Story*, by Stanley Green. The famous team of Rodgers & Hart was personified in the 1948 film *Words and Music*, with Tom Drake as Rodgers and Mickey Rooney as Lorenz Hart. To sum up, it's obvious that these great writers have attained star status in the world of music, and this book would do very little to enhance their image. Although I had to make an arbitrary decision to exclude them, I think it was a reasonable one. I hope you agree.

This book is not intended as a discography. Although recordings may often be mentioned in the narrative, labels and record numbers may not always be included. In any case, recordings that are listed, in accordance with the time span of most of the text, are the original 78 rpm records. If I know of a later reissue on LP or CD, sometimes I will point it out, but no effort has been made to provide this information.

Acknowledgments

I want to express my appreciation for the great help and support I received in researching and writing this book. First, I must acknowledge the generous and unselfish contributions of my good friend John Maimone, who patiently set and reset the text on his computer and gave support in countless ways. Next, I must thank Vince Giordano and John Miller, again for their patience and generosity in making available their extensive files on songs, composers, and recordings and for taking the time and trouble to comply with my tiresome demands. Tex Wyndham also deserves a bow for providing information from his sheet music collection.

And this acknowledgment wouldn't be complete without mention of the invaluable help provided by the following:

ASCAP Biographical Dictionary. 4th ed. New York: R. R. Bowker, 1980.

Kinkle, Roger D. *The Complete Encyclopedia of Popular Music and Jazz 1900–1950*. New Rochelle, N.Y.: Arlington House, 1974.

Lissauer, Robert. *Lissauer's Encyclopedia of Popular Music in America: 1888 to the Present*. 3 vols. New York: Facts-on-File, 1996.

Rust, Brian. *The American Dance Band Discography 1917–1942*. New Rochelle, N.Y.: Arlington House, 1975.

———. *Jazz Records 1897–1941*. New Rochelle, N.Y.: Arlington House, 1978.

Not to be forgotten is the help from my British friends Clarrie Henley, Derek Coller, Bert Whyatt, Charlie Crump, and David Griffiths. Nor the great cooperation of Ed Berger and Dan Morgenstern at the Rutgers Institute of Jazz Studies.

Special mention must be accorded the astute and generous contributions of those who gave their time and effort in researching the career and compositions of Peter Mendoza—Clarrie Henley, Maureen Mendoza, Peter Mendoza Jr., Dave Cooper, Arthur Badrock, Dave Griffiths, Derek Coller, and Bill Hebden.

My sincere and heartfelt gratitude to you all.

Warren Vaché, Sr.

Maurie Abrams

Maurie Abrams, one of Tin Pan Alley's pioneers, was born Maurice Abrahams in Russia, March 18, 1883. Coming to the United States at an early age, he wrote special material for vaudeville entertainers, especially his wife, Belle Baker, who was a headliner. By 1923 Abrams had established his own publishing firm and went on to become a talent agent. During his songwriting career he collaborated with Grant Clarke, Edgar Leslie, and Lewis Muir.

Most of Abrams's songs haven't survived the years, but a few are well known and are frequently revived, especially *Ragtime Cowboy Joe*, which Abrams wrote with Grant Clarke and Lewis Muir and published in 1912. Besides being featured on recordings by artists as diversified as Jo Stafford and the Chipmunks, this tune was sung by Alice Faye, Jack Oakie, and June Havoc in the 1943 movie *Hello Frisco, Hello*, and again by Betty Hutton, portraying Texas Guinan of "Hello, Sucker" fame, in the movie *Incendiary Blonde* a year later.

A genuine vintage piece depicting the trials and troubles of the owners of early automobiles, *He'd Have To Get Under*, a collaboration with Grant Clarke and Edgar Leslie in 1913, also survives as a typical novelty of the era. *Kitchy-Koo*, a song with words by L. Wolfe Gilbert and music by Maurie Abrams and Lewis Muir, was intended as a ragtime entry but received a swinging treatment on English Decca in the forties by a group from the Bert Ambrose band billed as the "Embassy Rhythm Eight."

Other titles credited to Maurie Abrams are *When the Grown-up Ladies Act Like Babies; Pray for Sunshine, but Always Be Prepared for Rain; I'll Always Think I'm in Heaven When I'm Down in Dixieland; Take Me to That Midnight Cakewalk Ball; High, High Up in the Hills; Pullman Porter's Parade; At the Cotton Picker's Ball; Everybody Loves My Gal;* and *Is There Still Room for Me.*

Maurie Abrams died in New York City on April 13, 1931.

Tom Adair

Lyricist Thomas Montgomery Adair was born in Newton, Kansas, June 15, 1913, but migrated to Los Angeles, where he graduated from John C.

Fremont High School and went to Los Angeles Junior College. Besides writing song lyrics he was a very successful scriptwriter for television shows such as *My Three Sons, The Munsters, My Favorite Martian,* and other situation comedies. He also wrote for movies and the stage and for some time was associated with Disney productions. He collaborated with Matt Dennis on those great tunes, with clever and humorous lyrics, associated with Tommy Dorsey and Frank Sinatra in the early forties, to be specific: *Let's Get Away from It All; Everything Happens to Me; Violets for Your Furs; Nine Old Men; Will You Still Be Mine?*; and *Free for All.* Adair and Dennis also collaborated on another great song, *The Night We Called It a Day*, but for some reason this partnership, which showed such great promise, wasn't continued, and both men went in different directions. Adair and bandleader D'Artega turned out a nice tune, *In the Blue of Evening*, in 1942, and later Adair collaborated with Gordon Jenkins on the score of a Broadway musical, "Along Fifth Avenue," but this was at the beginning of the falling market for good songs, and none of the tunes from the show went anywhere. Adair wrote for some movies and then continued writing special material for TV shows, such as *This Is Your Life,* the *Ann Sothern Show*, the *Tennessee Ernie Ford Show, Mickey Mouse Club*, and others.

Stanley Adams

Stanley Adams, onetime president of ASCAP and a native New Yorker, was born in Manhattan on August 14, 1907. He studied to be a lawyer, but an early success writing material for a revue at the famous nightclub Connie's Inn lured him into further work in films and Broadway musicals. He collaborated with a number of top melody writers, including Hoagy Carmichael, Fats Waller, Louis Alter, Milton Ager, Abel Baer, Ray Henderson, Victor Herbert, and Sigmund Romberg. He started out in 1930 with a Fats Waller tune, *Rollin' Down the River*, which I have on a contemporary Leo Reisman recording when Eddy Duchin and Nat Brandwynne were on twin pianos in the band and with a bass-baritone vocalist who persists in "Rollin' down the reever." It's a good tune that Waller enthusiasts would do well to revive. In 1934, that gold mine year for pop songs, Stanley Adams's name was on several entries, particularly on three impressive hits, *I Couldn't Be Mean to You*, in collaboration with Jesse Greer; *My Shawl*, a rumba, with Xavier Cugat; and *What a Difference a Day Made*, with composer Maria Grever, of whom we know nothing. Adams's career continued until 1955, and other titles include *Seein' Is Believin'; Papa Tree Top Tall; Little Old Lady* (with Hoagy Carmichael); and *There Are Such Things.*

Throughout his career he was an active participant in organizations dedicated to improving and protecting the rights of songwriters and musicians. Stanley Adams died on January 26, 1994.

Harold Adamson

Lyricist Harold Adamson was born in Greenville, N.J., on December 10, 1906. His long and prolific career as a lyricist included working with many of the top composers, and his name is on some very prestigious titles—*Time on My Hands*, for instance, and *Manhattan Serenade.* He attended Kansas and Harvard Universities and started writing songs at that time, leaving for New York and a songwriting career directly from Harvard. His first published song, *Time on My Hands*, appeared in 1930 (the same year as Stanley Adams's *Rollin' Down the River*), and was a blockbuster success. His collaborators on the song were Vincent Youmans and Mack Gordon—the latter also working on the lyrics. Adamson went on to write with Hoagy Carmichael, Louis Alter, Peter DeRose, Walter Donaldson, Vernon Duke, Duke Ellington, and Victor Young. The list of his songs is too long to publish here, but here are some of the high spots: *Everything I Have Is Yours; Everything's Been Done Before; Did I Remember?; You Never Looked So Beautiful; Where the Lazy River Goes By; It's Been So Long; You're a Sweetheart; It's a Wonderful World; 720 in the Books; Daybreak; Manhattan Serenade; A Lovely Way to Spend an Evening; I Don't Care Who Knows It; It's a Most Unusual Day; Around the World.*

A master of his craft, Adamson created word pictures ideally suited to the melody they showcased that were at the same time easy to memorize and to sing. Without any obvious attempt to do so, his lyrics often have a poetic air of symmetry and imagery that elevates them far above mere words to a song. Harold Adamson was a fertile contributor of outstanding songs to the Golden Age. Many of his songs have become standards, and his lyrics are indelibly seated in the public's consciousness. You may not remember his name, but you remember his lyrics.

Basil G. (Buzz) Adlam

Basil G. (Buzz) Adlam was born in Chelmsford, England, but emigrated to Canada where he attended public schools and studied music with Herman

Guess and Albert Coates. A saxophonist, he went on to work with the bands of Ozzie Nelson and Phil Harris, then to arrange for Horace Heidt, and eventually to arrange and conduct on radio and TV.

Although his songwriting credits are not extensive, there are several tunes that are worthy of mention. *The House Is Haunted by the Echo of Your Last Goodbye*, a 1934 entry with lyrics by Billy Rose, was introduced by Jane Froman in the "Ziegfeld Follies" of that year and enjoyed frequent air play. It was also recorded by Ramona, the featured vocalist with Paul Whiteman's orchestra on Victor. *Say It*, another offering in the prime year of 1934, is a beautiful ballad that stands up well in comparison with the many other great songs published that year and was accorded outstanding treatment by the Isham Jones Orchestra on Victor. *My Galveston Gal*, with both words and music by Buzz Adlam, published in 1933, was well received by contemporary bandleaders and recorded by Harry Reser on Columbia, Joe Haymes on Bluebird (under the pseudonym of "Mike Doty and His Orchestra"), and the Allen-Hawkins group on Perfect.

Buzz Adlam did well with two other songs, *Poor Robinson Crusoe* and *With Thee I Swing*. The former, published in 1937, was recorded in England by the British answer to Louis Armstrong, Nat Gonella, on the Parlophone label and in the United States by Jay Freeman on the new, and short-lived, Variety label; Dick Porter on Vocalion; and Buzz Adlam's former boss, Ozzie Nelson, on Bluebird. *With Thee I Swing* received comparable treatment, with recordings by Dick McDonough's Orchestra for ARC, the Riley-Farley Onyx Boys on Decca, and Teddy Wilson's group with Billie Holiday on Brunswick.

Basil (Buzz) Adlam died in 1974.

Milton Ager

Milton Ager is one of those songwriters who started to write quality material early in the period I have designated as the Golden Age. His first published song appeared in 1918, a tune with a tricky title, *Everything Is Peaches Down in Georgia*. It enjoyed fair success, but as he continued to contribute hit tunes throughout the twenties and into the thirties, Milton Ager's songs lent a definite flavor of their own to the period. He was born in Chicago, October 6, 1893, and after graduating from high school began working as a pianist in silent movie houses and for vaudeville theaters accompanying singers and song-pluggers. In 1913 he traveled to New York and took a job as an arranger for the publishing firm of Waterson, Berlin, & Snyder. After a brief stint in the army during WWI, he worked as an arranger for George M. Cohan and at the same time began his own career as a composer with the 1918 entry mentioned above. The following year he scored again with a song that has been revived several times since, *Freckles*. In 1920 he branched out, writing the score for a Broadway musical, "What's in a Name," which included a song that can be considered a standard, *A Young Man's Fancy*. In 1921 he published a tune that would become a hit all over again in 1941, *I'm Nobody's Baby*. But it was in 1922 that Ager began to contribute the kind of songs that have come to typify the twenties. His first entry was *Lovin' Sam*, followed in 1923 by *Louisville Lou* and *Mama Goes Where Papa Goes*; both titles have survived through the years and lend themselves well to jazz treatment, as Sophie Tucker demonstrated on a Decca recording, with an Eddie Condon group backing her on *Louisville Lou,* and Kay Starr did on a Capitol recording of *Mama Goes Where Papa Goes.*

Ager, ably abetted in most of his efforts by lyricist Jack Yellen, continued to turn out hit songs year after year. In 1924 he produced *Hard-Hearted Hannah*, delineated many years later by drummer-bandleader Ray McKinley; *Big Boy*, forever immortalized as played by Bix Beiderbecke and the Wolverines; and a soggy ballad that seemed to strike home with those who liked their songs heavy on sentiment, *I Wonder What's Become of Sally*. For the next few years the Ager magic seemed to fade a little, with no important songs, but 1927 saw the debut of a tune that to many seems to identify the twenties, *Ain't She Sweet*. Two others also did well that year, *Crazy Words–Crazy Tune* and *Is She My Girl Friend?* Ager continued to write for stage shows in the waning years of the decade, turning out scores for "Rain or Shine" in 1928 and "John Murray Anderson's Almanac" in 1929. That same year he started to write for movies, beginning with a film called *Honky Tonk*, which starred Sophie Tucker. But the best song of the year for Ager was a freelance item called *Glad Rag Doll.*

The thirties started off well. Ager and Yellen wrote the score for the Paul Whiteman movie *The King of Jazz*, contributing four titles, including the outstanding *Happy Feet*. "Rain or Shine" was made into a movie with the original stage score, and another movie, *Chasing Shadows*, with Jack Benny and Marie Dressler, featured two Ager–Yellen songs. One became the unofficial rallying song of the Great Depression and the campaign song for Franklin Delano Roosevelt, *Happy Days Are Here Again*. The other, a ditty called *Lucky Me, Lovable You*, has faded away.

As can be noticed in the output of other composers of the period, the Ager songs from this point forward began to take on a more sentimental and melodic approach. Several influences probably brought this about. The stock market crash of 1929 and the resultant shock to the country's economy and sensibilities ushered in a sober mood. This in turn was tempered by the popularity of radio, which quickly became the prime source of entertainment, and the influence of an overnight sensation, a crooning bandleader named Rudy Vallee. Vallee favored sentimental ballads with catchy melody lines, and he made a number of songs into hits. A proliferation of singing bandleaders added impetus to the movement, and, in keeping with the trend, the popular songwriters began churning out ditties to fit the mode. However, although the trend was toward sentimentality, the public also became receptive to songs with greater sophistication, more advanced chordal structure, and unusual innovations in the melody.

Thus, the Milton Ager titles of the thirties have a different flair than his hits of the twenties. Now the titles reflect the new trend—*If I Didn't Have You* (1931); *Auf Wiedersehen, My Dear; So Ashamed* (1932); *Trouble in Paradise; If I Didn't Care* (1933); *I Hate Myself; In a Little Red Barn* (1934); *Seein' Is Believin'* (1935); *It's No Fun; You're Giving Me a Song and a Dance; You Can't Pull the Wool over My Eyes* (1936). Now a new influence entered the picture. Benny Goodman ushered in the swing era and began to play ballads with a rhythmic lift. Two Ager tunes received early treatment, *You Can't Pull the Wool over My Eyes*; and *You're Giving Me a Song and a Dance*, followed by still another in 1937, *You Can Tell She Comes from Dixie*. *Trust in Me*, another ballad of the same year, received a warm welcome. Ager had two songs in the market for 1938, *Sweet Stranger* and *There's Rain in My Eyes*, and then, as though signing off with a tender thought, his final entry in 1939 was *Sweet Dreams, Sweetheart.*

Although Jack Yellen was Ager's primary collaborator, he also wrote with Benny Davis, Grant Clarke, Joe Young, and Stanley Adams.

Milton Ager died in Los Angeles on May 6, 1979.

Fred E. Ahlert

Before you read any further, ask yourself this question: How many songs can I name by Fred Ahlert? Can't think of any? Or was your comment, "Fred Who?" Fred Ahlert is one more of those extremely talented composers of many of our favorite songs whose name gets lost in the overemphasis on Berlin, Gershwin, Kern, Rodgers and Hart, and others who wrote primarily for stage shows and movies, because much of his output didn't appear in either. Nevertheless, his career, almost from beginning to end, was peppered with hits, while others stand up well in the category of quality songs. Among them are quite a few that have become standards, as well as vehicles that performers rode to stardom, such as Bing Crosby's theme, *In the Blue of the Night*; Ruth Etting's hit, *Mean to Me*; Russ Columbo's *I Don't Know Why*; and Fats Waller's big one, *I'm Gonna Sit Right Down and Write Myself a Letter*. Oh, you've heard of those, have you? Well then, how about *I'll Get By; Love, You Funny Thing; Walkin' My Baby Back Home*? You know them too. Good. Now you know why Ahlert qualifies in our catalog of great songwriters.

He was born in New York City on September 19, 1892,went to CCNY and Fordham Law School, but instead of taking up the practice of law he went to work for a song publishing firm and wrote special material for vaudeville entertainers. He started songwriting early in this period but really turned to it as a career in the early twenties with the publication of tunes with tricky titles like *I'd Love to Fall Asleep and Wake Up in My Mammy's Arms* and *I Gave You Up Just Before You Threw Me Down*, but by the middle of the decade he was beginning to develop more sophisticated themes. He had a fair hit in *There's a Cradle in Caroline*, immortalized for jazz record collectors by Bix Beiderbecke and the Broadway Bell Hops and again by Frank Trumbauer's Orchestra. It was also recorded by several other bands in this country, along with several sides in England that feature Sylvester Ahola, America's gift to the great British dance bands of the twenties and thirties.

In 1928 and 1929, though, Ahlert shifted into high gear with *I'll Get By; Evening Star; The One That I Love Loves Me; To Be in Love*; and *I'll Never Ask for More*. All of these were excellent songs and enjoyed considerable success in the highly competitive market where even the big hits had an expected life of only six weeks. At any rate, they apparently were good enough to bring Ahlert to the attention of Hollywood, and in 1930 he wrote tunes for three movies, contributing one song to each: *It Must Be You; The Whole Darned Thing's for You*; and *We're Friends Again*. Either he didn't care for a screen career, or the moderate success of his songs didn't impress the Hollywood moguls, because in the following year he was working independently again and scoring big. In quick order he turned out *Walkin' My Baby Back Home; I Don't Know Why; Can't You See*; and *In the Blue of the Night*. In 1932, the next year, he offered *Just a Little Home for the Old Folks; Love, You Funny Thing*; and *I'll Follow You*. *I Wake Up Smiling*, an unpretentious little waltz, was his big hit of 1933, and *The Moon Was Yellow* and *I Still Do* were back-to-back successes in 1934. *Sweet Thing*, which came along in 1935, was again tapped for immortality by two recordings, one by Fats Waller and another by Dick Porter's Orchestra with Eddie Condon, Jonah Jones, Joe Marsala, and George Wettling. In 1936 he wrote the famous *I'm Gonna Sit Right Down*, among others, and the next year produced some very pretty tunes that rate revival, *The Image of You; There's Frost on the Moon*; and *To a Sweet Pretty Thing*. His last published song appeared in 1945, *In the Middle of May*.

Fred Ahlert was an active member of ASCAP, served on its board of directors for a time, and was president from 1948 to 1950. He died in New York on October 20, 1953. So the next time anybody wants to know what songs were written by Fred Ahlert, don't forget *I'll Get By; Mean to Me; I'm Gonna Sit Right Down. . . .*

Harry Akst

Harry Akst was born in New York City on August 15, 1894, and his formal education was confined to the public schools. But he was a talented product of the times and while still in grade school performed a piano recital at Mendelsohn Hall. Then, wasting no time, he organized an orchestra bureau and went on to an exciting career as accompanist to the popular vaudeville headliner and stage star Nora Bayes for four years. When the First World War came along he saw some military service at Camp Upton, N.Y., where he met and became associated with Irving Berlin. After the war he worked for Berlin, interspersed with leading a dance band and writing songs.

Nowadays, whenever hit songs are the subject of conversation it's hard to overlook one that has been a favorite of jazz musicians ever since it first appeared in 1925. It has been recorded hundreds of times, and yet, if you were to ask, practically nobody remembers who wrote it. "The name of this song is *Dinah*!" as they sing on some of the old records, and it was written by Harry Akst, who also gave us *A Smile Will Go a Long, Long Way; Dearest; Baby Face; Am I Blue?; Guilty*; and a number of other fine songs throughout the twenties and thirties.

In his book *American Popular Song*, Alec Wilder placed *Dinah* in his chapter on outstanding individual songs and had this to say about it: "I love it because it's so relaxed and without pretense. I love it for its absolute naturalness. It's almost as if it simply happened rather than was written. The jazz men must have felt good about it, too, for they've been having fun with it for over forty years." This description fits much of the music of Harry Akst, especially the songs he wrote in the twenties. If one word could be used to characterize them, it would be "happy." They were happy melodically, and this feeling must have rubbed off on the lyricists, because most of the words and titles are happy too. So we have *Everything's Gonna Be All Right; No Wonder I'm Happy; Nothing's Too Good for My Baby*; and *What a Perfect Combination*, among other optimistic songs, and just enough wistfully blue ones like *Guilty; Am I Blue?*; and *Can't Get Mississippi off My Mind* to prove that Akst had unhappy feelings like everybody else.

The Akst composing cycle began early with the publication of *Home Again Blues* in 1921. In 1923 he had two outstanding hits, *A Smile Will Go a Long, Long Way* and *Dearest, You're the Nearest to My Heart*; 1925 brought the aforementioned *Dinah*. *Baby Face* was the main entry for 1926, and then Akst began to write for stage shows and movies. The 1929 Ted Lewis movie *Is Everybody Happy?* introduced the Lewis standard *I'm the Medicine Man for the Blues,* and another movie, *On with the Show*, included two hits, *Am I Blue?* and *Birmingham Bertha.* Akst continued to write for movies, but nothing of importance came along until 1931, when three freelance tunes all scored well—*Guilty; I Can't Get Mississippi off My Mind*; and *Nothin's Too Good for My Baby. Look What You've Done*, a song featured in the Eddie Cantor movie *The Kid from Spain*, was a collaboration with Bert Kalmar and Harry Ruby and Irving Caesar in 1932, along with *What a Perfect Combination*, and both were successful in that highly competitive year.

Harry Akst remained an active composer well into the fifties, and his last published song was a memorable one, *Anema E Core*. He died in Hollywood on March 31, 1963. He wrote for shows, wrote for the movies, was a professional pianist in his teens, and led dance bands, but his legacy to us is in the songs he left behind. Now, remember, if anybody should ask, *Dinah* was written by Harry Akst.

Steve Allen

Steve Allen was born in New York City, December 26, 1921, the son of vaudeville performers Belle Montrose and Billy Allen. As a result, Steve traveled all over the country with his parents and received a thorough grounding in show business. A man of many talents, he is an accomplished musician, a writer, an entertainer, an actor, and a well-known personality, but here it is his career as a composer that is the main interest.

This Could Be the Start of Something Big, with both words and music by Steve Allen, was introduced in 1956 on his Sunday night TV show by Les Brown's Orchestra and then was adopted as the theme. It went on to become a favorite with "society" bands, was also played on a number of records, and is now considered a standard. The remarkable thing about this is that the market for quality songs was very small by the time *Something Big* was published, and yet the song became a success strictly on its own merit without the help of a hit recording by a name artist. A jazz pianist of considerable merit, Steve Allen's work often reflects his jazz influences as evident in *An Old Piano Plays the Blues* and *Meet Me Where They Play the Blues*. At the same time he was able to take advantage of the new market created by the demand for "themes" in the movies. His best-known contribution to this was the theme from *Picnic*. Others include the title songs for *Houseboat*, *On the Beach*, *Sleeping Beauty*, and *Bell, Book and Candle*.

In my opinion, Steve Allen would have been a major songwriter if he had been around in the thirties and forties. He is a prime example of a great talent going to waste in the desert of rock.

Louis Alter

That gracious and multitalented lady of the keyboards Jane Jarvis has made it known that Louis Alter is a personal favorite of hers, and in response to her request here is a long overdue tribute to Mr. Alter.

Louis Alter was born in Haverhill, Mass. on June 18, 1902. He was educated at the New England Conservatory of Music and at the tender age of thirteen was already playing piano in movie theaters for silent films. From this he moved on to being accompanist to some very famous names, starting with Nora Bayes, with whom he toured both the United States and abroad, and Irene Bordoni, Helen Morgan, and Bea Lillie. Like so many other songwriters, he went to work for publishing firms—mainly as an arranger—and had his first song published in 1926, a tune called *Hugs and Kisses*. This kicked off a career highlighted by a number of contributions to stage shows and movies. The 1928 Earl Carroll version of "Vanities" featured songs by a number of composers, but I fondly remember the Louis Alter song *Blue Shadows*, a tune well worth reviving by some enterprising person. However, a little-known show of the same year, "Paris," introduced a melody that was eventually to become one of Louis Alter's biggest and best-known songs, *Manhattan Serenade*. Its success, however, was postponed until 1942 when it was revived, with lyrics by Harold Adamson.

Alter wrote *Love Ain't Nothin' but the Blues*, a 1929 entry, plus a couple of fairly successful songs for movies of the period and had a very nice hit with *Overnight*, a superior contribution to the stage show "Sweet and Low" in 1930. In the next year he had two more hits in the stage show "Ballyhoo"—*No Wonder I'm Blue* and *I'm One of God's Children Who Hasn't Got Wings*. Only one entry appeared in 1932, a tune called *What a Life*, but in 1933 the movie *Take a Chance* inspired a title lifted from a famous Mae West line,

Come Up and See Me Sometime; there were two other fine songs that year, *Morning, Noon, and Night* and *What Have We Got to Lose*. *I've Got Sand in My Shoes* was the only Alter entry in 1934, and nothing is listed for 1935, but in 1936 he contributed compositions to three movies. *Trail of the Lonesome Pine*, as comedian George Gobel was fond of pointing out, was the initial starring vehicle for Fred MacMurray, and it featured two Alter songs, *A Melody from the Sky* and *Twilight on the Trail* (sung, if I remember correctly, by Fuzzy Knight, former bandleader). *Rainbow on the River* starred singing juvenile Bobby Breen and included three Alter songs, *Rainbow on the River; A Thousand Dreams of You*; and *You Only Live Once*. Finally, *Sing, Baby, Sing*, a movie with Alice Faye and Tony Martin, included *You Turned the Tables on Me*, which the Benny Goodman band, with Pee Wee Erwin and Chris Griffin in the lineup and making the most of a Fletcher Henderson arrangement, recorded for posterity. Another movie, *Make a Wish*, came out in 1937 with two Alter tunes, *Make a Wish* and *Music in My Heart*, but again there is a lapse until 1940, when a very respectable hit came out, *The Sky Fell Down*. The following year Alter was responsible for two important songs in the score of a movie called *Las Vegas Nights*, in which the Tommy Dorsey band was featured. The two big tunes were *Dolores* and *Moments Like This*. Two others, *I Gotta Ride* and *Mary, Mary Quite Contrary*, were incidental.

Louis Alter continued to write good songs, but perhaps his biggest contribution to the library of jazz came from the songs written for the movie *New Orleans*, which appeared in 1947. Of course, the standard *Do You Know What It Means to Miss New Orleans* is from that score, along with two other titles, *Endie* and *Blues Are Brewin'*. *Nina Never Knew*, which was an entry in 1952, has been picking up steam ever since and is well on the way to becoming another standard. Alter also wrote "serious" works, including *Manhattan Moonlight; Metropolitan Nocturne; Side Street in Gotham; Manhattan Masquerade; American Serenade*; and *Jewels from Cartier Suite*. He saw military service in World War II, coordinating entertainment for air bases on the West Coast. His collaborators included some of the best lyricists of all time—Raymond Klages, Jo Trent, Oscar Hammerstein II, Charlotte Kent, and Sidney Mitchell.

Arthur Altman

Arthur Altman, a Brooklyn boy, was born there on October 28, 1912. He studied violin and played in dance bands early in his career but also attended St. John's School of Law. Altman devoted a large portion of his musical career to developing themes for movies and TV game shows and also functioned as staff librarian for CBS. He entered the songwriting field in 1932 with a collaboration with Jack Lawrence and Emery Deutsch, *Play, Fiddle, Play*, a tune that was well accepted and one of the lucky ones recorded by Ray Noble's New Mayfair Orchestra for the British HMV label. For some unexplained reason six years went by before the next Altman composition appeared. This had lyrics by Frank Loesser, and Manning Sherwin shared composer credit. The title was *I Fall in Love With You Every Day*, and it was introduced in the movie *College Swing* by John Payne and Florence George. It fared well in the recording market too, spanning all the major labels—Larry Clinton on Victor, Jimmy Dorsey on Decca, Dolly Dawn with George Hall's Orchestra on Vocalion, Horace Heidt on Brunswick, and Abe Lyman on Bluebird.

During Frank Sinatra's brief period as the vocalist with Harry James's new band, they recorded *All or Nothing at All*, an Altman song with lyrics by Jack Lawrence, and nothing much happened. Then Sinatra went on to overnight success, and in 1943 the record was reissued and sold over a million copies. *All or Nothing at All* automatically became Altman's biggest hit. He didn't have another until 1950, when again Sinatra played a big part in popularizing a collaboration with Hal David and Redd Evans, *American Beauty Rose*. The Sinatra recording with Mitch Miller's band on Columbia promoted the tune into a hit.

Arthur Altman continued to write songs, and very likely some of them would have been successful in an earlier time, but the dwindling market for quality songs in the fifties most likely cheated both Altman and that segment of the American public still able to appreciate them.

Harry Archer

Bandleader-composer Harry Archer was born in Creston, Iowa, on February 21, 1888. His well-rounded education included attendance at the Michigan Military Academy, Princeton University, and Knox College. A talented musician, he mastered all brass instruments with the exception of the French horn. He organized his own dance band and for several years made records for Brunswick and Vocalion. Starting in 1912 he wrote scores for Broadway musicals and in 1923, with lyricist Harlan Thompson, composed the all-time hit *I Love You* for the stage show, "Little Jessie James." Paul Whiteman had the best-selling record, but other contemporary sides were made by Carl Fenton, Ohman & Arden, Vincent Lopez, Ben Selvin, and others. The song has been recorded frequently through the years and was featured in the war film *Stalag 17* in a barracks scene in which the entire cast plays and sings the song.

In 1924 Archer and Thompson wrote *You and I* for the show "My Girl" and followed through in 1925 with *It Must Be Love*, for "Merry Merry." *I'd Rather Be the Girl in Your Arms* was the Archer–Thompson entry for 1926. Harry Archer and His Orchestra recorded it for Brunswick, but the song attained all-time distinction as recorded by the Jean Goldkette Orchestra. As such it has been reissued many times and also recreated. Harry Archer continued to write well into the thirties. Other songs include *A Girl Like You; Before the Dawn; Anything Your Heart Desires; Pretty, Petite, and Sweet; White Sails; Suppose I Had Never Met You; I'm Goin' to Dance with the Guy What Brung Me; Rainbow; Alone in My Dreams; The Sweetest Girl This Side of Heaven*; and *My Own.*

Harry Archer died in New York City on April 23, 1960.

Harold Arlen

The prolific composer of many of America's favorite songs, Harold Arlen was born Hyman Arluck in Albany, New York, on February 15, 1905. He attended the public schools but received a thorough musical training from Arnold Cornelissen and Simon Bucharoff. A talented youngster, he sang in the synagogue choir where his father was cantor when he was only seven years old, and by the time he was fifteen was already playing as a professional pianist in clubs and on lake steamers. In the mid twenties, aware of the greater opportunities to be had in New York City, he made the move and was soon singing, playing, and arranging with various dance bands in the city and was a member of Arnold Johnson's pit orchestra for the stage show "George White's Scandals of 1928." Following this, he worked as a rehearsal pianist for the show "Great Day," toured Loew's vaudeville circuit as a singer-pianist, and started composing.

Right from the start his songs were featured in movies and stage shows, beginning in 1929 with the movie *Rio Rita* and his early effort *Long Before You Came Along* and into the next year when *Hittin' the Bottle* was part of the score for "Earl Carroll's Vanities of 1930." But his first big hit was a freelance entry that same year, *Get Happy*. It was a sensational start and was quickly followed by more solid strikes. In 1931 the stage show "You Said It" included the Arlen tunes *Sweet and Hot* and *Learn to Croon,* while his freelance offerings included the perennial *Between the Devil and the Deep Blue Sea* and the title featured by the King of Hi-de-ho, Cab Calloway,

Kickin' the Gong Around. In fact, this worked so well that Arlen wrote another Calloway special which became a hit in 1932, *Minnie the Moocher's Wedding Day*. But it wasn't the only Arlen title. The song that trombonist Jack Teagarden adopted as his theme, *I Gotta Right to Sing the Blues*, came from "Earl Carroll's Vanities of 1932," and one of the nicer of the Arlen songs, *Music, Music, Everywhere*, also made a modest impression.

1933 was a banner year for the young composer, with no less than three destined-to-be standards in the running. *It's Only a Paper Moon* made its debut in the movie *Take a Chance,* and *Stormy Weather* and *I've Got the World on a String* were from the famous Cotton Club revues. The trend continued. *Ill Wind* and *As Long As I Live* were from the "Cotton Club Parade of 1934," and if these big hits weren't enough, the stage show "Life Begins at 8:40" provided *You're a Builder Upper; Fun to be Fooled; Let's Take a Walk around the Block*; and *What Can You Say in a Love Song?*, while the movie *Let's Fall in Love* included the popular title song, plus *Love Is Love Anywhere*. The Arlen output for the next few years was consistent and moderately successful, and then in 1939 came *The Wizard of Oz*, with the sensational *Over the Rainbow* and other well-known songs such as *Ding Dong the Witch is Dead* and *We're Off to See the Wizard*.

Buds Won't Bud was a worthy entry in 1940, starting the new decade off right, with the uptrend continuing the following year with the movie *Blues in the Night*, scoring a hit with the title song and *This Time the Dream's on Me*. Both songs had lyrics by Johnny Mercer, and *Blues in the Night* was nominated for an Academy Award, losing out to the Jerome Kern entry *The Last Time I Saw Paris*. Another Arlen–Mercer collaboration, *That Old Black Magic*, was introduced by singer Johnny Johnson in the 1942 movie *Star Spangled Rhythm* and went on to be recorded by practically every big star of the era. Still another, the title song from the movie *Captains of the Clouds*, was adopted by the Royal Canadian Air Force as its official song.

The Arlen–Mercer team penned still another Academy nominee in *My Shining Hour*, which was introduced by Fred Astaire in the movie *The Sky's the Limit*, but their other song in the movie, *One for My Baby (And One More for the Road)*, proved to be a durable property reappearing in several other movies, including *Young at Heart*, with Frank Sinatra, in 1954. *Happiness Is Just a Thing Called Joe* was another 1943 Arlen release, with lyrics by E. Y. Harburg, in the movie *Cabin in the Sky*. The stage show "Bloomer Girl" offered two Arlen–Harburg collaborations in 1944, *Evelina* and *Right as the Rain*. That same year the movie *Here Come the Waves* featured still another Arlen–Mercer contender for an Academy Award, *Accent-tchu-ate the Positive*, which was in the competition for 1944.

Harold Arlen continued to write for shows and movies well into the sixties, contributing a number of good songs in the process, among them *Now I Know; Come Rain or Come Shine*; and *The Man That Got Away*. For the most part, however, the songs, while important to the productions, suffered from the growing public apathy toward quality music.

Lil Hardin Armstrong

Lil Hardin was born in Memphis, Tennessee, February 3, 1902. She studied music at Fisk University, and in 1917 her family moved to Chicago, where early in her career she played sheet music in music stores. An accomplished jazz pianist, she soon began working with the better jazz bands in the city, including those of Freddie Keppard and King Oliver, where she met trumpet player Louis Armstrong and married him. It is generally conceded that Lil was a great influence on Armstrong and strongly contributed to his success. Although they were divorced in 1938, Lil continued to use the name Armstrong for the rest of her life. In 1927 they recorded a series of records for Okeh which have become jazz classics, including the standard *Struttin' with Some Barbecue*, on which they shared composer credit. Lil Armstrong continued to compose and in 1939 published her most outstanding song, *Just for a Thrill*, which is gradually assuming the status of a standard. *Brown Gal*, which she recorded with an all-star group on Decca, is another original, and the recording of this cute little tune also serves to demonstrate her talents as a vocalist, pianist, and bandleader.

Lil Armstrong succumbed to a fatal heart attack on August 17, 1971, while playing a concert dedicated to the memory of Louis, who had died the previous July.

Gus Arnheim

Just by being the peculiar beast it is, the songwriting business sometimes leaves itself wide open to difficult questions. One of the more serious is how do you go about correcting the misleading listings of certain big-name entertainers or bandleaders on songs they never wrote? For various business reasons, and often at the urging of the real composers, this was an accepted practice because it was common knowledge that, first of all, a song with a big name on it was easier to get accepted and published, and second, the big name also fostered sales. Then again, the problem gets more complicated by the fact that quite often the entertainers and bandleaders *were* involved with composing some songs, while only taking credit for others. In this case, how do you determine which is which? The unfortunate aspect of the whole thing is that some doubt is bound to attend all such listings, and the unrestrained egotism of people like Al Jolson and Irving Mills, who insisted on putting their names on every song within reach, makes that doubt justified.

Bandleader Gus Arnheim is an excellent example of the above confusion. There is no question that he and fellow bandleader Abe Lyman deserve full recognition for the standard *I Cried for You*, which was published in 1923, when Arnheim was playing piano in Lyman's orchestra. Most likely they also merit the rights to *Mandalay*, a 1924 title that also carried the name of another bandleader, Earl Burtnett. But now we come to the song that was used by the Arnheim band as a theme, blossomed into one of the biggest hits of 1931, and went on to become an all-time standard, *Sweet and Lovely*. Two of the names credited with this great song are familiar, Gus Arnheim and Harry Tobias, but who is Jules Lemare, the third party? Harry Tobias was a lyricist. Did Gus Arnheim have a hand in writing the melody, or was it actually the work of Jules Lemare, the unknown? Gus Arnheim's name also appears on *It Must Be True*, along with that of Harry Barris and Gordon Clifford. Clifford wrote the words. Did Arnheim assist Barris in writing the music?

More than likely the most important factor here was the promotional value of the Arnheim band, which in the early thirties was a fixture at the famous Cocoanut Grove in Los Angeles, enjoyed a lot of radio time, and recorded for Victor records with both Bing Crosby and Russ Columbo as vocalists. Gus Arnheim was a talented and competent bandleader, and his band was one of the best of the era. It's very possible that he actually had a hand in composing the songs in question, and it isn't my intention to belittle his contributions to two great songs. However, I think it is important to be aware of this aspect of the music business and to take it into consideration in evaluating the work of our composers.

Arshawsky, Arthur

See Artie Shaw.

Gene Austin

At a period in our musical history when the present and upcoming generations have difficulty remembering Bing Crosby, it's probably too much to expect anybody to recall one of the biggest stars of the twenties, Gene

Austin. Nevertheless, before Crosby broke all previous sales records with *White Christmas*, Gene Austin led the pack with his 1927 hit recording of *My Blue Heaven*, and he was one of the most popular entertainers of the decade—a crooner before the age of crooners. He was born in Gainesville, Texas, on June 24, 1900, but grew up in Louisiana. At age fifteen he ran away from home to join a circus and learned to play the calliope. After a stint of military service during the First World War, he went into vaudeville, touring with a partner, Roy Bergere. In 1924 they composed the hit song of the year, *How Come You Do Me Like You Do*. Austin recorded the tune for Victor, and it gave a ready boost to a career that saw him quickly become one of the most popular entertainers of the twenties.

In the same year (1924), Gene Austin, Jimmy McHugh, and Irving Mills combined on another tune destined to be a standard, *When My Sugar Walks Down the Street*. In 1928 Austin teamed with bandleader Nat Shilkret, and they turned out *The Lonesome Road*, which was featured in the 1929 first movie version of *Show Boat*. This, too, has achieved immortality as a standard. Austin performed bit parts in the movies himself in the early thirties, and while working on the film *Klondike Annie*, he composed *I'm an Occidental Woman in an Oriental Mood for Love*, as a feature for the star of the movie, Mae West.

Although he never regained the popular status he held in the twenties, Gene Austin remained a consistent performer throughout his career, working clubs, featured for awhile on the Joe Penner radio show, and even running his own club, Blue Heaven, in California. In 1934 he worked with still another collaborator, Carmen Lombardo, on a tune that enjoyed a very respectable rating in view of the fantastic competition in the song market that year, *Ridin' Around in the Rain*. It received first-class treatment on records by Bing Crosby, Glen Gray, and Isham Jones—and by Gene himself on Victor 24663. Most likely the final Gene Austin contribution to our heritage of popular songs was a worthy but overlooked entry in the early forties, *Take Your Shoes Off, Baby (And Start Running Through My Mind)*, for which he wrote both words and music. The tune was recorded by the popular Artie Shaw Orchestra on Victor 27719, beyond the ordinary because it featured a vocal by trumpeter "Hot Lips" Page. The flip side of the record offered an Artie Shaw original, *I Ask the Stars*, also a nice ballad. Neither song got much attention.

The Gene Austin bequest is not extensive, but it's impressive. *How Come You Do Me Like You Do; The Lonesome Road; When My Sugar Walks down the Street*; and *Ridin' Around in the Rain* comprise a short list, but the first three must be considered standards. The last was more than just an average hit in its days.

Austin died in Palm Springs, California, on January 24, 1972.

Abel Baer

Abel Baer was one of those composers who wrote songs that either became some of your all-time favorites, or ditties that you would prefer to forget. For example, he wrote *June Night,* one of the most delightful songs of the twenties, but he was also responsible for *I Miss My Swiss* and *My Mother's Eyes,* the tearjerker made forever infamous after countless renditions by George Jessel. Abel Baer was born in Baltimore, Maryland, on March 16, 1893. He started out to be a dentist, but was sidetracked by the First World War, and after it was over wound up leading a dance band. In 1920 he gravitated to New York City and went to work for a music publisher, with the inevitable result that he began to write songs himself.

In 1923 he collaborated with lyricist Cliff Friend on a tune that was introduced and featured by Sophie Tucker, *Mama Loves Papa,* and in the following year they hit again with *June Night,* this one plugged into popularity by the man with the battered top hat, Ted Lewis. At this point, Baer changed partners, and he teamed with L. Wolfe Gilbert for *I Miss My Swiss* (*My Swiss Miss Misses Me*), for which he must be forgiven, and still later, the tearjerker, *My Mother's Eyes,* which had the misfortune to be introduced by George Jessel in a movie. He adopted it as his own, and proceeded over the years to grind it into inanity by countless renditions. Baer and Gilbert also doodled around with things like *Lucky Lindy* and *Hello, Aloha, How Are You?,* but with the advent of the thirties Baer moved into the fast lane with a number of superior songs. With a variety of collaborators, including Dave Oppenheim, Charles Tobias, Sam M. Lewis, Stanley Adams, and George W. Meyer, Baer made the decade notable with such contributions as *It's the Girl* (1931); *Sweet Thing* (1935); *The Last Two Weeks in July* (1939); and to cap it all off, the song that made the Hit Parade for eighteen weeks in 1942, *There Are Such Things.* You can hear these for yourself on a few eminent 78 rpm contemporary discs such as Br 6150 by the Casa Loma Orchestra, on which Joe Hostetter vocalizes *It's the Girl*; Victor 25196, with Fats Waller and His Rhythm rendering *Sweet Thing* with authority and conviction; Decca 2770, on which "Bon Bon" Tunnell nostalgically recalls how it was during *The Last Two Weeks in July,* with Jan Savitt's Top Hatters; Victor 25486, with that great Benny Goodman band of 1936 backing Helen

Ward on *Gee, but You're Swell;* and finally Victor 27974, Tommy Dorsey's Orchestra with ol' Blue Eyes and the Pied Pipers doing *There Are Such Things*. Five records to make any songwriter proud.

Throughout his career, Abel Baer was an active protagonist for the rights of songwriters. As such he served on the ASCAP Board of Appeals for twelve years and as treasurer of the Songwriters of America for nineteen years. In 1955 he managed a stage show put together by ASCAP and the USO to entertain the armed forces in Germany and from 1955 to 1957 served as president of the American Guild of Authors and Composers.

He died in New York City on October 5, 1976.

Dave Barbour

Dave Barbour was born in Flushing, N.Y., on May 28, 1912. He attended the local schools and studied music privately. A fine rhythm guitarist, he started his professional career in small jazz bands like Wingy Manone's and Red Norvo's and then went on to work with the larger orchestras of Hal Kemp, Raymond Scott, and eventually Artie Shaw and Benny Goodman. It was during his tour with the Goodman band that he met vocalist Peggy Lee, and they were married. After Peggy Lee left Goodman to pursue a career as a star soloist, Dave Barbour led the groups that accompanied her, especially on recordings for Capitol records, and the couple combined in writing songs designed to showcase Peggy's intimate singing style. They shared equal credit for the words and music.

The clever *Mañana* was their most successful song, but they came close with *It's a Good Day* and *I Don't Know Enough about You.* To the large number of Peggy Lee fans, in which I include myself, some of the other titles are classics: *Just an Old Love of Mine; You Was Right, Baby; What More Can a Woman Do; Everything's Movin' Too Fast;* and *Don't Be So Mean, Baby*. The partnership came to an end when the couple divorced, and although Dave Barbour continued in music, leading bands, and even working in movies, he apparently did no more writing for the popular song market.

He died in Malibu, California, on December 11, 1965.

Harry Barris

Harry Barris is a name familiar to record collectors and those movie buffs concerned with Bing Crosby's early career, but even though he was responsible for several songs that have become part of the standard repertoire, it's safe to say that most people at this period of time have never heard of him. Barris was born in New York City on November 24, 1905, but grew up in Denver, where he attended public school. His musical talent developed early, and when he was only fourteen he was working as a professional pianist. When he was seventeen, he toured Asia with his own band.

In 1926 he teamed up with Al Rinker and Bing Crosby as a vocal feature attraction with the Paul Whiteman organization, the Rhythm Boys. As a vocal group they were undoubtedly the best of their era, and although the Crosby personality and vocal styling can be given much of the credit for this, Harry Barris was an equal factor because of the original material he wrote for the trio, some of which is still with us. *So the Bluebirds and the Blackbirds Got Together; What Price Lyrics;* and *Sweet Lil* were novelty tunes that helped the group to their well-earned success, but others of the period—*From Monday On* and *Mississippi Mud*—were big hits of the time, well remembered, and still played.

But it was in the early thirties that Barris really hit his stride. For some unknown reason he composed few songs compared to some other writers, but those he turned out for a few brief years are positive gems of the songwriting craft and typify the superior material that made the period the Golden Age of songwriting. Many of these are associated with Harry's friend Bing Crosby. They were invaluable tools in promoting the Groaner's success as a single—in particular, two songs, *I Surrender Dear* and *Wrap Your Troubles in Dreams*. Both of these are well known to everybody, and important numbers in the standard library of American popular songs.

Though possibly not as well remembered by the general public, Barris also wrote *It Must Be True; At Your Command; Lies; It Was So Beautiful; Let's Spend an Evening at Home; I'm Satisfied;* and *Thrilled*—all beautiful tunes that enjoyed considerable success in spite of their unusual character and originality.

In *American Popular Song* Alec Wilder singled out the delightful *It Must Be True* for this comment: "Whenever I see a song which seems free of strict commercialism, and has the quality of having been fun to write as opposed to having been ground out, I am impelled to mention it." Commenting on *It Was So Beautiful,* he said, "It's notey. But that's part of its charm. And played or sung not too fast, it's a very sweet song. The release is most unusual, being a series of octave drops which ascend chromatically each measure."

The songs of Harry Barris have always been great favorites with musicians and still continue to be, possibly because they were written by a fellow musician. Long before he joined the Rhythm Boys he was making a living as a professional pianist and for most of his life was a bandleader. The Rhythm Boys were featured in the Whiteman movie *The King of Jazz* (in my opinion the best thing in it), but afterwards they left Whiteman and went to work for Gus Arnheim, who had a very popular band at the prestigious Cocoanut Grove in Los Angeles. It was here Barris met Loyce Whiteman, who sang with the Arnheim band, and they eventually married. Also during this time, Bing Crosby began to build a career as a single, and this led to the breakup of the trio.

Harry Barris continued to write songs well into the thirties, scoring well with each new entry. Besides the recordings turned out by Crosby of Barris tunes like *I Surrender Dear; Let's Spend an Evening at Home; At Your Command;* and *Wrap Your Troubles in Dreams,* the Barris output was usually accorded very respectable treatment from contemporary bandleaders and recording artists. Following is a representative list.

Gus Arnheim Vic 22561 *It Must Be True* (vcl Bing Crosby) (1931)
Tom Coakley Vic 24610 *I'm Satisfied* (1934)
Abe Lyman Br 6142 *At Your Command* (1931)
Mildred Bailey Vic 22880 *Lies* (1931)
Ozzie Nelson Br 6347 *It Was So Beautiful* (1932)
Guy Lombardo *A Little Dutch Mill* Br 6781 (1934)
Henry King Col 3042-D *Thrilled* (1935)

Songwriting was only one facet of the Harry Barris personality. From time to time he worked as a vocalist, led dance bands, appeared on radio shows, and acted in movies, usually playing the part that came naturally to him, a musician or a bandleader. Of this stage of his career Roger Kinkle, in *The Complete Encyclopedia of Popular Music and Jazz,* wrote, "Barris played small, slick, jive-talking personality, fit perfectly Hollywood's idea of typical band musicians. Usually played role of rehearsal pianist, bandsman or bandleader. Better roles in *Hollywood Party* (1934), *Double or Nothing* and *Something to Sing About* (1937), *Some Like It Hot* (1939)." During World War II he accompanied comedian Joe E. Brown on overseas tours to entertain the troops and afterwards led a big band on a tour of one-nighters, featuring his wife, Loyce Whiteman, on vocals.

Harry remained active into the fifties. He died in Burbank, California, on December 13, 1952. Harry Barris—pianist, vocalist, entertainer, actor—but above all, songwriter. Look for him the next time you watch the late, late show, and remember him the next time you hear *Wrap Your Troubles in Dreams.*

William (Count) Basie

William (Count) Basie, also known as "the Kid from Red Bank," was born in that New Jersey town on August 21, 1904. His mother was his first music teacher, and later he took lessons from Fats Waller. He played in and led local groups for several years* and then began touring in vaudeville shows. In 1927 he found himself stranded in Kansas City and for a time played the organ in a theater there. A short time later he joined bassist Walter Page's Blue Devils and from there moved on to the well-established and popular Bennie Moten Kansas City Orchestra, which recorded for Victor. He worked with the band until Moten's death in 1935.

Organizing a small group, which later became the nucleus of his big band, he went into a place called the Reno Club, which had a radio wire, and it was during one broadcast that John Hammond, the jazz promoter, heard them. Through his efforts the band was brought to New York in 1936 and after some rough going managed a successful booking at the Savoy Ballroom. Meantime, in 1937 the band started to record for Decca, and in July of that year they waxed the Basie original that brought them to national attention and became the band's theme song, *One O'Clock Jump*. It was the start of a series of jazz instrumentals that were either written by the Count or on which he collaborated. Fans of the Basie band will have no trouble remembering *Every Tub; Jumpin' at the Woodside; John's Idea; Good Morning Blues; Blue and Sentimental; Basie Boogie; Swingin' the Blues; Miss Thing; Riff Interlude; Shorty George; Out the Window; Sent for You Yesterday; Red Bank Boogie;* and other titles less well known. Working with the Count as collaborators were Jimmy Rushing, Lester Young, Eddie Durham, Jerry Livingston, and Mack David. The latter two were involved with *Blue and Sentimental,* which the band recorded as a moody instrumental featuring the liquid tenor saxophone of Herschel Evans. Although the Basie compositions were always associated with the Basie band, they also attained wide popularity during the swing era and were frequently played by other bands.

Count Basie died in Hollywood, Florida, on April 26, 1984.

---

*In *Crazy Fingers,* my biography of bandleader Claude Hopkins, he mentions playing an audition against a Bill Basie group in Asbury Park, N.J. in 1925 (pp 11–12).

Billy Baskette

Billy Baskette, one of the early contributors to Tin Pan Alley's fame, was born in Henderson, Kentucky, on October 20, 1884. A man of many talents, he played brass bass (in a circus band) and performed as a dancer and pianist in stock companies and in vaudeville. When radio came along, he worked as an entertainer and became a staff composer for music firms in New York and Chicago. Most likely his most famous song is *Waitin' for the Evenin' Mail,* which can be heard in classic recorded renditions by Red Nichols; on a 1931 Brunswick by the Five Pennies, with a vocal by the ebullient Johnnie "Scat" Davis; and again on an early Capitol by Johnny Mercer. However, those of us with some longevity and long memories may recall that one of the hit tunes during World War I was *Goodby, Broadway, Hello, France;* and when Prohibition became the law of the land, Billy Baskette complained, *Everybody Wants a Key to My Cellar*. Billy's other songs have been lost in the mists of time, but I recall one of those sleepers from the thirties that I liked very much, *That's When I Learned to Love You.* It had the good fortune to be recorded by the hit maker of the era, Rudy Vallee.

Billy Baskette died in Culver City, California, on November 8, 1949.

Ray Bauduc

Drummer Ray Bauduc, acclaimed for his fine drumming and as a mainstay in the Bob Crosby band of the forties, was born in New Orleans, Louisiana, on June 18, 1906. He reached professional ability very early, and by age thirteen was playing drums in silent movie houses. Then he went on to play in jazz bands and for awhile was a member of the Scranton Sirens and the Dorsey brothers' Wild Canaries. Later on he played in the orchestras of Joe Venuti, Freddie Rich, and Ben Pollack. It was the Pollack crew that wound up as a cooperative unit fronted by Bob Crosby and became one of the name bands of the period. In the excellent rhythm section Bauduc was teamed with bassist Bob Haggart and guitarist and fellow New Orleans native Nappy Lamare. Bauduc and Haggart collaborated on several songs that were recorded by the band, especially the dixieland standard *Rampart Street Parade*. According to Haggart, they sketched the song out on a tablecloth in a restaurant, and when they left they took the tablecloth with them. They also developed the drums and bass routine that became *The Big Noise from Winnetka* and *Smokey Mary,* dedicated to a train of that name. Bauduc is also credited as the composer of *Louise, Louise; The Big Crash from China; Big Tom;* and *Mardi Gras Parade.*

Ray Bauduc died on January 8, 1988.

Phil Baxter

Phil Baxter was a well-known and popular bandleader in the Midwest and the South during the twenties and thirties. A native Texan, he was born in Navarro County, September 5, 1896, and died in Dallas, November 21, 1972. His band, the Texas Tommies, was a highly versatile group, playing straightforward jazz tempered by entertaining novelties. One musician, a highly talented showman and trombonist, Al Jennings, hailed from a town in Arkansas named Dumas, so Baxter wrote a novelty feature for him, *I'm a Ding Dong Daddy from Dumas.* The tune was a big success and led the way to the production of a number of hot dance tunes designed to showcase the bands. With his old friend Joe Haymes writing arrangements for the Ted Weems band in Chicago, it wasn't surprising that several of the Baxter compositions wound up as specialties for the Weems Orchestra. The first one, *Piccolo Pete,* as recorded for Victor, proved to be the biggest hit the band ever had and was followed by more Baxter titles: *Harmonica Harry* and *The One Man Band.* When Joe Haymes launched his own band a short time later, he continued to record Phil Baxter songs, including *Let's Have a Party* and *Uncle Joe's Music Store.*

Phil Baxter also had a ballad hit in 1931, the wistful *A Faded Summer Love,* and followed up with another in 1934, *Have a Little Dream on Me.* Of recent years the comparatively few sides the Baxter band recorded for the OKeh and Victor labels have become prized collector's items. Other Baxter compositions are *Going, Going, Gone; 'Leven Miles from Leavenworth; Smile for Me; Five Piece Band;* and *You're the Sweetest Girl.*

Leon Bix Beiderbecke

Legendary cornetist and pianist Bix Beiderbecke was born in Davenport, Iowa, on March 10, 1903. Mainly a self-taught musician, he started out on the piano but switched to the cornet when he was only fourteen. His subsequent career is one of the great stories of jazz. He has been the subject of books and movies, and his records are prized collector's items around the world and have been reissued many times over. Bix never wrote songs for the popular market, and it's actually due to the devotion and admiration of arranger Bill Challis, who is responsible for transcribing the Beiderbecke piano improvisations to paper, that we have them to appreciate.

The jazz standard *Davenport Blues,* recorded for the first time by Bix and His Rhythm Jugglers on the Gennett label in January of 1925, is Bix's earliest effort at composing. Since Bix was unable to read music at the time, it was most likely improvised at the session. Tommy Dorsey, who was one of the Jugglers, gave the tune its title. It wasn't copyrighted until 1927. Recorded many times since, it was featured on outstanding sides by Red Nichols, Bunny Berigan, Tommy Dorsey, and Adrian Rollini, now collector's items in their own right. *In a Mist* was recorded as a piano solo for the OKeh label by Bix under the title *Bixology,* in September 1927. It's the only one of his piano compositions he recorded. The other titles, *Flashes; Candlelights;* and *In the Dark,* were painstakingly transcribed to paper by Bill Challis as he listened to Bix improvise on the piano. As Bill told me many years ago, this wasn't easy because Bix never played the same phrase the same way twice, and Bill had a hard time persuading him to pick one he liked and stay with it.

Although they were written for the piano, these compositions have been orchestrated from time to time and recorded as instrumentals. Bunny Berigan, for instance, waxed all five Beiderbecke titles in two succeeding sessions for Victor in 1938, and prior to that, Red Norvo made *In a Mist* as a xylophone solo, accompanied by Benny Goodman, Artie Bernstein, and Dick McDonough on a Brunswick record in November 1933. A year later Frankie Trumbauer and his orchestra made it for the same company. In 1935 the incomparable Jess Stacy recorded *In the Dark* and *Flashes* as back-to-back piano solos first issued in England on the Parlophone label and then later on American Decca, and in 1939 he made *Candlelights* for Milt Gabler's Commodore label.

But it remained for that marvelous underrated genius from Wales, Dillwyn O. Jones, to showcase the complete Beiderbecke repertoire of originals, which he did on a Chiaroscuro LP (CR 112) in 1972. The album, *Davenport Blues,* was subtitled "Dill Jones Plays Bix." The producers of the record stated in the liner notes,

> Chiaroscuro Records is most appreciative of Bill Riddle's original suggestion that someone should get Dill Jones to record Bix Beiderbecke piano pieces. We feel that his interpretations are eminently successful and make available for the first time on one record all of Beiderbecke's piano compositions, as well as some songs associated with him.

Bix Beiderbecke died in New York City on August 6, 1931.

Bennie Benjamin

Bennie Benjamin was born in Christiansted, St. Croix, Virgin Islands, November 4, 1907; although this makes him a contemporary of many of the songwriters of the twenties and thirties, he had to wait until the forties to be recognized. He made his way to New York in 1927, studied banjo and guitar with Hy Smith, and then began to work in dance bands. With fellow collaborators Sol Marcus, George Weiss, Eddie Seiler, and Eddie Durham, working in various combinations, Benjamin tried repeatedly to get songs published without success, until *I Don't Want to Set the World on Fire* was accepted. The tune caught on, and resulted in the biggest-selling record the Tommy Tucker band ever had.

From that point on the team, working together or in pairs, was able to produce a number of hits—*Strictly Instrumental,* which became a big-selling record for the Harry James band; *When the Lights Go On Again (All over the World),* featured on a record by Vaughn Monroe; *Oh, What It Seemed to Be,* which received the Top Writers Award for 1946; *I Want to Thank Your Folks,* respectfully rendered by the King Cole Trio on Capitol; *Rumors Are Flying,* another award title; and *I Don't See Me in Your Eyes Anymore,* a better than average ballad that deserved more attention than it got. Bennie Benjamin and his friends continued to turn out songs, and Bennie and George Weiss struck paydirt twice in the fifties. Kay Starr's Capitol recording on *Wheel of Fortune* sold over a million copies and so did the Pattie Page rendition of *Cross over the Bridge.* Both songs seem indicative of the changing taste of the musical public.

Felix Bernard

Felix Bernard was born in Brooklyn, New York, on April 28, 1897. Like so many other songwriters he was a musical prodigy and after taking lessons from his father, went on to a professional career as a pianist at a very early age. He toured in vaudeville in both the United States and abroad and wrote special material for such headliners as Nora Bayes, Sophie Tucker, Eddie Cantor, and Al Jolson. Along the way he found time to work for music publishers, play in dance bands, and write and produce his own radio show.

One of his earliest songs has become an all-time standard and generated a 1919 million-seller record by Ben Selvin's Novelty Orchestra on Victor, and sheet music sales to match. However, the song, *Dardanella,* was involved in some controversy. As Robert Lissauer relates the story in his

Encyclopedia of Popular Music in America, the song was originally published under the title of *Turkish Tom Tom,* a piano rag composed by Johnny S. Black. Fred Fisher, who published the tune, wrote new lyrics and gave it a new title, but when the song appeared, composer Felix Bernard laid claim to the melody. By way of settlement, both Black and Bernard were given equal credit as composer, and Fisher for the lyrics. It can be safely assumed that all did very well on the proceeds. Bernard continued to compose, but considerable time elapsed before he had another hit—1934, to be exact, and the song is *Winter Wonderland,* with lyrics by Richard B. Smith. A hardy perennial, the tune has been recorded dozens of times and turns up every year as the Christmas season approaches. In 1941 lyric writer Raymond Klages teamed with Bernard to turn out one of the few memorable tunes of World War II vintage, *Twenty-one Dollars a Day—Once a Month,* a sharp reminder of the generous pay for an army draftee.

Felix Bernard died in Hollywood, California, October 10, 1944.

Ben Bernie

Ben Bernie, better known to two decades of loyal radio listeners as the Old Maestro and as leader of a popular dance band, is also recognized as a violinist and a composer. He was born in New York City, May 30, 1891, and attended City College and the New York College of Music. He organized his first dance band in 1922 and for a time toured with Maurice Chevalier. Then as time went on he became a well-known radio personality, with a broadcasting career that spanned over twenty years. As such, his name had a prime market value, and it appears on several major songs in collaboration with other recognized composers. Keeping in mind the fact that it was a common practice to credit a big-name bandleader as a cocomposer in order to take advantage of his popularity, nevertheless, the individual is entitled to the benefit of the doubt, and we can't overlook Ben Bernie's contribution to our musical heritage.

The two most outstanding titles are *Sweet Georgia Brown* and *Strange Interlude*. The first has become a standard, especially in the repertoires of jazz bands, and Ben shares composer credit with Maceo Pinkard and Ken Casey. Bernie's Orchestra introduced the song, and one of the rarest of sound films, estimated as dating to 1925, and now available on video tape,* shows the

**At the Jazz Band Ball,* Yazoo #514. Shanackie Corporation, 37 Clinton Street, Newton, N.J. 07860.

Bernie Orchestra playing *Sweet Georgia Brown,* featuring a sizzling saxophone chorus by the legendary Jack Pettis. *Strange Interlude* is one of those hauntingly beautiful ballads that characterized the early thirties, and this time Bernie shares credit for writing the lyrics with Walter Hirsch. The melody was composed by Phil Baker, better known as a comedian in Broadway musicals and for playing the accordion. His association with Bernie started when they toured vaudeville as a team. The title *Strange Interlude* was borrowed from the Eugene O'Neill play of that name, and the song did well in the heavy competition of 1932. It never achieved the status of a standard, but acquired a period of well-deserved longevity as the theme song of Bill McCune's popular dance band.

Bernie, Isham Jones, and Charles Newman are the composers of record of the 1932 hit *I Can't Believe It's True,* and this conflicts slightly with a memory I have held for many long years of something I heard Ben say on a radio broadcast during which he featured the song. Rather than taking credit himself, he said that his brother, Dave Bernie (also a bandleader), helped write the song, and that he, Ben, was inclined to go along with the song's title—"I Can't Believe It's True." Then again, memory can be tricky, and it's Ben and not Dave who gets official recognition with Charles Newman for the lyrics. Nobody, *but nobody,* helped Isham Jones write a song.

Who's Your Little Who-zis was a cute little ditty that was introduced by the Bernie band in 1931. It was composed by Al Goering, the pianist in the organization, and again Ben shared credit with Walter Hirsch for the words. He is also listed as a collaborator on a number of other titles, including *Holding My Honey's Hand; A Bowl of Chop Suey and Youey; After the Dance Was Over; Was Last Night the Last Night; Ain't That Marvelous (My Baby Loves Me);* and *I Can't Forget That You Forgot about Me.*

Ben Bernie was a highly respected and well-liked man, with a reputation for generosity and probity. He died in Beverly Hills, California, on October 20, 1943.

Buddy Bernier

Lyricist Buddy Bernier was born in Watertown, N.Y., on April 21, 1910. Although information about him is scarce, and his career not extensive, he wrote the lyrics to several important songs, and his work demonstrates superior talent. Most likely the best-known title is *Poinciana (Song of the Tree),* a collaboration with composer Nat Simon. This 1943 entry received first-class treatment and resulted in hit records by Bing Crosby, Benny

Carter, and especially David Rose, who showcased the tune in an outstanding instrumental arrangement for his orchestra. Bernier wrote the words to *Hurry Home,* a 1935 Joseph Meyer composition that also rated full representation on records, notably by the Bob Crosby band on Decca, Jan Savitt on Bluebird, Kay Kyser on Brunswick, Al Donahue on Vocalion, and Sammy Kaye on Victor. With Bob Emmerich, Bernier had three successful songs. In 1937 it was *The Big Apple,* a tune tied in with a dance of the same name, and in the following year, *This Time It's Real,* a pleasant ballad that got respectful treatment by the Tommy Dorsey Orchestra and vocalist Jack Leonard. Tommy Dorsey also had the main recording of the 1939 hit *Our Love,* with bandleader Larry Clinton sharing composing credit with Bernier and Emmerich.

In 1948 Bernier teamed with composer Jerry Brainin, and they turned out the title song for a movie, *The Night Has a Thousand Eyes.* This is not to be confused with an earlier song with the same name, by Irving Taylor and Vic Mizzy, which was recorded by Carl Ravazza and his orchestra for Bluebird in 1940. Oddly enough, the reference books have compounded this mistake by attributing the Ravazza record to the later song by Bernier and Brainin and completely omitting any reference to the Taylor–Mizzy composition. In 1950 Vaughn Monroe recorded *Bamboo,* written by Buddy Bernier and Nat Simon, and this appears to be the last of Bernier's output.

Irving Bibo

Irving Bibo was born in San Francisco, California, August 22, 1889, and died in West Los Angeles, California, on May 2, 1962, but into those seventy-two years he packed several careers. For awhile he headed his own song-publishing firm. He wrote songs for Broadway shows and movies and special material for stars like Marlene Dietrich, Ann Sheridan, Jim Burke, and Billy Gilbert. He was a member of the American Guild of Authors and Composers and director of ASCAP from 1924 to 1927. In the meantime he wrote some songs, collaborating with Al Piantadosi, Leo Wood, and Don George. An early effort (1921) with words by Leo Wood had a one-word name for a title that was almost magical in its popularity with the post–World War I public, *Cherie.* In addition, the hit recording was by the big name in orchestras of the period, Paul Whiteman on Victor.

Writing both words and music, Irving Bibo came up with a song that pleased the hit maker of the early thirties, Rudy Vallee, who recorded it and plugged it on his radio broadcasts. The song has a pleasing melody, and the lyrics were in the sentimental mode of the day. The title is *Huggable Kissable You.* Bibo wrote other ballads for a time and then began to specialize in songs for schools and colleges. Among these are *The Stanford Scalp Song; Sing UCLA;* and *Fight On Michigan State.*

Eubie Blake

Eubie Blake, who lived to be one hundred years old, was born in Baltimore, Maryland, on February 7, 1883. A graduate of New York University, he also studied music privately and was an accomplished pianist and organist. As a teenager he played in sporting houses and for rent parties, theaters, and vaudeville. While working in vaudeville he met and teamed with Noble Sissle, who sang in a high tenor, and after World War I they toured the United States with Jim Europe's band. With Noble Sissle writing the words and Eubie Blake the music, they composed the score for the Broadway show "Shuffle Along," which had a long run and included the hit *I'm Just Wild about Harry*—a tune adopted many years later as a campaign song for Harry Truman. Sissle and Blake continued to write, but split up in 1928. In 1930 Blake collaborated with lyricist Andy Razaf for the stage show "Blackbirds of 1930," and although it only lasted for twenty-six performances, the score included the perennial *Memories of You* and the excellent *You're Lucky to Me.*

Along with writing popular songs, Eubie Blake composed a number of piano rags, but without any doubt he will be best remembered for the three great songs mentioned here. Born in the month of February, he died in the same month only five days after his birthday, on February 12, 1983.

Ralph Blane

Lyricist Ralph Blane Hunsecker, who wrote songs as Ralph Blane, was born in Broken Arrow, Oklahoma, July 26, 1914. He attended elementary schools in Broken Arrow but graduated from high school in Tulsa and attended Northwestern University. A vocalist, he met his songwriting partner Hugh Martin when they were both in the cast of the Broadway show "Hooray for What," in 1937. They formed a vocal quartet, the Martins, and sang on Fred Allen's radio program, also providing background for Mickey Rooney and Judy Garland in *The Wizard of Oz.* The team began writing songs and produced a hit score for the 1941 Broadway musical "Best Foot Forward." They then moved on to Hollywood and wrote for the movies. Blane was twice nominated for Academy Awards. As time went on, he also collaborated with other composers, including Harry Warren, Harold Arlen, and Josef Myrow.

Blane's best-known songs were written with Hugh Martin, especially those for "Best Foot Forward," and "Meet Me in St. Louis." *Ev'ry Time* was introduced by Maureen Cannon in the 1941 stage production of "Best Foot Forward" then repeated by Rosemary Lane. Virginia Weidler sang it in the 1943 movie version. Nancy Walker, who played in both, recorded it for the Bluebird label. Two other successful songs came from the same show and film, *Buckle Down, Winsocki* and *Shady Lady Bird.* The Benny Goodman band recorded them both. Other recordings were made by Art Jarrett and Fred Waring, of the first title.

Blane and Martin hit it big again in 1947, with three songs in the movie *Meet Me in St. Louis,* starring Judy Garland, *The Trolley Song; The Boy Next Door;* and the delightful *Have Yourself a Merry Little Christmas.* Judy Garland recorded them all. *Pass That Peace Pipe,* with Roger Edens helping in the composition of the melody with Hugh Martin, was a 1947 entry heard in the movie version of "Good News." It was nominated for an Academy Award. Bing Crosby and Margaret Whiting had the top records.

Ralph Blane continued to write well into the fifties.

Rube Bloom

Rube Bloom was born in New York City on April 24, 1902, and died there March 30, 1976. His education was confined to public schools, but his musical talent was evident at an early age; he toured vaudeville as an accompanist to singers. If for no other reason, he will always occupy a special niche in the annals of jazz for half-a-dozen sides issued on the classic black Columbia label by Rube Bloom and His Bayou Boys, which featured Benny Goodman, Manny Klein, Adrian Rollini, and Tommy Dorsey. As might be expected with such a lineup, these are gems that will remain bright forever, but they present only one aspect of a man who was a very talented musician in his own right and an accomplished composer of material in both the popular and semiclassical veins. Rube Bloom was also a very successful freelance pianist who can be heard on records as a soloist (quite often playing his own compositions), backing some of the famous vocalists of the twenties and thirties, and as a member of some of the most famous recording groups in jazz, such as the Tennessee Tooters, the Red Heads, the Sioux City Six, and Joe Venuti's Blue Six.

Many of his compositions were written for the piano—*Soliloquy; Spring Fever; Sapphire; Serenata; Silhouette*—and his prize-winning piece written in 1928, *Song of the Bayou,* was much admired in the early thirties for its moody musical portrayal of the bayou country. But Bloom wasn't confined to turning out such serious material, as attested to by his collaboration with Harry Woods on *The Man from the South,* one of the most frantic sides by the Bayou Boys. He could also be melancholy, as with the 1934 standard *Out in the Cold Again,* one of the year's biggest hits, or predicting the coming age of swing with *Truckin',* which appeared in 1935. In 1937, 1938, and 1939 he had top contenders with *Is This Gonna Be My Lucky Summer* (recorded by Tommy Dorsey's Clambake Seven, with Pee Wee Erwin, on Victor 25610); *Feelin' High and Happy* (on Victor 25840 by Benny Goodman with Martha Tilton); *Don't Worry 'Bout Me* (on Vocalion 4734 by Count Basie with Helen Humes). In 1940 he came up with a mild blockbuster, *Fools Rush In,* and the following year offered *Good for Nothing, Joe.* Bing Crosby featured a song written by Rube Bloom with Harry Ruby (Decca 23469, *Give Me the Simple Life,* with Jimmy Dorsey's Orchestra and Lou Carter on piano, 1945), and Woody Herman did full justice to the 1947 *Maybe You'll Be There,* a beautiful ballad. Other Rube Bloom compositions include *Lost in a Dream; Day In Day Out; Here's to My Lady; Got No Time; I Can't Face the Music; Stay on the Right Side, Sister; The Ghost of Smokey Joe; Love is a Merry-Go-Round; What Goes Up Must Come Down.* All very worthy contributions to the American song bag.

Clay Boland

If Hollywood ever gets around to making good musicals again, there's always the remote chance that somebody with an eye and ear for quality will rediscover the life and career of Clay Boland, because here was a man of many dimensions. His songwriting activity was brief but brilliant and at that was most likely more of an avocation than a full-time occupation, because Clay Boland was a certified practicing dentist—among other things we will speak of later on. He was born in Olyphant, Pennsylvania, on October 25, 1903. He studied dentistry at Scranton and Pennsylvania Universities and then went on to postgraduate work at Bryn Mawr and Pennsylvania Hospitals. While in college, just to keep from being bored by the inactivity, it would seem, he taught himself how to play piano and worked in dance bands.

Possibly for similar reasons, in 1936 he began directing and writing songs for the University of Pennsylvania's Mask and Wig Show, and one of his first contributions for the production "Red Rumba" was a little gem called *Too Good to Be True*. This was promptly slated for immortality with an outstanding recording by the Benny Goodman Trio featuring Helen Ward on the vocal. The original Victor 78 rpm record was reissued on Volume II of the complete LP collections of Goodman. Boland was responsible for both words and music for *Too Good to Be True,* but he teamed with lyricist Moe Jaffe later in the year for the Mask and Wig show "This Mad Whirl," which resulted in two more excellent songs, *An Apple a Day* and *Something Happened to Me*. Hal Kemp's band with Skinny Ennis recorded them back-to-back on Brunswick 7775. The following year Jaffe and Boland had only one entry, another one of those sleepers that made the thirties great but went almost entirely ignored. Nevertheless, Tommy Dorsey knew a good song when he heard one, and the composers knew a helpful hand when it was offered, so Tommy's name is listed as one of the writers of *The Morning After*. The Dorsey orchestra recorded the song for Victor, but Lennie Hayton, his piano, and his orchestra turned out a very tasty platter for Decca.

In 1938 Clay Boland found a new partner in Bickley Reichner, another talented gentleman who dabbled in songwriting in his spare time, and they started things off with *Stop Beatin' around the Mulberry Bush,* which received loyal treatment by Tommy Dorsey and his band, and then followed through with a whole series of tunes, all of which were well received and recorded by the top artists of the day. *The Gypsy in My Soul,* featured in the Mask and Wig production "Fifty-Fifty," with words by Moe Jaffe, ran the gamut of recording labels with discs by Jan Savitt, Mildred Bailey, and Margaret Whiting, among others. *I Live the Life I Love,* another solo effort by Boland, was waxed by Jan Savitt, with the usual appealing vocal by Bon Bon, and by Richard Himber, with Stuart Allen delivering the words. Both were recorded on Victor. *There's No Place Like Your Arms,* a "Bix" Reichner collaboration, rated top honors, with recordings by Savitt, Tommy Dorsey, and—strange as it may seem—Arthur Godfrey. *When I Go A-Dreamin',* a product of the same pair, fared even better, with Martha Tilton singing and the Benny Goodman band swinging it, plus other renditions by Kay Kyser, Jan Savitt, and the popular singer Dick Todd. Also meeting with some popular approval in 1938 were *Midnight on the Trail; Button, Button; Ya Got Me;* and *Stompin' at the Stadium.* Altogether, Clay Boland had nine songs published in one year, no mean accomplishment for any writer.

Two entries in 1939 attained rather unique status. *Stop! It's Wonderful* was picked by bandleader Orrin Tucker as a logical follow-up to his hit record of *Oh, Johnny,* featuring vocalist Wee Bonnie Baker, and *How I'd Like to be with You in Bermuda,* a very attractive idea and song, made its debut along with Glenn Miller as his band's first recording for the Bluebird label. Two other Boland songs came out that year, *When I Climb Down from My Saddle* and *Delightful Delirium. Tell Me at Midnight* was the final offering by Boland and Reichner, published in 1940 and recorded by the still faithful Tommy Dorsey with a vocal by the new boy in the band, Frank Sinatra. Besides the songs mentioned above, Clay Boland is credited with the following: *Havana; I Like It Here; Holiday; Not So Long Ago; I've Got My Eye on You;* and *Christmas Eve.*

At this point Clay Boland's efforts took a more serious turn. He served in the navy as a commander during WWII, and as a captain in the Korean War. He died in Queens, New York, on July 23, 1963.

Brooks Bowman

The story of Brooks Bowman is a brief and tragic one. The tragedy applies not only to Brooks Bowman, who was cheated out of what every indication foretold as a brilliant career, but to all of us who were deprived of his great talent. He was born in Cleveland, Ohio, on October 21, 1913. He first attended Stanford University and then moved on to Princeton University. As a senior he wrote three songs for the Princeton Triangle Show "Stags at Bay," a 1935 production. All three songs were successful—*Love and a Dime; Will Love Find a Way;* and *East of the Sun*—but the last named was a big hit and went on to become a standard. Bowman's exceptional talent was instantly recognized, and he was offered a contract to write songs for the movies after he graduated. On the way to California he was killed in an automobile accident.

He died in Garrison, New York, October 17, 1937, just four days before his twenty-fourth birthday.

James Brockman

James Brockman was born on December 8, 1886. He was educated at the Cleveland Conservatory and in private study and, like many of his peers, got his early training in the entertainment world in vaudeville and musicals. From there it was customary to step to working with a song publisher and eventually to Hollywood. Among his early efforts was participation in the lyrics for the big hit of 1919, *I'm Forever Blowing Bubbles.* The music for this song was written by John W. Kellette, but the words are credited to a

"Jean Kenbrovin." It seems that no less than three men claimed rights to them, with the result that their names, James Kendis, James Brockman, and Nat Vincent, were condensed into "Kenbrovin." It's safe to assume that the *Bubbles* song generated enough money to keep everybody happy.

Feather Your Nest, a 1920 entry, was another cooperative venture, with both words and music credits shared by James Kendis, James Brockman, and Howard Johnson. Brockman alone, however, was responsible for the words to the most enduring of the songs he was associated with, *Down Among the Sheltering Palms,* which dates from 1915 and was composed by Abe Olman. This song was revived by Keenan Wynn in the movie *That Midnight Kiss* in 1949 and again as the title song of another movie starring Gloria DeHaven, Mitzi Gaynor, and William Lundigan in 1952. The 1959 movie *Some Like It Hot* was the last time the song was featured in a film, but it took on the added dimension of jazz immortality with a Decca recording by Eddie Condon and His Orchestra, a session that included Wild Bill Davison, Jack Teagarden, Pee Wee Russell, Gene Schroeder, Morey Raymond, and Johnny Blowers.

James Brockman died in Los Angeles on May 22, 1967.

Harry Brooks

Pianist-composer Harry Brooks was born in Homestead, Pennsylvania, on September 20, 1895, and if anybody deserves to be included in this book as an "unsung" songwriter, it would be hard to find a more worthy candidate, as you will see. Details of his career are sparse, but it appears that he graduated from high school, took private music lessons from a Walter Spriggs, and then went to work as a pianist in dance bands. He also functioned as a staff composer for music publishing firms. One of his early composing efforts was a song called *Saturday,* with lyrics by Sidney D. Mitchell, published in 1921. It was introduced by the vaudeville star Nora Bayes in a musical revue called "Snapshots of 1921," and she recorded it for Columbia. It's interesting that there is no mention of this collaboration in the biographical sketch for Sidney D. Mitchell in the *ASCAP Biographical Dictionary.*

It's likely that Brooks continued to write songs during the twenties, but 1929 was the banner year that should have established his reputation. Along with Andy Razaf, who wrote the words, Brooks is credited as cocomposer with Fats Waller of two very famous songs, *Ain't Misbehavin* and *Black and Blue,* both of which were part of the score for the musical "Hot Chocolates." Two other songs were included, *Song of the Cotton Fields* and *Sweet*

Savannah Sue. The latter tune enjoyed quite a success in its own right, rating contemporary recordings by Louis Armstrong, Mill's Hotsy Totsy Gang, Fats Waller (as a piano solo), and Fess Williams. Without any intention of diminishing the well-deserved reputation of Fats Waller it must be pointed out that there is a mystery here. Roger Kinkle in Volume I, *Music Year by Year* of his wonderful work *The Complete Encyclopedia of Popular Music and Jazz 1900–1950* lists Andy Razaf as writer of the book and lyrics for "Hot Chocolates," the revue staged at Connie's Inn, the Harlem nightclub. Fats Waller and Brooks share composing credit. However, Brooks isn't even mentioned in connection with the show *or* the tunes in *Ain't Misbehavin'*, the Eddie Kirkeby biography of Fats, nor in *Fats Waller,* by Maurice Waller and Anthony Calabrese.

Although the foregoing indicates that Brooks had nothing whatever to do with "Hot Chocolates," or with writing the songs that were featured in it, his name appears on the copyrights, and such being the case he rates part of the glory for writing some important songs. Not only that, but he went on to write more songs. One, a 1939 collaboration with two very respected writers, Irving Taylor and J. Russel Robinson, was *Swing, Mr. Charlie,* a bouncy item recorded by Bunny Berigan and His Boys for Vocalion; Judy Garland, backed by Bob Crosby's band; and Louis "King" Garcia on Bluebird, with Adrian Rollini and Joe Marsala in the lineup. Other titles penned by Brooks include *Low Tide; Rockin' in a Rockin' Chair; When the Sun Sets South; Strictly from Dixie;* and *On the Loose.*

Harry Brooks died in Teaneck, New Jersey, on June 22, 1970.

Shelton Brooks

Shelton Brooks, composer of a trio of songs that have become all-time standards in the catalog of jazz, was born in Amesburg, Ontario, May 4, 1886. At an early age he gravitated to Detroit, working as a pianist in cafés. From there he went into vaudeville, touring the United States and Canada for what must be something of a record, forty-five years. In 1923 he was with Lew Leslie's Blackbirds, touring Europe and playing a command performance for King George and Queen Mary.

He wrote songs for Nora Bayes, Al Jolson, and Sophie Tucker, and it was the last-named performer who adopted *Some of These Days* as her personal song and over the years plugged it into one of the best-known popular compositions. It was published in 1910, with words and music by Shelton Brooks, and he repeated the feat again with the 1917 offering *Darktown Strutters Ball.*

Sophie Tucker is again mentioned as helping the song become a hit. The third Shelton Brooks standard is a favorite of jazz bands, *Walkin' the Dog*. This time Brooks shares composing credits with the unknown Guy Shriglev. Other titles include *All Night Long; Jean; You Ain't Talking to Me; Honey Gal;* and *If I Were a Bee and You Were a Red-Red Rose.*

Still performing, in later years Shelton Brooks was a member of Ken Murray's Blackouts. He died in Los Angeles on September 6, 1973.

Lew Brown

Lyricist Lew Brown, at one important stage of his prolific career a member of the famed songwriting team of DeSylva, Brown, and Henderson, collaborated with other composers both before and after this association. Only a few writers, it is safe to say, have their names on more hit songs. He was born in Odessa, Russia, on December 10, 1893. His parents brought him to the United States when he was only five years old, and they settled in New York City, where the boy attended DeWitt Clinton High School. As a teenager he began writing parodies and lyrics and had his first hit at age nineteen in a collaboration with veteran composer Albert Von Tilzer on the 1912 song *I'm the Lonesomest Gal in Town.* This durable ditty was recorded by the excellent vocalist Teddy Grace on Decca 3428 in the forties, backed by an all-star group that included Bobby Hackett and Don Watt, and in the fifties by Kay Starr for Capitol.

In 1916 Brown and George W. Meyer wrote a song called *If You Were the Only Girl.* In the same year Clifford Grey and Nat D. Aver composed *If You Were the Only Girl in the World,* which was revived and popularized by Rudy Vallee in the thirties. One of those strange circumstances that seem to be part of the songwriting business. Brown and Albert Von Tilzer continued to work together for several years, with a hit song for each one. In 1919 it was *Oh! By Jingo* and in 1920, *Chili Bean* (not to be confused with *Jelly Bean (He's a Curbstone Cutie),* another entry for the same year) and *I Used to Love You (But It's All Over),* a vengeful sentiment enthusiastically delineated by George Brunies and His Jazz Band on Commodore 606 in 1946. *Dapper Dan,* the last title in the Von Tilzer collaboration, came out in 1921 and was recorded by the contemporary Joseph Samuels Jazz Band on OKeh. Seventeen years later, Bob Howard revived it on a Decca recording in 1938.

In 1923 Brown wrote the words for *Last Night on the Back Porch (I Loved Her Best of All).* Recorded by Paul Whiteman's Orchestra, and the novelty duo of Jones & Hare, the song was very popular. The music was composed by a man named Carl Schraubstader, a businessman who apparently never wrote another song. Another unusual combination in 1924 resulted in the all-time favorite *Shine*. The music was composed by bandleader Ford Dabney, and the lyrics are credited to Brown and Cecil Mack. Robert A. King and Ray Henderson were Brown's other partners for *Why Did I Kiss That Girl?* The association with Henderson appears to have started earlier, when they submitted a song, *Georgette,* to the "Greenwich Village Follies of 1922," and it seems to have worked out well, because they produced another hit in 1925, *Don't Bring Lulu*. Billy Rose shared lyrics credit with Brown on this one. Brown, however, still freelancing, teamed with composer Cliff Friend and lyricist Sidney Clare on *Then I'll Be Happy* that same year, and Clare and Brown also produced *I'd Climb the Highest Mountain* in 1926, sharing equal credit for both words and music. Then, as though just to make sure everybody shared in the pie, Lew Brown joined with Cliff Friend on *I'm Tellin' the Birds, I'm Tellin' the Bees.*

Clare and Brown combined with composer Harry Warren on the 1927 tune *One Sweet Letter from You*. Meanwhile, in 1925 Buddy DeSylva, a successful lyricist in his own right, had joined Brown and Henderson to submit a score to "George White's Scandals of 1925." Nothing great resulted from this first effort, but for the "Scandals of 1926" the team hit three home runs, *Birth of the Blues; Black Bottom;* and *Lucky Day*. From that point on until 1931 the team of DeSylva, Brown, and Henderson was a major factor in the world of popular music, writing for stage shows, movies, and turning out one hit after another. (*See* Buddy DeSylva; Ray Henderson).

In 1931 Buddy DeSylva left the team to go into movie producing, but Lew Brown and Ray Henderson continued to work together and turned in an outstanding group of tunes for "George White's Scandals of 1931," all of which were popular hits of the day: *My Song; This Is the Missus; The Thrill Is Gone; Life Is Just a Bowl of Cherries;* and *That's Why Darkies Were Born.* Of course, it didn't hurt that a member of the show's cast was Rudy Vallee, who proceeded to plug the tunes on his radio broadcasts and record most of them. Brown and Henderson wrote for "Hot-Cha," a stage show which featured comedian Bert Lahr, the following year and scored again with two outstanding songs, *There I Go Dreaming Again* and *You Can Make My Life a Bed of Roses*. In 1933 it was "Strike Me Pink," this one starring the irrepressible Jimmy Durante, and more hits: *Strike Me Pink; Restless;* and *Let's Call It a Day*. The score included two other good tunes too: *Love and Rhythm* and *It's Great to Be Alive*.

In 1934 the long-term partners parted company. Brown and Harry Akst wrote the score for the show "Calling All Stars," and Ray Henderson worked with Ted Koehler for "Say When." Both scores, though adequate, were not exceptional. Brown went on to write for movie musicals and in 1937 penned the great standard *That Old Feeling*. His final composition, released in 1950, bore the melancholy title, *On the Outgoing Tide*.

Lew Brown died in New York City on February 5, 1958.

Nacio Herb Brown

The name Brown, like Smith and Jones, is so common that a person tends to get lost in the crowd, so it is understandable why a caring parent might dub an infant Nacio in order to make him stand out among the myriad Browns of the world. The sad truth is that in this case it was only partly successful. Nacio Herb Brown was a very successful songwriter, but so was Lew Brown, lyricist in the famous team of DeSylva–Brown–Henderson, and through the years people have been mistaking one for the other. It doesn't help the situation, either, that Nacio Herb Brown wrote some songs in collaboration with Buddy DeSylva. Nevertheless, Nacio Herb Brown wrote a number of memorable songs, many of them well-known standards, and is entitled to stand alone in the rank of songwriters who have made outstanding contributions to our musical heritage.

He was born February 22nd, 1896, in the little town of Deming, New Mexico, but his family moved to Los Angeles while he was still a youngster, and he grew up there. He learned to play piano and became an accompanist, making several road tours in that capacity, and tried his hand at songwriting. He did fairly well with two tunes in the early twenties, *Coral Sea* and the perennial *When Buddha Smiles,* and again in 1927 with a novelty favored by piano players, *Doll Dance;* but it wasn't until 1929 that he hit his stride and became one of the most prolific composers turning out material for Hollywood musicals. In that year alone he had four hits in the movie *Broadway Melody*—the title song; *You Were Meant for Me; The Wedding of the Painted Doll;* and *The Boy Friend.* That same year *Singin' in the Rain* appeared in the movie *Hollywood Revue of 1929. Chant of the Jungle* was the hit of *Untamed,* and *Pagan Love Song* entered immortality as the theme of *The Pagan.*

From then on Brown turned out a steady stream of superior songs year after year. Here are some you may remember: *The Moon Is Low; Should I?; Eadie Was a Lady; You're an Old Smoothie; Love Song of the Nile; Temptation; Beautiful Girl; All I Do Is Dream of You; You Are My Lucky Star; I've Got a Feelin' You're Foolin; Yours and Mine; Smoke Dreams; You*

Stepped Out of a Dream; Love Is Where You Find It. His last effort was *Make 'Em Laugh* performed by Donald O'Connor for the movie *Singin' in the Rain* in 1952, the famous vehicle for Gene Kelly, which utilized Brown's old hit as the title song and also featured a number of his other songs. Nacio Herb Brown died in San Francisco on September 28, 1964.

Alfred Bryan

Pioneer lyrics-writer Alfred Bryan was born in Brantford, Ontario, Canada, on September 15, 1871. He received his early education in parochial schools and while still a young man went to work as a staff writer for various New York publishing firms. Later on in his long career, he wrote for Warner Brothers in California. Bryan wrote the words to dozens of songs with a wide variety of composers. He was especially active in the early years of the century, beginning in 1904, when he collaborated on what must have been a stinging sensation, *When the Bees Are in the Hive,* with composer Kerry Mills. From that point on he had songs published every year until 1918. Although most of them have been forgotten, a couple have survived, notably *Peg O' My Heart,* written with Fred Fisher in 1913, revived in 1927 and now considered a standard, and the still earlier (1910) *Come, Josephine, in My Flying Machine,* also a Fred Fisher melody, which has achieved respect as a vintage example of the era. A pre-World War I title, *I Didn't Raise My Boy to Be a Soldier,* with composer Al Piantadosi in 1915, expressed a commonly held opinion and enjoyed considerable success. It also had problems, as so many of the early songs did, concerning rights to the melody. A composer named Cohalen sued for plagiarism and won. Later, when America was overcome by patriotic fervor, Bryan's lyrics underwent a lot of criticism.

Bryan continued to produce prolifically, and in 1925 he and George W. Meyer wrote *Brown Eyes (Why Are You Blue),* which offered a catchy melody along with clever lyrics and was one of the hits of that year; and two years later he teamed with the other Meyer, Joseph, for *Blue River.* This has achieved a measure of immortality by having the good fortune to be recorded by the Jean Goldkette Orchestra, with Bix Beiderbecke in the band and an arrangement by Bill Challis. Bryan's term writing for Hollywood is represented by the 1929 song from the movie *Drag, My Song of the Nile,* with George M. Meyer, and *Miss Wonderful,* from the 1930 movie *Paris.* The Eddie Ward tune *Miss Wonderful,* a sprightly thing, was appropriately delivered by the great Ted Weems organization of the period, with a vocal by Parker Gibbs. *Lonesome Lover,* with music by James V. Monaco, was another successful title for that year, nicely rendered by Bert Lown's Orchestra and vocalist Elmer Feldkamp on Victor 22602.

Bryan had two more fine songs in the thirties. *Give Me Your Affection, Honey,* a 1931 song, with a cooperative melody by Carmen Lombardo and Pete Wendling, for some strange reason was never recorded by the Guy Lombardo Orchestra. Nevertheless, it was a worthy contender for popularity in that highly competitive year when good songs were the norm, not the exception. Then, in 1933, Bryan and Lou Handman offered *Puddin' Head Jones,* a pleasing novelty that struck the fancy of Rudy Vallee, who proceeded to record it and plug it into popularity. *Wintertime Dreams,* published in 1936 and written with Felix Bernard, appears to be Alfred Bryan's last effort and from all indications was largely ignored. I'm sure, however, that by then Bryan, with over fifty songs to his credit, was beyond worrying about such things.

Alfred Bryan died in Gladstone, New Jersey, on April 1, 1958.

Gene Buck

Gene Buck, a charter member of ASCAP and a man with an illustrious career in show business, was born in Detroit, Michigan, on August 8, 1885. A talented artist and designer, he started out designing sheet music covers. In 1907 he moved to New York to design and direct a stage presentation for Lillian Russell and from there moved on to work as chief writer and assistant to Florenz Ziegfeld. From 1912 until 1926 he directed and originated shows for Ziegfeld. The list of his collaborators reads like a "Who's Who" of the most distinguished members of the musical world—David Stamper, Rudolf Friml, Jerome Kern, Mischa Elman, Fritz Kreisler, Augustus Thomas, Werner Janssen, James Hanley, Ray Hubbell, Victor Herbert, Louis Hirsch. However, most of the songs they wrote were incidental to the shows they were featured in—especially the yearly editions of Ziegeld's "Follies." Probably the best known is *Hello, Frisco,* a collaboration with David Stamper from the "Follies of 1915." The song commemorated the new coast-to-coast telephone service. *Have a Heart,* written with Jerome Kern, was introduced in the 1916 edition. *Sally, Won't You Come Back* registered a fair success in 1921, even to the point of being recorded by the man with the battered top hat, Ted Lewis.

After leaving Ziegfeld in 1926, Gene Buck went on to produce shows in the United States and England. He died in Great Neck, New York, on February 25, 1957.

Walter Bullock

Lyricist Walter Bullock was born in Shelburn, Indiana, on May 6, 1907, and attended DePauw University. He started writing for the movies in 1936 and collaborated with many of the top composers. Two of the songs he wrote in that first year, *Magnolias in the Moonlight,* with Victor Schertzinger, and *When Did You Leave Heaven?,* a collaboration with Richard Whiting, were well received. In the following year he wrote the words to Harold Spina's melody for *I Still Love to Kiss You Goodnight* and Allie Wrubel's *The You and Me That Used to Be*. Although his most prolific year was 1938, and the songs were important in the movies they were in, it wasn't until 1940 that Bullock shared credit for more big songs. That year he and Jule Styne won an Academy Award nomination for *Who Am I?,* and teaming again with Allie Wrubel, Bullock scored well with *Where Do I Go from You?,* which was recorded on all the major record labels.

Walter Bullock continued to write for the movies, but again the songs were of local interest. He died in Los Angeles, California, on August 19, 1953.

Joe Burke

Joe Burke was a product of Pennsylvania from start to finish. He was born in Philadelphia on March 18, 1884, was educated at the University of Pennsylvania, and died in Upper Darby, on June 9, 1950. As we have noticed so often with songwriters, Burke served his apprenticeship in New York publishing houses and then started his own career as a composer in the midtwenties—1925, to be exact—and made a deep impression with two immediate hits, *Oh, How I Miss You Tonight* and *Yearning*. If you don't remember these tunes, dig into your Tommy Dorsey reissues for *Yearning,* which the band recorded in 1938; a friendly collector may have a copy of Dick Robertson's Decca 1951 recording of *Oh, How I Miss You Tonight.*

Nothing else very exciting came from Burke's pen, however, until 1929, when he wrote for the movie *Gold Diggers of Broadway* and once again had twin hits, *Tiptoe Through the Tulips with Me* and *Painting the Clouds with Sunshine. Tiptoe Through the Tulips with Me* was the big song for crooner-guitarist Nick Lucas in the movie and was a respectable ditty until self-styled "Tiny Tim" came along in the seventies and turned it into a caricature. Nevertheless, Burke's estate probably collected the royalties without complaint. *Painting the Clouds with Sunshine,* on the other hand, picked up a prestigious discography. They seemed to like the song particularly well in England, and it was recorded by the crack Bert Ambrose band, with Sylvester Ahola leading the brass team, and by the Rhythmic Eight, a recording group that also included Ahola, along with fellow American Danny Polo. On this side of the big puddle, the California Ramblers made sure they did justice to both tunes, recording them twice; once for the Harmony label and again for Edison. As a matter of fact, they made two versions of *Painting the Clouds with Sunshine* for Edison, and both were issued. Sammy Fain made records as the Crooning Composer, and one of them was *Painting the Clouds with Sunshine.* Other records included a Jean Goldkette coupling directed by Victor Young and a studio group for Grey Gull.

Burke continued to write for movies, and his songs enjoyed moderate success. He seemed especially lucky with waltzes (*Dancing with Tears in My Eyes; The Kiss Waltz; Carolina Moon; Many Happy Returns of the Day*), but in 1935 he had another big one, *Moon over Miami,* along with two others you may remember, *A Little Bit Independent* and *On Treasure Island.* In 1936 he contributed to the Ziegfeld "Follies" of that year and came up with two more winners: *Cling to Me* and *Robins and Roses.* In the following year he had another moderately successful pair, *Getting Some Fun Out of Life* and *It Looks Like Rain in Cherry Blossom Lane.* The same was true in 1938, when *At a Perfume Counter; Sailing at Midnight;* and *Somewhere with Somebody Else,* did rather well. Then Joe Burke went back to writing waltzes. *Rainbow Valley* had its debut in 1939; 1940 brought *Dream Valley;* and 1943, *By the River of the Roses. Rambling Rose* was the sole offering for 1948, and in 1950, the year Burke died, his final song was published, *It Couldn't Happen to a Sweeter Girl.*

Johnny Burke

Just to set the record straight, *Joe* Burke was a well-known composer of popular songs from the twenties into the forties. His contemporary, *Johnny* Burke was twenty-four years younger (Joe Burke was born in 1884; Johnny Burke in 1908) and a lyricist. This may not seem important until you realize that composer credits are often confined to last names only, especially on phonograph records, and the two J. Burkes are often confused for each other. Johnny Burke will probably be best remembered for the songs he wrote with composers James V. Monaco and Jimmy Van Heusen for Bing Crosby movies. Burke's lyrics were ideally suited to the Groaner's easygoing and relaxed style. *Pennies from Heaven* is typical.

Burke was born in Antioch, California, on October 3, 1908, but grew up in the Midwest, where he attended Crane College and the University of Wisconsin. As so many budding composers did, he went to work for a publishing firm in Chicago, then one in New York, and began turning out his own material in the early thirties. His first published song was written in collaboration with Steve Nelson, a composer who apparently didn't continue in the business but came up with a very nice melody for this tune, *Yours and Mine,* which was among the many fine entries for 1930.

From that point on Burke's lyrics were part of a long string of excellent songs, many of them big hits of the day, and quite a number of them well-known standards in the American heritage of great songs. To list them all would take pages, so here are some of the highlights: 1930—*Yours and Mine.* 1933—*Annie Doesn't Live Here Any More; Shadows on the Swannee.* 1934—*Beat O' My Heart; It's Dark on Observatory Hill.* 1935—*Love Dropped in for Tea; My Very Good Friend the Milkman.* 1936—*Pennies from Heaven; So This Is Heaven; Too Much Imagination.* 1937—*The Moon Got in My Eyes; On a Typical Tropical Night.* 1938—*On the Sentimental Side; I've Got a Pocketful of Dreams; Don't Let That Moon Get Away.* 1939—*East Side of Heaven; An Apple for the Teacher; You Crazy Moon; Scatter-brain; What's New?* 1940—*Do You Know Why?; That's for Me; Only Forever; Polka Dots and Moonbeams; Imagination.* 1941—*It's Always You; You Lucky People You.* 1942—*Got the Moon in My Pocket; Moonlight Becomes You.* 1943—*Sunday, Monday or Always.* 1944—*Going My Way; Swinging on a Star; Sleigh Ride in July; Like Someone in Love; Suddenly It's Spring.* 1945—*Aren't You Glad You're You.* 1946—*Welcome to My Dream; Personality; It's Anybody's Spring; So Would I.* 1947—*My Heart Is a Hobo; Country Style; But Beautiful; Apalachichola, Fla; Experience.* 1948—*The Friendly Mountains; The Kiss in Your Eyes* (lyrics written to *The Emperior Waltz* title song of the movie). 1949—*Busy Doin' Nothing; Once and for Always.* 1950—*High on the List.* 1951—*This Is My Night to Dream.* 1952—*Chicago Style; Moonflowers.* 1953—*Here's That Rainy Day.* 1954—*Misty.*

The above is an impressive list for any tunesmith, and if you remember the lyrics to any of these songs—and you *must* be familiar with quite a few—you know they are exceptional—everything from spritely novelties to sentimental ballads, and all in good taste. Burke wrote lyrics for many of the country's finest composers, including Jimmy Van Heusen, with whom he partnered in a song publishing firm and who became his chief collaborator; James Monaco; Arthur Johnston; Victor Schertzinger; Bob Haggart; Errol Garner; and Harold Spina.

Johnny Burke died in New York on February 25, 1964. And what a legacy he left us!

Earl Burtnett

Bandleader-pianist-composer Earl Burtnett was born in Harrisburg, Pennsylvania, on February 7, 1896, and was educated at Penn State College. During the early twenties he played in various dance bands and then organized his own, taking up a long residency at the Los Angeles Biltmore Hotel and recording prolifically, mostly for Brunswick. Toward the end of the decade he joined Art Hickman's Orchestra as pianist and arranger and on Hickman's death took over the band. They continued to record, and the band was popular on the West Coast and in the Midwest, playing top hotels and leading ballrooms and a stint at the Drake Hotel in Chicago; but Burtnett died on January 2, 1936, only thirty-nine years old, and the band's career ended.

His earliest published composition was *Canadian Capers,* a 1915 song for which he wrote the words. The music was a committee effort by three men, Gus Chandler, Bert White, and Henry Cohen. It was a popular entry, and although never quite a standard, it has been played often through the years. In the thirties it was the theme song of bandleader George Haefely, who called his band the "Canadian Capers." *Do You Ever Think of Me?,* which was published in 1920, is a Burnett melody with lyrics by John Cooper and Harry D. Kerr. A popular song when it came out, it has retained its favor with jazz musicians. It received special treatment by the Bob Crosby Bobcats on Decca 3040 in 1940, featuring Irving Fazola on clarinet, and this established the song as a jazz standard.

Mandalay, a 1924 item, teamed Burtnett with two other talented bandleaders, Gus Arnheim and Abe Lyman, and they took equal shares for the composition. Al Jolson recorded it and helped to make it popular. In collaboration with Jess Kilpatrick, Bert White, and Bill Grantham, Burtnett is credited with the 1930 tune *'Leven Thirty Saturday Night.* It was recorded by several bands, including Burtnett's, but the most outstanding treatment came from the band of Bert Ambrose on HMV in England in a swinging arrangement by pianist Lew Stone, with Sylvester Ahola sparking the brass and Danny Polo the reeds.

Earl Burtnett composed a number of other songs during his brief career, but the foregoing titles are the best known and the most enduring. The next time you hear *Do You Ever Think of Me?* it would be nice if you had a kind thought for Earl Burtnett.

Nat Burton

Lyrics writer Nat Burton was born in New York City on November 20, 1901, was educated in the public schools, and broke into the music business writing special material for vaudeville. Active through the thirties and forties, he teamed with several important composers including J. C. Johnson, George Whiting, Arthur Altman, Walter Kent, Basil Adlam, and David Rose. However, there is a mystery, or at the very least, some confusion, regarding his work. That is, either there were times when Burton wrote under the name of Nat Schwartz, or he is credited with songs he didn't write. The problem crops up early with two songs published in 1935, *Believe It, Beloved* and *Rhythm and Romance*. The music for both was written by J. C. Johnson. The lyrics are credited to George Whiting and Nat Schwartz. The same trio composed the 1934 title *Don't Let Your Love Go Wrong,* incidentally, but the difference here is that the first two titles are attributed to Nat Burton in the *ASCAP Biographical Dictionary*. Nat Schwartz is also listed as cowriter of the 1936 song *You Stayed Away Too Long,* with J. C. Johnson and George Whiting. Now before going any further, it should be pointed out that there is no biography for a Nat Schwartz in the ASCAP dictionary. In addition, there is no mention of a Nat Schwartz as a collaborator in the biography for J. C. Johnson, but Nat Burton is listed. Then again, if Nat Burton did not help write *Believe It, Beloved* or *Rhythm and Romance* with J. C. Johnson, he shouldn't be listed as a collaborator.

Aside from these controversial titles, Burton definitely wrote the lyrics for Basil (Buzz) Adlam's beautiful song *Say It!,* a 1934 entry that received appropriate treatment by the Isham Jones band. With composer Walter Kent, Burton hit the jackpot in 1941 with *The White Cliffs of Dover*. They repeated the next year, offering *When the Roses Bloom Again*. In 1934 Burton added words to Rose's melody for *Our Waltz,* which had been the theme song of Rose's radio program. Other titles attributed to Nat Burton are *Somebody Loses, Somebody Wins; The Secret of My Success; Two Seats in the Balcony;* and *You're the Dream, I'm the Dreamer*.

He died in Hollywood, California, on May 21, 1945.

Val Burton

Val Burton was born in London, England, on February 22, 1900, and was educated at Oundle School. He served his composing apprenticeship writing songs for some of the C. B. Cochrane revues and then sailed for the

United States in 1921. His American songwriting career began in 1930 with one of the tunes in the movie *Puttin' on the Ritz, Singing a Vagabond Song.* In 1932 he wrote the all-time standard *When We're Alone,* better known as *The Penthouse Serenade,* and in the same year a very good song, *If It Isn't Love.* He continued to write songs during the thirties but also wrote screenplays and radio shows (including the Henry Aldrich show). Other moderately successful songs were *Isn't This a Night for Love?; Roof Top Serenade; The Big Bad Wolf Is Dead;* and *Dilly Dally.*

Henry Busse

Trumpeter-bandleader Henry Busse was born in Magdeburg, Germany, on May 19, 1894. As a member of Paul Whiteman's Orchestra from 1918 to 1928, he was featured on some big-selling records, especially the Whiteman recording of *Hot Lips,* a 1922 song. Busse shared composer credit on the tune with Henry Lange and Lou Davis. In later years when the trumpeter organized his own orchestra, he used *Hot Lips* as his theme song and recorded it for Decca Records. While still with Whiteman, Busse collaborated with two other members of the band, clarinetist Gus Mueller and trombonist Buster Johnson, to write the music for *Wang Wang Blues.* Leo Wood added the lyrics. Both Whiteman and Busse recorded the song. Whiteman in 1920 and Busse in 1934. In the interim the song became a jazz standard. Published in 1921, it was immediately recorded by a number of bands both here and abroad, including the English answer to Paul Whiteman, Jack Hylton, and since then it has received notable treatment from top-name artists such as Duke Ellington, Fletcher Henderson, Ben Pollack, Les Brown, and Benny Goodman. Busse fared pretty well again in 1931, when he paired with Walter G. Samuels and Leonard Whitcup to produce *Fiesta.* He was also instrumental in writing two other songs, *Horn Tootin' Blues* and *Haunting Blues.* The latter made it into musical history with an all-star version by Red Nichol's Five Pennies on Brunswick 6234, recorded in 1931.

Henry Busse died in Memphis, Tennessee, on April 23, 1955.

Irving Caesar

Librettist and lyricist Irving Caesar was born in New York City on July 4, 1895. He attended the New York public schools and graduated from City College. During World War I he served as the official stenographer aboard the Henry Ford Peace Ship and after his return to the States started to write songs and scores for shows. With composer George Gershwin he scored big in 1919 with a song that Al Jolson made popular, *Swanee,* the first big hit for both Gershwin and Caesar. Caesar went on to write scores for Broadway musicals and to organize the Songwriters Protective Association, serving as its president for a time. In writing for shows Caesar collaborated with many of the most prestigious composers in the field, including Vincent Youmans, with whom he wrote *Tea for Two* and *Sometimes I'm Happy* for the 1925 production "No, No, Nanette" and *I Want To Be Happy,* which was part of the score for "Hit the Deck" in 1927. He also teamed with Victor Herbert, Sigmund Romberg, and Rudolf Friml.

In 1928 Caesar penned the lyrics for *Crazy Rhythm,* composed by band-leader Roger Wolfe Kahn and Joseph Meyer; and in 1931 provided the English lyrics for *Just a Gigolo,* which started out as a popular song in Vienna and was introduced in the United States by Irene Bordoni. The 1936 hit song *Is It True What They Say about Dixie?,* with music by Gerald Marks, had shared credit for the words by Irving Caesar and Sonny Lerner. Irving Caesar wrote for the movies as well as the stage, and with composer Cliff Friend contributed *Sweethearts Forever* to *The Crooner* in 1932 and in the same year combined with Harry Ruby and Bert Kalmar to turn out three songs for the Eddie Cantor movie *The Kid from Spain, Look What You've Done; What a Perfect Combination;* and *In the Moonlight.* All were successful. The 1935 movie *Curly Top,* which starred seven-year-old Shirley Temple, included three songs turned out by Caesar in cooperation with Ray Henderson and Ted Koehler, *Animal Crackers in My Soup; The Simple Things in Life;* and *It's All So New to Me.* Caesar continued to write well into the fifties. Besides writing for shows, movies, and popular songs, he authored a series of songs for children under the titles, "Sing a Song of Safety," "Sing a Song of Friendship," and "Songs of Health."

Irving Caesar died in New York City on December 17, 1996, at the age of 101.

Sammy Cahn

Anyone with the slightest interest in the popular songs of the forties and fifties has to be familiar with the name of Sammy Cahn. A four-time Academy Award winner, he collaborated with outstanding composers like Saul Chaplin, Jule Styne, and Jimmy Van Heusen to produce a long list of exceptional songs. He was born in New York on June 18, 1913. He attended local schools, studied the violin as a youngster, and by the time he was a teenager was playing in dance bands. Collaborating with Saul Chaplin, he turned out special material for vaudeville acts. One of their earliest successes was *Rhythm Is Our Business,* theme song of the Jimmie Lunceford band. The team moved on to Hollywood to write for the movies but broke up after several pictures failed to produce any hit tunes. Each of the partners went on to very successful careers.

Cahn teamed with Jule Styne, and together they wrote songs for nineteen films from 1942 to 1951. Outstanding titles by the team include *It's Magic; I've Heard That Song Before; Let It Snow! Let It Show! Let It Snow!; I'll Walk Alone; Five Minutes More; Time After Time; Saturday Night Is the Loneliest Night of the Week; It's Been a Long, Long Time;* and *I Fall in Love Too Easily.* The latter title was a hit record by Frank Sinatra. Cahn also worked with four other composers in the forties, and in each instance the result was a hit. With Axel Stordahl and Paul Weston he wrote *Day by Day* and *I Should Care* (two more hit records for Frank Sinatra) and with Gene DePaul, *Teach Me Tonight.* The fourth collaboration with Nicholas Brodzsky resulted in Mario Lanza's big hit, *Be My Love.*

When Jule Styne decided to concentrate on Broadway musicals, Cahn began a full-time association with Jimmy Van Heusen, concentrating on writing material for Frank Sinatra. The association was highly successful for all concerned, resulting in a long list of titles well known to Frank Sinatra fans—*All the Way; High Hopes; Call Me Irresponsible; The Second Time Around; My Kind of Town; The Tender Trap; Come Fly with Me; Come Dance with Me; Jealous Lover,* and more.

Cahn served on the ASCAP Board of Directors and as president of the Songwriters' Hall of Fame. In 1974 he published his autobiography, *I Should Care.* He died in Los Angeles, January 15, 1993. Sammy Cahn was a musician's writer, with a basic understanding of rhythm patterns in his lyrics and the shaping of a lyrical phrase to conform to a singer's voice. He could tackle any mood and any situation and meet them head-on with an appropriate twist of words or a sincere thought beautifully expressed. For illustration, consider the clever lyrics of *High Hopes* and the poignancy of *The Second Time Around.*

William D. Carey

William Carey, who had a varied career as a band singer (with Ben Bernie and Ted Fio Rito), an actor in movies, radio, and nightclubs, and a songwriter, was born in Hollister, California, on May 20, 1916. He started writing lyrics in the thirties, collaborating with composers Gene Howard, Don Kahn, and Henry Mancini, but in 1942 he and composer Carl Fischer combined to turn out three songs that were all successful as the result of outstanding renditions on recordings. Kay Kyser's band started the year off with an unusual arrangement of *Who Wouldn't Love You?* on Columbia 36526. In addition, a song that had been recorded by the fine Harry James band the prior October with vocalist Dick Haymes on Columbia 36412 and has since become a minor classic, *You've Changed,* was officially released and instantly became a best-seller. Then, as though to round things off, in July Victor released the Tommy Dorsey record of *It Started All Over Again,* with Frank Sinatra and the Pied Pipers (Victor 20-1523).

Other titles attributed to William Carey include *The Day Isn't Long Enough; Weep They Will; What's It Gonna Be; Summer Love; Promise; When You Trim Your Xmas Tree; The Sun Forgot to Shine This Morning;* and *To Know You Is to Love You.*

Frankie Carle

Frankie Carle (Francis Nunzio Carlone) was born in Providence, Rhode Island, on March 25, 1903. He received his early musical training from his uncle, the well-known pianist Nickolas Colangelo, and by the time he was eighteen years old was playing professionally. He worked in vaudeville as an accompanist, played in dance bands, and for a time was a member of the prestigious Edward J. McEnelly Orchestra, which enjoyed an excellent reputation in New England. In the early thirties he joined Mal Hallett's band, becoming a featured performer and assistant leader. In 1935 he joined Horace Heidt's popular unit, remaining until 1943, building a reputation for his piano stylings, and starting a very successful composing career. In 1937 he scored fairly well with a song called *Georgianna,* but *Sunrise Serenade,* a 1939 entry, was an outstanding hit, quickly followed by another respectable hit, *Shadows.* The next year Carle had two more hits, *Falling Leaves* and *A Lover's Lullaby.*

In 1944 Carle launched his own big band, using *Sunrise Serenade* as his theme song, while continuing to write for the popular market. In 1946 he produced *Oh, What It Seemed to Be,* which sold well but musically wasn't up to the quality of his earlier efforts. This also applies to three songs he published in 1947, *Roses in the Rain; Dreamy Lullaby;* and *Moonlight Whispers.* Other Carle titles are *Lollipop Ball; Carle's Boogie; I Didn't Know; Sunrise Boogie; Sunrise in Napoli; The Golden Touch; Blue Fantasy;* and *The Apple Valley Waltz.*

Like so many of our popular songwriters, Carle did his best work in the thirties, although the overall quality of his music stands up well in comparison to the competition. During the period just before, during, and after World War II the musical taste of the nation underwent several changes, and the cycle that created the atmosphere of the Golden Age ended. The big bands—those that continued for a time, as Frankie Carle's did—were no longer the prime hit-makers or the heaviest influence on creating hits. The baton had been passed to another generation.

Robert L. (Bob) Carleton

Bob Carleton, who wrote the words and music to the hardy jazz perennial *Ja-Da,* was born in St. Louis, Missouri, on November 8, 1896. He was educated in the public schools and during the First World War was stationed at the Great Lakes Naval Training Station. *Ja-Da* was published in 1918, a catchy melody with nonsense words, and it caught on. It has been featured in movies several times and recorded frequently over the years. It lends itself well to jazz treatment, and there have been some unusual developments. In 1938, the Bob Cats, the small unit within the Bob Crosby band, recorded a song they called *Slow Mood,* with tenor saxophonist Eddie Miller as composer and soloist. Miller's melodic line is based on the chord progressions of *Ja-Da.* In 1947 Johnny Mercer added words to *Slow Mood,* and it became *Lazy Mood.* As such, it was introduced on record by Matt Dennis and enjoyed a popular life of its own.

Eddie Miller wasn't the only jazz musician to realize the potential of the song played at a slower tempo. The tune was a favorite vehicle for Bobby Hackett's marvelous improvisations; the first recorded evidence of this was on the 1938 Commodore record (500), by an all-star group that included Bud

Freeman, Pee Wee Russell, Jess Stacy, Eddie Condon, George Wettling, Artie Shapiro, and, of course, Bobby Hackett. The session for this took place in January, two months before the Miller record, which was recorded in March. In the following year, Hackett waxed the song again, this time with his short-lived big band, and he slowed the tempo even further. All three recordings, Miller's and Hackett's, are classics.

Although Carleton is credited with several other songs, including *Teasin'; I've Spent the Evening in Heaven;* and *I've Got to Break Myself of You,* it wasn't until 1947 that he again surfaced with anything outstanding. This time, with words contributed by Cliff Dixon, it was a song introduced by Louis Armstrong and his band in the movie *New Orleans,* with the appropriate title *Where the Blues Were Born in New Orleans.* Phil Harris delineated it nicely on Victor 20-4342.

Bob Carleton died in Burbank, California, on July 12, 1956.

Hoagy Carmichael

There are songwriters, and then there are songwriters, but Hoagy Carmichael occupies a very special niche in the annals of American popular music—something like that of a favorite son. Howard Hoagland Carmichael was born in Bloomington, Indiana, November 22, 1899. He attended local schools and graduated with a law degree from Indiana University. He led his own band while in college, became a fervent fan of the Wolverines, the band that included Bix Beiderbecke, and took part in several early recordings on the Gennett label. Not only is he enshrined forever as the composer of the immortal *Stardust,* he became an intimate and close friend of Bix Beiderbecke in the golden years of the Wolverines, has a number of classic jazz records to his credit from the vintage twenties, was featured on radio, TV, and records as a pianist-singer-entertainer, and even carved himself quite a respectable career as a movie actor. He also wrote two autobiographies, *The Stardust Road* and *Sometimes I Wonder.* In other words, Carmichael was a multitalented man who could do almost everything well if he put his mind to it, and whatever he did, it somehow retained the Carmichael stamp. In songwriting, for instance, the Carmichael stamp has a definite tinge of his appreciation for jazz. His compositions incorporate features that are particularly attractive to musicians and jazz buffs. A Carmichael tune, besides an unusually appealing and memorable melody, almost always includes chords that seem to inspire improvisation, along with a naturally rhythmic lift that instrumentalists instinctively appreciate. This is particularly true of his earlier songs, such as

Riverboat Shuffle; Georgia on My Mind; and *Rockin' Chair,* but is still evident years later in tunes like *New Orleans* and *Skylark.*

A lot of songs have been written since 1927, the year he wrote *Stardust,* and 1931, the year it appeared with lyrics by Mitchell Parish to become a hit record by Isham Jones. The tune has been played and recorded so many times and in so many ways since then that it's difficult to realize at this stage how unique and original this melody was in comparison to other tunes of the period. In fact, the story goes that it was considered so advanced that the publisher left it on the shelf for four years, convinced that the public would never accept it. That it became such a tremendous hit is a great tribute to the taste of the American people of that generation and without question this acceptance opened the door for a host of other superior songs that might never have made it otherwise.

Aside from appreciating the exceptional beauty and originality of most of Carmichael's songs, jazz fans and record collectors have had the privilege of being privy, in several instances, to the source of their inspiration. One of the earliest examples of this is the Gennett recording of Hoagy's composition *Washboard Blues* by the Happy Harmonists (Gen 3066). He plays piano on this side, recorded on May 19, 1925, and his solo is an almost note-for-note forecast of his 1933 collaboration with Johnny Mercer, *Lazybones.* In fact, he must have been fond of this little improvisation, because he repeated it on the twelve-inch Victor recording by Paul Whiteman's Concert Orchestra of *Washboard Blues* as arranged by Bill Challis and recorded in 1927, two years later (Vi 35877).

He does it again, even more completely, on a recording for Brunswick by the Hotsy Totsy Gang made in January 1930 (Br 4920). The title on the record is *Barbaric.* It's an instrumental and starts off at a fast tempo and a melody line in keeping with the title, but then the key changes, the tempo slows, and the melody resolves into the memorable strain of *In the Still of the Night,* the lovely ballad that was published under that title in 1932 with lyrics by Jo Trent. A little irony enters here because this particular worthy contribution by Carmichael is completely neglected in all the reference books, overshadowed by the much later (1937) Cole Porter tune with the same title. With very few exceptions, a Carmichael song is a quality item, and again it is ironic that a few of his finest received only casual attention. Those that come to mind are the delightful *Ballad in Blue,* completely ignored except for a fine record by the Benny Goodman band (1935); *Vagabond Dreams,* a real sleeper that was recorded by several of the big bands in 1939, and featured nice lyrics by Jack Lawrence, but never rated as highly as it deserved; and *Kinda Lonesome,* a 1938 collaboration with Leo Robin and Sam Coslow. It was introduced by

Maxine Sullivan in the movie *St. Louis Blues,* and she recorded it for Victor. Like the title, it has a wistful but appealing melody.

Carmichael teamed with Frank Loesser on the hit novelty *Small Fry,* featured in the Bing Crosby movie *Sing You Sinners* and immortalized by a snappy-patter duet by Crosby and Johnny Mercer on a Decca recording in 1938 (De 1960). But the tune attained new heights as interpreted by Bobby Hackett on a Vocalion side with the Adrian Rollini Quintette, backing a vocal group called the Tune Twisters (Vo 4212). Discussing this record in an interview, Hackett recalled that Carmichael told him that after hearing the side he went out and bought a dozen copies to give away to friends.

Although Carmichael maintained a high level of quality in his writing through the years, it is possible to detect a change in his approach to his music when he started to write for movies in 1936. From his earliest compositions dating to 1925—*Riverboat Shuffle; Washboard Blues; Boneyard Shuffle*—to those of 1935—*Ballad in Blue; Down t' Uncle Bill's*—there is a strong jazz influence. This is so evident that most of the songs have become standards and favorites of jazz musicians, and the list of titles offers the most convincing evidence: *Rockin' Chair* (1930); *Stardust; Georgia on My Mind; Lazy River* (1931); *Thanksgivin'; Come Easy Go Easy Love; Sing It Way Down Low* (1932); *Lazybones; Old Faithful; Snowball* (1933); *Judy; Moon Country; One Morning in May* (1934); and the forementioned *Ballad in Blue* and *Down t' Uncle Bill's* (1935).

In 1936 Hoagy wrote a good one for the movie *Anything Goes, Moonburn,* which received treatment from Bing Crosby, but from this point forward, although there is no letup in superior construction or originality, the effort seems more tailored to the popular market. Here is a partial list of the more successful Carmichael titles: *Sing Me a Swing Song* (1936); *Little Old Lady* (1937); *Jubilee; New Orleans; Two Sleepy People; Small Fry; Kinda Lonesome; Heart and Soul* (1938); *Blue Orchids; I Get Along without You Very Well; Vagabond Dreams; Hong Kong Blues* (1939); *I Should Have Known You Years Ago; I Walk with Music; Ooh, What You Said; Can't Get Indiana off My Mind; Poor Old Joe; The Nearness of You* (1940); *Skylark* (1942); *The Old Music Master* (1943); *How Little We Know* (1944); *Memphis in June; Baltimore Oriole* (1945); *Doctor, Lawyer and Indian Chief; Ole Buttermilk Sky; Ivy* (1947). He continued to write all through the fifties and into the sixties, but aside from *In the Cool, Cool, Cool of the Evening,* which again got an able assist from Bing Crosby, none of the songs approached the success of his earlier efforts, no doubt due to the decline in the demand for quality music in the popular market.

Carmichael died December 27, 1982.

Harry Carroll

ASCAP charter member Harry Carroll was born in Atlantic City, New Jersey, on November 28, 1892. A pianist and composer, he served as a director of ASCAP from 1914 to 1917 and carried on a career working in theaters, vaudeville, and nightclubs and as arranger for music publishers. As a "contract writer" for Winter Garden Productions, he wrote material for the "Ziegfeld Follies" of 1921 and 1922 and for the "Greenwich Village Follies." Carroll wrote the music for a large number of songs, collaborating with lyricists Joseph McCarthy, Ballard MacDonald, Harold Atteridge, and Al Bryan. Oddly enough, his most famous compositions were written early in his career, and the most popular, *I'm Always Chasing Rainbows,* was based on a phrase in Chopin's *Fantasie Impromptu in C# Minor*. Nevertheless, this song has been performed in a number of movies, including *Rose of Washington Square* (1938); *Ziegfeld Girl,* with Judy Garland (1941); *Nobody's Darling* (1943); *The Merry Monahans* (1944); and *The Dolly Sisters* (1944). Perry Como recorded it in 1946, and the hit record propelled the song on the "Hit Parade" for twelve weeks. Joseph McCarthy wrote the words for the tune, which was published in 1917.

Three earlier titles have also survived the test of time, especially the appealing *Trail of the Lonesome Pine,* with lyrics by Ballard MacDonald, a 1913 entry. A hardy perennial, it was a favorite of radio personality Arthur Godfrey, who often sang it on his program, and it received classic treatment in the Laurel & Hardy epic *Way Out West,* with a fabulous duet by "the boys." Both the song and the movie have achieved immortality. Carroll and Ballard MacDonald scored twice in 1913. They had another popular number, *There's a Girl in the Heart of Maryland (With a Heart That Belongs to Me).* This song has also managed to hang on in the category of singable oldtimers. Then in 1914 Carroll and Harold Atteridge penned another hit, *By the Beautiful Sea.* All of the Harry Carroll songs are recalled whenever an "old-timers" revue is staged.

Harry Carroll died in Santa Barbara, California, on December 26, 1961.

Benny Carter

Bennett Lester (Benny) Carter was born in New York City on August 8, 1907. In the *ASCAP Biographical Dictionary* it is stated that he attended Wilberforce University, where he studied theology. However, Roger Kinkle's biographical sketch mentions that Carter intended to enroll at Wilberforce, but instead he joined Horace Henderson's Wilberforce Collegians, a college band, to play in New York. A highly respected and multitalented member of the jazz world of music, much admired for his distinctive style and tone on the alto saxophone, Carter is also recognized as an excellent arranger and composer. As musician, bandleader, and arranger, he has had a distinguished career both here and abroad, can be heard on numerous recordings as a soloist, and with his own bands.

In this instance we're mainly concerned with his composing efforts. Along with a number of things written for the movies, he is also responsible for some swinging jazz instrumentals and a respectable selection of high-quality popular songs. Among the instrumentals are *Hot Toddy; Shoot the Works; Everybody Shuffle; Lonesome Nights; Harlem Mood; When Lights Are Low;* and *I'm in the Mood for Swing*. Most of them can be heard on recordings by Carter, but *I'm in the Mood for Swing,* presented in a typically outstanding arrangement by him, and featuring his alto in the sax section, was played by an all-star aggregation on Victor 26011 under the leadership of Lionel Hampton in 1938. It's a swing classic, re-created many years later by Bob Wilber for his Phontostic label.

In the popular field Carter has scored several times, beginning with the 1931 hit *Blues in My Heart,* with lyrics by the ubiquitous Irving Mills. The tune got a swinging send-off by the Fletcher Henderson band. The melodic *Blue Interlude* came out in 1933, and this time Irving Mills shared credit for the words with Manny Kurtz. A recording unit under Carter's direction, the Chocolate Dandies, introduced the song on Decca 18255 in that year, and vocalist Chuck Richards, backed by a jazz group led by Red Allen, recorded it for Vocalion (2877) in 1934. Two years later Carter, working with the Kai Ewens Orchestra, recorded the tune in Copenhagen, Denmark (HMV 4699); after another two year gap, Cab Calloway recorded it for Vocalion (4538), and Benny Goodman waxed it for Victor (26021).

Benny Carter introduced *When Lights Are Low* on a recording by his Swing Quartet in London, June 1935, for the British Vocalion label (S-16) and in August recorded it again with the Kai Ewens band in Copenhagen. The side was coupled with *Blue Interlude* on HMV X-4699. The vocal on the record was by Carter, singing the Spencer Williams lyrics. In 1939, with his own band, Carter recorded the tune, which was released on a Columbia LP, CL-2162; and in the following month, September, he joined the Lionel Hampton group to record it for Victor (26371). *Melancholy Lullaby,* a collaboration with Edward Heyman, was introduced by the Carter band on Vocalion 4984 and Glenn Miller for Bluebird. *Cow Cow Boogie,* a popular entry for 1942, was written with Don Raye and Gene DePaul and became a hit record on Capitol by Ella Mae Morse.

Benny Carter continued to write, arrange, record, and tour and at the present time (1999) is still active.

James Cavanaugh

Author James Cavanaugh was born in New York City, and he died there on August 18, 1967. Not much is known of his early career, except that he worked in vaudeville and wrote his own material. During his songwriting career he teamed with several top composers, including Harry Barris, Vincent Rose, Russ Morgan, Nat Simon, and Dick Robertson. It appears his first effort was contributing the words to the Harry Barris melody for *Mississippi Mud,* the hit song of 1928, which was destined for immortality by being played and sung by Bix Beiderbecke and Bing Crosby. For some reason there is a big gap between that effort and Cavanaugh's next published song, the 1933 entry *I Like Mountain Music,* but this seems to characterize his work. The following year he teamed with Frank Weldon on the very successful *Neighbors,* which was featured and recorded by the Isham Jones Orchestra. Then along with Al Hoffman and Nat Simon he worked on the parody of old-time stage villains, *You're in My Power (Ha! Ha! Ha!),* which gave Ozzie Nelson a chance to emote on Brunswick.

In 1935 the sole offering was *Why Have a Falling Out?,* an inconsequential thing, and this was followed by another time gap. The next song, *The Umbrella Man* (1938), written with Vincent Rose and Larry Stock, although a mediocre melody, was promoted into popularity with recordings by Guy Lombardo, Connee Boswell with Woody Herman's Orchestra, Kay Kyser, and Lawrence Welk. With all that exposure it could hardly miss. At any rate, it probably inspired Cavanaugh to try to repeat its triumph in 1939 with *The Man with the Mandolin,* this time sharing credit for the lyrics with John Redmond, with music by Frank Weldon. The attempt succeeded so well that it probably even surprised the writers, with best-selling records by Glenn Miller on Bluebird and Horace Heidt on Brunswick. The tune even made it to *Your Hit Parade,* the influential radio program, and held the number two position for ten weeks.

Crosstown, published in 1940, a collaboration with John Redmond and Nat Simon, also merited a Glenn Miller treatment on Bluebird and an equally pleasant one by Dick Jurgens on OKeh. This was the most prolific year for Cavanaugh, with his name appearing on four other songs, *The Gaucho Serenade; On a Simmy Summery Day; The Sidewalk Serenade;* and *Goody Goodbye*. The latter was accorded special attention by the Smoothies, the singing group with Hal Kemp's band.

Once again a few years roll by fallow, and then in 1944 Cavanaugh had two songs in the running. *I'm a Little on the Lonely Side* didn't attract much attention, but a collaboration with bandleader Russ Morgan and composer Larry Stock, *You're Nobody 'Til Somebody Loves You,* hit the right button and besides attaining popularity in the usual channels, became a favorite with country–western fans. Other Cavanaugh titles, issued in the years 1945, 1947, and 1948, include *I'd Do It All Over Again; That Feeling in the Moonlight; Dreams Are a Dime a Dozen; The Man on the Carousel;* and *A Lovely Rainy Afternoon.* James Cavanaugh seems to have stopped writing after the last date.

Saul Chaplin

Like a number of other writers of hit songs, Saul Chaplin pursued a career of many facets. A Brooklyn boy, he was born there on February 19, 1912, and taught himself to play piano. Later on he extended that into arranging. He attended the New York University School of Commerce, but music had a stronger appeal. He co-led a dance band with friend Sammy Cahn, wrote material for vaudeville, and in the mid-thirties began writing songs. Working with Sammy Cahn for the most part, he turned out a very respectable list of hits. Their first effort, written in 1935 with bandleader Jimmie Lunceford, was *Rhythm Is Our Business,* which Lunceford parlayed into a best-selling record and the theme song of his band. It was an encouraging start, and the next year Chaplin and Sammy Cahn took full advantage of the opening by coming up with three outstanding tunes, *Shoe Shine Boy; Until the Real Thing Comes Along;* and *Rhythm Saved the World.*

Shoe Shine Boy, which is still performed enough to give it the rating of a semistandard, was introduced by Louis Armstrong and his band in a revue staged at the Harlem nightclub Connie's Inn. The Mills Brothers had the best-selling record. It was the first big hit for Chaplin and Cahn. *Until the Real Thing Comes Along* proved to be a big recording for the Andy Kirk band on Decca 809. Kirk also used it as a theme song. The Kirk outfit, originally from Kansas City, featured the piano stylings of Mary Lou Williams and vocals by Pha Terrill. Oddly enough, *Rhythm Saved the World* was accorded the most exposure on recordings. Bunny Berigan made it for Vocalion, where it was coupled with his first version of *I Can't Get Started;* Louis Armstrong waxed it for Decca; Tommy Dorsey and the Clambake Seven made it for Victor; the Mills Brothers offered a second version for Decca; and the irrepressible Wingy Manone recorded it on Bluebird.

Chaplin and Cahn were also involved with the blockbuster hit of 1937, combining to write the English lyric for *Bei Mir Bist Du Schoen.* This song originated in a Yiddish musical, with lyrics by Jacob Jacobs and music by Sholem Secunda. Introduced by the Andrews Sisters on Decca, backed by the Decca house band, it became an instant hit, helped along, no doubt, by the fun people had in paraphrasing the song title into *Two Beers Mister Shane, My Dear Mister Shane,* and similar versions. The record also marked the debut into the recording world of young Bobby Hackett, making his first contribution as a member of the Decca house orchestra.

Not content with one hit for 1937, Chaplin and Cahn had several originals that offered superior melodies and lyrics. Tommy Dorsey, who knew a good tune when he heard one, managed to record four of them for Victor. *Dedicated to You; If It's the Last Thing I Do; Just a Simple Melody;* and *If You Ever Should Leave,* the latter poignantly expressed by Edyth Wright with the Clambake Seven. When it came to starting the New Year off right, the duo rang the bell repeatedly, especially with *Please Be Kind,* which was an immediate hit as sung by Mildred Bailey with Red Norvo's Orchestra and further promoted on records by Benny Goodman, Bob Crosby, the recreated Original Dixieland Jazz Band, and various other artists. Another worthy entry, *Saving Myself for You,* turned into a good side by Fletcher Henderson on Brunswick. The great success of *Bei Mir Bist Du Schoen* was probably the inspiration for *Joseph! Joseph!,* another adaptation by Cahn and Chaplin of a Yiddish melody by Nellie Casman and Samuel Steinberg. This too was recorded by the Andrews Sisters but fell far short of the first song.

The melodies contrived by Saul Chaplin were always pleasant and memorable. In 1939 there were two, *It's Easy to Blame the Weather,* tastefully rendered by Jack Leonard with the Tommy Dorsey band, and *It's My Turn Now.* The latter title was recorded by Woody Herman for Decca and by Roy Eldridge for Varsity in 1939, the year of official publication, but was previewed considerably earlier by Ella Fitzgerald and her Savoy Eight on Decca 1596, recorded in December 1937 and apparently rereleased as Decca 2803 in 1939. One excellent song was the output for Cahn and Chaplin in 1940, *I Could Make You Care,* from the movie *Ladies Must Live* and a swooner for Frank Sinatra with Tommy Dorsey on Victor. Other movie songs in following years were unimportant, but in 1946 Chaplin teamed with Al Jolson on *The Anniversary Song,* which was used in the movie *The Jolson Story,* recorded by Jolson for the soundtrack and transcribed to a record as a huge success. By this time Saul Chaplin had become an active producer and director of movie musicals, writing the scores for many of them. In 1968 he produced the movie *Star.*

Newell Chase

Newell Chase, who combined a songwriting career with leading dance bands, conducting theater orchestras, and playing the organ, was born in West Roxbury, Massachusetts, on February 3, 1904. He received a thorough education, including attendance at Boston University and Harvard University and musical study with distinguished instructors. His early experience including playing the organ in church and the piano in dance bands. Later on he became assistant conductor of the Capitol Theater orchestra in New York and doubled as solo pianist for the Roxy Gang. Moving on to Hollywood, he scored for the movies, taking time out to serve as a lieutenant in the army during WWII.

Although Newell Chase had a number of songs published over the years, it has to be admitted that his chief claim to fame rests on two songs he wrote in collaboration with Leo Robin, who wrote the words, and Richard Whiting, who combined with him in composing the music. Both songs were introduced by Maurice Chevalier in the 1930 movie *Playboy of Paris*. The songs are *My Ideal,* which is a standard favorite, and *It's a Great Life If You Don't Weaken.* Other compositions include *Weather Man; Sweet Like You; Never Say Die;* and *Just a Kiss in the Moonlight.*

Newell Chase died in New York City on January 26, 1955.

Sidney Clare

Sidney Clare was born in 1892 in New York and enjoyed a productive career that started in the early twenties and continued well into the thirties. His collaborators included Oscar Levant, Con Conrad, Cliff Friend, Harry Akst, and Richard Whiting. The list of his credits is long, but here are some of the most outstanding titles: *Then I'll Be Happy; I'd Climb the Highest Mountain* (reputed to be Pee Wee Russell's favorite song); *Miss Annabelle Lee; Keepin' Myself for You; Please Don't Talk about Me When I'm Gone; You're My Thrill.*

Sidney Clare died in California on August 29, 1972.

Grant Clarke

Grant Clarke was born in Akron, Ohio, May 14, 1891, and had a brilliant career cut short by an early death at age forty, but in his active years from 1912 to 1931, he managed to leave us a number of well-known standards, along with some lesser-known but still very respectable tunes. His 1912 contribution is one you all know, *Ragtime Cowboy Joe,* followed the next year by that tribute to the driver of early automobiles, *He'd Have To Get Under—Get Out and Get Under*. The 1916 entries were *The Honolulu Blues* and *There's a Little Bit of Bad in Every Good Little Girl.* Later titles include *My Little Bimbo Down on the Bamboo Isle; Second Hand Rose; Blue (And Broken Hearted); Mandy, Make Up Your Mind; Am I Blue;* and *Thanks To You* (a classic by Bing Crosby from his early years with Gus Arnheim's band at the Coconut Grove in California). Grant Clarke was a charter member of ASCAP.

Michael H. Cleary

Michael H. Cleary was born in Weymouth, Massachusetts, on April 7, 1902, and received his major education at the United States Military Academy at West Point. For a time he performed as the organist in the Catholic chapel and wrote material for the academy shows. In 1926 he left the army and took a job as a newspaper reporter in Boston. His next move was into writing scores for Broadway stage shows, movies, and special materials for nightclub entertainers. He reentered the army for WWII as a captain and retired as a major.

Cleary's songwriting career predated his army service. After the war he never returned to it. Nevertheless, for a brief period he managed to turn out some nice songs that were accorded special attention on records, and one or two may even evoke pleasant memories. Probably the earliest effort was *Singin' in the Bathtub,* a 1929 offering that was introduced by Winnie Lightner in a movie, *The Show of Shows*. Herb Magidson and Ned Washington shared credits with Cleary.

In 1932 Cleary and lyricist Maurice Sigler did rather well with *Here It Is Monday and I Still Have a Dollar,* a cheerful sentiment that found favor with Rudy Vallee, who plugged it into a passing popularity; the following year, Sigler and Cleary combined again on a song that musically was one of their best, *Deep in the Blue*. Rather overcome by the heavy competition of the period, it nevertheless resulted in a nice recording by Don Bestor's Orchestra on Victor (24422). *When a Lady Meets a Gentleman Down South,* with words and music by Cleary, Jacques Krakeur, and David Oppenheim, is most likely Cleary's best-known composition, mainly due to a swinging version by the Benny Goodman band with a vocal by Helen Ward. The Goodman outfit was riding high in 1936, and everything it did sold well. Other Cleary songs include *Is There Anything Wrong in That?; It's in the Stars; My Impression of You;* and *Ten O'Clock Town.*

Michael Cleary died in New York City on June 15, 1954.

Gordon Clifford

Gordon Clifford was born in Providence, Rhode Island, on March 28, 1902. He attended Pawtucket High School and studied the violin privately. Eventually making his way to Hollywood, he acted bit parts in the movies. In the early thirties he teamed with Harry Barris and wrote the words to two of Barris's most famous songs, *It Must Be True* and *I Surrender Dear*. Both songs were recorded by the popular Gus Arnheim band, with vocals by Bing Crosby, and were big hits. *I Surrender Dear* became a standard associated with Crosby and in 1947 was the title song for a movie.

In 1930 Clifford and Nacio Herb Brown composed the waltz *Paradise,* another highly successful song that ran the gamut of recordings with waxings by Russ Columbo, Guy Lombardo, Phil Spitalny, and Morton Downey. In later interpretations it has gone the route of stars from Frank Sinatra to Eddy Howard and many more in between. In addition it has been featured in at least four movies. Clifford didn't write many songs. Other titles include *Who Am I?; Somebody's Birthday; Sahara Nights;* and *The Golden Years.* Nevertheless, there aren't many lyric writers who wouldn't be delighted to take credit for *I Surrender Dear*.

Gordon Clifford died in Clark, Nevada, on June 11, 1968.

Larry Clinton

Multitalented Larry Clinton (musician-arranger-composer-bandleader) was born in Brooklyn, New York, on August 17, 1909. A jazz trumpet player, he started arranging in the early thirties and soon acquired a reputation for excellent work. Among the bands he serviced were those of Isham Jones, Tommy and Jimmy Dorsey, Claude Hopkins, and Bunny Berigan. With the advent of swing he began writing instrumentals that were featured by the top orchestras and also incorporated into stock arrangements for the lesser lights. In 1937 he had three big hits, *Satan Takes a Holiday* (also recorded as *Spooky Takes a Holiday); The Dipsy Doodle;* and *A Study in Brown.* The latter was such a success that it was followed by a series dedicated to color, *A Study in Blue; A Study in Green;* and *A Study in Red.* Another composition in 1937 was *Dusk in Upper Sandusky,* a collaboration with Jimmy Dorsey. The Dorsey band recorded it for Decca in a Clinton arrangement.

Later in the year Clinton organized his own band and began a successful recording career for Victor records. His arrangements on the classics *Martha* and *I Dreamt I Dwelt in Marble Halls* were outstanding best-sellers. He also had a hit record with *My Reverie,* a song based on *Reverie* by the French composer Claude Debussy. As Robert Lissauer relates in his *Encyclopedia of Popular Music in America,* Clinton and his publisher thought that the Debussy composition was in the public domain. It wasn't, and after Clinton's recording with a vocal by Bea Wayne became a sensational hit, the Debussy estate sued for copyright infringement. They were awarded $60,000, a large settlement for the time, and more money than Debussy made in his entire life from his compositions.

In 1942 Clinton became an air force pilot, serving until 1946. He reorganized his orchestra after the war, but as other bandleaders were finding out, the old days were over, and he never regained his early popularity. For a while he owned and operated his own publishing company and record business, and then became an Artists and Repertoire man for Kapp records. Other songs and instrumentals credited to Clinton include *Midnight in a Madhouse; My Silent Mood; An Empty Ballroom; The Campbells Are Swinging; Dodging the Dean; Strictly for the Persians;* and *Our Love.*

Larry Clinton died in Green Valley, Arizona, on May 2, 1985.

George L. Cobb

George Cobb was born in Mexico—Mexico, New York, that is—on August 21, 1886. He was a graduate of Syracuse University and a staff composer for a Boston music publisher. His chief collaborator was Jack Yellen, and together they discovered that writing songs about the South could be very profitable. They published two in 1915 that did very well, *Alabama Jubilee* and *Are You from Dixie ('Cause I'm from Dixie Too).* The success of these songs led to more of the same: *All Aboard for Dixieland; See Dixie First; Listen to That Dixie Band; Mississippi Volunteers,* etc.

George Cobb died in Brookline, Massachusetts, on Christmas Day 1942.

Will D. Cobb

Lyricist Will Cobb was born in Philadelphia, Pennsylvania, on June 6, 1876. He attended Girard College in New York and before his success as a songwriter worked as a clerk in a department store. He began collaborating with composer Gus Edwards, and they wrote a series of tunes that are well remembered, among them, *In a Little Red Schoolhouse; School Days; Goodbye, Little Girl, Goodbye; Waltz Me Around Again; Willie; Sunbonnet Sue;*

and *Yip-I-Addy-I-Ay*. The stage star Anna Held featured the Will Cobb song *I Just Can't Make My Eyes Behave*.

Will Cobb died in New York City on January 20, 1930.

Richard Coburn

Richard Coburn was born in Ipswich, Massachusetts, on June 8, 1886. Although he wrote songs for popular revues, and also has a number of titles to his credit, his most outstanding composition was a collaboration with Vincent Rose and John Schonberger, the 1920 super hit *Whispering,* which sold over a million records for Paul Whiteman. Other than that, Richard Coburn had the unfortunate habit of picking song titles that were more successful by other composers, such as *Oriental; Tell Me Why; Nightingale; Day by Day;* and *Day Dreaming*. It's almost a certainty that the songs you have in mind with these titles were not written by Richard Coburn.

He died in Phelan, California, on October 27, 1952.

George M. Cohan

George Michael Cohan was born in Providence, Rhode Island, on July 3, 1878, into a theatrical family. At the age of nine he joined the family act, which included his sister Josephine, and they toured vaudeville as the Four Cohans. He wrote songs and sketches for the act and then went on to do it for others. Eventually he wound up on Broadway as a featured performer in stage musicals and later became a producer. In the early years of the twentieth century he dominated the American theater, pioneering in shows with a strong American flavor and a patriotic flair. Among other songs he wrote the most popular of World War I tunes, *Over There,* for which he received the Congressional Medal of Honor.

Cohan wrote both words and music for his songs, many of which are recognized standards in our musical heritage. Among the better known are *The Yankee Doodle Boy; Give My Regards to Broadway* (1904); *Mary's a Grand Old Name; You're a Grand Old Flag* (1906); and *Harrigan* (1908). In 1942 actor James Cagney won an Oscar for his portrayal of Cohan in the movie *Yankee Doodle Dandy,* and in 1968 a Broadway musical, "George M." was also based on his career. Both productions featured Cohan songs.

George M. Cohan died in New York City, on November 5, 1942.

Russ Columbo

Russ Columbo, who for a very brief period rivaled Bing Crosby as a popular singing star, was born in 1908. A talented youngster, he was an accomplished violinist by the time he was seventeen, also playing accordion, and during the twenties he worked as a violinist-vocalist with California dance bands. Eventually, he wound up in the band of Gus Arnheim, then playing at Hollywood's prestigious Cocoanut Grove in 1929. As it had been for Fred MacMurray and Bing Crosby, the Arnheim band was a springboard to better things. Columbo played some bit parts in movies and then, like Crosby, landed his own radio program. As a theme song, he featured the song he wrote in collaboration with Con Conrad, Gladys DuBois, and Paul Gregory, *You Call It Madness.* Both Columbo and the song were overnight hits, and he had the best-selling record on Victor. Other contemporary sides were made by the bands of Smith Ballew, Bert Lown, and Phil Spitalny, and Kate Smith also recorded it. In a spate of revival many years later, it again sold well on platters by Richard Himber, Nat "King" Cole, and Dick Stabile.

Columbo went on to front his own orchestra, touring the United States and part of Europe, and he is credited with collaborating on several more good songs. Of these, the best known is another 1931 entry, *Prisoner of Love,* with words by Leo Robin and Clarence Gaskill aiding with the music. Again, Russ Columbo had the best-selling contemporary record, but in 1946 it proved to be a major hit for another singer whose last name begins with a C and ends with an O, Perry Como. Not only was it again a best-seller on Victor, the song made *Your Hit Parade* for fifteen weeks. Seventeen years later James Brown recorded it on the King label, and it made the top twenty list. Of course, both *You Call It Madness* and *Prisoner of Love* must be considered all-time standards.

Russ Columbo's life and career were cut tragically short on September 2, 1932, when he was accidentally killed by an "unloaded" dueling pistol in a friend's collection, so there is no way of knowing to what heights he may have gone as both a highly talented vocalist and a songwriter. However, he did leave behind a small but quality legacy of songs. Besides the two already mentioned, he can be credited for *Let's Pretend There's a Moon; Too Beautiful for Words; My Love; When You're in Love;* and *Just Another Dream of You.* He recorded most of these, but friendly rival Bing Crosby also recorded *My Love* (just as Columbo waxed *In the Blue of the Night).* The Columbo version of *My Love,* by way of coincidence, is backed on the Victor recording by the Waller–Conrad song *Lonesome Me.*

Betty Comden

Betty Comden was born on May 3, 1915, in New York City, but her stage and lyricwriting activities began in the forties when she teamed with Adolph Green to write the books and lyrics for Broadway musicals, working with composers Jule Styne and Leonard Bernstein. Comden and Adolph Green were also performers and appeared in shows as a team. They wrote the show "On the Town" with Leonard Bernstein in 1945, from which came *New York, New York,* and with Jule Styne they had the 1956 hit "Bells Are Ringing," which contributed *Just in Time* and *The Party's Over*. The 1961 stage show "Do Re Mi" included another hit tune, *Make Someone Happy*. The team also wrote for the shows "Billion Dollar Baby," with Morton Gould (1946); "Bonanza Bound," with Saul Chaplin (1947); "High Button Shoes," with Jule Styne (1947); "Two on the Aisle," (1951); "Peter Pan," (1945); "Say Darling," (1958); "Subways Are for Sleeping," (1961); "Fade-In–Fade Out," (1964); and "Hallelujah Baby" (1967).

Edward E. (Zez) Confrey

"Zez" Confrey was born Edward E. in Peru, Illinois, on April 3, 1895. Where he acquired the unusual nickname of Zez is anybody's guess. He received his musical training at the Chicago Musical College and developed a highly individualistic piano style. Early in his career he made a large quantity of piano rolls. After a stint in the navy during WWI, he organized his own orchestra and toured vaudeville and played in nightclubs. The band played on the radio and made recordings that were very popular.

Confrey was a prolific composer, especially in writing pieces for solo piano. Most likely his best-known piece is *Kitten on the Keys,* which was published in 1921. Confrey recorded it twice that year, once for Victor and again for Columbia, and his recordings were a big influence in making the tune popular. It became a proficiency test for aspiring young pianists. The following year Confrey scored heavily with the great favorite *Stumbling,* providing both words and music for the clever ditty. It has never quite died out, and jazz bands frequently play it, but it got an added push on the revival path from the movie *Thoroughly Modern Millie* in 1967. *Dizzy Fingers,* another exercise in keyboard technique, made its appearance in 1923, and the composer had a hit record playing it on Victor in 1927. Years later Benny Goodman converted the tune into a tour de force for clarinet, performing it in concerts and radio broadcasts.

Confrey kept writing, and the list of his compositions is fairly long, but it wasn't until 1934 that he had another outstanding success. This time Byron Gay wrote the words, and the song was *Sittin' on a Log (Pettin' My Dog).* Introduced by the band of Jack Denny, it also received top recorded performances by Isham Jones, with the irrepressible Eddie Stone on the plaintive vocal; Anson Weeks, featuring young Bob Crosby in one of his earliest recorded efforts; and Sammy Robbins's band. The Confrey composition *Grandfather's Clock,* another wistful ditty, told the story of the grandfather's clock that stopped when the old man died. It deserved more attention than it was accorded the first time around, but Gene Krupa saw fit to arrange and revive it for Brunswick in 1938. Other compositions include *Buffoon; Jack in the Box; Dumbell; Mississippi Shiver; Nickel in the Slot; Charleston Chuckles; Humorestless; Poor Buttermilk;* and *Parade of the Jumping Beans.*

Zez Confrey died in Lakewood, New Jersey, on November 22, 1971.

Larry Conley

Lyricist Larry Conley was born in Keithsburg, Illinois, on November 29, 1895. He became a trombonist and in the early twenties was a member of the Gene Rodemich Orchestra, which recorded prolifically for the Brunswick label. In fact, one of Conley's earliest compositions, *Tia Juana,* was a collaboration with Rodemich. The Rodemich band recorded it for Brunswick in 1924, but it achieved status as a jazz classic as played by Bix Beiderbecke and the Wolverines on Gennett and by Jelly Roll Morton, who recorded it as a piano solo for the same label. In 1940 Bud Freeman and his Summa Cum Laude Orchestra made an album for Decca Records reprising the songs played by the Wolverines, including *Tia Juana;* with the advent of the LP record, pianist Ralph Sutton recreated the solo mood on his album for Columbia, *Piano Moods* (CL 6140). Of course, the original sides by Bix and Jelly Roll have been reissued countless times. Another Conley–Rodemich entry in 1924 was *Shanghai Shuffle.* It was recorded that year by the Fletcher Henderson Orchestra in an arrangement by Don Redman, with a solo by Louis Armstrong. Ten years later, Fletcher Henderson wrote his own arrangement of the tune and recorded it for Decca. In the same year (1934), Buster Bailey, with an all-star group he called "Seven Chocolate Dandies," waxed *Shanghai Shuffle* for Columbia, and the master made the rounds of all the affiliated labels throughout the world.

Conley's list of famous songs isn't long, but his outstanding ability with words is demonstrated on two fine ones. The first, *A Cottage for Sale,* was one of composer Willard Robison's most successful songs. It was published in 1930, and there is no question that although the melody is outstanding, the unusual and expressive lyrics made it a favorite with vocalists. Among the first records were sides by Ruth Etting, Guy Lombardo, Paul Small, and Bernie Cummins. However, it is said that Conley's favorite recording of the song was by Gracie Fields on the HMV label in England. Billy Eckstine's 1945 rendition on the National label sold a million copies.

In 1936 Conley teamed with composer Johnny Marks to write another delightful song, *Summer Holiday*. It didn't do as well in the highly competitive market of that year as it deserved, but it did get two treatments on records, both worthwhile in their own way. The Dick McDonough Orchestra, with Adrian Rollini in the line-up and Buddy Clark as the vocalist, recorded it on ARC 6-09-07; Wingy Manone manonized it on Bluebird B-6473. Other Conley titles include *Easy Melody; My Sweetheart; Guess There's an End to Everything; My Love for You; Dim the Harbor Lights; Crying for the Moon;* and *Let's Have an Old Fashioned Christmas*.

Larry Conley died in Lindenhurst, New York, on February 29, 1960.

Joseph P. Connor (Pierre Norman)

Joseph P. Connor, who composed under the names of Pierre Norman and Pierre Norman Connor, was born in Kingston, Pennsylvania, on November 16, 1895. He attended the Wyoming Conservatory, where he studied with Ergildo Martinelli, and St. Bonaventure College, where he earned B.A., M.A., and Mus.D. degrees. He served as the pastor of St. John's Church in Cliffside, N.J., and as chaplain to the New Jersey State Police and the New Jersey National Guard. Although many of his composing efforts in the latter part of his career were of a religious nature, at an earlier time he collaborated with Sammy Fain and Irving Kahal on two very important songs, *You Brought a New Kind of Love to Me,* which was introduced in the 1930 movie *The Big Pond* by Maurice Chevalier and has since become a well-loved standard, and *When I Take My Sugar to Tea,* a hit song in 1931. This tune was featured in the movie *Monkey Business* that year and on a hit recording by Glen Gray and the Casa Loma Orchestra, with a vocal by Pee Wee Hunt. It has since been recorded many times.

Pierre Norman Connor also contributed a number of themes to movie scores, including *The Big Pond; Young Man from Manhattan; The Perfect Fool; Blood and Sand;* and *Stars on Ice*. Other song titles are *The Golden Dawn; Lilies of Lorraine; The Far Green Hills of Home; Little Black Dog;* and *Miracle of the Bells*.

Joseph (Pierre Norman) Connor died in Teaneck, New Jersey, on March 31, 1952.

Con Conrad (Conrad K. Dober)

Conrad K. Dober, much better known by his professional name, Con Conrad, was born in New York City, on June 18, 1891. His early education took place in a military academy, but judging by his subsequent career, he had other ideas. As many of his contemporaries did, he started out as a pianist in silent movie houses and then toured in vaudeville in the United States and Europe. His first published song, *Oh! Frenchy!* with words by Sam Ehrlich, was a timely ditty that referred to American soldiers having the pleasure of meeting French girls. It was a good start, but just a warm-up, because in 1920 Con Conrad and his friends hit three home runs, *Margie; Palesteena;* and *Singin' the Blues (Till My Daddy Comes Home). Margie,* with words by Benny Davis and music by Conrad and J. Russel Robinson, was the kind of hit songwriters dream of. *Palesteena,* composed by Conrad and Robinson without Benny Davis, was a clever novelty that developed survival power; and *Singin' the Blues,* a very good song, was elevated to the status of a jazz classic after Bix Beiderbecke and Frankie Trumbauer recorded it in 1927. As it is, all three songs are standards and have been played and recorded countless times.

The same can be said for the song Conrad and Sidney Clare wrote for the Eddie Cantor stage show "Midnight Rounders of 1921," *Ma! (He's Makin' Eyes at Me).* It became the title of a movie in 1940; and in 1946 Judy Canova sang it in the movie *Singin' in the Corn.* And that's not all. Eddie Cantor dubbed it on the soundtrack of *The Eddie Cantor Story* in 1953. Meanwhile, it is played every time a band gets requests for old-time favorites. In 1923 Conrad and Billy Rose cashed in with *Barney Google (With the Goo Goo Googly Eyes);* but from the standpoint of durability they did even better with *You've Got to See Mamma Ev'ry Night (Or You Can't See Mamma at All).* It was initially featured and recorded by Sophie Tucker, but it was still being sung by Kay Starr, Dolly Kay, and Carol Channing many years later.

The success of *Ma!* in the stage show "Midnight Rounders of 1921" may have opened a few doors for Conrad, and by 1924 he was actively contributing to Broadway productions. Oddly enough, for the first four years he turned out nothing memorable, and the one hit song of 1925, *Lonesome and Sorry,* written with Benny Davis, was a freelance entry. However, the situation changed drastically when Conrad began writing for the movies, starting with the *Fox Movietone Follies of 1929*. Working with Archie Gottler on the music and Sidney D. Mitchell on the lyrics, he had three hit songs in the picture, *Big City Blues; Breakaway;* and *Walking with Susie*. Another tune, *Hittin' the Ceiling,* from the movie *Broadway,* also a Conrad–Gottler–

Mitchell creation, did well that year, but from my viewpoint the best team effort, *(Oh, Baby,) Look What You've Done to Me,* appeared in an obscure movie, *Don't Leave Home.* A quality song, it was recorded by contemporary artists like Leo Reisman's Orchestra and vocalists Irving Miller and Vaughn De Leath and then forgotten, but it enjoyed a pleasant resurrection by the King Cole Trio on Capitol 20064, a record that was also included in the album BD-29, *The King Cole Trio, Volume Two.*

Conrad continued to write for movies with some success but also continued the peculiar trait of achieving his biggest hits as freelance submissions. In 1931 he was part of the group undertaking that composed *You Call It Madness,* the song that was associated with singer Russ Columbo and is now a standard. Along with Conrad and Russ Columbo, other writer credits go to Gladys DuBois and Paul Gregory. In 1932 he combined with Andy Razaf and Fats Waller on *Lonesome Me,* a superior ballad that earned respectful treatment from buddy Russ Columbo and others but was then neglected for many years. Since then it has made something of a comeback in the ongoing research and performance of Waller's music. This was followed the next year with another pretty song, *I May Be Dancing with Somebody Else,* which enjoyed the usual brief success that was common at the height of the Golden Age, when the average life of a hit song was judged to be six weeks.

Two other fine tunes, *Blue Sky Avenue* and *Talking to Myself,* appeared in the movie *Gift of Gab,* and Conrad had two outstanding songs in the Fred Astaire–Ginger Rogers film *The Gay Divorcee, The Continental,* and *Needle in a Haystack.* Conrad and his cohorts had several other successful songs in the midthirties—*The Continental; The Champagne Waltz;* and *Here's to Romance*—but although he had a very respectable track record in the thirties, there is no doubt that Con Conrad's early compositions are those that have earned him a niche in the Songwriter's Hall of Fame.

Conrad Dober died in Van Nuys, California, on September 28, 1938.

J. Fred Coots

A name like J. Fred Coots somehow doesn't suggest great artistic talent, and it probably never will become a household favorite, but the owner of that handle was responsible for some lovely melodies during his long career, and if you've been around for longer than the rock blight you'll be familiar with many of them. Coots was born in Brooklyn, on May 2, 1897, and in his early years got his training as a song plugger. Then he graduated to playing piano in vaudeville and nightclubs, writing songs on the side, and got his first break with the Broadway musical "Sally, Irene and Mary" in 1922. He continued to write for shows during the twenties and had mild success with a few free-lance items, notably *Doin' the Raccoon; It Was the Dawn of Love;* and *A Love Tale of Alsace Lorraine,* all from 1928; and a number that has become associated with the Coon–Sanders Orchestra of the era, *Here Comes My Ball and Chain,* which came out in 1929.

Active as he was, he had to wait until 1930 to score with his first big hit, *I Still Get a Thrill,* but repeated the strike in 1931 with another all-time favorite, *Love Letters in the Sand.* It was an auspicious start for the Golden Decade, and Coots went on to a respectable showing for the rest of it. In 1932 he had two excellent entries, *Here's Hoping* and *Strangers.* Four titles made it for 1933, *I Want to Ring Bells; One Minute to One; This Time It's Love;* and *Two Tickets to Georgia.* The foregoing were all good songs and did well enough to be considered successful, but Coots was just warming up. In 1934 he entered the superior *For All We Know,* backed it up with *I Knew You When,* and capped off the year with his biggest moneymaker, *Santa Claus Is Coming to Town.*

In the next two years, 1935 and 1936, Coots hit his peak, loading the market with one hit song after another. Here are the high-powered entries he fielded in the heavy competition of the time: *Louisiana Fairy Tale; It Never Dawned on Me; Things Might Have Been So Different; Whose Honey Are You?; Is It Just a Summer Romance?; I'll Stand By; I'm Grateful to You; Isn't Love the Strangest Thing?; The More I Know You; Why Do I Lie to Myself About You?;* and *You Started Me Dreaming*—plus seven or eight songs of less importance. In other words, Coots had more hits in those two years than most songwriters have in an entire career, and he wasn't finished. In 1937 his top song was *My Day Begins and Ends with You,* accompanied by *In Your Own Little Way* and *Alabama Barbecue;* although these were decent submissions, they didn't compare to those that topped the list for 1938, *You Go to My Head; There's Honey on the Moon Tonight;* and *Summer Souvenirs.* These appear to have topped Coots's career. In 1939 he only entered one title, *Let's Stop the Clock,* a fitting suggestion for the end of the decade, and while he continued to write through the forties and into the early fifties, there were no more hits.

By any standards, including those of the highest order, this is a very respectable list. So remember that name—J. Fred Coots.

Sam Coslow

Sam Coslow may not be a name you instantly recognize as one of the giants in the long list of Tin Pan Alley greats, but he rates right up there just the same both as a composer and as a lyricist. His credits include a number of your favorite songs, all-time standards, and the only problem is that without the original music, or some other means of knowing, it's difficult to determine if he wrote the music or the words. He was born in New York City on December 27, 1902, and started writing songs right after graduating from high school. Among his earlier songs was the hit *Bebe,* in 1923, and in 1928 he contributed *Lonely Melody,* which achieved immortality in an arrangement by Bill Challis recorded by the Paul Whiteman Orchestra featuring Bix Beiderbecke.

Like most songwriters of the Golden Age, he gravitated to Hollywood a short time later and began writing for the movies. Early examples of this period are *True Blue Lou* and *Just One More Chance.* With Arthur Johnson doing the composing, Coslow worked on the scores for Bing Crosby's first two starring movies, *College Humor* and *Too Much Harmony,* resulting in the Crosby classics *Learn to Croon; Moonstruck; Down the Old Ox Road; Thanks; The Day You Came Along; Black Moonlight;* and *I Guess It Had to Be That Way.* Almost at the same time, he contributed the memorable *Moon Song* to Kate Smith's movie *Hello, Everybody.*

The following year (1934), Mae West benefited from *My Old Flame,* which appeared in her movie *Belle of the Nineties,* and *Murder at the Vanities* was blessed with two hits, *Cocktails for Two* and *Live and Love Tonight.* In 1936 he teamed with composer Harry Woods for *I Nearly Let Love Go Slipping through My Fingers,* which appeared in the movie *It's Love Again* but turned out the title song all by himself. He continued to write prolifically through the thirties and forties and into the fifties, when he retired. Other superior songs: *After You; You Took My Breath Away; Turn Off the Moon; True Confession; Every Day's a Holiday.*

A triple-threat talent, Sam Coslow was a talented vocalist, with several records on Vocalion and Victor made in the thirties. In the early forties he partnered with Col. James Roosevelt in founding "Soundies," the coin-operated movie machines that featured many of the bands of the era and are responsible for many of the films we have of them.

Noël Coward

Playwright, actor, composer Noel Coward was born in Teddington, England, on December 16, 1899. As a playwright he was witty and brilliant, as an actor he epitomized the polished and sophisticated man-about-town, and as a songwriter he wrote melodic and memorable songs, mostly waltzes, that were as popular in the United States as they were in England. He started writing for stage shows in 1924 but had his first hit song the following year in the "André Charlot Revue of 1925," *Poor Little Rich Girl.* Gertrude Lawrence introduced the song in the show and recorded it for Columbia. A catchy tune, it adapted well to a swinging approach, as Larry Clinton and his band demonstrated on a recording for Victor in 1929. Judy Garland made it for Decca. In 1975 Tammy Grimes sang the song in the stage musical "A Musical Jubilee."

Off to a flying start, Coward kept a string of hits intact year after year, writing his own plays and musicals and starring in most of them. In 1928, "This Year of Grace" opened on Broadway, with book, lyrics, and music by Coward, and starring Coward and Beatrice Lillie. Two songs were popular, *A Room with a View* and *Dance Little Lady.* Ben Selvin had the hit contemporary record on Columbia of *A Room with a View,* and Tommy Dorsey revived it in 1939 on a Victor record with Jack Leonard on the vocal. In England both titles were recorded for Brunswick by Fred Elizalde and His Hot Music in 1928. Coward sang *Dance Little Lady* in the show. "Bitter Sweet," with book, lyrics, and music by Coward, opened on Broadway in November 1929, and played to 159 performances. It introduced two outstanding waltzes that have since become standards, *I'll See You Again* and *Zigeuner.* An especially beautiful song, the latter title adapted well to swing treatment by the Artie Shaw band on a Bluebird recording in 1930, and a small jazz group led by violinist Eddie South waxed it for Columbia the following year.

Noel Coward starred in his play "Private Lives" in 1939 and penned another waltz *Someday I'll Find You,* as a vocal duet in the production featuring himself and Gertrude Lawrence. For "The Third Little Show," which starred Beatrice Lillie and offered a variety of music by several composers, Noel Coward contributed the satiric *Mad Dogs and Englishmen,* which Rudy Vallee promoted on radio broadcasts. The "Ziegfeld Follies" of that year also included a Coward song, *Half-Caste Woman.* It bore a family resemblance to *Limehouse Blues.* The Ambrose band did it full justice.

In 1932 Ray Noble's new Mayfair Orchestra recorded Coward's somber *Mad about the Boy,* a rather peculiar ditty that stomps along like a march. He did better the next year with *Twentieth Century Blues,* and again Ray Noble with Al Bowlly had the definitive recording. The song was featured in the movie *Cavalcade.* "Conversation Piece," another stage show with book, lyrics, and music by Coward, did well on Broadway and included two successful songs, *I'll Follow My Secret Heart* and *Nevermore.* Then in 1936 he presented another stage production, "Tonight at 8:30," which consisted of nine one-act plays, three of which were presented each evening, and one as a musical. Coward starred in the show with Gertrude Lawrence and contributed one of his best songs, *You Are There.*

Additional songs by Coward include *The Younger Generation; There's Life in the Old Girl Yet; The Roses Have Made Me Remember; If Love Were All; Weary of It All; Never Again; I've Been to a Marvelous Party; The Stately Homes of England; The Party's Over Now; Sail Away; Later Than Spring; Go Slow; Johnny; Something Very Strange; Where Shall I Find Him?; I've Been Invited to a Party; Lonely; This Time It's True Love; I'll Remember Her; Here and Now; My Family Tree; Any Little Fish;* and *Lover of My Dreams.*

Noel Coward died in Jamaica, West Indies, on March 26, 1973.

Henry Creamer

Henry Creamer was born in Richmond, Virginia, on June 21, 1879. An old-time vaudevillian, he toured Europe and the United States as a song and dance man, mostly working with pianist Turner Layton. With Creamer writing the words and Layton the music, they succeeded in turning out several of the most enduring standards in the history of popular music. However, Creamer's first song was a collaboration with the famous comedian Bert Williams and was called *That's A-Plenty*. It was a fairly popular song of its day, but it shouldn't be confused with the 1914 entry with the same title, composed by Lew Pollock, which became a famous jazz classic.

Not that the team of Creamer and Layton were concerned, because beginning with *After You've Gone* in 1918, they proceeded to turn out one hit standard after another. *After You've Gone,* which has been played and recorded countless times through the years, was given a big send-off by Al Jolson at the Winter Garden and Sophie Tucker in vaudeville. Off to a great start, in 1921 Creamer and Layton reworked the old spiritual *Deep River* and came up with *Dear Old Southland.* Paul Whiteman had a successful recording of it, and years later, singer-composer Gene Austin and his trio revived it on a Decca record. The next year, Creamer and Layton wrote the music and starred in the all-black Broadway show "Strut Miss Lizzie." Creamer also wrote the book. The title song was brought back to life by Eddie Condon and His Band on an early side for Milt Gabler's Commodore label (#530) and has since been a favorite of jazz groups.

In 1922 the team contributed another all-time standard *Way Down Yonder in New Orleans*. Oddly enough, this had been written for the show "Strut Miss Lizzie" but was turned down. They resubmitted it to another musical,

"Spice of 1922," and the rest is history. The song was promoted and recorded by the star performer Blossom Seeley and also by Paul Whiteman's Orchestra. Among hundreds of other renditions, in a movie Fred Astaire and Ginger Rogers danced to it (*The Story of Vernon and Irene Castle,* 1939); Bob Haymes sang it in *The Ted Lewis Story* (*Is Everybody Happy?,* 1943); Betty Hutton, portraying Blossom Seeley, did it in *Somebody Loves Me,* in 1952; and it was performed as an instrumental in *The Gene Krupa Story,* 1960. In 1923 Creamer and Layton penned *Down by the River,* which enjoyed some popularity, and they wrote other songs too, but nothing big happened. Other compositions of Henry Creamer and Turner Layton include *Everybody's Gone Crazy Bout the Doggone Blues; Sweet Emalina, My Gal;* and *Whoa, Tillie, Take Your Time.*

In 1926 Creamer found a new partner, father of the stride piano style, James P. Johnson, and together they produced *Alabama Stomp.* Bandleader Red Nichols liked this so much that he recorded it three times. This was just a warm-up, because in 1930 the new partners collaborated on *If I Could Be With You One Hour Tonight.* Recorded by Louis Armstrong for OKeh and by McKinney's Cotton Pickers on Victor, it also received heavy radio play and was one of the big hits of the year. Later on it became a stand-by favorite of Jack Teagarden, who performed it many times.

Henry Creamer died in New York City, on October 14, 1930.

Mann Curtis

See Manny Kurtz.

Charles Neil Daniels (Neil Moret)

Charles Neil Daniels was born in Leavenworth, Kansas, on April 12, 1878. He attended the public schools of St. Joseph and Kansas City, Missouri, and studied piano as a youngster, also taking lessons in composition and arranging. Daniels started composing as a teenager and had his first song published at age eighteen. This was the beginning of a career that spanned fifty years as a composer and music publisher. In 1901 he composed a song he called *Hiawatha,* an instrumental that was introduced by John Philip Sousa's band. It was intended as a tribute to the Kansas town where his sweetheart lived, but in 1903 lyricist James O'Dea added words to the tune, and it became a hit.

The following year Daniels established the Daniels & Russell Publishing Company in St. Louis. From there he moved on to Detroit to manage the office of Jerome H. Remick & Company, where he stayed for eight years. He continued to compose, and in 1908, under the pseudonym he was to use frequently from then on, Neil Moret, he wrote a song that is still being played, *You Tell Me Your Dream* (*And I'll Tell You Mine*). Two years later he scored again with *On Mobile Bay*. In 1914 Daniels moved on again, this time to San Francisco, where he established the firm of Daniels & Wilson, song publishers. But it wasn't until 1918 that "Neil Moret" had another hit. This time it was a sentimental ballad with words by Harry H. Williams called *Mickey,* a very early example of a song written to publicize a movie, a silent film starring Mabel Norman.

In 1924 Daniels became president of Villa Moret in San Francisco and the next year composed one of his most popular songs, *Moonlight and Roses,* with lyrics by Ben Black. This was the start of his most prolific period. In 1926 he wrote both words and music to a song that has become a favorite of jazz musicians and has attained the status of a jazz standard, *Song of the Wanderer*. His other entry for that year, *Don't Say Aloha When I Go,* hasn't survived. Daniels had two successful songs in 1927. The first, *Chloe,* with lyrics by Gus Kahn, has a beautiful and memorable melody but a somber and unusual theme. The lyrics describe the plight of a girl lost in a swamp. A popular song, it never quite died out, and it was revived with a smash in 1944 with the Victor recording by Spike Jones and His City Slickers. Spike turned the gloomy lyrics into a travesty but made the song a bigger hit than when it first was published. The Jones crew repeated their epic rendition in the 1945 movie *Bring on the Girls*. Gus Kahn also wrote the words to *Persian Rug,* the second offering in 1927, and this is a familiar title to Fats Waller collectors, because it was recorded by the Louisiana Sugar Babes on Victor, with Waller in the group. It achieved further immortality with records by the Dorsey Brothers Orchestra (OKeh) and Jack Teagarden (Brunswick).

A third submission in 1927, *Sluefoot* became a specialty for the Coon–Sanders Orchestra, a logical development, since Joe Sanders is listed as the cocomposer with Neil Moret. The band also recorded and featured *Ready for the River,* a 1928 Charles Daniels song with Gus Kahn lyrics. Ted Lewis made a major production out of his rendition of *She's Funny That Way,* which has words by Richard Whiting, an unusual thing in itself. But Lewis was just one of many. Gene Austin also recorded it for Victor, but the tune has proved very durable through the years. It was featured in the Lana Turner–John Garfield movie *The Postman Always Rings Twice* in 1946 and Frank Sinatra sang it in *Meet Danny Wilson.* Not to be outdone, Frankie Laine performed it in *Rainbow 'Round My Shoulder* in 1952.

Here You Come With Love, with lyrics credited to Harry Tobias and Jo Trent, made its debut in 1933 and did fairly well, with recordings by Leo Reisman, Bert Lown, and Freddy Martin on the major labels and Walter Feldkamp's Orchestra on the ill-fated Crown label. *Wild Honey,* a typically superior song of the thirties, was introduced by George Hamilton's Orchestra, and Hamilton shared credit with Henry Tobias for the lyrics to Neil Moret's melody. The song was well represented on records by Jan Garber, Joe Haymes, Dick Jurgens, and Archie Bleyer but never achieved the popularity it deserved. It was the last song of importance written by Daniels. He had one other published that year (1934), *A Pretty Girl—a Lovely Evening* and still another in 1937, *Lovely Debutante.* Among his lesser songs are *Silver Heels; Moonlight Poppies;* and *Heartsease.* Although Daniels didn't compose as prolifically as many of his contemporaries, his output for the most part involved high quality songs.

Neil Moret (Charles Neil Daniels) died in Los Angeles, California, on January 23, 1943.

Hal David

Hal David and Mack David are brothers. Hal is the younger one, born May 25, 1921, also a New York City native, and has been writing since the midforties. His best-known songs include *Four Winds and the Seven Seas; Walk On By; Alfie; Raindrops Keep Fallin' on My Head; Do You Know the Way to San Jose;* and *What the World Needs Now.*

Mack David

Lyricist Mack David, born July 12, 1912, in New York City, attended Cornell University and St. John's Law School and began writing in the early thirties. In fact, he had his first hit in 1932, *Rain, Rain Go Away,* a Johnny Green melody, on which he shared lyric credit with Edward Heyman. It was recorded by the popular bands of Ted Black and Art Kassel. It was an auspicious start to a long list of important titles. 1938 was an important year for David. Working with Haven Gillespie, he penned the words to *There's Honey on the Moon Tonight,* one of those gems by J. Fred Coots that was overlooked by most recording artists but got respectful treatment by Fats Waller and His Rhythm on Victor. David and Jerry Livingston then teamed with bandleader Count Basie for the wistful *Blue and Sentimental,* which became a Basie classic as performed by tenor star Herschel Evans. From the commercial aspect, however, the big moneymaker was *Moon Love,* an adaptation by André Kostelanetz of the first theme from the second movement of *Symphony #5 in E Minor* by Tchaikovsky. Mack David and Mack Davis provided the lyrics. Heavy exposure on the radio, plus top-selling records by Glenn Miller, Paul Whiteman, and others, pushed this entry into twelve weeks on *Your Hit Parade,* in the number one spot for four. The next year David joined Frankie Carle to produce *Falling Leaves.* It was introduced and recorded by the Horace Heidt Orchestra, in which Carle played piano, and was also waxed by Glenn Miller, Jimmy Dorsey, and Wayne King.

With the advent of the new decade, David teamed with Sammy Mysels and Dick Sanford on *The Singing Hills.* Bing Crosby had the top recording, followed by Dick Todd, Eddy Howard, and Gene Autry. In 1941 David worked with Larry Shayne in writing *A Sinner Kissed an Angel,* which received a double plug from Harry James, who recorded it with a vocal by Dick Haymes, and Tommy Dorsey, who made it with Frank Sinatra. Shayne, a music publisher, used the pseudonym Ray Joseph. Trombonist-bandleader Russ Morgan composed the music for the 1942 hit *Sweet Eloise,* with words by David. Morgan recorded it with his band on Decca, but Glenn Miller had the best-seller with Ray Eberle and the Modernaires on Victor. Les Brown made it for Columbia. In that same year Mack David wrote the lyrics to Rube Bloom's song *Take Me,* which also picked up top renditions by Tommy

Dorsey, with a vocal by Frank Sinatra; Jimmy Dorsey, with Helen O'Connell singing; and Benny Goodman, with Dick Haymes. *Don't You Know I Care?,* with music by Duke Ellington, was the Mack David entry for 1944. The Duke recorded it, and so did Paul Weston.

In 1950 David wrote English lyrics to a French song. Originally called *You're Too Dangerous,* it was introduced in this country by Edith Piaf, who also wrote the French lyrics to a melody by Louiguy. Her recording sold a million copies. As *La Vie En Rose,* with words by David it was a hit all over again, and popular records were released by Bing Crosby, Louis Armstrong, Tony Martin, and Paul Weston's Orchestra. *My Own True Love,* a 1954 release, had words by David to Max Steiner's famous theme for *Gone with the Wind, Tara's Theme.* Johnny Desmond recorded it for Coral, and Leroy Holmes's orchestra made it for MGM.

Other titles by Mack David include *Candy; Quicker Than You Can Say Jack Robinson; Just a Kid Named Joe; Sixty Seconds Got Together; What Do You Know About Love?; On the Isle of May; Do You Believe in Fairy Tales?; I'm Just a Lucky So and So; Chi-Baba Chi-Baba; Don't You Love Me Anymore?; A Dream Is a Wish Your Heart Makes; I Don't Care If the Sun Don't Shine;* and *Cherry Pink and Apple Blossom White.* Mack David also contributed lyrics for a number of stage shows and movies and is responsible for an unusual number of title songs, including *The Hanging Tree* (1956); *Bachelor in Paradise* (1961); *Walk on the Wild Side* (1962); *Hud* (1963); *Hush, Hush, Sweet Charlotte* (1965); *Cat Ballou* (1965); *Hawaii* (1966); and *The Dirty Dozen* (1967).

Benny Davis

Tin Pan Alley pioneer Benny Davis was born in New York City on August 21, 1895. He attended public schools, but by the age of fourteen he was performing in vandeville. He toured the country with Benny Fields as accompanist to Blossom Seeley. His first hit song came out in 1917, *Goodbye Broadway, Hello France,* a collaboration with C. Francis Reisner and Billy Baskette, written for "The Passing Show of 1917." In 1920 he wrote the words to *Margie,* a catchy tune concocted by J. Russel Robinson and Con Conrad, introduced and recorded by the Original Dixieland Jazz Band on Victor. Gene Rodemich's band made it for Columbia. In the next year Eddie Cantor sang the song in "The Midnight Rounders" at the Winter Garden in Manhattan. A longtime standard, the song was later used in several movies.

Still hitting bullseyes, in 1921 Davis teamed with Milton Ager and Lester Santly to turn out *I'm Nobody's Baby*. The popular favorite has been recorded many times, and in 1940 it was sung by Judy Garland in the film *Andy Hardy Meets a Debutante*. Her recording on Decca, along with others by top stars, revived the song, and it made *Your Hit Parade* for eleven weeks. The next year David and Georgie Price contributed the words to the Abner Silver ditty *Angel Child*. Price sang it in the stage musical "Spice of 1922," and Al Jolson recorded it for Columbia. In 1940 the song enjoyed a brief revival with good records by Glenn Miller, Sammy Kaye, and Kay Kyser.

Harry Akst wrote the music and Davis the words for *A Smile Will Go a Long, Long Way,* one of a batch of songs Davis worked on in 1923. Contemporary sides were made by Ted Weems (Victor), the Peerless Quartet (Victor), Sam Lanin (OKeh), and Bailey's Lucky Seven (Gennett). In 1935 it was reprised by Wingy Manone on a record for Vocalion and on another by Vic Berton for the same label. Davis and Akst also had another fine song that year, *Dearest (You're the Nearest to My Heart)*. Paul Whiteman recorded it for Victor, and Nora Bayes made it on Columbia. However, the player piano was a fixture in American homes in those days, and the song did very well on music rolls.

Nothing much happened in 1924, but Davis made up for it with two big ones in 1925, *Yearning* and *Oh! How I Miss You Tonight*. *Yearning,* a collaboration with Joe Burke, was a popular offering and was well represented on contemporary platters by Roger Wolfe Kahn on Victor, Harry Reser for Columbia, and Bill Wirges on Perfect. Gene Austin also made it for Victor. Tommy Dorsey, with Jack Leonard singing, revived the song in 1938, also on Victor. *Oh! How I Miss You Tonight,* a waltz, was written by Davis and Burke with the addition of Mark Fisher to the team. Benny Davis featured it in vaudeville. Georgie Price recorded it in 1925, Dick Robertson made it for Decca thirteen years later.

The hits continued to flow for Benny Davis. In 1926, among other songs, he hit big with *Baby Face,* a Harry Akst tune, and *Lonesome and Sorry,* with Con Conrad. *Baby Face* became a perennial. A hit the first go 'round, it was recorded by Jan Garber (with a vocal by Davis), Ben Selvin, and Sam Lanin (as the Ipana Troubadours). In 1948 it was recorded by Art Mooney's band for MGM, sold over a million copies, and put the song on *Your Hit Parade* for nine weeks. An interesting twist to the story is the coincidence that in 1926 "Whispering" Jack Smith recorded the song for Victor, and in 1948 another Jack Smith, The Voice with a Smile, made it for Capitol. And there's more. In 1958 the song made the charts with a record by Little Richard; in 1969 Bobby Darin repeated the feat; and in 1976, a group called the Wing and a Prayer Fife and Drum Corps did it again. The song was sung by Mary Eaton in the 1930 film *Glorifying the American Girl;* by Al Jolson dubbing for Larry Parks in *Jolson Sings Again* in 1949, and by Julie Andrews in *Thoroughly Modern Millie* in 1967. For those who prefer their music with a little heat, *Baby Face* received the jazz treatment from the Buffalodeons on Columbia, and by Joe Candullo on Pathe/Perfect. J. C. Flippen vocalized it backed by a hot group that included Red Nichols and Miff Mole, also on Pathe/Perfect.

I'm Gonna Meet My Sweetie Now, with music by Jesse Greer, was the Davis opus for 1927. A happy tune, it was recorded on Columbia by Kate Smith, but the immortal version was cut by the Jean Goldkette band in an arrangement by Bill Challis. As a Bix Beiderbecke classic, it was available in two takes. Take two was issued in 1927. Take three in 1936. In 1930 Davis and J. Fred Coots wrote a ballad that typified the great songs that would come along in the next few years, *I Still Get a Thrill (Thinking of You).* Guy Lombardo recorded it for Columbia, and Ted Weems for Victor. It was Ozzie Nelson's first recording for Brunswick. In later rejuvenations platters were made by Harry Belafonte, Francis Craig, Art Lund, and Dean Martin. Dick Haymes had a hit recording of it in 1950 for Decca.

In 1936 Davis again got together with the prolific J. Fred Coots, and the result was a spate of excellent songs, all published in that same year. Following is the list:

I'm Grateful to You. This title, a fine example of the pleasant melodies that J. Fred Coots turned out, seemingly without effort, was accorded appropriate treatment on records by Dick McDonough (with Bunny Berigan on trumpet and a vocal by Buddy Clark) on the ARC labels; Willie Bryant on Bluebird; Jimmie Grier on Brunswick; and Jan Garber for Decca.

In My Estimation of You. For some unknown reason this good song didn't get much attention. Carmen Lombardo shared in its composition, usually a certain indication that the Lombardo band would record it, but not this time. Sherman Keene and His Orchestra made it for ARA.

Isn't Love the Strangest Thing is a song that has been rediscovered in recent years, especially by jazz-oriented groups, and is well deserving of the new interest. Contemporary sides were made by Eddy Duchin on Victor and Duke Ellington, with the vocals by Ivie Anderson, on Brunswick. Wingy Manone gave it his inimitable vocal treatment on Bluebird.

Why Do I Lie to Myself about You is another gem of the period, also getting latter-day recognition. Fats Waller made a classic recording of it. Jan Garber recorded it for Decca; Johnny Johnson for ARC; and Mal Hallett for Vocalion.

You Started Me Dreaming was a popular radio number. It was recorded with enthusiasm by Wingy Manone on Brunswick, and other sides were made by Tommy Dorsey on Victor and Henry King for Decca.

Ted Fio Rito worked with Davis and Coots on *Yours Truly Is Truly Yours,* and he recorded the song for Decca. Gene Kardos made it for ARC.

Copper Colored Gal was made on sides by Fats Waller on Victor, Cab Calloway for Brunswick, and Gene Kardos for ARC.

Doin' the Susie-Q, a swingy thing, was waxed by Lil Armstrong on Decca, with a fine tenor sax solo by Chu Berry. Joe Haymes recorded it for Vocalion; Jerry Freeman for ARC.

I'll Stand By apparently was viewed as a worthy sentiment by bandleaders, because it was recorded by Jimmy Dorsey (Decca), Eddy Duchin (Victor), Joe Haymes (ARC), Henry King (Decca), and George Hall (Bluebird).

Fats Waller recorded *The More I Know You.*

Oscar Levant joined Davis and Coots to produce *Until Today,* and it made the rounds of the record labels—Vincent Lopez for ARC, Nat Brandwynne for Brunswick, Red Allen for Vocalion, and Ted Weems for Decca.

Who Loves You?, a pertinent question, was asked by Dolly Dawn, singing with George Hall's orchestra on Bluebird. Rudy Vallee recorded it for ARC; Reggie Childs for Decca.

Other Benny Davis titles include *Make Believe; Say It While Dancing; First, Last, and Always; Indiana Moon; Are You Sorry?; If I'd Only Believed in You; Somebody's Lonely; That's My Girl; Gorgeous; It's a Million to One You're in Love; No Wonder I'm Happy; Mary Ann; Who Wouldn't be Blue; That's How I Feel about You; Cross Your Fingers; You; It's You I Love; Red Hot and Blue Rhythm; Carolina Moon; Takes You; All That I'm Asking Is Sympathy; If You Haven't Got a Girl; Little Mary Brown; Nothing's Too Good for My Baby; I'm Happy When You're Happy; So Ashamed; There Goes My Heart; I Hate Myself; Chasing Shadows; That's What You Mean to Me; A Little Robin Told Me So; Alabama Barbecue; My Day Begins and Ends with You; Let This Be a Warning to You; Baby; I'm Madly in Love with You; This Is No Dream; To You; Sweet Dreams, Sweetheart;* and *All I Need Is You.*

Eddie DeLange

Those of you who grew up in the swing era ushered in by Benny Goodman's great success may recall a fine band that made a brief appearance on the scene in the late thirties, the Hudson–DeLange Orchestra, co-led by songwriter-arranger Will Hudson and lyricist-vocalist Eddie DeLange. The band recorded for Brunswick and the short-lived Master label and turned out some very worthwhile sides. The Hudson–DeLange collaboration also resulted in one of the most outstanding songs of the thirties, *Moonglow*. Eddie DeLange was born on January 4, 1904, in Long Island City, N.Y., attended the University of Pennsylvania, and then went to Hollywood to become an actor. He played bit roles in several movies and then returned to New York to try his hand at songwriting. *Moonglow,* written with Will Hudson, was one of his early and successful efforts, followed the next year (1935) by another outstanding hit, *Solitude,* with Duke Ellington. The Hudson–DeLange band broke up when the partners had the usual disagreements in musical matters, and each went on to lead separate bands for awhile. DeLange continued to write lyrics, and Hudson to compose and arrange.

DeLange collaborated with a number of fine composers—Josef Myrow, Jimmy Van Heusen, Louis Alter, Joseph Meyer, and Sam H. Stept—and through the years produced some excellent lyrics to quality songs. Besides the aforementioned *Moonglow,* 1934 saw the introduction of the very clever *I Wish I Were Twins,* and along with *Solitude,* 1935 produced *Haunting Me.* A few years later DeLange scored with four very respectable hits—*At Your Beck and Call; So Help Me; Deep in a Dream;* and *This Is Madness*—only to continue the next year (1939) with *All I Remember Is You; Can I Help It?; Heaven Can Wait;* and *Darn that Dream.* These are all titles any songwriter would be glad to claim, and there are more—*All This and Heaven Too; And So Do I; Flower of Dawn;* and the outstanding *Shake Down the Stars* (from 1940); *A String of Pearls* (1941); *Just as Though You Were Here; Velvet Moon* (1941); *Along the Navajo Trail* (1945); and in 1947 another blockbuster, *Do You Know What It Means to Miss New Orleans?*

Eddie DeLange was a highly talented man, a personable bandleader, actor, vocalist, and writer. Along with his other credits, he contributed the lyrics to the music for the Broadway show "Swingin' the Dream," which featured, among other outstanding musical organizations, the Benny Goodman Sextet. The show, unfortunately, only lasted for an unlucky thirteen performances. However, *Darn That Dream,* a tune from the musical, enjoyed a hit-life of its own and is still frequently heard.

Eddie DeLange was active as a lyricist well into the forties. He died in Los Angeles, on July 13, 1949.

Milton DeLugg

Back in the dim and almost forgotten days when television screens were only black and white, NBC presented a new program for late night viewers called *Broadway Open House*. It was the forerunner of the *Tonight Show,* and it featured the antics of a zany extrovert named Jerry Lester, who improvised a lot of the show's action on the spot. The little band that provided the music was led by an accordion player named Milton DeLugg, and Lester often involved him in the comic situations. One night they pretended to write a song. Sheer mayhem followed as lyrics were supposedly invented to fit the melody developed by DeLugg, and when the fun was over the result was a catchy little tune called *Orange Colored Sky*. A collaboration between DeLugg and William Stein, the song was off to a good start and went on to become quite popular. Jerry Lester recorded it on Coral; Nat King Cole, backed by Stan Kenton's orchestra, made it on Capitol; and it received suitable treatment by Betty Hutton on Victor. Although not up to the quality of *Orange Colored Sky,* another song, *Hoop-De-Doo,* had the added prestige of Frank Loesser's name as cowriter, and it was also given a send-off on *Broadway Open House* in 1950. This time all the big guns were brought to bear, and it made the rounds of the record labels—Perry Como on Victor, Kay Starr on Capitol, Russ Morgan for Decca, and Doris Day on Columbia.

The next year DeLugg paired with Bob Hilliard, and they turned out the clever and imaginative *Shanghai*. This worthy effort was recorded by Doris Day on Columbia, Bing Crosby on Decca, and by Bob Crosby and his orchestra for Capitol. *Be My Life's Companion* was the DeLugg–Hilliard composition in 1952, and it did rather well as rendered by the Mills Brothers with Sy Oliver's Orchestra on Decca and Rosemary Clooney on Columbia. In 1953 DeLugg, with still another partner, Sammy Gallop, submitted *My Lady Loves to Dance,* which Julius LaRosa recorded on the new Cadence record label. Other compositions by DeLugg are *Just Another Polka; Be-Bop Spoken Here; A Poor Man's Roses;* and *Send My Baby Back to Me*.

Milton DeLugg was born in Los Angeles, but there seems to be some disagreement about the date. ASCAP mentions December 2, 1921. Roger Kinkle makes it December 2, 1918. This aside, DeLugg received his education at John Marshall High School in Los Angeles and then went on to UCLA. He studied harmony, piano, and accordion privately and while still in school performed as a soloist on major radio programs. In 1938 he joined Matty Malneck's fine orchestra, which was part of the Broadway production of "Very Warm for May." DeLugg performed as an actor and soloist. He also played parts in several movies. In 1942 he enlisted in the air corps and was assigned to a radio production unit. He worked for Frank Loesser on a number of movies. Out of the service in 1946, he led a combo on the West Coast backing singer Frankie Laine and then became arranger and conductor of the Abe Burrows radio show. With the advent of TV he worked on a number of West Coast programs and then moved on to New York, starting with *Broadway Open House* and the *Herb Shriner Show,* and eventually moving to the *Tonight Show* with Johnny Carson. He is still active in TV.

Paul Denniker

Pianist-composer Paul Denniker was born in London, England, on May 30, 1897. He was educated at the Dover School in Wellington, England, and studied with Samuel Coleridge-Taylor. He served in the British army during WWI. In 1919 he immigrated to the United States and for awhile led his own band in vaudeville and nightclubs. In the early thirties he arranged and played piano in Will Osborne's orchestra and then went on to write for musical revues in Chicago's Grand Terrace and New York's Apollo Theater. In between his other activities he wrote songs, special material for performers, and radio commercials. His sojourn with Will Osborne resulted in the band's early theme, *Beside an Open Fireplace,* which enjoyed a reasonable degree of popularity in 1929. However, in that same year he and lyricist Andy Razaf published a tune called *S'posin'*. It caught the fancy of Rudy Vallee, who plugged it on his popular radio program and recorded it with his Connecticut Yankees for Victor; and it was also waxed by Seger Ellis on OKeh and others. But radio was king in those days, and the tune got frequent airing from the many dance bands broadcasting. It attained hit status and never quite died out, being recorded every now and then through the years. Donald O'Connor gave it a lift in 1948 by singing it in the movie musical *Feudin', Fussin', and A-Fightin'*. It achieved immortality by being recorded by Fats Waller in 1936.

Paul Denniker's other important compositions are both theme songs that served for years to identify two famous programs of radio station WNEW in New York. Both were written with Andy Razaf and were products of 1936. *Make Believe Ballroom,* recorded by Charlie Barnet's band with the vocal by the Modernaires on Bluebird, became Martin Block's theme, and *The Milkman's Matinee,* recorded by the same artists, was the long-standing signature of the all-night program of the same name.

Matt Dennis

Unlike most of the songwriters in this book, Matt Dennis didn't start turning out songs at an early age. He didn't start to write hit songs until the forties. He was born in Seattle, Washington, on February 11, 1914, the son of vaudeville entertainers, and learned to play piano as a youngster. He played with dance bands in the thirties, including a stint with Horace Heidt and then began to work as a single in clubs, becoming an excellent pianist and entertainer with a very pleasant vocal style. This led to playing and writing material for singers, including Martha Tilton, the Merry Macs, Six Hits and a Miss, and eventually the Pied Pipers. He was with them when they joined the Tommy Dorsey organization, where he began to function as a voice coach, arranger, and composer.

Most of his hit songs are associated with the Dorsey band—which recorded them all—and Frank Sinatra and are notable for the clever lyrics penned by Tom Adair, which were as important to the success of the songs as the catchy melodies. The list isn't long, but it's impressive: *Will You Still Be Mine?; Let's Get Away from It All; Everything Happens to Me; Nine Old Men; Violets for Your Furs; The Night We Called It a Day. Show Me The Way to Get Out of This World,* with words by Les Clark, was a top ten record by Peggy Lee with Dave Barbour in 1950; *Angel Eyes* was introduced by Matt himself in the 1953 movie *Jennifer*. Earl Brent did the lyrics.

There are other songs, but those listed here are enough to qualify Matt Dennis for the Songwriter's Hall of Fame. And if you would like to recall what he sounds like, try spinning the 78 rpm Eddie Miller Capitol of *Lazy Mood,* or better still, find a copy of Matt's RCA–Victor LP *Dennis Anyone?* You won't be disappointed.

Gene DePaul

Gene DePaul was born in New York City on June 17, 1919. He attended Benjamin Franklin High School and took private piano lessons. Early in his career he played piano in dance bands and then toured as a singer-pianist and arranged material for vocal groups. Working with lyricist Don Raye, he began writing songs right at the beginning of the forties. Their first song appeared in 1940, *Your Red Wagon,* based on a blues record by Richard M. Jones, with whom they shared composer credit. In the following year the pair began to write for the movies, and in the film *Keep 'Em Flying,* which starred Abbott & Costello, they had two successful songs, *Pig Foot Pete* and *You Don't Know What Love Is. Pig Foot Pete,* which was nominated for an Academy Award, was sung by Martha Raye in the movie and recorded by Dolly Dawn for Bluebird, Ella Mae Morse for Capitol, and Freddie Slack on Decca. *You Don't Know What Love Is* was introduced by Carol Bruce in *Keep 'Em*

Flying, and she gave it an encore in another movie the next year, *Behind the Eight Ball.* She also recorded it for Columbia, as did Dick Haymes. Other records were made by Ella Fitzgerald on Decca, Billy Eckstine with Earl Hines on RCA–Victor, and Dinah Washington for Mercury. That same year DePaul and Raye did nicely with the wistful *Starlight, Starbright,* which was featured in the movie *In the Navy.* The 1942 film *Behind the Eight Ball* also included the novelty *Mr. Five by Five*—which achieved some popularity, but the movie *Ride 'Em Cowboy* introduced the outstanding ballad *I'll Remember April,* with Don Raye sharing credit with Patricia Johnston for the words.

The 1943 Red Skelton film *I Dood It* offered another gem by DePaul and Raye, *Star Eyes,* and *Follow the Band* included *He's My Guy.* DePaul and Raye teamed with the great Benny Carter that year in adapting a theme by Cow Cow Davenport and producing *The Cow Cow Boogie.* Ella Mae Morse had the hit record on Capitol. DePaul and Don Raye continued to write for the movies, and then DePaul began working with Johnny Mercer. This resulted in scores for the movie *Seven Brides for Seven Brothers* and the stage show, followed by the movie *L'il Abner.* In 1954 Gene DePaul and Sammy Cahn, working as freelancers, wrote *Teach Me Tonight,* one of the better tunes of that year and a hit as recorded by Jo Stafford on Capitol.

Peter DeRose

Those who remember when radio was the king of home entertainment may possibly recall Peter DeRose and the Ukulele Lady, May Singhi Breen, a husband-and-wife team who were part of broadcasting for many years, starting in the pioneering days. They were a talented pair, and in addition to being an accomplished pianist, Peter DeRose wrote songs that were usually far above the average Tin Pan Alley potboilers. A number of these are still with us, and others that have been neglected deserve better consideration. If the popular market ever returns to an appreciation of superior songs, there is much to recommend in the output of Peter DeRose.

He was born in New York City on March 10, 1900. He attended public schools and graduated from DeWitt Clinton High School. He took piano lessons from his sister and began writing songs while still in his teens. His first hit song was *Muddy Water,* with words by Jo Trent, which was introduced and popularized by the headliner Harry Richman in 1926. This was followed by another hit in 1928, *I Just Roll Along,* also with Jo Trent, but like many other writers, DeRose seemed to hit a new stride with the advent of the thirties. To start the decade off he worked with Charles Tobias to produce *When Your Hair Has Turned to Silver,* a song that found favor with those who liked waltzes. Other outstanding songs in the thirties were *Somebody Loves You,* another collaboration with Tobias, and *Nightfall,* one of those delightful little ballads that seem to get better with each hearing, with lyrics by Harold Lewis. Both of these appeared in 1932. In the next year DeRose scored again with *Have You Ever Been Lonely* (lyrics by Billy Hill under the pseudonym of George Brown) and *Louisville Lady,* a torchy ballad also penned with Billy Hill that was more than adequately recorded by the bands of Isham Jones, Joe Haymes, and Anson Weeks.

In 1934 Hill and DeRose contributed the creaky *Wagon Wheels* to the "Ziegfeld Follies" of that year but redeemed themselves somewhat by also offering *Rain, Moonlight and Magnolias. Close to Me* and *So Little Time* were DeRose entries that did fairly well in the market, but in 1939 he struck pure gold. *Deep Purple,* which he had originally written as a piano solo in 1934 and was recorded as an instrumental by the Paul Whiteman Orchestra (Victor 36131), acquired lyrics by Mitchell Parish and became the top hit of 1939. There was more to come. Parish and DeRose joined Bert Shefter in adapting a melody by Maurice Ravel to a popular format and came up with the beautiful *The Lamp Is Low*. Then DeRose and Parish pulled out another DeRose piano solo, added lyrics, and foaled another hit, *Lilacs in the Rain.*

It was a sensational wind-up for the decade, but Peter DeRose was far from finished. He continued to write songs well into the fifties, with some notable titles: *Starlit Hour; The Moon Fell in the River; On a Little Street in Singapore; Moonlight Mood; Autumn Serenade; Who Do You Know in Heaven?;* and others. DeRose died in New York City, his birthplace, on April 23, 1953. He had just started to write for movie musicals when his career was cut short. Not all of his songs are of uniform quality, and many were obviously written to make money, but there are enough outstanding ones to qualify Peter DeRose as a worthy contributor to our musical heritage.

Buddy DeSylva

Whether or not you're old enough to remember the twenties, or even if you think DeSylva, Brown, and Henderson is the name of a law firm, unless you were born on Mars you have to be familiar with their music. Although there have been several successful songwriting teams in the history of American music, none of them have come close to the impressive record set by this one, and a list of their songs reads like an all-time hit parade. Ray Henderson was the man who wrote the music, but Buddy DeSylva and Lew Brown provided many of the ideas and the lyrics, and as a team they were so integrated that even now it's difficult to separate them. All of the men were successful in their own right, but as a team they seemed invincible, coloring an entire decade, the twenties, with their music. Together they turned out tunes that were so perfectly attuned to the pulse of the Roaring Twenties that to many they represent the music of the era. They were the pop tunes of the time, but an amazing number have become standards in the libraries of jazz bands. There are many others that should be. Lew Brown and Ray Henderson can be found in their own sections in this book; here I am going to concentrate on the third member of the team, Buddy DeSylva.

Buddy DeSylva was born in New York on January 27, 1895, but grew up in California. He attended USC for awhile and began writing lyrics. He had an early association with Al Jolson, who brought him back to New York to contribute several songs to the Broadway show "Sinbad" in 1918. Jolson and DeSylva wrote several hit songs together, and DeSylva worked with other writers in producing a number of respectable hits early in his career, among them *April Showers; Avalon; Look for the Silver Lining; A Kiss in the Dark; Alabamy Bound; Somebody Loves Me; If You Knew Susie;* and *California Here I Come*. DeSylva also wrote the lyrics for *Do It Again; Oh Baby; When Day Is Done; Minnie the Mermaid; You're an Old Smoothie;* and *Wishing*—to mention those most people remember. Al Jolson shared credit on the lyrics for *Avalon,* a 1920 song by Vincent Rose. It was introduced by Al Jolson at the Winter Garden and became a hit, but an infringement suit was brought by the composer Puccini and his publisher, claiming the tune was stolen from an aria in his opera *Tosca*. The suit was successful, and the claimants were awarded $25,000 and all future royalties. Considering that the song has long been a standard, played and recorded countless times and interpolated in a number of movies, the suit had long-range, expensive consequences.

In the following year DeSylva teamed with the venerable Jerome Kern on *Look for the Silver Lining*. He had better luck with this one. It was introduced by Marilyn Miller and Irving Fisher in the stage musical "Sally" in December of 1920 and went on to become a hit the next year. Then in 1929 Marilyn Miller and Alexander Grey sang it in the movie version of "Sally," and it was part of the music in the Jerome Kern biographical film *Till the Clouds Roll By,* as sung by Judy Garland. June Haver, in the role of Marilyn Miller, carried on the tradition of a vocal duet with Gordon MacRae in the 1949 film *Look for the Silver Lining*.

April Showers, a song associated with Al Jolson, was another entry in 1921. DeSylva wrote the words and Louis Silvers the music. Jolson sang it in "Bombo" at the Winter Garden and recorded it for Columbia. It became a hit. He sang it on the soundtracks of *The Jolson Story* in 1946 and *Jolson Sings Again* in 1949. The record he made for Decca in 1946 sold more than a million copies. And the song kept going. It was the title song of the movie musical *April Showers* starring Ann Sothern and Jack Carson in 1948. Still freelancing, Buddy DeSylva worked with Victor Herbert in 1922 on the waltz *A Kiss in the Dark*. It was introduced by Edith Day in the stage show "Orange Blossoms," the last to be produced while Victor Herbert was still alive. Mary Martin sang it in the movie *The Great Victor Herbert* in 1939, and Gordon MacRae sang it, and June Haver danced to it, in *Look for the Silver Lining* in 1949.

Al Jolson shared credit with DeSylva on the words to the Joseph Meyer song *California, Here I Come* in 1924. Another huge success, the song has a long and prestigious history. Jolson included it in the road tour of "Bombo" and used it again in another show, "Big Boy." He recorded it on Brunswick, and Georgie Price made it for Victor. As a movie feature it was heard in *Lucky Boy,* sung by George Jessel (1929); in *Hollywood Hotel,* played by the Benny Goodman band (1937); sung by Jolson in *Rose of Washington Square* (1939); again by Jolson with Evelyn Keyes in *The Jolson Story* (1946); and still again in *Jolson Sings Again,* where his voice was dubbed on the soundtrack for Larry Parks (1949). A chorus sang it in a medley of songs in the movie *With a Song in My Heart* (1952). If that isn't enough, consider that it has been recorded dozens of times through the years, and it was Abe Lyman's theme song. On radio and TV the opening strains are often used to introduce a scene or situation pertaining to California.

It was a very good year for DeSylva. With fellow lyricist Ballard MacDonald he shared credit for the words to George Gershwin's *Somebody Loves Me*. This perennial was introduced by Winnie Lightner and Tom Patricola in the stage presentation of "George White's Scandals of 1924." It has been recorded numerous times and frequently used in movies. Lena Horne sang it in *Broadway Rhythm* in 1943; Oscar Levant and Tom Patricola did it in *Rhapsody in Blue* in 1945. It was in *Lullaby of Broadway* in 1951; sung in the Blossom Seely biographical film, and the title song, *Somebody Loves Me* in 1952; and featured in the Jack Webb film, *Pete Kelly's Blues* in 1955, in which it was given a jazz treatment by Matty Matlock's band and also sung by Peggy Lee. Paul Whiteman had a contemporary record of the tune in 1924, with many others through the years. In his *Jazz Records 1897–1942,* Brian Rust lists sixteen sides alone, and this is far from all-inclusive. As a standard, it is still frequently played, not only as a ballad, but as a jazz selection. The Jack Webb film demonstrated both.

The association with Al Jolson continued, and in 1925 DeSylva and Joseph Meyer submitted a song to him called *If You Knew Susie (Like I Know Susie).* He tried it out in the stage show "Big Boy," but after a brief run he dropped it. The writers then took the song to Eddie Cantor, who recorded it and featured it in vaudeville and promoted it into a big hit. The song has been associated with him ever since. Like the other songs we've mentioned, this one also had a long screen pedigree. In 1936, Buddy Doyle, impersonating Cantor, sang it in *The Great Ziegfeld.* In 1945 Frank Sinatra and Gene Kelly sang it in *Anchors Aweigh.* It was the title song of the film *If You Knew Susie,* produced by Eddie Cantor in 1948. He starred in the movie and sang the song under the credits. He repeated the performance for the biographical musical *The Eddie Cantor Story,* in which his voice was dubbed on the soundtrack for Keefe Brasselle (1953). Also in 1925, DeSylva worked with Ray Henderson for the first time. With Bud Green they wrote *Alabamy Bound,* another standard, that was readily adopted and featured by Al Jolson and Eddie Cantor, has been recorded many times and, like the others, used repeatedly in movies. In *The Great American Broadcast,* a 1941 film, it was sung by the Ink Spots, and the Nicholas Brothers danced to it. In 1942 it was heard on the soundtrack of *Broadway* and again the next year in *Is Everybody Happy?* Eddie Cantor sang it in the 1944 film *Show Business,* and a chorus performed it in *With a Song in My Heart* in 1952. Like *Somebody Loves Me, Alabamy Bound* adapts easily to jazz treatment, is a favorite of musicians, and has been played and recorded steadily over the years.

In that momentous year of 1925, DeSylva joined with Ray Henderson and lyricist Lew Brown to create a songwriting team, and the combination of their talents created a fantastic output of songs, many of which have become standards. A complete list of titles would be far too long, but almost certainly you'll recognize many of the following: *Birth of the Blues; Black Bottom; The Best Things in Life Are Free; Varsity Drag; Lucky in Love; Broken Hearted; It All Depends on You; You're the Cream in My Coffee; Pickin' Cotton; Sonny Boy; Together; Button Up Your Overcoat; If I Had a Talking Picture of You; I'm a Dreamer—Aren't We All; My Sin; Just a Memory.* The team turned out scores for Broadway shows and movies from the midtwenties into the thirties and for awhile had their own publishing firm. DeSylva became a movie producer and left the team in 1931, but Brown and Henderson went on to write music for hit shows.

Buddy DeSylva died in Los Angeles, California, on July 11, 1950.

The team of DeSylva, Brown, and Henderson wrote good songs, and all three were exceptionally talented men. Their output includes a number of today's standards, but there are still many of their songs well worth playing that have been neglected, such as *Just Imagine; It Won't Be Long Now; Magno-*

lia; and *One More Time;* good material for those ambitious enough to look into it. They may be gone, but their songs have brought them immortality.

Emery Deutsch

Emery Deutsch was born in Budapest, Hungary, on September 10, 1907. He studied at the Royal Conservatory in Budapest and after coming to the United States continued his education at Fordham University and the Juilliard School of Music. During the thirties he organized and led his own dance band, which was featured in hotels and nightclubs and enjoyed frequent radio time. He served as music director at CBS for twelve years and in 1942 entered the U.S. Maritime Service as a musical conductor. After the war he reorganized his dance band and continued to record and broadcast well into the fifties. As a songwriter he can be credited with three respectable titles. *Play, Fiddle, Play,* with lyrics by Jack Lawrence, was a very successful entry in 1932 (and Jack Lawrence's first hit song). In 1935 he composed *When a Gypsy Makes His Violin Cry,* which he recorded and used as the theme song of his orchestra. The lyrics appear to have been a committee affair, with Dick Smith, Frank Winegar, and Jimmy Rogan all sharing the credit. The song was also recorded by Enric Madriguera's orchestra on Victor and the Pickens Sisters for Columbia. In 1937 Deutsch and Jimmy Rogan published a song that did very well in the popular market, *Stardust on the Moon.* The Deutsch Orchestra had the hit recording. Other compositions by Emery Deutsch include *My Gypsy Rhapsody; Moon of Desire; Stars and Soft Guitars; No Wonder You're Blue;* and *The Old Gypsy Fiddler.*

Dorothy Dick

See Dorothy Dick Link.

Howard Dietz

Howard Dietz was born in New York on September 8, 1896, and became one of Broadway's most important lyricists beginning in the early twenties and continuing well into the sixties. Before the First World War he wrote newspaper columns and advertising copy. He saw military service in the war and in 1924 began a long association with M-G-M as publicity director. Years later he did the same job for Loew's Inc. In the meantime he teamed with composer Arthur Schwartz, and together they turned out scores for a number of successful Broadway shows, notably "The Little Show" (1929); "Three's A Crowd" (1930); "The Band Wagon" (1931); "Flying Colors" (1932); "Revenge with Music" (1934); "At Home Abroad" (1935); "Between the Devil" (1938); and "Inside USA" (1948).

Dietz also teamed with other composers, including Jerome Kern, Vernon Duke, Jimmy McHugh, and Ralph Rainger. His credits include some of the best-known songs in the American heritage of popular music. In the following condensed list of titles you are bound to find many of your favorites.

I Guess I'll Have to Change My Plan; Moanin' Low (1929); *The Moment I Saw You; Something to Remember You By* (1930); *Dancing in the Dark; I Love Louisa; High and Low; White Heat; Sweet Music* (1931); *Louisiana Hayride; A Shine on Your Shoes; Alone Together* (1932); *You and the Night and the Music; If There Is Someone Lovelier Than You; Born to Be Kissed* (1934); *Got a Bran' New Suit; Love Is a Dancing Thing* (1935); *I See Your Face before Me; By Myself; You Have Everything* (1938); *The Love I Long For* (1944); *Rhode Island Is Famous for You; Haunted Heart* (1948); *That's Entertainment* (1953); *Where You Are* (1963).

One of the most distinguished lyricists and librettists in the history of American music, Howard Dietz died in 1983. A more detailed history of his life and career is available in *Song by Song,* by Caryl Brahms and Ned Sherrin (Bolton, England: Ross Anderson Publications, 1984).

Mort Dixon

Another native New Yorker, Mort Dixon was born there on March 20, 1892, and started out as a vaudeville actor. After service in World War I he began songwriting, collaborating with some of the best, including Harry Woods, Ray Henderson, Harry Warren, and Allie Wrubel. Dixon started off with *That Old Gang of Mine,* a big hit in 1923 and still well remembered, and then went on in successive years with *Follow the Swallow* (1924); *Bam, Bam, Bamy Shore; If I Had a Girl Like You* (1925); *Bye Bye Blackbird; Under the Ukulele Tree* (1926); *Cover Me Up with Sunshine; I'm Looking Over a Four-Leaf Clover; Just Like a Butterfly* (1927); *Nagasaki; Old Man Sunshine* (1928); *Would You Like to Take a Walk?; He's Not Worth Your Tears* (1930); *I Found a Million Dollar Baby; You're My Everything; Oooh! That Kiss; River, Stay 'Way from My Door* (1931); *The Lady in Red; Mine Alone; I Live for Love; So Nice Seeing You Again* (1935); *Did You Mean It?; Every Once in Awhile* (1936); *I Can't Lose That Longing for You* (1937); *Tears from My Inkwell* (1938).

Mort Dixon died on March 23, 1956, in Bronxville, N.Y., just three days past his sixty-fourth birthday.

Conrad K. Dober

See Con Conrad.

Robert Emmett Dolan

Robert Emmett Dolan was born in Hartford, Connecticut, on August 3, 1906. A highly talented youngster, he studied piano, first with his mother, then attended Loyola College on a scholarship, and continued further study with such savants as Mortimer Wilson and Joseph Schillinger. He went on to compose and direct for radio and in 1941 became musical director for MGM. As a conductor for Broadway musicals, he was associated with some of the most successful shows ever staged—"Good News," "Follow Through," "Flying Colors," "Strike Me Pink," "May Wine," "Leave It to Me," "Very Warm for May," "Louisiana Purchase," and many others. In this regard, his main claim to fame is his work as a conductor, but he also found time to write songs. In 1929 he collaborated with radio personality Walter O'Keefe on *Little by Little,* a pleasant little tune that was quickly adopted by pianist-bandleader Little Jack Little as his radio theme. Other songs include *Hullabaloo; At Last I'm in Love; Song of the Highwayman; Out of the Past;* and *Your Heart Will Tell You So.*

In 1936 Dolan teamed with Johnny Mercer to write the scores for two Broadway musicals, "Texas Li'l Darlin' " and "Foxy." Songs from the former included the title tune and *Big Movie Show in the Sky; Horseshoes Are Lucky; They Talk a Different Language;* and *It's Great to Be Alive.* The Dolan–Mercer composition *Talk to Me, Baby* was revived in 1996 by cornetist Warren Vaché Jr., both as the title for his Muse CD (MCD 5547) and played and sung by him therein.

Robert Emmett Dolan died in California on September 26, 1972.

Walter Donaldson

You may not be aware of it, but there's a strong possibility that Walter Donaldson is your favorite composer. One thing is certain, he wrote a lot of your favorite songs, spanning a long and prolific period from 1915 into the early forties. However, unlike many of his contemporaries, who seem to have hit their stride in the thirties, Walter Donaldson had early attained his prime in the twenties, turning out a steady stream of hits and quality songs, both for stage shows and as a freelancer. It might even be said that Donaldson, more than any other single composer, captured the spirit of the twenties. Even today his songs seem to evoke the excitement and the adventure of the decade.

Walter Donaldson was born in Brooklyn, New York, on February 15, 1893. He attended public schools and for awhile worked for a Wall Street brokerage firm. He moved on to playing piano for a music publisher and during World War I was involved as an entertainer at Camp Upton. This led to his joining the staff of Irving Berlin Music. He began composing in 1915 and kicked off his musical tributes to the period as early as 1919 with *How Ya Gonna Keep 'Em Down on the Farm,* a testimonial to the wider horizons that opened up after the war. From that point on he continued with one hit after another. In 1920 he penned the little gem *My Little Bimbo Down on the Bamboo Isle* and followed it in 1921 with the expressive *Down South.*

A good start, but he was only getting warmed up. In 1922 he struck gold with *Carolina In the Morning; My Buddy;* and *On the 'Gin, 'Gin, 'Ginny Shore*. In 1923 he had *Mindin' My Business* and *Beside a Babbling Brook,* with two more big ones the next year, *My Best Girl* and *Oh, Baby.* Every year the list of hits grows longer. In 1925 we were endowed with *I Wonder Where My Baby Is Tonight; That Certain Party; Let It Rain, Let It Pour;* and *Yes, Sir, That's My Baby. After I Say I'm Sorry* and *Thinking of You* are just a pair of the hits that came out in 1926, and they were only a prelude to 1927, which produced three standards: *At Sundown; Changes;* and *My Blue Heaven,* not to mention a handful of others that will be familiar to jazz buffs and record collectors (*Dixie Vagabond; He's the Last Word; My Ohio Home; A Shady Tree;* and *Sam, the Old Accordion Man*).

In 1928, for Eddie Cantor's stage show "Makin' Whoopie," Donaldson cranked out the title song (now a perennial); *I'm Bringing a Red, Red Rose; Love Me or Leave Me; My Baby Just Cares for Me;* and *Come West, Little Girl, Come West.* Of course, it didn't hurt a bit that the lyricist was that other stalwart, Gus Kahn. But then—as though just to prove he didn't require outside help—Donaldson packed four more freelance titles into the year, writing both words and music for *Because My Baby Don't Mean Maybe Now; Just Like a Melody Out of the Sky; Out of the Dawn;* and *Say "Yes" Today.*

The transition year of 1929 was rather quiet, with Donaldson only scoring with a couple of tunes, one to become a Bix Beiderbecke–Bing Crosby classic as recorded by the Paul Whiteman organization, *Reaching for Someone,* but he started off the new decade with a tune that rocketed to the top, *You're Driving Me Crazy.* While all the tunes from "Whoopie" were being revived and recorded in a movie of the stage show, he again demonstrated there was still a lot more where they came from, with hit after hit: *Kansas City Kitty; Little White Lies; Sweet Jennie Lee; Tain't No Sin;* and *There's a Wah Wah Girl in Agua Caliente*. The following year saw *Hello, Beautiful* and *Without That Gal,* among others, and 1932 brought *My Mom* and 1933 *You've Got Everything*. Donaldson had another bonanza year in 1934. The movie *Hollywood Party* featured the outstanding ballad *I've Had My Moments;* another Eddie Cantor epic, *Kid Millions,* was a handy vehicle for *Okay, Toots; An Earful of Music;* and *When My Ship Comes In*. The same year also brought *A Thousand Goodnights; Sleepy Head;* and *Riptide*.

In keeping with the emerging pattern of off years, 1935 produced only *Clouds,* to be immortalized by Django Reinhardt and the Quintette of France, and *Tender Is the Night*. For the rest of his career Donaldson was busy writing for the screen, and a string of hits emerged—*You Never Looked So Beautiful; Did I Remember?; I'd Be Lost Without You; It's Been So Long; Why'd Ya Make Me Fall in Love?; Cuckoo in the Clock; Gotta Get Some Shut-eye; Mister Meadowlark;* and finally, in 1943 for the movie *What's Buzzin', Cousin,* the haunting *Nevada*. Besides Gus Kahn the other distinguished lyricists who worked with Donaldson are Joe Young, Sam M. Lewis, Edgar Leslie, Harold Adamson, and Johnny Mercer.

Walter Donaldson died in Santa Monica, California, on July 15, 1947, leaving a legacy of superior songs for us to relish and revere in almost every category of songwriting—romantic ballads, rhythm tunes, novelty tunes, melodic tunes—and many of them such gems of simplicity, seemingly so uncomplicated, they disguise the touch of genius that it took to fashion them.

After the original of this article appeared in *Jersey Jazz,* the publication of the New Jersey Jazz Society, I received a letter from Jane Cole of Watchung, New Jersey, who identified herself as Walter Donaldson's niece. She wrote,

Dear Mr. Vaché,

Thank you so much for the copy of *Jersey Jazz* and the article about Uncle Walter. I enjoyed it thoroughly and have sent copies to several cousins, including Ellen, Uncle Walter's youngest daughter, because I know she'll appreciate it too.

My mother was the first one to sing his music, "Little Jennie Donaldson," and I think was the one for whom he wrote *Oh, Gee, Jennie* and *Sweet Jennie Lee*. He told me he was dedicating *Nevada* to me although there is no inscription on the sheet music.

I thank you again for your thorough and perceptive article.

Sincerely,

Jane Cole

Jimmy Dorsey

Bandleader and alto sax virtuoso Jimmy Dorsey was born in Shenandoah, Pennsylvania, on February 29, 1904. Like brother Tommy, he was a musical prodigy, taking lessons from his father. As a saxophonist he was in demand and played and recorded with many of the most famous orchestras in jazz and dance music history: the Scranton Sirens, Jean Goldkette, the California Ramblers, the Original Memphis Five, Sam Lanin, Paul Whiteman, etc. In later years he and Tommy organized their own band but had a falling out, and Jimmy wound up taking the band over. It recorded for Decca Records from 1935 into the fifties. As a composer Dorsey has a number of fine titles to his credit, including the beautiful theme for his band, *Contrasts,* which he originally called *Oodles of Noodles* and recorded as a saxophone solo for Brunswick in July 1932. The record (6352) was backed by another original composition, *Beebe.* Years later an alternate take of *Oodles of Noodles* was issued on Columbia 36063. Jimmy composed the music for the excellent popular song *It's the Dreamer in Me* (1938), which was also exceptional for having lyrics by Jimmy Van Heusen.

Over a period of many years he is listed as the collaborator on a long series of titles, especially instrumentals. However, it must be kept in mind that his name carried a lot of prestige in the market place, and it's certain that there were times when he was named as cocomposer purely for the sales potential. I know this to be true in regard to the beautiful *I'm Glad There Is You,* which was entirely the work of Paul Madeira Mertz, the one-time pianist with Jean Goldkette. Jimmy agreed to let Paul put his name on the music to help get it published. Which isn't to imply that Dorsey didn't contribute to other titles that bear his name, and the roll of credits is long, starting in the twenties with a tune called *The Pay Off* that was recorded in 1927 by a segment of the California Ramblers. The next year Jimmy and Howdy Quicksell, the legendary banjo player, combined on another in the same gloomy mood, *The Panic.* Although published, it appears that nobody recorded this one. In March 1933 a recording unit billed as the Dorsey Brothers Orchestra recorded *Mood Hollywood,* a collaboration between Jimmy and pianist Lennie Hayton. It was backed by *Shim Sham Shimmy,* another tune Jimmy had a hand in writing. Both sides were reissued on Columbia 36066. It's one of those typical little ironies of the songwriting business that Lennie Hayton tried twice to record *Mood Hollywood* with his own group and both takes were rejected.

After the Jimmy Dorsey Orchestra became well established as one of the big "names" in the music business, Jimmy began to compose prolifically. In the beginning most of his efforts went into jazz instrumentals for the band. One of the band's earliest hit records was *Parade of the Milk Bottle Caps,* a showpiece for the soloists. Originally recorded on Decca 941, it reappeared some years later on Decca 3334. Jimmy wrote the tune with Pat McCarthy. They were also responsible for a later and less successful effort, *Serenade to Nobody in Particular.* Dorsey and fellow bandleader Larry Clinton are credited with two titles in 1936, *Dorsey Stomp,* which later evolved into *Dusk in Upper Sandusky,* and *Dorsey Dervish,* which also developed an alter ego as *Waddlin' at the Waldorf. John Silver,* another Dorsey standard, written with Ray Krise, came out in 1938. It was issued on Decca 1860, again on Decca 3334, and performed by the Jimmy Dorsey Orchestra in an Abbott & Costello movie, *Lost in a Harem,* in 1944. With the advent of the forties the pace increased, and Jimmy's collaborators included Sonny Burke, Toots Camarata, Dick Jacobs, Marvin Wright, Dave Mann, John Gillespie, Herb Ellis, and Lou Carter, among others. Song titles are *Grand Central Gateway; Outer Drive; Clambake for Saxes; Hip Hop; Farewell to Ebb; The Champ; A Bundle of Beats; I Bought a Wooden Whistle; Dixieland Detour; Hep Te Hootie;* and *Major and Minor Stomp.*

Jimmy Dorsey died in New York City, on June 12, 1957.

Tommy Dorsey

Tommy Dorsey, Jimmy's younger brother, was born in Shenandoah, Pennsylvania, on November 19, 1905, and with Jimmy got his early training and experience in music from his father. They played in their father's band playing parades and concerts and had their own dance band. Tommy also put in time with the Scranton Sirens and the California Ramblers. The brothers went to New York and as freelance studio men made countless recordings with a variety of leaders and eventually organized their own orchestra. After an argument about tempo, Tommy walked off the bandstand one night and proceeded to organize another band. Jimmy continued with the original group. Both became very successful and were consistently at the top of the most popular dance bands. Tommy's trombone stylings were always the feature of his orchestra, in the same way Benny Goodman's clarinet was the key factor in his popularity.

Although not as prolific a composer as Jimmy, Tommy is credited with cocomposing three excellent songs, all from 1939 and all recorded and promoted by the Tommy Dorsey Orchestra, with vocals by Jack Leonard. *To You* and *This Is No Dream* were written in collaboration with Benny Davis, who wrote the words, and Ted Shapiro. They were issued back-to-back on Victor 26234. *To You* was also featured on records by Glenn Miller, Al Donahue, and Paul Whiteman and enjoyed frequent radio play. *You Taught Me to Love Again,* another superior entry, was the work of lyricist Charlie Carpenter, with Henri Woode and Tommy Dorsey sharing composing honors. Besides the usual Dorsey recording for Victor, it was waxed by Gene Krupa's band on Columbia and Jan Savitt on Decca, with Bon Bon Tunnell making it all sound believable.

Tommy Dorsey died on November 26, 1956, in Greenwich, Connecticut.

Dan Dougherty

Dan Dougherty was born in Philadelphia, Pennsylvania, on July 17, 1897. Other than that, there isn't much information on his early days except that he started out like so many others of his generation by writing special material for vaudeville. One of his more familiar efforts of this kind is *Mr. Siegel, Make It Legal,* a lament associated with Sophie Tucker. He served as director on the Pathé movie lot and later on as an assistant director for Columbia. He started writing songs early in the twenties, usually in collaboration with lyricist William Tracey, and in 1922 they had a popular entry that found favor with the headliner team of Van & Schenk, who recorded it for Columbia. It had the catchy title *You Can Have Him, I Don't Want Him, Didn't Love Him Anyhow Blues.* Mamie Smith and Her Jazz Hounds also waxed it for OKeh.

In 1926 Dougherty, Bud Green, and Harry Warren combined to produce a sentimental thing called *Wimmin! Aaa!* William Tracey came back for the words to *Sing, Katie (But Leave the Piano Alone),* and then Dougherty and Tracey, aided by Sam Ehrlich, wrote *Out in the New Mown Hay* and *Short & Sweet.* William Tracey, who went on to work with some top-notch writers like Maceo Pinkard, George Meyer, and Nat Vincent and became a charter member of ASCAP, was still working with Dougherty in 1927. They had two songs that year, *All in Fun* (with bandleader Ernie Golden sharing lyric credit) and *I'm Walkin' on Air.* After that Tracey was replaced by other writing partners, mainly Jack Yellen, with whom Dougherty wrote his most successful songs. It may be just a strange coincidence, but Dougherty isn't mentioned as a collaborator in the biographies of either William Tracey or Jack Yellen.

Phil Ponce wrote the words for *Oh! You Have No Idea,* published in 1928. The tune was recorded a number of times both here and in Europe, and Paul Whiteman apparently considered it important enough to assign Bill Challis to arrange it for the Columbia recording. Then Jack Yellen combined with Ponce for the lyrics to *I'd Rather Cry over You (Than Smile at Somebody Else),* which achieved modest success, following which Ponce dropped out. In the same year Dougherty worked briefly with Edmund Goulding in writing three songs for the movie *The Grand Parade. Moanin' for You* and *Alone in the Rain* were both recorded for Victor by the Coon–Sanders band. The third title, *Molly,* didn't make it. However, an outstanding recording of *Moanin' for You* was made by the great Bert Ambrose band for HMV in England, featuring the Fabulous Finn from Gloucester, Massachusetts, Sylvester Ahola, on trumpet.

Glad Rag Doll was the name of a movie in the doleful year of 1929, and Jack Yellen and Milton Ager contributed the lyrics to the song, which is probably Dougherty's biggest hit. It was extensively recorded and has become a semistandard, especially with Dixieland jazz bands. Yellen and Dougherty had another song in the movie *Call of the West, Sittin' on a Rainbow,* a pleasant tune that got the usual showcase treatment from Ray Noble and the New Mayfair Orchestra on a recording for HMV. Obviously trying to repeat the success of *Glad Rag Doll,* Dougherty and Yellen offered *Dance Hall Doll* as an encore in 1930, without much luck. But the following year they struck paydirt with four very respectable titles—*After Tonight; Alone in a Corner; There's No Depression in Love;* and *Let's Get Friendly.* They had one song in 1932, *You're Still in My Heart,* and it appears that after that Dan Dougherty stopped writing.

He died in New York City, on June 13, 1955.

Horace Kirby (Saxie) Dowell

Saxie Dowell was a mainstay in the reed section of the Hal Kemp Orchestra for fifteen years, and his composing ability was an important factor in the band's long-lasting popularity. He was born in Raleigh, North Carolina, on May 29, 1904. He attended the University of North Carolina, where he met Kemp and began their long association. Besides being featured on tenor sax, he often sang novelty vocals. One of his early efforts in composing, *I Don't Care* (not to be confused with the song made famous by Eva Tanguay), lent itself well to the band's penchant for ensemble vocals as delineated by their theme, *How I'll Miss You (When the Summer Is Gone).*

Dowell had two hits songs while he was with Kemp. In 1939 *Three Little Fishies,* with the vocal by Saxie and the Smoothies, was not only a best-seller for the Kemp band but made hit records for Kay Kyser and Paul

Whiteman and especially for Mildred Bailey with Red Norvo's Orchestra. Mildred's "little girl" impression was very suitable to the song. Still writing both words and music, Dowell scored again the next year with *Playmates*. This time the Kay Kyser recording, with Harry Babbitt doing his incredible imitation of a child's voice, was the top seller.

When WW II came along to ruin the band business, Dowell joined the navy and became the bandmaster on the USS *Franklin* until it was sunk in the South Pacific Ocean in 1945. After the war he tried reorganizing his band but ran into the postwar world of shrinking bookings and heavy expenses, so he gave it up to become a disc jockey on the Chicago radio station WGN. In 1948 he became a song plugger and worked at it for several years. His other compositions include *Tonight I'm Thinking of You; V for Victory; Rugged But Right; She Told Him Emphatically, No; All I've Got Is Me; Oo–Goo the Little Worm; I Don't Know If I'm Comin' or Goin'*.

Saxie Dowell died in Scottsdale, Arizona, on July 22, 1974.

Walter Doyle

Walter Doyle was born in Scranton, Pennsylvania, on July 8, 1899. Very little is known of his early years except that he attended public schools and taught himself to play the piano. During WW I he served with the marines. Doyle didn't write many songs—that is, those that succeeded in getting published—but he had three hits in 1929 and the early thirties, and he wrote both words and music for two of them. All three were recorded by the excellent Ted Weems band of the period, which specialized in up-beat tunes with clever lyrics. It appears that Doyle had a close association with the Weems organization and at one point collaborated with Ted Weems in composing two songs, *The Toyland Band* and *I'll Never See My Baby Any More*. Weems recorded both titles, but for some reason they were rejected by Victor.

Collegiate Love, with lyrics by Bobby Heath, came out in 1929 and got the full Weems treatment on Victor, with a Joe Haymes arrangement and the vocal by Country Washburne and Art Jarrett. It enjoyed moderate success. *Mysterious Mose* and *Egyptian Ella* were published in 1930 and were solo efforts by Doyle, who wrote the words as well as the music. Again they were recorded by Weems, with Parker Gibbs relating the story of *Mysterious Mose,* but the tune achieved jazz immortality on the Columbia record by composer Rube Bloom and His Bayou Boys, a recording group that included Manny Klein, Benny Goodman, Tommy Dorsey, and Adrian Rollini. Discographer Brian Rust mentions in his Ted Weems listing that the Victor files state that the vocalist on *Egyptian Ella* is the composer, Walter Doyle, but the credits on the record label name Country Washburne. Both songs received frequent radio play, which was the most important outlet in those years, and have become staples in the category of novelty songs. Other Doyle titles include *Sweet Dixie Lady; No One;* and *When I Think of You.*

Walter Doyle died in Millville, New Jersey, on March 30, 1945.

Milton Drake

Lyricist Milton Drake was born in Brooklyn, New York, on August 3, 1916. He graduated from NYU with degrees in business administration, an education he didn't immediately take advantage of. Instead he became a radio entertainer and announcer on NBC and the Mutual networks and started writing songs for the stage and screen. In 1932 he teamed with Walter Kent in writing the words to a melody by Abner Silver, and the result was *Puleeze, Mr. Hemingway,* a slightly daring but successful little novelty. It was especially favored in England, getting showcase treatment from the Bert Ambrose band. The following year Drake combined with new partners, Duke Enston and Harry Stride, to write *Bless Your Heart.* It was well accepted and recorded. The excellent band of Ernie Holst included it as one of seven titles all recorded in one session for Bluebird.

The *Champagne Waltz,* title song of a 1934 film, was the product of still another combination, Drake, Ben Oakland, and Con Conrad. In an era when waltzes were still popular, it did very well. But it appears that a number of years went by before Drake was involved with another hit. In 1941 he penned the lyrics to a melody by Ben Oakland, and it caught the public's fancy. The tune was *Java Jive,* a big-selling record by the Ink Spots on Decca. Possibly aware that clever novelties had a big market, Drake and partners Al Hoffman and Jerry Livingston struck twice in 1944, with *Fuzzy Wuzzy* and the smash hit *Mairzy Doats.* Again, Decca had the best-seller as recorded by the Merry Macs.

Kiss Me Sweet, with both words and music by Drake, was published in 1949. It was recorded by Sammy Kaye on Victor and Mitch Miller on Columbia. Then a few more years rolled by, and Drake contributed the fine lyrics to a Louis Alter melody that resulted in *Nina Never Knew.* Now in the class of a semistandard, the song was first popularized by Joe Mooney, singing with the Sauter–Finnegan Orchestra on Victor. In 1959 Drake gave up writing songs and went back to the work he was trained for—business. He organized an independent marketing firm specializing in electronics.

Other songs in the Milton Drake list of titles include *Pardon My Love,* a collaboration with Oscar Levant in 1933; *I'm a Big Girl Now; Instant Love;* and *Heaven Only Knows,* a Harry Stride tune, and one of those great songs that got bare attention in the terrific competition of the thirties but managed to reach posterity on a record by Will Osborne. Then we have *The Man with the Weird Beard; If Wishes Were Kisses; She Broke My Heart in Three Places;* and *Wake Up and Dream.* Not a bad record for a businessman.

Paul Dresser

Paul Dresser, a man of many talents, was born in Terre Haute, Indiana, on April 21, 1857. His real name was Dreiser, and he was the brother of the famous novelist Theodore Dreiser. Paul changed the spelling when he decided to become an entertainer. He was educated at St. Meinrad's and trained to become a priest, but while still a teenager he left to join a medicine show; later on he toured in vaudeville and performed as an "end man" in the Billy Rice Minstrels.

In 1886 he wrote his first song, *The Letter That Never Came,* and it was such a success that it convinced him to forget performing and to concentrate on songwriting. A sampling of the titles gives an indication of the public taste of the times: *The Convict and the Bird; The Lone Grave; The Pardon Came Too Late; He Fought for a Cause He Thought Was Right.* However, Dresser managed to compose two songs that are implicit in the standard catalog of American songs, *On the Banks of the Wabash,* written in 1897 and the official state song of Indiana, and *My Gal Sal,* published in 1905. In 1942 a movie with the same title, based on Dresser's life and career, starred Victor Mature in the role of the composer.

Paul Dresser died in New York City on January 30, 1906. He didn't live to see his song *My Gal Sal* become a runaway best-seller.

Dave Dreyer

Dave Dreyer, another Brooklyn boy, was born there on September 22, 1894. Information is scarce about his early years, but as a pianist he worked for a music publishing firm and also accompanied vaudeville headliners like Belle Baker, Sophie Tucker, Al Jolson, and Frank Fay. He started writing songs in the twenties, collaborating with a number of partners, and in 1947 founded his own publishing company. Dreyer, although most likely not recognized in the front runners of popular music composers has to be recognized, nevertheless, as contributing a number of outstanding songs. In 1925 he wrote the music and Herman Ruby the words for *Cecilia,* a tune that was promoted into a hit by the singer-pianist Whispering Jack Smith, who recorded it for Victor. In 1940 it was revived by Dick Jurgens with a vocal by Ronnie Kemper and still later by Parke Frankenfield and his band. The next year Billy Rose turned out the lyrics and Al Jolson took credit with Dreyer for the music of *Me and My Shadow,* a tour de force for bandleader Ted Lewis. Jolson plugged the song too. It turned into a hardy perennial, recorded a number of times and performed by the Ted Lewis band in the movie *Hold That Ghost* in 1941. Donald O'Connor performed it in *Feudin', Fussin' and A-fightin* in 1948. It was played in the film *Funny Lady,* the life and career of Fanny Brice, in 1975, and recorded by Sammy Davis Jr. and Frank Sinatra in 1962.

A 1927 entry by the same writers, *Four Walls,* enjoyed a reasonable success, was recorded for Victor by the popular Johnny Johnson band and again plugged by Al Jolson. The combination of Dreyer, Jolson, and Billy Rose continued into 1928, contributing *There's a Rainbow 'Round My Shoulder* to the Jolson movie *The Singing Fool,* along with *Golden Gate*. The latter title took on still another collaborator, Joseph Meyer. Dreyer, Jolson, and Rose turned out another hit that year, *Back in Your Own Backyard.* The tune was accorded exceptional treatment by the Paul Whiteman organization as arranged by Bill Challis and recorded for Victor with the full orchestra, featuring Bix Beiderbecke. The original record was made from take three of the session. The reissue in 1941 was from take four. It was also recorded by the bands of Gus Arnheim and Jan Garber and vocalized by Ruth Etting. In 1929 Jolson sang it in another movie, *Say It With Songs*. Through the years the tune has moved into the category of a jazz standard, frequently played by traditional jazz bands.

With the coming of the new decade, Dreyer began to freelance, working with a variety of partners. In 1930 he worked with Ballad MacDonald to produce the perky *I'm Following You,* introduced by the popular Duncan Sisters in the movie *It's a Great Life*. In 1931 he really broadened out and with Cliff Friend wrote *I Wanna Sing About You,* recorded by Bert Lown, Paul Tremaine, and others, and combined with tenor Morton Downey on the hit waltz *Wabash Moon*. With Vee Lawnhurst he composed the music to words by Lucy Bender Sokole for *I'm Keepin' Company,* a pleasant little ballad that was recorded and featured on the radio by Rudy Vallee. Other titles by Dave Dreyer include *In a Little Secondhand Store,* written with Harry Pease and Ed Nelson; *You Can't Be True, Dear; The Wall; Next Stop Paradise; Hold My Hand; What Am I Supposed to Do; Honey Babe;* and *I'll Never Let You Go*.

Al Dubin

In combination with composer Harry Warren, Al Dubin wrote an amazing number of tunes that have become lasting treasures in the American heritage of popular songs. Dubin was born in Zürich, Switzerland on June 10, 1891, but came to this country at the early age of two and went to live in Pennsylvania. He went to school at Perkiomen Seminary and then, like so many other songwriters, gravitated to New York to work for publishing houses. World War I interrupted his career, and he served in the military before returning to songwriting.

Before his eventful teaming with Harry Warren he worked with other composers, including Victor Herbert, J. Fred Coots, Sammy Fain, Mabel Wayne, Burton Lane, Jimmy McHugh, Irving Mills, J. Russel Robinson, and Joe Burke. He was moderately successful with some tunes beginning in 1917, but in 1925, in collaboration with Jimmy McHugh and Irving Mills, he contributed several numbers to the "André Charlot Revue of 1925," including *A Cup of Coffee a Sandwich and You; The Lonesomest Girl in Town;* and *Nobody Knows What a Red-Headed Mama Can Do,* all of which enjoyed reasonable acceptance. The following year he and McHugh turned out *My Dream of the Big Parade*. In 1927, with bandleader Roger Wolfe Kahn, he wrote *All by My Ownsome*. Four tunes appeared in 1928, two of them with J. Russel Robinson, *Half-Way to Heaven* and *Memories of France,* one with Al Sherman, *I Must Be Dreaming,* and then his first collaboration with Harry Warren, *Along Came Sweetness*.

Dubin continued to work with other composers and in 1929 turned out several ditties with Joe Burke, including the big hit *Tiptoe Through the Tulips With Me*. By this time Dubin was already working in movies, and *Tiptoe* was part of the score for *Gold Diggers of Broadway*. The next year the picture was *Hold Everything,* which featured comedienne Winnie Lightner, Joe E. Brown, and Abe Lyman's Orchestra. Dubin and Burke rang the bell with *To Know You Is to Love You*. They didn't do badly either with two free-lance offerings, *Dancing with Tears in My Eyes* and *The Kiss Waltz*. Dubin and Burke continued to pair off in 1931 with three successful songs, *Crosby, Columbo and Vallee,* a tribute to the leading crooners of the day; *Many Happy Returns of the Day;* and *When the Rest of the Crowd Goes Home*. Dubin and Warren got together again, and the result was *The River and Me*. This was the start of a long-lasting association and a list of titles that approach the unbelievable. Here are some of the highlights:

Three's a Crowd; Too Many Tears (1932); *No More Love; Build a Little Home; Shuffle off to Buffalo; You're Getting to Be a Habit with Me; The Gold*

Digger's Song; I've Got to Sing a Torch Song; The Shadow Waltz; Pettin' in the Park (1933); *Why Do I Dream Those Dreams; Boulevard of Broken Dreams; Coffee in the Morning; Song of Surrender; I'll String Along With You; I Only Have Eyes for You* (1934); *About a Quarter to Nine; Lulu's Back in Town; You Can Be Kissed; Sweet Music; Where Am I?* (1935); *I'll Sing You a Thousand Love Songs* (1936); *September in the Rain; With Plenty of Money and You; Remember Me?; The Lady Who Couldn't Be Kissed* (1937); *Garden of the Moon; Love Is Where You Find It; Confidentially* (1938).

In 1939 Dubin wrote lyrics to an old Victor Herbert melody, and the result was the hit *Indian Summer.* He again teamed with Jimmy McHugh to turn out music for a stage show featuring Abbott & Costello, Bobby Clarke, and a cast of stars, "Streets of Paris." This produced two excellent songs, *Rendezvous Time in Paree* (one of Benny Goodman's first recordings for the new Columbia Record Company) and *South American Way.* The next year Dubin and Howard Dietz got together to write the book and lyrics for another hit stage show, "Keep Off the Grass," with Jimmy Durante, Ray Bolger, Jane Froman, Ilka Chase, and Larry Adler. Jimmy McHugh was the composer, and the tunes were *Clear Out of This World* and *A Latin Tune, A Manhattan Moon and You.*

But Dubin wasn't locked in any longer on any permanent associations, and in that same year (1940) he worked with composer Will Grosz and another lyricist, Edwina Coolidge, to write the title song for the movie *Along the Santa Fe Trail* and then with a composer named W. Franke Haring, wrote *Where Was I?* for another movie *Till We Meet Again.*

Al Dubin continued to write in the forties and with James V. Monaco turned in a score for the wartime movie *Stage Door Canteen,* but this was almost his last effort. In 1945 he and Burton Lane contributed *Feudin' and Fightin'* to the Olsen and Johnson stage show "Laffing Room Only," and on February 11, 1945, Al Dubin died in New York.

Vernon Duke

Vernon Duke was born Vladimir Dukelsky in the Russia of the czars on October 10, 1902. When the revolution came along he fled with his parents to the United States. He had received a thorough musical education in Russia, attending the musical conservatory in Kiev, but he was disappointed by the lack of appreciation and success in America, so in 1923 he returned to Europe and launched a substantial career writing for London musicals. No doubt encouraged by this success, he returned to the States in 1928, and, most likely due to the reputation he had established abroad, this time he was able to break the ice. His first published song, *I'm Only Human After All,* appeared in the "Garrick Gaieties" for 1930 and enjoyed fair popularity.

As time went on, he continued to write for stage and screen, and a select number of his songs have become all-time favorites—becoming part of that rare list of tunes that have been played and recorded countless times over—*April in Paris; I Can't Get Started; What Is There to Say; Autumn in New York; Taking a Chance On Love;* and *This Is Romance*. Paradoxically, his other compositions have been mostly forgotten. *April in Paris,* of course, was a tremendous hit in 1932, when it was featured in the stage show "Walk a Little Faster," and was already a standard long before the Count Basie band's "One More Time!" recording, but *Autumn in New York,* which was introduced in the stage show "Thumbs Up" in 1935, made no such impression, and, as the old saying goes, thereby hangs a tale. A personal anecdote, that is.

In 1947, or thereabouts, my good friend Ross Doyle, a pianist and composer in his own right, was performing double duty as Tommy Dorsey's band manager and manager of the Dorsey music publishing house. In the latter capacity he was entitled to a tiny office in Manhattan's Brill Building with a piano and a few chairs. The chairs were usually occupied by song pluggers from other publishing firms hopeful of persuading Ross into persuading Tommy into playing the latest gem on their push lists. So it was on the day I decided to drop in to see Ross, and before long I was in conversation with a man I had never met before about the great songs of the past, spurred along by the mutual concurrence with comic George Gobel that "They don't hardly write 'em like that no more." During this spirited exchange the man put his heart into a comment that went something like this: "What a great tune *April in Paris* was! I'd give my right arm to have another Vernon Duke tune like that one!"

"Yes, it is a great tune," I agreed, "but Duke wrote another one that I like just as well, and it has been completely forgotten. In fact, it was hardly recorded at all. The only reason I know about it is because I happen to have an old Victor record of it by Richard Himber's band."

The man's head came up like a rabbit sniffing a carrot. "That so?" he asked eagerly. "What's the name of it?"

"Autumn in New York."

He reached into an inside pocket of his jacket and brought out a little black notebook and after running a finger down one of the pages, nodded his head in satisfaction.

"We've got it!" he announced delightedly. He stood up, acknowledged my contribution with a quick "thanks" and left.

I never ran into the man again, but shortly afterwards it seemed that *Autumn in New York* was being played by every band still lucky enough to have a radio broadcast, recordings of it were being made by both bands and singers, and all at once the tune attained the hit status it had never achieved in 1935. Which only goes to prove, I guess, that of such chance conversations great hits are made. I can only hope that Vernon Duke appreciated the revival of his lovely composition, even if he never knew what brought it about. As for me, I'm satisfied. It's nice to know I had something to do with the preservation of a beautiful song.

Duke continued to compose, including the writing of some so-called "serious" works, but none of his later songs attained hit status. Which is not to say they didn't deserve it. Maybe some day—as with the late blooming of *Autumn in New York*—somebody will rediscover the delightful melody *The Love I Long For,* which Duke wrote for "Sadie Thompson" in 1944.

Vernon Duke died on January 16, 1969, leaving behind just enough classic melodies to earn him a permanent niche in the hall of fame of American popular music.

Gus Edwards

Gus Edwards, the man who made an indelible impression on the art of songwriting with his own approach to show business in the early years of the twentieth century, was born in Hohensaliza, Germany, on August 18, 1879. Brought to this country as an infant, he grew up in New York and attended the public schools. At an early age he started singing in vaudeville and later organized and produced his own vaudeville act featuring talented children. In the process he is credited with discovering and promoting the careers of many of the biggest names in entertainment, among them Eddie Cantor, George Jessel, Georgie Price, Walter Winchell, Lila Lee, Elsie Janis, the Duncan Sisters, Sally Rand, Jack Pearl, Eleanor Powell, the Lane Sisters, Ina Ray Hutton, Mae Murray, Eddie Buzzell, Groucho Marx, Phil Silvers, Bert Wheeler, Mervin LeRoy, Ricardo Cortez, and Helen Menken.

The Edwards productions were headliners, playing the best theaters, including the fabled "Palace" in New York. At one stage he established the Gus Edwards Music Hall in New York, opened his own music publishing house, and produced revues. At a period in our history when radio was still to come and the phonograph little more than a novelty, sheet music was the barometer of a song's popularity. The Edwards song *School Days,* with words by Will Cobb, written as the title song of the Edwards vaudeville act featuring child stars, sold over three million copies. This 1907 hit has never quite died out and gained an additional push toward immortality in 1939 when Bing Crosby, playing the role of Edwards in the movie based on his life, *The Star Maker,* sang it in the film. It was also featured in the 1954 movie *Sunbonnet Sue,* sung by Gale Storm and Phil Regan. *Sunbonnet Sue,* of course, was the title of another Will Cobb–Gus Edwards collaboration published in 1906. In 1923 it became the title song of a Broadway show, eventually getting the same treatment for the movie. Bing Crosby also sang it in *The Star Maker.*

Most likely Edward's earliest hit song was *Goodbye, Little Girl, Goodbye,* with Will Cobb, published in 1904. It was perpetuated on a Columbia record by Bryron G. Harlan and, in a move predating by many years the latter-day effort to erase the pain of the market takeover by the more compact disc (CD) with the simultaneous issue of cassette recordings, the recording also came out on cylinder. In 1905 Gus Edwards teamed with a new partner, Vincent P. Bryan, to write another perennial, *In My Merry Oldsmobile.* The song, originally intended to commemorate a record-breaking (for the time) auto trip to publicize the car and honor the Lewis and Clark Expedition, was adopted by General Motors and used as a radio and TV theme for Oldsmobile commercials. But from the standpoint of our musical heritage it achieved immortality much earlier when GM commissioned the Jean Goldkette band to make a "special record" of the tune on Victor for their 1927 convention in Detroit. As arranged by Bill Challis, the record features Bix Beiderbecke in the ensemble. It has been reissued in Beiderbecke anthologies a number of times.

Working with Will Cobb again, Edwards penned the song that came to be associated with the star Anna Held, *I Just Can't Make My Eyes Behave,* in 1906. In 1909 Edwards hit it big again in collaboration with lyricist Edward Madden and a tune introduced by George Price in one of Edwards's child revues, *By the Light of the Silvery Moon.* Later that year it was featured in the "Ziegfeld Follies of 1909." In 1952 it was the title song of a film starring Gordon MacRae and Doris Day and has also been played and sung in more than a half-dozen other movies.

Jimmy Valentine, written with Edward Madden, was the successful entry for 1911. The lyrics were based on a short story by O. Henry, "The Retrieved Information." It became the theme of the 1928 movie *Alias Jimmy Valentine,* and Bing Crosby sang it in *The Star Maker* in 1939. Edwards composed quite a number of songs, and most of them were at least moderately successful. A partial list includes *If I Was a Millionaire; I Can't Tell You Why I Love You, but I Do; I'll Be With You When the Roses Bloom Again; Orange Blossom Time;* and *Strolling Through the Park One Day.*

Gus Edwards died in Los Angeles, California, on November 7, 1945.

Raymond B. Egan

Raymond B. Egan was born on November 14, 1890. A Canadian by birth, he grew up in Detroit, Michigan, and started out as boy soprano in St. Johns Episcopal Choir. After attending the University of Michigan, he worked as a bank clerk for awhile, and then—in what seems to be an inevitable move for budding songwriters—he joined the staff of a music publishing company. He began to write lyrics in the teens, and continued well into the thirties, collaborating with top composers, including Walter Donaldson, Ted Fio Rito, and Richard Whiting. His first big hit, written with Richard Whiting, was *Till We Meet Again,* published in 1918, one of the most popular songs associated with the First World War. Easily adapted to four-four time, it is a favorite of jazz musicians and has been recorded in a jazz arrangement several times. An outstanding example is the "Pete Kelly's Big 7" version on Capital 1780. The tune has also surfaced in a 1942 movie with Judy Garland, *For Me and My Gal* and *On Moonlight Bay,* a 1951 film starring Doris Day and Gordon MacRae.

In 1920 Egan had two big hits back-to-back. With Dick Whiting the entry was *Japanese Sandman,* a harmless little ballad that was introduced by Nora Bayes and successfully recorded by Paul Whiteman. During World War II it fell into disfavor due to the efforts of overzealous patriots, but its status as a standard has been restored since. The other song was the enthusiastic *I Never Knew (I Could Love Anybody),* on which Egan teamed with Tom Pitts and Roy Marsh, two gentlemen who seem to have no other songs to their credit. Popular through the years and frequently recorded, it received exceptional treatment in an arrangement by Joe Haymes for his band, recorded for RCA–Victor, and was released on the Bluebird label. Originally Bluebird B-5178, it was reissued on the two-record LP album *Joe Haymes and His Orchestra 1932–1935.*

The following year Egan was back working with Richard Whiting, abetted by Gus Kahn, and they came up with the slightly satiric *Ain't We Got Fun.* It did well on an early recording for Columbia by the popular team of Van & Schenk, and was featured by Ruth Roye in vaudeville. It was played in the movie *On Moonlight Bay* and was sung by Doris Day and Gordon MacRae in the 1952 film *By the Light of the Silvery Moon.* It has been recorded many times since then. *Sleepy Time Gal,* another perennial favorite, came along in 1925. Egan and Joseph R. Alden wrote the words to music by Ange Lorenzo and Richard Whiting. In these cases it's easy to suspect that Alden and Lorenzo may have been the primary composers, with Egan and Whiting providing the necessary prestige and know-how to get the song published, but regardless, it's a great song. Ben Bernie had an early hit record of it, and it has been recorded dozens of times since. In 1942 it was the title song of a movie starring Judy Canova and Tom Brown, and Frances Langford sang it in the 1943 film *Never a Dull Moment.*

Egan and Ted Fio Rito combined to write *Three on a Match,* a fine song that was used in a movie starring Robert Montgomery, Marion Davies, Jimmy Durante, and Billie Dove, *Blondie of the Follies.* It came out in the fruitful year of 1932, one of the most prolific in the production of good songs, and managed to hold its own against the strong competition. Paul Whiteman recorded it, with a vocal by the up-and-coming singing star Red McKenzie, on Victor; Will Osborne did it for Melotone; and Anson Weeks made it for Brunswick. Freddy Martin, destined to make dozens of records in his long career, included *Three on a Match* in his very first session, a date for Columbia. Other Egan compositions include *They Called It Dixieland; Somebody's Wrong; Some Sunday Morning; Where the Morning Glories Grow; Tell Me Why You Smile, Mona Lisa; Downstream Drifter;* and *Knick Knacks on the Mantle.*

Raymond Egan died in Westport, Connecticut, on October 13, 1952.

Edward Eliscu

Edward Eliscu, a native New Yorker, was born in the big city on April 2, 1902, and if there ever was such a thing as a triple-threat man in the entertainment business, he would qualify. Besides writing lyrics for songs, he was a playwright, an actor, and a producer—and successful in each capacity. As a songwriter he collaborated with a number of the finest composers, including Vernon Duke, Johnny Green, Jay Gorney, Billy Hill, and Franz Lehar, but his most important contributions were made with Vincent Youmans, with some help from Billy Rose and Gus Kahn. "Great Day!" a stage musical produced in 1929, only lasted for thirty-six performances, but it introduced three songs that have become standards, the title song, *Without a Song,* and *More Than You Know.* All three were composed by Vincent Youmans, with lyrics by Eliscu and Billy Rose. The beautiful *More Than You Know* has been recorded countless times, especially by vocalists; Benny Goodman gave it special treatment on a twelve-inch Columbia, arranged by Eddie Sauter, with a vocal by Helen Forrest (CO 55002/264015). It has also been featured in several movies: *Hit the Deck* in 1930 and again in the 1955 remake; *The Helen Morgan Story* in 1957; and *Funny Lady* in 1974.

Without a Song has also had a distinguished career. Introduced in the short-lived "Great Day," it was sung by Lawrence Tibbett in the movie *The Prodigal* and was associated with him. It has also been recorded and sung by Bing Crosby, Perry Como, Nelson Eddy, Jan Peerce, and Frank Sinatra, among others, and also waxed by Ray McKinley, Rex Stewart, Wild Bill Davis, and Eddie Heywood. The title song *Great Day,* although not as illustrious as the first two songs, got off to a good start on the road to immortality by being paired with *Without a Song* on Paul Whiteman's Victor recording, both sides featuring Bing Crosby vocals. In later reincarnations it was featured in the 1974 film *Funny Lady* and *A Musical Jubilee* in 1975.

Eliscu supplied the words for the delightful *You Forgot Your Gloves,* a 1931 entry with music by Ned Lehac. It was introduced by Constance Carpenter and Carl Randall in the stage production of "The Third Little Show," and treated to a swinging revival by Les Brown and his "Band of Renown" on Coral 60785. Eliscu teamed with Vincent Youmans again in 1933, aided and abetted by Gus Kahn, and they turned out four songs for the movie *Flying Down to Rio,* which starred Fred Astaire and Ginger Rogers. The titles were *Orchids in the Moonlight; Carioca; Music Makes Me;* and the title song, *Flying Down to Rio*. This was Vincent Youmans's last published score.

Edward Eliscu continued to write but had no more timeless hits. His other titles include *They Cut Down the Old Pine Tree; Damn the Torpedoes; It's No Fun Eating Alone; It's the Same Old South; A Kiss to Remind You; The Four Rivers;* and *You're Perfect.*

Duke Ellington

One of the first and most eminent names to be enshrined in the "American Jazz Hall of Fame" by the New Jersey Jazz Society, in cooperation with Rutgers University, was that of Duke Ellington. An unquestioned giant in American music, he had a long and influential career that covered all facets of the art. He was an excellent pianist, a superb arranger, a personable and colorful bandleader, and a highly original composer. A number of books that explore his life in detail have been written, including the biography *Music Is My Mistress,* published in 1973, but in this case I'm going to confine the scope to his work as a composer, particularly in regard to his popular songs. Even that presents problems, because the Duke composed two ways, music designed for his orchestra and music intended for the popular song market. In many instances the pieces he wrote for the orchestra were developed and modified into popular songs. Nevertheless, the Ellington stamp was unmistakable, because one of his greatest talents was the ability to write prolifically in a style that was entirely his own, harmonically and melodically.

For the most part, Ellington wrote all his music with the orchestra in mind, often composing pieces designed to showcase the great individual soloists in the band who made the Ellington Orchestra a musical organization far superior to the average dance band. In writing material for the orchestra he was a master of moods, spanning everything from rhythm numbers that rocked the band to soulful tone poems. In between were songs for every tempo, every mood, every occasion, and everyone, for the Duke touched all bases, and there isn't anyone who doesn't have at least one favorite in the Ellington songbook. He started writing in the twenties, turning out successful instrumentals that became standards in themselves and long-lasting trademarks of the Ellington Orchestra—*East St. Louis Toodle-Oo* (which became the band's theme); *Birmingham Breakdown; Black and Tan Fantasy; Washington Wobble; Creole Love Call; The Mooche; Misty Morning*—but it wasn't until 1931, when *Mood Indigo* was published with lyrics, that an Ellington composition became a popular song. Originally this collaboration with Barney Bigard was entitled *Dreamy Blues,* and some recordings issued in 1930 have this name on the label. It was renamed and lyrics were added by Mitchell Parish, but due to a typical Mills publishing contract, Parish received no credit or royalties from the song, and Irving Mills's name is listed with Ellington and Bigard as cocomposer.

From then on, Ellington continued to write instrumentals through the years, and his contributions to the popular market resulted in hits that often became standards. Even a partial list is impressive: *It Don't Mean a Thing; Sophisticated Lady; In My Solitude; In a Sentimental Mood; I Let a Song Go Out of My Heart; Prelude to a Kiss; All Too Soon; I Got It Bad (And That Ain't Good); Don't Get Around Much Any More; Do Nothin' Till You Hear from Me; I Didn't Know About You; I'm Beginning to See the Light; Satin Doll.* In typical Ellington fashion, three of these songs were adaptations of instrumentals. *Do Nothin' Till You Hear from Me,* with lyrics by Bob Russell, came from *Concerto for Cootie,* which the Duke wrote to feature trumpeter Cootie Williams. *Don't Get Around Much Any More,* also with words by Russell, was originally *Never No Lament. I Didn't Know about You* started out as *Sentimental Lady.* Again Bob Russell added the skillful lyrics.

In addition to these, there is a long list of Ellington compositions with beautiful melodic lines that seem to cry out for lyrics to further delineate the titles and the moods they create—*Awful Sad; Azure; Delta Serenade; Dusk; Warm Valley;* and many others. Duke Ellington also composed extended orchestral works. Probably the best known of these is *Black, Brown and Beige.*

He was born in Washington, D.C., on April 29, 1899, and died in New York City on May 24, 1974.

Mercer Ellington

Mercer Ellington was born in Washington, D.C., on March 11, 1919. He was educated at Columbia University and Juilliard and pursued a career in music. As to be expected, he worked closely with his father Duke Ellington, writing material in a similar vein. Many of his songs were recorded by the Ellington Orchestra. Mercer led his own band for several years, served as manager and played trumpet in the Cootie Williams Orchestra, and, after the Duke's death in 1974, took over as leader of the Ellington Orchestra. His two best-known compositions are probably *Moon Mist* and *Things Ain't What They Used to Be*. Others include *Blue Serge; Jumpin' Punkins; Happy-Go-Lucky Local; John Hardy's Wife;* and *The Girl in My Dreams Tries to Look Like You.*

Mercer Ellington died in Copenhagen, Denmark, on February 8, 1996.

John M. (Jack) Elliott

Lyricist John M. (Jack) Elliott was born in Gowanda, New York, on May 7, 1914. He graduated from high school and then toured in vaudeville as a singer, later performing in nightclubs, theaters, and on the radio. Like so many other budding writers, he wrote special material for other acts besides his own and in 1940 started writing songs. Eventually this led to working in the movies, writing background scores and conducting on soundtracks. In 1941 he teamed with pianist Lew Quadling to turn out the superior ballad *Do You Care?* It was accorded equally superior treatment by Dinah Shore on Bluebird; Sam Donahue's band, with a vocal by Irene Daye (also on Bluebird); and Bob Crosby's orchestra on Decca. A decade later it was recorded by Frances Wayne vocalizing with Neal Hefti's orchestra on Coral.

Sam's Song, a 1950 Elliott–Quadling offering, enjoyed the unique position of being recorded on Decca by "Gary Crosby and Friend," a tasty duet by Bing and his oldest son that was an instant hit. Once again, over a decade later, Dean Martin and Sammy Davis Jr. reprised it on Reprise. That same year (1950) Jack Elliott and composer Harold Spina gave Dinah Shore another song ideally suited to her styling, *It's So Nice to Have a Man Around the House*. Then, as though not to appear playing favorites, they wrote *Be Mine,* a successful recording for Mindy Carson on Victor and June Hutton with Vic Schoen's band on Decca. Elliott continued to write songs, but he had other business interests, such as producing TV commercials. Then too, the fifties saw the end of the demand for superior songs. Other titles to his credit include *I Think of You; I Don't Wanna Be Kissed by Anyone but You; A Weaver of Dreams; Funny Melody;* and *Summer Vacation.*

Jack Elliott died in Los Angeles, California, on January 3, 1972.

Vivian Ellis

British pianist, composer, and writer Vivian Ellis was born in Hampstead, London, England, on October 29, 1904. His grandmother was a member of the Royal Academy, a friend of Sir Arthur Sullivan, and composer of a successful opera; and his mother was an accomplished violinist. As a boy Ellis was already so advanced as a pianist that when concert pianist Myra Hess heard him play, she immediately took him as a student. However, rather than a concert pianist, Ellis decided to become a composer and with this in mind went to work for a music publisher and while still in his teens began contributing material to musical revues. In 1929 he had two successful songs in the show "Mr. Cinders," *Spread a Little Happiness* and *I'm a One Man Girl*. Both songs were recorded back-to-back by the New Mayfair Orchestra on English HMV, probably under the direction of Carroll Gibbons, who preceded Ray Noble as "Light Music Director" with the company.

The following year Ellis started a long association with the producer C. B. Cochran and wrote the score for "Cochran's 1930 Revue," which also included additional songs by Rodgers and Hart. Most importantly, this show produced the song that, in my estimation, is not only the best Ellis ever wrote, but one of those gems that deserve much greater recognition, *The Wind in the Willows*. It was sung in the revue by Leslie Hutchinson and recorded in the United States by Rudy Vallee for Victor and Ben Bernie for Brunswick in January 1931. The lyrics were by Desmond Carter, and their wistful delineation of loneliness and regret was probably inspired by the gentle melancholy of the melody. Words and music are an excellent match. Ellis, now recognized as a talented writer of quality songs, next wrote the entire score for "Follow a Star," including three songs for Sophie Tucker, *I Can Never Think of the Words; That's Where the South Begins;* and *If Your Kisses Can't Hold the Man You Love*. Ray Noble, directing the New Mayfair Orchestra, recorded the music from this show on HMV C2020, a twelve-inch record with both sides presenting the score in overture format. The rather staid performance gets a sudden jolt of hot jazz in the rendition of *If Your Kisses Can't Hold the Man You Love,* with a scorching chorus by the young trumpet player Norman Payne.

Ellis continued to write for successful shows, and his songs were very popular in England. In 1930 he also wrote for "Little Tommy Tucker" and in the first month of 1931 contributed to three shows: "Folly to Be Wise," "Blue Roses," and "The Song of the Drum." Later that same year he contributed material to the Jack Buchanan show "Stand Up and Sing." Overexposure cut the demand for his composing efforts, so he began writing books. Then a reunion with C. B. Cochran a few years later put him back in the running, and he wrote for more shows. World War II put a temporary end to his career, and for five years he served in the British navy. Once again reunited with C. B. Cochran, Ellis, with A. P. Herbert writing the lyrics, had more hit shows to his credit. One of these, "Bless the Bride," had nearly nine hundred performances.

In 1973 Vivian Ellis was presented with the Ivor Novello Award for Outstanding Services to British Music.

Bob Emmerich

Robert D. Emmerich was born in New York City, July 26, 1904. He attended Horace Mann High School and business school, but show business exerted the greatest attraction. He played piano in vaudeville, nightclubs, and on the radio. Later on he became a newspaper columnist and advertising director. He started writing popular songs in the midthirties. One of his early efforts, *Darling,* a collaboration with Dave Oppenheim, came out in 1935 and was recorded by the great Isham Jones Orchestra on Decca. The vocalist was the new boy in the band, Woody Herman. *Woe Is Me,* a sprightly little ditty in spite of the title, got more attention in England than it did here and was recorded by Bert Ambrose and Harry Leader. Fats Waller gave it his inimitable attention on Victor. James Cavanaugh wrote the song's words.

In 1937 Emmerich and Buddy Bernier composed *The Big Apple,* a song designed to be played and sung in conjunction with the dance of the same name. Both were successful to some extent. The song was recorded by the bands of Tommy Dorsey, Clyde Lucas, and Frankie Froeba—the latter with a vocal by the Al Rinker Trio. The association with Buddy Bernier continued, and in 1938 they scored big with *Hurry Home,* a ballad that got full treatment on recordings by Al Donahue, Sammy Kaye, Bob Crosby, Jan Savitt, and Gene Krupa, thus spanning all the major labels. *This Time It's Real,* another nice song, rated two very musical renditions on records, Tommy Dorsey's band with Jack Leonard on Victor, and Ella Fitzgerald and the "Savoy 8" on Decca. *Our Love,* one of the biggest hits of 1939, was the combined effort of Emmerich, Buddy Bernier, and bandleader Larry Clinton and was adapted from Tchaikovsky's *Romeo and Juliet Fantasy Overture.* Tommy Dorsey had the hit recording. Possibly influenced by its success, Emmerich and Bernier reworked another importation in 1939, this time a Viennese composition, *Hear My Song, Violetta.* Glenn Miller had the best-selling record on Bluebird.

Other titles by Bob Emmerich are *If I Were You; I'd Love to Make Love to You; The American Way; Up in New Hampshire; You Went to My Head; Gandy Dancer; Believing; So Lovely; I Haven't Got a Hat; No Wonder;* and *Lost in the Shuffle.*

Ernie Erdman

Ernie Erdman, composer, was born in Pittsburgh, Pennsylvania, October 23, 1879. Details of his early life are sparse, but it is known that he was the house pianist at Schiller's Café in Chicago and played with Johnny Stein's "Dixie Jazz Band." He was also involved in the fiasco resulting in the suit over composing credit of *Livery Stable Blues*. In *The Story of the Original Dixieland Band* by H. O. Brunn (Louisiana State University Press, Baton Rouge, 1960), the author relates that Erdman suggested the title for the song, but when Nick LaRocca requested that he appear as a witness to verify this, Erdman refused to do so unless he received one-sixth of the royalties. Erdman also functioned as professional staff pianist for a Chicago music publisher. He is listed as co-composer of several big songs published in the early twenties, notably *Toot Toot Tootsie, Goodbye,* on which he shares credit with Ted Fio Rito, Gus Kahn, and Robert A. King; *No No Nora,* by the same team; and *Nobody's Sweetheart,* a collaboration with Elmer Schoebel, Billy Meyers, and Gus Kahn.

Toot, Toot Tootsie, Goodbye, a 1922 entry, was introduced by Al Jolson in the Broadway show "Bombo," and it was an instant hit. He went on to record it for Columbia, and the song became identified with him. He sang it again in the pioneering sound movie *The Jazz Singer* in 1927; the movie *Rose of Washington Square* (1939); *The Jolson Story,* the film based on his life (1946); and finally *Jolson Sings Again* in 1949. In the last two his voice was dubbed in on the soundtrack for Larry Parks. *No No Nora,* although not so well documented, was a hit song in 1923, the year it was published. Erdman again teamed with Gus Kahn and Ted Fio Rito on this one, and page eighty-seven of *Bix, Man & Legend* (Evans and Sudhalter, Arlington House, 1974) mentions that Beiderbecke was very fond of the song, with its "ever-shifting chord sequence which lent itself well to Bix's piano variations." *Nobody's Sweetheart,* of course, is the standard so favored by jazz bands. Published in 1924, it was another team effort, with composing credits shared by Erdman, Elmer Schoebel, Gus Kahn, and Billy Meyers. Although it never completely died out, it was handed a new lease on life by the Mills Brothers in 1932 on their first recording, which sold over a million copies. Since then it has been played and sung in a number of movies, especially the Gus Kahn biography, *I'll See You in My Dreams* (1952), with Doris Day singing it.

Erdman composed or cocomposed a respectable number of other songs, including *Jean; Underneath Hawaiian Skies; Ireland and Someone I Love; The Waltz That Made You Mine; Sail On, Silv'ry Moon; I'm Going Back, Back, Back to Carolina;* and *The Little Red School.*

Ernie Erdman died in Rockford, Illinois, November 1, 1946.

Ray Evans

Ray Evans will most likely be familiar to the casual listener of popular songs because his work is recent and most of it was connected with movies. In collaboration with composer Jay Livingston he turned out a number of successful titles. He was born February 4, 1915, in Salamanca, N.Y., attended the Wharton School and the University of Pennsylvania, and played clarinet and sax in college and dance bands. He met Jay Livingston, a pianist, in college, and later on they teamed to write songs. Getting started in the highly competitive field wasn't easy, and Evans had to work as a clerk and accountant. However, a big break came with the commission to write special material for the Olsen and Johnson hit show "Hellzapoppin'," and then again for another one, "Sons O' Fun." The team had their first hit in 1941, *G'Bye Now,* but then Livingston entered military service. On his return they landed a movie contract and from 1945 on began to turn out tunes for the movies. Among the better-known titles are *To Each His Own; Golden Earrings; The Streets of Laredo; Song of Surrender; Buttons and Bows; Mona Lisa;* and *Tammy.*

Redd Evans

Redd Evans was born in Meridian, Mississippi, on July 6, 1912. His education included a stint at the University of Arizona and Kent College. He started out as a singer and a soloist on the ocarina but graduated to the clarinet and saxophone, working in dance bands. Among the bands he worked with were Teddy Wilson's and Horace Heidt's. He also formed his own publishing house. Evans was a comparative latecomer to the ranks of popular songwriters in the traditional idiom, and the list of his titles isn't extensive, but it includes some important songs, especially in the World War II years. Probably his earliest hit, *Let Me Off Uptown,* was written with bandleader Earl Bostic (with whom he also wrote *The Major and the Minor*). The former, a 1941 submission, was promoted into a hit by the Gene Krupa Orchestra, with a duet by Roy Eldridge and Anita O'Day.

In 1943 Evans worked with John Jacob Loeb to turn out *Rosie the Riveter,* a song that appealed to the patriotic fervor of women working in defense plants. It was recorded by the Four Vagabonds on Bluebird and then featured in a movie, *Follow the Band,* as sung by the King Sisters with Alvino Rey's band. In the following year Evans had a song that helped add to the rising popularity of bandleader Vaughn Monroe, *There, I've Said It*

Again. Frim Fram Sauce developed into a hit record by Nat Cole in 1946; Ella Fitzgerald and Louis Armstrong turned it into a duet on Decca. The tune was a collaboration with Joe Ricardel. Evans had another hit in 1950, combining with Hal David and Arthur Altman on *American Beauty Rose*. Frank Sinatra had the big-selling record, with Eddy Howard not far behind. Vaughn Monroe entered the picture again in 1956 with a successful recording of *Don't Go to Strangers*. This time Evans contributed the lyrics, and Arthur Kent and Dave Mann wrote the music. Dave Mann and Evans came up with the song that is the most musical of the Evans output, *No Moon at All*. Although it was published in 1963, rather late in the season for a quality song, it was featured on two excellent records, one by the King Cole Trio, the other by the Ames Brothers with Les Brown's band on Coral. Other titles include *Pushin' Along; He's A-1 in the Army; Are You Livin', Old Man; Unconditional Surrender; This Is the Night; Made Up My Mind; Gobs of Love;* and *Birmingham Jailhouse*.

Redd Evans died in Scarsdale, New York, on August 29, 1972.

Sammy Fain

Sammy Fain probably comes as close as anybody ever will to the characterization of a songwriter the movies have led us to expect—the combined pianist, singer, composer with a long list of hits to his credit. Among the hits are many of your favorite songs—and some others that you can't help wishing you could forget—all the result of a long and prolific career. He was born in New York City on June 17, 1902, and early in his career went to work for a song publisher. He also worked as a pianist and a singer and even made records as a vocalist. His songwriting began in 1925 with *Nobody Knows What a Red-Headed Mama Can Do,* which enjoyed a fair success, and was followed in the next couple of years by *I Left My Sugar Standing in the Rain* (made immortal by the Rhythm Boys—Crosby, Rinker, and Barris) and *Let a Smile Be Your Umbrella,* but he really hit it big in 1929 with *Wedding Bells Are Breaking Up That Old Gang of Mine.*

The thirties—that golden era for songwriters which offered an unprecedented market for superior songs—saw him start off with a blockbuster, *You Brought a New Kind of Love to Me,* for the movie *The Big Pond,* starring Maurice Chevalier, and from then on he contributed to film scores for over thirty years. Among his better-known songs are *When I Take My Sugar to Tea; Hummin' to Myself; Was That the Human Thing to Do?; Am I Gonna Have Trouble with You; That Old Feeling; Don't You Know or Don't You Care?; I Can Dream, Can't I?: I'll Be Seeing You; Secret Love; Love Is a Many-Splendored Thing*; and *A Very Precious Love*. Fain also wrote for stage shows, contributing songs to successes like "Hellzapoppin'," "George White's Scandals of 1939," "Sons O' Fun," and "Alive and Kicking," among others, and a number of movie musicals, including *Alice in Wonderland, Peter Pan,* and *The Jazz Singer*. In later years he wrote title songs for others—*Love Is a Many-Splendored Thing; April Love; Tender Is the Night*. He had a consistent track record for hits, but as is usually the case, some of his better songs are only remembered by those who were around when they came out, tunes like *When Tomorrow Comes; Ev'ry Day; That Never-to-Be Forgotten Night; Who Blew Out the Flame*; and

Are You Havin' Any Fun. Altogether, some worthy contributions to our musical heritage.

Sammy Fain died in Tucson, Arizona, in 1983.

Arthur Fields

Arthur Fields, who can still be heard singing on countless old 78 rpm records, was born in Philadelphia, Pennsylvania, on August 6, 1888. He started out singing and acting in minstrel shows, then toured in vaudeville, and was an early radio star. At a later period he partnered with bandleader Fred Hall in a music publishing firm. One of his earliest songs, *On the Mississippi,* was a collaboration with lyricist Ballard MacDonald, Arthur Fields sharing composing credit with Harry Carroll. The year was 1912, and the song was featured in two stage musicals, "The Whirl of Society," and "Hanky Panky." It was revived decades later to be heard in the 1946 movie *The Dolly Sisters* and again in 1953, with Mitzi Gaynor in the role of Eva Tanguay singing it, in another movie, *The I Don't Care Girl.*

Aba Daba Honeymoon, with words and music by Fields and Walter Donovan, was a 1914 composition introduced by Ruth Roye at New York's famed Palace Theater, the apex of the vaudeville circuit. The vocal duet of Arthur Collins and Byron Harlan performed it on a hit record for Victor. It was revived thirty-six years later in the movie *Two Weeks with Love,* sung by Debbie Reynolds and Carleton Carpenter. They recorded it for M-G-M Records in 1951. It sold over a million copies, and the song made the Hit Parade for nine weeks. *Auntie Skinner's Chicken Dinner,* with words and music by Fields, Ted Morse, and Harry Carroll, was another 1914 entry. Collins and Harlan again had the big record. The tune has enjoyed a revival on the West Coast with traditional jazz bands and is frequently played at festivals.

Fields continued to write, and in 1929 he had another hit in the novelty *I Got a Dode Id by Dose,* a cooperative offering with Fred Hall and Billy Rose. Fred Hall and His Sugar Babes recorded it for OKeh, and just to make it complete, the vocal was by Arthur Fields. Fields and Hall struck again the following year with *Eleven More Months and Ten More Days,* a sad tale relating the plight of a jailbird doing a one-year term. Vernon Dalhart recorded it on the Harmony label disguised as "Mack Allen," and in England the Rhythmic Eight thought enough of the opus to make it into a two-sided recording for Zonophone. Other titles credited to Fields are *There's a*

Blue Sky 'Way Out Yonder; Our Hometown Mountain Band; Who Else but God; and *There Shall Be No More Tears.*

Arthur Fields died in Largo, Florida, on March 29, 1953.

Arthur B. (Buddy) Fields

Arthur (Buddy) Fields was born in Vienna, Austria, of American parents on September 24, 1889. He attended public schools in Chicago, and in WW I was a member of the 133 Machine Gun Battalion of the Thirty-Sixth Division. After the war he performed in vaudeville and clubs and then gave it up to become a theatrical agent. Although he can't be described as composing any sensational hits, he did collaborate on a number of successful songs in the twenties and thirties. One of his earliest efforts appeared in 1922, a collaboration with Will Collins and A. Cameron called *Falling*. In 1924 he worked with Seymour Simons on a tune called *Remember* that was recorded by Jean Goldkette's Orchestra on Victor with a vocal by none other than Seymour Simons. The song is not to be confused with the Berlin melody of the same name that was a super hit in 1925.

In 1926 Buddy Fields and Sam Lerner composed a ditty called *The Pump Song, or It's Hard to Tell the Depth of the Well by the Length of the Handle on the Pump*. It found favor with Irving Aaronson's Commanders on Victor, and the popular duo of Jones and Hare, among others. The title may not be the longest for a popular song, but it must be close to it. What's more, it's memorable. I recall hearing the tune on the radio when it first came out, and I have never forgotten it. I always did have an ear for the classics. Seymour Simons returned to collaborate with Fields on the 1930 song *Chinnin' and Chattin' with May*. For some reason this one appealed to jazz musicians. Bubber Miley's Mileage Makers recorded it for Victor, and an Eddie Kirkeby group, the Hot Air Men, waxed it for Columbia.

Gerald Marks wrote the music for another long-winded Fields title in 1941, *With You on My Mind (I Can't Write the Words)*. A Ben Selvin recording unit including Bunny Berigan, Benny Goodman, and other top-notch studio men of the time made this under one of the more popular pseudonyms that Selvin used to disguise his activity, "Roy Carroll and His Sands Point Orchestra." A pleasant song and gently sentimental, it rated top treatment. It must be one of the many little ironies of the songwriting business that two of Fields's collaborators, Seymour Simons and Gerald Marks, got together without him and produced the all-time standard *All of Me,* one of the biggest hits of 1931. Fields and Marks continued to work together for awhile, and in 1932 they had two entries. The first I'll mention, *Night Shall Be Filled with Music,* is among my favorite songs and to my mind typifies the high quality, both in melody and lyrics, of the average songs of that year. I use the word "average" here not to disparage the quality of the song, but to point out that as fine as it is, it was average for that period of the Golden Age. It was given fair playing time on radio but little attention on records. The Lou Gold Orchestra recorded it on Perfect, and the Harold Van Enburgh Orchestra made it for Crown. The song deserved much better representation.

While *Night Shall Be Filled with Music* was mostly overlooked, another Fields and Marks offering in the same year with the delicate title of *You're the One (You Beautiful Son-of-a-Gun)* got more attention than it rated. It was used by entertainer Harry Richman in the revue "George White's Music Hall Varieties," plugged by Rudy Vallee on his radio broadcasts, and recorded by Richman on Brunswick and the Fred Waring organization on Victor. Robert Lissauer, in his *Encyclopedia,* relates that Marks originally wrote the tune as a schottische, but Fred Waring overheard him demonstrating it at the publisher's office and suggested the tempo be changed to 6/8. Marks made the change and the song was successful. *Night Shall Be Filled with Music* is a much better song in my opinion.

In 1933 Fields joined with Al Sherman and Al Lewis for the collegiate-sounding *You Gotta Be a Football Hero*. Ben Bernie and All the Lads had fun with it, and Harry Reser and his Eskimos added the rest of the tune's title, *To Get Along with the Beautiful Girls,* on their version, which spanned all the ARC labels, Perfect, Conqueror, Banner, Melotone, and Oriole. The side eventually wound up on Royal. Other titles by Fields are *By the Sign of the Rose; Indoor Outdoor Girl; By a Campfire; If It Wasn't for You; How Can I Be Anything but Blue*; and *I'll Get Along Somehow*.

Buddy Fields died in Detroit, Michigan, on October 4, 1965.

Dorothy Fields

A New Jersey native, Dorothy Fields, one of our most prolific lyricists, was born in Allenhurst, July 15, 1905. She was the daughter of Lew Fields, half of the famous vaudeville comedy team of Weber & Fields. Most of her work was done with composer Jimmy McHugh, but she also collaborated with Jerome Kern, Oscar Levant, Arthur Schwartz, Fritz Kreisler, Sigmund Romberg, Morton Gould, Burton Lane, and her brother Herbert Fields. She is also the first woman to be elected to the Songwriters Hall of Fame. Fields's career was long and fruitful, starting in 1928 when she combined with Jimmy

McHugh to write material for the show "Blackbirds of 1928," which produced *I Can't Give You Anything but Love; Diga Diga Doo; I Must Have That Man; Porgy; Doin' the New Low Down; Baby*; and *Bandana Babies*. In 1929 the show "Hello Daddy" included *In a Great Big Way; Let's Sit and Talk about You; Out Where the Blues Begin*; and *Futuristic Rhythm*. It starred Lew Fields, the book was by Herbert Fields, and lyrics were by Dorothy Fields. (You might say it was a Fields day. *Sorry, couldn't resist it.)* Jimmy McHugh was the composer.

But Fields and McHugh were just warming up. In 1930 they wrote for the Lew Leslie stage show "The International Revue" and turned out the all-time standards *On the Sunny Side of the Street* and *Exactly Like You*. Another show in that same year, "Vanderbilt Revue," was a flop, but out of it came Wild Bill Davison's favorite song, *Blue Again*. In 1933 the team worked on a movie, *Dancing Lady,* which starred Joan Crawford, Clark Gable, and Franchot Tone, and scored again with *Don't Blame Me; My Dancing Lady; Dinner at Eight*; and *Hey, Young Fella*. Then, possibly just to prove they didn't need shows or movies to write hits, in 1934 they free-lanced two of them, *Lost in a Fog* and *Thank You for a Lovely Evening*.

The following year they were writing for the movies again. *Nitwits,* a Wheeler–Woolsey classic, offered the lovely *Music in My Heart,* and the Fred Astaire–Ginger Rogers hit *Roberta* included two Fields–McHugh songs, *Lovely to Look At* and *I Won't Dance*. But that isn't all. Another movie, *Every Night at Eight,* introduced *I'm in the Mood for Love; I Feel a Song Coming On; Speaking Confidentially*; and *Take It Easy*. *Hooray for Love* included the title song plus *Living in a Great Big Way; I'm in Love All Over Again*; and *You're an Angel*. You might think this was enough, but for good measure the team published *Every Little Moment*. And that's not all! In that same year of 1935 Fields branched out for the first time and with Oscar Levant wrote three songs for a Ginger Rogers–George Brent movie, *In Person*. The titles were *Don't Mention Love to Me; Out of Sight, Out of Mind*; and *I've Got a New Lease on Love*. Then she paired with Jerome Kern and for *I Dream Too Much* wrote the title song, plus three others, and for the movie *Alice Adams* penned *I Can't Waltz Alone* with Max Steiner.

Thc Rogers–Astaire hit *Swing Time* came in 1936, and the Jerome Kern–Dorothy Fields score included *The Way You Look Tonight; A Fine Romance; Pick Yourself Up; Bojangles of Harlem; Never Gonna Dance*; and *Waltz in Swing Time*. That same year *The King Steps Out* featured two songs by Fields with Fritz Kreisler, *Stars in My Eyes* and *Madly in Love*. *When You're in Love,* a 1937 screen entry, with Cary Grant and Grace Moore, put Fields back with Jerome Kern for two songs, *Our Song* and *The Whistling*

Boy—a rather quiet year for our heroine, but by this time she could afford to rest a bit on her laurels. The team was only getting ready for 1938 and *Joy of Living,* one of those films where they couldn't seem to get anybody and had to wind up with Irene Dunne, Douglas Fairbanks Jr., Alice Brady, Guy Kibbee, Lucille Ball, Jean Dixon, Eric Blore, and Warren Hymer. This time the tunes were *You Couldn't Be Cuter; Just Let Me Look at You; What's Good about Good-Night*; and *A Heavenly Party.* "Stars in Your Eyes," a title obviously cadged from the Fritz Kreisler–Dorothy Fields song of 1936, was a stage show starring Ethel Merman and Jimmy Durante, and teamed Fields with still another composer, Arthur Schwartz. The collaboration produced *This Is It; It's All Yours; Okay for Sound*; and *The Lady Needs a Change.*

The new decade opened slowly, with only one song of note in 1940, *You and Your Kiss,* with Jerome Kern for the Abbott & Costello opus *One Night in the Tropics.* Fields was beginning to relax a bit, and a couple of years slid by fallow, but in 1945 she was back stronger than ever, collaborating with her brother Herbert on the book for "Up in Central Park," and writing the music with Sigmund Romberg. The songs were *Close As Pages in a Book; When You Walk in the Room*; and *It Doesn't Cost You Anything to Dream.*

Dorothy Fields continued to write well into the seventies, contributing lyrics to stage shows and movies, but the public's appreciation for quality songs had waned by this time, and aside from Cy Coleman's *Big Spender,* which enjoyed modest success in 1965, none of the songs could be termed hits. She died in New York City on March 28, 1974, leaving us a rich heritage of outstanding lyrics.

Carl Theodore Fischer

Carl Theodore Fischer was born in Los Angeles, California, on April 9, 1912. His early education included private music study, and it resulted in employment as a pianist in the film studios. During WW II he served as assistant orchestra leader in both the navy and the marines. After the war he became conductor–accompanist for singer Frankie Laine, a span from 1946 until Fischer's death in 1954. Fischer didn't write many songs, but the odd circumstance is that his three best compositions were all published in 1942, with hit recordings for everybody involved. Bill Carey was the lyricist.

Probably the best known of the three is *You've Changed.* Oddly enough, the Harry James recording, with the vocal by Dick Haymes, was made in 1941 and started off slowly, but the fine arrangement of an outstanding song eventually was recognized. The recording is still considered one of the band's finest. The song had two later waxings, one in 1949 by Russ Case, and another in 1954 by Connie Russell with Harold Mooney's Orchestra. It is now considered a standard. *It Started All Over Again,* sung by Frank Sinatra and the Pied Pipers with Tommy Dorsey's band on Victor, was another big-seller. The Fischer melody was an ideal vehicle for the fast-rising singer, and the song has become identified with him. The third song, *Who Wouldn't Love You?,* although not as well known, lacks none of the quality of the first two, and it resulted in a very successful record for the popular Kay Kyser band with the vocal by Trudy and Harry Babbitt. The arrangement was a big asset, well played with a light swing and a clever flurry of rimshots at the beginning of each phrase of the song. In 1945 Fischer and Frankie Laine wrote a good song, *We'll Be Together Again.* Laine introduced it and recorded it for the Mercury label, and the Pied Pipers with June Hutton made it for Capitol, as did the Four Freshmen.

Even without any further hits, the above songs would speak well for the talent of any composer. However, there are other Fischer titles: *Promise; Could Ja; Give Me a Kiss for Tomorrow; Black Lace; Baby, Just for Me.*

Carl Fischer died in Sherman Oaks, California, on March 28, 1954.

Doris Fisher

Songwriting, a strange combination of creative artistry and commercial endeavor (like the rest of the music business, for that matter), is seldom confined to strict guidelines. That is, every so often it's hard to divide collaboration into a neat category where one partner is clearly designated as the composer, and the other—or others—as the lyricist(s). When the subject is multitalented, as many songwriters are, the dividing line gets very blurry. Such is the case with Doris Fisher and Dave Franklin. Although they wrote the words to songs by a number of famous composers, they sometimes also contributed to the composition of the melodies.

Fisher was born in New York City on May 2, 1915, and is best known for her work with composer Allan Roberts in the forties. The daughter of another well-known songwriter, Fred Fisher, her first hit song was in collaboration with her father, the 1940 hit that did so much to further the career of the Ink Spots, *Whispering Grass.* However, Doris Fisher went on to an almost exclusive partnership with Allan Roberts and with him shared credit for both music and lyrics on some respectable hits. Among these are *Into Each Life Some Rain Must Fall; You Always Hurt the One You Love;*

Tampico; Good, Good, Good; You Can't See the Sun When You're Crying; Put the Blame on Mame.

In addition to her songwriting talents, Fisher was an accomplished vocalist who performed in nightclubs, was featured for awhile with Eddy Duchin's band, and later formed her own vocal group, recording with it as "Penny Wise & Her Wise Guys."

Fred Fisher

A legendary figure in the history of popular songwriting, Fred Fisher was born of American parents in Cologne, Germany, on September 30, 1875. He was educated in Germany and served in the German army. As if this wasn't enough, he joined the French Foreign Legion. He came to the United States in 1900. He began his songwriting career in Chicago, moved on to New York, and took over as manager of a music publishing house. This led to the next step, founding his own publishing company in 1918. Fisher wrote both words and music, usually collaborating with others, but sometimes performing both chores. The list of his songs is extensive. He wrote prolifically from 1904 until 1940, the year his last song, *Whispering Grass,* was published, with words to the melody by his daughter Doris.

Fisher had an impressive number of hits in the early 1900s, including another contender for long titles, *Any Little Girl That's a Nice Little Girl Is the Right Little Girl for Me,* with words by Thomas J. Gray in 1910; *Come, Josephine, in My Flying Machine,* a vintage item of the era, with lyrics by Alfred Bryan; and *Ireland Must Be Heaven, for My Mother Came from There.* The last is a Fisher melody with words by Joseph McCarthy and Howard Johnson. *Peg O' My Heart,* one of Fisher's more enduring songs, with words by Alfred Bryan, first appeared in 1913. It was featured in the "Ziegfeld Follies of 1913," and Charles Harrison, on Victor, and Henry Burr, on Columbia, had hit records. The song surfaced again in 1933 as the title of a movie starring Marion Davies and was played in *Oh, You Beautiful Doll,* the movie based on Fisher's life, with S. Z. ("Cuddles") Sakall portraying the composer. In 1947 the Harmonicats had a big-selling record of the tune, and so did singer Buddy Clark on Columbia, but the classic rendition was waxed in 1944 on Milt Gabler's Commodore label. Trombonist Miff Mole and his Nicksieland Band, with Bobby Hackett, Pee Wee Russell, and kindred all-stars, were accorded a twelve-inch platter in order to do the song full justice—and they did. In the 1943 movie *For Me and My Gal,* Gene Kelly gave his rendition of *They Go Wild, Simply Wild, Over Me,* a

Fisher song with words by Joe McCarthy that first was heard in 1917. It was featured by the popular Marion Harris, who also recorded it for Victor.

Fisher reversed his songwriting talent in 1919, penning the lyrics to *Dardenella,* one of the biggest hits in the history of the business. The melody created a controversy. Fisher, by then a song publisher, added new words to a piano rag by Johnny S. Black called *Turkish Tom Tom.* After this, Felix Bernard claimed to have written the music, so to avoid further problems both composers shared credit. Ben Selvin had the first smash record, which sold over a million copies, and the sheet music sales were even higher. It has been recorded countless times since but achieved immortal treatment by Bill Challis in his arrangement for the Paul Whiteman Orchestra, recorded on Victor featuring Bix Beiderbecke.

Chicago, with both words and music by Fisher, came out in 1922, and again the sheet music sales were over a million. It has since gone on to become a standard with a distinguished career. Fred Astaire and Ginger Rogers danced to it in the 1939 movie musical *The Story of Vernon and Irene Castle.* It was part of the score of *Oh, You Beautiful Doll* in 1949; dubbed by singer Jane Froman on the soundtrack of the movie based on her life, *With a Song in My Heart,* with Susan Hayward mouthing the words on screen; and sung by Frank Sinatra in *The Joker Is Wild,* a 1957 film, and so on. Unofficially it has become the city's theme song, getting played as background music whenever Chicago is the site of a movie or a play. Jazz musicians like it because it lends itself well to improvisation. Other outstanding titles by Fisher include *When I Get You Alone Tonight,* a 1912 collaboration with Joe McCarthy and Joe Goodwin reprised by Dick Robertson and the Decca house band in 1940; *Fifty Million Frenchmen Can't Be Wrong,* a 1927 offering introduced and recorded by Sophie Tucker, with words by Willie Raskin and Billy Rose; and *There Ain't No Sweet Man Worth the Salt of My Tears,* a tender sentiment with words and music by Fisher, sympathetically expressed by Bing Crosby and the Rhythm Boys with Paul Whiteman's Orchestra in 1928. Kay Starr had a convincing version for Capitol some twenty years later.

Fisher, the consummate professional, had no problem making the change to more sophisticated ballads in the thirties. In fact, he got a jump start on the trend in 1929 when he wrote the lyrics for a melody by Martin Broones to produce *I Don't Want Your Kisses (If I Can't Have Your Love).* The song was featured in the movie *So This Is College,* which starred Robert Montgomery. Parker Gibbs sings it on the Victor record by the Ted Weems band, but doesn't seem too concerned about the situation. *Blue Is the Night*—another solo effort by Fisher—a little melancholy but not too sad, came out in

1930. It was the theme of the movie *Their Own Desire,* starring Norma Shearer. Then, just to prove he hadn't lost his sense of humor, he and Ada Benson turned out a ditty that Fats Waller developed into a hit record, *Your Feet's Too Big*. The 1936 novelty was offset by the moody *Moon Rose* of the same year. In 1938 Fisher wrote the music and Maurice Spitalny the words for *Angels with Dirty Faces;* the next year he worked the same way with Stella Unger on *Two Fools in Love. Whispering Grass,* his final song, with lyrics by daughter Doris, came out in 1940.

Fred Fisher's other compositions include: *Every Little Bit Helps; And a Little Bit More; Oh! You Chicken; I'm on My Way to Mandalay; Norway; Siam; There's a Broken Heart for Every Light on Broadway; There's a Little Bit of Bad in Every Good Little Girl; Lorraine, My Beautiful Alsace-Lorraine; Oui, Oui, Marie; Daddy, You've Been a Mother to Me; Savannah; If All the Stars Were Pretty Babies; Georgia Rockin' Chair; And the Band Played On*; and *I'd Rather Be Blue.*

Fred Fisher died in New York City, January 14, 1942.

Mark Fisher

Mark Fisher, bandleader, vocalist, and composer, was born in Philadelphia, Pennsylvania, March 24, 1895. The reference books offer no further information, other than that he led his own dance band in nightclubs and hotels. This is verified to some extent by two records made for Columbia on February 2, 1933, by Mark Fisher and His Edgewater Beach Hotel Orchestra. I also recall hearing the band on radio broadcasts from this Chicago hotel. As a composer Fisher was involved in the writing of three well-known popular songs. The first, a collaboration with two veterans of the business, Benny Davis and Joe Burke, was a certified tearjerker in 1925, *Oh! How I Miss You Tonight.* A waltz, it was introduced by Benny Davis in his vaudeville act and rendered with proper pathos by George Jessel on record.

Everywhere You Go, a tune that Guy Lombardo made into a hit recording in 1949, was written by Fisher, Larry Shay, and Joe Goodwin and made its first appearance in 1927. Moderately successful at the time, it was a new song to a later generation. Doris Day's record for Columbia helped in the big revival. The trio of Fisher, Shay, and Goodwin had their most important song published in 1928, one that is still with us with every indication that it will be around for a long time to come, even serving as background music for a toothpaste commercial on TV. The song is *When You're Smiling (The Whole World Smiles with You).* Louis Armstrong kicked it off with a hit recording for OKeh, and it has been played and recorded countless times since. It's a particular favorite of jazz bands.

Other titles credited to Fisher include *Who Wants a Bad Little Boy; Don't Forget to Remember; Dear One; You're Too Much; Heart Breaker*; and *Take Me Back to the Garden of Roses.*

Mark Fisher died in Long Lake, Ingleside, Illinois, on January 2, 1948.

Dave Franklin

Dave Franklin may not be considered a household name in the songwriting field, although his name is on the credits of some well-known titles. For me he occupies a special place in the pantheon of great songwriters because he collaborated on a number of songs that are among my favorites—songs that never made anybody's hit parade (thank goodness) but are fine examples of the craft at its best. Franklin was born in New York City, September 28, 1895, and wasted no time in starting his musical career. Leaving school at the tender age of thirteen to (you guessed it!) take a job playing piano for a song publishing house, he went on to tour in vaudeville, accompanying performers; made a wide swing of nightclubs, both here and abroad; and began dabbling in songwriting in the early thirties. Meanwhile, he penned special material for the revues at the famous Connie's Inn and the Paradise Restaurant, for bandleader Ben Bernie.

His first published song has long been forgotten but the title is still intriguing—*Isadore the Toreador*—but it wasn't until 1934 that he hit big. First, it was with a song he wrote alone—both words and music—*I Ain't Lazy—I'm Just Dreamin',* a tour de force for the irrepressible Eddie Stone, the vocalist with the great Isham Jones band of the period who made the "I-Don't-Care" attitude of the lyrics sound very convincing. Immediately after this, Franklin teamed with Islam Jones to turn out one of those songs among my favorites, *It's Funny to Everyone but Me.* The following year Franklin performed solo again, writing words and music for a very respectable hit, *I Woke Up Too Soon,* then repeated his collaboration with Isham Jones on *Give a Broken Heart a Break,* which, in spite of the catchy title, didn't do very well.

In 1936 he teamed with Cliff Friend, a prolific composer, and they struck pay dirt immediately with *When My Dream Boat Comes Home.* Then, as though to prove once more that he didn't need outside help, Franklin penned words and music for *I Hope Gabriel Likes My Music,* recently revived by Marty Grosz on an LP of the same title. However, 1937 proved to be a banner year for the team of Franklin and Friend, starting off with one of those favorites I told you about earlier, *Everything You Said Came True*. This was followed by *The Merry-Go-Round Broke Down; Never Should Have Told You* (a Benny Goodman sleeper); *Two Dreams Got Together*; and *You Can't Stop Me from Dreaming,* which was immortalized by Teddy Wilson on one of his classic Brunswicks. The next year the team had two contenders, *I Must See Annie Tonight* and *There's a Brand-new Picture in My Picture Frame.* Then in 1939 Franklin did it again, contributing one of my favorites to the Kay Kyser movie *That's Right—You're Wrong, Happy Birthday to Love,* which received exceptional treatment on a recording by the Smoothies, the vocal group with Hal Kemp's band.

When Franklin did so well writing songs by himself, it's hard to understand why he didn't do it all the time, but that same year he turned out three more rather mediocre titles with Cliff Friend, *Concert in the Park; I'm Building a Sailboat of Dreams*; and *You Don't Know How Much You Can Suffer*. For some unknown reason, 1940 was a fallow year, but when Franklin's next composition was published in 1941, he was teamed with Al Dubin on what is probably the biggest moneymaker of his career, *The Anniversary Waltz*. This was to be the last hit song for him, although Franklin continued to write well into the fifties; a very respectable career.

He died in Los Angeles, California, on February 3, 1970.

Arthur Freed

Arthur and Ralph Freed, as you may have suspected, were brothers. Between them they are responsible for the lyrics of so many songs in the standard library of our musical heritage that it would seem they should be household names. Instead, it's very likely that the average person would be unable to name one title in their long list of compositions. Arthur Freed was born on September 9, 1894, in Charleston, N.C., but grew up in Seattle. Early in his career he went into vaudeville, where he became acquainted with top performers of the day such as Gus Edwards, for whom he wrote special material. He also teamed with Lou Silvers and later on collaborated with him on material for New York nightclub revues. This was interrupted by service in the military in World War I, but upon discharge Arthur went back into vaudeville.

His songwriting career began around this time, with his first published title a collaboration with Nacio Herb Brown and somebody calling himself "King Zany" on the standard *When Buddha Smiles* in 1921. Brown was to be his principal collaborator, but Freed's next effort was with the rather unique team of two bandleaders, Gus Arnheim and Abe Lyman, the 1923 release *I Cried for You,* which underwent a well-deserved revival in the forties. A 1924 effort, *In the Land of Shady Palm Trees,* has been long forgotten, and it wasn't until 1929 that another Freed song came out; in the meantime he was busy producing shows in a Los Angeles theater. The 1929 return, however, was something of a blockbuster, with Freed reuniting with Nacio Herb Brown and entering a new career writing for movie musicals. Their first score for *Broadway Melody* produced several hits, including the title song, *You Were Meant for Me,* and *The Wedding of the Painted Doll.* The team also contributed a song to another movie, *Hollywood Revue of 1929,* which was not only the hit of the day, but went on to become the title song for the 1952 Gene Kelly classic *Singin' in the Rain.* But Freed wasn't through with 1929. Two other movies featured Brown–Freed songs—*Marianne,* which produced *Blondy,* and the Joan Crawford–Robert Montgomery steamer *Untamed,* which included the equally steamy *Chant of the Jungle.*

Montana Moon, another Joan Crawford entry (1930), included a pleasing score by Brown and Freed and the outstanding title *The Moon Is Low. Lord Byron of Broadway* offered the hit perennial *Should I?* And just possibly to prove he didn't need Brown to turn out hit songs, Freed teamed with composer Joseph Meyer, and they contributed *You're Simply Delish* to the score of the movie *Those Three French Girls.* The following year *The Big Broadcast of 1932* introduced the Harry Barris hit *It Was So Beautiful,* with lyrics by Arthur Freed, and Freed also had a hand in writing the sprightly *Fit as a Fiddle,* with Al Goodhart and Al Hoffman.

Freed continued to write for the movies throughout the 1930s and sporadically into the forties and fifties, teaming at times with composers Burton Lane, Harry Warren, and Roger Edens. Even a partial list of titles is impressive: *After Sundown; Temptation; Beautiful Girl* (1933); *All I Do Is Dream of You; From Now On; A New Moon Is over My Shoulder* (1934); *Alone; You Are My Lucky Star; I've Got a Feelin' You're Foolin* (1935); *Would You?* (1936); *Yours and Mine; Smoke Dreams* (1937); *Our Love Affair* (1940); *This Heart of Mine* (1945).

Arthur Freed died in Los Angeles on April 12, 1971.

Ralph Freed

Ralph Freed was born May 1, 1907, in Vancouver, British Columbia, Canada, and like brother Arthur, grew up in Seattle. However, for some reason he didn't begin writing lyrics for songs until 1934, when he followed in his brother's footsteps and teamed with Harry Barris to turn out *A Little Dutch Mill* and with Goodhart and Hoffman for the sardonic *Who Walks in When I Walk Out?* In 1935 he collaborated with Bonnie Lake on *Sandman,* which the Dorsey Brothers adopted as the theme of their short-lived orchestra, and in 1936 worked with Burton Lane on the pleasing *Guess Who?* Then with Johnny Noble, and somebody with the authentic-sounding name of "Leleiohako," Freed turned out the English lyrics for *Hawaiian War Chant.* In 1937 Ralph, too, went into writing for movies and continued to do so well into the fifties. A sampling of titles includes *Blue Danube Waltz; Smarty; Stop, Look, and Listen* (1937); *Lovelight in the Starlight; You Leave Me Breathless; You and Me* (1938); *I'll Remember* (1939); *Love Lies* (1940); *How About You?* (1941); *Madame, I Love Your Crepe Suzettes* (1943); *In a Moment of Madness*; and *Young Man with a Horn* (1944).

Ralph Freed died on February 13, 1973, in California.

Cliff Friend

Composer, pianist, and lyricist Cliff Friend was born in Cincinnati, Ohio, on October 1, 1893. He was educated at the Cincinnati College and Conservatory. Early in his career he worked as a test pilot at Wright Field. Then for three years he toured in vaudeville as accompanist to Harry Richman. A classic record in the long list of sides in the career of Joe Tarto is the unique version of *June Night,* which features Cliff Edwards (Ukulele Ike) backed by nothing but Joe's tuba. The tune was a big hit in the twenties and is now back into favor with jazz bands and musicians who are constantly looking for something good in the fantastic list of yesterday's favorites. It is just one of the many likely candidates for this treatment composed by the prolific Friend. Others worth investigating are *Mama Loves Papa; There's Yes Yes in Your Eyes; Tamiami Trail; Give Me a Night in June; Bashful Baby; Everything You Said Came True*; and *When My Dream Boat Comes Home,* just a sampling of the many songs he wrote over a period of more than forty years, including many for stage shows and movies.

Friend began writing for stage shows and for publication in 1921, but his first hit was probably the novelty *You Tell Her—I Stutter,* a big moneymaker, obviously a lesson he never forgot because although he could, and did, write many memorable and superior ballads—*The Same Old Moon; Then I'll Be Happy; I Wanna Sing about You; Just Because You're You*—periodically he hit the jackpot with novelties that are still remembered—*It Goes Like This; The Broken Record; Wah-hoo; The Merry-Go-Round Broke*

Down; and *I Must See Annie Tonight.* Along the way he contributed tunes that furthered the careers of stars like Eddie Cantor and Rudy Vallee and managed to add a number of those forgotten but personal favorites that, it can always be hoped, will be rediscovered some day, like *Never Should Have Told You* (a familiar title to early Benny Goodman fans) and *Time Waits for No One.* Other songs by Friend are *Love Sick Blues; Blue Hoosier Blues; Big Butter and Egg Man; Hello Bluebird; When the Pussy Willow Whispers to the Catnip; Where the Lazy Daisies Grow; Bigger and Better Than Ever; My Blackbirds are Bluebirds Now; Trade Winds; We Did It Before and We Can Do It Again; Don't Sweetheart Me; You Missed the Boat*; and *Old Man Time.*

Cliff Friend died in Las Vegas, Nevada, June 27, 1974.

Rudolf Friml

Composer Rudolf Friml, famous for his contributions to the American musical stage, was born in Prague, Czechoslovakia, on December 7, 1879. He was educated at the Prague Conservatory and studied with Dvorak and Jiranck to become a concert pianist. He toured Europe with violinist Jan Kubelik and in 1901 came to the United States for five years of successful tours, deciding to stay. His first big break as a composer came when he was asked to substitute for Victor Herbert in writing the score for the 1912 musical "The Firefly." The show was a success (in 1937 it was a popular movie, starring Jeanette MacDonald and Allan Jones) and launched his career as a composer of Broadway shows. Friml's background and training strongly influenced his composing. His songs, written for stage productions in the tradition fostered by the works of Victor Herbert and Sigmund Romberg, have the flavor of European light opera. The majority of Friml's songs never became well known beyond the context of the productions they were written for, but a respectable number have become popular hits, and a few are standards.

One of the most durable is a melody that is flexible enough to fit into any musical mold, *Allah's Holiday,* with lyrics by Otto Harbach, part of the score of the stage show "Katinka." At least two recordings illustrate the song's adaptability, the 1929 Brunswick by Red Nichols and the 1930 Ray Noble arrangement recorded by the Nightclub Kings on HMV. *You're in Love,* from the show of the same name, was the Friml hit song of 1917; this time Otto Harbach shared credit with Edward Clark on the words. But it wasn't until 1922—many songs later—that Friml scored with another favorite. Oddly enough, this was one of the very few songs not written for a show, and the lyrics are by a lady who may never have written another song. The title is *L'Amour, Toujours, L'Amour* (Love Everlasting), and the lady's name is Catherine Chisholm Cushing. In its prime it was recorded by "trained" singers like Jessica Dragonette and Lily Pons. It received more intimate treatment by Maxine Sullivan on a 1939 Victor recording directed and arranged by Claude Thornhill. In 1936 it was featured in the movie *Cain and Mabel,* starring Clark Gable and Marion Davies, and again in 1944, when it was sung by Susanna Foster in *This Is the Life.*

Otto Harbach and Friml struck gold in 1924. The show was "Rose-Marie," and two of the songs in it were outstanding successes, *Rose-Marie,* the title song, and *Indian Love Call.* Oscar Hammerstein II helped Harbach on the lyrics for the latter tune, which was introduced by Mary Ellis and Dennis King in the stage show. Years later, in the movie *Rose Marie* (without the hyphen), it was sung by Jeanette MacDonald and Nelson Eddy. They recorded it in 1936, and the record, with an orchestra directed by Nat Shilkret on Victor, hit the million mark. And that's not all. In the 1954 remake of the movie, the tune was sung by Fernando Lamas and Ann Blythe. From the jazz standpoint, it fared even better on the Bluebird record by Artie Shaw's hard-swinging band in 1938. It made the country–western hit parade in 1952 with a million-seller by Slim Whitman.

Rose-Marie didn't do badly either. Introduced in the show by Dennis King and Arthur Deagan, it was sung in the movie by Nelson Eddy. Howard Keel sang it in the remake movie of 1954, and Slim Whitman slipped in a repeat hit.

"The Vagabond King" was the stage offering for 1925, starring the swashbuckling Dennis King, with the book and lyrics by Brian Hooker and W. H. Post. All four songs in the show were popular, *Song of the Vagabonds; Only a Rose; Some Day*; and *Huguette Waltz.* Dennis King had two shots at *Song of the Vagabonds.* He introduced it in the stage show and sang it in the first movie version (1930). It was featured in still another remake in 1956. *Only a Rose,* performed as a duet by Dennis King and Carolyn Thompson in the show, was sung by King and Jeanette MacDonald in the 1930 movie. In the 1956 remake it was sung by Oreste and Kathryn Grayson. *Some Day* went through the same process, plus a hit recording by Tony Martin on Victor in 1952 followed with another by Frankie Laine in 1954 for Columbia. *Huguette Waltz* was introduced in the stage show by Jane Carroll. In the 1930 movie it was sung by Lillian Roth and in the 1956 remake by Rita Moreno.

Friml wrote the music for a piano solo in 1923 called *Chanson.* With lyrics added by Dailey Paskman, Sigmund Spaeth, and Irving Caesar, it became *Chansonnette* and was featured in the "Ziegfeld Follies." When "The Firefly" was made into a movie in 1937, the song was reworked, with new words by Robert Wright and George Forrest and melodic changes by Friml and Herbert Stothart. It became the *Donkey Serenade,* a feature in the movie for Allan Jones associated with him thereafter. He recorded it and so did vocalists Frank Parker and Lanny Ross. Artie Shaw recorded it for Bluebird, Horace Heidt for Columbia. Vaughn Monroe joined the parade in 1940 with another record for Bluebird.

The foregoing represents Rudolf Friml's best known songs. He composed many others, including *Sympathy; Something Seems Tingle-ingling; You're in Love; The Door of My Dreams; March of the Musketeers*; and *Ma Belle.*

He died in Hollywood, California, on November 12, 1972.

John Collins (Jack) Fulton

Jack Fulton was born in Phillipsburg, Pennsylvania, on June 13, 1903. A trombonist, he started playing with local bands and then joined George Olsen as a trombonist-vocalist early in 1926. Later in the year he joined the Paul Whiteman organization and was a featured member all through the prime years of the band's popularity, until 1934. During that time his distinctive high-tenor voice became familiar to radio listeners and record buyers all over the world. After he left Whiteman he performed as a single and for a time led a band to accompany Sophie Tucker. In the midforties he joined the staff at WBBM in Chicago, the CBS radio outlet, and remained there for twenty years.

Fulton doubled as both a composer and a lyric writer, beginning this second career in the early forties. Although his output wasn't extensive, he and his partners managed to turn out some successful songs. *My Greatest Mistake,* written with Jack O'Brien (probably the pianist with Ted Weems's band), was a 1940 entry and made it into the top ten. The vocal group the Ink Spots had the best-selling record on Decca. Musically, the best record was on Victor by the Duke Ellington Orchestra. Two years later Fulton teamed with Moe Jaffe and Nat Bonx on an adaptation of Rubenstein's piano piece *Romance,* and they produced *If You Are but a Dream.* Jimmy Dorsey recorded it on Decca with a vocal by Bob Eberle, and it did fairly well. In 1945 Frank Sinatra reprised it on a Victor recording, with Alex Stordahl arranging and directing, to still greater success. Bob Crosby collaborated with Fulton on a pleasant song entitled *Until* in 1948. Tommy Dorsey recorded it with a vocal by Harry Prime. But 1954 was the big one for Fulton. With Lois Steele he wrote *Wanted.* Perry Como recorded it on Victor with Hugo Winterhalter's Orchestra, and it sold a million copies. Other Jack Fulton songs include *Say a Prayer Every Day; Wanting You; Let's Return to God; Moody; Ivory Towers; Silence Is Golden; Mrs. Santa Claus*; and *Keep Your Promise, Willie Thomas.*

Sammy Gallop

A latecomer to the songwriting business, composer-lyricist Sammy Gallop put in most of his career as a surveyor and draftsman, but in the early forties he gave it up to become a full-time songwriter. During a short but very prolific career he collaborated with some of the best craftsmen in the business—Peter DeRose, David Rose, Guy Wood, Jerry Livingston, Rube Bloom, Jimmy Van Heusen, and Dick Jurgens, among others. As it has been demonstrated in this book many times, the best way to start a songwriting career is with a big hit, and Gallop was no exception. His first entry in 1941 was *Elmer's Tune*. This was followed in 1943 by another major strike, *Holiday for Strings,* with the eminent David Rose, and Sammy was off (to coin a title) and running. The forties were good for Gallop, and in quick succession he had solid hits with *There Must Be a Way; Autumn Nocturne* (1945); *Shoo Fly Pie and Apple Pan Dowdy* (1946); *Maybe You'll Be There* (featured in an outstanding recording by Woody Herman on Decca) (1947)—but then, although Sammy continued to write to the midfifties, there were no more outstanding hits. He then put in time writing scores for New York nightclubs and material for minor Broadway shows.

Born March 16, 1915, in Duluth, Minnesota, he died in Hollywood, California, on February 26, 1977 at the rather young age of sixty-two.

James Kimball (Kim) Gannon

Kim Gannon, who wrote the words to a number of hit songs in the forties and fifties, was born in Brooklyn, New York, on November 8, 1900. He graduated from St. Lawrence University with a B.S. degree and went on to study law at Albany Law School. He was admitted to the New York bar in 1934. He began writing lyrics to songs in 1939 and in 1940 had two very successful ones. *Five O'Clock Whistle,* a collaboration with Josef Myrow and Gene Irwin, got the full treatment on recordings. Marion Hutton sang it on MGM; Ella Fitzgerald made it for Decca; Duke Ellington worked with Ivy Anderson for Victor; Ray McKinley recorded it with the Will Bradley band on Columbia; and Erskine Hawkins and His Orchestra played it as an instrumental on Bluebird. Not as widely recorded but, nevertheless, a big-seller on Decca by the Jimmy Dorsey Orchestra with vocalist Bob Eberly, was *I'll Understand,* a happy partnership with Mabel Wayne.

Paula Kelly sang Gannon's lyrics on the Artie Shaw Victor record of *Make Love to Me,* written to music by Paul Mann and Stephen Weiss and published in 1941. Anita Boyer recorded it for OKeh. But 1942 was a banner year for Gannon, with three important songs in the running. *Always in My Heart,* with a melody by Ernesto Lecuona, was the title song of the movie in which it was introduced by Gloria Warren. The song was nominated for an Academy Award. Glenn Miller recorded it, with Ray Eberle on the vocal, and Jimmy Dorsey, not to be outdone, waxed it for Decca with brother Bob Eberly singing it. *Moonlight Cocktail,* a delightful idea, was Gannon's inspiration to a melody by pianist Luckey Roberts, an adaptation of his own composition written for piano, *Ripples of the Nile.* Glenn Miller had the big record on Bluebird. *Autumn Nocturne,* another beautiful song, was the work of Josef Myrow, and although Gannon got credit for the lyrics the outstanding record was by Claude Thornhill, who chose to treat it as an instrumental featuring his unique piano styling.

The perennial holiday standard *I'll Be Home for Christmas,* published in 1943 when thousands of servicemen couldn't be, was recorded by Bing Crosby, and the disc sold over a million that year. With the memorable melody by Walter Kent and Buck Ram, it has long since become a standard, including use in a TV commercial Christmas message for Anheuser-Busch. *It Can't Be Wrong* was the theme of the movie *Now, Voyager,* starring Bette Davis. Gannon wrote the words to the melody by Max Steiner. It was on the Hit Parade for twenty weeks and a hit record by Dick Haymes and the Song Spinners on Decca.

It was 1949 before the Gannon magic worked again. Pairing with Mabel Wayne once more, he produced *Dreamer's Holiday,* a solid strike for Perry Como on Victor, closely followed by Buddy Clark on Columbia. Gordon Jenkins also recorded it for Decca, and Ray Anthony waxed it for Capitol. In 1953 Gannon wrote English lyrics to a French song with a melody by Hubert Giraud, and it became *Under Paris Skies.* The original title was *Sous le Ciel de Paris,* the same as the movie it came from. It did well in that waning period for good songs and received acceptable, if highly commercial, treatment on records by Mitch Miller (Columbia), Georgia Gibbs (Mercury), and the Three Suns (Victor). Gannon also collaborated with J. Fred Coots and Jule Styne. Other titles include *For Tonight; Angel in Disguise; Be Fair; The Singing Sands of Alamosa; Three Dreams Are One Too Many; Sweet Dreams, Sweetheart;* and *Reciprocity.*

Kim Gannon died in Lake Worth, Florida, on April 29, 1974.

Clarence Gaskill

Clarence Gaskill didn't write many songs, but he managed to turn out some important ones. He was born in Philadelphia, Pennsylvania, on February 2, 1892, and was educated at St. Johns School, Friends School. He studied music with his mother and private teachers, and when he was only sixteen was playing piano in local theaters. When he was twenty-one he had his own music publishing firm. During the First World War he served as a machine gunner and was awarded the Purple Heart. He later toured in vaudeville as the "Melody Monarch." He had his first song published in 1919, but his first big hit didn't come along until 1924. That year he and Will Donaldson wrote the novelty *Doo Wacka Doo,* putting the words to the music by George Horther. Both Isham Jones (Brunswick) and Paul Whiteman (Victor) recorded it.

In 1925 Gaskill wrote both the music and lyrics for the successful "Earl Carroll's Vanities of 1925," which included over twenty songs. None of them became popular. In 1927 he collaborated with composer Jimmy McHugh on the all-time standard *I Can't Believe That You're in Love With Me.* It was recorded on Victor by Roger Wolfe Kahn's Orchestra when it first came out, but it soon became a favorite of jazz musicians and arrangers. Through the years it has been played and recorded by many of the biggest stars, including Louis Armstrong, Benny Goodman, Artie Shaw, Teddy Wilson, Lionel Hampton, Adrian Rollini, Jesse Stacy, and Count Basie. It has since been featured in several movies.

In 1928 Gaskill had a hit all by himself, composing both words and music to the novelty *I'm Wild about Horns on Automobiles (That Go Ta-Ta-Ta-Ta).* Fred Hall and His Sugar Babes had fun with it on a recording for OKeh. Back to working with others, Gaskill had a big year in 1931. With Cab Calloway he composed *Minnie the Moocher,* a big hit for Cab, who recorded it for Columbia after introducing it at the famous Cotton Club in New York. He went on to perform it with his orchestra in the movie *The Big Broadcast of 1932* and continued to feature it throughout his career. Leo Robin wrote the words, and Gaskill and Russ Columbo the music, for *Prisoner of Love,* a romantic ballad that was featured and recorded by Russ Columbo on Victor and did a lot to promote his popularity. It never really died out, but in 1946 it came back stronger than ever with a best-selling record by Perry Como, also for Victor. The song made the Hit Parade for fifteen weeks. Other Gaskill songs include *Another Perfect Day Has Passed Away; Swanee River Rhapsody;* and *Still I Love Her.* He also wrote material for nightclub revues.

Clarence Gaskill died in Fort Hill, New York, April 29, 1947.

Lewis E. Gensler

Lewis E. Gensler was born in New York City on December 4, 1896. He attended public schools, graduated from high school, and studied music privately with Louis Oesterle. He started composing in the twenties and had two successful songs in 1925. *Fond of You,* with lyrics by Buddy DeSylva, was recorded by four of the big names of the day, Ben Bernie, Harry Reser, George Olsen, and Sam Lanin. But the big song was *Smiling at Trouble,* again with words by Buddy DeSylva. Al Jolson also had his name on the song, and he introduced it in the stage show "Big Boy." Then just to make sure, he sang it again in the movie *The Singing Fool* in 1928. The song was a particular favorite of the great tenor saxophonist Bud Freeman, who recorded it twice in a jazz format. The first session took place in New York on December 4, 1935, but was initially issued in England on the Parlophone label and only came out on the Decca Red label series some years later. In the meantime, Freeman, along with a trio including Jess Stacy on piano and drummer George Wettling, waxed the tune again on Commodore in 1938.

Buddy DeSylva and Gensler were still working together in 1926, and they came up with the pleasant offering *Cross Your Heart.* It was featured in the movie *Queen High* and recorded by the orchestra of Roger Wolfe Kahn on Victor and by the vocal duet of Vaughn DeLeath and Ed Smalle on Columbia. It also came in for a latter-day jazz treatment by Artie Shaw and His Gramercy Five on Victor. Gensler went to Hollywood and became a producer, writing for Paramount, including the films *Big Broadcast of 1937* and *Artists and Models.* He also wrote for the Broadway stage. In 1935 he teamed with lyricist Leo Robin, and the result was the standard *Love Is Just Around the Corner.* It was sung by Bing Crosby in the movie *Here Is My Heart.* A popular entry when it was first introduced, it has never died out and is a favorite of jazzbands. Other titles by Gensler include *Me Without You; It's a Great Life; When You Are in My Arms; Boys Will Be Boys; Old Man Rhythm; I Never Saw a Better Night; Riddle Me This; Will You Remember;* and *You Need Someone.*

Lewis Gensler died in his hometown, New York, on January 10, 1978.

Don George

Lyricist Don George, who collaborated with some of the most famous names in the music world, was born in New York City on August 27, 1909, was educated in the public schools, and became a songwriter for the stage and films. Among other things, he wrote special material for Ida Lupino, Patti Page, and Nat "King" Cole and a biography of Duke Ellington entitled *Sweet Man*. He began writing popular songs in the forties. With Mack Davis sharing credit on the words and Walter Kent composing the music, he had a fairly successful song in 1943, *I'll Never Mention Your Name*. Former Tommy Dorsey vocalist Jack Leonard had a nice record of the song, backed by Ray Bloch's Orchestra on OKeh, and Dick Haymes recorded it for Decca with the Song Spinners.

But 1944 was the big year, with one of those "committee" written songs, *I'm Beginning to See the Light*. Composer credit for this super hit included George, Harry James, Johnny Hodges, and Duke Ellington, with the prize going to Harry James, who also had the best-selling record. It was also recorded by Ella Fitzgerald, the Ink Spots, and Duke Ellington. The song was on the Hit Parade for eleven weeks. George also teamed with Duke Ellington on *It Shouldn't Happen to a Dream,* a typically superior melody by the Duke, with exceptional lyrics. Ellington recorded it, but the platter was issued on Musicraft, a company that seemed to make a specialty of surface noise, and it didn't do justice to anybody involved. George wrote with Nat "King" Cole, turning out at least two titles, *Calypso Blues* and *My Mother Told Me*. Cole recorded them both for Capitol.

In 1965 George revamped an old minstrel tune dating back to Civil War days, and it was published as *The Yellow Rose of Texas*. Not exactly in the class of popular songs otherwise mentioned in this book, and a far cry from qualifying as jazz, it nevertheless appealed to the music-buying public of the fifties. Characteristically, Mitch Miller had the big-selling record. Other Don George compositions include *I Ain't Got Nothin' but the Blues; The Beautiful Blonde from Bashful Bend; Two Thirds of the Tennessee River; How Bitter, My Sweet;* and *Coal Dust on the Fiddle*.

Gene Gifford

Gene Gifford, guitarist, composer, arranger, and for many years an important member of the famous Casa Loma Orchestra, was born in Americus, Georgia, on May 31, 1908, but grew up in Memphis, Tennessee. He learned to play the banjo as a youngster and toured the southwest with several dance bands, including his own for a time. While on a date in Detroit, he was hired by the Jean Goldkette organization to write arrangements for the various units in their stable. This led to his joining the Orange Blossoms, the band led by Henry Biagini, which evolved into the Casa Loma Orchestra and later still, the Glen Gray Casa Loma Orchestra. Gifford played guitar with the band for quite some time, and his composing and arranging talent was instrumental in forming the band's style and success. Outstanding among his many compositions is the beautiful *Smoke Rings,* which became the band's theme. He also wrote the moody *Paramour* and collaborated with Joe Bishop on the very advanced (for the time) *Out of Space.*

In the early thirties, before Benny Goodman introduced the world to swing, Gifford wrote instrumentals for the Casa Loma band that established it as a pioneer in the hot style. These included *Maniac's Ball; Casa Loma Stomp; Black Jazz; Dance of the Lame Duck; San Sue Strut; Blue Jazz;* and others. Eventually, he left Glen Gray to become a freelance arranger and performed this function for Freddy Martin, Jimmy Joy, Tommy Reynolds, and Mal Hallett, later joining the Bob Strong band as guitarist-arranger. After another stint with Glen Gray, he retired to Memphis to pursue a career in teaching music.

In the midfifties Glen Gray assembled a band of all-star studio musicians to recreate the Casa Loma sounds for Capitol Records, utilizing the original arrangements. In the process, an excellent representation of Gifford's compositions was committed to high-fidelity recording and issued on long-playing records. On *Casa Loma in Hi-Fi* (Capitol W-747), the following can be heard: *White Jazz; Maniac's Ball; Casa Loma Stomp; Dance of the Lame Duck; Black Jazz;* and *Smoke Rings.* On *Casa Loma Caravan* (Capitol T-856) the Gifford compositions are *Paramour* and *Out of Space.*

Gene Gifford died in Memphis on November 12, 1970.

L. Wolfe Gilbert

Lyricist L. Wolfe Gilbert was born in Odessa, Russia, on August 31, 1886. When he was only one year old he was brought to this country. He grew up in Philadelphia, where he attended the public schools. He started his career by singing in amateur contests, then went into vaudeville and worked as a nightclub entertainer. At one time he toured with the prizefighter John L. Sullivan. He started composing and in 1912 had two hit songs, *Waiting for the Robert E. Lee* and *Hitchy-Koo.* The first song, with music by Lewis F. Muir, has a long success story. It was introduced by Al Jolson at the Winter Garden in New York and also promoted in vaudeville by the headliner Ruth Roye. It was featured in *The Jazz Singer,* a 1927 movie, and Fred Astaire and Ginger Rogers danced to it in *The Story of Irene and Vernon Castle* in 1939. Judy Garland sang it in *Babes on Broadway* in 1941, and Al Jolson supplied the dubbed-in vocal track for *The Jolson Story* in 1946. In the meantime, it has been recorded numerous times, including a version by Louis Jordan and his Tympany Five on a 1940 waxing for Decca (3360). *Hitchy-Koo,* a ragtime piece, was revived in a swinging arrangement by the Embassy Eight, an all-star jazz unit comprised of musicians from the Bert Ambrose band, for the English Decca label in 1935 (DeE F-5435). It was released in this country on the short-lived Champion label (40068). On this one, Lewis Muir shared the music credit with Maurice Abrahams. In 1928 Gilbert teamed with orchestra leader Nat Shilkret on the waltz *Jeanine, I Dream of Lilac Time,* the theme of the movie *Lilac Time,* which starred Gary Cooper. It was recorded on several big-selling records, including one by Gene Austin, another by Nat Shilkret and the Victor Orchestra, and still another by John McCormack. All three were Victor records. *Marta (Rambling Rose of the Wild Wood)* was a Cuban import with music by Moises Simons. Gilbert gave it English lyrics, and it became the famous theme song of Arthur Tracy, the Street Singer. Tracy recorded it several times and sang it in the movie *The Big Broadcast of 1932.* Other Gilbert titles include *Oh, Katherina; Lucky Lindy; Mama Inez; Ramona; Green Eyes; Mama Don't Want No Peas and Rice and Cocoanut Oil; Take Me to That Swannee Shore; La Golondrina; Chiquita.*

L. Wolfe Gilbert died on July 12, 1970.

Haven Gillespie

Haven Gillespie was born in Covington, Kentucky, on February 6, 1888, and started writing songs around 1924. Although not exactly what you might call a household name, he is credited with some important titles. Primarily a lyricist, he collaborated with a number of master songsmiths, including J. Fred Coots, Richard Whiting, Larry Shay, Seymour Simons, and Egbert Van Alstyne. Gillespie was a journeyman printer working on newspapers such as the *New York Times,* and it isn't clear how and why he started writing songs, but his first entry, *You're in Kentucky, Sure as You're Born,* a Larry Shay composition, bears up well today and proved to be a favorite of small British groups like Nat Temple and His Club Royal Orchestra, who recorded it for English Decca. Gillespie also struck gold with his 1925 number *Drifting and Dreaming,* written with three composers claiming credit, Egbert Van Alstyne, Erwin Schmidt, and Loyal Curtis. Not to be regarded as a mere flash in the pan, Gillespie repeated in 1926, with Seymour Simons at his elbow, turning out the lyrics for Richard Whiting's standard, *Breezin' Along with the Breeze*. Haven Gillespie continued to write well into the fifties, and even if you don't remember his name, you'll remember some of his songs—*Beautiful Love; Santa Claus Is Comin' to Town; Louisiana Fairy Tale; It's the Little Things That Count; You Go to My Head;* and *There's Honey on the Moon Tonight.*

Haven Gillespie died in Las Vegas, Nevada, on March 14, 1975.

Al Goering

See Jack Pettis & Al Goering.

John Golden

John Golden was born in New York City on June 27, 1874, attended New York University, and went on to become an actor, reporter, playwright, and producer. As a songwriter his output was scarce, but he wrote the words to one of the most enduring popular songs, *Poor Butterfly*. A collaboration with Raymond Hubbell in 1916, introduced in "The Big Show" on the stage of the Hippodrome Theater in New York, this song has never lost its luster through the years and has been recorded by a variety of artists, both as an instrumental and as a vocal. It was a particular favorite of the great cornetist Bobby Hackett, who recorded it several times and played it frequently in concerts. John Golden also wrote the words to a popular entry for 1914, *Goodbye Girls, I'm Through,* featured in the show "Chin Chin." The melody was composed by Ivan Caryll. Other Golden titles are *Willie Off the Yacht; I'm Growing Fond of You; I Can Dance With Everybody but My Wife;* and *You Can't Play Every Instrument in the Band.*

John Golden died in New York City on June 17, 1955, just ten days after his birthday.

Al Goodhart

Al Goodhart, one of those composers who helped make the thirties and early forties the Golden Age of songwriting, was born in New York City on January 26, 1905. His early career included a stint playing piano in vaudeville, writing special material, radio announcing, and performing on radio in a two-piano team. He started writing songs in 1930, contributing two tunes to the movie *Dangerous Nan McGrew* and in 1931 had his first big hit, *I Apologize,* a collaboration with Al Hoffman and Ed Nelson. He was to work with Hoffman frequently from then on. Bing Crosby introduced the song, and it enjoyed renewed popularity in 1951 as recorded by Billy Eckstine.

The team of Goodhart, Hoffman, and Nelson scored again in 1932, with *Auf Wiedersehen, My Dear,* which received a successful push from Russ Columbo. But the big song was *Fit as a Fiddle,* with Arthur Freed joining Goodhart and Hoffman in the composition. The lyrics made good use of two then current slang phrases, "Hey-nonny-nonny," and "hot-cha-cha," which make the song sound very dated today but were one of the big reasons for its popularity. *Roll Up the Carpet,* a familiar title to the many fans of Ray Noble and Al Bowlly, came out in 1933, and Goodhart and Hoffman again welcomed another member to the team, lyricist Raymond Klages.

Goodhart and Hoffman went to England around 1934 and picked up another collaborator, Maurice Sigler. This resulted in several tunes. One of the nicest was *I Saw Stars*. Ray Noble missed this one, for some strange reason, but it merited full attention in this country, with records by Paul Whiteman, Joe Haymes, and Freddy Martin. *Who Walks In When I Walk Out?,* a paranoic sentiment with words penned by Ralph Freed, was another Goodhart–Hoffman entry for 1934, and this time Ray Noble gave it full treatment. His arrangement accorded the musicians wide latitude in improvisations, so that two distinctive takes were made and released. The year 1936 was a busy one for Goodhart and Hoffman, and with Maurice Sigler back on board, they wrote several hit songs for English movies and stage shows. For "This'll Make You Whistle," a stage show, they turned out *Crazy with Love; I'm in a Dancing Mood; There Isn't Any Limit to My Love;* and *My Red Letter Day*. They wrote the title song for the British movie *She Shall Have Music,* and it was popularized in America by the English bandleader Jack Hylton, who was touring the country at that time. His recording, along with one by Rudy Vallee, was a best-seller. Another British movie starring Jessie Matthews featured two songs that were successful that year, *Everything's in Rhythm with My Heart* and *Say the Word and It's Yours*. Goodhart and his friends continued to compose until 1950, but the foregoing songs represent the cream of his output. Other titles are *Why Don't You Practice What You Preach?; Your Guess is Just as Good as Mine; My First Thrill; I Can Wiggle my Ears; Where There's You There's Me; There's Always a Happy Ending; Johnny Doughboy Found a Rose in Ireland;* and *Serenade of the Bells*.

Al Goodhart died in New York City on November 30, 1955.

Benny Goodman

Benny Goodman was born in Chicago, Illinois, on May 30, 1909. As a jazz clarinetist and bandleader he became internationally famous, known as the King of Swing. Without an intention of retelling the story of his life and career, which has been well-covered in book and film, I think it is important to recognize that his name is on a number of musical works, some of which became very popular. At the same time, as I have with other famous bandleaders, I must point out that it was common practice to list one as a co-composer in order to sell a song to a publisher, besides getting the prestige and promotion this entailed. There is no question of Goodman's musical ability, or that in a number of instances he contributed to the composing of some songs, but this peculiar fact of the songwriting business should be kept in mind.

Pianist Artie Schutt is listed as cowriter with Goodman of the 1934 instrumental *Georgia Jubilee*. In that pre-swing year Benny recorded it for Columbia with an all-star group, in an arrangement by Artie Schutt. The great Isham Jones band made it for Victor. In that same year, Chick Webb recorded two instrumentals written and arranged by Edgar Sampson. *Stompin' at the Savoy* was waxed for Columbia, and *Don't Be That Way* for Decca. Composer credit for *Stompin'* lists Andy Razaf for the words and Chick Webb, Edgar Sampson, and Benny Goodman for the music. Sampson arranged the Goodman recording for Victor in 1936, which was a big hit. The Goodman Quartet recorded it again in 1937, also for Victor. The tune became a swing standard and has been played and recorded by a number of top artists. On the 1934 Chick Webb recording of *Don't Be That Way,* Edgar Sampson is the only composer, and he also arranged it. In 1938 Mitchell Parish added lyrics to the song, it was recorded by the Goodman Orchestra and, again, was a big hit. Benny's name was included as cocomposer.

In 1938 another hit record was *If Dreams Come True,* with Irving Mills taking credit for the words and Goodman and Sampson sharing the music. Ella Fitzgerald sang it with Chick Webb on a Decca disc in 1937, and it went on to pick up a prestigious pedigree, with records by Bobby Hackett, Teddy Wilson, and Andy Kirk. It has since become a standard. That same year the Goodman Orchestra recorded *Lullaby in Rhythm,* a catchy but slightly tricky melody which was written by pianist Clarence Profit. The final credits include lyricist Walter Hirsch, Edgar Sampson, and Benny Goodman. Besides the hit Goodman recording, Nan Wynn sang it on Vocalion, Woody Herman made it for Decca, and Harry James for Brunswick.

The swing standard *Flyin' Home* made its debut in 1939 as recorded by the Goodman Sextet on Columbia, featuring Lionel Hampton. Hampton and Goodman share the music credit and Sid Robin the words, which were added later. It has been recorded many times since, and Hampton has adopted the song as his theme. *Air Mail Special,* an instrumental by the Goodman band on Columbia in 1941, cocomposed by Goodman, Jimmy Mundy, and Charlie Christian, started out as *Good Enough to Keep,* recorded by the Goodman Sextet. Among the many groups who perpetuate the Goodman repertoire, it's a standard. Goodman's name also appears on the following: *Dizzy Spells; Seven Come Eleven; Three O'Clock Jump; Four Once More;* and *The Kingdom of Swing.*

Benny Goodman died on June 20, 1986.

Joe Goodwin

Lyricist Joe Goodwin was born in Worcester, Massachusetts, on June 6, 1889, and attended the public schools. He toured in vaudeville as a monologist, and during WW I wrote shows for the 81st Wildcats. Later he wrote material for films and English revues. He also worked as a talent agent and owned his own music publishing firm. Goodwin started writing songs early in the century, and his ASCAP membership dates to 1914. A number of his songs have been successfully revived, and are therefore well known—possibly more now than when they were first published. A prime example is *Billy (For When I Walk),* published in 1911, with Goodwin collaborating with James Kendis and Herman Paley. Revived by Orrin Tucker with a vocal by Bonnie Baker on a Vocalion record in 1939, it was carried along to success by the sensational *Oh Johnny, Oh, Johnny, Oh!* that Tucker and Baker recorded a few months later for Columbia. In 1919 Goodwin, Ballard MacDonald, and James F. Hanley combined their talents on *Breeze (Blow My Baby Back to Me),* a tune that has endeared itself to jazz musicians with its interesting and moving melodic line and its hospitality toward improvisation. Illustrating this is the Bluebird recording by the irrepressible Wingy Manone. Wingy sings the words to a half chorus of the song and then drops out.

When I Get You Alone Tonight, with words by Goodwin and music by James F. Hanley, is another early bird, dating to 1912. Singer Dick Robertson, in his long series of Decca recordings aimed at the jukebox trade, revived it in 1940, and it did very well. That same year Teddy Grace, one of the better female vocalists, recorded *Gee, I Hate to Go Home Alone,* also for Decca, a 1922 collaboration between Goodwin, Joseph M. McCarthy, and Fred Fisher. Teddy Grace is backed by the classic Summa Cum Laude band led by Bud Freeman. The trend continued, and in 1949 Guy Lombardo revived *Everywhere You Go,* a song written by Goodwin with Larry Shay and Mark Fisher, published in 1927. Doris Day also had a big-selling record of it. *When You're Smiling,* written by Goodwin, Mark Fisher, and Larry Shay, published in 1928, never had to be revived because it never died out. Introduced by Louis Armstrong, it quickly became a standard and has been played and recorded ever since. It was the title song for a 1950 movie, and Frank Sinatra sang it in the film *Meet Danny Wilson* in 1952.

Joe Goodwin died in the Bronx, New York, on July 31, 1943.

Irving Gordon

Irving Gordon was born in New York City on February 14, 1915. A composer as well as a fine lyric writer, two of his best songs were solo efforts, the melodic *Be Anything (But Be Mine)* and the unforgettable *Unforgettable,* the latter rendered immortal by Nat "King" Cole's vocal with Nelson Riddle's orchestra on Victor in 1951. Of more recent times this has been turned into a duet with daughter Natalie Cole through the magic of modern electronics. *Be Anything (But Be Mine)* was introduced and recorded by Eddy Howard on the Mercury label. Peggy Lee made it for Decca, and Helen O'Connell for Capitol. For a quality song in 1951, it did very well.

Of course, Gordon served his apprenticeship at a much earlier time and was fortunate in working with top composers. One of his early efforts is the lilting *Me, Myself and I,* written with Al Kaufman and Allan Roberts. A 1937 entry, it received top treatment on radio and did well on records, with platters by Billie Holiday, Joe Haymes, and Bob Howard. Across the ocean, Nat Gonella recorded it. Over fifty years later, jazz vocalist Terry Blaine included it in a collection of thirties songs for Jukebox Jazz she called *Whose Honey Are You?,* a scintillating rendition of music from the classic period (JJZ-9201). *What Will I Tell My Heart?* also came out in 1937. This time Gordon teamed with Peter Tinturin and Jack Lawrence, and the tune got heavy attention on records. Bing Crosby had the big record, but not far behind were Eddy Howard, Hal Kemp, Andy Kirk, and Art Tatum.

The next year Gordon and the ubiquitous Irving Mills shared recognition for the lyrics to two great Duke Ellington songs, *Prelude to a Kiss* and *Pyramid. Prelude to a Kiss* has become a classic in the Ellington songbook. The Ellington Orchestra recorded both songs, as did Johnny Hodges with an Ellington unit. *Moments in the Moonlight* came out in 1940, with bandleader Richard Himber's name on the music along with Gordon's and Al Kaufman's. Himber recorded it, but so did Glenn Miller, Bob Crosby, Tommy Reynolds, and Gene Krupa. A typically nice thirties ballad, the tune did quite well. Other titles attributed to Irving Gordon include *The Band Played On and On; Nine Little Broken Hearts; Stevedore's Serenade; Gypsy Without a Song; Mister and Mississippi;* and *Save a Little Sunbeam.*

Mack Gordon

Lyricist Mack Gordon was born in Warsaw, Poland, on June 21, 1904. Brought to the United States as a youngster, he grew up in Brooklyn and the Bronx. He was educated in the public schools, but started his career in the music business as a boy soprano in a minstrel show. From there he went on to become a singer-comedian in vaudeville. He began writing songs in the early thirties, mostly collaborating with Harry Revel, and the team was successful right from the start. From then until 1939 they practically dominated the movie musicals, and together they turned out one hit after another.

However, Gordon's first important title was the all-time favorite *Time on My Hands,* on which he shared credit with Harold Adamson for the words to the music by Vincent Youmans. It was introduced in the 1930 stage production "Smiles" and has since been featured in films and recorded countless times. That same year Gordon paired with Max Rich, and they turned out a song that was a feature for Helen Kane in the movie *Pointed Heels*. The tune was *Ain' Cha?,* and Kane also recorded it. In 1931 Gordon got together with Harry Revel, and history in the field of quality popular song hits was made. *Help Yourself to Happiness,* written for the "Ziegfeld Follies of 1931," in which it was introduced by Harry Richman (who also took some composing credit for the music), was Harry Revel's first big song. It was recorded by Glen Gray and the Casa Loma Orchestra on Brunswick, and Smith Ballew sang it on a Columbia side by a Benny Goodman group.

In 1932 the team wrote for a couple of unsuccessful shows but did well with a flurry of freelance titles: *And So to Bed; A Boy and a Girl Were Dancing; I Played Fiddle for the Czar; Listen to the German Band;* and *Underneath the Harlem Moon.* All were recorded, but more important in those days, they were frequently heard on the radio. But this was just the preview. The ball started rolling in 1933. Two hit songs, *Doin' the Uptown Lowdown* and *You're My Past, Present, and Future,* were featured in the movie *Broadway through a Keyhole,* which referred, of course, to columnist and radio commentator Walter Winchell. In addition, there were four more freelance items in the high-quality tradition of the era: *It Was a Night in June; An Orchid to You; It's Within Your Power;* and *A Tree Was a Tree.*

Now the floodgates were open, and in the following year Gordon and Revel, working in Hollywood, were responsible for one major hit song after another. From the film *Shoot the Works* came *With My Eyes Wide Open I'm Dreaming;* from *Sitting Pretty* we had *Did You Ever See a Dream Walking?; You're Such a Comfort to Me; Many Moons Ago;* and *Good Morning Glory.* The Bing Crosby picture *We're Not Dressing* gave us *May I?; Love Thy Neighbor; She Reminds Me of You; Goodnight, Lovely Little Lady;* and *Once in a Blue Moon. The Gay Divorcee* included *Don't Let It Bother You;* and a second Crosby epic, *She Loves Me Not,* offered *Straight from the Shoulder; I'm Hummin', I'm Whistlin', I'm Singin';* and *Put a Little Rhythm in Everything You Do. College Rhythm,* which starred the comedian with the duck, Joe Penner, padded out the year's score with three more hits: *Stay As Sweet As You Are; Take a Number from One to Ten;* and *Let's Give Three Cheers for Love.*

Love in Bloom, a movie that starred the future Mrs. Bing Crosby, Dixie Lee, kicked off the action in 1935. Burns and Allen were also in the film, and Gracie sang the hit song, *(Lookie, Lookie, Lookie) Here Comes Cookie.* The other two songs, *Got Me Doin' Things* and *My Heart Is an Open Book,* were recorded for Decca by Dixie Lee accompanied by the Orville Knapp Orchestra. Bing was also busy, and Gordon and Revel, who knew how to write songs that suited him, turned out some more for the movie *Two for Tonight: Without a Word of Warning; Two for Tonight; From the Top of Your Head; I Wish I Was Aladdin; Takes Two to Make a Bargain. Paris in the Spring* and *Stolen Harmony* were two more films that offered songs by Gordon and Revel that year. In the first it was the title song. In the second, which featured Ben Bernie's Orchestra and George Raft, it was *Would There Be Love?* Singers Morton Downey (on Melotone) and Gertrude Niesen (on Columbia) recorded the last mentioned, and the bands of Will Osborne (Banner) and Paul Pendarvis (Columbia) also made it.

In 1936 it was the movie *Collegiate* with one of those typical thirties casts that seem so fabulous—Jack Oakie, Joe Penner, Betty Grable, Frances Langford, Ned Sparks, Lynne Overman, and Betty Jane Cooper—that started the Gordon–Revel hit parade for the year: *You Hit the Spot* and *I Feel Like a Feather in the Breeze.* Then two Shirley Temple movies, *Poor Little Rich Girl* and *Stowaway,* were the vehicles for more: *When I'm With You; But Definitely; Goodnight, My Love; A Star Fell Out of Heaven;* and others. All good songs, but the outstanding *Goodnight, My Love* created a minor controversy when it was recorded by the Benny Goodman band with the vocal by Ella Fitzgerald. Ella was under contract to Decca at the time, and they protested so strongly that Victor withdrew the side, along with two others made at the same session. Those that managed to escape to the public became coveted collector's items. In the sixties the sides were made available again in the Goodman reissue series.

The Gordon and Revel caravan rolled on unabated, and in the 1937 film *Wake Up and Live* they contributed the title song and *Never in a Million Years; There's a Lull in My Life; It's Swell of You;* and *I'm Bubbling Over.* Ozzie Nelson had a good record of *Never in a Million Years* on Brunswick. Vocalist Helen Ward recorded *There's a Lull in My Life* and *It's Swell of You* in two classic sides by a Teddy Wilson group that included Harry James. Then Gordon and Revel went international, and for the Jessie Matthews English film *Head over Heels in Love* they wrote *Head over Heels in Love; Looking Around Corners for You; There's That Look in Your Eyes Again;* and *May I Have the Next Romance with You?* The British dance band of Bert Ambrose nicely recorded them all. Back in the States they wrote the score for the movie *You Can't Have Everything,* a film that immediately canceled the sentiment in its title by featuring a cast that seemed to offer everything—Alice Faye, Don Ameche, the Ritz Brothers, Charles Winninger, Tony Martin, Gypsy Rose Lee, Rubinoff, Phyllis Brooks, Arthur Treacher, and Louis Prima's band. The songs were *You Can't Have Everything; Afraid to Dream; The Loveliness of You;* and *Danger, Love at Work.*

The team's last big year was 1938, and although the songs continued to do well and some of them were of excellent quality, there were no outstanding hits. For the movie *In Old Chicago* they had two fine titles, *In Any Language* and *Where in the World;* both of which were accorded nice treatment on Victor by the Hal Kemp Orchestra. For *Love and Hisses,* they penned *Sweet Someone* and *I Wanna Be in Winchell's Column.* These two were waxed for the ARC labels by the Isham Jones band that he put together following his first "retirement." For the movie *Thanks for Everything,* Gordon and Revel wrote the title song (also recorded by Isham Jones); and for *Love Finds Andy Hardy,* they offered *Meet the Beat of My Heart; What Do You Know about Love?;* and *It Never Rains but It Pours.* Then, in quick succession came *My Lucky Star—I've Got a Date With a Dream; Could You Pass in Love?; By a Wishing Well; This May Be the Night; The All American Swing—Sally, Irene, and Mary—Sweet As a Song; Got My Mind on Music*—and *Rebecca of Sunnybrook Farm—An Old Straw Hat.* All of these were tuneful ditties that deserved more attention than they got.

The final year was 1939, with sparse material. For the film *Rose of Washington Square,* the Gordon–Revel song was the exceptionally fine *I Never*

Knew Heaven Could Speak. They wrote the title song for *The Rains Came.* The team parted in 1940. Mack Gordon began working with Harry Warren, and another long string of hits began—mostly for movies—and these will be discussed when we take up the career of Harry Warren. Toward the end of his career Gordon also wrote some songs with other composers, the most notable being *The Girl Next Door,* a collaboration with Josef Myrow, but for the most part the songs are unimportant.

Mack Gordon died in New York City on March 1, 1959.

Jay Gorney

Composer, writer, and producer Jay Gorney was born in Bialystok, Russia, December 12, 1896. He came to the United States when only ten years old and grew up and was educated in Detroit. He attended the University of Michigan, earning several degrees, and also studied music with Earl Moore. He started composing in college and wrote a number of student musicals. He started writing for stage musicals in the early twenties, beginning with the "Greenwich Village Follies of 1924," and continued to write for shows without scoring an outstanding song until 1929, when *What Wouldn't I Do for That Man,* with lyrics by E. Y. Harburg, was introduced by Helen Morgan in a movie called *Applause.* The singer repeated the performance in another movie the very next year, *Glorifying the American Girl.* Helen Morgan recorded it, as did several other singers of the time, but it is significant that jazz musicians recognized the song's superior structure, and two hot groups recorded it. Frankie Trumbauer made it on OKeh, with a vocal by Smith Ballew; and the Charleston Chasers, with Phil Napoleon, Miff Mole, and young Benny Goodman in the lineup, waxed it for Columbia. The song has been played and recorded many times since and is now a semistandard.

In 1932 Harburg and Gorney collaborated on a song that delineated the despair of the Depression, which seemed to be getting deeper that year, *Brother, Can You Spare a Dime?* It was introduced by Rex Weber in the stage musical "Americana" but owed its subsequent popularity to countless renditions on the radio. It was also recorded by Bing Crosby, Rudy Vallee, and Leo Reisman, but in 1932 not many people could afford to buy records. Again, the song has achieved semistandard status and is revived every now and then. *Ah! But Is It Love?* was sung by Roger Pryor and Lillian Miles in the movie *Moonlight and Pretzels* in 1933. Again the lyrics were by E. Y. Harburg, the melody was catchy and very singable, and the song was a hit. Freddy Martin's band, which was in the enviable position of getting all the best songs of the thirties to record for Brunswick and affiliated labels, also got this one. Martin also made a promotion record for *Moonlight and Pretzels.*

Sidney Clare was the word man for *You're My Thrill,* the Gorney entry for 1934. A beautiful ballad, with just a slight touch of the dramatic, it was recorded by Isham Jones on a contemporary Victor record and by Lena Horne with Charlie Barnet's band in 1941. Bobby Hackett, a man who knew a good song when he heard it, recorded it several times on LPs. Gorney continued to write for stage and screen but produced no more hits, although a few of his songs enjoyed moderate success, such as *Baby, Take a Bow* and *The Stars Remain.* Other compositions include *Dance Your Way to Paradise; A Girl in Your Arms; Gabriel Is Blowing His Horn; Knee Deep in Daisies; Hot Moonlight; This Is Our Last Night Together; I Found a Dream;* and *Damn the Torpedoes—Full Speed Ahead.*

Jay Gorney died in New York City on June 14, 1990.

Archie Gottler

Archie Gottler was born in New York City, May 14, 1896. He was educated at City College of New York and the Long Island Business College. Like many of his contemporaries, he started his musical career playing the piano in silent movies. Later on, when sound movies came along, he pioneered in them as both a composer and director. During World War II he produced training films for the signal corps. Gottler started composing in 1915, and one of his first songs was a big hit in that year of high patriotic fervor, *America, I Love You,* with lyrics by Edgar Leslie. The tune was revived in the 1940 movie *Tin Pan Alley,* starring Alice Faye.

The "Ziegfeld Follies of 1918" produced another song that was retreaded years later, *Would You Rather be a Colonel With an Eagle on Your Shoulder or a Private With a Chicken on Your Knee?* Sidney D. Mitchell wrote the words, and the song was introduced by Eddie Cantor in the "Follies." It was briefly revived in the early years of World War II. *I Hate to Lose You (I'm So Used to You Now),* with lyrics by Grant Clarke, also came out in 1918 but enjoyed much greater exposure and popularity in the 1944 movie *The Merry Monahans,* starring Jack Oakie, Donald O'Connor, Ann Blyth, Peggy Ryan, and Rosemary DeCamp. In 1947 Benny Goodman recorded *I Hate to Lose You* in a big band session for Capitol Records.

"The Fox Movietone Follies of 1929" included two songs by Gottler, with lyrics by Sidney D. Mitchell and Con Conrad helping with the music, *Big City Blues* and *Walking with Susie.* The first title rated a lot of attention and was recorded by the bands of Bert Lown, George Olsen, Lou Gold, and Arnold Johnson and by vocalist Annette Hanshaw. *Walking with Susie* was also waxed by George Olsen on Victor, Milt Shaw for Columbia, and Hal Kemp (as the Carolina Club Orchestra) for OKeh. Gottler teamed with George W. Meyer on the music for *To Whom It May Concern,* a very pretty song with rather clever lyrics by Sidney Mitchell that deserved better attention than it got in the gloomy year of 1930, a record by Ben Bernie's band on Brunswick. Quite a few years elapsed before Gottler had another success—1939 to be exact—and the song was *Baby Me,* written in conjunction with Lou Handman and Harry Harris. Glenn Miller had the big record of this one, featuring Kay Starr on the vocal.

Archie Gottler died in California on June 24, 1959.

Chauncey Gray

Chauney Gray was born in Rock City Falls, New York, on January 5, 1904. He studied piano with Professor Gene Somers and, while still in high school and short pants, organized his first dance band. Gray developed a highly individual piano styling and by 1929 was playing and recording with Bert Lown's band in New York. It was while still with the Lown band that Gray wrote, or was instrumental in the writing of, three songs that were closely identified with the band, *Bye Bye Blues,* the band's theme; *By My Side;* and *You're the One I Care For. Bye Bye Blues,* of course, was the biggest hit and has since become a standard. It became a hit all over again in the fifties as performed by Les Paul and Mary Ford as one of the famous sides in their series for Capitol. In my profile of Bert Lown I give him credit as a cocomposer of the above titles, because he is so listed. However, just who wrote what in composing the songs is hard to determine, with one notable exception—Chauncey Gray's name is on all three.

Bye Bye Blues, in particular, has a very interesting chronology. It was published in 1930, with "words and music" by Bert Lown, Chauncey Gray, Fred Hamm, and Dave Bennett, but the song's history goes back much earlier. Fred Hamm was a bandleader, and in 1925 both Dave Bennett—who played clarinet and alto sax—and Chauncey Gray were members of Fred Hamm's Orchestra when it made the trip to Camden in order to record for Victor. Nothing unusual about that, except this band may have established a high-water mark for rejected takes. As noted by Brian Rust in his *American Dance Band Discography, 1917–1942,* in the month of April, after three successive sessions (twenty-one, twenty-seven, thirty) and an almost unbelievable number of takes, only one was accepted, and this was number nine of *Stomp Off, Let's Go*. More important here, *Bye Bye Blues,* with a vocal by leader Fred Hamm, was recorded four times at the first session, three times on the second, and *five* on the third. All were rejected. Finally, on May 1, take number thirteen was approved and released on Victor 19662. Composer credit went to Fred Hamm and Dave Bennett. The next step brings in Bert Lown, who is listed with the Hamm Orchestra for a Victor session later in the year. I suspect that *Bye Bye Blues* went through a number of metamorphoses before it evolved into the moody theme song of the Lown band, and that Gray was mainly responsible for its transition. Lown's name, most likely, was included for its business value.

You're the One I Care For was also published in 1930. This time Harry Link wrote the words and Bert Lown and Gray the music. Thanks to lots of radio coverage, the tune did very well, and the Lown recording with Elmer Feldkamp's vocal was the definitive version. *By My Side,* third in the trilogy, came out in 1931. The Lown band was at its height and again was able to plug the tune into a hit. Bert Lown, Gray, and Harry Link are joined by a lady named Dorothy Dick, actually the wife of Harry Link, with quite a respectable list of songs to her credit. As a team, they performed with quiet efficiency.

Gray went on to play with Ozzie Nelson, and still later, Dick Stabile, but finally settled on his own band, putting in a long tenure at the El Morocco in New York. This stay is conserved for posterity on a ten-inch Decca LP (DL 5436), *A Night at the El Morocco*. Other compositions by Chauncey Gray are *No More Rain* and *I Had Too Much to Dream Last Night*.

Jerry Gray

Jerry Gray was born in East Boston, Massachusetts, on July 3, 1915. He graduated from high school and studied music with Ondricek. At age thirteen he performed with the Boston Junior Symphony as solo violinist. He formed his own orchestra to play in nightclubs but in 1936 he joined the Artie Shaw Orchestra as first violinist and arranger. Still later he performed the same function for André Kostelanetz and eventually the Glenn Miller band. It was during his stint with Miller that he wrote and arranged the instrumentals that became synonymous with the Miller organization: *String of Pearls; Pennsylvania 6-5000; I Dreamt I Dwelt in Harlem; Sun Valley Jump;* and *The Spirit Is Willing*.

String of Pearls was published with words by Eddie DeLange, but as an instrumental composed and arranged by Gray it was one of the most successful Miller recordings, unique because the orchestration included a remarkable ad lib chorus by Bobby Hackett. As later published in a stock arrangement, the Hackett solo was included note-for-note, was played by hundreds of trumpet players, and almost became trite. For that reason, years later when the musicians were recruited to record remakes of the Miller charts in high fidelity, Hackett took particular delight in playing the solo backwards. *Pennsylvania 6-5000,* a title taken verbatim from the phone number of the Hotel Pennsylvania in New York, where the Miller band was playing, was an earlier entry by Gray (1940), with words attributed to Carl Sigman. Said "words" consisted of the band chanting "Pennsylvania 6-5000" in assorted ways, including "Pennsylvania Six-Five-Oh-Oh-Oh." A popular Miller trademark, the tune was incorporated in the movie *The Glenn Miller Story* in 1954.

I Dreamt I Dwelt in Harlem was a collaboration between Gray, Ben Smith, and Leonard Ware, with lyrics by Robert B. Wright. Played and recorded by the Miller band, it's one of the most swinging instrumentals in the book. It came out in 1941. *Sun Valley Jump* and *The Spirit Is Willing,* both Gray originals, came along a little later, adding still more flavor to the Miller legend that persists to the present. Other compositions include *Crew Cut; Keep 'Em Flying;* and *The Man in the Moon'.*

Jerry Gray died in Dallas, Texas, on August 10, 1976.

Bud Green

Bud Green, a lyricist with several memorable titles to his credit, was born in Austria in 1897 but was brought to this country while still an infant. He grew up in New York, went the familiar route of becoming a staff writer for a music publisher, and saw his first song published in 1923, the not memorable but attention-getting *Whose Izzy Is He?* In the next year he struck pay dirt with a tune that can be considered a standard, *Alabamy Bound,* penned with Ray Henderson and Buddy DeSylva, and followed through with another hit in 1925, *I Love My Baby (My Baby Loves Me),* in collaboration with Harry Warren. The entries for 1926, *Ya Gotta Know How to Love,* and for 1927, *Away Down South in Heaven,* were fair performers, but his 1928 title panned pure gold, *That's My Weakness Now,* written with Sam H. Stept.

In 1929, with Stept and Herman Ruby, he contributed two songs to the movie *Syncopation,* which featured tenor Morton Downey, Barbara Bennett, and the Fred Waring Orchestra—*I'll Always Be in Love with You* and

Do Something. (This film should not be confused with the 1942 movie of the same title, which starred Jackie Cooper and featured Benny Berigan on the soundtrack.) In the same year he and Sam Stept produced one of my personal favorites, a sleeper named *Good Little Bad Little You,* which got fine treatment from Ukulele Ike (Cliff Edwards), with Joe Venuti and Eddie Lang backing him up and by the New Mayfair Orchestra, directed by Carroll Gibbons, on HMV in England.

Bud Green continued writing not only song lyrics, but special material for performers like Sophie Tucker and Winnie Lightner and a book called *Writing Songs for Fame and Fortune*. In 1937, possibly to prove he knew what he was writing about, he teamed with Michael Edwards on the hit *Once in Awhile;* with Chick Webb, Ella Fitzgerald, and Teddy McRae, he wrote *You Showed Me the Way,* recorded by Webb and Fitzgerald on Decca 1220 (for those discographically inclined). In 1938 he gave us *Day after Day* (with Richard Himber); *The Flat Foot Floogie* (with Slim Gaillard and Slam Stewart); and *More Than Ever,* a beautiful song by Isham Jones. With another bandleader, Little Jack Little, Bud Green wrote the 1940 title *Honestly* and with still another leader, Tommy Tucker, *The Man Who Comes Around.* The eventful year of 1944 seems to mark his final contribution, but it's one you will most likely be well acquainted with, no matter how old you are, *Sentimental Journey,* in collaboration with still another bandleader, Les Brown, and Ben Homer.

Johnny Green

Everybody knows *Body and Soul; Out of Nowhere;* and *I Cover the Waterfront*. And some of you with longevity and long memories may also remember *I'm Yours; You're Mine You; Easy Come, Easy Go,* and a long list of similar examples of the songwriting art, such as an obscure but beautiful little gem called *Hello, My Lover, Goodbye*. They're all the work of John W. Green—sometimes known as Johnny Evergreen because so many of his tunes have withstood the test of time. Johnny Green, a native New Yorker, was born October 10, 1908, and graduated from Harvard in 1928. At college he majored in economics but was much more interested in the musical activities on campus. In his junior year he even made a summer trip to Cleveland to arrange for the Guy Lombardo Orchestra, at that time just beginning to achieve national recognition. While he was there he collaborated with Carmen Lombardo and Gus Kahn in the writing of the hardy perennial *Coquette,* his first hit song. This gave him a taste of the sweet life, and shortly after graduating from Harvard he rebelled against the Wall Street career his father had planned for him and decided to become a professional musician.

Body and Soul, his next big milestone, was written as special material for Gertrude Lawrence while he was working as her accompanist and was first published in England in 1931. He moved on to a job as a rehearsal pianist at the old Paramount Studio in Astoria, Long Island, which led to his becoming staff arranger, then assistant conductor, and finally full arranger-conductor of the staff orchestra. Later he became arranger and accompanist for Ethel Merman and, at that time, popular tenor James Melton. It was during this period—1930 to 1933—that he turned out *I'm Yours; Out of Nowhere; Rain, Rain, Go Away; I Wanna Be Loved; I Cover the Waterfront;* and others. *Body and Soul* was introduced in America by Libby Holman in the show "Three's a Crowd" and became an instant hit.

Although a successful songwriter, Green still followed a very busy career as a musician and arranger-conductor. At one time he put in a stint as pianist with Buddy Rogers's orchestra. In 1932 he was commissioned by Paul Whiteman to compose "The Night Club Suite" and appeared with the Whiteman Orchestra as soloist when the suite was performed in a series of concerts that included Carnegie Hall and Symphony Hall, the latter in Boston. In 1933 he went to London to compose the score for *Mr. Whittington,* which starred Jack Buchanan and included *Weep No More, My Baby,* and on his return to the States immediately began another career in radio, conducting orchestras on many of the top shows of the time and working with stars like Ruth Etting and Fred Astaire. After a few years of this he decided to write a symphony and took a year off to work on it. He turned out a fantasia for piano and orchestra called *Music for Elizabeth.* Following this he reorganized a band for the Philip Morris radio show, which aired three times a week for two solid years, but broke it up to compose the score for George Abbot's *Beat the Band.* From there he went into the pit to direct the orchestra for *By Jupiter* and as a direct result of this was signed to go work for MGM in California. Here he continued to compose scores for the movies, conduct concerts, and maintain a very active and illustrious musical career.

Johnny Green's songs, particularly those of the thirties, are exceptional for their highly original melodies and sophisticated chord structures. Each is a polished example of the songwriting craft at its best. Green in later years, with his eyes on more ambitious composing, tended to deprecate his early efforts, but it is more than likely that, like George Gershwin, Dana Suesse, Peter DeRose, and others who attempted to write serious music, he will be best remembered for his fine popular songs.

Mort Greene

Mort Greene was born in Cleveland, Ohio, on October 3, 1912. His education included the University of Pennsylvania and the University of Akron. He started out as a contract writer for movies, and then became an associate publisher at 20th-Century Fox. Still later he became a writer and producer for TV shows, contributing special material and songs for a variety of artists, including Bob Cummings, Herb Shriner, Bob Crosby, Red Skelton, Johnny Carson, and others. Through the years he collaborated with many of the foremost composers. One of his earlier efforts was the lyrics for *Thrilled,* the fine Harry Barris song of 1935. But he really hit his stride in the early forties with a cluster of very successful tunes.

Greene had his name on three good songs in 1941, *Sleepy Serenade,* which had a dreamy kind of melody by Lou Singer; *Heavenly, Isn't It?;* and *When There's a Breeze on Lake Louise,* the latter two from the RKO film *The Mayor of 44th Street,* with music by Harry Revel. *Sleepy Serenade* was treated as an instrumental by both Claude Thornhill, who recorded it for OKeh, and Woody Herman, who made it on Decca, but the Andrews Sisters saved the day for Greene by singing his words in the movie *Hold That Ghost,* backed by Ted Lewis and His Band, and then recording the song for Decca. Freddy Martin saxed *Heavenly, Isn't It?* and *When There's a Breeze on Lake Louise,* and the two songs were released back-to-back on a Bluebird disc, with Eddie Stone marveling at how heavenly it was and Clyde Rogers admiring the breeze.

The delightful *Nevada,* with lyrics by Greene, was featured in the film *What's Buzzin', Cousin,* in 1943. The melody was by Walter Donaldson and was his last published song. In 1945 Greene wrote the English words to a Mexican melody he called *Stars in Your Eyes*. The original title was *Mars,* and the music was composed by Gabriel Ruiz. It was introduced and featured in the movie *Pan-Americana*. Mort Greene also collaborated with Allie Wrubel, Leigh Harline, and Lew Pollack. Other titles include *A Full Moon and Empty Heart; Sing Your Worries Away; The Circus Is Coming to Town; Nocturne;* and *I Want You from This Day Forward.*

Jesse Greer

Composer Jesse Greer was a native New Yorker, born in 1896, and he took what appears to be the standard route for budding songwriters, playing piano in theaters and clubs and working for a music publishing house. He is assured immortality for two reasons. For one thing, his 1927 title *I'm Gonna Meet My Sweetie Now,* with lyrics by Benny Davis, received a classic treatment by the Jean Goldkette Orchestra, with Bix Beiderbecke, and a 1929 entry, which was featured in the movie *Marianne, Just You, Just Me,* developed into a jazz standard. Most people would be satisfied to have those two tunes to their credit, but Greer can claim a few more worthy items in the American library of standard songs—not necessarily classics, but well-seated moneymakers in their day, such as *Kitty from Kansas City,* which Rudy Vallee plugged into a hit. Rudy did well with another Greer title, too, *Sleepy Head,* a tune which that connoiseur of great songs Bobby Hackett later used as the radio theme for his band on broadcasts from Nick's, the jazz club in Greenwich Village.

On the Beach With You was a respectable seller for Ozzie Nelson, and *I Lost My Gal Again* was a typical tour de force for Parker Gibbs with the Ted Weems band on Victor 22637. In 1936 Greer published the excellent song *Did You Mean It?,* which immediately received superior treatment at the hands of Benny Goodman's band with Ella Fitzgerald singing the Mort Dixon lyrics. The recording turned out to be one of the sides Victor had to withdraw when Decca Records claimed Ella's vocals constituted a breach of contract.

Another sleeper was introduced in 1937, *I Can't Lose That Longing for You,* again with lyrics by Mort Dixon, and one of the excellent titles recorded by Dick McDonough and an all-star group on ARC 7-03-12. Bunny Berigan is reputed to be present. There are other Jesse Greer titles, none of them bad, but not particularly memorable. However, it's pretty obvious he has nothing to apologize for.

Clifford Grey

Clifford Grey was born in Birmingham, England, on January 5, 1887. He was educated at King Edward VI School and then at Cambridge. An accomplished sportsman, he won medals at the 1928 and 1932 Olympics. He started his career as an actor but soon switched to writing. As a lyricist-librettist he was an important contributor to the Broadway stage in the twenties and still later, the movies. Among his collaborators were many of the most famous composers in the history of American popular music: Jerome Kern, J. Fred Coots, Vincent Youmans, Jay Gorney, Sigmund Romberg, Rudolf Friml, Lew Gensler, Johnny Green, Oscar Levant, Leo Robin, Victor Schertzinger, and Richard Myers. While still in England, Grey teamed with Sonny Miller to write the words to music by Jack Waller and Joseph Tunbridge for a song they called *Got a Date with An Angel.* Ray

Noble recorded it on HMV with the New Mayfair Orchestra, but it turned out to be a hit song in this country recorded by Hal Kemp and His Orchestra, with a vocal by drummer Skinny Ennis. The song was a big factor in the band's success. Kemp referred to it as "Our lucky song." When Ennis had his own band years later, he used the song as a theme.

Most likely Grey's first hit song was the well-known *If You Were the Only Girl in the World,* a waltz, with music by Nat D. Ayer, published in 1916. Like a cat with nine lives, this tune surfaces every so often to become a hit once more. Rudy Vallee modified the framework of the song by playing it in half-time and featured it in his first movie, *The Vagabond Lover*. He also recorded it for Victor, and it made the Hit Parade and came back again in 1952 in the movie *By the Light of the Silvery Moon,* sung by Doris Day and Gordon MacRae. *Wild Rose* and *Sally* were both in the stage musical "Sally," which starred Marilyn Miller in 1921. Jerome Kern wrote the music. They were heard again in the movies. Marilyn Miller sang *Wild Rose* in the film *Sally* in 1929; and June Haver, portraying Miller in *Look for the Silver Lining,* reprised the performance in 1949.

In 1926 a short-lived Broadway musical named "This Merry World" included a song by Grey and J. Fred Coots called *Sunday*. It was recorded by the Jean Goldkette Orchestra, thus picking up the mantle of immortality, and as a favorite of jazz musicians has been recorded frequently ever since. Grey and Leo Robin provided the words to *Hallelujah,* one of the big songs from the stage show "Hit the Deck." Vincent Youmans wrote the music. In the 1929 movie version, it was sung by Marguerite Padula and in the 1959 remake by Tony Martin, Russ Tamblyn, and Vic Damone. Rudolf Friml wrote the music for the 1928 musical "The Three Musketeers," starring Dennis King. Grey provided the lyrics for *Ma Belle,* and he and P. G. Wodehouse made up the words for the stirring *March of the Musketeers*. The next year the production was *The Love Parade,* a movie musical starring Maurice Chevalier and Jeanette MacDonald in her film debut. Victor Schertzinger wrote the music, and the songs were *My Love Parade* and *Dream Lover*.

Clifford Grey wrote many songs for stage and movie musicals that were important to the plays but went no further. He died in Ipswich, England, on September 24, 1941.

Jimmie Grier

Jimmie Grier was born in Pittsburgh, Pennsylvania, on March 17, 1902. He grew up in California and was educated at the Los Angeles Polytech

High School. An accomplished musician, he studied a variety of instruments, as well as arranging, and worked with several dance bands during the twenties. As a member of Gus Arnheim's band he arranged the popular theme *Sweet and Lovely*. In 1931 he formed his own orchestra, following Arnheim into the famed Cocoanut Grove in Los Angeles, and began a successful period of radio broadcasting and recording for Brunswick Records. His band opened broadcasts with the theme *Music in the Moonlight* and closed with *Bon Voyage (To Your Ship of Dreams),* both composed by Grier.

Besides making records of its own, the Grier band made a number of sides backing Bing Crosby. It also made a few with Pinky Tomlin, who sang with the band for a time, and collaborated with Jimmie Grier on several popular songs. The most successful of these was *The Object of My Affection,* a 1934 offering with words and music by Grier, Tomlin, and lyricist Coy Poe. Grier and Tomlin had the best-selling recording on Brunswick, but the song was covered by every label and performed by top artists. Glen Gray and the Casa Loma Orchestra made it for Decca; the Boswell Sisters waxed it for Brunswick; Jan Garber for Victor; Archie Bleyer, Vocalion; Paul Pendarvis, Columbia; and Joe Reichman, on the various ARC labels. It was incorporated into the movie *Times Square Lady* in 1937. Lionel Hampton obligingly recorded it for Victor that year. The Dorsey band played it in the 1947 movie *The Fabulous Dorseys*.

What's the Reason (I'm Not Pleasin' You), with composer credits as above plus the addition of Earl Hatch, was introduced by Pinky Tomlin in *Times Square Lady* and again was recorded by Grier and Tomlin for Brunswick. Fats Waller had his usual fun with it on Victor, but Decca gave it all-out treatment on recordings by Guy Lombardo, the Mills Brothers, and Jimmy Dorsey and His Orchestra. *Don't Be Afraid to Tell Your Mother,* another collaboration of Tomlin, Grier, and Poe, also came out in 1935. Tomlin sang it on the Grier recording for Brunswick, and it did well on records by the Mills Brothers on Decca, Little Jack Little on Columbia, and Charlie Barnet for Bluebird.

During the thirties the Jimmie Grier Orchestra was often heard on coast-to-coast radio, especially in broadcasts by Burns & Allen, Jack Benny, and Joe Penner. It appeared in movies and musical shorts and recorded for Brunswick at first, and then Decca. After a stint leading a coast guard band during World War II, Grier reorganized his band and continued to perform into the fifties. Other Grier compositions include *Remember Cherie; Hollywood at Vine; Silver River; Anitra's Boogie;* and *Ivy-Covered Arbor*.

Jimmy Grier died in California on June 4, 1959.

Ferde Grofé

Ferde Grofé was born Ferdinand Rudolph Von Grofé in New York City on March 27, 1892, but grew up in California. A highly talented youngster, he studied piano and viola and was a member of the Los Angeles Symphony for ten years. At the same time he played in and arranged for dance bands and in 1920 joined Paul Whiteman's Orchestra. His arrangement of George Gershwin's *Rhapsody in Blue,* which was performed by the Whiteman Orchestra at Aeolian Hall in New York on February 12, 1924, launched the trend to "symphonic jazz," which Grofé and Whiteman pioneered.

Although Grofé is not generally thought of as a writer of popular songs, he composed several, and others evolved as excerpts from his longer works. In 1922 he collaborated with Peter DeRose to turn out a song in the then-popular oriental mode, *Suez,* and in that same year, composed the hit waltz *My Wonderful One,* with lyrics by Theodora Morse under the pseudonym of Dorothy Terriss. The melody was adapted from a theme by Marshall Neilan. Paul Whiteman made a successful recording of the tune. Years later Judy Garland sang it in the 1940 movie *Strike Up the Band,* and it was also heard in *Margie,* another film that year. The following year it was used in "The Great American Broadcast."

On the Trail, a selection taken from Grofé's *Grand Canyon Suite,* entered the popular market in 1933. A highly descriptive piece, it was recorded by the Whiteman organization and then became the theme of the Philip Morris radio program. When Grofé organized his own orchestra later, it became his theme. Harold Adamson added words, and Kay Kyser recorded it with a vocal in 1946. That same year Grofé teamed with Irving Caesar and Edgar Guest, and they contributed the words to his melody for *Count Your Blessings.* A pleasant song with typically up-beat Edgar Guest sentiments, it did rather well in that year of heavy competition, with records by Grofé's Orchestra on Columbia, Freddy Martin on Brunswick, Harry Sosnik on Victor, and Henry King on Vocalion.

Daybreak, a very memorable song that is still heard at various times, was another adaptation, this time from the *Mardi Gras* theme of Grofé's *Mississippi Suite.* With lyrics by Harold Adamson, it was a successful entry in 1942. Kathryn Grayson sang it in the film *As Thousands Cheer,* and it received excellent representation on records. Tommy Dorsey's disc, with the vocal by Frank Sinatra, was probably the best-seller, but Harry James and Jimmy Dorsey also did well. In 1955 Al Hibbler recorded the song. Besides writing extended musical works—*Mississippi Suite; Grand Canyon Suite;*

and *Death Valley Suite,* Ferde Grofé scored for films, including *The King of Jazz; Time Out of Mind; The Return of Jesse James;* and *Minstrel Man.*

He died in Santa Monica, California, on April 3, 1972.

Walter Gross

Walter Gross was born in New York City on July 14, 1909. He graduated from high school and studied music privately. At the age of ten he gave a piano recital and then went on to a professional career. He played with a number of the top orchestras in concerts and on the radio and established an excellent reputation. After military service during WW II, he worked as musical director for CBS and Musicraft Records and acted as conductor and arranger on records, backing such artists as Frank Sinatra, Mel Tormé, Sarah Vaughan, Buddy Clark, and Gordon MacRae.

His most outstanding composition is the standard *Tenderly,* written in 1946. In those days my good friend Ross Doyle, also a piano player and songwriter, was in charge of Tommy Dorsey's publishing firm, and every day he would meet Walter Gross and they would have lunch together. Since both had songs published about the same time, they made a small bet with each other as to whose song would be the most popular. Gross's entry was *Tenderly.* Sorry to say, I don't remember the title of Ross's tune. The lyrics for *Tenderly* were written by Jack Lawrence. It was introduced on a Capitol recording by Clark Dennis, and Sarah Vaughan recorded it on Musicraft. In 1952 Rosemary Clooney made a record of it for Columbia that went on to be a million-seller. The song was also used in the 1953 movie *Torch Song,* starring Joan Crawford. Walter Gross composed other songs and piano pieces, including *Your Love; To Be Worthy of You; A Slight Case of Ivory; I'm in a Fog about You; Just a Moon Ago; Creepy Weepy; Please Remember; How Will I Remember You?; Mexican Moon; Improvisation in Several Keys;* and *It's Somebody Else That You Love.*

He died in Los Angeles, California, on November 27, 1967.

Wilhelm Grosz (Hugh Williams)

Concert pianist and composer Wilhelm Grosz was born in Vienna, Austria, on August 11, 1894. He graduated with honors from the Staatsakadamie for Music, and then took further studies at the music department of the University of Vienna. For awhile he served as conductor at the Operahouse in Mannheim, Germany, and then toured Europe as a concert pianist. From 1927 to 1933 he was the musical director for Ultraphone Gramaphone Company in Berlin and then, returning to Vienna, performed the same duty for the Kammerskiele. In 1934 he moved to England and a short time later began composing songs for the popular market. With lyricist Jimmy Kennedy, he had two hit songs in 1935, *Isle of Capri* and *Red Sails in the Sunset*.

Isle of Capri was an international hit, and as sometimes happens with such blockbusters, a dispute arose regarding its origins. Shortly after the song was published in London, a song with a similar melodic line was published and performed in a revue in Vienna. Paul Reif, one of the composers of this song, brought suit and won a settlement, claiming *Isle of Capri* was an infringement on his melody. The story is, he regretted the settlement after coming to this country and realizing how big the song had become. He would have made a better deal by insisting on composing credit and royalties. Written as a tango, the song was a big record for Latin bandleader Xavier Cugat and others of the more commercial dance orchestras of the era, but far removed from the element of jazz. So far, in fact, that most jazz musicians had a very low opinion of the tune. One in particular was trumpeter Wingy Manone, who never hesitated to express his opinion on such things. At the time he was making records for Vocalion. On learning how much Wingy hated the *Isle of Capri,* the musicians in his band decided to turn it into a practical joke. They told him they had overheard the executives at Vocalion making plans to have Wingy record the song. At first Wingy was outraged. Then thinking it over, he decided to take matters in his own hands and record the song in his own way. Nobody will ever know what Will Grosz thought of this irreverent treatment of his composition, but for Wingy it resulted in a hit record.

Red Sails in the Sunset was also an English importation, not quite as schmaltzy as the *Isle of Capri* but with the same commercial appeal. It sold well in sheet music, got a lot of radio play, and was plentifully recorded by a wide variety of artists—Bing Crosby, Louis Armstrong, the Mound City Blue Blowers, Guy Lombardo, Frances Langford, etc. In line with the well-known cliche that you can't argue with success, Kennedy and Grosz returned to the well one more time, and in 1937 they produced another tale of woe, *Harbor Lights*. Again they hit the target, and the song made the prestigious Hit Parade for ten weeks. Rudy Vallee plugged the tune, and other bands and singers gave it a lot of radio attention. It sold well on records by Claude Thornhill, Roy Fox, Rudy Vallee, and Emery Deutsch. And that wasn't the end of it. Revived in 1950, it soared to number one again, and this time resulted in big-selling records for Sammy Kaye, Guy Lombardo, Ray Anthony, Ralph Flanagan, and Bing Crosby. Ten years later the Platters had a top ten record of it on Mercury.

In the interim, Grosz emigrated to the United States, and in 1940 in collaboration with Al Dubin and Edwina Coolidge, who provided the words, *Santa Fe Trail*, his last song, was published. In my humble opinion this is the best of his output. It received topflight attention by Glenn Miller on the Bluebird label. The song was featured in the movie with the same title. Other songs by Will Grosz (Hugh Williams) include *Bird on the Wing; Tomorrow Night; Tina; In an Old Dutch Garden;* and *Poor Little Angeline.*

Will Grosz died in New York City, December 10, 1939.

Theodore (Ted) Grouya

Composer-author-pianist Ted Grouya was born in Bucharest, Roumania, July 31, 1910. He attended local schools and then went to Paris to study at the Sorbonne and the Ecole Normale de Musique, where he studied piano with Alfred Cortot and harmony with Nadia Boulanger. In this country he performed as pianist, songwriter, and public relations man, and became head of the Robbins-Feist & Miller subsidiary of MGM. His collaborators are among the top names in the business: Sammy Cahn, Ira Gershwin, Frank Loesser, Johnny Mercer, Ed Heyman, Eddie DeLange, Nat Burton, Paul Francis Webster, Ned Washington, Ed Anderson, and Don George.

Most likely Grouya's most popular and enduring song is *Flamingo,* with words by Ed Anderson, introduced on a Victor recording by Duke Ellington, the vocal by Herb Jeffries. But 1943 was the top year for him, because he had two entries that did rather well, *In My Arms,* with words by Frank Loesser, and *I Heard You Cried Last Night,* a collaboration with Jerrie Kruger. *In My Arms* was featured in the film *See Here, Private Hargrove*. Dick Haymes had the best-selling record. *I Heard You Cried Last Night* got sympathetic treatment from Harry James on Columbia, with Helen Forrest providing appropriate emotion. The song came from another movie, *Cinderella Swings It.* Other compositions include *When Am I Gonna Kiss You Good Morning?; Ballade New Yorkaise; Don't Ever Change; Two Heavens; Since You Went Away; Will You Remember Me?;* and *The Road I Didn't Take.*

Albert Gumm

See Albert Von Tilzer.

Harold Gumm

See Harry Von Tilzer.

Bob Haggart

Bassist-arranger-composer Bob Haggart was born in New York City on March 13, 1914, but grew up in Douglaston, Long Island. He attended Great Neck High School and Salisbury Prep School. He studied a number of instruments and underwent intense musical training. He played with the Bob Sterling Orchestra in the midthirties and then joined the newly constituted Bob Crosby band. As a member of this organization from 1935 to 1942, he performed his most important work as an arranger and composer. His arrangements fashioned a good portion of the band's most important work and gave it a distinctive flavor. This can also be said of his compositions, because he arranged them all and the band recorded them.

The first of these was *Dixieland Shuffle,* with Gil Rodin, Nappy Lamare, and Matty Matlock listed as collaborators, recorded in March 1936 for Decca Records. The band was to stay with this label until it broke up in 1942. The all-time jazz standard *South Rampart Street Parade* was recorded at a session in November 1937. Haggart and Ray Bauduc conceived the tune while sitting at a restaurant table, sketching the music on the white tablecloth. When they left they took the tablecloth with them. The Haggart arrangement, put together with the aid of Deane Kincaide, was recorded on a twelve-inch record and quickly became a best-seller. *Dogtown Blues,* a Haggart original, was waxed at the same session. Decca later issued ten-inch edited versions of *South Rampart Street Parade.*

In 1938 Haggart and Ray Bauduc recorded the novelty they had worked up for bass and drums, *The Big Noise From Winnetka,* which has long since become a tour de force for Haggart. He has performed it hundreds of times. Only a short time later the Crosby band recorded two more of his originals, *I'm Prayin' Humble* and *I'm Free.* The latter, with lyrics by Johnny Burke, went on to become the well-known standard *What's New?* As such, it has had a distinguished career, performed on superior recordings by Billy Butterfield (who used it as the theme song of his band), Benny Goodman, Bing Crosby, Stan Getz, Maynard Ferguson, among others, and saw a revival in the pop market in 1983 on an LP record by Linda Ronstadt. At the risk of sounding like a proud father, I would also like to point out that it received masterful treatment by Warren Vaché Jr. on an album produced by Les Paul for Atlantic Records in 1985, starring pianist Joe Bushkin, *Play It Again, Joe*.

In the same month (October) of 1938, the Crosby band cut another Haggart composition, *My Inspiration*. On the original record Irving Fazola was the featured player on clarinet. In May 1930, an all-star jazz group that included Haggart on bass turned out a CD for George Buck's Jazzology label, with Allan Vachi on clarinet, rendering another outstanding performance. Like most of the Haggart compositions, *My Inspiration* shows every evidence of becoming a standard. Early in 1938 the Crosby crew recorded a collaboration attributed to Haggart, Ray Bauduc, and Matty Matlock, *Smokey Mary,* an instrumental dedicated to a railroad train of the same name and made another recording of *South Rampart Street Parade*. Other Haggart instrumentals include *The Mark Hop; Chain Gang;* and *Swingin' at the Sugar Bowl*.

Bob Haggart died in Florida on December 2, 1998.

George (Spike) Hamilton

George (Spike) Hamilton, bandleader and composer, was born in Newport, Vermont, January 13, 1901. He was educated at Dartmouth College. For awhile he led the Barbary Coast Orchestra and for four years conducted the orchestra at the Chicago Opera. Still later he led dance bands in hotels around the country. He also appeared in the movies—*George White's Scandals* and *A Night at the Trocadero*. As a songwriter he was only moderately successful, but he did have two successful songs. The first, *Bye Bye, Pretty Baby,* written with Jack Gardner, was a hit in 1927 and well represented on recordings by Nathan Glantz, Abe Lyman, Jan Garber, Ben Selvin, and Frank Crumit. A typical song of the carefree twenties, it can still be heard in medleys of "oldtimers."

In 1934 Hamilton collaborated with Harry Tobias and Neil Moret to write the delightful *Wild Honey*. It was only one of many great songs in that bounteous year, but it received across-the-board attention on records by Dick Jurgens, Joe Haymes, Jan Garber, and Archie Bleyer. In the late forties it was revived on a record by Don Darcy. Other Hamilton compositions include *Here Comes Your Pappy (With the Wrong Kind of Load); Lovely While It Lasted; I Feel Sorry for the Poor People; There's Never Been a Love Like Ours; Hat Check Girl; You Can Say That Again;* and *Iowa Corn Song*.

George Hamilton died in New York City, on March 31, 1957.

Oscar Hammerstein II

In a biographical sketch of Oscar Hammerstein II, Roger Kinkle commented, "Except for Irving Berlin, most prolific lyric writer of all time." Although this is a very big statement, I'm not about to argue with it. Such judgments are always arbitrary, but the fact remains that Oscar Hammerstein II collaborated with many of our foremost composers, turning out a list of songs that approaches the unbelievable and is bound to include some of your favorites. A native New Yorker, Oscar Hammerstein II was born on July 12, 1895, into a prestigious show business family. His father was manager of the historic vaudeville theater the Victoria in Manhattan, and his grandfather, the first Oscar, was an opera impresario and theater builder.

Oscar II went to Columbia University and to law school, but the stage was in his blood. He wrote and acted in college plays, and afterwards worked as a stage manger for his uncle, Arthur Hammerstein. His attempts to write plays were unsuccessful. During the twenties he joined fellow lyricist-librettist Otto Harbach to write material and songs for Broadway shows. After a slow start they were very successful. In 1924 they collaborated with Rudolf Friml and Herbert Stothart on the hit musical "Rose Marie" and in the following year repeated the trick with Jerome Kern, providing the music, for "Sunny." In 1926 the show was "The Desert Song," with music by Sigmund Romberg.

The association with Otto Harbach dissolved, and in 1929 Hammerstein worked with Frank Mandel and Laurence Schwab on the book and lyrics for "New Moon." Sigmund Romberg was the composer. Oscar II then went on to writing the book and the lyrics all by himself for the sensational hit show "Show Boat," with music by Jerome Kern. Following the death of Lorenz Hart he worked with Richard Rodgers. He also collaborated with George Gershwin and Vincent Youmans. In a number of instances the stage shows he wrote—and sometimes produced—went on to second lives as important movies. He was twice awarded the Pulitzer Prize for his collaboration with Richard Rodgers on "Oklahoma" (1944), and "South Pacific" (1950).

A complete list of Hammerstein songs would probably put you to sleep, but even a partial is impressive. Here are some highlights: *Rose Marie; Indian Love Call; Sunny, Who?; The Desert Song; One Alone; The Riff Song; Brown Eyes; Make Believe; Why Do I Love You; Old Man River; Bill; Can't Help Lovin' That Man; Lover, Come Back to Me; Softly, as in a Morning Sunrise; Why Was I Born; Don't Ever Leave Me; The Night Is Young; When I Grow Too Old to Dream; All the Things You Are; The Last Time I Saw Paris; The Surrey with the Fringe on Top; June Is Bustin' Out All Over; It*

Might As Well Be Spring; Some Enchanted Evening; Younger Than Springtime; This Nearly Was Mine; Getting to Know You; Hello, Young Lovers—and many more.

Oscar Hammerstein II died in Doylestown, Pennsylvania, on August 23, 1960. His lyrics assure him a niche of immortality in the annals of great songwriters.

Lou Handman

Composer Lou Handman was born in New York City on September 10, 1894. At age seventeen he was already a professional pianist and toured in vaudeville, including Australia. Following the path of many of the early songwriters, he went to work for a music publishing firm and in 1920 started composing his own songs. *Blue (And Broken Hearted),* published in 1922, was Lou Handman's first hit, with words by Grant Clarke and Edgar Leslie. It was introduced by the popular recording artist Marion Harris, and other contemporary records were made by the California Ramblers, the Virginians, McMurray's California Thumpers, and Fletcher Henderson. A well-liked song, it never completely died out. Earl Hines recorded it twice, once in 1934 and again in 1935. Vic Berton also waxed it in 1935, and five years later Jimmy Dorsey had a big-selling record with vocals by both Helen O'Connell and Bob Eberle. Not to be outdone, Mildred Bailey did equally well on her version.

In the happy year of 1923 Handman had two outstanding titles, *My Sweetie Went Away (And She Didn't Say Why),* a catchy tune with lyrics by Roy Turk, and *Lovey Came Back.* It's hard to say which came first, but the first tune, which still gets played, was introduced by Aileen Stanley, along with being recorded by Ben Bernie, Billy Murray, and Ed Smalle. *Lovey Came Back* did well on piano rolls and sheet music but is sharply etched in my mind as recorded by the Georgians, directed by Frank Guarante. I think this was my first introduction to jazz. *I'm Gonna Charleston Back to Charleston* was a timely entry in 1925, also with words by Roy Turk, but nothing compared to the song the pair published in 1927. This was *Are You Lonesome Tonight?,* a tune that resulted in hit records for Vaughn DeLeath, Henry Burr, and Little Jack Little. Revived in 1960, it provided Elvis Presley with a number one record and another for Donny Osmond in 1973. It was used in the 1979 movie *Elvis,* with the soundtrack dubbed in by Ronnie McDowell for Kurt Russell, who had the title role.

A few years elasped after this megamonster, and the next Handman song is one that had no relationship with his earlier work, but was more of a novelty, *Puddin' Head Jones.* Alfred Bryan wrote the words, which tell a fanciful tale, and the tune found favor with Rudy Vallee, who featured it on the air and recorded it. The Joe Haymes band waxed it too. A short time later Handman teamed with a new lyricist, Walter Hirsch. In 1936 they produced *Me and the Moon,* which was nicely recorded by Jimmie Lunceford, Richard Himber, and Shep Fields; the next year they had a very pretty ballad featured in the movie *Rhythm in the Clouds.* The song is *Don't Ever Change,* and it can be heard on contemporary records by Dick McDonough and Will Osborne. *Was It Rain?,* another offering that year, was introduced by Frances Langford and Phil Regan in the film *The Hit Parade.*

Baby Me, a melodic swinger with collaborators Harry Harris and Archie Gottler taking credit for the lyrics, was Handman's last hit. It was a big record for the Glenn Miller band. Other Handman compositions are *Give Me a Smile and a Kiss; Twelve O'Clock at Night; When I Was the Dandy and You Were the Belle; I Can't Get the One I Want; Love Is Good for Anything That Ails You; Last Night I Dreamed of You; Let This be a Warning to You, Baby; I Solemnly Swear; What Good Would It Do?; Is My Baby Blue Tonight?; No Nothing;* and *Fill Your Glasses with Kisses.*

Lou Handman died in Flushing, New York, on December 9, 1956.

William Christopher (W. C.) Handy

William Christopher (W. C.) Handy was born on November 16, 1873, in Florence, Alabama. As a young man he taught school and also worked in a steel mill for a time. He played cornet and in 1893 organized a quartet to play the Chicago World's Fair. Later he performed as a bandmaster in Henderson, Kentucky, and then went on an extensive tour as cornet-director of Mahara's Minstrels. Still later he taught music in Clarksdale, Mississippi. Known as the "Father of the Blues," mainly through the tremendous popularity of his biggest hit, *St. Louis Blues,* the story goes that Handy jotted down the songs he heard being sung by black workers and entertainers and used them as inspiration for his compositions. His first published work, *Memphis Blues,* was popular in 1912 and 1913, and he immediately ran into royalty problems; in 1913 he formed his own publishing company.

Memphis Blues, with lyrics by George A. Norton, was originally an instrumental called *Mr. Crump,* and Handy wrote it as a campaign song for Edward A. Crump, who was running for election as mayor of Memphis. Norton added the lyrics in 1913. Now a standard, the tune has been recorded and played countless times. Bing Crosby sang it in the 1941 movie *Birth of the Blues,* and it was also used in the film *Belle of the Nineties* (1934) and again in *St. Louis Blues,* the film based on Handy's life. The renowned *St. Louis Blues,* probably the most popular and most-played blues of all time, was published in 1914. This time Handy wrote both words and music. Aside from being recorded by just about every name artist since (Brian Rust lists over 150 waxings in his *Jazz Records, 1897-1941),* the song has been featured in a half-dozen films. In 1929 it was played by Ted Lewis and His Band in *Is Everybody Happy?* It was sung by Nan Wynn in the 1943 movie, with the same title, based on Lewis's life and career. It was the title of two movies named *St. Louis Blues,* the first one in 1939 with Maxine Sullivan, and the second in 1958, with Nat "King" Cole portraying Handy. Then, in 1954, it became the *St. Louis Blues March* as arranged and conducted by Glenn Miller in *The Glenn Miller Story.*

Handy continued to compose prolifically. *Yellow Dog Blues* was also published in 1914 but most likely was overwhelmed by the success of *St. Louis Blues* and had to wait until 1928 to be rediscovered. It still managed to gain enough attention to be recorded by some eminent names—Duke Ellington, Bessie Smith, Ted Lewis, and even Handy himself. In 1915 Handy released *Hesitation Blues.* It was recorded by a number of contemporary artists, including the Victor Military Band in 1916. Muggsy Spanier brought it to more recent attention as recorded by his big band on Decca in 1942.

Ole Miss, the favorite of Dixieland bands, made its debut in 1916, followed by *Beale St. Blues* in 1917. The latter has been treated to classic performances by Jelly Roll Morton (and his Red Hot Peppers) on Victor (reissued several times on LP) in 1927; Joe Venuti–Eddie Lang and Their All-Star Orchestra—originally on Vocalion, but also reissued many times (1931); and more recently, Bob Crosby's Orchestra (1935) and Wingy Manone in 1939. Wingy also recorded *Hesitation Blues* in a 1936 session.

Aunt Hagar's Blues, one of Jack Teagarden's specialties, came out in 1920, and in the following year *Loveless Love,* sometimes called *Careless Love,* appeared. *Atlanta Blues* dates to 1923. Sara Martin recorded it with Clarence Williams. In 1939 Eddie Condon made an album for Decca called *Jazz Concert,* which included *Atlanta Blues,* now more familiar to jazz fans as *Make Me a Pallet On the Floor.* All of the foregoing Handy compositions are standards in jazz, frequently heard and often recorded.

In 1941 the augmented Artie Shaw Orchestra recorded *Chantez Les Bas (Sing 'Em Low),* which Handy wrote ten years earlier, a classic in itself. Among the very many other compositions credited to Handy are *Friendless Blues; Joe Turner Blues; Harlem Blues; Basement Blues;* and *Wall St. Blues.*

W. C. Handy died in New York City on March 29, 1958.

Bernie Hanighen

Bernie Hanighen was born in Omaha, Nebraska, on April 27, 1908. He attended Harvard, where he was president of the Harvard Dramatic Club, and wrote for the Hasty Pudding and Pi Eta club shows. He went on to a varied career as musical director for record companies and contributed special material to stage shows and orchestras. The list of his compositions isn't long, but it's distinguished not only for superior melodies, but excellent lyrics by the genius Johnny Mercer. The collaboration started out in 1934, when the pair turned out three fine titles: *Fare-Thee-Well to Harlem; Here Come the British;* and *When a Woman Loves a Man. Fare-Thee-Well to Harlem* was recorded by the Paul Whiteman Orchestra for Victor, with a vocal duet between Jack Teagarden and Johnny Mercer. Then Teagarden recorded it with his own band for Brunswick. The novelty *Here Come the British* also rated a Whiteman rendition, this time Johnny Mercer abetted by Peggy Healy and Johnny Hauser. It got other top treatments by Eddie Stone, vocalizing with Isham Jones on Decca, and by Pee Wee Hunt and the Casa Loma Orchestra on Columbia. *When a Woman Loves a Man,* with words by Johnny Mercer, was a collaboration between Hanighen and Gordon Jenkins on the music. It became a particular favorite of Bobby Hackett, who recorded it at least twice.

This penchant of jazz musicians to like Hanighen songs carried over into the next group of titles in 1935. These include *The Dixieland Band,* an early Benny Goodman hit with vocalist Helen Ward, recorded several times; *If the Moon Turns Green,* with words by Paul Coates, one of four sides turned out by Taft Jordan and the Mob, the great little band put together by trumpeter Taft Jordan to record for the American Record Company, with Teddy Wilson, Johnny Mince, and Ward Silloway in the lineup; and *Yankee Doodle Never Went to Town,* this one with lyrics by Ralph Freed, accorded over-all treatment by Pee Wee Hunt with Casa Loma, Helen Ward with Benny Goodman, and other sides by Joe Venuti and Teddy Wilson. *Bob White* was the Bernie Hanighen–Johnny Mercer entry in 1937, and of the many treatments on records, the Bing Crosby–Johnny Mercer side was outstanding. Mildred Bailey worked her magic on *The Weekend of a Private Secretary* in 1938, and Johnny Mercer scored again with the vocal on the Goodman recording of *Show Your Linen, Miss Richardson* in 1939.

Jack Teagarden, Bob Crosby, and Larry Clinton were among the bandleaders who had fun with the Hanighen–Harold Adamson novelty *The Little Man Who Wasn't There* in 1939. Nothing happened in 1940, but you may remember Charlie Butterworth as the inspiration for the rather doleful *Poor*

Mr. Chisholm in the Artie Shaw movie, *Second Chorus,* which came out in 1941, the same year for another independent entry, *The Air-Minded Executive. House of Joy* was the only Hanighen offering in 1945; he turned lyricist and collaborated with Raymond Scott to provide the music for the Broadway production of "The Lute Song." Other Hanighen titles are *Me and the Ghost Upstairs; Two Little Fishes and Five Loaves of Bread; 'Round Midnight; Tired Teddy Bear; Mountain High, Valley Low; See the Monkey; Where You Are; My Old Man; Blue Fool;* and *Baby Doll.*

James F. Hanley

Although you may be skeptical about it, because it is very possible you have never heard of James F. Hanley, he wrote some of your favorite songs. What's more, these are songs that are so firmly entrenched in the American standard library that they will never die as long as there is a musician still around to play them. What are the songs? *Indiana; Rose of Washington Square; Secondhand Rose; Just a Cottage Small; I'm in the Market for You; Zing! Went the Strings of My Heart.* James F. Hanley was born in Rensselaer, Indiana, on February 17, 1892, and had his first song published in 1917. Following this, he wrote prolifically for twenty-five years, including material for stage shows and movies, but his promising career was cut short by his death, which also took place in February only a few days before his birthday. He died on February 8, 1942, in Douglaston, New York. Two of Hanley's songs, *Rose of Washington Square* and *Secondhand Rose,* were featured in early Ziegfeld shows (1919, 1920, 1921) and were hits for the talented comedienne Fanny Brice. Her life and career were portrayed by Barbra Streisand in the movie *Funny Girl,* and the songs enjoyed a well-deserved revival period.

Hanley's first published song, with lyrics by Ballard MacDonald, was the all-time standard *(Back Home Again in) Indiana.* A favorite of jazz musicians, it is sure to be played at every jazz festival at least once. It has also been featured in several movies, including the one based on the life and career of Red Nichols, *The Five Pennies,* another fantasy, *The Gene Krupa Story,* and *With a Song in My Heart,* based on the life of singer Jane Froman.

Another collaboration with Ballard MacDonald produced *Breeze (Blow My Baby Back to Me),* which also takes well to jazz treatment, as demonstrated by the irrepressible Wingy Manone on Banner 33356 and related labels.

In the twenties and thirties Hanley composed quite a large number of songs, mostly for stage shows and movies, but he also managed to squeeze in some freelance material every now and then, such as *Sing Song Girl,* which achieved a degree of immortality as recorded by the Ben Pollack band with Benny Goodman, Jack Teagarden, Eddie Miller, and Charlie Spivak. The 1930 movie *High Society Blues* offered three excellent songs by Hanley. The title song, *High Society Blues,* got noble treatment from Ray Noble in England, who was just starting out on his illustrious career as musical director for HMV. Here in the United States, *Just Like in a Storybook* and *I'm in the Market for You* were nicely paired and played by the all-star studio orchestra of Bob Haring on Brunswick 4782. The great Ambrose band with Sylvester Ahola recorded *I'm in the Market for You* on HMV B5824 in England; not to be outdone, over here a young fellow named Louis Armstrong waxed the title on OKeh 41442. The stage show "Thumbs Up," produced in 1935, included one of Hanley's biggest hits, *Zing! Went the Strings of My Heart,* which has been recorded innumerable times. Perhaps the most prophetic title of all of his songs was his final published work, which appeared in 1940—*You Forgot About Me.* Other songs by James F. Hanley include *One Day in June; From Your Heart to Mine; The Magic Kiss; Melancholy Blues; Gee! But I Hate to Go Home Alone; Bamboo Babies; At the End of the Road; The Little White House at the End of Honeymoon Lane; No Foolin'; Every Little Thing You Do; Nice Baby; Heading for Harlem; Little Log Cabin of Dreams; Sleepy Valley; The Cute Little Things You Do;* and *There's Music in My Heart Cherie.*

Otto Harbach

Characterizing Otto Harbach as an "unsung songwriter" is like calling Mount Rushmore a pile of rocks, but although this famous lyricist-librettist was responsible for the words to some very famous songs—not to mention the books for successful Broadway shows that very often, in turn, became equally successful movies—it's more than likely that most people are not aware of it. For instance, did you know that Harbach wrote the lyrics for *Cuddle Up a Little Closer?* You did! I didn't! Harbach was born in Salt Lake City on August 18, 1873, and he died in New York City on January 24, 1963. In between those dates he fashioned a brilliant career in show business, but it seems this wasn't his original intention. He was educated at Collegiate Institute in Salt Lake City and Knox College and then went on to become a professor of English at Whitman College from 1895 to 1901.

For most people this would have been a career choice, but for some reason Harbach wasn't satisfied, and by 1902 he was in New York City working as a newspaper writer and from there went into advertising. This stage in his life lasted until 1910, but in the meantime, in 1908, he met a composer named Karl Hoschna, and they collaborated on the score for a Broadway show, "The Three Twins," which turned out to be very successful and included Harbach's first hit, the aforementioned *Cuddle Up a Little Closer.* The team went on to write other shows, but in 1911 Hoschna died, so Harbach began working with Rudolph Friml. As time went by, he collaborated with many of our most famous composers and playwrights—Harry Tierney, Vincent Youmans, George Gershwin, Sigmund Romberg, Jerome Kern—and the list of hit shows he was involved in, sometimes as lyricist, but often as librettist or both, reads like a history of Broadway's greatest hits.

In 1910 the stage show "Bright Eyes" produced the song of the same name, and that same year *Every Little Movement* was a memorable part of another show, "Madam Sherry." These established Otto Harbach as a successful writer, and every year without a break, until a brief hiatus in 1932, he was involved with a major stage production or a movie. Since our main concern is with his career as a lyricist, here are some of his best-known songs: *Bright Eyes; Every Little Movement; Allah's Holiday; The Love Nest; Wildflower; Bambalina; Rose Marie; Indian Love Call; Sunny; Who?; The Desert Song; The Riff Song; One Alone; Brown Eyes; The Same Old Moon; The Night Was Made for Love; She Didn't Say "Yes"; Try to Forget; Smoke Gets in Your Eyes; The Touch of Your Hand; You're Devastating; Yesterdays.*

E. Y. (Yip) Harburg

After eulogizing Otto Harbach, it's rather a shock to realize that the next subject in line is one of the heaviest hitters ever to put a set of lyrics together, E. Y. "Yip" Harburg. A list of Harburg's titles is equivalent to an all-time hit parade. A native New Yorker, he was born in the big city on April 8, 1898, and after attending CCNY went into the appliance business. Just how he made the transition to writing song lyrics isn't clear, but apparently he skipped the usual routine of apprenticeship in a music publishing firm; when he started writing in 1929, he jumped in with both feet. First he contributed to the current Earl Carroll's "Sketchbook" and then for the movie *Applause,* collaborating with composer Jay Gorney on the hit song *What Wouldn't I Do for That Man?* After this kick-off "Yip" Harburg never looked back.

Roger D. Kinkle, in his comprehensive *The Complete Encyclopedia of Popular Music and Jazz, 1900–1950,* traces Harburg's career year by year, through every stage show and movie he wrote for; the long list is impressive, to say the least. So is the roster of composers he worked with: Harold

Arlen, the aforementioned Jay Gorney, Johnny Green, Vernon Duke, Burton Lane, and Jerome Kern. As you can see, the former appliance dealer moved right into the major league. Harburg's contributions to the great heritage of the American popular song put him in the first rank. After you read the following partial list of his songs, take the time to play some of them on your phonograph or current reproducing equipment—It will be an enjoyable experience.

Here we go: *What Wouldn't I Do for That Man; I'm Yours; If I Didn't Have You; Thrill Me; Brother, Can You Spare a Dime; April in Paris; Ah! But Is It Love; It's Only a Paper Moon; Isn't It Heavenly; What Is There to Say; You're a Builder Upper; Down with Love; Over the Rainbow; Tampico; Evelina; How Are Things in Glocca Morra; That Old Devil Moon; When I'm Not Near the Girl I Love.*

Of course, this is a mere sampling. E. Y. Harburg wrote dozens of songs that were important in the scores of stage productions and movies but never became popular hits. Nevertheless, if his reputation only depended on the songs in the last paragraph, it would still be fantastic.

Frank W. Harling

Composer-conductor Frank W. Harling was born in London, England, on January 18, 1887, but came to the United States in 1888. He received part of his education at the Grace Church Choir School in New York City and then attended the London Academy of Music, where he studied with Theodore Ysaye. In 1907 and 1908 he was organist and choir director at the Church of the Resurrection in Brussels and served at the U.S. Military Academy for two years. He composed the West Point songs *The Corps* (a hymn) and *West Point Forever,* the official march. He wrote incidental music for plays, composed operas and tone poems, and collaborated in the writing of some excellent popular songs.

The most productive year for Frank Harling was 1930. With veteran songsmith Richard Whiting he collaborated on the music for two songs, both with lyrics by Leo Robin and introduced by Jeannette MacDonald in the film *Monte Carlo,* which also starred Jack Buchanan. The songs were *Always in All Ways* and *Beyond the Blue Horizon.* The latter tune has attained the status of a standard and received classic jazz treatment by the Artie Shaw Orchestra on Victor in 1941. In the same year, Harling and Sam Coslow turned out *Sing You Sinners.* The song was featured in the movie *Honey,* sung by Lillian Roth. Vaudeville star Bell Baker featured it on stage and recorded it, but it was heard frequently on the radio and made a moderate hit. It was accorded a second life in the fifties on a recording by Tony Bennett and through inclusion in two movies, *Cruisin' Down the River,* in which Billy Daniels sang it (1953), and *I'll Cry Tomorrow,* the Lillian Roth bio film, with Susan Hayward portraying Roth (1955) and reprising the vocal.

Where Was I?, a very pretty ballad with music by Harling and words by Al Dubin, was in the 1940 movie *Till We Meet Again* and became so popular that it was included in *Your Hit Parade,* the prestigious radio program, for ten weeks. Charlie Barnet had a big-selling record, and Jan Savitt and Sammy Kaye had successful discs, but the most musical was the Columbia recording by Ray Noble's Orchestra, with Larry Stewart on the vocal.

It appears this was the last song Harling composed for the popular market. He died in Sierra Madre, California, November 22, 1958.

Charles K. Harris

Charles K. Harris was born in Poughkeepsie, New York, May 1, 1867. He started out as a banjo player, touring in vaudeville and writing special material. Later on he became a music publisher in Chicago, then New York, and also wrote scripts for plays and silent movies. His autobiography is entitled *After the Ball: Forty Years of Melody,* echoing the fame and popularity of his greatest song hit, *After the Ball,* for which be wrote both words and music. This sentimental tearjerker, an ideal entry for its time, was introduced in 1892 by J. Aldridge Libby in Milwaukee and in a stage musical called "A Trip to Chinatown." Another entertainer, May Irwin, followed through at Tony Pastor's in New York, and then John Philip Sousa played it at the Chicago World's Fair. Robert Lissauer, in his *Encyclopedia of Popular Music in America,* states that in its initial surge of popularity, the song sold five million copies of sheet music. Contemporary recordings in that infant industry—one by a whistler, the other by an Irish tenor—also sold well.

So the song was well established in the popular music of a generation, but it didn't end there. It has enjoyed a steady round of revivals since. In 1927 it was sung by Norma Terris in the theater production of "Show Boat" and later on by Irene Dunne, who took her place in the show and went on to sing it again in the movie production in 1936. Alice Faye sang it in the 1940 film *Lillian Russell,* Scotty Beckett in *The Jolson Story* (1946), Gloria Jean in *There's a Girl in My Heart* (1950), and Kathryn Grayson in the 1951 movie version of *Show Boat.* In addition to its legitimate life, the song is familiar to a countless horde of kids who early on learned the words to the parody that starts, "After the ball was over, Maggie took out her glass eye, put her false teeth in water, hung up her hair to dry. . . ." In the long run this may be the best-remembered version of the tune.

Harris had another big hit in 1897, *Break the News to Mother,* a sorrowful ditty that took the public fancy as a result of the Spanish–American War. And he kept on going. In 1905, the popular entertainer Bryon G. Harlan recorded and featured the Harris song *Would You Care?,* and it was quite popular. Then, in 1909, another tune in a similar vein, *Nobody Knows, Nobody Cares,* also did well, and in 1911, *There'll Come a Time* followed right along. Harris's fame and reputation will most likely rest upon his composition of *After the Ball,* but even though he worked alone, he turned out a very respectable list. Here are some of them: *I'm Trying So Hard to Forget You; Better Than Gold; Just Behind the Times; I've Just Come to Say Good-bye; Mid the Green Fields of Virginia; For Old Time's Sake; I've a Longing In My Heart for You, Louise; Hello Central, Give Me Heaven; Always in the Way; The Best Things in Life;* and *Songs of Yesterday.*

Charles K. Harris died in New York City, on December 22, 1930.

Clarence Leonard (Clancy) Hayes

Clarence Leonard "Clancy" Hayes was born on November 14, 1908, in Caney, Kansas, the seventh son of a seventh son. He was the complete songwriter, handling both the music and the lyrics in a variety of styles. With one outstanding exception, his songs never got the exposure they deserved, and Clancy's real claim to fame came as a musician and singer. Had he not been so gifted a performer, he might have concentrated more on composing and getting his efforts before the general public. His own recorded versions of his songs bear lasting testimony to the quality of his work. *Ten to One It's Tennessee* must surely qualify as one of the best "hometown" songs ever written, raising this hoary old theme to new heights of finesse and sensitivity. *When the One You Love Is Gone* reveals a poignancy and sense of drama that few can match, while *Swingin' Doors* is a catchy foot-tapper with penetrating lyrics that will bring a smile to any face. June King shared composer credits on these last two, and she also teamed with Clancy on a Latin swinger called *In New Orleans.* It was a team that produced compositions of consistently high quality and variety—but which lacked the killer instinct when it came to marketing the product.

Clancy was equally adept on his own, penning the catchy *Travellin' Shoes; Gettin' My Boots;* and the happy-yet-melancholy *Glad to Be Me.*

Charles Conlin joined him on *Parsons, Kansas Blues,* which effectively employed a repetitive bass line to simulate locomotives leaving Parsons on the KMT (Kansas, Missouri, Texas) Line. There are other songs, such as *Hassan the Man; I'm Going Steady with Eddie;* and *Nothing's Gonna Stop Me Now,* which exist only on private recordings, suggesting that a rich vein of Hayes material may still be lying untapped. The big irony of Clancy's career was that when he teamed with Kermit Goell to write a song that was to become a big international success, rival versions and not Clancy's own recording set the cash registers jingling. Hoagy Carmichael's Indiana drawl was almost made-to-measure for *Huggin' and Chalkin',* which produced a big hit for Decca, while Johnny Mercer also chalked up huge sales for Capitol and Kay Kyser scored for Columbia.

As a musician, Clancy was exceptionally versatile and unique in that he specialized on the six-string banjo but also played guitar, piano, and drums. In 1923 he joined Ham Crawford's Blue Devils, which boasted Wingy Manone on trumpet, and in 1928 contracted to NBC in San Francisco—a move which put him in contact with trumpeter Lu Watters. When Watters formed the Yerba Buena Jazz Band in the late thirties, Clancy joined, becoming an integral part of the great traditional jazz revival. Late in 1949, Bob Scobey broke from Watters to start his own band, and Clancy went with him to form a memorable team, Scobey showcasing Clancy's vocals against a velvet backdrop and his own trumpet. They made many albums together, including one with Bing Crosby, who named Clancy as his own favorite male singer. The jazz world was stunned in 1960 when Hayes split with Scobey to go out as a single before joining Yank Lawson and Bob Haggart in the World's Greatest Jazz Band.

Clancy's death was agonizingly tragic, for he was struck with near blindness before cancer attacked this warm-voiced and most engaging singer in the throat. He fought both afflictions with courage and defiance until he succumbed on March 3, 1972, in San Francisco.

Neal Hefti

Neal Paul Hefti was born in Hastings, Nebraska, October 29, 1922. He attended North High School in Omaha and then went on to study at the Juilliard School of Music, taking trumpet lessons from Jimmy Smith. Serving his apprenticeship as a trumpet player in high school and in other bands, he joined Woody Herman's Orchestra in 1944 and started to write arrangements. Several of these were popular favorites as recorded by Herman's

"First Herd," *Apple Honey; Wild Root;* and *The Good Earth.* Later on he contributed charts to the Count Basie band that helped maintain the band's popularity, at the same time becoming standard instrumentals in the repertoire of many big bands. Among the better known: *Cute; Lil Darlin'; Coral Reef; Buttercup; Cherry Point; The Kid from Red Bank; Girl Talk.* Other compositions include *Plymouth Rock; Two for the Blues; Blowin' Up a Storm; Why Not?;* and *Lake Placid.*

Ray Heindorf

Ray Heindorf was born in Haverstraw, New York, on August 25, 1908, and was educated at the Troy Conservatory. As a composer, arranger, and conductor, he contributed scores and musical backgrounds for a number of top motion pictures and in the process has produced several superior songs. In 1945 the song was *Some Sunny Day,* with words by Ted Koehler and music written in collaboration with M. K. Jerome. It was introduced by Alexis Smith in a movie starring Errol Flynn, *San Antonio,* and was nominated for an Academy Award. Helen Forrest and Dick Haymes recorded it with Gordon Jenkins's Orchestra, and Louis Prima also made it.

Five years later Heindorf wrote *Melancholy Rhapsody,* with lyrics by Sammy Cahn. The song was based on the theme he wrote for the movie *Young Man with a Horn,* which starred Kirk Douglas in the role of a jazz trumpet player, with Harry James providing the soundtrack. Another five years later (1955) for another movie about a jazz trumpet player, *Pete Kelly's Blues,* with Jack Webb in the title role, Heindorf composed the title song, *Pete Kelly's Blues.* In the film it was sung by Ella Fitzgerald. One of the best films ever made about jazz musicians, the film also featured a jazz band led and arranged by Matty Matlock. The all-star group made LP records for Victor, Decca, and Columbia of the music from the movie. On the Columbia LP, Heindorf conducts a large orchestra playing *Pete Kelly's Blues.* Sammy Cahn wrote the words for this great song, which is again performed by Ella Fitzgerald on the Decca album *Songs From Pete Kelly's Blues,* where she is backed by an instrumental quartet. Peggy Lee, accompanied by an orchestra directed by Harold Mooney, sings other songs from the film on the same LP. Jack Webb also produced and starred in a television series called *Pete Kelly's Blues,* with the song as the theme of the program. A Warner Brothers LP called *Pete Kelly's Blues* was made at this time. The jazz band on this album, which includes the same personnel as on the Victor and Columbia LPs, has Dick Cathcart designated as leader.

Charles Henderson

Charles Henderson was born in Boston, Massachusetts, on January 19, 1907. He was educated at the Roxbury Latin School and then went on to graduate from Harvard University. A pianist, he arranged for vocalists and orchestras, wrote special material for radio and stage productions, and eventually became a TV producer. Although not a prolific composer, he was responsible for several excellent songs, at least two of which are still being played.

In 1929 Henderson wrote *Deep Night,* a melody with a dark but romantic mood. Rudy Vallee, just at the beginning of his sensational career, wrote the words and recorded it for the first side on his new Victor contract. He also plugged the song on his popular radio broadcasts, and it became a hit. In 1957 the song was sung by Gogi Grant, dubbed in for actress Ann Blyth on the soundtrack for the movie *The Helen Morgan Story*. The next year (1930), Charles Henderson combined with singer Tom Waring and Pat Ballard to compose the words and music to *So Beats My Heart for You,* which the Fred Waring organization proceeded to record for Victor and also feature on radio broadcasts. Among contemporary recordings was a Columbia rendering by Will Osborne. The song has been waxed many times since and can be considered a semistandard.

Carefree, a beautiful melody, has lyrics by Edward Heyman, and it was the theme song of the *Chesterfield Radio Hour* in 1934. The Orville Knapp Orchestra recorded it for Decca in 1935, but for some unknown reason, this record—backed by the excellent Harry Barris tune *Thrilled*—was never released, the only Knapp recordings that weren't. A test pressing was made, and some privately made tapes exist that were dubbed from a copy in very poor condition. Other songs by Henderson are *This Is a Chance of a Lifetime* and *Hold Me in Your Arms.*

Charles Henderson died in Laguna Beach, California on March 7, 1970.

Fletcher Henderson

Fletcher Henderson was born in Cuthbert, Georgia, on December 18, 1898. He attended Morehouse College in Atlanta and graduated with a degree in chemistry. In 1920 he went to New York, planning for further study, but instead took a job in a publishing house demonstrating songs. One thing led to another, and for awhile he was the house pianist for the new Black Swan record company, recording with many of the famous blues singers of the period, including Bessie Smith and Ma Rainey. In 1923 he took his first band into a new nightspot called the Club Alabam and started making records immediately. Through the following years, he had several bands with personnels that read like a jazz "Who's Who," subsequently launching the careers of musicians who took their turns at greatly influencing the music—Don Redman, Coleman Hawkins, Louis Armstrong, John Kirby, Benny Carter, Rex Stewart—the list is long and impressive.

Henderson didn't write arrangements until after he lost the services of Don Redman, who left to become the leading light with McKinney's Cotton Pickers. In a comparatively short time, Henderson had developed a style that was eventually to become a major factor in the success of the Benny Goodman band. Although seemingly simple in structure, the Henderson charts were able to assert the melody line with a drive and a swing, along with wide latitude for individual solos, in a way that seldom has been equalled. Henderson was especially adept at articulating clarinets and saxes, achieving voicings and harmonies that were highly original. As a composer, Henderson's work may not be in the strict category of popular songwriting, but in the annals of swing and big band music, most of his original instrumentals were and are very popular. These include *Stampede* (an early barn burner); *Wrappin' It Up; Down South Camp Meetin* (two bestsellers for the Goodman band); *Bumble Bee Stomp; Hotter Than 'Ell; No, Baby, No;* and *It's Wearing Me Down.*

Fletcher Henderson died in New York City on December 29, 1952.

Ray Henderson

Earlier in this book, in profiling Buddy DeSylva and Lew Brown, I have mentioned the songwriting team of DeSylva, Brown, and Henderson. In this very successful trio DeSylva and Brown were the lyricists, and Ray Henderson the composer. Working together they contributed a plethora of songs to the American library of standards. Because of this, it is often overlooked that all three collaborated with other songwriters. Ray Henderson, in particular, wrote a number of hits before the team was organized and continued to do so after it broke up. In light of his prolific career he must be considered one of the giants in the field, on par with many of the more recognized composers of our music.

Ray Henderson was born in Buffalo, New York, on December 1, 1896. His education included the Chicago Conservatory, after which, like so many of his peers, he served an apprenticeship as a pianist in dance bands, toured in vaudeville, and then went to work as an arranger and song plugger for New York music publishers. Early in the twenties he began to work with Lew Brown, and they turned out one hit after another. Many of these are still familiar to contemporary ears—*That Old Gang of Mine* (1923); *Alabamy Bound; Follow the Swallow; Why Did I Kiss That Girl* (1924); *Five Foot Two Eyes of Blue; Don't Bring Lulu; If I Had a Girl Like You; I'm Sitting on Top of the World* (1925); *Bye-Bye Blackbird* (1926); *Cover Me Up With Sunshine* (1927).

In 1925 DeSylva, Brown, and Henderson began to work as a team and continued to do so until 1931. Henderson and Brown collaborated afterwards, but at the same time Ray Henderson wrote with other lyricists, especially for the movies, a distinguished crew including Mort Dixon, Sam M. Lewis, Joe Young, Jack Yellen, Ted Koehler, Billy Rose, and Irving Caesar. Henderson and Brown collaborated on the score for the Broadway musical "George White's Scandals of 1931," which produced a basketful of hits: *My Song; The Thrill Is Gone; That's Why Darkies Were Born; Life Is Just a Bowl of Cherries;* and *This Is the Missus*. In the next year, for the stage show "Hot-cha," they combined on *There I Go Dreaming Again* and *You Can Make My Life a Bed of Roses*. In 1933, for the show "Strike Me Pink," they wrote the title song plus *Let's Call It a Day; Love and Rhythm; Restless;* and *It's Great to Be Alive*.

For "Say When," a 1934 musical that starred Harry Richman and Bob Hope, Henderson paired with Ted Koehler on two songs, *Say When* and *When Love Comes Swinging Along*. Then, in the same year, he worked with Jack Yellen and Irving Caesar on the score for the movie *George White's Scandals of 1934*. It included *Nasty Man; Hold My Hand; My Dog Loves Your Dog; Sweet and Simple; So Nice;* and *Six Women*. The film starred Rudy Vallee, Alice Faye, Jimmy Durante, and Cliff Edwards. Henderson and Ted Koehler combined again for the Shirley Temple movie *Curly Top* in 1935, providing the title song: Henderson with Ed Heyman for *When I Grow Up,* and with Koehler and Irving Caesar on *Animal Crackers in My Soup; The Simple Things in Life;* and *It's All So New to Me*.

"George White's Scandals of 1936" was a stage show that year, with Rudy Vallee, Willie and Eugene Howard, Bert Lahr, Cliff Edwards, and others. Henderson and Jack Yellen composed the songs: *Life Begins at Sweet Sixteen; I'm the Fellow Who Loves You; Cigarette; Anything Can Happen;* and *I've Got to Get Hot*. For good measure, that year Henderson and Mort Dixon turned out the delightful *Every Once in Awhile,* just in time for Wingy Manone to turn it into a personal classic on a record for Bluebird (B-6393). With the advent of the forties Henderson's musical activities began to taper off, and although a few songs appeared early in the decade, they are not memorable. However, this is a good place to offer a reminder of some of the great titles credited to the team of DeSylva, Brown, and Henderson: *Birth of the Blues; Black Bottom; Lucky Day; The Best Things in Life Are Free; Varsity Drag; Lucky in Love; Just Imagine; Broken Hearted; It All Depends on You; Just a Memory; You're the Cream in My Coffee; To Know You Is to Love You; Pickin' Cotton; I'm On the Crest of a Wave; Button Up Your Overcoat; My Lucky Star; I Want to be Bad; You Wouldn't Fool Me, Would You?; Sunny Side Up; If I Had a Talking Picture of You; Turn On the Heat; I'm a Dreamer, Aren't We All; My Sin; Don't Tell Her What Happened to Me;* and many more.

Ray Henderson died on New Year's Eve 1970, in Greenwich, Connecticut, leaving us a heritage of wonderful songs. To many people, the songs of DeSylva, Brown, and Henderson symbolize the best of the twenties and seem to capture the essence of the decade in tunes that will live on long after the twentieth century becomes ancient history.

Victor Herbert

Victor Herbert, father of the operetta-styled Broadway musical, was born in Dublin, Ireland, February 1, 1859. He pursued his early music studies in Germany. A virtuoso on the cello, he played with symphony orchestras in Germany and Austria and for five years led the Court Orchestra in Stuttgart. He married an operatic soprano, Therese Forster, who received an offer to join the New York Metropolitan Opera. She signed the agreement, with the stipulation that Victor Herbert would play cello in the pit orchestra. They came to the United States in 1886, and Forster sang at the Met for a time but then retired. Herbert continued to play in the orchestra and became a featured cellist in concerts.

He started composing and writing scores for stage musicals. For several years he met with mediocre success but finally made it in 1897 with "The Serenade," although nothing sensational happened with the music. It wasn't until the next year, with a new show, "The Fortune Teller," that he had his first hit song, *Gypsy Love Song*. He continued to write and compose prolifically and had a very successful show in 1903, the perennial "Babes in Toyland," which brought him recognition as the foremost Broadway composer.

Victor Herbert also continued as a musician-conductor, playing concerts for more than twenty years all over the country. In 1914 he was active in the group that organized ASCAP. Later in his career, as his own shows lost appeal, he began to contribute freelance compositions to other productions.

Ironically, after his death in 1924, his shows and scores attained the status of classics and have often been revived, as well as converted into movies. Two of these, "Naughty Marietta" and "Sweethearts," brought stardom to the singing team of Jeannette MacDonald and Nelson Eddy. In 1939 a movie based on Victor Herbert's life and career, with Walter Connolly portraying the composer and also starring Allan Jones and Mary Martin, was made, *The Great Victor Herbert.*

Victor Herbert wrote dozens of songs, many of no consequence beyond the stage productions they were written for, but a very well-known selection of titles has come down through the years: *Kiss Me Again; Ah! Sweet Mystery of Life; Toyland; Gypsy Love Song; In Old New York; I'm Falling in Love with Someone; A Kiss in the Dark; Thine Alone*. In addition, two songs written early in his career, with added lyrics, became latter-day hits, especially *Indian Summer,* now a standard. Herbert wrote the melody as a piano solo in 1919. Twenty years later Al Dubin put words to it, and it became number one on the Hit Parade, with best-selling records by Tommy Dorsey and Glenn Miller. The second tune, *Yesterthoughts,* was a 1940 follow-up, with Stanley Adams providing the lyrics to a forty-year-old instrumental by Victor Herbert. Again Glenn Miller had a hit record.

Victor Herbert was active right up to the end. He died suddenly of a heart attack on May 24, 1924, in New York City.

Woodrow (Woody) Herman

Woody Herman, one of the most famous, respected, and well-liked bandleaders in the history of American music, was born in Milwaukee, Wisconsin, on February 9, 1914. An accomplished reed player and a versatile vocalist who could handle ballads as well as novelties and jazz, he started out with Tom Gerun's band and then joined Isham Jones's Orchestra in the latter part of 1935, coming aboard only a short time before Jones decided to retire and left the band high-and-dry. When the nucleus of the band (less strings) decided to stay together as a cooperative unit, they elected Woody to front the group; thus began his long and successful career as a bandleader.

The first band was known as "The Band That Plays the Blues," and one of the members was Joe Bishop, composer of *Blue Prelude* and *Blue Lament*. He and Woody collaborated on a number of originals that the band recorded, which helped in establishing its style and reputation. The most important of these, most likely, is *At the Woodchopper's Ball* (1939). Herman also shared credit with Toby Tyler for the popular *Blues On Parade,* another

1939 entry. In the following year the partnership of Bishop and Herman published and recorded five titles: *Whistle Stop; Herman at the Sherman; Bessie's Blues; Jukin';* and *Music By the Moon.* All did well and were identified with the Herman band. The foregoing were all recorded by the first band on the Decca label. With another band and for another label (Columbia), in 1945 Woody recorded the instrumental *Apply Honey,* for which he took full credit. The band also played it in the movie *Earl Carroll's Vanities* that same year. Still later, in 1949 Herman is listed as cowriter with Ralph Burns of the hit song *Early Autumn.* This was adapted from an earlier Burns composition, *Summer Sequence.* The first record by the band featured Stan Getz on tenor in an instrumental. Johnny Mercer added lyrics to the song in 1952, and it went on to a second life as a popular hit.

Woody Herman continued to play and lead a band until his death in Los Angeles on October 29, 1987.

Edward Heyman

Possibly one of the most unappreciated lyricists, Edward Heyman nevertheless had a fantastic and brilliant career writing scores for stage shows and movies, at the same time collaborating with the most talented and prolific composers of the thirties and forties. Possibly the last is the reason for his comparative obscurity in the songwriting profession. Although he wrote the words to a lot of famous songs, many of them standards, the composers get most of the credit. Here are some examples of the high-powered names I refer to: Johnny Green, Rudolf Friml, Jimmy Van Heusen, Sigmund Romberg, Dana Suesse, Arthur Schwartz, Vincent Youmans, Nacio Herb Brown, Ray Henderson, and Victor Young. Here are some of the titles they turned out with Ed Heyman: *Body and Soul; Out of Nowhere; My Darling; My Silent Love; Rain, Rain Go Away; I Cover the Waterfront; You're Mine, You; I Wanna Be Loved; This Is Romance; You Oughtta Be in Pictures; Blame It On My Youth; Boo Hoo; Have You Forgotten So Soon; They Say; Love Letters; Bluebird of Happiness.*

Edward Heyman was born in New York City on March 14, 1907, but grew up in Chicago. He attended the University of Michigan, where he wrote for college musicals, and this led logically to a professional career. With a forgotten composer, Ken Smith, he contributed one song, *I'll Be Reminded of You,* to the Rudy Vallee movie *The Vagabond Lover.* Vallee recorded it for Victor, and thanks to his popularity and promotion, the song was a moderate success. Heyman's career was off to a good start.

In 1930, a collaboration with composer Johnny Green and two other lyricists (Robert Saur and Frank Eyton)—at least that's how the credits read—resulted in the smash hit *Body and Soul*. The song was introduced in England by Gertrude Lawrence on a BBC radio broadcast. She was heard by Bert Ambrose, the bandleader, who recorded it and had a big selling side. Then Max Gordon, the American producer, secured rights to include the song in his stage musical "Three's a Crowd," where it was performed by singer Libby Holman and dancers Clifton Webb and Tamara Geva, and it was well on the way to becoming the standard it is. Contemporary records were made by Libby Holman (Brunswick) and Paul Whiteman, but the song has been recorded countless times since. In 1939 tenor saxophonist Coleman Hawkins turned it into a jazz classic with his rendition on a Bluebird record.

The next year, 1931, was another good one for Ed Heyman. With Dana Suesse he wrote *Ho-Hum!*, a clever little ditty that was popular for a season, and then, rejoining Johnny Green, penned the words to another evergreen, *Out of Nowhere*. Guy Lombardo and the Royal Canadians introduced this one. It has been recorded dozens of times since and featured in quite a few movies. In 1932 Heyman and Vincent Youmans wrote the score for a stage show, "Through the Years." It only played for twenty performances, but it offered two well-conceived songs, *Through the Years* and *Drums in My Heart*. With Richard Myers, Heyman had two songs in "Earl Carroll's Vanities of 1932," *My Darling* and *Forsaken Again*. The first title did well. But the big song of the year for Heyman was another collaboration with Dana Suesse, *My Silent Love*. Another standard, it has a distinguished history. Heyman and Johnny Green, assisted by lyricist Mack David, also turned out another success, *Rain, Rain, Go Away*.

"Murder at the Vanities," a variation on the usual Earl Carroll title, included several hit songs, two of them with Heyman lyrics: *Me for You Forever,* written with Richard Myers, and *Weep No More, My Baby,* with Johnny Green. In fact, 1933 was a banner year for Heyman (as it was for many songwriters), and his name is on some very fine songs. *I Cover the Waterfront,* another Johnny Green perennial, was written to promote a movie with the same title. Ben Bernie's band recorded it, and the song became so popular that the movie soundtrack was rescored to include it as the film's theme. It is one more standard in the Johnny Green–Edward Heyman catalog, and they wrote two others that year that should rate the same status: *You're Mine, You* and *I Wanna Be Loved*. Not playing any favorites, Heyman worked with Vernon Duke to produce another classic, *This Is Romance*.

Heyman wrote lyrics for two songs by Harden Church for a 1934 stage production, "Caviar," which added nothing to anyone's reputation, but he had two solid entries in the Ziegfeld "Follies" for that year, *The House Is Haunted,* written with Buzz Adlam, and the clever *You Oughtta Be in Pictures,* with Dana Suesse. *Blame It On My Youth,* with Oscar Levant, was another contender in 1934, and "Murder at the Vanities" enjoyed new life as a movie. Then, just to round out the year, Heyman and Johnny Green came up with *Easy Come, Easy Go.* Heyman continued to write for shows and movies, and in 1936 he and Hoagy Carmichael added one song to the Cole Porter score for "Anything Goes" when it was made into a movie starring Bing Crosby. The tune, well known to any Crosby fan, was *Moonburn.*

In 1939 Heyman wrote the words for Benny Carter's great melody *Melancholy Lullaby,* and in 1940, with Louis Alter, he contributed *The Sky Fell Down.* In 1945 he partnered with Victor Young on a theme for the movie *Love Letters.* The song, with the same title, was nominated for an Academy Award. Dick Haymes had the hit record. Heyman wrote for productions at Radio City Music Hall, and while in the army during World War II, he wrote "At Your Service." Afterwards, he went on to produce shows in Mexico City. His songwriting career continued well into the fifties, and he collaborated with Victor Young on the theme for the TV show *Medic, Blue Star.*

DuBose Heyward

Author-playwright DuBose Heyward was born in Charleston, South Carolina, August 31, 1885. His education came mostly from public schools, but in later years he received honorary degrees from the University of North Carolina, the College of Charleston, and the University of Southern California. As the author of the book for the 1935 stage production of "Porgy and Bess," he shares credit with Ira Gershwin for the lyrics to the songs that George Gershwin composed for the famous score. The songs include *Summertime; I Got Plenty O' Nuttin'; It Ain't Necessarily So; I Loves You, Porgy; Bess, You Is My Woman Now; My Man's Gone Now; Where Is My Bess?; A Woman Is a Sometime Thing;* and *There's a Boat Dat's Leavin' Soon for New York.*

DuBose Heyward died in Tyron, North Carolina, on July 16, 1940.

Eddie Heywood Jr.

Pianist-composer Eddie Heywood Jr. was born in Atlanta, Georgia, on December 4, 1915. He took piano lessons from his father, a well-known artist who worked and recorded with blues singers in the twenties and thirties. At age fourteen young Eddie was already playing theater jobs in Atlanta, also in his father's and other local bands. During the thirties he toured with dance bands, including a stint with Clarence Love in Kansas City and later with Benny Carter in New York. In 1943 he formed his own combo and the following year recorded *Begin the Beguine* for Milt Gabler's Commodore label. The arrangement, and Heywood's unusual and distinctive approach to the keyboard, caught on, launching a successful recording career.

In the midfifties Heywood started to compose, and the result was several superior songs that managed to become popular in spite of a failing market for such things. In several instances, Heywood's recorded renditions of his own compositions were the important factors in promoting the songs. *Land of Dreams,* with lyrics by Norman Gimbel, came out in 1954. It was introduced by Eddie Heywood playing piano with Hugo Winterhalter's Orchestra on RCA–Victor. A good song, it was a forecast of better things to come. Norman Gimbel also wrote the words for *Canadian Sunset,* a truly beautiful song and Heywood's biggest hit, which came out in 1956. The big record was again Heywood, at the keyboard with Hugo Winterhalter's Orchestra, playing the tune as an instrumental; but singer Andy Williams also did well on a vocal version. The song is well on the way to becoming a standard and has been played and recorded frequently since it was introduced. *Soft Summer Breeze,* with lyrics by Judy Spencer, also came out in 1956. Heywood recorded it as an instrumental for Mercury, and the record made the top twenty category. The Diamonds had the best-selling vocal recording. *I'm Saving Myself for You* is another pleasant song by Heywood.

Eddie Heywood Jr. died in Palm Beach, Florida, on January 3, 1989.

Art Hickman

Pioneering orchestra leader Art Hickman was born in Oakland, California, June 12, 1886. He organized his orchestra in 1915 and began experimenting with instrumentation and arrangements that utilized sections, harmonic backgrounds, and voicings that were to become basic in dance bands that were to follow. His band was a staple attraction at San Francisco's St. Francis Hotel, which became its home base for many years. In 1920 he was invited to take part in the Ziegfeld "Follies," thus becoming the leader of the first dance band to play in a Broadway production. He composed his theme song, *Rose Room,* in 1918 and introduced it in New York at the New Amsterdam Roof, where the "Ziegfeld Midnight Frolic" was performing. An all-time standard, the song has been a favorite of jazz bands for years, played and recorded countless times, and featured in several movies.

Hickman toured and recorded in England in the early twenties then returned to California, where he led a big band and broadcast on radio. Ill health forced his retirement in the late twenties. He died in San Francisco, on January 16, 1930. Other titles by Art Hickman are *Hold Me; Dry Your Tears; Without You; Come Back to Georgia; Love Moon; June, I Love No One But You; Dream of Me;* and *My Midnight Frolic Girl.*

Alex Hill

Pianist-composer-bandleader W. Alexander Hill was born in Little Rock, Arkansas, on April 19, 1906. College educated and well trained, as a youngster he had his own orchestra, even appearing with it in silent movies. Pianist in a number of dance bands, he finally wound up in New York and developed a prominent career as an arranger, contributing charts to many of the name bands, including those of Cab Calloway, Duke Ellington, Benny Goodman, and Claude Hopkins, as well as his own units. During the musical thirties, Hill had a hit song almost every year, performing the roles of composer, lyric writer, or both. In 1931 he contributed the words for the romping Fats Waller ditty *I'm Crazy 'Bout My Baby (And My Baby's Crazy 'Bout Me).* Waller recorded it for Columbia that year, and the tune logged a lot of airtime too; it was very successful in a highly competitive market. Waller was to record the song again several times.

The next year Hill aided and abetted Claude Hopkins in the composition *I Would Do Anything for You,* which became the popular theme song of Claude's orchestra on frequent radio broadcasts and has since become a standard. The Hopkins band recorded the tune for Columbia, but it has had innumerable renditions since. *Delta Bound,* a very lyrical and pensive ballad entirely the work of Hill, also came out in 1932. It was recorded by the Duke Ellington Orchestra and also by that ARC standby, Chick Bullock. In recent years it has seen some revival activity, notably by singer Banu Gibson. Hill published another original in 1933, *Dixie Lee.* Although it wasn't a great hit, it still merited respectable records by the Casa Loma Orchestra and the aforementioned Chick Bullock.

In 1934, Hill turned out *Armful O' Sweetness,* memorable mainly for the Waller treatment it promptly received on Victor. It was accompanied by *Long About Midnight,* and this Hill tune rated the royal carpet provided by Cab Calloway, Frankie Trumbauer, Mildred Bailey, Willie Bryant, and

Louis Prima. Needless to say, it did rather well. A personal favorite of mine, *Devil in the Moon,* made its debut in 1935 on a "sleeper" recording by Taft Jordan and the Mob. Released on the ARC labels with little notice and no fanfare, this all-star disc has since become a classic, automatically elevating the song to similar status. They both deserve it. *Our Love Was Meant to Be,* another collaboration with Fats Waller, dates to 1937. Waller recorded it, of course, but Alex Hill wasn't around to hear it. He died in North Little Rock, Arkansas, February 1, 1936.

Billy Hill

Billy Hill was born in Boston, Massachusetts, on July 14, 1899. He attended public schools and took violin lessons from Carl Muck. He also played piano. As a young man he traveled through the west, working as a cowboy and with surveyors in Death Valley. He worked as a violinist or piano player in dance bands and eventually led his own in Salt Lake City. He started writing in the thirties, and some of his earliest songs were under the pseudonym of "George Brown." It is said that Hill sold a number of his early compositions outright. He composed both words and music for many of his songs. On others, Peter DeRose collaborated on both. Hill anticipated by several decades the public's fondness for western sentimentality and nostalgia, and once he discovered the formula—as indicated by the success of his first big hit, *The Last Roundup*—he made repeated trips back to the money well.

One of his earliest efforts was a collaboration with Edward Eliscu and Willie Raskin, and a forerunner of this trend, *They Cut Down the Old Pine Tree,* a mournful ditty that was published in 1930. Then in 1932, still hiding under the George Brown name, he wrote the words to Victor Young's music for *The Old Man of the Mountain.* A catchy tune, with interesting lyrics, it was a hit record for the Mills Brothers, with other sides by Fred Waring's Pennsylvanians, Joe Haymes, and vocalist Lee Wiley. *The Last Roundup,* a solo effort, came out in 1933, and was introduced by Joe Morrison with the George Olsen Orchestra on the stage of New York's Paramount Theater. They also recorded it, but when the song hit, others quickly followed, including Bing Crosby, Rudy Vallee, Arthur Tracy (the Street Singer), and even Conrad Thibault. In the following year it gained added impetus by being included in the Ziegfeld "Follies." In 1941 it made the movies, with Gene Autry singing it on the ground in *The Singing Hills,* and Roy Rogers intoning the deathless lyrics in the 1961 film *Don't Fence Me In.*

Besides scoring big with *The Last Roundup* in 1933, Hill came close again with *The Old Spinning Wheel,* providing both words and music, recorded by two widely divergent talents, Frank Parker and Riley Puckett, and *There's a Cabin in the Pines.* The latter tune was introduced on the radio by George Hall's Orchestra with Loretta Lee singing, and was recorded by Mildred Bailey. But the song had the good fortune to be selected by Ray Noble for his usual exceptional treatment and was recorded by his New Mayfair Orchestra HMV in England and also released on Victor in the United States. *Louisville Lady,* a collaboration with Peter DeRose, was still another entry for 1933, and it received wide attention, with records by Joe Haymes, Isham Jones, Paul Ash, and Anson Weeks.

Hill continued to write prolifically. In 1934 he had a number of successful songs (besides *The Last Roundup,* which was getting another go around in the "Follies"), *Wagon Wheels,* another pairing with Peter DeRose; *The Old Covered Bridge;* and *Night on the Desert.* The last two were entirely by Hill, and all three were recorded by Ray Noble in England to their great benefit. *Rain,* a departure from the Hill format, had music by Peter DeRose and was recorded by the bands of Jan Garber, Don Bestor, and Larry Funk (with a vocal by Vaughn Monroe). *Lights Out* was Billy Hill's big song for 1935. The melody, which invokes the sound of "taps," was given a radio send-off by Ozzie Nelson and his orchestra, with Harriet Hilliard singing, and among the many subsequent recordings was waxed by Eddy Duchin, Dick Robertson, Little Jack Little, and Victor Young. Other Hill contributions that year were *The Oregon Trail; Put On an Old Pair of Shoes; When Love Knocks at Your Heart;* and *Alone at a Table for Two.* Although he continued to collaborate on some songs, he was most successful on his own.

Empty Saddles, a melancholy ditty, was introduced in the 1936 movie *Rhythm On the River,* with Bing Crosby doing the honors. The words by J. Keirn Brennan were based on a poem he wrote. Billy Hill again stepped out of character to write a very pleasant ballad, *The Scene Changes.* It didn't get the attention his money makers did, but it rated at least one fine recording by an all-star group under the nominal leadership of Dick McDonough on the ARC labels. Much more consideration was given to *In a Chapel in the Moonlight,* which was recorded by the popular band of Shep Fields, vocalist Ruth Etting, and enjoyed fourteen weeks on the Hit Parade, finally making it to number one. Nor was this the only hit Hill had that year. *The Glory of Love* was still another. It was recorded and plugged by Rudy Vallee, and Benny Goodman's version, with Helen Ward on the vocal, did very well. In 1967 it was heard in the movie *Guess Who's Coming to Dinner,* and Bette Midler revived it again in the 1988 film *Beaches.*

In 1937 Hill went continental for a brief stint, collaborating with Jimmy Kennedy and Will Grosz on *The Miller's Daughter Marianne*. Other titles that year included *Timber; On a Little Dream Ranch;* and *Till the Clock Strikes Three. All Ashore,* still another solo flight by Hill, was the big one for 1938. Sammy Kaye and Paul Whiteman had successful records. *When Twilight Comes,* written with Peter DeRose, was recorded by Will Osborne and by Jan Savitt's band. Billy Hill kept composing right up to the last year of his life, and in 1940 had two good songs. *Call of the Canyon,* which he authored himself, was recorded across the board for every major label by Glenn Miller, Guy Lombardo, Kay Kyser, and the King Sisters. *On a Little Street in Singapore* was a final collaboration with Peter DeRose. Jimmy Dorsey had the top recording, with vocalist Bob Eberle. But in 1944 Columbia Records released a record Frank Sinatra had made with the Harry James band in 1939, and the tune made another hit.

Thus ended the career of a very successful songwriter who early on discovered the right button to push in order to reach the ears of the general public. Billy Hill died in his native Boston on December 24, 1940.

Bob Hilliard

One of the most clever lyricists of recent years, Bob Hilliard was born in New York City on January 28, 1918. It appears that he made his debut as a songwriter in 1946 with *The Coffee Song (They've Got an Awful Lot of Coffee in Brazil)*. A collaboration with composer Dick Miles, this tune was introduced in a revue at the Copacabana in New York. Recorded and featured by Frank Sinatra, it developed into a hit. The next year was a big one for Hilliard. Working with Carl Sigman, he scored with the novelty *Civilization (Bongo, Bongo, Bongo),* introduced by Elaine Strich in the stage show, "Angel in the Wings." It was picked up and recorded by Danny Kaye and the Andrews Sisters; also Louis Prima, Ray McKinley, Woody Herman, and Jack Smith with Frank DeVol's Orchestra. From the same revue came *The Thousand Islands Song (I Left My Love on One of the Thousand Islands),* which turned out to be a best-selling record for Arthur Godfrey. Johnny Mercer, who knew and appreciated clever lyrics even when they were written by somebody else, also recorded the song. A third entry in 1947 was *Red Silk Stockings and Green Perfume,* Hilliard working with the team of Dick Sanford and Sammy Mysels. Ray McKinley did well with it on the Majestic label with his new band, and it was also waxed by Sammy Kaye and by Tony Pastor. The trio of Hilliard, Sanford, and Mysels was also responsible for *Mention My Name in Sheboygan,* a hit recording for the Gay Nineties specialist Beatrice Kaye. Altogether, Hilliard scored four hits in 1947.

Careless Hands, a 1949 collaboration with Carl Sigman, was a successful song and well covered by hit records from Mel Tormé, Bob Crosby, and others. But in 1950 Hilliard changed partners again. With Sammy Fain he wrote *Dear Hearts and Gentle People,* which turned out to be a million-seller for Bing Crosby on Decca, with Dinah Shore on Columbia and Gordon McRae on Capitol also doing well. The song title was based on a note written by Stephen Foster and found in his pocket after his death. Hilliard then worked with David Mann to produce *Dearie,* a tune that became a popular recorded duet for Ray Bolger and Ethel Merman, backed by Sy Oliver's Orchestra. It was also recorded by Guy Lombardo and by Jo Stafford and Gordon MacRae.

Returning to the clever lyric, Bob Hilliard and Milton DeLugg turned out the superior tune *Shanghai* in 1951, and it immediately received proper treatment from top artists of the day: Doris Day, Bing Crosby, Bob Crosby, and the Billy Williams Quartet. All seemed to take particular delight in the "turn-around" phrase, "I'm just around the corner in a phone booth." Hilliard and DeLugg penned *Be My Life's Companion* in 1952, and it did well with records by the Mills Brothers and by Rosemary Clooney; but it wasn't until 1955 that Hilliard came up with another notable song. This was *In the Wee Small Hours of the Morning,* written with David Mann, an unusual sentiment for Hilliard, who generally saw the world from a happier viewpoint. Nevertheless, Frank Sinatra gave it respectful treatment. *My Little Corner of the World,* with music by Lee Pockriss, came out in 1960, the start of the Dark Decade for quality songs. It was recorded by Anita Bryant. Other Hilliard titles include *The Big Brass Band from Brazil; A Strawberry Moon; Don't Ever Be Afraid to Go Home; How Do You Speak to an Angel?; Somebody Bad Stole de Wedding Bell; Our Day Will Come, My Summer Love; Moonlight Gambler; Seven Little Girls;* and *Sailor Boys Have Talk to Me in English.*

Bob Hilliard died in Los Angeles, California, on February 1, 1971.

Richard Himber

Richard Himber was born in Newark, New Jersey, on February 20, 1907. He attended college and studied music privately. A violinist, at age thirteen he was already playing a summer job at Coney Island. This was followed by other dates around New York in small clubs and restaurants, and he was heard by Sophie Tucker, who hired him to take part in her act. They toured vaudeville, and during this period Himber became interested in magic, eventually becoming a talented amateur. Himber went on to become a band manager, for a time performing this service for the Buddy Rogers and Harry Barris bands in the early thirties and then Rudy Vallee. He formed his own orchestra in 1933 and opened at the swank Essex House in New York.

The band's theme song on radio broadcasts was the beautiful *It Isn't Fair*. Himber is credited with collaborating with two others, Frank Warshauer and Sylvester Sprigato, on the melody and with writing the lyrics. Besides the recording by the Himber Orchestra it received quality treatment from the bands of Hal Kemp, Jack Fulton, and Elmer Feldkamp. For a song introduced in the depth of the Depression, this was high praise and appreciation. In 1950, Sammy Kaye, at the height of his popularity, revived the song on a Victor recording featuring his vocalist, Don Cornell, and the song enjoyed another round of popularity, being listed on the Hit Parade for twelve weeks. Just to help it along, it was also recorded by Benny Goodman, Les Brown, and Russ Case.

Although it may not be significant, the profile of Frank Warshauer in the *ASCAP Biographical Dictionary,* while listing *It Isn't Fair* as one of his compositions, does not mention Richard Himber as a collaborator. Sylvester Sprigano is not in the dictionary.

Day After Day, which came out in 1938, had music by Himber and words by Bud Green. The Himber Orchestra recorded in on Victor, and vocalist Barry Wood sang it on Brunswick. A very nice song, *Moments in the Moonlight,* was a committee composition in 1940, with "words and music" by Himber, Irving Gordon, and Al Kaufman. It was dutifully introduced by Richard Himber and His Orchestra, and obligingly waxed by Glenn Miller for Bluebird, Gene Krupa for Columbia, Bob Crosby for Decca, and Tommy Reynolds for Vocalion. Other Himber compositions include *After the Rain; Am I Asking Too Much?;* and *Time Will Tell.*

Richard Himber died in New York City on December 11, 1966.

Earl Hines

Earl Hines, the acknowledged "Fatha" of modern jazz piano, was born in Duquesne, Pennsylvania, December 28, 1905. As early as 1918 he was working with dance bands in the Pittsburgh area. In 1922 and 1923 he worked and toured with the singer Lois Deppe and then again led dance bands in Pittsburgh and Chicago. From time to time he performed as a soloist. In 1928 he recorded a series of classic jazz sides with Louis Armstrong, and in December of the same year he waxed eight piano solos for the rare QRS label in Long Island City. During this same critical period he organized a band to play the famous Grand Terrace in Chicago, a stint that lasted for ten years. Hines led bands and groups for the rest of his busy career and has left a huge legacy of recordings as a testimonial to his great contributions to American music. He made significant offerings in the form of musical compositions, including a number of piano solo pieces and some popular songs that have become standards.

One title fits into both of these categories, *A Monday Date*. This originated as a piano solo, and Hines recorded it as such on his historic QRS session in December 1928; nevertheless, earlier in the year it got instrumental and vocal treatment from Louis Armstrong's Hot Five and as such, has been played and recorded many times over the years. However, from the standpoint of a popular song, there's no question the honors go to *Rosetta,* a collaboration with arranger Henri Woode that came out in 1933. Hines recorded this gem a number of times, but long ago it attained the status of a standard and has been recorded by just about every name attraction in the music business. To mention only a few: Benny Goodman, Muggsy Spanier, Teddy Wilson, Art Tatum, and Charlie Shavers. In 1932, Hines combined with Charles Carpenter and Luis Dunlap to compose *You Can Depend On Me,* and although it will never approach the importance of *Rosetta,* it has become a favorite in the jazz band lexicon and has traveled the rounds of recording luminaries. *When I Dream of You,* another collaboration with Charles Carpenter, is one of those songs you can't help but wonder why it never became more popular. A beautiful ballad with a highly original melody line, it's one of the Fatha's best, but just never caught on.

Through the years, Hines composed prolifically, turning out dozens of pieces for the piano and, in collaboration with his talented arrangers, a number of swinging instrumentals for his orchestra. An excellent representation of his activity, both as composer and bandleader, is presented by the Epic LP *Hines Rhythm: Earl "Fatha" Hines and His Orchestra* (EE 22021). A cross section of sides recorded in the thirties and several made in 1968, it includes sixteen tracks, with eleven of them either Hines originals or collaborations, as follows: *Rosetta* (Woode–Hines), recorded Feb. 13, 1933; *Cavernism* (Hines–Mundy), recorded Feb. 13, 1933; *Mad House* (Mundy–Hines), recorded March 26, 1934; *Darkness* (Hines), recorded March 27, 1934; *Swingin' Down* (Hines), recorded March 27, 1934; *Flany Doodle Swing* (Hines), recorded Feb. 10, 1937; *Pianology* (Hines), recorded Feb. 10, 1937; *Rhythm Sundae* (Hines), recorded Feb.

10, 1937; *Inspiration* (Hines), recorded Feb. 10, 1937; *Hines Rhythm* (Hines), recorded Aug. 10, 1937; *Ridin' a Riff* (Hines), recorded Aug. 10, 1937.

Other Hines titles include *Deep Forest* (theme song); *One Night in Trinidad; Straight to Love; Piano Man; Everything Depends On You; Jelly Jelly; Stormy Monday Blues; Ann; Love at Night (Is Out of Sight); Jitney Man; The Fatha Jumps; Fatha Steps In; Blues in Thirds; Brussels Hustle; Cannery Walk; 57 Varieties;* and *Stanley Steamer.*

Earl "Fatha" Hines died in Oakland, California, on April 22, 1983.

Louis A. Hirsch

Louis A. Hirsch was born in New York City on November 28, 1887. He attended CCNY and studied music in Germany, preparing for a career conducting and composing. Later he worked as a pianist for New York publishing houses and wrote special material for minstrels. From 1912 to 1914 he was a staff composer for the Schubert Brothers. Later, he became a partner in the Victoria Publishing Company. Although from the standpoint of memorable songs, Hirsch hasn't left us many, as the composer of early stage shows he was a prolific contributor right up until his death. In the process, he wrote a lot of songs that were important in the productions and worked with noted collaborators, including Irving Caesar, Otto Harbach, Gene Buck, Harold Atteridge, Con Conrad, Melville Gideon, and David Stamper.

One of the more durable titles in the Hirsch list is *Hello, Frisco,* a 1915 ditty written as an unofficial salute to the newly inaugurated cross-country telephone service, with lyrics by Gene Buck. It was introduced in the Ziegfeld "Follies" of that year by Ina Claire. Revived in 1943 as *Hello, Frisco, Hello,* it became the title song of a movie in which it was sung by Alice Faye, John Payne, Jack Oakie, and June Havoc. Recorded as a sprightly novelty by the Merry Macs on Decca, it became one of their best-selling discs. And that's not all. In 1953 the song was heard in the movie *The I Don't Care Girl* based on the life and career of Eva Tanguay.

More in the ballad tradition is the hit song and standard *The Love Nest.* With words by Otto Harbach, it was introduced in the 1920 Broadway production "Mary." In 1953 it gained new life in the movie *The Helen Morgan Story,* and even better, it became the theme song of the long-running *Burns and Allen Show* on television. Aside from these credits, the song is frequently played and recorded on its own merit. Other well-known Hirsch songs are *The Tickle Toe* and *The Gaby Glide,* both associated with dance steps.

Louis Hirsch died in his native New York City, on May 13, 1924. In December of that year, his last show, "Betty Lee," opened on Broadway.

Walter Hirsch

In keeping with the title of this book, the odds are that our next candidate for overdue recognition will be unfamiliar to all except those involved in the songwriting business. He is lyricist Walter Hirsch, born in New York City on March 10, 1891. Other details about his career and personal life are sparse, but his contributions to our musical heritage during the thirties include some of my favorites (yours, too, I believe) and entitle him to a solid niche on our songwriters' honor roll. We can begin with the beautiful theme, *Out of the Night,* which identified Ted Weems and his band on radio broadcasts. Hirsch wrote the words to the melody by bandleader-composer Harry Sosnik. From there it's an easy move to 1926 and the popular jazz standard *'Deed I Do,* a collaboration with Fred Rose.

Hirsch had his name on some prestigious songs in the thirties. In 1931 he worked with Frank Magine and Phil Spitalny to compose the popular *Save the Last Dance for Me,* and in that same year he combined with pianist-composer Al Goering and bandleader Ben Bernie on the hit song *Who's Your Little Who-siz?,* which the Bernie band helped to make popular. In 1932 he again paired with Ben Bernie to pen the words to comedian-accordionist Phil Baker's wonderful *Strange Interlude. Don't Ever Change* was a collaboration with Lou Handman in 1937, and the pair also contributed three songs to the movie musical *The Hit Parade, Was It Rain?; Love Is Good for Anything That Ails You;* and *Last Night I Dreamed of You.* In the following year Hirsch wrote the words to pianist Clarence Profit's swing classic *Lullaby in Rhythm.* On this they were aided and abetted by Benny Goodman (whose band recorded and promoted the song into a hit) and arranger-composer Edgar Sampson, both of whom claimed cowriting credit.

The next time you attend a jazz concert and the band plays *'Deed I Do,* have a kind thought for Walter Hirsch.

Johnny Hodges

Johnny Hodges was born in Cambridge, Massachusetts, on July 25, 1907. He attended public schools and learned to play the saxophone, developing a highly individual style with readily recognized tone and technique. In 1927 he joined the Duke Ellington Orchestra, beginning a lifetime association. As a featured member of the Ellington band, Johnny Hodges made dozens of recordings as a soloist with the full orchestra, but he also made a series of records under his own name, utilizing Ellington musicians in small groups. This was an Ellington policy. Billed as "An Ellington Unit," very often with Ellington included, the key soloists in the band—Hodges, Rex Stewart, Cootie Williams, Barney Bigard—all made records under their own names.

Hodges, sometimes in collaboration with Duke Ellington, composed a number of original instrumentals for his recording sessions. Among the titles written with the Duke are *Jeep's Blues; Hodge Podge; The Jeep Is Jumpin'; Jitterbug's Lullaby; Wanderlust; Swingin' in the Dell; Mood to be Wooed;* and *It Shouldn't Happen to a Dream.* Working on his own, Hodges wrote *Truly Wonderful; My Heart Jumped over the Moon; The Rabbit's Jump;* and *Going Out the Back Way.* In addition, he is listed, along with Ellington, Don George, and Harry James, as cocomposer of the 1944 superhit, *I'm Beginning to See the Light.*

A major voice in the world of jazz, Johnny Hodges was active right up until his death in New York City on May 11, 1970.

Al Hoffman

Al Hoffman was born in Minsk, Russia, September 25, 1902, came to this country at an early age, and attended Franklyn High School in Seattle, Washington. A drummer, he played in local dance bands and for awhile led his own. In 1928 he made his way to New York, working as a drummer in nightclubs, and began composing in collaboration with other lyricists and composers, turning out a long list of excellent songs. From 1934 to 1937 he worked in England with Al Goodhart and Maurice Sigler, writing scores for stage shows and movies. Among his other well-known collaborators were Ed Nelson, Sammy Lerner, Dick Manning, Jerry Livingston, Milton Drake, Mack David, Leon Carr, Walter Kent, Mann Curtis, and Leo Corday.

I Don't Mind Walking in the Rain (When I'm Walking in the Rain With You), a song with words by Hoffman and music by Max Rich, was an important entry in 1930 and a rather fateful title in that it was one of the last songs recorded by Bix Beiderbecke (Victor 23008) and one of the first in the career of Ozzie Nelson (Brunswick 4897). It was also a prodigious score for Al Hoffman, and he made the most of it. In the next couple of years he struck repeatedly. In 1931 he wrote the melody to John Klenner's words for the hardy perennial *Heartaches*. Guy Lombardo introduced the tune, but Ted Weems had the super-hit, more or less by luck. The Weems band recorded it in 1931, with Elmo Tanner whistling a chorus, but records in 1931 were no big factor in the music market. Then for some reason they recorded the arrangement again in 1937, this time for Decca. As before, it made no great waves, but ten years later a disc jockey on a radio station in North Carolina came across the record, liked it, and started to play it on his program. It caught on, Decca reissued it, and *Heartaches* became number one on *Your Hit Parade*.

A similar episode pertains to *I Apologize,* which came out in the same year. Introduced by Bing Crosby, it enjoyed good airtime and was also recorded by Kate Smith, Nat Shilkret, and Phil Spitalny; however, 1931 was a year loaded with good songs, and even good ones didn't stay on top very long. But the story doesn't end there. In 1951 Billy Eckstine recorded the tune with Pete Rugolo's Orchestra backing him on an M-G-M platter, and it was a bigger hit than the first time around. The song was a team effort, Hoffman working with Al Goodhart and Ed Nelson on the words and music. Another Al Hoffman ballad in 1931, written with Jack Murray and Barry Trivers, *Oh! What a Thrill (To Hear It From You),* deserved more attention than it received, but the competition was tough that year.

Hoffman continued to write with whoever was willing to collaborate or had a good idea for a song and did very well in 1932. With Ed Nelson, Al Goodhart, and Milton Ager, he came up with *Auf Wiedersehen, My Dear,* which Russ Colombo recorded. The song became identified with the singer, who had a brilliant but tragically brief career. Probably the most outstanding Hoffman title that year was a collaboration with Al Goodhart and Arthur Freed. The song was *Fit as a Fiddle,* a happy and sprightly ditty that benefited tremendously from a lyric break that comes at the end of the release, utilizing a phrase that was in vogue at the time, "With a hey-nonny-nonny and a hot-cha-cha." The song got a lot of airplay, the most important factor of the era, and still gets played. It rated a further lift by Donald O'Connor and Gene Kelly in the movie *Singin' in the Rain* (1952).

Hoffman's stay in England is commemorated by two exceptional songs that stand out in a period of prolific output. One of these is *Roll Up the Carpet,* with lyrics by Raymond Klages and music by Hoffman, Klages, and Goodhart. Recorded in England by Ray Noble, with vocalist Al Bowlly, it's a minor classic. The other, *I Saw Stars,* by Hoffman, Maurice Sigler, and Goodhart, did very well in 1934, with plenty of recorded attention by Paul Whiteman, Joe Haymes, Freddy Martin, and Morton Downey. In that same year, Hoffman published a cluster of songs, all of which were moderately successful: *Little Man You've Had a Busy Day; Jimmy Had a Nickel; Who Walks In When I Walk Out?; Why Don't You Practice What You Preach?; Your Guess Is As Good As Mine; You're in My Power*.

For the next few years the Hoffman talent was devoted to writing for English movies, with some titles making an international impression, such as *I'm in a Dancing Mood; She Shall Have Music; My First Thrill; Everything's in Rhythm with My Heart;* and *Say the Word and It's Yours*. This was followed by a lean period, with only one song per year for several years, but Hoffman, teaming with Jerry Livingston and Mann Curtis, had a winner in the 1942 offering *The Story of a Starry Night,* an adaptation of a theme by Tchaikovsky. Glenn Miller had the hit record. Hoffman hit paydirt again in 1944, this time with Jerry Livingston and Milton Drake on the novelty *Mairzy Doats*. Then, with Mack David replacing Drake, they repeated the win in 1947 with *Chi-Baba, Chi-Baba*. Perry Como's recording sold over a million copies. Peggy Lee did well also. For the animated cartoon *Cinderella,* Hoffman, Livingston, and David provided *A Dream Is a Wish Your Heart Makes; So This Is Love; Bibbidi Bobbidi Boo;* and *The Cinderella Work Song*. Then, just to make sure 1949 wasn't a wasted year, Hoffman got together with Leon Carr and Leo Corday, and they performed a few magic tricks with the old Italian song *O Sole Mio*. The result was *There's No Tomorrow,* which turned out to be a big hit for singer Tony Martin, who not only recorded it, but sang it in the 1951 movie *Two Tickets to Broadway*. Still trading partners, Hoffman, with Bob Merrill and Clem Watts, penned the clever novelty *If I Knew You Were Comin', I'd've Baked a Cake*. Eileen Barton's record of this 1950 ditty was a number one best-seller on the National label. The phrase itself enjoyed a vogue as an informal greeting.

Al Hoffman died in New York City on July 21, 1960, but he continued to work and write and turn out hit songs as late as 1959. In 1953 it was *Takes Two to Tango*. In 1954 it was *Papa Loves Mambo*. In 1956 it was *Hot Diggity*. And in 1958, it was the *Hawaiian Wedding Song,* for which he and Dick Manning wrote English lyrics to the original Hawaiian melody by Charles E. King, composed in 1926. Andy Williams had the hit record. *La Plume De Ma Tante,* possibly Hoffman's final song, was published in 1959. The other songs credited to Hoffman make up a long list. Here are some of them: *If You Haven't Got a Girl; Makin' Faces at the Man in the Moon; Happy-Go-Lucky You; It's Winter Again; Meet Me in the Gloaming; Two Buck Tim from Timbuctoo; Black-Eyed Susan Brown; There Isn't Any Limit to My Love; Everything Stops for Tea; On the Bumpy Road to Love; Close to You;*

Wherever You Are; I'm Gonna Lasso a Dream; Don't You Love Me Anymore?; I'm Gonna Live Till I Die; I Ups to Her and She Ups to Me; Fuzzy Wuzzy.

Mann Holiner

Lyricist-actor Mann Holiner was born in Brooklyn, New York, on June 7, 1897. He was educated at Cornell University and studied at the American Academy of Dramatic Arts. As an actor he performed in stock, in vaudeville, and on Broadway. He also wrote special material. In collaboration with his wife, composer Alberta Nichols, Holiner is credited with a number of good songs in the thirties, including *You Can't Stop Me From Loving You* (1931); *Your Mother's Son-in-Law* (1933); *I Just Couldn't Take It, Baby* (1934); and *Until the Real Thing Comes Along* (1936). On the latter song the couple shared composing credit with Sammy Cahn, Saul Chaplin, and L. E. Freeman.

You Can't Stop Me from Loving You was intended for the Billy Rose revue "Corned Beef and Roses," but the show never made it to Broadway, closing in Philadelphia. The song got a second chance in Lew Leslie's "Rhapsody in Black," with the aid of Ethel Waters and Blue McAllister. Several contemporary artists recorded it, including Ethel Waters, who waxed it for Columbia. Others were Cab Calloway, Chick Bullock, and the Washboard Rhythm Kings. Jay Wilbur's band recorded it in England. *Your Mother's Son-in-Law* was introduced in Lew Leslie's "Blackbirds" (1933–1934). Seventeen-year-old Billie Holiday recorded it for Columbia, backed by Benny Goodman and an all-star studio group.

I Just Couldn't Take It, Baby, one of the best in the Holiner–Nichols output, was also from Lew Leslie's "Blackbirds," and this one was recorded by Ethel Waters with Benny Goodman's band, in the same session that produced the Billie Holiday side. A much better song, *I Just Couldn't Take It, Baby* was a popular item and rated considerable attention on radio and records. Jack Teagarden made it for Brunswick, and Eddy Duchin for Victor. This is one of those songs that musicians appreciate, and it resurfaces every now and then. Later records were made by the Hal Kemp band, Lionel Hampton, and Neil Hefti, with Mabel Wayne singing. *Until the Real Thing Comes Along* was introduced on a hit record by the Andy Kirk band, with a vocal by Pha Terrell. It became so identified with Kirk that the band adopted it as a theme song. Other Holiner–Nichols compositions include *There Never Was a Town Like Paris;*

Sing a Little Tune; Come On and Make Whoopie; What's Keeping My Prince Charming?; I'm Walkin' the Chalk Line; A Love Like Ours; and *Why Shouldn't It Happen to Us?*

Mann Holiner died in Hollywood, California, on October 29, 1958.

Fred Hollander

Composer Fred Hollander was born in London, England, on October 18, 1896, but was educated in Germany. He attended German primary schools and the Berlin Conservatory of Music. At eighteen he was already an associate conductor at the Prague Opera House. In 1931 he scored the music for the German film *The Blue Angel,* which starred Marlene Dietrich. Her throaty rendition of the Hollander song *Falling in Love Again* attracted worldwide attention, made the song a big hit, and launched her screen career. It also brought Hollander to Hollywood, where he began writing for more films and turning out a list of successful songs.

In 1936 the movie *Anything Goes* starred Bing Crosby and featured the Hollander song *My Heart and I,* with lyrics by Leo Robin. The next year, Hollander and Robin contributed *Moonlight and Shadows* to the Dorothy Lamour movie *The Jungle Princess* and *Whispers in the Dark* to *Artists and Models.* Connee Boswell sang it in the movie and also recorded it with Ben Pollack's band on Decca. Both tunes were well represented on records. *True Confession,* a big song in 1937, had words by Sam Coslow and was the title song of a movie starring Carole Lombard and Fred MacMurray. Among the many recordings (Dorothy Lamour, Don Bestor, Larry Clinton, Sammy Kaye, Russ Morgan), the most unusual was by the Adrian Rollini Quintette, which featured a young genius on cornet named Bobby Hackett.

Ralph Freed was the lyricist for Hollander's 1938 entry, *You Leave Me Breathless.* It was introduced by Fred MacMurray and Harriet Hilliard in *Cocoanut Grove,* a movie musical, and Harriet went on to record the tune with husband Ozzie Nelson's band. Other recordings were made by Tommy Dorsey, with Jack Leonard; George Hall with Dolly Dawn; and Jimmie Grier. Dorothy Lamour and her sarong came back in *Her Jungle Love,* a 1938 film, and the Hollander song was *Lovelight in the Starlight,* again with lyrics by Ralph Freed. Dorothy recorded it with Herbie Kay's Orchestra, where her career started, and it was covered by all the major labels with discs by Jan Savitt, Horace Heidt, Buddy Rogers, and Ruby Newman.

The Jimmy Stewart opus *Destry Rides Again* featured *See What the Boys In the Back Room Will Have,* as performed by Marlene Dietrich. The lyrics were by Frank Loesser. Vocalist Teddy Grace recorded it for Decca backed by Bud Freeman's Summa Cum Laude Orchestra in 1940. Frank Loesser is also responsible for the clever lyrics for *Li'l Boy Love,* from the 1940 movie *A Night at Earl Carroll's*. Benny Goodman gave it all-out treatment on a Columbia platter featuring Helen Forrest in the vocal. Other Fred Hollander titles are *You and Me: Naughty Lola; The House Jack Built for Jill; It's Raining Sunbeams; Beside a Moonlit Stream; That Sentimental Sandwich; Strange Enchantment;* and *The Melody Has to Be Right.*

Claude Hopkins

Composer-pianist-bandleader Claude Hopkins was born in Alexandria, Virginia, on August 24, 1903. His mother and father were employed at Howard University, in Washington, D.C., where Claude grew up and attended public school. He enrolled at Howard, majoring in music, and received a thorough grounding in classical music and developed his talent for the piano. While in college he began to take outside work in nightclubs as a pianist, assimilating a jazz background and eventually organizing his own band. With Sidney Bechet in the line-up, his band was part of the musical revue "Revue Negre," which toured Europe and brought Josephine Baker into international prominence. Hopkins and Spencer Williams wrote the music for the show.

In New York the Hopkins Orchestra became a steady feature at the famous Roseland Ballroom, with frequent radio broadcasts that made it a popular attraction. It also made numerous road tours. Claude continued to write material for the band, and most likely his most famous composition is *(I Would Do) Anything for You,* a 1932 collaboration with Alex Hill and Bob Williams. This was the Hopkins radio theme, and the band recorded it for Columbia. It has since become a standard, often played and recorded. Other compositions by Hopkins include the melodic *Crying My Heart Out for You* and *Blame It On a Dream;* but Hopkins primarily wrote instrumentals for his band or piano solos. In the former category are *Sweet Horn; Everybody Shuffle; Hopkins' Scream;* and *Washington Squabble*. In the latter are *Late Evening Blues; Low Gravy; 58th Street Blues; Safara Stomp;* and *Crazy Fingers*. I borrowed the last title as the name for my biography of Claude Hopkins, published by the Smithsonian Institution Press in 1992. Hopkins also composed *Vamping a Coed; Count Off; Dancing to the Hop; Deep Dawn; Sand Fiddler; Is It So?; That Particular Friend of Mine;* and *Thru With Love Affairs*.

Claude Hopkins died in Riverdale, New York, on February 22, 1984.

Karl Hoschna

Composer Karl Hoschna was born in Kuschwarda, Bohemia, on August 16, 1877. He studied music at the Vienna Conservatory and played oboe in the Austrian army band. He came to this country in 1896 and for two years played in the Victor Herbert Orchestra and arranged for Witmark Music. He wrote scores for early Broadway musicals beginning in 1908 and was well on the way to a successful career when it was cut off by his death on December 22, 1911, in New York City. Although Hoschna wrote prolifically for Broadway shows, and it appears that the shows were successful, his reputation today is based on the longevity of two songs, *Cuddle Up a Little Closer, Lovey Mine* and *Every Little Movement (Has a Meaning All Its Own). Cuddle Up a Little Closer* came out in 1908 and was written for the musical "The Three Twins." It was one of Hoschna's earliest efforts, and the first hit song for Otto Harbach, who still spelled his name as Hauerbach. Besides being frequently recorded through the years, the song has been featured in a number of movies as performed by stars like Mary Martin (*Birth of the Blues*, 1941); Betty Grable (*Coney Island,* 1943); Bob Haymes (*Is Everybody Happy?,* 1943); Fred Astaire and Ginger Rogers (*The Story of Vernon and Irene Castle,* 1939); and Gordon MacRae (*Moonlight Ray,* 1951).

The Ben Pollack Pick-a-Rib Boys, with Muggsy Spanier on trumpet, serve up a hot jazz version of the tune on Decca 1546, recorded in 1937. *Every Little Movement* was part of the score for the stage show "Madam Sherry" in 1910. It also has lyrics by Otto Harbach and like *Cuddle Up a Little Closer* has had a long and distinguished career, both on recordings and in movies. Connie Gilchrist and Judy Garland sang it the 1943 film *Presenting Lily Mars;* Robert Alda did the same in *April Showers,* in 1948; and Jack Smith in *On Moonlight Bay* in 1951; and to top it all off, it was given an instrumental treatment in the 1946 movie *The Jolson Story.* To coin a cliché, not many songs can say that.

Eddy Howard

Popular singer and bandleader Eddy Howard was born in Woodland, California, on September 12, 1914. He attended San Jose State College and Stanford University Medical School. But medicine was not to be his life's work. A guitarist, he started working and singing with dance bands, including stints with Ben Bernie, Tom Gerun, and Eddie Fitzpatrick. In 1934 he joined the Dick Jurgens band and began a six-year association that was mutually beneficial. Howard's intimate vocal style was important in building the band's popularity, and as a featured vocalist, he gained the attention that eventually made it possible for him to go out on his own, first as a single, then with his own band.

The Jurgens band and Howard shared in the success of three hit records in 1939. *My Last Goodbye,* with both words and music by Howard, was awarded heavy play on the nation's jukeboxes, and so was *If I Knew Then,* a title with Dick Jurgens listed as cocomposer. But one of the top records of the year was *Careless,* which garnered a host of best-selling records by Jurgens, Tommy Dorsey, Glenn Miller, Phil Harris, Tony Martin, and others. In his *Encyclopedia of Popular Music in America,* Robert Lissauer tells about the circumstances involved in the song's publication. The composer credits included Lew Quadling, the band's arranger; Eddy Howard, the vocalist; and Dick Jurgens, the bandleader. They submitted the tune to the Irving Berlin publishing company. Berlin overheard Dave Dreyer, his manager, running over the melody on the piano and investigated. They liked the melody, but were unhappy with the title and the lyrics but at the same time wary of turning the song down. Dick Jurgens led a popular band with a lot of airtime, and the thought surfaced that he might not waste any of it on Berlin-published tunes if his song wasn't one of them. Irving Berlin took the song home, gave it a new title, *Careless,* and a set of lyrics to match. His company published the tune, but Berlin received no credit or royalties for the song, which went on to become a huge success.

The trio of Howard, Jurgens, and Quadling scored again in 1940 with *A Million Dreams Ago,* an excellent ballad and best-selling record for Dick Jurgens as sung by vocalist Harry Cool. Howard, by this time, was working as a single. He formed his own dance band in 1941, using *Careless* as his theme song. With some interruption due to poor health, he led a band well into the sixties. His other compositions include *Now I Lay Me Down to Dream; Something Old—Something New; So Long for Now; For Sale; Lonesome Tonight.*

Eddy Howard died in Palm Desert, California, on May 23, 1963.

Joe Howard

Singer-composer Joe Howard was born in New York City on February 12, 1878. He toured in vaudeville as a boy soprano when he was only eleven years old. He acted in stock companies and played a song-and-dance man in vaudeville and nightclubs. A prolific songwriter, his chief collaborators were Will N. Hough, Frank Adams, and Harold Orlob, who worked with him on his most successful and memorable song, *I Wonder Who's Kissing Her Now,* published in 1909. Howard introduced this song himself in the stage musical "The Prince of Tonight," and it went on to sell over three million copies of sheet music. It was the title song of the Howard biographical film starring Mark Stevens as Howard in 1947. Buddy Clark's voice was dubbed over Stevens's for the singing role. Howard was also part of the popular radio program *Gay Nineties Revue,* with Beatrice Kay, in 1930 and 1940. Among the long list of titles credited to Howard during his long career writing for stage shows are *Hello Ma Baby* (1899), his first hit song; *Goodbye, My Lady Love;* and *Tonight Will Never Come Again.*

Joe Howard died in Chicago, on May 19, 1961.

Raymond Hubbell

Composer Raymond Hubbell was born in Urbana, Ohio, June 1, 1879. He attended public schools and studied music in Chicago. Early in his career he led a dance band and then worked as a staff composer for a Chicago publishing firm. Moving on to New York, he began writing scores for musical shows, including Ziegfeld's "Follies," and carved out a successful career. Unfortunately for his reputation with the general public, most of his songs were important only to the themes of the shows. However, he is responsible for one of the most popular songs of all time, *Poor Butterfly,* which was published in 1916 with words by John Golden and introduced in the production of "The Big Show" at the Hippodrome Theater in New York. This is most likely one of the most recorded songs in the history of American music, with renditions by a variety of artists, but long ago it established itself as a favorite of jazz musicians. In *Jazz Records 1897–1942,* Brian Rust indexes sixteen versions on 78 rpm records alone. The song was a special favorite of lyric cornetist Bobby Hackett, who recorded it several times and featured it in concerts.

Hubbell was one of the nine original founders of ASCAP, and served as a director from 1914 to 1941. He was treasurer of the organization from 1917 to 1928. Other Hubbell titles include *The Ladder of Roses; Hello, I've Been Looking for You; Jealous Moon; Chu Chin Chow; Just My Style; Little Girl in Blue; Look at the World and Smile;* and many others.

Raymond Hubbell died in Miami, on December 13, 1954.

Will Hudson

Back in the thirties, when the summer season started new dance bands would suddenly appear in new locations with a radio wire, and listeners' horizons would brighten up. This is how it was in 1934, when Bert Block's brand-new band, sparked by such talented youngsters as vocalist Jack Leonard and arranger Axel Stordahl, opened at a Long Island location called the Roadside Rest. As its theme song the band introduced a song that was to take the country by storm. It was called *Moonglow,* and the composer was the well-known arranger and future bandleader Will Hudson. Hudson was born in Barstow, California, on March 8, 1908, but attended high school in Detroit. He studied arranging and cut his teeth in the business writing charts for McKinney's Cotton Pickers, the Erskine Tate Orchestra, and other bands in the area. Cab Calloway thought so highly of his work that he brought him to New York. Hudson immediately began writing for all the top bands—Benny Goodman, Fletcher Henderson, Earl Hines, Don Redman—and then started to compose.

Moonglow, a collaboration with Eddie DeLange and Irving Mills, caught on quickly and has long ago become a standard. In the process it has been recorded by top bands and performers, including Glen Gray and the Casa Loma Orchestra, Guy Lombardo, Artie Shaw, Cab Calloway, Benny Goodman (both with the full band and with a quartet), the King Sisters, Art Tatum, Art Mooney, and Ethel Waters. In 1956 it was combined in counterpoint with *The Theme from Picnic,* heard as background music in the movie *Picnic.* As such, it was a hit all over again, resulting in big-selling records for Morris Stoloff and His Orchestra (Decca) and George Cates and His Orchestra (Coral). Hudson was also responsible for two successful instrumentals recorded by the Jimmie Lunceford band, *White Heat* and *Jazznocracy.* Ray Noble's composition *Cherokee,* as recorded by the Ray Noble Orchestra on Brunswick, was a Will Hudson arrangement.

In 1935 he organized a dance band with Eddie DeLange as coleader. Its theme song was *Sophisticated Swing,* composed by Hudson, with lyrics by Mitchell Parish. They recorded it for Brunswick. Other sides were made by Les Brown, Bunny Berigan, and Ozzie Nelson. When the partnership with DeLange dissolved, Hudson continued leading a band until thc calamitous year of 1941, when the usual problems with travel restrictions and the draft made it impractical to go on. Other Will Hudson compositions include *Eight Bars in Search of a Melody; The Moon Is Grinning at Me; Organ Grinder's Swing; Mr. Ghost Goes to Town; You're Not the Kind; Tormented;* and *That's My Desire,* the latter not to be confused with the Helmy Kresa song made popular by Frankie Lane and others.

Herman Hupfeld

"Play It Again, Sam!" has become a catch phrase of recent times, erroneously attributed to Humphrey Bogart as a line from the movie *Casablanca,* as a request to pianist Dooley Wilson to repeat a chorus of the old song *As Time Goes By*. More than likely, due to the movie, anybody over the age of fifteen is familiar with the song, but it is just as likely they have never heard the name of the man who wrote it, Herman Hupfeld. Hupfeld wrote both words and music to the song, and it was introduced in the 1931 theater musical "Everybody's Welcome" by Frances Williams. In its original inception, it was moderately successful on radio broadcasts and a Victor recording by Rudy Vallee, but its elevation to a standard had to wait until 1942 and *Casablanca.*

In 1942 I was working as an outside salesman for Decca Records, which maintained its sales offices on West Fifth-fourth Street in Manhattan. At the time James Caesar Petrillo, president of the American Federation of Musicians, had imposed his first recording strike, and no new records were being made. When *Casablanca* was released it created a tremendous demand for the song *As Time Goes By,* and every one of my dealers kept asking me if I had a recording. Decca as a company dated from 1932, so it had no records of the tune on its own label, but when the assets of the American Record Company were sold, the sale included the rights to the old Brunswick masters. Up to a certain date they were sold to Decca, and from there on to Columbia. Complicating the situation was the shortage of shellac, the material used to make records in those days, brought about by Japan's invasion of India, the prime source. This necessitated the reclaiming of the shellac in old records in order to make new ones, and all the companies instituted a drive to collect old records for scrap. In the warehouse of the Fifth-fourth Street office were stacks upon stacks of old records waiting to be broken up for scrap, and I was certain that buried in them somewhere was a Brunswick recording by somebody of *As Time Goes By*.

At a sales meeting I suggested a search be made for the record, and since it would be in the period of Brunswick sides now the property of Decca, it could be rereleased. The idea was greeted with considerable skepticism, but I won permission to conduct the search, and after turning over a few hundred old platters, I found what I was looking for. It was Brunswick 6205, *As Time Goes By,* recorded by Jacques Renard and His Orchestra, with a vocal by Frank Munn. On playing the record, not one of Brunswick's better efforts, nor Frank Munn's for that matter, we were disappointed by the quality. At the same time, there could be no denial that it was a recording of *As*

Time Goes By, and it was decided that the demand warranted reissuing the side. But since there was some objection to putting it out as a Decca recording, a compromise was reached. It was the only Decca record to have a green label, and it was priced at fifty cents instead of the regular Decca black label price of seventy-five cents. As a favor to Frank Munn, possibly to avoid a suit, his name was left off the label. I never knew how many copies of this hybrid were sold, and in typical Decca fashion I never received any financial recognition of my suggestion. It was intimated I could be proud of "the feather in my cap." Composer Herman Hupfeld never knew what I did for him, but I'm sure he enjoyed the resulting boost in royalties.

One of New Jersey's native sons, Hupfeld was born in Montclair on February 1, 1894. In *The Songwriter's Showcase* for February 1995, editor-publisher Bob Allen credits Steven Sharf, a member of the New York Sheet Music Society, for providing information on Hupfeld's life and career. Sharf states that music was important in the Hupfeld household and when Herman was only nine he was sufficiently proficient on the piano and violin to be sent to Germany for further training. He turned down a scholarship in Germany in order to return to Montclair, where he attended the high school and was active in music, learning to play the saxophone. During World War I he played in the navy band. Afterwards he worked as a performer, playing and singing his own songs, and then toured as an accompanist for Irene Castle and Julia Sanderson.

In 1930 and 1931 he contributed to the "Little Shows," including a novelty, *When Yuba Plays the Rumba on the Tuba.* This caught the attention of Rudy Vallee, who recorded and plugged it into some popularity. Vallee also recorded *As Time Goes By* for Victor as a vocal, which was reissued during the recording ban in 1942 in response to the great demand created for the song by *Casablanca.* The story goes that even this was a near thing, because Max Steiner, the film's musical director, didn't like the song and wanted to substitute one of his own.

Hupfeld is credited with over one hundred songs, but *As Time Goes By* was his only major hit. However, he did write three other pleasant and memorable songs that were moderately successful: *Sing Something Simple; Night Owl;* and *Let's Put Out the Lights (And Go to Sleep).*

Herman Hupfeld died in his hometown of Montclair, New Jersey, on June 8, 1951.

Roy Ingraham

Composer-bandleader Roy Ingraham was born in Whiting, Indiana, December 6, 1895. A child prodigy on the violin, he had his own orchestra at age eight and played in the Whiting Theater when he was ten. He toured in vaudeville, and had his first song published when he was seventeen. After some time spent in Los Angeles, he took a job in New York as a contract writer for Berlin, Inc., and Witmark & Sons.

Ingraham also possessed a pleasant singing voice, and in the wake of the great success of crooner Rudy Vallee, he opened with his own orchestra in the grillroom of the Hotel Paramount in New York, broadcasting regularly on the CBS network. The band recorded for Brunswick, including the song *Deep in the Arms of Love*, its theme. The exceptional melody was composed by Ingraham, with lyrics by Lou Davis, which Ingraham vocalizes on the record (Br 4544). In 1936 Ingraham, working with Harry Tobias, composed the hit song *No Regrets,* a worthy entry in the Golden Era tastefully recorded by Billie Holiday, Artie Shaw, Tommy Dorsey, Joe Haymes, and Wingy Manone, among others on the contemporary scene. The tune has achieved semistandard acceptance and is frequently played and recorded.

Roy Ingraham went on to write for the movies and special material for stars like Sophie Tucker and Marion Harris. Other titles to his credit include *Topper; Music; I've Got a Cross-Eyed Papa (But He Looks Straight to Me); Love Is a Beautiful Thing; A Girl Like You, a Boy Like Me; Sunny Side of the Rockies*; and *Stars over the Desert.*

Moe Jaffe

Moe Jaffe was born in Vilna, Russia, on October 23, 1901. The next year he was brought to this country. He was educated at the Wharton School then attended the University of Pennsylvania. Most likely Jaffe's first hit song was *Collegiate,* written in 1925 with Nat Bonx. Right in tune with the spirit of the times—the fascination with college football, coed flappers, hip flasks, and raccoon coats—the song was an instant success. It was introduced and recorded by Fred Waring's Pennsylvanians. It also enjoyed an afterlife in three movies, the 1929 musical *The Time, the Place, and the Girl* and two Marx Brothers epics, *Animal Crackers* (1930) and *Horse Feathers* (1932).

In the late thirties Jaffe teamed up with composer Clay Boland in writing shows for the Mask and Wig productions at the University of Pennsylvania, and they turned out some excellent songs. In 1936 it was *An Apple a Day* and *Something Has Happened to Me,* both recorded by the Hal Kemp band for Brunswick; and in 1937 the song was *The Morning After,* delightfully delineated by Lennie Hayton's Orchestra on Decca 1443 and by the Tommy Dorsey organization on Victor 25703. Dorsey shared composing credit for the song. The biggest hit, if not the best song, from this collaboration, is *The Gypsy in My Soul,* from the Mask and Wig production "Fifty-Fifty" in 1938. This was accorded full treatment on records by Jan Savitt, Mildred Bailey, and Margaret Whiting.

Jaffe also worked with other writers, and in 1942 he and his old friend Nat Bonx combined with Jack Fulton to produce *If You Are But a Dream,* an adaptation from Rubenstein's piano composition *Romance, No. 1 in E Flat.* Jimmy Dorsey's band had the contemporary recording, but two years later Frank Sinatra had a big-selling record with an arrangement by Axel Stordahl. In 1948, Jaffe and Dwight Latham turned out the delightful novelty, *I'm My Own Grandpaw.* Guy Lombardo recorded it, with a vocal by Don Rodney, and Tony Pastor made it with the Clooney Sisters, Rosemary and Betty. Jo Stafford, with Paul Weston's Mountain Boys, turned it into a pseudo-country tune on Capitol as *I'm My Own Grandmaw.* Other compositions by Jaffe are *If I Had My Life to Live Over Again; Oh You Sweet One; Actions Speak Louder Than Words; High School; These Things Are Known; Watch That First Step;* and others.

Moe Jaffe died in Creskill, New Jersey, on December 2, 1972.

Will Jason

Composer-lyricist Will Jason was born in New York City on June 23, 1910. His composing partner was Val Burton, and although they wrote comparatively few songs, they turned out some very good ones. Foremost of these is the standard *Penthouse Serenade,* sometimes called *When We're Alone*. Initially published in 1932, it became a standard and was featured in several movies, including *Sweetheart of Sigma Chi* (1946); *Sarg Goes to College* (1947); and *Beau James* (1957). Among the many recordings of the song are discs by Bob Crosby, Errol Garner, Eddie Heywood, and Sarah Vaughan. Jason and Val Burton also wrote for the movies, and in 1933 they contributed *Isn't This a Night for Love* to the film *Melody Cruise,* which starred Phil Harris and Charles Ruggles. The following year, the Wheeler and Woolsey comedy *Cockeyed Cavaliers* included *The Big Bad Wolf Was Dead,* which was recorded by the Joe Haymes band and by Ted Fio Rito's Orchestra.

Other Jason–Burton songs are *If It Isn't Love,* which was recorded by Fats Waller; *Dilly Dally,* another recording by Joe Haymes; *Buy a Kiss,* waxed by Henry King's Orchestra; *It Can Happen to You,* recorded by Red Norvo on Brunswick and by Wingy Manone on Bluebird; plus *Out of the Blue;* and *Sincerely Yours*.

Gordon Jenkins

A man of many talents, Gordon Jenkins was born in Webster Grove, Missouri, on May 12, 1910. He started his musical career as a banjo player in dance bands then for a time worked as a staff pianist on radio. In the early thirties he joined the great Isham Jones band as a pianist-arranger and during this period collaborated with Joe Bishop on the outstanding *Blue Prelude* (1933). Jenkins went on to arrange for other leading orchestras of the era, including those of Benny Goodman, Paul Whiteman, André Kosterlanetz, and Vincent Lopez, and composed the famous closing theme *Goodbye* for the Goodman band. It has since became a standard. He served as arranger-conductor for the Broadway musical "The Show Is On" in 1937 and then moved on to serve as musical director for NBC radio on the West Coast. In the meantime, he wrote music for movies, radio, and nightclubs. For awhile he was musical director for Decca Records, accompanying many of the big-name stars on recordings.

The Jenkins list of songs is not as long as that of some composers, but few offer the consistent quality his does, and in many instances he wrote both the music and the words. In 1934 he teamed with lyricist Johnny Mercer, and the result was three superior titles that are still being played: *P.S. I Love You; You Have Taken My Heart;* and *When a Woman Loves a Man.* Rudy Vallee was responsible for making the first tune a big hit, Glen Gray and the Casa Loma Orchestra the second, and Billie Holiday the third. In 1943 Jenkins provided words and music for *San Fernando Valley,* which turned out to be a number one seller for Bing Crosby. Johnny Mercer also recorded it for Capitol. Roy Rogers not only recorded it but went on to sing it in the 1944 movie that borrowed the same title, *San Fernando Valley.* Then Jenkins arranged and conducted the Frank Sinatra recording for Columbia of *Homesick—That's All,* his offering for 1945. Still writing words and music, Jenkins struck gold in 1963 with the eloquent *This Is All I Ask,* an exceptional offering in the desert of rock that has since become a standard. Other Jenkins tunes include *Blue Evening; When You Climb Those Golden Stairs; Tomorrow; Sally Doesn't Care; Saddest Man in Town; The Best Time of the Day; I Love Love in New York;* and *Goin' Back to Brooklyn.*

Gordon Jenkins died in 1984.

M. K. Jerome

Composer and music publisher M. K. Jerome was born in New York City on July 18, 1893. In high school, he took private music lessons and while still in his teens worked as a pianist in vaudeville and silent movie theaters. This led to a job as staff pianist for Waterson, Berlin & Snyder. He founded his own publishing firm in New York in 1911 but in 1929 moved on to Hollywood to write for the movies. He was with Warner Brothers for eighteen years.

Jerome's first hit song was *Just a Baby's Prayer at Twilight,* a 1918 ballad with words by Sam M. Lewis and Joe Young. A song in tune with the war anxieties of the country, it sold a million records for singer Henry Burr. Two years later Jerome, who usually worked alone writing music, teamed with Otto Motzan on the melody for *Bright Eyes,* with lyrics by Harry B. Smith. A sprightly tune, it was recorded by the Paul Whiteman and Leo Reisman Orchestras as an instrumental and was in direct contrast with the other Jerome song of that year, *Old Pal, Why Don't You Answer Me?* Lewis and Young wrote the words for this attempt to repeat the success of *A Baby's Prayer at Twilight.* Singers Ernest Hare and Henry Burr both made records for Victor of this ballad of bereavement.

Jerome continued to write for movies. In 1931 he did well with *I Idolize My Baby's Eyes,* which had lyrics by Joan Jasmyn; and in 1936, Jack Scholl wrote the words for *Thru the Courtesy of Love,* a song featured in the movie *Here*

Comes Carter. *My Little Buckeroo* was in the 1937 movie *Cherokee Strip,* and *You, You Darlin'* was a 1940 entry that did well. *Sweet Dreams, Sweetheart,* with lyrics by Ted Koehler, was introduced by Kitty Carlisle and Joan Leslie in the movie *Hollywood Canteen* in 1944. Kitty Carlisle recorded it, as did Ray Noble's orchestra. In the following year Jerome contributed *The Wish That I Wish Tonight* to *Christmas in Connecticut.* Jack Scholl returned to do the lyrics, and the bands of Russ Morgan and Ray Noble made the records. In 1946 the Jerome offering was *Some Sunday Morning* for the film *San Antonio,* as performed by Alexis Smith. Ted Koehler wrote the words, and Ray Heindorf assisted with the melody. Vocalist Dick Haymes had a good record, accompanied by the Gordon Jenkins Orchestra on Decca. Louis Prima had another. Other songs by M. K. Jerome are *Mary Dear; Dream Kisses; Jose O'Neill, the Cuban Heel; The Old Apple Tree; Knock on Wood; Would You Believe Me?; Don't Throw Cold Water on the Flame of Love,* and many more.

William Jerome

Lyricist William Jerome was born in Cornwall-on-the-Hudson, New York, on September 30, 1865. Early in his career he performed in minstrel shows. A charter member of ASCAP, he served as a director from 1914 to 1925. As a music publisher his main claim to fame was the great World War I song *Over There*. As a lyric writer he has a number of famous songs to his credit. One of these is the all-time jazz favorite *Chinatown, My Chinatown,* written with composer Jean Schwartz. Published in 1906, the song was promoted into a hit by the 1910 stage show "Up and Down Broadway." Aside from being played and recorded countless times since, it was also incorporated in a number of movies: *Bright Lights* (1931); *Is Everybody Happy?* (1943); *Jolson Sings Again* (1949); *The Seven Little Foys* (1955); and *Young Man with a Horn* (1950).

In 1912 Jerome and James V. Monaco combined on the hit song of the Ziegfeld "Follies" of that year, *Row, Row, Row*. It enjoyed an afterlife in *The Incendiary Blonde,* a 1944 film starring Betty Hutton; *The Eddie Cantor Story* with Eddie Cantor's voice dubbed on the soundtrack for Keefe Braselle (1953); and Bob Hope with a chorus of juveniles in *The Seven Little Foys* (1955). Also in 1912, Jerome penned the words to the Harry Von Tilzer novelty *And the Green Grass Grew All Around*. Jerome and Andrew B. Sterling wrote the words to another Von Tilzer song in 1913, *On the Old Fall River Line*. Other Jerome titles include *Bedelia; Get Out and Get Under the Moon; Mr. Dooley; My Pearl Is a Bowery Girl; Picture Me Down Home in Tennessee; Old King Tut;* and *That Old Irish Mother of Mine*.

William Jerome died in New York City on June 25, 1932.

Howard E. Johnson

Howard E. Johnson was born in Waterbury, Connecticut, June 2, 1887. While in high school he studied music privately. Like many of his contemporaries, he played piano in silent movie houses and then went to work as a staff pianist for a New York publishing house. In World War I he served in the navy. Johnson shares credit for quite a few songs that have become standards or semistandards in our musical heritage, especially for a group published in the twenties. *Feather Your Nest,* for instance, a collaboration with James Kendis and James Brockman and a 1920 entry that has eclipsed the years and is still played. An even earlier tune, *What Do You Want to Make Those Eyes at Me For?,* which made its debut in 1916, surfaces every now and then in rollicking versions like that of Bob Howard on Decca in 1937. Johnson and Joe Young wrote the words, James V. Monaco the music. Donald O'Connor and Peggy Ryan sang the song in *The Merry Monahans* (1944), and in the same year it was interpolated in *The Incendiary Blonde,* the biographical movie about Texas Guinan starring Betty Hutton.

Sweet Lady, with music by entertainer Frank Crumit and Dave Zoob and lyrics by Johnson, was one of the better offerings for 1921. In the following year Johnson teamed with Walter Donaldson to produce *Georgia.* Paul Whiteman and Carl Fenton had the best-selling records. A decade later Johnson and composer Harry Woods came up with *When the Moon Comes Over the Mountain.* Kate Smith recorded it and adopted it as her radio theme song. She also sang it in the 1932 movie *The Big Broadcast.* Other Johnson songs include *Ireland Must Be Heaven for My Mother Came from There; I Scream, You Scream, We All Scream for Ice Cream; M-O-T-H-E-R; What Do We Do on a Dew Dew Dewy Day?; Where Do We Go from Here, Boys?; There's a Broken Heart for Every Light on Broadway; I Don't Want to Get Well; Love Me or Leave Me Alone;* and *Am I Wasting My Time On You?*

Howard E. Johnson died in New York City on May 1, 1941.

J. C. (Jimmy) Johnson

This Jimmy Johnson, not to be confused with James P. Johnson of stride piano fame, was a very versatile and successful musician and composer in his own right. He was born in Chicago, Illinois, on September 14, 1896. He attended Phillips High School and in his early years worked as a pianist and bandleader. He began making records in the twenties, accompanying blues singers, sometimes writing the songs they sang. From there he went on to writing for nightclub revues, including material for Texas Guinan, the "Nightclub Queen."

It appears that his first published song, *You Can't Do What My Last Man Did,* a 1923 entry, created a mild sensation. It was recorded by a galaxy of blues and jazz stars on as many labels. J. C. Johnson was one of them, accompanying Ethel Waters on Black Swan. She recorded the song again two years later for Columbia. Fats Waller was the pianist for Alberta Hunter on two takes made and released on Paramount; then the obliging Fats did the same for Anna Jones. Fletcher Henderson played piano for singer Maggie Jones on the Pathe and Perfect labels and then followed through accompanying George Williams in a duet with Bessie Brown for Columbia, but the side was rejected. Mamie Smith and Her Jazz Hounds waxed the tune for OKeh, and to top things off in grand style, fellow composer and pianist James P. Johnson played it as a solo on Victor 19123. What budding composer could ask for more?

In 1926 Johnson had two titles: *I Need Lovin'* and *Alabama Stomp. I Need Lovin'* was recorded by Fletcher Henderson for Columbia; the Goofus Five on OKeh; and the Coon–Sanders Orchestra for Victor, a pretty fair representation, but nothing compared to the reception accorded *Alabama Stomp.* This went the rounds of the labels. The Gus Edwards Orchestra made it for Victor; a Red Nichols group did it for Pathe–Perfect, and Red and Miff's Stompers for Edison. Leo Reisman's Orchestra, oddly enough, recorded it on Victor, and overseas Jack Hylton reciprocated on HMV. Fletcher Henderson's group, disguised as The Dixie Stompers, made a side for Harmony; Harry Pollock's Maurice Club Diamonds for Gennett; and in 1927 vocalist Charles Kaley waxed it for Columbia, backed by Red Nichols and Rube Bloom.

Johnson was off to a flying start. He had no entries in 1927, but he must have been working because he more than made up for the lapse in the following year. *Dusky Stevedore,* with lyrics by Andy Razaf, has become a jazz classic as recorded for OKeh by Frankie Trumbauer's Orchestra featuring Bix Beiderbecke. Razaf also wrote the words to *Take Your Tomorrow,* which Trumbauer also recorded later in the year, but he shared credit with Bob Schafer on the words to *Louisiana* and *When,* two famous records by the Paul Whiteman Orchestra of the period, with Bix Beiderbecke in the band. *Louisiana* rated an outstanding arrangement by Bill Challis. Young Bing Crosby was featured in the vocal group. Tom Satterfield arranged *When,* another excellent presentation. Songwriter Harry Barris is in the vocal quartet backing Jack Fulton.

Guess Who's in Town, another collaboration with Andy Razaf, didn't get much attention that year, but Ethel Waters recorded it for Columbia accompanied by James P. Johnson. An excellent song, it has received latter-day appreciation. In 1988 Bobby Short made it the title song for an album. *Empty Bed Blues,* with both words and music by J. C. Johnson, was recorded for Columbia by Bessie Smith on a two-sided rendition that has become another classic. *Trav'lin' All Alone* came out in 1930, another solo effort by Johnson. The Isham Jones band had a good contemporary record for Brunswick. Billie Holiday and her orchestra recorded it for Vocalion in 1937.

Dip Your Brush in the Sunshine was a natural for that perennial optimist Ted Lewis, who recorded it for Columbia in 1931. Snooks and His Memphis Stompers made it on Victor. But it wasn't until 1934 that Johnson again hit the jackpot, and he did it twice. *Believe It, Beloved* was a big record for Fats Waller. It was also recorded by Isham Jones and Red Allan, plus enjoying considerable airtime. A collaboration with George Whiting, it was joined by *Don't Let Your Love Go Wrong*. On the latter Nat Schwartz shared lyrics credit, and again Isham Jones and Red Allen recorded it along with the Boswell Sisters on Brunswick and the Gene Kardos band on Victor.

J. C. Johnson also collaborated with Fats Waller and Nat Burton. Other titles are *Somebody Loses, Somebody Wins; Rhythm and Romance; Crying My Heart Out for You; The Joint is Jumpin'; That Was My Heart; Patty Cake, Patty Cake; The Spider and the Fly; My Particular Man; Yankee Doodle Tan; How Long Is the Journey; Inside This Heart of Mine;* and others.

Johnson was in the service during World War II and then went on to become a civic leader in Harlem, but most likely he will be best remembered for his songs.

James P. Johnson

The grand old man of Harlem stride piano, James P. Johnson is well represented in the American library of standard songs, with some hardy perennials that everybody knows, even if they don't know—or care—who wrote them. He was born in New Brunswick, New Jersey, on February 1, 1891, but apparently moved to New York City at an early age, because he attended public school there, studying music privately. By 1904 he was already working as a professional pianist, and by thc time the twenties rolled in, he had his own band. He toured Europe with the show "Plantation Days" and then put in a period as accompanist to singers, including Bessie Smith, Ethel Waters, Trixie Smith, and Laura Smith, often recording with them. His composing career started early. In 1923 he wrote the music for the show "Runnin' Wild," which featured an all-black cast, and in 1929 repeated the effort for the show "Messin' Around."

Probably the best-known composition by Johnson is *Charleston,* a collaboration with Cecil Mack for the show "Runnin' Wild" and the song associated with the dance that became a sensation and the representative symbol of the twenties. The song is one that is readily recognized even by today's generation. Not one of Johnson's best musical efforts, nevertheless, when the characteristic Charleston rhythm is disregarded, the tune lends itself well to jazz interpretation. A better example of the Johnson–Mack partnership is *Old Fashioned Love,* also from "Runnin' Wild." This standard has been recorded frequently over the years, but those familiar with the recorded history of the great Joe Haymes band of the thirties will recognize this as a classic rendition of the tune, the first recording of the band on Victor. Along with a masterful arrangement by Haymes, it features two talented youngsters who would become star performers—Pee Wee Erwin and Johnny Mince.

In the category of songs that seem to be specifically written for the lazy, down-home delivery of vocalist Jack Teagarden is *If I Could Be With You*—so much so, that the great trombonist's early recording of the song with the Whoopie Makers is a jazz classic. Other James P. Johnson standards are *A Porter's Love Song to a Chambermaid; Snowy Morning Blues*—a great favorite of the late Dick Welstood, who recorded it a number of times—*Carolina Shout;* and *Keep off the Grass*. In addition to the popular compositions mentioned here, Johnson wrote extensive instrumental work and several books, including two autobiographies. He died in New York City on November 17, 1955.

Arthur Johnston

Arthur Johnston's songwriting career was mainly confined to the thirties, and many of his best-known compositions were written in collaboration with Sam Coslow. He was responsible for a number of successful scores for movie musicals early in the decade, and many of his tunes are associated with Bing Crosby, including one of Bing's greatest hits, *Just One More Chance*. Johnston was born in New York City on January 10, 1898, and attended public schools. He went the classic route of so many tunesmiths, playing piano for silent movies and then working with a song publisher as an arranger and song plugger. For awhile he was Irving Berlin's personal pianist and stage director.

In 1929 he went to Hollywood and began writing for the movies, especially a string of Bing Crosby films, *College Humor; Too Much Harmony; Thanks a Million; Pennies from Heaven;* and *Double or Nothing*. These spanned a period from 1933 to 1937, and all were loaded with well-remembered songs—the title tunes from *Thanks a Million* and *Pennies from Heaven,* plus *Learn to Croon; Down the Old Ox Road; Thanks; The Day You Came Along;* and a number of others less well known. Johnston also wrote two gems of the period that are treasured by all those who appreciate the outstanding songs of the Golden Era. Both have lyrics by Sam Coslow. *Moon Song* was introduced by Kate Smith in her movie *Hello, Everybody.* She recorded it for Brunswick, and the song was represented on all the major record labels. However, it was in later years that it began to be fully appreciated and has been accorded the status of a standard. *My Old Flame* was featured in the Mae West film *Belle of the Nineties* and was sung by the star accompanied by Duke Ellington's Orchestra. Ellington recorded it with Ivie Anderson, and it has since been reprised many times on records. Other fine Johnston songs include *Cocktails for Two; Live and Love Tonight; Sing, Brother, Sing; One, Two, Button Your Shoe; The Skeleton in the Closet;* and *All You Want to Do Is Dance.*

Arthur Johnston died in Corona Del Mar, California, on May 1, 1954.

Al Jolson

The famous entertainer Al Jolson was born Asa Yoelson in St. Petersburg, Russia, on March 26, 1886. In 1890 he was brought to the United States and was educated in the public schools of Washington, D.C. His father, a rabbi, wanted him to become a cantor in his synagogue, but the boy joined a burlesque troupe as a stooge. Later on he developed into a singer, touring in vaudeville and also working in minstrels. In his stage career he often performed in blackface.

Jolson had a long and successful career on the stage, in the movies, and on records and radio. He performed and promoted a number of songs into popular hits, and he is included as a cocomposer on many of them. Although it is likely that in some cases he did contribute to their composition, it is also common knowledge that he insisted on having his name included as the price of promoting a song. Nevertheless, he is credited with collaborating on some very important ones. These include *Avalon; Yoo Hoo; California, Here I Come; Keep Smiling at Trouble; Me and My Shadow; Four Walls; Back in Your Own Backyard; Golden Gate; Sonny Boy; There's a Rainbow 'Round My Shoulder; Little Pal; I'm in Seventh Heaven; Used to You;* and *The Anniversary Song.* These were all hit songs in their day, and quite a few have become standards. Other Jolson titles are *'N Everything; I'll Say She*

Does; You Ain't Heard Nothin' Yet; Stella; Miami; Why Can't You?; Evangeline; A Year From Today; The Egg and I; and *All My Love.* In addition, Jolson is associated with songs he made famous—*Swanee; April Showers; Rock-a-bye Your Baby With a Dixie Melody; My Mammy; Toot, Toot Tootsie;* and *I'm Sitting on Top of the World.*

Al Jolson died in San Francisco, California, on October 23, 1950.

Isham Jones

One of the most prolific of the freelance songwriters, pioneer bandleader Isham Jones has left us a wonderful legacy of his original compositions, along with an extensive list of outstanding recordings by the bands he led during a long and illustrious career. Some of the best of these feature Isham Jones tunes. Like his contemporaries Duke Ellington and Ray Noble, he was fortunate in having his own fine orchestra to showcase his work. Jones was born January 31, 1984 in Coalton, Ohio, a mining town, and one not very conducive to a musical career, but he grew up in Saginaw, Michigan, and learned to play the saxophone. At an early age he made a wise move to Chicago and began a long and very lucrative musical career, leading successful bands and writing highly successful songs. One of his earliest hits is still with us and a favorite of jazz groups, *On the Alamo,* which dates to 1922. In the following year he came through with another, *Swingin' down the Lane.*

In spite of the successes of his career, Isham never forgot his frugal upbringing and was always a very careful man with money. The story goes that he walked home every night from where his band was playing at the College Inn and on the way always stopped to look in the window of a piano store to admire the beautiful grand piano on display, but could never bring himself to spend the money to buy it. So on his thirtieth birthday in 1924 his wife bought it for him as a present, and the evening of the day it was delivered Isham worked at the keyboard until he had written three songs that he hoped would offset the cost of the piano and make the purchase worthwhile. You can judge for yourself if he succeeded. The tunes were *The One I Love Belongs to Somebody Else; Spain;* and *It Had to Be You. Spain,* which has seen a bit of revival locally thanks somewhat to the solo efforts of tenorman Nick Sassone, started out as a tango, which was a very popular dance in 1924 due to the sensational career of Rudolph Valentino. The tune was a big hit internationally and was a smash in the country it was named for, to such an extent that the Spanish government seriously considered adopting it as the national anthem and made inquiries of the publisher. When they found out it had been written by a man named Jones they lost all interest. Jones didn't let three outstanding hits dampen his efforts, though. In 1924 he had several more tunes published and among them were *I'll See You in My Dreams; Gotta Get a Girl;* and *Why Couldn't It Be Poor Little Me*. Without missing a beat he turned out hit tunes every year, maintaining a prolific output. In 1929 he contributed *Song of the Blues,* in 1930 the exceptional *What's the Use* (a favorite of the late Bobby Hackett as recorded on Milt Gabler's Commodore 507), and in 1931 three great songs that are worthy of greater attention, *I Keep Remembering; I Wouldn't Change You for the World;* and the one that became the theme song of the marvelous dance band Isham led in the early thirties, *You're Just a Dream Come True.*

One of the most piquant of my musical memories dates back to the early days of radio, when one of the popular hobbies of the time was known as DX-ing. This entailed waiting until the local broadcasting stations went off the air for the night and carefully tuning your radio to bring in the most distant station you could find. I still recall the thrill when I heard the announcer's faint voice impart the information: "You are listening to the music of Isham Jones and his world-famous orchestra broadcasting from . . ." I forget where it was from, but this was the first time I ever heard the Isham Jones band, and I never forgot it. It was that kind of a musical organization, like its leader, unique and one of a kind.

Some years ago I was delighted to get a small reel of recorded tape in the mail. It was a voice letter from Eddie Stone, the violinist-vocalist who was a mainstay in the Jones Orchestra for eight years, adding a lot to its distinctive personality. On the tape he reminisced briefly, saying that when he auditioned for "Mr. Jones," and was hired, he was told that he had to have a tuxedo to wear on the bandstand. He passed on the information to his father, who took him to a second-hand store where they bought a tux for $4.50. The first year the band played the Ritz-Carlton Hotel in Atlantic City, Eddie recalled, he and Saxey Mansfield, who played tenor in the band, and Isham donned bathing suits for a dip in the surf. "A big speedboat came in and Saxey, Ish, and I climbed in and went for a ride. Then on the way back he pulled up into the waves, and we got out and swam ashore—that is, Saxey and I. We were younger than Ish, and we buzzed right to shore. And when we turned around, there was Ish—his big Irish face was really red, and he was huffin' and puffin'. So we swam back to him, and Saxey got on one side and I got on the other, and we said, 'Are you all right, Ish?' 'Take me to shore! Take me to shore!' he gasped. So I told him, 'Well, just stand up and walk, will ya!' Then he got up enough nerve to put his feet down. Saxey and I were standing there holding him. He walked to the beach, but that was the last time we saw Ish in the water at Atlantic City."

As it was for many other songwriters, the decade of the thirties presented just the right atmosphere for Isham Jones, and the demand and acceptance for superior ballads inspired him to write one outstanding song after another. In 1932 alone he published *I Can't Believe It's True; Let's Try Again; Let That Be a Lesson to You; If You Were Only Mine; I'll Never Have to Dream Again; The Wooden Soldier and the China Doll; I Only Found You for Somebody Else;* and *One Little Word Led to Another*. With the exception of *Wooden Soldier,* the Jones Orchestra made exceptional recordings of all of these songs, now coveted collector's items. Odds are that among these is at least one of your favorites. The year 1933 was notable in the Jones songbook for two big hits, *Why Can't This Night Go On Forever* and *You've Got Me Crying Again,* plus a lesser known but delightful ballad, *Honestly;* and 1934 for three other gems, *All Mine—Almost; You're Welcome;* and *It's Funny to Everyone but Me*. More than likely Isham's last big hit was *There Is No Greater Love,* which appeared in 1936, just prior to his first retirement, and introduced the voice of young Woody Herman as the vocalist on the Jones recording for Decca. Isham wasn't finished, however. He reorganized in 1937, and in the next two years penned three more exceptional songs that he recorded for Vocalion, *Thanks for Everything; Just to Remind You;* and *More Than Ever,* which were moderately successful. *More Than Ever,* in particular, is every bit up to the Jones standard for a quality ballad.

He continued to write until the fifties, by which time the market for a good song was rapidly waning. He died on October 19, 1956, in Hollywood, California, leaving us an inheritance of wonderful songs, and a long and fruitful output of recordings—both major contributors to our musical heritage. In the opinion of many musicians, the dance band that Isham Jones fronted from 1928 to 1936 was the best ever organized, with outstanding arrangers in Gordon Jenkins, Joe Bishop, Jiggs Nobee, and Victor Young—and the great songs of Isham Jones.

Dick Jurgens

Bandleader and composer Dick Jurgens was born in Sacramento, California, on January 9, 1910. He attended local schools and spent one year at the University of California, Berkeley and then devoted himself to a career as a professional musician and trumpet player. His composing efforts started early. He wrote the melody for *Day Dreams Come True at Night* as a course project while still a student at the Sacramento Junior College. The song later became the famous theme for his very successful band.

The Jurgens output, as a matter of fact, stems from the period of the band's greatest popularity, when Eddy Howard and Ronnie Kemper were still part of it. In 1939 they produced three hit songs with hit recordings to match. The biggest of the three was *Careless,* attributed to Jurgens, Eddy Howard, and Lew Quadling. Submitted to Irving Berlin's publishing company, it underwent a revision of title and lyrics by Berlin and then went on to become a number one song, without any recognition of his contributions. (*See* Eddy Howard.) Eddy Howard and Dick Jurgens followed through with *If I Knew Then,* a popular hit not only for the band but for Howard himself, who sang on the recording. Then Jurgens and Ronnie Kemper combined to write *It's a Hundred to One,* giving them another hit record, along with others by Jack Teagarden, Jan Savitt, the Tommy Dorsey Clambake Seven, and Dick Todd. Eddy Howard and Lew Quadling were still with Jurgens to compose the lovely *A Million Dreams Ago,* but before it was published Howard had departed to work as a single, so the excellent recording of the tune by the Dick Jurgens Orchestra had Harry Cool on the vocal. Glenn Miller also had a fine recording of the 1940 song.

With his old friends now out on their own, Jurgens found new collaborators, and in 1941, working with Elmer Albrecht and Sammy Gallop, he shared credit for *Elmer's Tune.* Arranger Lew Quadling scored the tune for the Jurgens band, and they recorded it as an instrumental. It remained for Glenn Miller to make a record with the words sung by Ray Eberle and the Modernaires, and the song soared to number one in popularity and fifteen weeks on *Your Hit Parade. One Dozen Roses,* so the story goes, was written by Jurgens in honor of his brother-in-law, who was a florist. However, Dick had considerable help with this 1942 ballad. The lyrics are credited to Roger Lewis and Country Washburne, and Walter Donovan is included for work on the music. Again, Jurgens scored big, and the song was on *Your Hit Parade* for fourteen weeks, twice in the number one spot. The Jurgens band, with a vocal by Buddy Moreno, had the top seller, but it was closely followed by Harry James. Dinah Shore and the Glen Gray Casa Loma Orchestra also had successful sides. Other songs by Dick Jurgens are *I Guess I'll Be on My Way; Knit One, Purl Two;* and *I Won't Be Home Anymore When You Call.*

Irving Kahal

Lyricist Irving Kahal was born in Houtzdale, Pennsylvania, on March 5, 1903. He attended Cooper Union on an art scholarship and then went into show business as a child performer in Gus Edwards's famous troupe. Most of Kahal's songs, over a long career that continued well into the forties, were written with Sammy Fain, the Crooning Songwriter. A partial list of Kahal titles is still very impressive: *I Left My Sugar Standing in the Rain; It Was Only a Sunshower* (1927); *Let a Smile Be Your Umbrella* (1928); *Wedding Bells Are Breaking Up That Old Gang of Mine* (1929); *You Brought a New Kind of Love to Me* (1930); *Moonlight Saving Time; When I Take My Sugar to Tea* (1931); *Three's a Crowd* (1932); *By a Waterfall; Sittin' on a Backyard Fence* (1933); *How Do I Know It's Sunday; Simple and Sweet; Spin a Little Web of Dreams; When Tomorrow Comes* (1934); *Ev'ry Day; There's a Different "You" in Your Heart; Ballad in Blue* (written with Hoagy Carmichael) (1935); *Lazy Weather; The Night Is Young and You're So Beautiful* (1936); *Don't You Know, or Don't You Care* (1937); *I Can Dream, Can't I; I'll Be Seeing You* (1938); *Such Stuff as Dreams Are Made Of; I Want to Live* (1940); *Love Song of Renaldo* (1941); *Old Sad Eyes* (1942).

Irving Kahal died in New York City on February 7, 1942.

Gus Kahn

This time our accolades go to one of the most eminent lyricists in the history of American popular music, Gus Kahn. Born in Coblenz, Germany, on November 6, 1886, he accompanied his parents to this country in 1891 and grew up in Chicago. He began composing songs shortly after graduating from high school, and after a period without any success, he got his first break in a collaboration with Egbert Van Alstyne on a tune called *My Dreamy China Lady,* published in 1906. Two years later he scored again with a song written by his future wife, Grace LeBoy, called *I Wish I Had a Girl,* and with another by Van Alstyne, *It Looks Like a Big Night Tonight.*

These songs enjoyed moderate success but created little excitement. Neither did another LeBoy tune, *Moonlight on the Mississippi,* or Van Alstyne's

Sunshine and Roses, which came out in 1913, or two more LeBoy entries for 1914 called *Everybody Rag with Me* and *On the Good Ship Mary Ann.* However, Van Alstyne and Kahn finally found the right combination the following year with *Memories,* which not only became a hit but, like other perennials such as *Goodnight, Sweetheart; The Party's Over; A Pretty Girl*—songs that are adaptable to certain situations and set a theme—it still enjoys a solid niche in our musical heritage. The team did well again in 1916, turning out the blockbuster *Pretty Baby,* followed by a quiet entry, *Just a Word of Sympathy*. But in 1917 Kahn began to broaden his outlook. He combined with Al Jolson and Buddy DeSylva on a composition called *'N Everything;* teamed again with Van Alstyne for *Sailin' Away on the Henry Clay;* and then joined with Richard Whiting and lyricist Raymond B. Egan to turn out *Some Sunday Morning*—a song that saw a successful revival many years later—and *Where the Morning Glories Grow.*

The year 1918 was mainly devoted to a hit show starring Al Jolson, "Sinbad," which included a lot of music, much of which is still with us in songs like *Rock-a-bye Your Baby With a Dixie Melody; My Mammy;* and *Swanee,* but also a couple of the Jolson–DeSylva–Kahn collaborations, *'N Everything* and *I'll Say She Does*. Kahn continued to diversify, combining with Van Alstyne for a contribution to "Ziegfeld's Midnight Frolics" of 1919, *Baby;* working with a new name, Walter Blaufuss, on *My Isle of Golden Dreams* and *Your Eyes Have Told Me So;* then switching over to the Jolson–DeSylva combination for *You Ain't Heard Nothin' Yet.*

The year 1920 slid by without an entry, but 1921 opened with a solid strike with Richard Whiting and Raymond Egan, *Ain't We Got Fun,* followed by another fair success, *Bimini Bay*. "The Passing Show of 1922" staged a sensational cast that included Willie and Eugene Howard, Fred Allen, Ethel Shutta, and the beginning of an important collaboration between Walter Donaldson and Gus Kahn on a song called *Carolina in the Morning*. They followed through with a tune called *Dixie Highway* that has since been forgotten, but Gus Kahn couldn't have been too badly discouraged, because a first-time outing with Isham Jones resulted in *On the Alamo,* and then he and Donaldson recouped their fortunes with *My Buddy*. Kahn even found time to join forces with Ted Fio Rito, Robert King, and Ernie Erdman on *Toot Toot Tootsie*. So, all in all, 1922 wasn't a bad year.

By this time Kahn was an established name in Tin Pan Alley, well respected and with a reputation for writing hit songs. But what had gone before was only a prelude to a career that not only spanned the Golden Era, but went a long way in creating it. You will probably recognize many of the songs in the following list and may include a number of them in your personal library of favorites. At the same time, just to emphasize the fantastic contribution to our heritage of popular songs made by Gus Kahn, you might keep in mind that this is just hitting the high spots.

1923: *Beside a Babbling Brook; Mindin' My Business; Sittin' in a Corner; When Lights Are Low; Swingin' Down the Lane.*

1924: *Charley, My Boy; Gotta Get a Girl; I'll See You in My Dreams; Spain; It Had to Be You; Nobody's Sweetheart; The One I Love; Why Couldn't It Be Poor Little Me.*

1925: *I Never Knew; I Wonder Where My Baby Is Tonight; Old Pal; That Certain Party; Ukulele Lady; Yes Sir, That's My Baby.*

1926: *Barcelona; A Bird's Eye View of My Old Kentucky Home.*

1927: *He's the Last Word; Chlo-e; Persian Rug; My Ohio Home.*

1928: *Makin' Whoopie; Love Me or Leave Me; My Baby Just Cares for Me; Beloved; Coquette; Ready for the River; Where the Shy Little Violets Grow.*

1929: *Liza; Here We Are.*

1930: *Sweetheart of My Student Days; Around the Corner; The One I Love Can't Be Bothered with Me.*

1931: *Dream a Little Dream of Me; Guilty; The Hour of Parting; I'm Thru with Love; Now That You're Gone; Old Playmate; The Waltz You Saved for Me; You Gave Me Everything but Love.*

1932: *Goofus; I'll Never Be the Same; A Little Street Where Old Friends Meet; Lovable; A Million Dreams; Was I to Blame?; So at Last It's Come to This.*

1933: *Flying Down to Rio; Carioca; Sweetheart Darlin'; You've Got Everything.*

1934: *Waitin' at the Gate for Katy; Wine Song; I've Had My Moments; An Earful of Music; Okay Toots; Your Head on My Shoulder; One Night of Love; Tonight Is Mine; Sleepy Head.*

1935: *Thanks a Million; Sugar Plum; New Orleans; Love Song of Tahiti; You're All I Need.*

1936: *Let's Sing Again; With All My Heart; Gone.*

1937: *All God's Chillun Got Rhythm; Tomorrow Is Another Day; Josephine.*

1938: *The One I Love; Shadows on the Moon; Who Are We to Say?*

1939: *Honolulu; This Night; How Strange.*

1940: *Blue Lovebird; Waltzing in the Clouds.*

1941: *You Stepped Out of a Dream; Day Dreaming.*

In the latter years of his life he wrote mostly for the movies, and many of the songs, although important in context, were not great hits. Nevertheless, he was active during the most productive period in songwriting history and had the great fortune to work with many of our foremost composers. Besides those previously mentioned, he collaborated with Neil Moret, Vincent Youmans, George and Ira Gershwin, Harry Woods, Harry Warren, Harry Akst, Sigmund Romberg, Victor Schertzinger, and others. In the 1951 movie *I'll See You in My Dreams,* based on Kahn's life and music, Danny Thomas played the great lyricist.

Gus Kahn died on October 8, 1941, in Beverly Hills, California.

Kalmar and Ruby

See Bert Kalmar.

Bert Kalmar

Although best known for his collaborations with composer Harry Ruby, lyricist Bert Kalmar had an interesting and exciting career long before they met. In fact, the 1940 movie *Tin Pan Alley* is loosely based on his life. It featured an all-star cast, including John Payne, Alice Faye, Jack Oakie, and Betty Grable. Ten years later another film, *Three Little Words,* portrayed the team of Kalmar and Ruby, with the roles of the songwriters played by Fred Astaire and Red Skelton. Bert Kalmar was born in New York City on February 16, 1884. When he was only ten years old he ran away from home. Then, achieving in real life the sort of adventure that many kids have fantasized for decades, he wound up traveling with a tent show and performing as a magician. When the show went broke he was paid in medicated soap and had to peddle it door-to-door to earn the trainfare back home. Later he tried working in a team of acrobats, went on to writing and singing song parodies, and became a "hoofer." This led to playing leads in musical comedy, where he met a talented tap and ballet dancer named Jessie Brown and teamed up with her to tour in vaudeville. They were headliners on the Keith and Orpheum circuits, and true to the script, they fell in love and got married.

When they were forced into temporary retirement because the partnership was about to be augmented into a trio, Kalmar decided to go into the song-publishing business, forming a partnership with fellow vaudevillian Harry Puck. It was at this time that the firm of Kalmar and Puck was approached by a young man who wrote song parodies and aspired to a job as a song plugger. Kalmar liked his work and hired him, but told him he was wasting his time writing lyrics. This initial association was short-lived. After Bert Kalmar Jr. arrived, Kalmar and his wife went back to headlining in vaudeville, and Ruby had to look for another job. This might have been the end of the team of Kalmar and Ruby before it ever got started if Kalmar hadn't had an accident that injured a knee and was once more forced into temporary retirement. At least, it was supposed to be temporary. He went back into songwriting, and this time was so successful he forgot about vaudeville.

Kalmar's first attempt at lyric writing was in 1911, a collaboration with veteran Ted Snyder on a ditty called *In the Land of Harmony,* but he did better with his partner Harry Puck in 1913 with *Where Did You Get That Girl?* A 1915 entry, written with a composer named Joe Cooper, still surfaces now and then as a novelty offering by dixieland bands, *I've Been Floating Down the Old Green River (On the Good Ship Rock 'n Rye*). His first song with Harry Ruby was *What a Girl Can Do,* for the 1918 Broadway show "Babies First," which also featured songs by the Gershwins. It was an inauspicious beginning, but a portent of better things to come. Kalmar and Ruby went on to compose the music for a number of Broadway shows, including "Animal Crackers" and "Five O'Clock Girl," and for an even greater number of movies. Whether by accident or deliberate intent, they seemed to specialize in films that starred famous comedians. For example, they wrote the score for *The Cuckoos,* which starred the comedy team of Wheeler and Woolsey; *Check and Double Check,* the Amos and Andy movie from which came the all-time standard *Three Little Words; The Kid from Spain,* an Eddie Cantor flick; and *A Night at the Opera,* with the Marx Brothers.

Kalmar also worked with other composers, including Ted Synder, Oscar Hammerstein II, Herbert Sothart, Harry Tierney, Harry Akst, Con Conrad, Edgar Leslie, Fred Ahlert, and Pete Wendling. His best-known songs are *Who's Sorry Now; Three Little Words; Nevertheless; Oh, What a Pal Was Mary; I Wanna be Loved by You;* and *I Love You So Much.*

Bert Kalmar died in Los Angeles, California, on September 18, 1947.

Bronislaw Kaper

Composer Bronislaw Kaper, best known for his scores for Hollywood movies, starting in the mid-thirties, was born in Warsaw, Poland, February 5, 1902. He received his education at the Warsaw Conservatory of Music and before coming to this country led an active career as a conductor and composer in the major cities of Europe. In the process of writing scores and background music for movies, he managed to write a respectable number of popular songs, collaborating with Walter Jurmann, Gus Kahn, and Paul Francis Webster.

You're All I Need, written for the 1935 movie *Escapade,* had lyrics by Gus Kahn. Walter Jurmann assisted with the music. It was recorded by the

Dorsey Brothers Orchestra shortly before their historic break-up and then by the Ted Fio Rito organization. More important at the time, it was accorded solid radio play. In the following year the same team produced the title song for the movie *San Francisco.* It was introduced in the film by Jeannette MacDonald. Later reincarnations included the 1943 musical "Hello, Frisco, Hello," with a chorus singing it; part of the background music in *Nob Hill,* a 1945 film; and the Gus Kahn film biography *I'll See You in My Dreams* in 1952. *All God's Chillun Got Rhythm* was a 1937 entry by the same trio of collaborators, and it was introduced by Ivy Anderson and a chorus in the Marx Brothers movie *A Day at the Races.* Anderson also recorded it, along with a veritable "Who's Who" of the music business of the day: Judy Garland (her debut recording); Bunny Berigan; Fletcher Henderson; Duke Ellington; and Artie Shaw, among others.

Kaper continued to write for films without a let-up, but a decade went by before he wrote the song that is probably his best, *On Green Dolphin Street,* an adaptation of the theme from the film *Green Dolphin Street,* a beautiful melody with words added by Ned Washington. A contemporary recording was made by the Jimmy Dorsey Orchestra, and Ralph Marterie, the fine Chicago trumpeter, chose it for his debut recording in high-fidelity. Oddly enough, the ballad took on a new character as interpreted by musicians playing in the style called bop, with accelerated tempo and improvisations on the melody and the chord structure. *Hi Lili, Hi Lo,* with words by Helen Deutsch and music by Kaper, was introduced by Leslie Caron and Mel Ferrer in the movie musical *Lili* in 1952. A hit single record was made from the soundtrack album. Other popular compositions by Bronislaw Kaper include *Take My Love; Tomorrow Is Another Day; Just for Tonight; The Next Time I Care; Cosi-Cosa; Follow Me;* and *Somebody Up There Likes Me.*

Art Kassel

Bandleader-composer Art Kassel was born in Chicago, Illinois, on January 18, 1896. He attended the Chicago Art Institute and saw military service in World War I. Afterwards he worked music jobs in Chicago and formed his first big band in 1924. A very young Benny Goodman was an occasional sideman. Although Kassel always led a commercially styled orchestra, his earliest hit composition, *Sobbin' Blues,* for which he wrote both words and music in 1922, was an instant favorite with jazz bands, recorded by the King Oliver Creole Jazz Band and the New Orleans Rhythm Kings on contemporary platters and in later years by the bands of Bunny Berigan and Artie

Shaw. A couple of years later Kassel got together with Mel Stitzel, pianist with the New Orleans Rhythm Kings, and they wrote the novelty *Doodle Doo Doo,* which the bandleader adopted as his theme song until 1932. At that time he wrote another striking novelty, *Hell's Bells,* and it became his new theme. A very interesting instrumental, it was also recorded by the bands of Jimmie Lunceford and Clyde McCoy.

In the meantime, Kassel and Gus Kahn had a popular entry in 1930 called *Around the Corner*. The Kessel band featured it on radio, the big outlet of the day, and so did Rudy Vallee. *Don't Let Julia Fool Ya* was the combined effort of Kassel, Burke Bivens, and Jerome Brainin in 1941. A nice melody with clever lyrics, it resulted in a good record by Skinnay Ennis and his band. Other titles by Kassel include *You Never Say Yes; Oh What I Know about You; Pennsylvania Dutch; Silvery Moonlight; Chant of the Swamp; Beautiful One; Golden Wedding Day;* and *Bundle of Blue*.

Art Kassel died in Van Nuys, California, on February 3, 1965.

James Kendis

Another of the Tin Pan Alley pioneers, charter ASCAP member James Kendis was born in St. Paul, Minnesota, on March 9, 1883. He attended the St. Paul schools. At various times he headed his own publishing companies. As both lyricist and composer, he is associated with some of the oldest standards in the music business. One of these was the 1919 super-hit of its day, *I'm Forever Blowing Bubbles*. Writer credits for this song are listed as "words by Jean Kenbroven, and music by John W. Kellette." Kenbroven is a pseudonym made up of the combined names of James Kendis, James Brockman, and Nat Vincent as a compromise over contractual conflicts. Ben Selvin's Novelty Orchestra had the best-selling record. The song never quite died out, and it was used in two movies in later years, *The Great American Broadcast* (1941) and *On Moonlight Bay,* as sung by Jack Smith (1951).

This wasn't the first successful song by Kendis, however. In 1910 he collaborated with lyrics writer Alfred Bryan and composer Herman Paley on *Angel Eyes,* which vocalist Billy Murray recorded on a popular Victor offering; and in 1913 he wrote the music, and Lou Klein the words, for *If I Had My Way*. The Peerless Quartet had the contemporary record, but the tune came roaring back in 1940 as the title song of the Bing Crosby film *If I Had My Way*. It also rated outstanding arranging by Ray Noble on a recording for Columbia that year. In fact, it did so well that it was included in another movie, *Sunbonnet Sue,* in 1945. *Feather Your Nest,* with words and music by Kendis,

Brockman, and Howard Johnson, came out in 1920. It got off to a good start as featured by the Duncan Sisters in the stage musical "Tip Top." It still surfaces occasionally. In 1924 Kendis introduced his new novelty song on radio. It had the interesting if misleading title *When It's Nightime in Italy, It's Wednesday Over Here* and was well received.

James Kendis died in Jamaica, New York, on November 15, 1946.

Charles Kenny

Charles Kenny broke into the songwriting business in 1931. Along with brother Nick, he wrote *Love Letters in the Sand,* a solid hit and perennial favorite. He was born in Astoria, New York, June 23, 1898, attended public schools, and then went to Longuelle College in Montreal. He majored in music at McGill University and while in the navy started writing shows for the battleship he was serving on. Back in civilian life he wrote material for Mills Music and Berlin & Feist, toured in vaudeville, wrote for more shows, and performed in some.

Love Letters in the Sand was a big success, and by a strange coincidence was recorded by Benny Goodman and an all-star jazz group for Columbia (2540D). However, the Kenny brothers made no pretense of writing jazz. They were only interested in the commercial aspect of songwriting, and succeeding titles reflect this attitude—*Every Minute of the Hour; Carelessly; Little Old Cathedral in the Pines; There's a Gold Mine in the Sky;* etc. A song a bit better than the others came out in 1939 and was made memorable on an outstanding record by Jan Savitt's band with Bon Bon singing the lyrics, *Running Through My Mind* (Decca 2614). After that came *Dream Valley; Make Believe Island; Violins Are Playing; Beyond the Purple Hill; Scattered Toys*—none of which made any great impression—and then in 1950, a final and quite respectable hit, *Gone Fishin'*. Most of Charles Kenny's songs were written with brother Nick, but from time-to-time he also teamed with others, including J. Fred Coots, Tommy Dennis, and Frank Perkins.

Nick Kenny

Songwriter-newspaperman Nick Kenny was born in Astoria, New York, on February 3, 1895. He was educated at Columbia University, and served in the navy during WW I. Early in his career he worked as a newspaper reporter and then became "radio editor" of the long-defunct *Daily Mirror,* a New York tabloid newspaper. He wrote a daily column, dabbled in homespun poetry, and even performed on radio shows—including an early amateur show. All of his songs were written in collaboration with his brother, Charles Kenny, including their first and most enduring hit, *Love Letters in the Sand.* Kenny's lyrics were characterized by heavy nostalgia mixed with strong sentiment, as evidenced in the titles to his songs. These include *There's a Gold Mine in the Sky; It's a Lonely Trail; Little Skipper; Every Minute of the Hour; Dream Valley; Make Believe Island; Beyond the Purple Hills; Drop Me Off in Harlem; Laughing at Life; Little Old Cathedral in the Pines; While a Cigarette Was Burning; When You're Traveling All Alone; Running Through My Mind; Leanin' on the Old Top Rail; Carelessly; A Letter From Home; Violins Were Playing; Paradise Valley; Save Me a Dream;* and his last title, which had a wide appeal, *Gone Fishin'.*

Walter Kent

Walter Kent, who had a number of successful songs in the thirties and early forties, both as a composer and lyricist, was born in New York City on November 29, 1911. He was educated at CCNY and studied at Juilliard on a scholarship. He took advanced violin lessons from Leopold Aver and Samuel Gardner and for a while led his own orchestra in theaters and on radio. He went to Hollywood as a freelance composer and wrote for films, including the score for Disney's *Johnny Appleseed,* which won the Critic's Circle Award.

His first important song is probably *Pu-leeze, Mr. Hemingway,* published in 1932. He collaborated on the words with Milton Drake to the melody by Abner Silver. The song was moderately successful in the United States but did even better in England, where it was recorded by Ambrose and His Orchestra, the top band of the time. In 1936 Kent and Richard Jerome did rather well with *Love Is Like a Cigarette.* Louis "King" Garcia and his jazz group recorded it for Bluebird, and the Riley–Farley Onyx Club Boys followed suit for Decca. But Kent and his partners hit their stride with the advent of the forties.

First came the 1941 entry *(There'll Be Bluebirds Over) The White Cliffs of Dover,* with words by Nat Burton and music by Walter Kent. Published during this bleak year of World War II, it struck a sympathetic response in the American public's hope and belief in the ultimate victory of the Allies and the survival of Britain. The song made it to *Your Hit Parade* for seventeen weeks and was in the number one spot six times. All the recordings did well, and it was covered on every label—Kay Kyser on Columbia, Glenn

Miller on Bluebird, Sammy Kaye on Victor, and Jimmy Dorsey on Decca. Kate Smith vocalized it on Columbia. However, for sheer staying power, the song that will probably be Kent's most memorable contribution to our musical heritage is the 1943 *I'll Be Home for Christmas*. On this, he collaborated with Kim Gannon and Buck Ram. Bing Crosby's recording sold over a million copies. With so many of the country's men in the service, the pleasant melody, coupled with words that expressed the thoughts of both the men away and those at home, had a wide appeal. And that basic feeling has withstood the test of time. The song has become a staple offering during the Christmas holiday season and for several years has been played as background music for an Anheuser–Busch TV commercial.

With the war years over, Kent and "By" Dunham combined on a tune that helped singer Frankie Laine in his rise to popular success. *Ah! But It Happened*. This 1948 entry was followed by another in 1950, also featured and recorded by Laine, *I'm Gonna Live Till I Die,* a collaboration with Al Hoffman and Mann Curtis. Walter Kent wrote the music and Kim Gannon the lyrics for the score of the stage show "Seventeen" in 1951. None of the songs were hits. Since Kent was a successful architect, it's very possible the waning market for good songs discouraged him from any further writing. Other titles to his credit include *Mama, I Wanna Make Rhythm; Isle of Pines; Once and for All; When the Roses Bloom Again; For Whom the Bell Tolls; Too Much in Love; Endlessly; The Last Mile Home;* and *I'm Gonna Cross My Fingers*.

Jack King

Jack (Albert) King was born in Tacoma, Washington, on May 6, 1903. He studied music abroad and toured Europe as a concert pianist, making his debut as a child prodigy at age ten and playing concerts until he was twenty-one. He performed as assistant director of the University of California Glee Club early in his career and then went on to tour in vaudeville and appear in nightclubs. Although King's song credits are limited, he was responsible for one of those songs that every other songwriter wistfully compliments with the words "I wish I wrote that." The song is the great standard *How Am I to Know?,* graced with lyrics by Dorothy Parker and introduced in 1929 by Russ Columbo in the movie *Dynamite*. Years later (1951) Ava Gardner sang it in the film musical *Pandora and the Flying Dutchman*. But more important are the outstanding instrumental recordings made through the years. Among these is a 1938 Victor record (25870) by Larry Clinton's Orchestra featuring a classic solo by tenor sax player Tony Zimmers. Another is the

Benny Goodman Sextet version recorded for Columbia in 1952, released on LP CL552. This exceptional side enjoyed an extensive reprise as background for a TV commercial in 1995. Smith Ballew had one of the early recordings, a good one, on OKeh; Glenn Miller, Stan Kenton, and Tommy Dorsey all waxed the song at one time or another.

For the 1930 movie *Paramount on Parade,* which featured over forty-five stars and music by several composers, King contributed *Any Time's the Time to Fall in Love,* with words by Elsie Janis. A good song, it was overlooked in this country but accorded respectful treatment by the New Mayfair Orchestra on HMV in England. In 1935 King teamed with Harold Adamson and Edwin H. Knopf on *Everything's Been Done Before,* a superior tune that was introduced in the film *Reckless,* with Virginia Verrill's voice dubbed in for the star, Jean Harlow. Freddy Martin and Guy Lombardo had contemporary sides, but after Art Jarrett took over leadership of the Hal Kemp band, following Kemp's tragic death in an automobile accident, he recorded the tune for Victor in 1941 and then adopted it as the band's theme. Other titles attributed to King are *Paramount on Parade; I'm True to the Navy Now; You Still Belong to Me; Live and Love Today; All I Know Is You're in My Arms.*

Jack King died in Hollywood, California, October 26, 1943.

Wayne King

Wayne King, well-known to radio audiences of the thirties as the "Waltz King," was born in Savannah, Illinois, on February 16, 1901. He was educated at Valparaiso University. Early in his career he played professional football and worked as a garage mechanic and an insurance salesman. A fair clarinetist, he played with the Del Lampe Orchestra in Chicago and then organized his own. Specializing in waltzes, the band was a fixture at the Aragon Ballroom for nine years, made a number of recordings, and was heard frequently on the radio.

King shares credit with Egbert Van Elstyne and Victor Young for composing the music to the 1931 waltz *Beautiful Love*. Haven Gillespie wrote the lyrics. This was Van Elstyne's last hit song, but the second one for Victor Young, who already had *Sweet Sue* to his credit. The song was introduced by Wayne King and recorded by James Melton for Columbia and Lewis James for Victor. In 1934 Victor Young finally got around to recording it with his orchestra on Decca, with Donald Novis as the vocalist. Pianist Art Tatum also made two takes of the song for Decca that year. Both were released as Decca 306.

The Waltz You Saved for Me was the theme song of the Wayne King Orchestra. Gus Kahn wrote the words, and King and Emil Flindt the music. King recorded it for Victor in 1930 and promoted it with frequent airtime on the radio. In the category of waltzes it has become a standard. In 1933 the King organization recorded a song from the Kate Smith movie *Hello, Everybody*. It was called *Twenty Million People* and was written by Arthur Johnston and Sam Coslow, who also contributed the wonderful *Moon Song* to the same film. The King recording was straightforward until the last chorus, at which point arranger Burke Bivens provided a delightful paraphrase of the melody. Four years later the arrangement reemerged as a new composition with words by Gus Kahn, with King and Burke Bivens sharing composing credit. In its reincarnation it was called *Josephine*. The King Orchestra recorded it, and it became the best-selling record they ever had. In addition, the song drew the attention of top recording artists, including Benny Goodman, Tommy Dorsey, Adrian Rollini (with Bobby Hackett), Milt Herth, and Frankie Froeba. Other compositions by King include *That Little Boy of Mine; Goofus; Blue Hours; Annabelle; Baby Shoes; With You Beside Me; So Close to Me; Corn Silk;* and *I'd Give My Kingdom for a Smile*.

Wayne King died on July 16, 1985.

Raymond Klages

Lyricist Raymond Klages was born in Baltimore, Maryland, on June 10, 1888. He was educated at Baltimore City College. In his early years he performed in minstrels and road shows and toured in vaudeville. He also wrote special material. During World War I he served in the field artillery. After the war he followed in the footsteps of many budding songwriters and went to work as a staff writer for a New York music publisher. He began writing in the early twenties.

In collaborating with many of the top composers, including J. Fred Coots, Louis Alter, Jesse Greer, Al Hoffman, Vincent Rose, and James V. Monaco, Klages wrote a variety of songs, ranging from novelty to beautiful ballads. One of his earliest efforts was the 1928 hit *Doin' the Raccoon,* written with J. Fred Coots, a musical comment on the college boy fad for raccoon coats. The song was popular on the radio and was recorded by George Olsen's Orchestra. It was also waxed for the inexpensive Harmony label by the upcoming crooning bandleader Rudy Vallee. *Blue Shadows,* one of those forgotten gems of the era, was one of two tunes by Klages and Louis Alter for the stage show "Earl Carroll's Vanities of 1928." The other title was *Once in a Lifetime*. The Johnny Hamp band recorded *Blue Shadows;* Johnny Johnson's Orchestra and the California Ramblers made *Once in a Lifetime*.

Klages moved on to Hollywood and in 1929 combined with Jesse Greer to produce the great standard *Just You, Just Me* for the movie *Marianne*. "Ukulele Ike," Cliff Edwards, had a popular contemporary recording. However, from the musical standpoint, the best record was by Smith Ballew's Orchestra, taking advantage of the superior quality of the OKeh recordings of the time. Other contemporary recordings were made by Johnny Johnson, Seger Ellis, and the California Ramblers. The song has enjoyed a long and illustrious career. In 1957 it was used in the movie musical *This Could Be the Night* and again in the 1977 picture *New York, New York*. Most important, it is a favorite of musicians, so it still gets frequently played and recorded.

Vincent Rose wrote the music, and Klages and Jack Meskill the words, for *Pardon Me, Pretty Baby,* a successful entry in 1931. The bands of Freddie Rich and Sam Lanin had concurrent records, but the most unique was the OKeh by Joe Venuti and his "Blue Four" (Venuti, Jimmy Dorsey, Frank Signorelli, and Eddie Lang), which featured a vocal by songwriter Harold Arlen. With the advent of the thirties and the trend to more melodic and sophisticated songs, Klages had two outstanding numbers in 1933. For the delightfully rhythmic *Roll Up the Carpet,* he not only wrote the words, but contributed to the melody line along with Al Hoffman and Al Goodhart. The song received classic treatment by Ray Noble's New Mayfair Orchestra with Al Bowlly on the vocal, and the recording was released both in England and the United States. The second title, *It Might Have Been a Diff'rent Story,* was composed by James V. Monaco, and Raymond Klages collaborated with Jack Meskill on the lyrics. Richard Himber recorded it for Victor, with Joey Nash on the vocal; Hal Kemp made it for Brunswick, with Skinnay Ennis singing.

It All Begins and Ends With You came out in 1936, a cooperative production by Raymond Klages, pianist-bandleader Frankie Froeba, and Jack Palmer. Froeba gave it a nice rendition on Columbia with a jazz band that included Bunny Berigan and Joe Marsala; and Red Norvo followed suit on Brunswick, with an arrangement by Eddie Sauter and Mildred Bailey on the vocal. With timely nicety Klages and Felix Bernard commemorated Uncle Sam's effort to build a citizen's army with *Twenty-One Dollars A Day—Once a Month*. It struck a responsive chord, you might say. Other songs by Klages include *Kiss by Kiss; I Wonder Why; Something in Here; Time Will Tell* (all for the stage show "Sally, Irene, and Mary," 1922); *Climbing up the Ladder of Love; One Step to Heaven; Low Down Rhythm;* and *Tonight or Never*.

Raymond Klages died in Glendale, California, on March 20, 1947.

John Klenner

Information is very scarce about pianist-composer-lyricist John Klenner. It is known that he was born in Germany, February 24, 1899, and that he died in New York City on August 13, 1955. In between those events he found time to write some excellent songs, in some cases composing the music, in others writing the words. Most likely his first successful song was the 1928 offering called *Japansy*. Klenner wrote the music for this one, and Alfred Byran the words. It rated top-notch attention as recorded by Guy Lombardo for Columbia, Johnny Hamp for Victor, and Jimmie Noone for Decca. In the following year Klenner and bandleader Rudy Vallee combined on *I'm Still Caring,* which the Connecticut Yankees dutifully recorded and plugged on radio broadcasts. Then Klenner reverted to the role of lyricist. With composer Pete Wendling he wrote *Crying Myself to Sleep,* a rather unhappy ditty that was recorded by the bands of Bert Lown and Ben Bernie, and with orchestra leader Nat Shilkret penned the words to the waltz *Down the River of Golden Dreams*. Both songs were published in 1930.

Moderately successful up to this point, Klenner changed hats again and wrote the music for *Just Friends,* with Sam M. Lewis adding the words. This 1931 song had instant appeal to the top vocalists of the day, and they all rushed to record the pretty song with the wistful words. It was introduced by Red McKenzie on Columbia, Russ Columbo made it for Victor and featured it on radio, Morton Downey waxed it for Perfect, and Art Jarrett recorded for Brunswick. Other contemporary discs were recorded by the bands of Jack Denny and Ben Selvin. Now a standard, it has been revived by Glen Gray and others on more recent recordings but has also undergone a strange metamorphosis. From being a ballad played in a slow or moderate tempo, it has been transformed by modern jazz musicians into a fast-paced vehicle for improvisation. In that same momentous year Klenner once again became a lyricist and with Al Hoffman wrote *Heartaches*. (*See* Al Hoffman.) Off to a fair start and then dormant for years, it came alive again in 1947 to the great benefit of all concerned.

It appears that in 1932 Klenner made a trip to England, where he collaborated with two gentlemen named Praeger and Quinto on the writing of a delightful tune called *With Love in My Heart*. It was published by the British firm of Campbell and Connolly, and Ray Noble, who never failed to appreciate a good song, recorded it for HMV. While it was not a big seller on its release, latter-day critics have come to appreciate the semi-hot jazz treatment of Noble's arrangement. In 1937 Klenner worked with Lloyd Shaffer and Ted Steele on a song that became the theme of the radio show called *The*

Chesterfield Supper Club. The song, *Smoke Dreams,* was introduced on the program by Jo Stafford, who also recorded it for Capitol. Other songs by John Klenner are *Window of Dreams; Don't Cry, Little Sweetheart; On the Street of Regrets;* and *Driftwood on the River*.

Johnny Kluczko (Johnny Watson)

Johnny Kluszko, arranger and composer who worked under the professional name of Johnny Watson, was born in Newark, New Jersey, on September 24, 1912. His education included graduating from the Curtis Music Institute in Philadelphia. Watson is only credited with cowriting three songs but has the unique standing of writing three hits. With lyricist Harold Adamson and bandleader Jan Savitt, he wrote two of the band's biggest hits, both in 1940. They are *It's a Wonderful World* and *720 in the Books*. The Savitt recordings, with vocalist Bon Bon Tunnell, were best-sellers and helped establish the band as a successful unit. Both songs have attained semistandard status. A short time later Johnny Watson moved on to join the newly organized Vaughn Monroe Orchestra as arranger and director, and early in 1941 the band recorded *Racing With the Moon,* with a melody by Watson, Vaughn Monroe sharing lyric credit with Pauline Pope. Again, the record was a big one for the band, and Monroe adopted it as his theme.

Johnny Watson died in Las Vegas, Nevada, on March 23, 1977.

Ted Koehler

Ted Koehler, one of the most prolific lyricists in the songwriting business, was born in Washington, D.C., on July 14, 1894. He was educated in the public schools and then trained in the highly skilled trade of photoengraving. But this, it would appear, failed to appeal to him, and he gave it up to play piano in theaters. He wrote special material for vaudeville and Broadway performers and pioneered in the plugging of songs in the better theaters. In his spare time he produced floor shows for nightclubs.

He started writing early in the twenties and had several successful songs, but it wasn't until the decade was almost over that he devoted himself to it full time. As it is, few writers would be able to point to a more consistent series of hit songs. Koehler really hit full stride in his collaborations with composer Harold Arlen; some of his nicest songs were also written with others.

A prime example of this is his first published song, *Dreamy Melody,* a collaboration with Frank Magine and C. Naset that came out in 1922. A waltz, it has the dreamy quality that Koehler mentions in the title, and it sold a lot of records for Art Landry's Orchestra, which recorded it on Gennett. The following year, Koehler and Gus Kahn combined on the words for the Ted Fio Rito song *When Lights Are Low,* which was featured and recorded by the Fio Rito Orchestra. In 1929 Frank Magine composed a delightful melody, and Koehler added the title and words. *Baby—Oh Where Can You Be?* was one of the better entries for the year and received thorough representation on records. Rudy Vallee was especially fond of the tune, plugging it on radio broadcasts and recording it for Victor. Among others it was waxed by Lou Gold, Dick Robertson, Sam Lanin, Fats Waller, and the Dorsey Brothers.

The association with composer Harold Arlen began in 1930 with Arlen's first hit song, *Get Happy*. Robert Lissauer relates how the song came to be written. Arlen was subbing as a rehearsal pianist for the Vincent Youmans musical "Great Day." He got tired of using the same two-bar vamp to start the musical numbers and began to improvise and experiment with a new approach. In the process, he created a new song. Koehler added lyrics, and as *Get Happy* he was able to have it included in a show called "Nine-fifteen Revue." The show was a flop, but Ruth Etting's rendition of the song was a hit. The tune went into the standard column many years ago and has been played and recorded countless times. It has also been featured in a number of movies. Koehler and Arlen were just getting warmed up. That same year they began writing for the revues staged at the Harlem nightspot the Cotton Club, and for the show "Rhythmania" contributed *Between the Devil and the Deep Blue Sea*. It was introduced in the show by Aida Ward. Like many other of the Arlen–Koehler songs, this one quickly became a favorite of the "hot" jazz fraternity. It has been recorded frequently over the years, including sides by Dick McDonough, Benny Goodman, the Boswell Sisters, Ben Selvin, Dicky Wells, Frankie Trumbauer, Teddy Wilson, Bob Zurke—and that's just a sampling.

Kickin' the Gong Around and *I Love a Parade* were both Koehler-Arlen songs introduced and recorded by Cab Calloway, from the 1931 edition of "Rhythmania." In 1932 Harry Richman sang *I Love a Parade* in "George White's Music Hall Varieties" and recorded it for Columbia. Movie star Winnie Lightner sang it in the film *Manhattan Parade*. The great standard *I Gotta Right to Sing the Blues* was introduced in the 1932 (tenth edition) "Earl Carroll's Vanities." Another favorite of jazz musicians, it became the theme song of Jack Teagarden's band and was recorded by Teagarden, Louis Armstrong, and a host of other people.

Koehler and Harold Arlen were "on a roll," as the saying goes. Every song they wrote was a success. In the meantime, Koehler took time out in 1931 to work with Billy Moll on polishing the lyrics to an outstanding song by Harry Barris, *Wrap Your Troubles in Dreams.* With a willing boost from Bing Crosby, this song was launched on a popular spiral that has never failed and, again, has been recorded many, many times.

The Cotton Club revues continued to promote Arlen–Koehler songs, and another title in 1932, tailored to the talent of Cab Calloway, was *Minnie the Moocher's Wedding Day.* As successful as Koehler and Arlen had been up to then, the best was still to come. In 1933, still writing for the Cotton Club, they had two blockbuster hits, *I've Got the World On a String,* introduced by Aida Ward in the revue "Cotton Club Parade," and *Stormy Weather.* The latter title was supposed to be for Cab Calloway, but when he was not in the 1933 edition, the song was passed on to Ethel Waters. But before the revue opened, Harold Arlen recorded the tune, singing with Leo Reisman's Orchestra, and it was an immediate hit. Nevertheless, the song has always been identified with Ethel Waters. *I've Got the World On a String,* a natural swinger, got off to a quick start with records by Bing Crosby, Louis Armstrong, and Cab Calloway. Like *Stormy Weather,* it long ago became a standard, has been recorded many times, and been performed steadily over the years. It was a favorite of Maxine Sullivan. *Happy as the Day is Long,* another song from the second edition of "The Cotton Club Parade," although not as big as the two just mentioned, was also a successful item and was recorded by a distinguished group. Duke Ellington, Fletcher Henderson, Adrian Rollini, and Joe Haymes all had good records.

Still riding high, in 1934 Koehler and Arlen came up with two more big ones for the Cotton Club, *As Long as I Live,* introduced by the beautiful, sixteen-year-old Lena Horne with Avon Long in the "Cotton Club on Parade," and *Ill Wind,* performed by Ada Ward in the revue and recorded for Victor by Harold Arlen. Both songs are standards. That same year Harold Arlen wrote his first song for a movie, with Koehler still adding the words. The song was *Let's Fall in Love.* Art Jarrett and Ann Sothern each sang it in the film of the same title, but that was just the beginning. Like a snowball rolling downhill, the tune went on to be performed in a long string of films and like the others, has become a standard.

Ted Koehler went on to collaborate with other composers. In 1936 he and Burton Lane wrote *Stop! You're Breakin' My Heart.* It was performed by Judy Canova and Ben Blue in the movie musical *Artists and Models,* and Hal Kemp, Claude Thornhill, and Maxine Sullivan had records. Then in the same year, Koehler teamed with Jimmy McHugh on *I'm Shooting High,* which was sung by Alice Faye in *King of Burlesque*. She also recorded it, and so did Louis Armstrong, Jan Garber, Lud Gluskin, Wingy Manone, and the Little Ramblers. Rube Bloom was the composer for the 1938 Koehler entry, *I Can't Face the Music (Without Singing the Blues),* a tune that was well received by some of the top names in the business, resulting in records by Mildred Bailey with Red Norvo's band, Nan Wynn with Teddy Wilson, June Richmond with Jimmy Dorsey, and Bea Wain with Larry Clinton. But Koehler and Bloom scored big with one in 1939, *Don't Worry 'Bout Me*. This one moved into the top ten and received diversified treatment on records by Count Basie, Horace Heidt, Bob Crosby, and Les Brown. Later sides were made by Teddy Wilson and by Zoot Sims, and the song promises to keep on going.

Koehler wrote the lyrics, and M. K. Jerome and Ray Heindorf the music, for the 1945 song *Some Sunday Morning*. It was introduced by Alexis Smith in the Errol Flynn movie *San Antonio* and was nominated for an Academy Award. Other Koehler titles include *Hittin' the Bottle; One Love; Tell Me With a Love Song; Music, Music, Everywhere; Stay on the Right Side of the Road; When Love Comes Swinging Along; Out in the Cold Again; The Simple Things in Life; Picture Me Without You; I've Got My Fingers Crossed; Too Good to Be True; When the Sun Comes Out; Sweet Dreams, Sweetheart;* and *Me and the Blues.*

Ted Koehler died in Santa Monica, California, on January 17, 1973.

Alex Charles Kramer

Alex Charles Kramer was born in Montreal, Quebec, on May 30, 1903. His education included private piano study with Dunev, Gardner, and Hungerford in Montreal. In his early years he played piano in dance bands and worked in nightclubs and hotels both home and abroad. For a time he was a vocal coach for singer Aileen Stanley then he led his own band, broadcasting on the Canadian network. With his wife and collaborator, Joan Whitney, he formed the Kramer–Whitney Inc. publishing company and the Whitney–Kramer–Zaret Music Co. As the above names imply, Kramer's working partners were usually Joan Whitney and Hy Zaret, with one exception we will get to shortly.

High on a Windy Hill, a descriptive ballad published in 1940, was the first hit song for Kramer and Whitney, and it met with kind acceptance, both on the airwaves and on recordings by Gene Krupa, Hal Kemp, Jimmy Dorsey, Vaughn Monroe, and Sammy Kaye. *So You're the One,* another title that same year, introduced Hy Zaret to the team, and again the song was well represented on recordings by Eddy Duchin for Columbia, Vaughn Monroe on Bluebird, and Hal Kemp on Victor, with the vocal by future movie star Janet

Blair. Off to a good start, the trio scored twice in 1941. *My Sister and I,* a title borrowed from the book by a Dutchman, Dirk von der Heide, who suffered from Nazi persecution, managed to hit number one on the weekly radio broadcast *Your Hit Parade* and resulted in top-selling records for Jimmy Dorsey, Bea Wain, Bob Chester, and Benny Goodman. The other song, *It All Comes Back to Me Now,* also scored in the top five for the year and again was recorded on every major label, with sides by Hal Kemp, Ted Weems (with Perry Como), Gene Krupa, and Eddy Duchin.

Mack David came aboard in 1944 in place of Hy Zaret, and the result was the sensational *Candy,* which has since become a standard. It was a great record for Johnny Mercer and for Jo Stafford and the Pied Pipers on Capitol, also for Dinah Shore, Johnny Long, and the King Sisters. Then, as though to prove they didn't need outside help, Kramer and Whitney came up with *Love Somebody,* a 1944 entry that was a top-seller on Columbia as performed by the duet of Doris Day and Buddy Clark. And in case somebody might consider this a fluke of chance, in 1949 they wrote *Far Away Places,* which spent nineteen weeks on *Your Hit Parade,* three of them as number one. Top ten records were turned out by Bing Crosby, Margaret Whiting, Perry Como, and Dinah Shore. The "Age of the Vocalists" had arrived. Other songs by Alex Kramer include *No Man Is an Island; Ain't Nobody Here but Us Chickens; It's Love, Love, Love; Money Is the Root of All Evil; That's the Beginning of the End; Curiosity; Why Is It?;* and *You'll Never Get Away.*

Zoe Parenteau Kramer (Joan Whitney)

Zoe Kramer, better known under her professional name of Joan Whitney, was born in Pittsburgh, Pennsylvania, on June 25, 1914. She is the daughter of composer Zoel Parenteau. Her education included Carnegie Tech in Pittsburgh and Finch College in New York. During her prolific career as a performer, she recorded with the bands of Leo Reisman, Will Osborne, and Enric Madriguera; appeared in the Broadway musical "The Great Waltz"; and had her own show on the CBS network. For a time she worked as a staff writer for Sun Music. Later she and husband Alex Kramer formed their own publishing companies. As outlined in the profile of Alex Kramer, they collaborated on a number of hit songs, sometimes working with Hy Zaret and Mack David. In addition to the titles attributed to Alex Kramer, Joan Whitney also has the following to her credit: *That's the Beginning of the End; Behave Yourself; Summer Rain; I Only Saw Him Once; The Way That the Wind Blows; Comme Ci, Comm Ça; Before I Loved You.*

Emanuel (Manny) Kurtz (Mann Curtis)

Manny Kurtz, who used the professional name Mann Curtis, was born in Brooklyn, New York, on September 15, 1911. He attended high school in Brooklyn and the Brooklyn Evening College. His early experience as a lyricist was as a staff writer for Vitaphone Studios. In a long and prolific career, Kurtz teamed with other composers for some excellent songs. One of these is the great Duke Ellington composition *In A Sentimental Mood,* published in 1936. Kurtz shared the mandatory credit for the lyrics with Irving Mills. Another was recorded by Fats Waller for Bluebird, *You Meet the Nicest People in Your Dreams,* a collaboration with Al Goodhart and Al Hoffman. The recording demonstrates that the tune deserved more attention than it received.

Al Hoffman and Jerry Livingston were Kurtz's partners for *The Story of a Starry Night,* a successful adaptation of Tchaikovsky's *Pathétique*. The 1942 song was a best-seller for the Glenn Miller Orchestra. Then in 1944 Kurtz got together with composer-arranger Vic Mizzy, and the result was *The Whole World Is Singing My Song,* which was accorded appropriate attention by Doris Day with Les Brown's band. Bob Eberle and Jimmy Dorsey recorded it too. Kurtz and Vic Mizzy came right back the next year with the delightful *My Dreams Are Getting Better All the Time,* which was introduced by Marion Hutton in the Abbott and Costello film *In Society*. Les Brown and Doris Day again had the best-selling record, with others by Johnny Long and the Phil Moore Four.

The team even made it into the forlorn fifties with *The Jones Boy,* a 1954 hit recording for the Mills Brothers on Decca. But not content with that, Mann Curtis (as he now called himself) worked with veteran Harry Akst on the English lyrics to an Italian song, *Anema e Core* (*With All My Heart and Soul*). The Italian words were by Tito Manlio, and the music by Salve d'Esposito. It was introduced in the Italian movie of the same title by Ferrucio Tagliavini. Eddie Fisher had the big-selling record in English. Other songs with lyrics by Manny Kurtz are *Let It Be Me; I'm Gonna Live Till I Die; Romance Runs in the Family; I Ups to Her and She Ups to Me; My Summer Colors; One Pair of Hands; I'm Still Not Thru Missing You; Pretty Kitty Blue Eyes; Look Out I'm Romantic; Did 'Ja Ever; Apple Blossoms and Chapel Bells; Play Me Hearts and Flowers;* and *A Prairie Fairy Tale*.

Burton Lane

Composer Burton Lane was born in New York City on February 2, 1912. He studied piano and composing, and his talent developed so quickly that at age fifteen he was working as a staff writer for Remick Music. After a rather small start as a composer, with the submission of two unimportant titles to the stage show "Three's a Crowd," he placed three songs in "Earl Carroll's Vanities of 1931"—*Love Came into My Heart; Heigh Ho! The Gang's All Here;* and *Have a Heart*. All had lyrics by Harold Adamson. Lane had still another in the 1932 musical "Americana." The last song had the provocative title *You're Not Pretty, but You're Mine.*

But 1933 was the turning point, and Lane had the hit song in the score for the movie *Dancing Lady,* which starred Clark Gable and Joan Crawford. The tune, *Everything I Have Is Yours,* has become a semistandard, to say the least, and it outclassed contributions to the movie by Rodgers and Hart and Jimmy McHugh and Dorothy Fields. Lane also did well with a freelance entry that year, *Tony's Wife,* a rumba. In 1934 Lane and Harold Adamson had two good songs in the film *Bottoms Up, Little Did I Dream* and *Turn On the Moon,* but for the next two years he returned to the freelance market and did rather well with three respectable titles: *Beyond the Shadow of a Doubt* (a solo effort); *Guess Who* (lyrics by Ralph Freed); and *'Taint't No Use* (with words by Herb Magidson). Benny Goodman fans may recall the comment on the label for Victor 25469: "Apologetically sung by Benny Goodman." In reference to the latter title, it seemed very appropriate.

A rash of titles for Hollywood movies appeared in 1937, none too impressive, but in 1938 Lane and Frank Loesser came up with *Says My Heart* for the movie *Cocoanut Grove,* starring Fred MacMurray and Harriet Hilliard. Then for *College Swing,* a feature starring Burns & Allen, Bob Hope, and former Hal Kemp drummer-vocalist Skinnay Ennis, Lane and Loesser contributed the outstanding *Moments Like This,* along with another good song, *Howd'ja Like to Love Me*. The year 1939 was memorable for the movie *Some Like It Hot* (not to be confused with the later film starring Marilyn Monroe, Jack Lemmon, and Tony Curtis), a Bob Hope epic that also featured the Gene Krupa Orchestra, and presented songwriter Harry Barris in a character role. Burton and Loesser contributed the title song, along with the excellent *The*

Lady's in Love With You. This time the Burton song got kinder treatment on a Benny Goodman recording, with the vocal by Martha Tilton.

In the forties Lane continued to write for shows and movies; some of his better songs include *I Hear Music; How About You; Poor You;* and *I'll Take Tallulah.* In 1947 he and E. Y. Harburg wrote the score for the hit show "Finian's Rainbow," which included *How Are Things in Glocca Morra; Old Devil Moon; If This Isn't Love;* and *When I'm Not Near the Girl I.Love.* Following this, for some reason Lane was absent from the music scene until 1951. That year he and Alan Jay Lerner combined on a score for the movie *Royal Wedding,* which included two excellent songs, *Too Late Now* and *You're All the World to Me.* Lane teamed with Lerner again in 1965 for the show, "On a Clear Day You Can See Forever." The result was the outstanding title song (more so, since by this time quality songs had become a novelty) and *Come Back to Me.*

John Latouche

Lyricist John Latouche was born on November 13, 1917, in Richmond, Virginia. He was educated at the Richmond Academy of Arts and Sciences and Columbia University. Although his songwriting output wasn't extensive, he collaborated with composers of top caliber, such as Vernon Duke, Duke Ellington, and Bronislaw Kaper, resulting in his name on some important songs. Probably the best known of these are *Cabin in the Sky,* and *Taking a Chance on Love,* written with Vernon Duke for the 1940 stage production of "Cabin in the Sky." Both songs were introduced by Ethel Waters in the theater production. In the show she sang *Taking a Chance on Love* with Dooley Wilson (of *As Time Goes By* fame). In the 1943 movie she performed both songs with Eddie "Rochester" Anderson. *Taking a Chance on Love* made a big comeback, inspired by the movie, and was on *Your Hit Parade* for seventeen weeks. The two songs were heavily recorded.

In 1953 Latouche and Marvin Fisher composed a song with an aptly descriptive title, *Strange*; and in 1954 Latouche worked with composer Jerome Moross to produce the unusual ballad *Lazy Afternoon.* It was introduced by Kaye Ballard in the stage musical "The Golden Apple." Other songs with lyrics by John Latouche are *Honey in the Honeycomb; Love Turned the Light Out; So What You Wanna Do?; Yellow Flower; Summer Is A-comin' In; Tomorrow Mountain; Just for Tonight; It's the Going Home Together; Wind Flowers;* and *My Love Is on the Way.*

John Latouche died in Calais, Vermont, on August 7, 1956.

Vee Lawnhurst

Vee Lawnhurst, pianist, singer, teacher, and composer, was born in New York City on November 2, 1905. A member of the original "Roxy's Gang" and a pioneer in radio broadcasting, she was half of the well-known piano team of Muriel Pollack and Vee Lawnhurst. Eventually she would form a partnership with lyricist Tot Seymour that produced a number of excellent songs, but her first collaboration of importance was with Dave Dreyer and Lucy Bender Sokole, who contributed the words to the 1931 song *I'm Keepin' Company*. Rudy Vallee recorded it and promoted it on radio broadcasts. In 1933 Lawnhurst and Roy Turk combined on the plaintive *I Couldn't Tell Them What to Do,* with the articulate Eddie Stone explaining why on the Isham Jones recording for Victor and Will Osborne following suit on the American Record Company labels.

The partnership with Tot Seymour was a huge success from the start. In 1935 the team had a bundle of entries on the song market. Among these is the lilting *And Then Some,* recorded by the bands of Ozzie Nelson, Bob Crosby, and Joe Reichman, and *Accent on Youth,* the title song of a film starring Herbert Marshall and Sylvia Sidney. It was well recorded by the Orville Knapp band, fast making a name on the west coast, and the Duke Ellington Orchestra, featuring Johnny Hodges. Most songwriting teams would have been content with these winners, but just for good measure Lawnhurst and Seymour offered *An Evening in June,* a song as pleasant as the title implies. Victor Young's Orchestra recorded it for Decca. Still another title was *No Other One,* a sprightly ditty, with records by Bob Crosby, Little Jack Little, and Putney Dandridge, offset a little bit by the rather forlorn *When the Leaves Bid the Trees Goodbye*. Dick Messner waxed that one.

Billie Holiday recorded *Please Keep Me in Your Dreams,* a Lawnhurst–Seymour entry for 1936, and it was also made by the Al Donahue Orchestra and by George Hall with vocalist Dolly Dawn. *Cross Patch,* published in the same year, was recorded by Louis Prima and by Willie Bryant, both for Brunswick. In addition, there was *Us on a Bus,* graphically rendered on record by Fats Waller, as well as Rudy Vallee and Shep Fields; *What's the Name of That Song?*, well covered on the radio and on records by Ozzie Nelson and Bob Crosby; and *The Bride Comes Home*. The last title was recorded by the Hal Kemp band with a Skinnay Ennis vocal, and apparently Hal Kemp liked the song so well that he rerecorded it for another label years later, this time sung by Bob Allen. Boyd Bunch shared composing credit with Lawnhurst for *The Day I let You Get Away,* still another item in 1936. The bands of Isham Jones and Nat Shilkret, and Tommy Dorsey's Clambake Seven, all recorded it.

Lyricist Ed Heyman helped Tot Seymour with the words to *Alibi Baby,* the Lawnhurst tune published in 1937. Again Tommy Dorsey's Clambake Seven gave it a working over, with Edyth Wright singing. Not to be outdone, Dolly Dawn performed the same duty with George Hall, and so did Teddy Grace with Mal Hallett. In 1941 Vee Lawnhurst worked with Mack David on songs for the movie *Pot O' Gold,* and among them was the engaging *Do You Believe in Fairy Tales?* Freddy Martin recorded it for Bluebird.

Jack Lawrence

Not too long ago at a luncheon of the Sheet Music Society in Manhattan, I had the pleasure of hearing Jack Lawrence sing a program of his hit songs. He has a pleasant baritone voice and sings with professional assurance. As with most "and then I wrote" routines, he sang the songs the majority of the audience would remember, thereby leaving out some of his best. A Brooklyn boy, Lawrence was born there on April 7, 1912, and he attended Long Island University. In his early years he sang on the radio. In the thirties he started writing lyrics, and his first published entry was a collaboration with composer Arthur Altman and bandleader Emery Deutsch, *Play, Fiddle, Play.* It did pretty well in 1932, a year still revered for its great crop of songs. Emery Deutsch promoted it in broadcasts by his orchestra, and Arthur Tracy the "Street Singer," had a hit record.

Five years later Lawrence hit his stride, pairing with composer Peter Tinturin on *Big Boy Blue; Foolin' Myself* (a Teddy Wilson classic on Brunswick with Billie Holiday); *Have You Ever Been in Heaven;* and *What Will I Tell My Heart?* The latter title was a big hit for Bing Crosby on a Decca record backed by the Richard Whiting–Johnny Mercer top contender *Too Marvelous for Words.* Nothing outstanding took place in 1938, but the slack was well taken up the next year with *If I Didn't Care,* a blockbuster for the Ink Spots, with both words and melody by Lawrence. In addition he wrote the lyrics to Frankie Carle's *Sunrise Serenade* and to Hoagy Carmichael's *Vagabond Dreams.* This fine song never got the appreciation it deserves but enjoys a special niche in jazz history. It was recorded by singer Buddy Clark on the short-lived Varsity label, accompanied by Bud Freeman and His Summa Cum Laude Band. Another song, *All or Nothing at All,* a collaboration with Arthur Altman, came out that year, and it was recorded on Columbia by Harry James with the vocal by Frank Sinatra. It had to wait until 1943 and Sinatra's overnight surge to the top of popularity to become a hit.

Jack Lawrence wrote an outstanding lyric for Ted Shapiro's lovely ballad

A Handful of Stars in 1940, along with a song by a newcomer, Clara Edwards, *With the Wind and the Rain in Your Hair*. Then he scored another solo bulls-eye with *Yes, My Darling Daughter,* recorded by the bands of Benny Goodman, Gene Krupa, and Glenn Miller, but a smash side for vocalist Dinah Shore. Lawrence topped off the year with composers Guy Hall and Henry Kleinkof on *Johnson Rag,* and Jimmy Mundy and Eddie White on *So Far So Good*. The last rated nice jazz treatment on a recording for Decca by Bob Crosby's "Bob Cats." Lawrence continued to write well into the sixties, until the blight called rock 'n' roll ended the demand for good songs. He still managed to contribute some excellent titles: *Sleepy Lagoon,* a big hit for the Harry James band and a collaboration with Eric Coates; *Symphony,* a French song by Alex Alstone, for which Lawrence wrote an English lyric; *Tenderly,* the Walter Gross standard; *Delicado;* and *The Poor People of Paris*.

Turner Layton

Turner Layton isn't a name you will hear every day—just to overstate the situation. More than likely, unless you happen to be a song nut or a collector of old sheet music, you have never heard of this pioneer songwriter. Yet I'm willing to bet that you know several of his songs almost as well—as the saying goes—as your own name. Jazz bands have always had a leaning toward them. Among the better known, and all in the category of standards, are *After You've Gone; 'Way Down Yonder in New Orleans; Dear Old Southland;* and *Strut Miss Lizzie*. In most cases, Layton's songs were written with words by Henry Creamer, his long-term partner in vaudeville. As a team, they toured the United States. Layton also played very listenable piano, but since he only recorded in England, this aspect of his talent isn't well known in his homeland. On the other hand, it isn't every songwriter who can lay claim to four all-time hits, and Turner Layton deserves greater recognition. So the next time the band plays *After You've Gone,* try to remember Turner Layton.

Peggy Lee

Singer-actress-composer Peggy Lee was born Norma Jean Egstrom in Jamestown, North Dakota, on May 26, 1920. As a youngster she started her singing career in the church choir and over the radio station in Fargo, North Dakota. In the midthirties she toured with Jack Wardlaw's dance band and then put in some time singing in nightclubs. After she did more work in nightclubs, bandleader Will Osborne hired her in the latter part of 1941. She left early the next year to join a trio singing in Chicago's swank Ambassador East hotel. The next step was a big one: she took a new name and joined the Benny Goodman band. This involved recording and appearing with the band in movies and also resulted in the hit record *Why Don't You Do Right?* which attracted very favorable comment in 1942.

Early in 1943 she left Goodman to marry guitarist Dave Barbour. The following year they signed a contract with Capitol Records and proceeded to write and record songs together. Peggy's jazz-tinged, sultry delivery was nicely complemented by clever lyrics and the tastefully arranged orchestral backgrounds provided by Barbour. This formula proved highly successful, and they had several hit records—sometimes singing other songs besides their own but still maintaining a high standard for everything they did. Most likely the most successful of their songs was the novelty *Mañana (Is Soon Enough for Me),* which came out in 1948 and promptly sold over one million copies. They also scored well with *I Don't Know Enough About You* and *Just An Old Love of Mine.* Some other outstanding Lee–Barbour compositions include *I Love Being Here with You; What More Can a Woman Do?; You Was Right, Baby; Everything's Movin' Too Fast; Don't Be Mean to Me, Baby;* and *It's a Good Day.*

After her divorce from Dave Barbour, Peggy continued to write with others, including Cy Coleman and Victor Young.

Carolyn Paula Leigh

Lyricist Carolyn Paula Leigh was born in New York City on August 21, 1926. She was educated at Hunter College, Queens College, and New York University and started writing in 1951. This makes her a latecomer compared to most of the writers who have created our great heritage of quality songs, but thanks to people like Frank Sinatra, Tony Bennett, and Lucille Ball, who still recognized a good song when they heard one, she had a number of successful titles throughout the fifties, mostly in collaboration with pianist Cy Coleman. One of her biggest hits—also one of the earliest—was *Young at Heart,* a 1954 collaboration with composer Johnny Richards. Leigh wrote new words to a melody that Richards had written fifteen years earlier. With Nelson Riddle providing the arrangement and the background, Frank Sinatra's recording of the tune on Capitol sold over one million copies. Since one success deserves another, the familiar title was adapted to a movie starring Sinatra and Doris Day in 1955, with the singer performing the song at the beginning and the end of the film.

In 1958 Leigh teamed with Cy Coleman, and they turned out two songs that Tony Bennett promoted into hits, *Firefly* and *Witchcraft*. He followed through for them the following year, too, with his recording of *The Best Is Yet To Come*. Then in 1960 Lucille Ball and Paula Stewart sang *Hey Look Me Over* in the musical "Wild Cat," and again Leigh and Coleman had a winner. Sid Caesar also did his part, rendering *A Real Live Girl* in the stage show "Little Me" in 1962. Altogether, Leigh and Coleman had a respectable score. Other songs with lyrics by Carolyn Leigh include *Pass Me By: Step to the Rear; How Little We Know; I've Got Your Number; On the Other Side of the Tracks; Here's to Us; A Doodlin' Song; It Amazes me; I've Gotta Crow; I Won't Grow up; I'm Flying; Stay with Me;* and many more.

Alan Jay Lerner

Alan Jay Lerner, a native New Yorker, was born on August 31, 1918, and is best known for his collaboration with composer Frederick Leowe on the scores for Broadway shows, especially the long-running adaptation of George Bernard Shaw's play "Pygmalion" as the musical "My Fair Lady." Other big stage successes were "Brigadoon," "Paint Your Wagon," and "Camelot." Lerner's best-known songs include *Almost Like Being in Love; The Heather on the Hill; They Call the Wind Maria; I Could Have Danced All Night; On the Street Where You Live; Gigi; Thank Heaven for Little Girls;* and *On a Clear Day*. My personal favorite is *You're All the World to Me,* from the movie *Royal Wedding,* one of those gems that have a habit of being rediscovered and coming to light many years later. It merits a long future.

Samuel Manuel (Sammy) Lerner

Sammy Lerner was born in Saveni, Romania, on January 28, 1903. How and when he came to this country isn't clear, but he was educated in Detroit at the Central High School and then attended Wayne State University. He became a writer of special material for vaudeville acts and wrote original scripts and songs for Paramount shorts. As a lyricist, he wrote for Broadway shows, London stage productions, and movies. His collaborators read like a list of famous composers—Hoagy Carmichael, Irving Caesar, Abel Baer, Gerald Marks, Richard Whiting, Al Hoffman, Al Goodhart, Burton Lane, Ben Oakland, Jay Gorney, Dana Suesse, Al Skinner—so it only follows that his name is on some important songs.

How important it is may be debatable, but Lerner wrote the slightly daffy words to *The Pump Song,* a gem from 1926, in collaboration with Arthur (Buddy) Fields and Richard Whiting, made more significant by its subtitle, *It's Hard to Tell the Depth of the Well by the Length of the Handle on the Pump.* This deep thought was given serious attention by the comedy vocal team of Jones & Hare and by the orchestras of Ben Selvin and Irving Aaronson. Lerner redeemed himself somewhat with the 1929 song *In the Hush of the Night,* a very nice tune written with Al Hoffman and recorded by the all-star Ben Pollock band for Victor and by Lou Gold for the Plaza labels. In 1931 Lerner wrote the English lyrics to *Falling in Love Again,* with music by Frederick Hollander. Featured in the German film *The Blue Angel,* it launched the career of Marlene Dietrich and has always been associated with her.

The thirties made up a good decade for Lerner. In 1934 he and Hoagy Carmichael brought out the tantalizing *Judy*—tantalizing because Lerner produced two sets of lyrics. In one version the young lady is a rather heartless flirt; in the other she's every man's dream girl. In each instance the lyrics cleverly outline the lady's character to a typically exceptional Carmichael melody. He did it full justice with an all-star group on a recording for Victor, backing it with another of his compositions, *Moon Country.* It has become a standard, recorded many times through the years. The next year Lerner, Irving Caesar, and Gerald Marks came up with another timely suggestion: *Oh Suzanna (Dust Off That Old Pianna).* Although it's doubtful if anybody named Suzanna was involved, it rated immediate attention from the New Orleans Rhythm Kings on Decca, Fats Waller on Victor, Ozzie Nelson on Brunswick, and George Hall with Loretta Lee and Sonny Schuyler on Bluebird, an across-the board sweep. But this songwriting team was just warming up. In 1936 they came back with two entries, *I don't Know Your Name (But You're Beautiful)* and *Is It True What They Say About Dixie?* Red McKenzie recorded the first title, but Rudy Vallee and Al Jolson promoted the second into a best-seller. It surfaced again in 1943 in a movie starring Deanna Durbin, *His Butler's Sister,* and again in the 1949 epic *Jolson Sings Again.* For Sammy Lerner *I Promise You,* written with Ben Oakland and recorded by Ozzie Nelson, was a fitting finale for the thirties. He continued to write for the movies, even contributing *I'm Popeye the Sailor Man,* the celebrated salt's theme song. Other Lerner titles are *Saskatchewan; You'll Never Get Up to Heaven That Way; Ev'rybody's Laughing; Intrigue; Sittin' in the Sand A-Sunnin'; By the Sign of the Rose; Lord and Lady Whoozis; The Rhyming Song;* and *The Eyes of the World Are on You.*

Edgar Leslie

One of the most prolific lyricists in Tin Pan Alley history—especially during the Golden Era of the thirties—Edgar Leslie was born in Stamford, Connecticut, on December 31, 1885. He was educated at Cooper Union, New York, and in his early years wrote special material for vaudeville headliners Nat Wills, Belle Baker, Lew Dockstader, and others. He was a charter member of ASCAP and, in addition to writing for the stage and screen, went on to become a producer and a publisher. Leslie began his long career in 1909 with four published songs in collaboration with three different composers. Two of the titles were written by another aspiring songsmith, Irving Berlin, *I Didn't Go Home at All* and *Sadie Salome, Go Home!* With George W. Meyer he wrote *Lonesome* and with Al Piantadosi *'Way Down in Cotton Town.* Not a bad start by any measure, but just an appropriate introduction to a lifelong production that wound up in 1949 with the pretty ballad *Lost in a Dream,* a Rube Bloom composition.

In the meantime, lots of good music would be crammed into the years, as Leslie collaborated with many of the top composers of the era. In addition to those mentioned above, the eminent list includes Joe Burke, Fred Ahlert, Harry Ruby, James V. Monaco, Walter Donaldson, Harry Warren, Archie Gottler, Maurie Abrams, Joe Young, E. Ray Goetz, and Pete Wendling. As you would expect, work with men of such exceptional talent was bound to result in some well-known songs—along with some that have been forgotten—but even the casual listener will remember most of these: *He'd Have to Get Under—Get Out and Get Under* (a tribute to the automotive problems of 1913): *America, I Love You* (1915); *For Me and My Gal* (1917, revived in 1942); *Oh What a Pal Was Mary; Take Your Girlie to the Movies* (1919); *Watcha Gonna Do When There Ain't No Jazz?* (1920, and a dire prophecy); *Blue and Broken Hearted); On the Gin, Gin, Ginny Shore; Rose of the Rio Grande* (1922); *Among My Souvenirs* (1927); *Me and the Man in the Moon* (1928); *My Troubles Are Over; Reaching for Someone* (1929); *I Remember You From Somewhere; Kansas City Kitty; 'Tain't No Sin (To Take Off Your Skin and Dance Around in Your Bones); Reminiscing* (1930); *By the River Sainte Marie* (1931); *Crazy People; You've Got Me in the Palm of Your Hand; I'm Yours for Tonight* (1932); *I Wake Up Smiling* (1933); *And I Still Do; The Moon Was Yellow* (1934); *A Little Bit Independent; Moon Over Miami; On Treasure Island; The Girl I Left Behind Me* (1935); *Midnight Blue; Cling to Me: Robins and Roses* (1936); *Getting Some Fun Out of Life; It Looks Like Rain in Cherry Blossom Lane* (1937); *At a Perfume Counter; Sailing at Midnight; Somewhere with Somebody Else* (1938); *Rainbow Valley* (1939); *Lost in a Dream* (1949).

Oh, and by the way, Edgar Leslie was responsible for the classic lyrics to Al Piantadosi's *Where Was Moses When the Lights Went Out?*

Oscar Levant

Concert pianist, composer, actor, and author Oscar Levant was born in Pittsburgh, Pennsylvania, on December 2, 1906. He was educated at the high school level and studied music privately with Sigismund Stojowski, Arnold Schoenberg, and Joseph Schillinger. As an accomplished concert pianist, he was a featured soloist with symphonies. As a personal friend and great admirer of George Gershwin, he presented frequent concerts of Gershwin's music. As an actor, he appeared in some important movies, including *Rhapsody in Blue, The Barkleys of Broadway, An American in Paris,* and *The Band Wagon.*

As a composer, his preference was writing works for the piano and string quartets but he also wrote for the stage and movies. Although his popular songs usually met with acceptance, I have always had the opinion that Levant wrote down to the popular market, and as a result—with only a few exceptions—his songs seem to lack the extra spark needed to create quality hits. His songs are all good, some are better, none are of standard rank. *If You Want the Rainbow (You Must Have the Rain)* was a collaboration with veterans Mort Dixon and Billy Rose. It was introduced by Fanny Brice in the 1928 movie *My Man.* She also recorded it for Victor, and Eva Taylor obliged for OKeh. Herb Gordon's Orchestra made it for Brunswick. In 1929 Sidney Clare and Levant contributed two songs to a movie called *Street Girl* that starred Jack Oakie and Betty Compton and included Gus Arnheim's Orchestra. The best of the two was *Lovable and Sweet,* which Arnheim recorded for Victor. The Charleston Chasers did it for Columbia. *My Dream Memory,* the second tune, rated dutiful treatment by Nat Shilkret for Victor with his All-Star Orchestra.

Irving Caesar wrote the words to *Lady, Play Your Mandolin,* a 1931 ditty aimed at the fad for Spanish-tinged songs, and it enjoyed good radio play. On records it was made for Victor by Nat Shilkret and by Will Osborne for Melotone. Adrian Schubert took care of it for Crown, and overseas Ambrose waxed it. Ray Noble recorded *We've Got the Moon and Sixpence* in 1932, a song featured in the English stage show "Out of the Bottle." Levant wrote the music; the lyrics were by Grey. In 1934, Edward Heyman provided the words to *Blame It on My Youth,* one of Levant's best songs, possibly because of the high quality of material for that year and the heavy competition. The Dorsey Brothers Orchestra recorded it on Decca, and Jan Garber did it for

Victor. Van Alexander revived it on a Capitol disc with Gordon MacRae some years later. *Don't Mention Love to Me* was sung by Ginger Rogers in the movie *In Person,* a 1935 film, and she also recorded it, as did Isham Jones for Decca and Kay Thompson for Brunswick. *Pardon My Love,* a Milton Drake twist on the more familiar "Pardon My Glove," was a Levant entry that same year. The melody line is one of his better efforts and deserved more attention than it got, but the irrepressible Fats Waller recorded it for Victor. It showed up years later on a transcription by the Isham Jones Orchestra, with a vocal by Eddie Stone. *Wacky Dust* was recorded by the Bunny Berigan Orchestra in 1938. Stanley Adams claimed the words.

Oscar Levant died in Beverly Hills, California, on August 14, 1972.

Jerry Levinson

See Jerry Livingston.

Al Lewis

Songwriter Al Lewis was born in New York City on April 18, 1901, and was educated at the University of Michigan. That sparse information, coupled with the designation "composer, author, publisher," constitutes the entire biographical material under his name in the *ASCAP Biographical Dictionary,* even though Lewis was a member from 1927. Nevertheless, his name is on a number of well-known songs, starting with that momentous year. At the same time, it isn't clear whether Lewis performed as lyric writer or composer, or both, because invariably the song credits read "Words and Music by." It can only be assumed he had a hand in both.

The 1927 tune mentioned above is *Gonna Get a Girl,* a collaboration with Howard Simon. This was Lewis's first hit song, and it did pretty well at that time, even getting international attention on records. In Paris it was recorded by Lud Gluskin and in London by the Gilt-Edged Four. Jackie Souders's band recorded it in Los Angeles. This tendency for jazz musicians to prefer the song still cropped up in 1947, with popular recordings by Benny Goodman on Capitol and Tony Pastor on Bluebird reviving the tune. In 1931 Lewis and Al Sherman combined to turn out a trio of successful songs: *Ninety-nine Out of a Hundred Wanna Be Loved,* which Rudy Vallee obligingly plugged into a hit; *Got the Bench, Got the Park (But I Haven't Got You),* a plaintive lament, with composer Fred Phillips lending a helping hand; and *Now's the Time to Fall in Love*. The second song was recorded in this country by Paul Whiteman, Noble Sissle, and Freddie Rich. Ray Noble gave it acknowledgment in his HMV medley of "holiday hits" in England. Eddie Cantor created a big thing out of *Now's the Time to Fall in Love,* making the best of the Depression by declaring "Potatoes are cheaper, tomatoes are cheaper . . ." and making it all sound believable. In 1946 he sang it on the soundtrack for *The Eddie Cantor Story,* dubbing in for Keefe Brasselle.

Buddy Fields joined Lewis and Sherman in 1933, and they declared, *You Gotta Be a Football Hero.* Ben Bernie and Harry Reser, among others, agreed and recorded the song. But only Lewis and Sherman were responsible for the pleasant 1934 ballad *Over Somebody Else's Shoulder,* which was sympathetically waxed by Isham Jones for Victor and by Will Osborne for the folks who could only afford to shop the five-and-tens. That same year Al Lewis worked with Tony Sacco and Richard B. Smith, and the result was one of the best songs of the year, *The Breeze (That's Bringin' My Honey Back to Me).* This drew wide coverage on records, with the Dorsey Brothers on Decca, Anson Weeks on Brunswick, Henry King for Victor, and Anthony Trini on Bluebird.

Still hitting home runs, Lewis paired with Tom Waring in 1935, and with the terrific support of brother Fred Waring, who plugged the song on his radio broadcasts, they offered *Way Back Home.* Fred even ran a contest on his network broadcast, asking for listeners to submit new lyrics to the song. The winners got to have their words sung on the air. *Blueberry Hill,* a rather mediocre song that received better attention than it deserved, both in 1940 when it came out and still later when the recording that Louis Armstrong made with Gordon Jenkins's Orchestra in 1949 was rereleased in 1956. In the first round Glenn Miller had the hit record; Connee Boswell and Sammy Kaye also made recordings of it. The song was on *Your Hit Parade* for fourteen weeks. It was sung by Gene Autry in his movie *The Singing Hills* (1941), and in 1956 Fats Domino had a million seller, the song again reaching the top ten. Decca reissued the Louis Armstrong version, and it sold in the top forty.

Meanwhile, Lewis and Charles Tobias put together a corny novelty called *Rose O'Day (The Filla-ba-dusha-Song)* and again saw it move into the top ten in all categories of sales. The 1941 chart buster resulted in big-selling records for Freddy Martin, Kate Smith, Woody Herman, and Alvino Rey. Even as late as 1958 Lewis was still trying. With Sylvester Bradford he wrote *Tears on My Pillow.* It was a hit record by Little Anthony and the Imperials. Other Lewis titles include *No, No, a Thousand Times No; Sweet Child; Slowly but Surely; All American Girl; Why Don't You Fall in Love with Me; Cincinnati' Dancing Pig; You're Irish and You're Beautiful; Invitation to a Broken Heart;* and others.

Al Lewis died in New York City on April 4, 1967.

Sam M. Lewis

Lyricist Sam M. Lewis was born in New York City on October 25, 1885. He was educated in the public schools. As a youngster, he worked as a runner for a brokerage house and sang in cafes. From there he went into vaudeville and began writing special material for performers like Van & Schenck and Lew Dockstader. His first published song came out in 1912, *That Mellow Melody,* and in 1914 he worked with composer George W. Meyer on the successful *When You're a Long Long Way From Home,* which was briefly revived in 1942.

In 1916, Lewis teamed with another lyricist, Joe Young, and they worked together until 1930, collaborating with a number of composers, including George W. Meyer, Jean Schwartz; Ted Snyder; Walter Donaldson, Fred Ahlert, M. K. Jerome, Ray Henderson, Harry Akst, Ted Fio Rito, Harry Warren, Oscar Levant, Victor Young, J. Fred Coots, and Pete Wendling. Lewis and Young dissolved their partnership in 1930, and each went his separate way, still very successful. A partial list of the songs Lewis and Young wrote together, includes *Where Did Robinson Crusoe Go With Friday on a Saturday Night; Arrah Go On, I'm Gonna Go Back to Oregon (1916); Huckleberry Finn; I'm All Bound 'Round with the Mason–Dixon Line (1917); Rock-a-bye Your Baby with a Dixie Melody; Hello Central, Give Me No Man's Land; My Mammy; Just a Baby's Prayer at Twilight* (1918); *How You Gonna Keep 'Em Down on the Farm; You're a Million Miles from Nowhere* (1919); *Old Pal, Why Don't You Answer Me; Singin' the Blues (Till My Daddy Comes Home)* (1920); *Cry Baby Blues; Tuck Me to Sleep in My Old 'Tucky Home* (1921); *Lovey Came Back* (1923); *Cover Me Up With the Sunshine of Virginia* (1924); *Dinah; Five Foot Two, Eyes of Blue; I'm Sitting on Top of the World* (1925); *In a Little Spanish Town; Take In the Sun, Hang Out the Moon* (1926); *There's a Cradle in Caroline* (1927); *In My Bouquet of Memories; King for a Day; Laugh, Clown, Laugh* (1928); *I Kiss Your Hand, Madame; Then You've Never Been Blue; I Used to Love Her in the Moonlight* (1929); *Have a Little Faith in Me; Cryin' for the Carolines; Absence Makes the Heart Grow Fonder* (1930).

After parting with Joe Young, Lewis collaborated on the following: *Song of the Fool; Telling It to the Daisies* (1930); *Just Friends; Too Late; I Lost My Gal Again* (1931); *Lawd, You Made the Night too Long* (1932); *One Minute to One; We Were the Best of Friends; Street of Dreams; This Time It's Love* (1933); *For All We Know* (1934); *I Believe in Miracles; Things Might Have Been So Different; It Never Dawned on Me* (1935); *A Beautiful Lady in Blue; Gloomy Sunday; Close to Me; I'm a Fool for Loving You;*

Love, What Are You Doing to My Heart; Now or Never (1936); *Don't Wake Up My Heart* (1938); *The Last Two Weeks in July* (1939).

Sam M. Lewis died in New York City on November 22, 1959.

Dorothy Dick Link

Dorothy Link (née Dorothy Dick) was born in Philadelphia, Pennsylvania, on November 29, 1900. Her education included the Sternberg School of Music, the Academy of Arts, and the Academy of Design. She married composer Harry Link and in many instances collaborated with him in writing songs, using the name Dorothy Dick. One of their early collaborations was with Carmen Lombardo in 1930, *Until We Meet Again, Sweetheart.* If memory serves correctly, this was a waltz, and it enjoyed moderate success and airtime. They worked together frequently the following year, and one of their compositions is a song I have always liked even though it merited little attention; to my knowledge it was only recorded by the Will Osborne Orchestra, *In a Boat Out to Sea.* Typically, in that era of great songs, it got lost in the shuffle.

But 1931 was a good year for the Links. Dorothy composed the English lyrics to the German song *Sag Mir Darling,* and as *Call Me Darling* it was recorded and popularized by crooner Russ Columbo and by Arthur Tracy, the Street Singer. The German composers were Bert Reisfeld, Mart Fryberg, and Rolf Marbet. Then Dorothy and Harry wrote *The Kiss That You've Forgotten,* another moderate success. But most important, 1931 was the year they teamed with bandleader Bert Lown and pianist Chauncey Gray on *By My Side.* The Lown band was at the peak of its popularity, with lots of airtime and a Victor recording contract. Both helped to promote the song into a hit. Harry Link had worked with Lown and Gray in 1930 on their other hit song, *You're the One I Care For.*

In 1933 Gene Gifford, guitarist and arranger for the Casa Loma Orchestra noted for his hot jazz compositions, wrote a waltz, *The Moment I Looked in Your Eyes,* with words by Dorothy Dick, and the band recorded it on Brunswick. Then with Ted Shapiro, of *If I Had You* fame, Dorothy shared credit for *Modern Melody,* which the Joe Haymes band recorded for Bluebird. The following year she worked with Nick Kenny and Al Vann to produce *Must We Say Goodnight So Soon?* Even in that dark year of the Depression it rated recordings by Russ Morgan, Richard Himber, and Eddie Stone. In 1937 Dorothy Dick wrote the lyrics to Max Steiner's melody for *A Star Is Born,* the title song for the film. Other titles by Dorothy (Dick) Link are *I Was Introduced to Heaven (When I Was Introduced to You); Kiss Me Once More; Let's Go*

Back to Where We Started; It's Love Time; You're Out of This World to Me; Peelin' the Peach; There Is No Breeze; All the World Is Mine; I May Hate Myself in the Morning; Please Tell Me That You Love Me; and *Remember Tonight.*

Harry Link

Harry Link was born in Philadelphia, Pennsylvania, on January 24, 1896. He was educated at the University of Pennsylvania. During his career as a composer, he also served as manager for various music publishing firms. He was married to Dorothy Dick. Our first song of any importance involving Link is the 1926 novelty *I'm Just Wild About Animal Crackers,* a collaboration with Sam Coslow and bandleader Freddie Rich. The song enjoyed some popularity for its humor at the time, but has been obligingly forgotten.

However, Link redeemed himself in 1929 by teaming with Fats Waller on the great standard *I've Got a Feeling I'm Falling.* They wrote the music, Billy Rose wrote the words. Helen Morgan sang it in the movie *Applause* that year. Nell Carter sang it in the stage show of Fats Waller's music, "Ain't Misbehavin'," in 1978. Jazz bands play it all the time. Link and Fats Waller, with Andy Razaf in place of Billy Rose, wrote another quality song in 1930, called *Gone.* For some reason it didn't receive much attention, although Nat Shilkret recorded it for Victor and Sam Lanin on Harmony, but it has been rediscovered, to a certain extent, in recent years. The Jim Cullum band in San Antonio, for example, feature it in its repertoire of Waller's music.

That same year Link changed hats and wrote the lyrics to *You're the One I Care For,* a very pretty song composed by pianist Chauncey Gray with bandleader Bert Lown. The Lown band had a lot of airtime, broadcasting from the Hotel Biltmore in Manhattan, and featured the tune as well as recording it on Victor. It did very well, so in 1931 the team came up with another that did even better, *By My Side.* This time they were aided and abetted by a young lady named Dorothy Dick, the future Mrs. Link. In 1935 Link worked with Bob Rothberg and David A. Pollack in the writing of *Nightwind,* a song that appealed to the jazz element in the music business. It was thus accorded thorough treatment by Taft Jordan and "the Mob" on the ARC labels, Fats Waller on Victor, Benny Goodman with Helen Ward on Columbia, the Dorsey Brothers, with vocalist Bob Crosby, on Decca, plus others. However, in spite of all the exposure, the song has languished.

Not so for the entry that Harry Link contrived in 1936 in association with Jack Strachey, with whom he wrote the music, and Holt Marvell (Eric Maschwitz), who wrote the words. This was the all-time favorite, *These*

Foolish Things, which was introduced in the London musical revue "Spread It Abroad," and they certainly did! With combined airtime, sheet music sales, and recordings, the song made it to the number one spot and *Your Hit Parade* for thirteen weeks. It has been recorded and rerecorded many times since, but contemporary waxings were made by Benny Goodman, Mark Warnow, Nat Brandwynne, Joe Sanders, and Lee Sims. The song also had an afterlife in the movies, being included in *A Yank in the R.A.F.,* starring Tyrone Power (1941); *Ghost Catchers,* with Olsen & Johnson (1944): and *Tokyo Rose,* a Humphrey Bogart film in 1949.

Harry Link died in New York City in June 1957.

Jack (Little Jack) Little

Jack Little, much better known as "Little" Jack Little, was born in London, England, on May 28, 1900. He came to the United States as a youngster and eventually attended the University of Iowa as a pre-med student. While there he organized a dance band, and this apparently was more to his liking than medicine. Throughout his long career as an entertainer, he alternated between performing as a single—playing piano and singing in an attractive and distinctively deep baritone—and leading dance bands. He was a star attraction on radio and made a number of recordings.

As a songwriter he made some very respectable contributions to our heritage. One of his early compositions is the standard *Jealous,* which he wrote in 1924, with lyrics by Tommy Mali and Dick Finch. He introduced the song, but it was also recorded by Marion Harris and by Ben Selvin's Orchestra. It enjoyed a successful revival in 1941, when it was recorded by the Andrews Sisters. Another entry from the twenties is the delightful little waltz *Ting-a-Ling (The Song of the Bells).* It came out in 1926, with words by Addy Britt.

With the coming of the thirties, Little was right in there with the competition. In 1932 he and Ira Schuster composed the music and Joe Young the words for *In a Shanty in Old Shanty Town.* It did pretty well. Little recorded it for Columbia and so did Ted Lewis. Singin' Sam, who worked in a style similar to Little's, made it on Oriole and associated labels, and Ted Black recorded it on Victor. However, all of these together couldn't equal the 1946 sensational hit of the tune by Johnny Long and His Orchestra for Decca. By paraphrasing the lyrics and having the band chant them in unison, Long created a novelty approach that was an instant winner. It also made the song a standard known to everybody.

Little entered two nice songs in the market in 1933. Collaborating with Ira Schuster and Dave Oppenheim, he wrote *Hold Me,* which was well presented on records by Eddy Duchin and Ted Fio Rito, and *I May Be Dancing With Somebody Else.* Will Osborne did justice to this one. What may well be Little's best song, *You're a Heavenly Thing,* came out in 1935, with lyrics by Joe Young. The Benny Goodman band recorded it and so did Orville Knapp's. *Honestly* was a 1940 offering, in collaboration with Bud Green. Again, Eddy Duchin's band recorded the best version. Other titles by Little include *I Promise You; After I've Called You Sweetheart; Ev'rybody Loves You; I Hope to Die (If I Told a Lie); You Broke the Only Heart That Ever Loved You; Oh My Achin' Heart; If I Could Be the Sweetheart of a Girl Like You; Would I Mind?; Raindrops.*

Little Jack Little died in Hollywood, Florida, on April 9, 1956.

Fud Livingston

Joseph Anthony (Fud) Livingston was born in Charleston, South Carolina, on April 10, 1906. A talented reed player, he started out with the band of Tal Henry. He went on to work with Jean Goldkette, Paul Whiteman, Ben Pollack, and other name bands of the twenties and thirties, contributing a respectable list of arrangements and original material. He also wrote a few more tunes for the pop market, but *I'm Thru with Love* remains his biggest hit.

Like most musicians, Pee Wee Russell wasn't offered too many opportunities for making a lot of money, and the memory of one of the few times that he was, which he turned down, stayed with him for the rest of his life. It happened during a lean period in the Chicago days, when fellow jazz clarinetist Fud Livingston, hard up for cash, offered Pee Wee a share in the song he had just written, but not yet published, for a pitiful five or ten dollars. Pee Wee, far from affluent himself and anxious to hang on to the little he had, refused to buy in. The song, *I'm Thru with Love,* which Fud wrote in collaboration with violinist Matty Malneck, with words by Gus Kahn, turned out to be the biggest hit of 1931, a year that was full of hits. But Pee Wee had good sound reasons to be skeptical of Fud's offer, because the tunes he usually wrote were not the kind designed for moonlight romancing or making high school girls' hearts flutter and had little appeal to the popular market. For the most part, they were rather complicated instrumentals that Fud framed in arrangements that were highly interesting to musicians of the jazz variety, but short on the kind of melodies adaptable to humming and whistling.

Nevertheless, these tune-arrangements, for that is what they are rather than conventional songs, have achieved a degree of immortality, because as long as there is a collector of Red Nichols's records they will continue to be played and heard. It's doubtful, however, if they were ever played very much outside of the recording studios and even more unlikely that Livingston ever made any money on them. In fact, on the original Brunswick issue of *Feelin' No Pain* the company didn't even take the trouble to list his name as composer, although this error was corrected on the reissue years later. He does receive credit on the Columbia contemporary recording, though, which is by the Charleston Chasers—one of the many pseudonyms for the Nichols groups, and the two records offer another interesting sidelight. It is Pee Wee's clarinet heard on the Brunswick and Fud's on the Columbia, with the two exhibiting an amazing similarity in styles and approach. Fud also led off on the Five Pennies Brunswick of *Imagination,* another of his originals, not to be confused with the pop hit that came along years later. Recorded in 1928, this is a musically intricate and harmoniously advanced piece for the period. Fud is featured again on *Harlem Twist,* made for Victor in the same year by Red Nichols and His Orchestra, where he shares composing credit with drummer Chauncey Moorehouse.

For the period, and from the jazz standpoint, these instrumentals are far superior to most pop tunes of the time and offer a much greater challenge to musicians. They were also direct reflections of Livingston's ability as a jazz clarinetist and his outstanding capabilities as an arranger. In the latter capacity, he contributed scores for many of the large bands of the twenties and was also responsible for the arrangement of *Singin' the Blues* on the all-time classic record by Bix Beiderbecke and Trumbauer. Later, he turned out scores for Paul Whiteman, Benny Goodman, Jimmy Dorsey, and many others and worked in movies and radio, but it is quite likely that his niche in musical immortality will be carved out by the fine clarinet solos he recorded in the twenties, the legacy of *I'm Thru with Love,* and the few "hot" instrumentals.

Fud Livingston died in New York City on March 25, 1957.

Jay Livingston

Jay Livingston was born in McDonald, Pennsylvania, on March 28, 1915. A graduate of the University of Pennsylvania, he studied piano with Harry Archer and orchestration with Harl McDonald. He also attended the University of California, where he studied orchestration and film scoring with Leith Stevens and Earle Hagen. While in college, he organized a dance band that played clubs and cruises. Still later he worked as a singer-pianist on radio and then wrote special material for the comedy team of Olsen and Johnson. For ten years, from 1945 to 1955, he was a contract writer for Paramount Pictures then went on to freelance for all the major studios.

Although he collaborated with a number of top composers during his career, his primary partner was Ray Evans, and as a team they wrote both lyrics and music, sometimes working with other writers, but often by themselves. Comparative latecomers in the songwriting field, they were very successful, winning Academy Awards and marketing songs that made a lot of money. Musically their material, while very good, doesn't measure up to the standards of the thirties. It is also significant that two of their best titles, from the musical standpoint, were collaborations. *The Song of Surrender* had music composed by Victor Young. *In the Arms of Love* was composed by Henry Mancini.

Nevertheless, as the old cliche has it, you can't argue with success, and Livingston and Evans started with a big one in 1941, albeit as part of a "committee." Along with Ole Olsen and Chic Johnson, who share composing credit, they had the big hit from Olsen and Johnson's "Hellzapoppin'," *G-Bye Now*. Woody Herman's Woodchoppers recorded it for Decca, with Bing Crosby vocalizing. Other sides were made by Horace Heidt, with former Dick Jurgens vocalist, Ronnie Kemper; Martha Tilton and Vaughn Monroe also recorded it. In 1945 Livingston and Evans were nominated for an Academy Award for their *The Cat and the Canary,* which was featured in the movie *Why Girls Leave Home*. In the same year, the King Sisters introduced *Stuff Like That There* in the film *On Stage, Everybody*. Betty Hutton had the best-selling record. Then in 1948 they won the coveted trophy when *Buttons and Bows,* featured in the Bob Hope movie *Paleface,* won the Academy Award. Dinah Shore had the best-selling recording of this pseudo-country and western ditty, backed by the Happiness Valley Boys. Other successful sides were made by the Dinning Sisters and by Betty Garrett.

In 1949 the aforementioned *Song of Surrender,* the title song of a film with the same name, was the Livingston and Evans collaboration with Victor Young. It was nicely treated on a record by Buddy Clark.

Then came 1950, and Livingston and Evans won another Academy Award for *Mona Lisa*. Although the song was never heard in its entirety in the movie *Captain Carey, U.S.A.,* as recorded by Nat "King" Cole, it sold over one million copies. *Silver Bells,* a sleeper that was introduced in the 1951 Bob Hope–Marilyn Maxwell film *The Lemon Drop Kid,* was recorded two years later by Bing Crosby and Carol Richards, and the best-selling platter made the song a Christmas standard. It has sold millions of copies of sheet music as well as records and is heard every year during the holiday season. *Almost in Your Arms,* also known as *Love Song,* made its debut in *Houseboat,* sung in the movie by Sophia Loren in 1958. The song received another nomination for an Academy Award. Johnny Nash had the best record. *In the Arms of Love,* an exceptionally well-put-together song for the time, came out in 1966. Livingston and Evans provided the words, and Henry Mancini the music, and the tune was heard in the movie *What Did You Do in the War, Daddy?* Andy Williams made it into a hit record for Columbia.

The list of other titles credited to Livingston is quite long: *Wish Me a Rainbow; As I Love You; Never Let Me Go; All the Time; You're So Right for Me; Red Garters; I'll Always Love You; His Own Little Island; Through Children's Eyes; Warm and Willing; Song of Delilah; Wait Until Dark; Dreamsville; A Thousand Violins; Home Cookin'; Surprise; Marshmallow Moon; Havin' a Wonderful Wish; Brave Man; A Dime and a Dollar!; Haven't Got a Worry; Just an Honest Mistake; Femininity; The Ruby and the Pearl; Streets of Laredo; A Square in the Social Circle; My Love Loves Me; Angeltown; The Morning Music of Montmarte; Maybe September;* and *Bye-Bye.*

In the process of writing these songs, Jay Livingston collaborated with Max Steiner, David Rose, Percy Faith, Neal Hefti, John Addison, Jimmy McHugh, Leith Stevens, Allan Sherman, Franz Waxman, and Sammy Cahn.

Jerry Livingston

In line with our discourse on bandleaders who have made substantial contributions to our heritage of popular songs, at this point we offer a prime example, Jerry Livingston. However, to avoid confusion it must be pointed out immediately that Jerry's real name is Levinson. He is not related to Jimmie Livingston (also a bandleader, brother of Fud Livingston, whose band made records for Bluebird in the thirties), nor to Jay Livingston, a songwriter of later years best known for his collaboration with Ray Evans. Jerry Levinson was born in Denver, Colorado, on March 25, 1909. As a youngster he learned to play piano and while still in high school worked with dance bands in the Denver area. As a student at the University of Arizona, he studied piano, harmony, theory, and composition as a music major and wrote scores for college musicals. He also organized and led his first dance band.

In the early thirties he gravitated to New York, playing piano in the bands of Art Landry and Teddy Brewer, and decided to try writing songs on the professional level. Still using his real name, he hit the jackpot in 1933 with four solid hits, written in collaboration with lyricists Marty Symes and Al Neiburg: *Darkness on the Delta; Under a Blanket of Blue; It's Sunday Down in Caroline;* and *It's the Talk of the Town.* Besides being a terrific boost to the composer's career, these songs went a long way toward establishing the popularity of three name bands of the period. *Under a Blanket of Blue* and *It's the Talk of the Town* were big records for Glen Gray's Casa Loma Orchestra, and *Darkness on the Delta* was a hit for Isham Jones. In England, Ray Noble's great arrangement of *It's Sunday Down in Carolina* was in the classic mold that is still so much admired and established the reputation that eventually brought him to the United States.

The following year saw the team score with three more excellent songs, not the heavy hits of the earlier ones, but still substantial entries in a year crowded with good songs: *Ol' Pappy; In Other Words We're Through;* and *Learning.* And in 1935 there were four more: *Stargazing; Where There's Smoke There's Fire; In a Blue and Pensive Mood;* and *I've Got an Invitation to a Dance.* If you know these songs you're well aware that up to this point Jerry was batting a thousand. All of the titles were well recorded by the name bands of the time; all were distinctive and original melodies; and they enjoyed the brief span of popularity allotted to all popular songs in the Golden Decade. In fact, although Jerry Levinson continued to compose as late as the sixties, and quite a few of his songs were hits and substantial money makers *(Mairzy Doats; Chi-Baba, Chi-Bada).* He never surpassed his early efforts. In the mid-thirties he went to Hollywood and turned out some tunes for the "Hollywood Revels of 1936," which included a nice ballad, *When April Comes Again,* but his freelance efforts were better—*Moonrise on the Lowlands; There Goes My Attraction;* the prophetic *Whatcha Gonna Do When There Ain't No Swing?*; and *A Little Bit Later On.*

In 1938 Jerry Levinson became Jerry Livingston and from then on composed and worked under that name. In that same year he collaborated with Mack David on the hit song *Just a Kid Named Joe* and with Count Basie and Mack David on *Blue and Sentimental,* which became a classic in the Basie band's history as a recorded feature for tenorman Herschel Evans. In 1942 Livingston teamed with Al Hoffman and Mann Curtis in reworking the second phrase of the second theme of the first movement of Tchaikovsky's *Pathetique,* from *Symphony no. 6 in B Minor.* The result was *The Story of a Starry Night,* a best-seller by the Glenn Miller band on Bluebird, with a vocal by Ray Eberle.

In the meantime, Livingston organized another dance band, which was heard on radio broadcasts frequently in the New York metropolitan area. But in 1949 he went back to Hollywood and wrote the score for the movie cartoon feature *Cinderella.* The songs were *Cinderella; A Dream Is a Wish Your Heart Makes; The Cinderella Work Song; So This Is Love;* and *Bibbidi*

Bobbidi Boo. Al Hoffman and Mack David were again involved. This was followed by scores for other movies, among them *At War With the Army, Sailor Beware, Those Red Heads from Seattle, The Hanging Tree,* and *Cat Ballou.* In addition Livingston is responsible for the TV theme songs of such shows as *Casper, the Friendly Ghost, 77 Sunset Strip, Bourbon St. Beat, Lawman, Hawaiian Eye, Surfside 6, The Roaring Twenties,* and *Bugs Bunny.*

Other songs by Jerry Livingston include *You're Looking for Romance; I've Got Rain in My Eyes; My Window Faces the South; Sweet Stranger; Sixty Seconds Got Together; What Do You Know about Love?; Take a Tip From the Whippoorwill; But It Didn't Mean a Thing; That Wonderful Worrisome Feeling; I Don't Want to Be Loved; Don't You Love Me Anymore?; If I Had Only Known; The Mill on the Floss; Unbelievable; Jesse James; Wake the Town and Tell the People; Dawn; Who Are We?; The Twelfth of Never; The Blues Country Style; I'd Give a Million Tomorrows; Fuzzy Wuzzy; I'm a Big Girl Now; Young Emotions.*

Other collaborators were Milton Drake, Sammy Gallop, Paul Francis Webster, Ralph Freed, Mitchell Parish, Milton Berle, Bob Merrill, and Allan Roberts.

John Jacob Loeb

Composer John Jacob Loeb was born in Chicago, Illinois, on February 18, 1910, and educated at Woodmere Academy in New York. Another one of those songwriters you seldom hear mentioned by name, Loeb started his career late in the twenties. However, if you were around in the thirties and forties, you may remember some of his songs. Even though few—with the bare exception of *Boo Hoo,* a collaboration with Carmen Lombardo—became big hits, they are usually very pleasant melodies that have survived the test of time in satisfactory shape. *Boo Hoo,* of course, was plugged into a hit by the Guy Lombardo band and is still associated with it.

Two Little Blue Little Eyes, which came out in 1931, was a clever little tune with lyrics by Paul Francis Webster that helped Rudy Vallee pile up his millions. Never bashful about such things, Rudy even put his name on the music as a co-lyric writer. *Reflections in the Water,* a moody but superior piece, also a Loeb–Webster effort, followed in 1933. David Rose revived and recorded it with a marvelous arrangement in the fifties. Billy Rose claimed a share with Webster in writing the words to *Got the Jitters,* a timely song for the Depression, which almost too realistically expressed the nervous anxiety of the times. It was counterbalanced a bit by the light and fluffy

Sweetie Pie, a solo entry by Loeb to which he wrote both words and music. Fats Waller turned it into a delightful romp on Victor 24737.

Boo Hoo was only one of several songs that appeared in 1937, a great year for Loeb. The best of these is probably the one that achieved immortality as played by the Benny Goodman quartet on a Camel Caravan broadcast, *A Sailboat in the Moonlight.* This gem has been reissued in recent years as part of the Goodman heritage. Carmen Lombardo wrote the lyrics, as he also did for *It's Never Too Late,* a moderately successful entry in 1939 when the competition was fierce. It's a melodically pleasant song as sung by Joe Sudy with His Orchestra on Bluebird B-10165. The glory of the war year 1943 was commemorated by Loeb in collaboration with Redd Evans on *Rosie the Riveter.* It's even possible that this soggy saga, which enjoyed considerable popularity, is the only song mentioned that you still remember.

Loeb again worked with Carmen Lombardo with a couple of worthy entries, *It's Easier Said Than Done,* a 1938 song that got tasteful treatment from the Bob Crosby band on Decca 1658, and *It Seems Like Old Times.* Besides getting a boost from the Lombardo band, *It Seems Like Old Times* became the Arthur Godfrey theme song, which meant it got radio exposure every day, plus TV time later on. Other Loeb compositions are *Masquerade; Everything Is Okey Doakey; Love Marches On; Maybe; You're Here, You're There; There Won't Be a Shortage of Love; Hereafter; Once Upon a Song; You'll Know When It Happens; Somebody Else's Picture; Get Out Those Old Records; Our Little Ranch House; Where You Gonna Be When the Moon Shines; Bubbles; My Sentimental Heart; The Kid in the Three-Cornered Pants; If My Heart Had a Window; Some Rainy Day; Boulevard of Memories; Horses Don't Bet on People; On the Waterfall; Ma, I Miss Your Apple Pie; Toodle-oo; Rosemary.*

John Jacob Loeb died in Woodmere, New York, on March 2, 1970.

Frank Loesser

Frank Loesser was born in New York City on June 29, 1910. He attended CCNY for awhile and wrote songs for the college shows. He worked as a newspaper reporter then toured in vaudeville as a pianist, singer, and caricaturist. For a time he wrote material for vaudeville acts then in the early thirties began to write lyrics. As a lyricist he collaborated with such highly talented people as Burton Lane, Hoagy Carmichael, and Jimmy McHugh and built up a long list of hits. Later in his career he composed the music as well as the words.

His first successful song was the sardonic *Junk Man,* written with Joseph Meyer in 1934 and featured on records by Benny Goodman, with the vocal by Mildred Bailey and by Isham Jones, with Eddie Stone chanting the words. Jack Teargarden liked the tune too and recorded it a couple of years later. But Loesser and Meyer had another popular entry in 1934, a favorite of jazz musicians, who have promoted it into the category of a standard. With additional help from wordsmith Eddie DeLange, who enjoyed his first hit, they came up with *I Wish I Were Twins.* A natural swinger, this happy tune was introduced by Fats Waller on Victor but was closely followed by Adrian's Ramblers (Rollini), Red Allen, and Coleman Hawkins on rival labels. In later years it was often featured in jazz concerts as a two-piano specialty by Dick Hyman and the late Dick Wellstood.

As did most of his contemporaries in the thirties, Loesser gravitated to Hollywood and started writing for films. By 1938 he was in full stride, associated with one hit song after another. In the movie *Cocoanut Grove, Says My Heart,* a collaboration with Burton Lane, was sung by Harriet Hilliard, who also recorded the song with Ozzie Nelson's Orchestra. Other records were made by Billie Holiday, Tommy Dorsey, Jimmy Grier, and George Hall with Dolly Dawn. For good measure, the tune made the top position on *Your Hit Parade* for twelve weeks. For *College Swing,* Loesser and Lane produced the wistful *Moments Like This,* introduced in the picture by Florence George and recorded by Maxine Sullivan, Dick Stable, and Teddy Wilson on contemporary discs, and many times since. For the same movie, Loesser teamed with composers Manning Sherwin and Arthur Altman to provide the words to *I Fall in Love With You Every Day.* Introduced in the film by John Payne and Florence George, it was recorded on successful records by Larry Clinton, Jimmy Dorsey, and George Hall with Dolly Dawn.

Small Fry, with words by Loesser and music by Hoagy Carmichael, was another entry for 1938, featured in the movie *Sing You Sinners,* and performed by Fred MacMurray and Donald O'Connor. Bing Crosby and Johnny Mercer had a hit record of it. But the inimitable Bobby Hackett turned it into a jazz classic on a recording by a vocal group called the Tune Twisters, backed by the Adrian Rollini Quintet. After hearing Hackett's trumpet solo on the record, Hoagy Carmichael immediately bought a dozen copies of the Vocalion disc to give to his friends. Loesser and Carmichael followed through with *Two Sleepy People,* a vehicle for Bob Hope and Shirley Ross in *Thanks for the Memory.* It was recorded by the pair on Decca, and Hoagy Carmichael and Ella Logan made it for Brunswick. Other contemporary sides were made by Fats Waller, Sammy Kaye, Lawrence Welk, and Kay Kyser. Bob Hope subsequently adopted the song as his theme. In 1987 it was featured in the Fats Waller musical "Ain't Misbehavin'."

A movie short entitled *A Song Is Born* introduced another Loesser–Carmichael composition, *Heart and Soul,* played by Larry Clinton's Orchestra. A year later it cropped up again in the film *Some Like It Hot,* performed by Gene Krupa's band. Also in that year of magic for Loesser, he worked with violinist-bandleader Matty Malneck on a song that has gained more respect and attention through the years than it enjoyed initially, *I Go for That.* It was sung by Dorothy Lamour in the movie *St. Louis Blues* but delightfully reprised by guitarist Steven Jordan many years later on his solo album for Fat Cats Jazz. Dorothy Lamour also introduced *Moon of Manakoora* in the film *Hurricane.* The Loesser lyric was set to music by Alfred Newman. Bing Crosby, Ray Noble, Van Alexander, and Ruby Newman all had records.

The Loesser stream of successful songs in 1939 continued with another outstanding collaboration with Burton Lane, *The Lady's in Love with You,* a Bob Hope–Shirley Ross number in *Some Like It Hot.* They also recorded it, and the Gene Krupa band, which backed them in the movie, also waxed it for Brunswick with a vocal by Irene Day. Benny Goodman had the usual swinger, with Helen Forrest singing, and there were other releases by Glenn Miller, Bob Crosby, and Nellie Lutcher. Other Loesser songs for the year included *Strange Enchantment; That Sentimental Sandwich; See What the Boys in the Back Room Will Have; Snug as a Bug in a Rug; Bubbles in the Wine* (the Lawrence Welk theme); and *Kiss Me with Your Eyes.*

Still combining his exceptional talent as a lyric writer with outstanding composers, in 1940 Loesser worked with Freidrich Hollender on *Li'l Boy Love* for the film *A Night at Earl Carroll's.* Other 1940 titles were *My! My!; Say It; My Kind of Country* (all with Jimmy McHugh for the Jack Benny movie *Buck Benny Rides Again*); *I Hear Music; Dancing on a Dime* (with Burton Lane for the film *Dancing on a Dime*); *I've Been in Love Before.* The forties were marvelous years for Frank Loesser. The big hit *Dolores* was introduced by Frank Sinatra in 1942 in the film *Las Vegas Nights.* A Louis Alter melody, it was recorded by Sinatra with Tommy Dorsey's Orchestra. Bing Crosby also had a big-selling record. The tune was nominated for an Academy Award. A collaboration with Victor Schertzinger produced three good songs for the Mary Martin film *Kiss the Boys Goodbye,* including the title song; *Sand in My Shoes;* and *I'll Never Let a Day Pass By*—all well covered by contemporary recordings.

I Don't Want to Walk Without You was one of the top songs of 1942. The Loesser lyric, eminently suited to the wartime atmosphere of the day, was matched by an excellent Jule Styne melody. It was introduced by Johnny Johnston in the movie *Sweater Girl* that year, and he sang it again two years later in *You Can't Ration Love.* Harry James had a top-selling record with Helen Forrest on the vocal; Bing Crosby and Dinah Shore were not far behind.

A semistandard, at least, the song still crops up and was successfully reprised by Phyllis McGuire on the label devoted to such things, Reprise. Barry Manilow did it again in 1980. The other Loesser blockbuster of that year was *Praise the Lord and Pass the Ammunition.* This was Loesser's first attempt at writing both words and music, and he based the lyrics on words spoken by navy chaplain William Maquire during the bombing of Pearl Harbor. Kay Kyser's recording was a million-seller. Other titles for the year include *Jingle, Jangle, Jingle,* with music by Joseph J. Lilley (this sleeper spent fourteen weeks on *Your Hit Parade* and hit number one five times; it was a smash record for the Merry Macs on Decca); *I Said No; You're in love with Someone Else; I've Got You; Now You See It.*

Although not as sprinkled with hits as the previous two years, 1943 was notable for several top titles with melodies by Jimmy McHugh. *Let's Get Lost; "Murder," He Says;* and *Can't Get Out of This Mood.* The first two were in the Mary Martin film *Happy Go Lucky.* Vaughn Monroe had the best-seller on *Let's Get Lost,* followed by platters by Kay Kyser and Jimmy Dorsey. Betty Hutton introduced *"Murder," He says. Can't Get Out of This Mood,* a superior ballad in every way, was introduced by Ginny Simms in the movie *Seven Day's Leave.* She was also in the group backing Harry Babbitt on the best-selling Kay Kyser recording of the song. Johnny Long's band also made it. Other titles for 1943 include *The Fuddy Duddy Watchmaker; A Touch of Texas; Soft Hearted; I Get the Neck of the Chicken; They're Either Too Young or Too Old; The Dreamer;* and *In My Arms.* Frank Loesser alone was responsible for *Spring Will Be a Little Late This Year,* the melodiously melancholy ballad he wrote for the Deanna Durbin film *Christmas Holiday.* It was his only submission for 1944, but one to be proud of.

Nothing much happened in 1945 and 1946, and only one song, *What Are You Doing New Year's Eve,* another solo effort by Loesser, was exceptional in 1947. Margaret Whiting had a good record, and so did Dick Haymes. But 1948 brought the Ray Bolger hit "Where's Charley?" The stage musical included songs by Loesser for which he wrote both words and music: *Once in Love With Amy; My Darling, My Darling; Make a Miracle;* and *The New Asmolean Marching Society Student's Conservatory Band.* And as though that wasn't enough, he capped off the year with the delightful *On a Slow Boat to China.* Kay Kyser is credited with the best-selling record, but sharing the hit were Benny Goodman, Freddy Martin, Eddy Howard, and Art Lund. Loesser continued to write for the stage and movies well into the sixties, and his output was prolific. However, as is often the case, the songs, while important to the production, made no outside impression. Of course, there were some exceptions: *Baby, It's Cold Outside* and *If I Were a Bell,* but the popular song market had changed. Good songs were no longer in great demand.

Frank Loesser died in New York City on July 25, 1969.

Frederick Loewe

Composer Frederick Loewe was born into a theatrical family in Berlin, Germany, on June 10, 1901. A child prodigy on the piano, at age fifteen he wrote the European song hit *Katrina.* In 1924 he immigrated to the United States and tried performing as a pianist, but with indifferent success, so he worked at odd jobs. Among other things, he worked as a ranch hand in the west and in professional boxing as a bantamweight. In the latter capacity he had the dubious honor of being knocked out by the legendary Tony Canzoneri.

Back in New York in the late twenties, he again tried playing the piano for a living and decided to try composing. With a lyricist, Earle Crooker, he turned out *A Waltz Was Born in Vienna* in 1936. Then two years later the pair collaborated on a more ambitious project, a Broadway show, "Great Lady," a short-lived production. They also wrote a musical for the St. Louis Opera. Loewe continued to work as a pianist. In the early forties he began to compose with librettist-lyricist Alan Jay Lerner, but for a time they weren't very successful. Two Broadway shows, "What's Up" (1943) and "The Day before Spring" (1945), had brief runs. But in 1947 they hit it big with "Brigadoon." One song from this production was a hit, *Almost Like Being in Love.* The other songs, while important to the story, failed to become popular. The same thing must be said for the successful "Paint Your Wagon," a 1951 production. From this score, only two songs enjoyed moderate success on the popular market, *I Talk to the Trees* and *They Call the Wind Maria.*

But then came 1956 and "My Fair Lady," a Broadway musical based on George Bernard Shaw's "Pygmalion." This show ran for a record-breaking 2,717 performances and included five hit songs: *On the Street Where You Live; I Could Have Danced All Night; I've Grown Accustomed to Her Face; Get Me to the Church on Time;* and *Wouldn't It Be Loverly.* In addition, two other songs were fairly successful, *The Rain in Spain* and *With a Little Bit of Luck.* Two years later, the team of Lerner and Loewe wrote a highly successful score for the movie *Gigi,* starring Maurice Chevalier. All of the songs were popular: *Gigi; I Remember It Well; Thank Heaven for Little Girls; I'm Glad I'm Not Young Anymore;* and *The Night They Invented Champagne.* In 1960 Loewe not only wrote the music, he coproduced another successful Broadway production, "Camelot." However, the songs, while receiving some attention, were never big hits. Nevertheless, four Lerner and Loewe shows were made into successful movies: "Brigadoon," "My Fair Lady," "Camelot, " and "Paint Your Wagon."

A graduate of New York University, Frederick Loewe received an Honorary Doctorate from his alma mater and another from Redlands University. As a pianist he gave a recital at Carnegie Hall in 1942. For "My Fair Lady" he received the New York Critics "Tony" Award in 1947; for *Gigi* the Academy Award in 1958; and for "Brigadoon," "Paint Your Wagon," and "Day before Spring," the Drama Critics Award in 1947. He died in 1988.

Carmen Lombardo

To a musician, a record collector, or most anyone with a fondness for great songs, quite often a certain melody is automatically associated with a recording. So it is that to my mind *Coquette* will always remind me of the Teddy Wilson recording with Benny Goodman and Harry James. *Freckle Face, You're Beautiful* suggests Al Bowlly singing with Ray Noble's New Mayfair Orchestra. *A Sailboat in the Moonlight* recalls a classic performance by the Goodman Trio transcribed from a radio broadcast. And *It Seems Like Old Times,* although probably best remembered as Arthur Godfrey's radio theme, is delineated for me in a sparkling interpretation by Bobby Hackett with Eddie Condon's NBC-TV Orchestra. Then there's Fats Waller's rendition of *Ooh, Looka There, Ain't She Pretty?* and some personal likes that probably nobody else remembers, such as Rudy Vallee's *Snuggled on Your Shoulder* and Will Osborne's *You're Beautiful Tonight, My Dear*. What do they all have in common? These are all songs composed or co-composed by Carmen Lombardo.

Carmen, one of the four Lombardo brothers who organized the Royal Canadians, one of the most popular and long-lived dance bands of all time, was born in London, Ontario, Canada, on July 16, 1903. As the lead saxophonist and vocalist he lent his own tonal personality to the band, exemplified by a wide vibrato. But he also enjoyed a very successful career as a songwriter and turned out a respectable list of fine tunes. In addition to those mentioned above, he can be credited with *Sweethearts on Parade* (heard in a latter-day transition as a dixieland jazz tune); *The Sweetest Music This Side of Heaven; In My Estimation of You; Boo-Hoo; It's Never Too Late;* and *Ridin' Around in the Rain.* Carmen's contributions to songwriting often included both words and music, but he also teamed with some of the top names in the business, among them John Jacob Loeb; Johnny Green, Joe Young, Gus Kahn, Cliff Friend, and Charles Newman.

Carmen Lombardo died in Miami, Florida, on April 17, 1971.

Ruth Lowe

Pianist-composer-lyricist Ruth Lowe was born in Toronto, Ontario, on August 12, 1914. She attended public schools and as a professional pianist performed on the Canadian Radio Broadcasting Commission and then joined Ina Ray Hutton's all-girl Orchestra, from 1937 to 1939. Although not a prolific composer, she penned both words and music to *I'll Never Smile Again,* the 1940 hit song. Recorded by the Tommy Dorsey Orchestra, with the vocal by Frank Sinatra and the Pied Pipers, it turned out to be the biggest record the band ever had. The song made the number one spot for twelve weeks. In his movie debut, Frank Sinatra and the band reprised the tune in *Las Vegas Nights* the following year. Collaborating with Stephen Weiss and Paul Mann, Lowe helped in the writing of *Put Your Dream Away for Another Day,* which Frank Sinatra adopted as his theme song. He recorded it with Axel Stordahl's Orchestra in 1945. Other Ruth Lowe titles include *Too Beautiful to Last; Ode to an Alligator; Won't Somebody Please Write a Song; A Touch of Love; A Short Short Story;* and *Take Your Sins to the River.*

Bert Lown

Bandleader Bert Lown was born in White Plains, New York, on June 6, 1903. After graduating from high school he became a salesman and sales executive. He taught himself to play piano and in 1926 opened a booking agency in New York in partnership with Rudy Vallee. The story goes that while sitting in the lobby of the Hotel Biltmore, he overheard the manager complaining about the quality of the dance band working at the hotel. He introduced himself as a bandleader, succeeded in getting an audition, and that evening on the telephone managed to put together a dance band that not only played the audition the next day, but landed the job playing in the hotel.

With plenty of airtime and a Victor recording contract, the band was a very successful unit in the early thirties. During that time it featured and recorded three songs that were popular, one of which has attained standard distinction, *Bye Bye Blues.* This was the band's theme song and composing credits include Bert Lown, pianist Chauncey Gray, another bandleader Fred Hamm, and Dave Bennett. Although published in 1930, the song was around for some time before that and was recorded by Fred Hamm's Orchestra on Victor 19662 in 1925. On the recording, Fred Hamm and Dave Bennett (who played clarinet and sax in his band) were listed as composers. Chauncey Gray was also in the Hamm Orchestra but wasn't listed as a cocomposer until the song was published. Thus the tune is an interesting example of the machinations that sometimes took place in getting a song published.

Lown is also listed in the credits for another 1930 entry, *You're the One I Care For.* The lyrics were written by Harry Link, and Chauncey Gray and Lown composed the music. In each case the Lown band recorded these songs and made them popular. In 1931, the tune was *By My Side,* and this time Lown and Gray shared authorship with Harry Link and Dorothy Dick. Lown also is listed as collaborating with Theodore Kurrus on *Tired,* which the Lown band recorded in 1932. Other credits include *I'm Disappointed in You; My Heart and I; Today and Tomorrow;* and *Let Me Fill Your Day With Music.*

Bert Lown died in Portland, Oregon, on November 20, 1962.

Abe Lyman

Abe Lyman, who led a very successful dance orchestra from the early twenties into the forties, was born in Chicago, Illinois, on August 4, 1897. A gifted drummer, at the age of fourteen he was already a professional playing in Chicago's Colonial Cafe. He worked in silent movie houses, played local music jobs, and even took outside jobs, including driving a taxi. In 1919 he went to California, and his drumming ability soon brought him work in the various restaurants; and he organized his own band. From 1921 to 1924 the band established a firm reputation at the famous Cocoanut Grove in Los Angeles. Gus Arnheim, who was to lead a band of his own later, was the pianist, and it was during this period that he collaborated with Lyman in composing the melody to the great standard *I Cried for You.* Arthur Freed wrote the words to the 1923 song. The Lyman Orchestra recorded and promoted the tune, and it did well. In 1938 it was revived by Glen Gray and the Casa Loma Orchestra, and in the following year it was sung by Judy Garland in the film *Babes in Arms.* As though this established a pattern, it was played by Harry James's orchestra, with Helen Forrest singing, in the 1944 movie *Bathing Beauty;* featured in the Blossom Seeley biographical film *Somebody Loves Me* in 1952; again in the 1955 *Love Me or Leave Me;* in the 1957 *The Joker Is Wild;* and the Billie Holiday bio *Lady Sings the Blues* in 1972. In the meantime, it has been played, sung, and recorded countless times. Lyman and Arnheim got together with another future bandleader, Earl Burtnett, who was playing piano and arranging for the Art Hickman band, and the trio came up with the words and music for *Mandalay,* a 1924 title that was recorded by the Abe Lyman orchestra with the vocal by Al Jolson. Paul Whiteman also recorded it.

Abe Lyman and His Californians played several long stints at the Cocoanut Grove, recorded steadily through the years—mostly for Brunswick, but later on Decca and Bluebird—and were featured in a number of movies. In 1926 Lyman and Walter Donaldson wrote another all-time standard, *After I Say I'm Sorry.* Again the Lyman band recorded it, and the song enjoyed contemporary popularity. Because bandleaders and musicians liked it, it never died out as most songs did. Then, in 1955 it was another Lyman tune featured in the movie *Love Me or Leave Me,* and it was accorded even greater attention in the Jack Webb film *Pete Kelly's Blues* that same year, resulting in several recordings of the music from the picture. *Mary Lou* was another entry for 1926, with Lyman and George Waggner contributing the words to the melody by J. Russel Robinson. It turned out to be a popular ditty of the day. The next year Lyman and Phil Silvers combined on the words to *Did You Mean It?*, which had music by the comedian with the accordion, Phil Baker. Silvers and Baker were starring in the Broadway revue "A Night in Spain," in which the song was featured. Marion Harris was also in the cast. The song received wide treatment on recordings by J. C. Flippen and His Gang, Seger Ellis and His Orchestra, and vocalist Marion Harris. This song is not to be confused with the 1936 composition by Jesse Greer and Mort Dixon with the same title which was recorded in a Jimmy Mundy arrangement by the Benny Goodman band with the vocal by Ella Fitzgerald. Other titles credited to Lyman include *Faithfully Yours; I Don't Want You to Cry Over Me;* and *In the Land of Shady Palm Trees.*

Abe Lyman died in Beverly Hills, California, on October 23, 1957.

Ballard MacDonald

Librettist and lyric writer Ballard MacDonald was born in Portland, Oregon, on October 15, 1882. A graduate of Princeton University, he wrote material for vaudeville early in his career and started composing in 1909. During his long ensuing career he wrote songs with a distinguished list of composers—George Gershwin, Sigmund Romberg, Walter Donaldson, James F. Hanley, Harry Carroll, Joseph Meyer—and starting in 1918 he wrote for the Broadway stage. In addition, he was librettist for the Broadway productions of "Battling Butler" (1923), "Padlocks of 1927," "Rufus Lemaire's Affairs" (1927), and "Hot Rhythm" (1930). MacDonald's first published song, *I Wish I Had My Old Girl Back Again,* appeared in1909, and he had other entries in 1910 and 1912; but 1913 was the year that established his reputation. He had three hits: *Nights of Gladness; There's a Girl in the Heart of Maryland;* and *The Trail of the Lonesome Pine.* The latter two, or course, were long ago established as all-time favorites, and both were collaborations with composer Harry Carroll.

Then in 1917 MacDonald wrote the words to a melody by James F. Hanley, and the result was one of those songs with a life of its own, so far above the average in popularity and acceptance that it is probably only surpassed by *Stardust.* The song is *Back Home Again in Indiana,* a perennial favorite with jazz musicians, most often called *Indiana.* Besides being played countless times and recorded almost as many, it has been featured in several movies. Red Nichols dubbed it on the soundtrack of his bio movie *The Five Pennies,* and Jane Froman did the same on her bio film *With a Song in My Heart.* It was also played in *The Gene Krupa Story.*

In 1918 MacDonald penned the words for the popular waltz *Beautiful Ohio.* The music was composed by Robert A. King under the name of Mary Earl, because he was under contract as a staff writer to his publisher. The problem was straightened out, and King collected full royalties for the song, which sold copies of sheet music in the millions. In the following year MacDonald and James F. Hanley struck again, this time with a song they contributed to the stage show "Ziegfeld's Midnight Frolics," *Rose of Washington Square.* It was sung by Fanny Brice, the popular comedienne, and the show and the song continued into the following year. Alice Faye sang it in the 1939 movie that adopted the same title, *Rose of Washington Square,* and in the stage show "To Broadway with Love," produced at the New York World's Fair in 1964, it was sung by Millie Slavin. Ann Dee reprised it in another movie in 1967, *Thoroughly Modern Millie.* Like *Indiana,* the song is a favorite of jazz musicians and is often heard at jazz festivals and concerts.

MacDonald continued to write for the stage. As often is the case, the songs, while important in the production, made no popular impression. However, in 1922 he wrote English lyrics to an imported song with an international background. Originally a German instrumental composition by Leon Jessel, *Die Parade der Holzsoldaten,* it picked up words in French by Victor Oliver and was performed in Paris by a Russian revue, "Chauve Souris," which introduced the song in the United States. It was a popular novelty and was recorded by Paul Whiteman, Carl Fenton, and Vincent Lopez. In 1924, MacDonald teamed with Buddy DeSylva on the lyrics to *Somebody Loves Me,* the George Gershwin song that was featured in the "George White Scandals" of that year. Now a standard, the tune has been recorded many times and has been performed in almost as many motion pictures: *Broadway Rhythm* (1943), *Rhapsody in Blue* (1945), *Lullaby of Broadway* (1951), *Somebody Loves Me* (1952), and *Pete Kelly's Blues* (1955). *Clap Hands! Here Comes Charley!* was a happy ditty with music by Joseph Meyer and words concocted by MacDonald in collaboration with Billy Rose. It made a hit in 1925 and has been recorded frequently over the years. MacDonald also worked with James F. Hanley on *At the End of the Road,* a pleasant ballad that was recorded on contemporary sides by Fred Waring's Pennsylvanians and by singer Lewis James.

MacDonald continued to write until 1935, the year of his death, and had other successful songs in *I'm Following You* (1930) and *Bend Down Sister* (1931). Ballard MacDonald died in Forest Hills, New York, on November 17, 1935.

Cecil Mack

Lyric writer Cecil Mack was born in Norfolk, Virginia, on November 6, 1883. He was educated at Norfolk Mission College, Lincoln University, and the University of Pennsylvania. He started out in show business writing special material for the comedy team of Bert Williams and George Walker and then went on to collaborate on songs and material for Broadway shows with composers Chris Smith, James P. Johnson, Ford Dabney, Eubie Blake, and Albert Von Tilzer. His three best-known compositions alone are enough to establish him in the songwriter's pantheon. The first two, *Charleston* and *Old Fashioned Love,* were collaborations with James P. Johnson for the 1923 stage production "Running Wild." *Charleston,* of course, was the song associated with the dance craze that colored the twenties and influenced the construction of other popular songs to conform to the Charleston format. *Old Fashioned Love* has been recorded many times and is a semistandard. An outstanding version is played by Joe Haymes and His Orchestra, as arranged by Haymes for the very first record made by the band. It was released on Victor and Bluebird under the pseudonyms of "Radio Rascals Orchestra" and "Harlem Hot Shots."

Shine, an uncontested standard, was a collaboration between Mack and Lew Brown on lyrics to the music by Ford Dabney. Associated with Louis Armstrong, who featured the song, it has also been recorded by other jazz artists, including Benny Goodman, Ella Fitzgerald, Jack Teagarden, Art Hodges, and Sidney Bechet. In the movies it has been featured in *The Birth of the Blues* (1941), *Cabin in the Sky* (1942), *The Benny Goodman Story* (1955), and *The Eddy Duchin Story* (1956). Other songs by Mack are *Good Morning, Carrie; Josephine, My Jo; I Take Things Easy; In the Shade of the Pyramids; Teasing; He's a Cousin of Mine; Down Among the Sugar Cane; You're in the Right Church but the Wrong Pew; If He Comes In I'm Going Out; That Minor Strain; Ginger Brown; Huggin' and Muggin'; By the Sweat of My Brow; Never Let the Same Bee Sting You Twice; All In, Down and Out; You for Me, Me for You; The Camel Walk; Little Gypsy Maid;* and *Look into Your Baby's Eyes and Say Goo Goo.*

Cecil Mack died in New York City on August 1, 1944.

Edward Madden

Lyric writer Edward Madden, a charter member of ASCAP, was born in New York City on July 17, 1877. He was educated at Fordham University, and early in his career he wrote special material for singers, including Fanny Brice. It appears that his first published song came out in 1903, and he also had entries in 1904; but it wasn't until 1905 that he had his first successful song, *Daddy's Little Girl,* written in collaboration with Theodore F. Morse. Other songs followed, of course, and in 1907 he started to write for stage shows. As is often the case, however, the songs were important to the productions but failed to become popular. In fact, Madden's first big hit, another entry with Morse, *Down in Jungle Town,* was an independent publication in 1908. This also applies to the song that came out the following year and has become a tried-and-true standard, *By the Light of the Silvery Moon,* written with Gus Edwards. Introduced in one of Gus Edwards's revues featuring children, it was sung by Georgie Price. Since then the song has been sung and recorded many times and has been featured in a number of movies, including becoming the title song for the 1952 film starring Doris Day and Gordon MacRae; *The Story of Vernon and Irene Castle* (1939); *Birth of the Blues* (1941); *Babes on Broadway* (1942); *Hello, Frisco, Hello* (1943); *The Jolson Story* (1946); *Always Leave Them Laughing* (1949); and *Two Weeks with Love* (1950).

Two years later Madden and Edwards combined on *Jimmy Valentine,* a tune based on an O. Henry story about a "sentimental crook." Years later (1928) it was used as the background theme in the movie *Alias Jimmy Valentine,* and Big Crosby sang it in the film *The Star Maker,* based on Gus Edwards's life, in 1939. In 1912 Madden and Percy Wenrich wrote another all-time winner, *Moonlight Bay.* A popular song with barbershop quartets through the years, like *By the Light of the Silvery Moon* it took on a new life in the movies in the forties. Alice Faye sang it in *Tin Pan Alley* (1940); it was played in *Is Everybody Happy* (1943); and it was sung by Doris Day in the film that adopted the title, *Moonlight Bay* (1951). Bing and Gary Crosby made a popular duet recording of it that year. The list of Madden titles is fairly long and includes collaborations with Jerome Kern, Ben Jerome, Joseph Daly, Julian Edwards, Louis A. Hirsch, and his wife, Dorothy Jardon.

Edward Madden died in Hollywood, California, on March 11, 1952.

Herb Magidson

Herb Magidson was born in Braddock, Pennsylvania, on January 2, 1906. He attended Braddock High School and then went on to study journalism at the University of Pittsburgh. A talented writer of special material, he was brought to New York by Sophie Tucker and went to work for a music publisher in 1928. The following year he moved on to Hollywood and began writing for movies, the beginning of a long and successful career contributing to stage and screen. He started writing in 1928, and during his long career he worked with many of the top composers of the era: Con Conrad, Allie Wrubel, Ben Oakland, Carl Sigman, Sam H. Stept, Sammy Fain, Michael Cleary, and Jule Styne. In the process he is credited with a long list of hit songs. Just skimming the highlights provides an overall perspective of a brilliant career.

In 1929 Magidson teamed with Michael Cleary and Ned Washington on the sprightly novelty *Singin' in the Bathtub,* which was introduced by comedienne

Winnie Lightner in the movie *Show of Shows*. In 1932, with Sammy Fain, it was *Hummin' to Myself,* with an assist on the lyrics from Monty Siegel. The song rated considerable airtime and popularity. The Joe Haymes band recorded it, but Victor saw fit to issue the side on the experimental Electradisk label, with little or no distribution. In 1934 Magidson and Con Conrad combined to turn out the first song to win an Academy Award, *The Continental*. It was featured in the film *The Gay Divorcée,* which starred Fred Astaire and Ginger Rogers. Conrad and Magidson followed through the next year with the title song for the film *Here's to Romance*. Magidson also collaborated with Joseph Meyer on *According to the Moonlight,* with an assist from Jack Yellen. It was sung and introduced by Alice Faye in the movie *George White's Scandals for 1935*. She also recorded it for Melotone, and Harry Richman did the same for Columbia. Victor Young's Orchestra waxed it for Decca.

The first songwriting team to hit on the idea of using the title of a popular book for a song, Herb Magidson and Allie Wrubel came up with *Gone With the Wind* in 1937. Whether or not the title had anything to do with it, the tune was a huge success, and has gone on to become a standard much admired and featured by jazz musicians and singers. Among those who have recorded it are Mel Tormé, Maxine Sullivan, Art Tatum, Claude Thornhill, Stan Getz, and others. The association with Allie Wrubel produced the big hit *Music, Maestro, Please* in 1938. This song, which has never really died out, and is still frequently heard, was on *Your Hit Parade* for twelve weeks, and made number one four times. Tommy Dorsey had a big-selling record, and so did Kay Kyser. In later editions the tune has been recorded by the Benny Goodman Quintet, Sammy Kaye's band, and Frankie Lane.

Not quite as big a smash, but still able to make the Top Ten for the year, *I'm Afraid the Masquerade Is Over* was the Magidson-Wrubel entry for 1939. It got top exposure on records by Jimmy Dorsey, Larry Clinton, and Horace Heidt. They got together again in 1940 for the nostalgic *I'm Stepping Out with a Memory Tonight,* another hit. It was introduced by Kate Smith on her radio program and, again, well represented on records by Glenn Miller, Kay Kyser, Tony Martin, and Al Donahue. In addition, the song was played in the 1942 movie *Footlight Serenade*. *I'll Buy That Dream* was the Magidson–Wrubel offering for 1945, and like their other collaborations, a quality song. It was introduced by Anne Jeffreys in the film *Sing Your Way Home,* and Helen Forrest, dueting with Dick Haymes and backed by Victor Young's Orchestra, had a big record for Decca. Kitty Kallen did the same for Columbia with Harry James.

Magidson and Ben Oakland had another hit in 1947, *I'll Dance at Your Wedding*. The catchy melody and clever lyrics were a big lift to the career of singer Buddy Clark who, abetted by Ray Noble's excellent arrangement, had the hit recording for Columbia. Tony Martin and Peggy Lee also had nice records. Peggy Lee did full justice to *Linger in My Arms a Little Longer, Baby,* a great tune perfectly suited to her sultry singing style. The 1946 song is unique for being one of the few compositions solely the work of Herb Magidson. Peggy's record for Capitol was made during her classic period with Dave Barbour. Still writing, in 1950 Magidson, with composer Carl Sigman, had the pleasure of enjoying the popularity of *Enjoy Yourself (It's Later Than You Think).* Guy Lombardo had the big record, but Doris Day wasn't far behind. Other titles by Herb Magidson are *H'lo, Baby; So I Married the Girl; I Beg Your Pardon, Mademoiselle; Blue Sky Avenue; Talkin' to Myself; I Knew You When; Midnight in Paris; 'Tain't No Use; Roses in December; Beau Night in Hotchkiss Corners;* and *How Long Has This Been Going On.*

Matty Malneck

Matty Malneck, a highly talented and versatile artist, was born in Newark, New Jersey, on December 19, 1903. He attended a manual training high school and studied accounting at the University of Denver. More importantly in regard to his career, he studied violin with Henry Ginsbury and by 1927 was playing in and arranging for the Paul Whiteman orchestra. He was part of the organization until 1938, but he also performed as a freelancer, especially on recordings, and eventually organized his own combos and orchestras. He was featured with them in a number of movies and on major radio programs.

His first published song, *Gypsy,* came out in 1928, and from that point forward few songwriters would be able to equal the list of excellent compositions he turned out year after year. In 1930 Malneck got together with two other bandleaders, Ozzie Nelson and Frank Signorelli, and the result was *And Then Your Lips Met Mine.* Nelson, enjoying the popularity created by frequent radio broadcasts, plugged the song on the air and also recorded it for Brunswick. Bert Lown recorded it for Victor. But Malneck was just getting started. In 1931, he and clarinetist-arranger Fud Livingston wrote music to words by Gus Kahn and produced the great standard *I'm Thru With Love.* Possibly the biggest hit of a year saturated with fine songs, it was recorded on contemporary sides by Bing Crosby for Brunswick, Henry Busse on Victor, and Don Voorhees for Hit-of-the-Week—and it kept on going. In 1938 Glen Gray and the Casa Loma Orchestra, with Kenny Sargent on the vocal, had a nice seller for Decca, and in 1941 Dinah Shore followed with one for Bluebird. In 1943 it was on the soundtrack of the movie *Honeymoon Lodge* and again in the Gus Kahn bio film *I'll See You in My Dreams,* in 1952. Bobby Van sang it in the 1953 movie *The Affairs of Dobie Gillis,* and Marilyn Monroe reprised it in *Some Like It Hot,* the hit comedy of 1959. Actually, the song has never died out, is frequently heard, and has been recorded around the world. In that same year—and without the able assistance of Fud Livingston—Malneck and Kahn published the wistful ballad *Old Playmate,* which Jack Fulton vocalized for a Paul Whiteman platter on Victor was tunefully rendered by Ozzie Nelson and his band on Brunswick, and painfully emoted by Ted Lewis for Columbia. The Jack Fulton–Whiteman recording was also part of a medley released on one of Victor's early experiments in a 33 ⅓ rpm long-playing record.

I'll Never Be the Same, one of the most beautiful songs in the American catalog of popular music, also had lyrics by Gus Kahn. The melody was a collaboration by Malneck and Frank Signorelli, and in its original form was an instrumental called *Little Buttercup,* which pal Joe Venuti promptly recorded with Frank Signorelli on piano on June 1931, for the OKeh label. Fortunately for the composers, Gus Kahn was invited into the picture to write the lyrics and promptly changed the title to *I'll Never Be the Same.* The rest is musical history. With a slower tempo, a new title, and lyrics by Gus Kahn, it was one of the highlights of 1932—a great song in a year of great songs. Mildred Bailey loved it, sang it on the radio with Paul Whiteman, and they recorded it. The popular Ruth Etting also recorded it, and so did Adelaide Hall. Guy Lombardo made it for Brunswick and The Embassy Orchestra waxed it on the Depression label Crown. A perennial favorite with musicians and bandleaders, it is still frequently recorded and in later renditions can be heard in outstanding sides by Artie Shaw, Teddy Wilson, Phil Napoleon, and Ziggy Elman.

Although not quite up to the standard of *I'll Never Be the Same,* two other very nice songs by Malneck were published in 1932. *So at Last It's Come to This,* another collaboration with Gus Kahn and Frank Signorelli, was recorded by Paul Whiteman with a vocal by Irene Taylor, but it deserved much better attention than it received, as did many songs of the era that got lost in the competitive rush. That year Malneck paid a visit to England and while overseas collaborated with the famous British songwriters and publishers James Campbell and Reg Connolly on another pleasant ballad, *Till Tomorrow,* and just to make sure this event wasn't overlooked, Mr. Malneck and his violin recorded it on an English Columbia record as a guest of Carroll Gibbons and His Boy Friends. Rudy Vallee made it for the domestic Columbia label.

For some reason Malneck had no entries for 1933, but he was back the following year with the man who would be his partner on a number of hit songs,

Johnny Mercer. They started out with two songs, *If I Had a Million Dollars,* which was introduced by the Boswell Sisters in the movie *Transatlantic Merry-Go-Round* and very adequately covered on recordings by Richard Himber, Joe Haymes, and Ozzie Nelson, among others, and the quirky novelty *Pardon My Southern Accent.* Johnny Mercer, more than just an adequate vocalist, had fun with his song on a Paul Whiteman Victor, Pee Wee Hunt did his best with Glen Gray on Brunswick, and the irrepressible Eddie Stone had his say on an Isham Jones Decca. In 1935, a very eventful year for Malneck, they repeated the success, and for another movie, *To Beat the Band,* they wrote *If You Were Mine; Eeny Meeny Miney Mo;* and *Santa Claus Came in the Spring. If You Were Mine* achieved classic status on the Brunswick recording by Teddy Wilson with Billie Holiday's vocal. Johnny Mercer introduced *Eeny Meeny Miney Mo* in the movie and recorded it in a duet with Ginger Rogers for Decca. The Bob Crosby band recorded it for Decca, Benny Goodman made it on Victor, and Teddy Wilson with Billie Holiday caught up with them a year later on Brunswick. *Santa Claus Came in the Spring* was recorded by the Goodman band, and the side is unique because it features a vocal by trombonist Joe Harris. In that same year Malneck and Frank Signorelli composed an instrumental suite they called *Park Avenue Fantasy.* As such, it was respectfully performed, but with limited acceptance. Then in 1939, the man with the magic pen, Mitchell Parish, added lyrics to the main theme of the suite, and as *Stairway to the Stars* it went on to become one of the top songs of the year. Matty Malneck and His Orchestra recorded it under the original title, but the big records were by Glenn Miller for Bluebird, Sammy Kaye on Victor, Kay Kyser on Brunswick, and Al Donahue on Vocalion. Martha Raye and Kenny Baker also recorded the tune as a vocal. *Stairway to the Stars* was featured on *Your Hit Parade* for twelve weeks, in the number one spot for four of them.

In the meantime, in 1936 Malneck and Mercer combined on the swingy *Goody-Goody,* which proved ideal for the Goodman interpretation with Helen Ward. Bob Crosby had a successful record too, and the tune enjoyed considerable airtime. As *Stairway to the Stars* would do three years later, *Goody-Goody* spent twelve weeks on *Your Hit Parade,* four of them in the number one spot. Malneck took another rest in 1937, but in 1938 he and Frank Loesser turned out a song for the film *St. Louis Blues* that was introduced by Dorothy Lamour, the clever *I Go for That.* They paired up again the next year, and this time it was *Snug as a Bug in a Rug.* Jan Savitt recorded it, and so did Jack Marshard. Then, of course, this was the year that *Stairway to the Stars* climbed to top honors.

Around this time Malneck left Whiteman in order to front his own group, and if you happen to see a rerun on TV of the Bing Crosby 1939 film *East Side of Heaven* or the Jack Benny picture *Man about Town,* you will hear the Malneck orchestra. However, neither film included one of his songs, although another movie, *Hawaiian Nights,* did—two tunes with Frank Loesser, *Hey, Good Looking; Snug as a Bug in a Rug;* and the beautiful *Stairway to the Stars*. Malneck used this from then on as his radio theme when broadcasting with his band. He continued to lead bands well into the forties, but his composing slacked off. Then in 1946 he and Robert Maxwell, who played harp in his orchestra, collaborated on *Shangri-La.* They recorded it for Columbia as a two-part instrumental. With lyrics added by Carl Sigman, it was revived as a vocal in 1957 by the Four Coins on Epic, and again by Vic Dana in 1964, and still again by the Lettermen in 1969.

Finally, for those of you who appreciate great jazz fiddle, you can hear Matty Malneck on such jazz classics as records by Annette Hanshaw, Irving Mills and the Hotsy Totsy Gang, the New Orleans Blackbirds, Jack Pettis, Frankie Trumbauer, Mildred Bailey, Paul Whiteman, Bing Crosby, and a whole series of recordings on Decca and Columbia under his own name. But if you can't remember him for anything else, keep in mind that he and Frank Signorelli wrote *I'll Never Be the Same* and *Stairway to the Stars.*

Bernard Maltin

Pianist-composer Bernard Maltin was born in New York City on June 17, 1907. He received his musical education at the Juilliard School of Music and went on to play piano in dance bands, including those of Ben Bernie and Ray Heatherton. He also served as accompanist to vocalist Connee Boswell and during WW II was in the USMS. Maltin's association with the Bernie organization resulted in his first published song in 1926, a ballad called *Afraid (Of Losing You),* a collaboration with Ken Casey. The Bernie Orchestra recorded it for Brunswick, and Bob Haring also waxed it for the Cameo label.

In 1935 Maltin teamed with Joe Young and Harry Stride on a pretty song, *Because of Once upon a Time,* which achieved immortality by being recorded by Fats Waller twice, once for Victor and again on transcription. Johnny Green's orchestra also made it for Columbia. With Harry Stride, but with Ralph Freed in place of Joe Young, Maltin had his best-selling song in 1936, *Don't Count Your Kisses.* Ozzie Nelson waxed it for Brunswick, and Red McKenzie made it for Decca with a group that included Bunny Berigan and Frank Signorelli. Other Maltin titles are *You Are Music; I'm Good for Nothing but Love; Dixie Vagabond; Little Shirley Temple;* and the fine piano solo and instrumental *Finesse.*

Bernard Maltin died in New York City on April 10, 1952.

Henry Mancini

Pianist-composer-conductor Henry Mancini was born in Cleveland, Ohio, on April 16, 1924. He received his basic musical education at Carnegie Tech Music School and Juilliard. Early in his career he played piano in dance bands then put in military service during WW II. In the late forties he worked as a pianist-arranger with Tex Beneke's band and then moved on to a staff job with Universal Pictures. At a period in popular music when quality songs were difficult to sell, Mancini found an outlet for his material by writing for movies and TV, and first attracted national attention in the late fifties with his scoring and composing for the TV series *Peter Gunn.* In 1960 he composed the theme for the TV series *Mr. Lucky* and had the hit record with his own orchestra on RCA.

The following year he wrote the music and Johnny Mercer the words to a song introduced by Audrey Hepburn in the film *Breakfast at Tiffany's, Moon River.* Not the greatest song either one ever wrote, it nevertheless scored big with the public. It collected an Academy Award, a Grammy Award, and again Henry Mancini and His Orchestra had the best-seller, followed by the vocal record by Andy Williams. Mercer and Mancini atoned for everything in 1962 by producing the excellent title song for the Jack Lemmon film *The Days of Wine and Roses.* This also drew top honors—an Academy Award and a Grammy—and again Mancini and Andy Williams had the best-selling records.

On a roll, Mercer and Mancini came up with still another title song, this one for the picture *Charade.* The usual Mancini and Williams records were augmented with one by Sammy Kaye, but this time no awards were forthcoming. Mancini justified this in the next year, though, by composing the theme for *The Pink Panther.* Winning a Grammy in 1964, the song ran through all the subsequent sequels to the original film and had another life in TV commercials for Owens-Corning insulation material. Other Mancini titles include *Palladium Patrol; Baby Elephant Walk; Dear Heart; The Sweetheart Tree;* and the title songs for a number of movies.

Johnny Mandel

Jazz musician-arranger-composer Johnny Mandel was born in New York City on November 23, 1925. A thoroughly schooled musician, he studied arranging with Van Alexander when only thirteen years old, and he also attended the Manhattan School of Music and Juilliard. Privately, he studied with Stefan Volpe, Bernard Wagner, Mario Castelnuovo-Tedesco, and George Trembly. He started out as a jazz trombonist and arranger for dance bands, including those of Joe Venuti, Jimmy Dorsey, and Alvino Rey, among others. In 1949 he arranged for Artie Shaw. Meanwhile, he wrote for radio and TV, especially *Your Show of Shows*. In 1953 he was with Count Basie as trombonist-arranger and contributed the instrumental *Straight Life*.

Settling on the West Coast, he began to write for movies, composing scores for some important pictures. Some of his credits include *You're Never Too Young; I Want to Live; The Americanization of Emily; The Sandpiper; The Russians Are Coming; Harper; An American Dream;* and *Drums of Africa*. Like Henry Mancini, he found an outlet for quality songs in films. In 1964 he wrote a theme for the James Garner film *The Americanization of Emily,* and with lyrics added by Johnny Mercer it became *Emily,* a beautiful song that resulted in a hit record for singer Andy Williams and became a staple item in the repertoire of Bobby Hackett. Hackett recorded it on a Project 3 LP in 1967 called *That Midnight Touch*.

Almost as though the producers didn't know what to do with the song, the wonderful *The Shadow of Your Smile* was played behind the closing credits in the movie *The Sandpiper* in 1965. With fine lyrics by Paul Francis Webster it went on to win an Academy Award and a Grammy and become a best-selling record for singer Tony Bennett. It has also assumed the role of a standard. Tony Bennett had another hit record with the Mandel–Webster song *A Time for Love,* introduced by Jackie Ward, whose voice was dubbed on the soundtrack of the movie *An American Dream* for actress Janet Leigh. The song was nominated for an Academy Award.

Other Johnny Mandel songs are *The Shining Sea; Close Enough for Love; Suicide Is Painless;* and *Not Really the Blues*.

David Mann

David Mann was born in Philadelphia, Pennsylvania, on October 3, 1916. He received his Master's degree from Villanova University and also attended the University of Pennsylvania and the Curtis Institute of Music. He began his professional career while still in high school, broadcasting on the radio and working in a piano duo known as Mann and Irwin. In the early forties he played piano in the bands of Jimmy Dorsey and Charlie Spivak, doubling as arranger. During a hitch in the army during World War II, he became President Harry Truman's official pianist.

After his discharge, he began a successful career as an arranger, writing for stars like Frank Sinatra, Ella Fitzgerald, Martha Tilton, and Billie Holiday and for bands like Ray Bloch's and Ray Noble's. In addition, he arranged for Broadway stage presentations, radio broadcasts, and movies. Then, just to be sure he covered all bases, he wrote newspaper editorials, and taught in the Walden School, New York, as head of the music department. He began songwriting in the early forties, and his first published song, *Made Up My Mind,* came out in 1941, but it wasn't until 1945 that he had a successful song. This was in collaboration with Redd Evans, and the tune was *There, I've Said It Again.* Oddly enough, the song had been recorded on Bluebird by Benny Carter's orchestra four years earlier, but Vaughn Monroe had the hit record in 1945 on Victor. Jimmy Dorsey also made a good-selling record for Decca, as did the Modernaires for Columbia.

Nevertheless, four more years went by before Mann had another hit. Redd Evans again was his partner, and they turned out the highly original *No Moon at All.* It was recorded by Nat "King" Cole, but once more it remained for the 1953 recording by the Ames Brothers with Les Brown's band on Coral to put the song on the charts. In the meantime, Mann teamed with Bob Hilliard on the 1950 novelty *Dearie (You're Much Older Than I),* which Ray Bolger and Ethel Merman recorded on a very successful record for Decca. Other hit records followed by Guy Lombardo and by Jo Stafford with Gordon MacRae. In 1954 Mann and Hilliard contributed a Calypso-styled song to the revue at the Copacabana nightclub, *Somebody Bad Stole de Wedding Bell (Who's Got de Ding Dong?).* Ertha Kitt had the big hit on RCA-Victor. Georgia Gibbs made it for Mercury.

Frank Sinatra had the definitive recording of *In the Wee Small Hours of the Morning,* the David Mann–Bob Hilliard offering for 1955. In the following year, Mann and Arthur Kent combined to write the music to Redd Evan's lyrics for *Don't Go to Strangers,* which was a successful record for Vaughn Monroe. Etta Jones revived the song in 1960 on a record for Prestige. Other songs by David Mann include *These Will Be the Best Years of Our Lives; Jealous Eyes; Downhearted; I'll Sing to You; Rhyme Your Name; I've Only Myself to Blame;* and *Passing Fancy.*

Paul Mann

Composer Paul Mann was born in Vienna, Austria, on September 3, 1910. He received his major education at the Academy of Music in Vienna and embarked on a career of composing songs for the stage and movies in Austria and Germany. He came to the United States in 1937, and almost immediately began writing a string of very successful songs. Possibly the most important song in his limited but brilliant output is the 1938 hit *They Say.*

This tune had a clever lyric by Edward Heyman, and Mann collaborated with Stephan Weiss on the music. Considering that it wasn't part of a movie or stage score, it enjoyed all-out acceptance and popularity and was recorded by a long list of the heaviest hitters in the field—Artie Shaw, with the vocal by Helen Forrest; Teddy Wilson, with Billie Holiday; Red Norvo, with Mildred Bailey; Connee Boswell with Woody Herman's Orchestra; plus the bands of Sammy Kaye and Ted Fio Rito. Blues singer Ethel Waters also made it. Eddie DeLange contributed the words to another big hit by composers Mann and Weiss, the 1940 entry *And So Do I*. Again, it rated very respectable treatment, with top records by the Jimmy Dorsey band with Helen O'Connell's vocal; Tommy Dorsey with Connie Haines singing; Raymond Scott with Nan Wynn; and Francis Langford accompanied by Victor Young's Orchestra.

Changing lyricists but still collaborating with Stephan Weiss, Mann scored again that year with *Angel in Disguise*. Kim Gannon wrote the words to the pleasant ballad, and it did well on records, too, with platters by Bob Crosby's band—Marion Mann on the vocal—singer Dick Todd, and the bands of Ozzie Nelson and Lou Breeze. The same team followed through the next year with *Make Love to Me*. This tune went the rounds of the record labels of the day—Artie Shaw with Paula Kelly on Victor, Teddy Powell with Ruth Gaynor on the vocal for Bluebird, the Harry James band with Helen Forrest on Columbia, and Ella Fitzgerald for Decca. Ruth Lowe penned the words for *Put Your Dreams Away,* the Mann–Weiss melody that became Frank Sinatra's theme song. They wrote the song in 1942, but it wasn't until 1945 that Sinatra recorded it with Axel Stordahl's orchestra for Columbia.

Paul Mann's other credits include *The Finger of Suspicion; Anybody's Love Song; When You Look in Your Looking Glass;* and *The Woodchuck Song*.

Sol Marcus

Pianist-composer-arranger Sol Marcus was born in New York City on October 12, 1912. He attended schools in Linden, New Jersey, and Columbia University. Marcus was a friend of mine. I didn't know him when he was writing his hit songs in the forties, but many years later we often worked together on music jobs. I enjoyed his company as a person and respected his ability as a pianist. One of my prized possessions from those years is a tape recorded at a senior prom dance at Kean College. When I put the band together for the date I decided to use two pianos, and since two baby grands were available, the instruments presented no problem. But very few places provide these facilities, piano players usually work alone and, as a result, don't get to work with and know other pianists. So on the night of the prom I introduced Sol Marcus to Ed Tompkins, who would man the other keyboard, and a memorable evening was had by all.

Marcus and his usual collaborators, Eddie Seiler and Bennie Benjamin, wrote a lot of songs and finally scored with a number of hits, but not every song got published; and even those that did were not always successful. This is especially true of a delightful little tune that went nowhere in popularity but did succeed in getting recorded in a virtuoso performance by Les Paul and His Trio on Decca 23444 as an instrumental. The title is *Dream Dust,* with Seiler and Guy Wood sharing composer credit with Marcus. I distinctly recall Sol's surprise the first time I asked him to play it. "How do you know about that one?" he wanted to know. "It never made it."

There were others that never got recorded, and as many an aspiring tunesmith has found out to his regret, it isn't easy getting a song published. Of course, the team of Marcus, Seiler, Benjamin, and Eddie Durham hit big in 1941 with *I Don't Want to Set the World on Fire,* the song that established them in the business, provided bandleader Tommy Tucker with the biggest record in his band's history, and went on to a fifteen-week spot on *Your Hit Parade,* four of them in the number one slot. But if you think this was a snap, you're wrong. The song was turned down repeatedly, and in at least one instance this illustrates that even experts can guess wrong. Sol told me that the team took the song to Benny Goodman, and Goodman asked his ace arranger, Fletcher Henderson, what he thought of it. Henderson's comment was less than enthusiastic, so Goodman decided not to record the song. Tommy Tucker, however, willingly recorded another Marcus-Seiler–Benjamin title that same year, *Cancel the Flowers.* The tearful ditty did fairly well.

Then came 1942, a gloomy year with a dire prospect, and Marcus and his friends did their best to cheer things up with *When the Lights Go On Again All Over the World.* Vaughn Monroe had a big-seller on Victor, with Les Brown right behind him on OKeh. Lucky Millinder recorded it for Decca. More important in those years, the song gained a lot of airtime on the radio. Marcus, Seiler, and Benjamin, aided and abetted by Edgar Battle, were also responsible for the Harry James hit instrumental *Strictly Instrumental.* It was listed on the charts for three months. In 1944 Marcus and Eddie Seiler worked with the English composer Guy Wood, and the result was *Till Then,* an immediate smash recording for the Mills Brothers. The Hilltoppers group managed to recapture some of the glory in 1954, with a chart record for the Dot label. Another juggling of the team in 1965 brought abut Bennie Benjamin and Marcus collaborating with Gloria Caldwell on the grammatical conundrum *Don't Let Me Be Misunderstood.* Appropriately, this was a hit record for M-G-M by the English group the Animals. Sol Marcus also had a hand in the following titles: *Ask Anyone Who Knows; You're Gonna Fall and Break Your Heart; Small World; Fishin' for the Moon; The Girl from Jones Beach; And Then It's Heaven; Because You Love Me; Lonely Man; Of this I'm Sure.*

Sol Marcus died in Linden, New Jersey, on February 6, 1976.

Paul Mares

Pioneer jazz cornetist, bandleader, and composer Paul Mares was born in New Orleans, Louisiana, on June 15, 1900. He was educated at the St. Aloysius School and served with the United States Marines in World War I. While in New Orleans he was an active musician on the local scene, working frequently with the talented clarinetist Leon Roppolo (sometimes spelled Rappolo) and the Brunies brothers. In 1919 he went to Chicago with Tom Brown, and after some mixup in the musical chairs, wound up organizing the Friars Society Orchestra, with Roppolo and trombonist George Brunies. (Brunies later changed his name to Brunis on the advice of a numerologist.)

Mares and his cohorts are not in the category of popular songwriters, but Mares, especially, is credited with cocomposing three very important jazz instrumental standards, staples in the repertoire of all traditional jazz bands, but also favorites of big band arrangers. The titles are *Milenberg Joys; Farewell Blues;* and *Tin Roof Blues. Farewell Blues,* a collaboration between Mares and pianist Elmer Schoebel, was written in 1922 and recorded by the Friars Society Orchestra (later and better known as the New Orleans Rhythm Kings) on Gennett. Among the countless records since are sides by Ted Lewis, Paul Whiteman, Cab Calloway, and Woody Herman.

Tin Roof Blues has the Mares name on it too, but this tune is more accurately credited to the entire personnel of the New Orleans Rhythm Kings, plus the added help of Walter Melrose, who wasn't a member of the band. The others were Leon Roppolo, George Brunis, Mel Stitzel, and Ben Pollack. The Kings kicked the tune off with a recording for Gennett, followed by the Memphis Five on Victor and the Original Indiana Five for Pathe/Perfect. When the famous Greenwich Village jazz club "Nick's" existed in the forties and fifties, *Tin Roof Blues* was the theme that was used as a bridge between sets, indicating that one band was winding up a set, and the next one was to take over the bandstand. In 1954 words were added by Bill Norvas and Allan Copeland to a watered-down version of the melody, and as

Make Love to Me it became a million-seller for vocalist Jo Stafford on Columbia. Nevertheless, as the venerable *Tin Roof Blues* it retains its immortality. *Milenberg Joys* is credited to Mares, Leon Roppolo, and Ferd "Jelly Roll" Morton. All three were members of the Kings in 1925, when the tune was published, and the band recorded it for Gennett no less than three times, all with piano solos by Morton. It has since undergone a lot of special treatment on records by Glen Gray, Tommy Dorsey, and Larry Clinton, just to mention a few.

Mares was active on the Chicago music scene well into the forties, leading jazz combos. In January of 1935 he recorded four sides for the original OKeh label with a group of Chicago jazz musicians under the name of Paul Mares and His Friars Society Orchestra. The titles were *Nagasaki; The Land of Dreams; Reincarnation;* and *Maple Leaf Rag*. Jess Stacy was the pianist on these records, and the story goes that Mares, knowing that Benny Goodman was looking for a pianist, recommended Stacy. Goodman listened to Stacy on the Mares records and was sold, and thus began the famous association.

Paul Mares died in Chicago on August 18, 1949.

George Marion Jr.

Lyricist-librettist-author George Marion Jr. was born in Boston, Massachusetts, on August 30, 1899. He was educated at the La Villa School in Lausanne, Switzerland, and Harvard University. In the thirties he wrote scenarios for sound movies, including *Love Me Tonight, The Big Broadcast of 1932, We're Not Dressing, The Gay Divorcee,* and *College Rhythm*. Then at the end of the decade and into the forties he wrote the librettos for Broadway shows such as "Too Many Girls," "Beat the Band," "Early to Bed," and "Marinka." As a lyricist, he collaborated with a distinguished list of composers—Fats Waller, Sammy Fain, Johnny Green, Emmerich Kalman—but his most memorable songs were written with Richard Whiting. An early example is *My Sweeter Than Sweet,* which was introduced by Nancy Carroll in the 1929 film, *Sweetie*. Leo Reisman recorded it for Victor, featuring a piano solo by future bandleader Eddy Duchin.

In 1930 Richard Whiting and Marion wrote two outstanding songs, both distinguished by excellent lyrics. *My Future Just Passed* was sung by Charles "Buddy" Rogers in the film *Safety in Numbers*. He also recorded it for Columbia, and the song enjoyed popularity on the radio. It did well on other recordings too, with Annette Hanshaw, Chick Bullock, the Boswell Sisters, and the California Ramblers all sharing the pie. In England it was a best-seller for Arthur Rosebery and his band. In the forties the song was revived by vocalist Dick Haymes on a Decca record, backed by the Les Paul Trio. The other 1930 gem is *It Seems to Be Spring,* which was featured in the film *Let's Go Native.* A delightful melody, the George Marion lyrics complement it perfectly, and the song is an ideal illustration of the high standard of popular songwriting of this era. At the same time, it must be admitted that it was not a great hit and, as I recall, was usually performed as an instrumental. It remained for that timely troubadour Clancey Hayes to reprise the song and its clever lyrics twenty years later.

Adorable was the title of a 1933 movie that starred Janet Gaynor, and Marion and Richard Whiting wrote the popular waltz that was the title song. It was featured and recorded by Wayne King, the Waltz King, and by pianist Lee Sims and the bands of Freddy Martin and Little Jack Little. In 1942 Marion paired with composer Johnny Green for the music, and with George Abbott on the book, for the stage show "Beat the Band." It didn't do too well, but one song got some attention, *The Steam Is on the Beam.*

Other George Marion titles are *Love Is a Random Thing; There's a Man in My Life; I Think You'll Like It; Prep Step; A Bee in Your Boudoir; My Mad Moment; Proud of You; Keep It Casual;* and *The Ladies Who Sing With a Band.*

Gerald Marks

Although the name Gerald Marks may not be one that falls into the classification of a household variety, it certainty should be a familiar one because Marks wrote a song that is most likely one of your favorites, *All of Me.* He also wrote one of mine, another of those great tunes from the early thirties that only managed to make a faint splash in the flood of wonderful songs of the era, *The Night Shall Be Filled with Music.* Gerald Marks was born in Saginaw, Michigan, in the portentous year of 1900, on October 11, and by the time the twenties were in full bloom he was playing piano in dance bands. He was playing piano at a resort in North Michigan when Seymour Simons, bandleader and lyricist, overheard him run over the melody of *All of Me,* which was still without a title or words. Simons like the tune, asked Marks to jot down the melody line, and only a short time later returned with the lyrics.

The team had faith in their newborn brainchild, but getting it published wouldn't be easy, and they knew it. I had the pleasure of hearing Marks tell the fabulous story of what took place from that point on, at a meeting of the New York Sheet Music Society, and as closely as I can remember, this is what he said.

"Since the most important music publishers were in New York, Seymour Simons insisted I take the song and make a personal circuit of Tin Pan Alley. I made the trip and faithfully made the rounds of all the publishing houses without any success. Discouraged I went back to Michigan. A bit later a friend mentioned that Belle Baker, an important star of vaudeville in those days, was appearing at a local theater, and suggested I ask to play the song for her. Sometimes a star could plug a song into a hit. I went to the theater, and at the stage door asked to see Miss Baker. There was no problem. I went right to her dressing room, and she was getting ready for her next show. As luck would have it, there was a little piano in the room, and when I told her why I was there, she pointed at the piano.

"'Bring it right over here, and play for me.'

"I rolled the piano right next to her dressing table, and started to play. I sang the words, and all at once I realized something was very wrong. Miss Baker was sobbing and crying, and altogether acting completely miserable. It wasn't until later that I found out she had just undergone a personal loss, and my song hit a sensitive nerve. I stopped playing, but she insisted I keep going, and I played the tune over several times. When I left she told me she would see what she could do. I thanked her, but as time went on and I didn't hear anything, I forgot about the whole thing.

"But a miracle was getting ready to happen. Belle Baker was interviewed on WOR, a radio station located in Newark, N.J., on a program that was aired at midnight. Midnight, mind you, because how many working people stayed up to listen to radio that late in those days, and how many could have heard the broadcast? Nevertheless, Belle Baker sang *All of Me* without any accompaniment, and somebody must have heard her, because the station began to get calls asking where they could buy the song. In turn, the station began calling the music publishers, and all at once *All of Me* was hot property—and none of them had it!

"I started to get telegrams: 'Dear Gerry, we knew you could do it. Have a great deal for you.' Suddenly we're on a first name basis. Anyway, I went back to New York—this time they wanted me—and the tune was published and became a hit."

Marks's songwriting career began with *All of Me* in 1931, but in that same year he scored again with a very respectable hit, *Can't Write the Words*. The next year only one song was published, *You're the One,* but Marks contributed some material to "Earl Carroll's Sketch Book" in 1935, one of which, *Dust Off That Old Pianna,* still gets played on occasion, and he did rather well with a freelance offering, *I Don't Know Your Name (But You're Wonderful)*. The following year, 1936, was a big one for Marks, because some of his songs were used in the movies, particularly *That's What I Want for Christmas,* which enjoyed the popularity so many Christmas songs did before the market potential was realized and we were overwhelmed with them. Marks struck it big with *Is It True What They Say About Dixie?* This was to be his last big hit, although he kept on writing, and in 1954 was part of the ASCAP group that toured U.S. army bases abroad. Among his special works are the *Songs of Safety* series for children.

Johnny Marks

Songwriter and publisher Johnny Marks was born in Mt. Vernon, New York, on November 19, 1909. He was educated at Colgate and Columbia Universities and studied music in Paris. He produced radio shows, coached singers, and produced army shows overseas during the Second World War. He was awarded the Bronze Star and four Battle Stars. In 1949 he organized St. Nicholas Music and edited the *Christmas Community Lyric Book.* That was the year his best-known song, *Rudolph, the Red-Nosed Reindeer* was published. Prior to this, he had several good songs published, notably *Summer Holiday,* a 1936 entry that was more than adequately treated by Dick McDonough and his all-start group on ARC, with a vocal by the still-to-be-recognized Buddy Clark. But none of them were hits. *Rudolph,* on the other hand, was a blockbuster and is still to be heard every holiday season. So writing Christmas songs became a career for Marks, and he has a long list to his credit—*Rockin' Around the Christmas Tree* (which did well in 1958, as synonymous with the current fad); *I Heard the Bells on Christmas Day; A Merry Merry Christmas; The Night before Christmas Song; Everyone's a Child at Christmas; When Santa Gets Your Letter; A Holly Jolly Christmas; Silver and Gold; The Most Wonderful Day of the Year;* and *Jingle Jingle Jingle.* Other titles include *Neglected; Don't Cross Your Fingers, Cross Your Heart; Address Unknown; Who Calls?; She'll Always Remember; What Have You Got to Lose (But Your Heart)?; Cane Bottom Chair; Happy New Year, Darling;* and *How Long Is Forever?*

Hugh Martin

Composer Hugh Martin was born in Birmingham, Alabama, on August 11, 1914. He was educated at Birmingham Southern College and studied with Edna Gussen and Dorsey Whittington. He met his collaborator, lyricist

Ralph Blane, when they were both in the cast of the stage show "Hooray for What?" in 1937. Martin was the vocal arranger for that and other shows, including "One for the Money," "Too Many Girls," Dubarry Was a Lady," "Louisiana Purchase," "Streets of Paris," and "Stars in Your Eyes." With Blane he formed a vocal quartet called the Martins, and they sang on the Fred Allen radio program.

The team of Martin and Blane started off big in 1941, providing the score for the successful stage musical "Best Foot Forward," which included three well-received songs, *Buckle Down Winsocki; Shady Lady Bird;* and *Ev'ry Time*. The first was recorded by the Benny Goodman band on Columbia. The second and the third were recorded back-to-back by Nancy Walker, who starred in the show. They did even better in 1944 with the music for the Judy Garland film *Meet Me in St. Louis*. This time the entries were *The Trolley Song; The Boy Next Door;* and *Have Yourself a Merry Little Christmas*. Judy Garland recorded all three. *The Trolley Song* got the most attention, was nominated for an Academy Award, and was recorded by the Pied Pipers, Vaughn Monroe, the King Sisters, and Guy Lombardo. It was on *Your Hit Parade* for fourteen weeks, five of them in the top spot. The songs were revived in the 1989 stage production of "Meet Me in St. Louis."

In 1947 another Martin–Blane song was nominated for an Academy Award, *Pass That Peace Pipe,* from the movie *Good News*. That same year they worked with Roger Edens to turn out the freelance tune *Connecticut,* which was a pleasant duet on Decca by Bing Crosby and Margaret Whiting. The Blane–Martin partnership ended that year, and Hugh Martin continued writing on his own and with others well into the sixties. Although the shows were successful, the songs didn't become popular. The following titles were also composed by Hugh Martin: *Who Do You Think I Am?; That's How I Love the Blues; The Joint Is Really Jumping; Carnegie Hall; Love; Tiny Room; If You'll Be Mine; I'm Not So Bright; The Little Boy Blues; The Way It Might Have Been; That Face!; When Does This Feeling Go Away?; What I Was Warned About; Over and Over; Paris, France; Love Can Change the Stars; You'd Better Love Me; Where Is the Man I Married?; Was She Prettier Than I?; Home Sweet Heaven; If I Gave You;* and *Forever and a Day*.

Joseph McCarthy

Lyricist Joseph McCarthy, a pioneer in the annals of Tin Pan Alley, was born in Somerville, Massachusetts, on September 27, 1885. Like Irving Berlin, McCarthy started out as a singing waiter and then took the usual path of budding songwriters, going to work for music publishers. He published his first song in 1910, a rather exotic title for anybody named McCarthy, *That Dreamy Italian Waltz.* In 1913 he and James Monaco wrote *You Made Me Love You,* a contemporary hit for Al Jolson, who recorded it for Columbia, and then incorporated it into his performances at the Winter Garden. Judy Garland sang it to a photograph of Clark Gable in the movie *The Broadway Melody of '38* and then recorded it as *Dear Mr. Gable* for a very successful Decca side. In 1941 Harry James, leaning heavy on the schmaltz, had a million-seller on Columbia.

I have an amusing recollection of an incident that took place around this time at Nick's, the jazz club in Greenwich Village. Somebody in the audience requested the band to play the song—disregarding the fact that it was not in the usual repertory—and they complied. Wild Bill Davison was the trumpet player, and he gave it his customary steam rendition. Then as the band was about to leave the stand for the intermission, I overheard him remark to one of the other musicians, "Hey, that tune ain't half bad when it's played like that. But have you heard that thing by Harry James?" Aside from Bill's opinion, the song kept on going. In 1946 Al Jolson reclaimed it for the movie *The Jolson Story,* and the soundtrack was used again in a montage effect for the 1949 film *Jolson Sings Again.* Doris Day, portraying Ruth Etting, sang it in *Love Me or Leave Me,* the 1955 biographical film.

With fellow lyricist Howard E. Johnson, McCarthy collaborated with James Monaco on the 1916 song, *What Do You Want to Make Those Eyes at Me For?* Billy Murray and Ada Jones had the contemporary recording on Columbia. In 1937 singer Bob Howard gave it a swinging treatment accompanied by an all-star studio group on Decca 1605. It was also featured in the Donald O'Connor–Peggy Ryan film *The Merry Monahans,* and again in the Betty Hutton movie *Incendiary Blonde,* the glorified screen bio of Texas Guinan. In 1918 McCarthy and composer Harry Carroll performed a little musical plagiarism for the Broadway musical "Oh, Look!", borrowing a little phrase from Chopin to come up with the hit song *I'm Always Chasing Rainbows.* In 1919 he collaborated with Harry Tierney on the music for the Broadway musical "Irene," writing the title song, another called *Castle of Dreams,* and the all-time hit *Alice Blue Gown.* In the 1940 movie revival of the show, the song was sung by Anna Neagle; in 1973 it was reprised by Debbie Reynolds in the stage revival.

McCarthy continued in a very successful career of writing for stage musicals, including "Kid Boots" (1924); "Rio Rita" (1927); and Cross My Heart" (1928). Then, just as though to prove they could do it, he and James Monaco penned the 1929 hit *Through (How Can You Say We're Through),* a freelance entry on the open market. It went the complete circuit of the record labels. Casa Loma recorded it for OKeh; Roger Wolfe Kahn for Brunswick; Ted Lewis on Columbia; and Leo Reisman on Victor. Vocalist Sid Gary made it for Perfect. *High Society Blues,* a movie starring Janet Gaynor and Charles Farrell, offered a score by James F. Hanley and Joseph McCarthy in 1930. Two titles, *High Society Blues* and *Eleanor,* were recorded by the New Mayfair Orchestra, directed by Ray Noble, on HMV, the English label. Two others, *Just Like in a Story Book* and *I'm in the Market for You,* received excellent treatment by Bob Haring's Orchestra on Brunswick. Louis Armstrong made *I'm in the Market for You* with his New Sebastian Cotton Club Orchestra for OKeh. *Sing Song Girl* was a popular 1931 entry, with James F. Hanley writing the melody, and in 1932 Joseph McCarthy wrote American lyrics for the British import *Underneath the Arches,* with words and music by Reg Connelly and Bud Flanagan. George Olsen had the best-selling record with a vocal by Ethel Shutta. In 1948 the song enjoyed a revival and made it to *Your Hit Parade.* In 1940 McCarthy wrote the words to Jimmy Van Heusen's music for the Billy Rose Aquacade. "Irene," with the original stage score, was made into a movie. "Rio Rita" followed suit in 1942.

Joseph McCarthy died in New York City on December 18, 1943.

Jimmy McHugh

Without any question, composer Jimmy McHugh is one of the giants of Tin Pan Alley. With a prolific output of material for stage, screen, and the popular market, plus a list of hits and standards that reads like an all-time hit parade, his credentials are overwhelming. Many of his songs have become fixtures in the jazz catalog, even though they were written as popular songs of the day; their merit is such that they will probably remain an integral segment of our musical heritage. Jimmy McHugh was born in Boston, Massachusetts, on July 10, 1894. He was educated at St. John's Prep and Holy Cross College. He started his musical career as a rehearsal pianist. His first hit song was written with popular singing star of the twenties Gene Austin and Irving Mills. The tune was *When My Sugar Walks Down the Street,* the year was 1924, and from that point on scarcely a year went by without at least one McHugh song success.

In 1925 the entry was *Everything Is Hotsy Totsy Now,* another collaboration with Irving Mills; in 1926 it was *My Dream of the Big Parade,* with Al Dubin, written as a promotional song for the movie *The Big Parade;* and in 1927 *I Can't Believe That You're in Love with Me,* in partnership with

Clarence Gaskill. In 1928 McHugh joined Dorothy Fields in writing music for the stage show "Blackbirds of 1928," with a resulting grand slam of hits—*I Can't Give You Anything but Love; I Must Have That Man; Diga Diga Doo; Doin' the New Low Down; Baby;* and *Bandanna Babies*. But this was just the beginning. In the following year the stage show was "Hello Daddy," and Fields and McHugh scored well again with *Let's Sit and Talk About You; Out Where the Blues Begin;* and *Futuristic Rhythm*. They then went on to do even better in 1930 for the "International Revue," a show that starred Gertrude Lawrence, Harry Richman, Jack Pearl, and other headliners, with two songs that were destined to become standards, *On the Sunny Side of the Street* and *Exactly Like You*.

There were no big hits in 1931, but the team still managed to turn out one of those "sleepers" I love so much, *It's the Darndest Thing,* which was featured in a movie called *Singin' the Blues*. There was only one entry the next year, but it proved to be an important one, *Goodbye Blues,* which the Mills Brothers sang in the film *The Big Broadcast of 1932* and then adopted as their theme song. *My Dancing Lady,* a movie starring Clark Gable and Joan Crawford, featured the title song by Fields and McHugh, but the really important titles for 1933 were both freelance compositions, *Dinner at Eight* and *Don't Blame Me*. For good measure, there was also *Hey, Young Fella*. Possibly the success of these songs encouraged the team to prove that freelance efforts could still pay off big, and in 1934 they again erased all doubts with *Lost in a Fog* and *Thank You for a Lovely Evening*.

Nevertheless, the following year they went back to writing for the movies, and for the George Raft–Alice Faye epic *Every Night at Eight* they contributed *I'm in the Mood for Love; Take It Easy; I Feel a Song Coming On;* and *Speaking Confidentially*. Another big movie that year was *Roberta,* a Fred Astaire–Ginger Rogers classic. Fields and McHugh added two new songs, *Lovely to Look At* and *I Won't Dance,* to the original score by Jerome Kern and Otto Harbach for the stage show. In 1935 the team began to drift apart. Although they worked together on the music for the Ann Sothern film *Hooray for Love,* coming up with the title song plus *Livin' in a Great Big Way; I'm in Love All Over Again;* and *You're an Angel;* and they also had a nice little song, *Music in My Heart,* in the Wheeler and Woolsey comedy *The Nitwits*. Dorothy Fields went on to collaborate with Oscar Levant, composing the music for *In Person,* a George Raft-–Ginger Rogers film. And with the advent of 1936, Jimmy McHugh began to work with other lyric writers. For the movie *Banjo on My Knee,* he teamed with Harold Adamson; for the Shirley Temple film *Dimples* and for *King of Burlesque,* he worked with Ted Koehler.

Jimmy McHugh continued to write prolifically through the rest of the decade and well into the fifties, working with a variety of lyric writers, including Johnny Mercer, Ned Washington, Al Dubin, and Frank Loesser. Quite a few of the songs they produced were composed for specific scenes in movies and relatively unimportant, but McHugh still came up with some excellent ones. Here are a few of the outstanding titles: *Where Are You; You're a Sweetheart* (1937); *Serenade to the Stars; My Own* (1938); *Rendezvous Time in Paree* (1939); *I'd Know You Anywhere; The Bad Humor Man* (1940); *Can't Get out of This Mood; Let's Get Lost* (1943); *I Couldn't Sleep a Wink Last Night; A Lovely Way to Spend an Evening; In a Moment of Madness* (1944); *I Walked In; I Don't Care Who Knows It* (1945); *I Didn't Mean a Word I Said* (1946); *You Say the Nicest Things, Baby* (1948).

Jimmy McHugh died in Beverly Hills, California, on May 23, 1969, but he left us a rich inheritance of wonderful songs. It's a comforting thought that those who appreciate good music will be able to enjoy them as long as there is someone able and willing to play them.

Theodore (Teddy) McRae

Theodore (Teddy) McRae was born in Philadelphia, Pennsylvania, on January 22, 1908. His education included North Philadelphia High School and Temple College, where he studied medicine. At the same time he took private music lessons. In 1928 he organized a dance band with his brothers which worked the local area. Then he moved on to New York where he went to work for Chick Webb as a sideman and arranger. When Chick Webb died, he continued on with Ella Fitzgerald and then went with Louis Armstrong.

Most likely his first published song was *You Showed Me the Way* (1937), on which he shared credit with Ella Fitzgerald, Chick Webb, and Bud Green. The quality song enjoyed fair success and was recorded and introduced by the Chick Webb band on Decca with Ella on the vocal, but it went the rounds on other labels as well. Billie Holiday sang it with Teddy Wilson's group on Brunswick; Fats Waller liked it so much he recorded it twice for Victor, once with a vocal, the other as an instrumental; Wingy Manone waxed it for Bluebird; Gene Kardos for the ARC labels; Frankie Newton for Vocalion; and in Paris, France, it was recorded by vocalist Edith Wilson. It was also recorded by Michael Warlop with Django Reinhardt and Stephan Grappelli. In 1938 and 1939 McRae collaborated with bandleader Artie Shaw on two instrumentals that were important ingredients in the success of the Shaw band, *Back Bay Shuffle* and *Traffic Jam*.

McRae's other titles include *Jumpin' in a Julep Joint; Broadway; All Night Long; Santa Rosa; You're Too Lovely to Last; Paper Boy; You're Too Sharp to Be Flat; Cincinnati; Daddy; Ding-Dong Boogie;* and *Bang Your Box.*

Walter Melrose

Walter Melrose, listed in ASCAP as "composer-author-publisher," was born in Sumner, Illinois, on October 26, 1889. He received a high school education and by 1912 was already active in the music business. During the First World War he served in the army. From the standpoint of meriting inclusion in this book, he shares credit as cocomposer on several important jazz standards. Since Melrose published the songs, this leads to the suspicion that it was his major contribution; nevertheless, as reported in the profile of Paul Mares, Walter Melrose is on record as a cocomposer of the jazz perennial *Tin Roof Blues,* which was published in 1923. His name is also on the 1924 hit *Copenhagen,* as the lyricist of the Charlie Davis instrumental; and in 1925 he performed the same service for King Oliver's *Dipper Mouth Blues,* which became *Sugar Foot Stomp* as the result of the new words. Melrose is purported to have had something to do with these other great jazz instrumentals, *Milenberg Joys; High Society;* and *Spanish Shawl.* Other titles are *That Same Old Way* and the popularized version of *Tin Roof Blues, Make Love to Me.*

Murray Mencher (Ted Murray)

Composer Murray Mencher, who sometimes wrote under the name of Ted Murray, was born in Boston, Massachusetts, on October 5, 1904. In his early years he played piano in vaudeville and recorded piano rolls. Still later he wrote material for nightclub acts and reviews and for awhile was a coach for Eddie Cantor. As many songwriters did, he went to work for a music publishing firm as a song plugger. His own career as a songwriter kicked off in 1930 with *I Want a Girl,* a heavy hit, and wound up in 1938 with a minor strike, *On the Bumpy Road to Love*. (An interesting sidelight on the latter title is that it is a rare Bobby Hackett side, because he is a member of the Adrian Rollini group backing the Tune Twisters, a vocal unit that recorded it for Vocalion.)

In between the aforementioned years, Mencher wrote some very tasty songs. *Under Your Window Tonight,* for example, was accorded excellent treatment on Columbia and Subsidiary labels by one of Ben Selvin's studio orchestras, with Benny Goodman in the lineup. Then in 1934 he scored rather well with *Alice in Wonderland,* after which he penned a really superior tune, *Throw Another Log On the Fire*. In the next year he contributed *Flowers for Madame* to Earl Carroll's "Sketch Book of 1935." In 1936 Benny Goodman returned in a big way for Murray Mencher, and with Pee Wee Erwin in the band recorded *You Can't Pull the Wool over My Eyes,* with a vocal by Helen Ward. The following November, with Chris Griffin on board, the band waxed *Take Another Guess,* with Ella Fitzgerald. This title, coupled with *Goodnight, My Love,* is famous in Goodman lore, because Fitzgerald was under exclusive contract to Decca records at the time. When Decca protested to Victor, the records were withdrawn. For years they were prized collectors items and have since been reissued. Lyricists collaborating with Murray Mencher include Charles Tobias, Benny Davis, Charles Newman, and Al Lewis.

Other Mencher songs are *Merrily We Roll Along; Don't Break the Heart That Loves You; I'll Follow the Boys; Whose Heart Are You Breakin' Tonight; Poor Cinderella; Ro Ro Rolling Along; I See God; Let's Swing It; Tonight's My Night; Sweet Varsity Sue; Moonlight and Violins;* and a number of songs for children.

Peter Hygham Mendoza (Peter Venning)

For many years I have been a fan of the great British dance bands of the thirties, especially those of Ray Noble, Roy Fox, Lew Stone, Bert Ambrose, and to some extent, Carroll Gibbons, Jack Jackson, and other lesser lights. At one time I had an extensive collection of their records and therefore came to hear and admire a number of fine songs briefly notated on the labels as written by Peter Mendoza. In particular, I have always been impressed by two that were recorded by Ray Noble's New Mayfair Orchestra on HMV which are showcased in typical Noble arrangements that are years ahead in conception, *My Sweet* and *The Echo of a Song*. Not only are the melodies unusual and appealing, the lyrics are, in turn, happy and optimistic and wistfully sad as though one song is the answer to the other. Since I considered these songs to be the equal of, in fact, better than, many being turned out by a lot of American writers, it seemed only logical to include the composer in this book. So I wrote to a few English friends and requested they do a little digging in reference books and provide me with material for a profile on Mendoza.

The replies were very discouraging at first. Although a few people were familiar with his songs, they didn't know anything about the composer, and none of the standard reference works offered any information. I considered this a case of incredible neglect and hard to understand. That a man of such obvious talent could be ignored and forgotten in his own country—especially when others of lesser talent are profiled in all the reference books—was not only a shame, it was downright ridiculous. I made up my mind that I would do all I could to remedy the situation and try to bring some overdue recognition to a composer who was obviously worthy of the title, "Unsung Songwriter." I wrote more letters, and like a tiny snowball rolling down a hill and getting bigger with every turn, things began to develop. My good friend Clarrie Henley, a seasoned journalist with some experience at uncovering facts, contacted the English equivalent of ASCAP, the Performing Rights Society, in London, but his polite queries drew limited response. The Society provided the birth and death dates for Peter Mendoza, and admitted they paid royalties to a "Mrs. Mendoza," but refused to provide any further information. Reporting this to me, Clarrie suggested that we both write letters to Mrs. Mendoza, explaining what we were trying to do and send them to her in care of the Performing Rights Society. Even though it seemed unlikely that Mrs. Mendoza was still alive at this late date, we wrote the letters. And only a short time later my phone rang and the caller turned out to be Clarrie, who started the conversation off with, "Guess who I just finished talking to on the phone?" I couldn't guess, but it was Mrs. Maureen Mendoza, and our pleading letters had convinced her to cooperate by giving us what information she could about her late spouse. She is the fourth Mrs. Mendoza, twelve years his junior. In several conversations with Clarrie she gave him considerable background on the composer and even provided a copy of the only extant photo of him. In the meantime she alerted her stepson, Peter Mendoza Jr., now living in Palm Beach, Florida, to our research project, and he volunteered to help, so she passed on his address and phone number.

Peter wasn't able to provide much more information on his father but stated that in spite of his father's handicap of only one hand, he rigged an ingenious contraption on his left arm that enabled him to play the bass notes on the piano and became so proficient that he performed on BBC radio. Peter Jr. pointed out that during World War II his father's tune *Don't Be Late In the Morning* was played on the British radio as a wake-up song for defense workers and as a tune to accompany calisthenics. Most important, Peter Jr. had a cassette tape he recorded some years ago when he lived in Australia. It was made from the 78 rpm records in his father's collection of his own songs, but even more interesting, it included a track of Peter Sr. playing piano and accompanying himself singing three of his songs. He said he would send me the tape to copy, and he did.

In the meantime, two letters came in from England. Dave Cooper enclosed a tape of three Mendoza titles recorded by the Roy Fox band, two of which were new to me, *One More Affair*—a beautiful piece very much in the Mendoza style—and *My Sweet.* I had never heard the Roy Fox interpretation of the second title. The third side, *Call It a Day,* was also welcome because my taped copy was incomplete. The second letter was a complete surprise, because it came from a stranger, a man named Arthur Badrock, who explained that our mutual friend Derek Coller had told him of my research, and he was sending along the biographical material on Peter Mendoza that he had found in his 1935 edition of *Who's Who in Music.* Besides providing some pertinent facts about Peter Mendoza's career, this offered a comprehensive list of his composing efforts, including work for stage and movies and songs he wrote under the name of Peter Venning. Mrs. Mendoza intimated that Venning was a family name, but Peter Jr. implied that his father made it up because he liked the sound of it.

The tape from Peter Mendoza Jr. contained several surprises, not the least of which is the aforementioned track of Peter Mendoza, Sr. playing piano and singing three of his songs. The piano playing is very professional, amazingly so for a man with only one hand, but the singing is adequate to the purpose of conveying the words to the very pleasant melodies. Most likely none of these, which are played in a medley—*Mine; You Danced Your Way into My Heart;* and *If I Thought*—were ever published. Three other titles are heard on the tape, *We Won't Make a Song and Dance,* sung by a male vocalist (Mendoza?) accompanied by an orchestra that sounds like the Roy Fox band; *Escape to Yesterday,* performed by a female singer in what appears to be a live appearance; and *Blue Moon in the Sky,* another side by Roy Fox, a waltz, not sung by Al Bowlly.

Thanks to all those who participated in the research, we now have a fairly complete picture of Peter Mendoza as a man, as a performer, and as a composer of excellent songs. After a lapse of some sixty years, he is finally getting some of the recognition he deserves.

Peter Hygham Mendoza was born in London, England, July 1, 1902. Of all the songwriters listed in this volume, Peter Mendoza is, without doubt, the most unsung of them all. A team of four experienced English researchers failed to turn up any reference to the elusive Mendoza, and even the giant EMI Corporation, which holds the copyright on many of his songs, could provide no biographical information. It was only by the diligence and clever detective work of journalist Clarrie Henley that his widow was traced and this amazing story compiled. The irony of all this is that Peter Mendoza was a man of rare talent who produced many memorable and lasting compositions, often writing his own lyrics. In addition, he led a full and adventurous life that sets him apart as a most remarkable man.

Although the name Mendoza is Spanish, several generations of the family lived in England before Peter was born in St. John's Wood, adjacent to the famous Lord's Cricket Ground, an Englishman through and through. He had no musical training but enjoyed a natural gift for music that revealed itself during his teenage years. He was educated at the famous Harrow public school, where he was the victim of a school bully who caused the loss of his favored left hand at the age of fourteen. The arm was badly damaged during a vicious beating, and young Peter tried to do the honorable thing by keeping his injury secret, steadfastly refusing to show the damage to the matron despite the urging of his pals. Eventually, the wound turned gangrenous, and the arm was amputated up to the elbow. It meant learning to write, and do everything, with his right hand. While such a tragedy would have left most teenagers full of self-pity, it didn't daunt Mendoza, although he was conscious of his loss and often did his best to conceal it. When he graduated from Harrow, he made light of his handicap, added an extra three years to his age, and somehow gained entry into the Royal Flying Corps towards the end of the First World War. He wasn't allowed to fly as he would have liked but was happy to work as a member of the ground staff. Military records show his year of birth as 1899, but it was really 1902, those "fake" years surely making him the youngest man ever to serve in the R.F.C.

On discharge, he embarked upon a musical career, composing at the piano with the aid of an ingenious extension to his arm that enabled him to add a basic bass while he explored melodic and harmonic possibilities with his right hand. He set about producing such distinguished songs as *My Sweet; The Echo of a Song; Gone For Ever; Escape to Yesterday; The Moment I Saw You; It's Always Goodbye; Don't Be Late in the Morning;* and *One More Affair*. These numbers were recorded by the popular orchestras of the day, among them those of Ray Noble, Roy Fox, and Harry Leader and Carroll Gibbons's Savoy Orpheans. They all enjoyed huge sales, with Leader's records on the budget Eclipse label being widely distributed through the Woolworth chain. For a man who taught himself everything he knew about the piano and music, and who suffered the affliction of having only one hand, such success was truly amazing. The financial rewards enabled the rising composer to buy a car, with the only restriction concerning his handicap demanding that the handbrake be mounted on the driver's right. The exotic and extravagant Bentley not only fulfilled this requirement, but also Mendoza's penchant for power, luxury, and sophistication. He loved the car, and it served him well for many years.

The film industry soon latched on to his talents, and it was not long before Mendoza was contracted to Alexander Korda, often being called to the Elstree Studios in the early hours to create instant music for the latest brainstorm. It was a challenge to which his talent could easily rise, and he composed a number of successful songs that first saw the light of day in films, as well as creating the incidental music. His Elstree work included the films *The Wedding Rehearsal, The Blarney Stone* (which included the lovely song *Someone to Share My Dreams*), and a saga on the Loch Ness Monster. For B.I.P. Film Productions he wrote the music to *Leave It to Me,* which included the successful song *Somebody,* and for London Film Productions he came up with the delightful melody of *Who Cares?* for the film *That Night in London.* Lyricist Arthur Wimperis collaborated on this one. While Mendoza usually wrote his own lyrics, there were occasional collaborations, Arthur Le Clerc penning the words to *Don't Be Late in the Morning,* a catchy piece more sprightly than Mendoza's usual melancholy romanticism. He also turned his hand to the theater and wrote music for the stage shows "Money for Jam" and the comedy "Six-Eight."

The stream of successful numbers seemed endless, and several songs were published under the fictitious name of Peter Venning, *Song without Words* being a notable example. Film work led him into contact with all sorts of people and helped to broaden an already extensive social life. A handsome, charming, and gregarious man, he knew Alfred Hitchcock and the actress Ann Todd and was a close friend of Roy Fox, Noël Coward, and Rex Harrison, often holidaying in the south of France with the latter two. In the midthirties, he decided to try his luck in the United States and worked for some five years in New York with moderate success. Despite his experience in films, he never went to Hollywood. He returned to England at the outbreak of World War II and joined the British army as a commissioned officer with the rank of captain. Although he had served with the flying corps in the earlier hostilities, he chose the army because he wanted to join the bomb-disposal team. But again his handicapped arm was against him, and he was consigned to a desk job that he positively hated.

A return to civilian life in 1946 found Mendoza struggling to maintain his earlier success. Times had changed, and so had tastes in music. The desire for memorable melodies, rich harmonies, and meaningful lyrics had given way to trite ditties, nonsense words, and sloppy sentimentality. It was not the world of Peter Mendoza. He embarked upon a new career on the stock exchange, and there he worked until his death from liver failure in 1968. He was married four times, the first and third being short-lived affairs and the second to a beautiful White Russian who was later to become Countess Olga, wife of the 3rd Earl of Cromartie. His fourth marriage was to the pretty, petite, and much younger Maureen Deborah Willets in 1961, and it survived until his death. The first marriage resulted in the birth of a son, Peter Mendoza Jr., who is not involved in the music business but who is justly proud of his father's many achievements. Mrs. Mendoza continues to live in London and takes great interest in the entertainment scene, but still muses over the mysterious disappearance some years ago of two trunks that contained almost all of her husband's published music, many recordings of the songs, photographs, and other memorabilia. So, somewhere there may be a treasure trove of information on Peter Mendoza, and whoever has possession of those two trunks probably has no idea of their intrinsic importance. Maybe their contents have already been scattered to the winds, thus adding to the string of events that continue to conspire against this talented composer, qualifying him, unquestionably, as the mystery man of popular music.

Other titles by Mendoza include *Call It a Day; Are You Prepared (To Be True); Ask Your Heart; Blue Moon in the Sky; Calm After the Storm; Hang On to Love; I'm Going to Lose My Heart to Someone; I've Got Two of Everything; Red Sky at Night; You Answer "No", Marie; We Won't Make a Song and Dance; Mine; You Danced into My Heart;* and *If I Thought.*

Peter Mendoza died in London on May 5, 1968.

Johnny Mercer

Johnny Mercer is credited with writing the lyrics to over a thousand songs, but that's only half the story, because in many instances he also wrote the music. At the same time, in his long and prolific career he managed to collaborate with a veritable "Who's Who" of fellow songwriters, including Hoagy Carmichael, Henry Mancini, Jerome Kern, Gordon Jenkins, Jimmy McHugh, Richard Whiting, Harold Arlen, Victor Schertzinger, Arthur Schwartz, Gene DePaul, Jimmy Van Heusen, Bernie Hanighan, and Matty Malneck.

Johnny Mercer was born in Savannah, Georgia, on November 18, 1909. He was educated at Woodbury Forest Prep, a Virginia school, where he took roles in little theater groups. When he got to New York in the twenties, he worked at a variety of jobs and had his first collaboration with a songwriter named Everett Miller. The song was *Out of Breath and Scared to Death of You,* and it was included in the score of the Broadway show "Garrick Gaieties of 1930."

Then, in what has become a time-honored tradition for budding songwriters, he went to work for a song publishing firm and by 1934 was an established and successful member of Tin Pan Alley. A quick look at some of the Mercer titles for those early years explains this: *It's About Time; Thanksgivin'; While We Danced at the Mardi Gras* (1932); *Lazy Bones; It Might Have Been a Different Story* (1933); *If I Had a Million Dollars; Fare Thee Well to Harlem; Moon Country; Here Come the British; Pardon My Southern Accent; Fool That I Am; When a Woman Loves a Man; P.S. I Love You; You Have Taken My Heart* (*all* published in 1934).

It's obvious that Mercer was off to a great start, but even more important, there were no dead spots from that point forward. A complete list of his songs would take a page by itself, but even a partial goes beyond merely impressive—it's fantastic! It will also include many of your favorites. Again, I'll list them year by year.

If You Were Mine; Eeny Meeny Miny Mo; Santa Clause Came in the Spring (1935); *I'm an Old Cowhand; Goody-Goody; Dream Awhile; Peter Piper; Lost; Welcome Stranger; I'm Building Up to an Awful Letdown* (1936); *Too Marvelous for Words; Just a Quiet Evening; Sentimental and Melancholy; Have You Got Any Castles, Baby?; Bob White* (1937); *Hooray for Hollywood; Silhouetted in the Moonlight; Let That Be a Lesson to You; Jeepers Creepers; Say It With a Kiss; Girl Friend of the Whirling Dervish; Confidentially; Day Dreaming; The Weekend of a Private Secretary; You Must Have Been a Beautiful Baby; Something Tells Me* (1938); *And the Angels Sing; Cuckoo in the Clock; You and Your Love; I Thought about You* (1939); *Ooh What You Said; I'd Know You Anywhere; The Bad Humor Man; Don't Think It Ain't Been Charming; Mister Meadowlark* (1940); *The Waiter and the Porter and the Upstairs Maid; Blues in the Night; This Time the Dream's on Me* (1941); *Tangerine; Arthur Murray Taught Me Dancing in a Hurry; I Remember You; That Old Black Magic; The Strip Polka* (1942); *My Shining Hour; One for My Baby; The Old Music Master; Trav'lin' Light; Harlem Butterfly* (1943); *Accent-chu-ate the Positive; I Promise You; Let's Take the Long Way Home; How Little We Know; GI Jive* (1944); *Out of This World; Dream; Laura* (1945); *Come Rain or Come Shine; On the Atcheson, Topeka, and the Santa Fe; Any Place I Hang My Hat Is Home* (1946); *Forever Amber; Midnight Sun* (1947); *In the Cool Cool Cool of the Evening* (1951); *Early Autumn; Glow Worm* (1952); *Something's Gotta Give; Autumn Leaves* (1955); *Satin Doll* (1958); *Moon River* (1961); *The Days of Wine and Roses* (1962).

Mercer continued to write songs well into the seventies, but this wasn't the full extent of his talent. He was a versatile performer as a vocalist and master of ceremonies and an astute businessman. In the latter capacity he founded Capitol Records, and in the former proceeded to record hit records that established the company.

He died in Los Angeles, California, on June 25, 1976.

Paul Madeira Mertz

Pianist-composer-arranger Paul Mertz was born in Reading, Pennsylvania, on September 1, 1904. His education included attendance at the University of Detroit, Texas A & M, and Los Angeles City College. An accomplished pianist, at eighteen he was already touring with dance bands, including the Dorsey Brothers' Wild Canaries. In the twenties he was a member of the Jean Goldkette Orchestra at the Greystone Ballroom in Detroit and arranged for Goldkette and Red Nichols groups. Later on he worked with Fred Waring's Pennsylvanians and Irving Aaronson's Commanders. For a time he was pianist and chief arranger with Horace Heidt and wrote for the movie studios of Paramount, MGM, and Columbia.

Although his output as a songwriter is not extensive, it does include one very fine composition, *I'm Glad There Is You,* which was published in 1942. Credits on the song list Paul Madeira for the lyrics and Jimmy Dorsey for the music, but the composition was entirely the work of Paul Mertz. For some reason he used his middle name on the copyright, and he enlisted Jimmy Dorsey's help and name to get the song published. One of his most treasured mementos was a letter from Cole Porter in which Porter praised *I'm Glad There Is You* as the best song of the year, but said he had a little trouble in tracing its origins to Paul because of the name Madeira. However, he wanted Paul to know how much he liked the song.

Other titles by Paul Mertz are *Merry Ann; Learn to Love; Goodbye Blues;* and the piano solos *Hurricane; Ennui;* and *Erratique.*

Jack Meskill

Lyricist Jack Meskill was born in New York City on March 21, 1897. He graduated from high school and then went on to write special material for vaudeville and movies, at the same time pursuing a career as a professional basketball player. Collaborating with composers like Jack Stern, Jean Schwartz, Al Sherman, Vincent Rose, and Raymond Klages, he turned out a respectable list of popular songs in the thirties. His later efforts in the forties and fifties didn't catch on. Meskill had a banner year in 1930. Teaming with Pete Wendling and Harry Richman, he shared credit for *There's Danger in Your Eyes, Cherie,* which Richman introduced in the film *Puttin' on the Ritz.* Richman recorded the tune for Brunswick, but the popular ballad was represented on all the other record labels by top talent of the day—Waring's Pennsylvanians (Victor); Guy Lombardo (Columbia); Ed Lloyd (Ted Wallace) with Smith Ballew singing (OKeh); plus vocalists Sid Gary (Harmony); James Melton (Victor), and Irving Kaufman (Columbia). (The song was reprised in 1951 by Danielle Darrieux in the movie *Rich, Young and Pretty*.)

That same year, Meskill and Jean Schwartz wrote *Au Revoir, Pleasant Dreams,* which bandleader Ben Bernie adopted as his closing theme for radio broadcasts and recorded for Brunswick, backing it with his opening theme, *It's a Lonesome Old Town* (Br 4943). Both songs enjoyed frequent airtime and popularity. And to top things off for Meskill, the famous recording unit the Charleston Chasers, with young Benny Goodman in the lineup, recorded his jazz-oriented effort with composer Con Conrad, *Here Comes Emily Brown,* for Columbia. The tune was accorded much more attention in England, where it could be had on most major labels. Jack Hylton made it for HMV; Jack Payne and His BBC Orchestra recorded it on English Columbia; and Philip Lewis for Decca.

Bing Crosby crooned *Were You Sincere?*, rendering the Meskill lyrics with appropriate sincerity on a Brunswick recording of the Vincent Rose melody in 1931. It did well for that gloomy year, but *Smile, Darn Ya, Smile,* a collaboration with Charles O'Flynn and Max Rich, pushed the right button in the public's reaction to the ever-deepening Depression, and its optimistic outlook was well represented on records by Ben Selvin (Columbia), Lawrence Welk (Broadway), Snooks and His Memphis Stompers (Victor), the Carolina Club Orchestra (Hal Kemp) (Melotone), and in England by Roy Fox (English Decca). *Pardon Me, Pretty Baby,* with words and music by Meskill, Raymond Klages, and Vincent Rose, was another 1931 entry, a song with happy lyrics and a sprightly melody that adapted well to jazz treatment. The latter is demonstrated on the contemporary Joe Venuti recording for OKeh which, among other hot choruses, exhibits a vocal by songsmith Harold Arlen. Other sides were made by Freddie Rich and by Sam Lanin. It received latter-day treatments by Bobby Sherwood and Benny Carter. The same trio combined on the 1932 song *Kiss by Kiss,* which rated well in radio renditions. It was recorded by Leo Reisman for Victor and by Marty Golden for the Crown label, but it should be kept in mind that in the early thirties, unlike the post-Depression years, records were not a true indication of a song's popularity. Radio exposure was much more important. Record sales were at their lowest ebb in the history of the business.

In 1935 Meskill and Jack Stern wrote the music for the Maurice Chevalier–Ann Sothern film *Follies Bergere,* producing four titles: *I Was Lucky; Rhythm of the Rain; Singing a Happy Song;* and *Au Revoir, L'Amour*. The Dorsey Brothers orchestra recorded *I Was Lucky; Rhythm of the Rain;* and *Au Revoir, L'Amour* for Decca. Benny Goodman, with Helen Ward on the vocal, made *I Was Lucky* for Victor.

Nineteen thirty-six may qualify as the peak year for Jack Meskill. With Al Sherman and Abner Silver, he penned the very popular *On the Beach at Bali Bali.* The song received heavy airplay and more than adequate treatment on records by Henry "Red" Allen (Vocalion); Shep Fields (Bluebird); Connee Boswell (Decca); Tommy Dorsey (Victor); and Jimmie Lunceford (Decca).

Meskill continued to write well into the fifties and has a considerable number of titles to his credit, but his work in later years failed to maintain the success of his early efforts. The list includes *One Little Raindrop; When the Organ Played "O Promise Me"; You'll Be Reminded of Me, My Fantasy* (based on Alexander P. Borodin melody); *Serenade; Don't Let This Waltz Mean Goodbye; I Sent a Letter to Santa; Oh Gee, Georgie; The Day You Said Goodbye to Old Hawaii; What, No Women; Adios, My Madonna; Cheer Up and Smile; Mama Macushla; Santa Claus Is Riding the Trail; I've Been Around; Burning Sands; Make with the Music; You'd Be a Vision in Television; Buenos Noches Mi Amor; June, July and Always; Nothing Ever Lasts Forever; It's Always June in Miami; St. Andrews by the Sea; Telling All My Troubles to the Daisies;* and *Pancho's Rancho.*

Jack Meskill died in California on May 18, 1973.

George W. Meyer

Composer George W. Meyer was born in Boston, Massachusetts, on January 1, 1884. He was educated at Roxbury High School and after graduation went to work as an accountant in department stores in Boston and then New York. A self-taught pianist, he turned to song plugging and then to songwriting. His collaborators, during a career that spanned almost four decades, included lyricists Alfred Bryan, Roy Turk, Edgar Leslie, Joe Young, Sam Lewis, Grant Clarke, Jack Drislane, and composer Pete Wendling. Meyer may be said to typify the songwriters who merit the title of this book. Although he composed quality songs, including a number of hits, it's a pretty safe bet that the proverbial man-on-the-street has never heard of him. This may be, as most often it is, because he didn't have too much to do with writing for the stage or movies, but regardless of the reason, he has never received the recognition his prolific output should merit.

He started writing as early as 1909, and had several songs published that year and in the next three, but in 1914 he teamed with Sam Lewis on *When You're a Long Long Way From Home.* The doleful ditty was successfully revived in 1942 on recordings by Harry James, Hal McIntyre, and Russ Morgan. Then in 1917, with Edgar Leslie and E. Ray Goetz framing the lyrics, he wrote *For Me and My Gal.* It was one of the biggest sheet music hits of the year, was recorded by the popular vaudeville team of Van & Schenk on Victor, and was featured by stars like Al Jolson, Eddie Cantor, Sophie Tucker, and Belle Baker. In 1942 the song was revived by Judy Garland and Gene Kelly in the film *For Me and My Gal,* became a hit all over again in 1943 and was on *Your Hit Parade* for seven weeks.

Continuing to turn out several songs each year, in 1918 Meyer worked with lyricist Grant Clarke to produce the wistful *In the Land of Beginning Again.* This was also destined for revival, this time by Bing Crosby, who sang it in *The Bells of St. Mary's* in 1945 and also recorded it for Decca. Sam Lewis and Joe Young wrote the words for *Tuck Me to Sleep in My Old 'Tucky Home* in 1921. Introduced by Al Jolson, it was also featured on popular records by Vernon Dalhart, Ernie Hare, and Billy Jones. It still gets heard in "old-timer" medleys. *Sittin' in a Corner* was a collaboration with Gus Kahn in 1923. Popular at the time, it was recorded by the Vagabonds on Gennett, Joseph Samuels on Banner, the California Ramblers for Columbia, and the Broadway Syncopators, a Ben Selvin unit, on Vocalion.

In 1924 Meyer, with Arthur Johnston, wrote the music for two songs that were featured in the stage musical "Dixie to Broadway." The lyrics were by Roy Turk and Grant Clarke and the songs were *Mandy, Make Up Your Mind* and *I'm a Little Blackbird Looking for a Bluebird.* Eva Taylor had a popular recording with Clarence Williams of the latter title. *Mandy, Make Up Your Mind,* on the other hand, was well represented on contemporary records by Fletcher Henderson, Clarence Williams, and the Russo–Fio Rito Orchestra. It came back to become a jazz standard in 1939 when it was one of "the Great Sixteen" by Muggsy Spanier and His Ragtime Band in a hit recording for Bluebird. Tommy Dorsey made it for Victor in 1942, and it has since been played and recorded many times.

A sprightly song with a clever title and lyrics by Alfred Bryan, *Brown Eyes (Why Are You Blue?),* was published in 1925. It received almost across-the-board treatment on records of the day, including one by the California Ramblers with Speigle Willcox in the band. Nathan Glantz made several records of the tune for as many labels, and other sides were pressed by Ben Selvin, Nick Lucas, Carl Fenton, Franklyn Baur, the Goodrich Silvertown Orchestra, the Honey Boys, Arthur Fields, and Harry Spindler's Orchestra. In other words, it was a very popular song, also doing well on sheet music and that forgotten but favorite form of entertainment in the twenties, the player piano roll. It has attracted occasional interest in latter times, such as inclusion in a medley on a *Songs of Our Times* album for Decca, but it deserves more frequent exposure. It's a very good song.

In 1926 Roy Turk and Paul Ash joined Meyer in composing *Someone Is*

Losin' Susan, a harmless little ballad that did pretty well in the marketplace. Ben Bernie, Phil Spitalny, Sam Lanin, and Harry Reser all recorded it. Meyer started the new decade with *To Whom It May Concern,* sharing the credit with Sidney Mitchell, who wrote the words, and Archie Gottler for help with the melody. A pleasant entry, it was nicely recorded by Ben Bernie, Sam Lanin, and Bert Lown.

In 1932 Meyer joined a new team, lyricist Charles O'Flynn and composer Pete Wendling, and the trio turned out the witty ditty *I'm Sure of Everything But You.* The vocal trio explained the problem on Guy Lombardo's Brunswick recording of the tune. But this was the year when exceptional songs were the rule rather than the rarity, so this excellent composition went largely unnoticed. The same may be said for the fine *We Were the Best of Friends,* which came out in 1933; this time Pete Wendling and Meyer worked with Meyer's early partner, Sam Lewis. Glen Gray and the Casa Loma Orchestra waxed it, and one of those wonderful records that somehow get lost in the shuffle is an all-star session labeled as "Steve Washington and His Orchestra" that took place in New York on November 22 for Vocalion. It should place both the song and the performance in the category of classics.

There were no Meyer entries for 1934, but he more than made up for it the next year with three very successful ones—*I Believe in Miracles; The Girl I Left Behind Me;* and *I'm Growing Fonder of You. I Believe in Miracles,* which has seen a well-deserved revival, was another Meyer, Wendling, and Lewis composition. It sold well on records by Fats Waller, the Dorsey Brothers, Don Bestor, and Little Jack Little. *The Girl I Left behind Me* was a Meyer melody with words by Billy Rose and Edgar Leslie, and the up-and-coming Orville Knapp band had a successful record on Decca. *I'm Growing Fonder of You,* a very nice sentiment as well as a song, also got recognition from Fats Waller, as well as Freddy Martin, Archie Bleyer, and Connee Boswell. It was a collaboration between Meyer, Pete Wendling, and lyricist Joe Young.

In 1942 three veteran songwriters got together—Meyer, Abel Baer, and Stanley Adams—and in the customary way of songwriters they wrote a song. It turned out to be the last big hit for all three, but it was a grand slam. The song was *There Are Such Things,* and the Tommy Dorsey recording with Frank Sinatra and the Pied Pipers was at the top of best-sellers for six months. For six weeks it was in the number one spot and spent sixteen weeks on *Your Hit Parade. In the Land of Beginning Again,* the song Meyer wrote in 1918, was revived in 1945 by Bing Crosby in *The Bells of St. Mary's,* and Meyer continued to write. In 1947 he submitted *If I Only Had a Match* in collaboration with Arthur Johnston and Lee Morris. It was introduced and recorded by Al Jolson for Decca. And in 1948 Vaughn Monroe and His Orchestra recorded *In a Little Bookshop*. The credit on this song goes to a new team, Kay Twomey and Al Goodhart with George W. Meyer. Besides the songs I have mentioned, Meyer is responsible for these: *I'm Awfully Glad I Met You; Lonesome; You Taught Me How to Love You, Now Teach Me to Forget; I've Got Your Number; Bring Back My Golden Dream; That Was Before I Met You; Honey-Love; In Dixie Land with Dixie Lou; Oh You Little Rascal; That Mellow Melody; Dear Old Rose; My Mother's Rosary; There's a Little Lane Without a Turning; Where Did Robinson Crusoe Go with Friday on Saturday Night?; If You Were the Only Girl; Bring Back My Daddy to Me; Everything is Peaches Down in Georgia; If He Can Fight Like He Can Love; Good Night Germany; Beautiful Anna Bell Lee; Now I Lay Me Down to Sleep; Cry Baby Blues; Cover Me Up with the Sunshine of Virginia; Her Beaus Are Only Rainbows; My Song of the Nile; I Love You, I Hate You; Did My Heart Beat, Did I Fall in Love?; Quicker than You Can Say Jack Robinson; Don't Wake Up My Heart.*

George W. Meyer died in New York City on August 28, 1959.

Joseph Meyer

Composer Joseph Meyer, most likely no relative of George W., was born ten years later, on March 12, 1894, in Modesto, California. He attended Lowell High School in San Francisco and then went to Paris to study the violin, harmony, and counterpoint. On returning home in 1908 he worked as a violinist in cafes. During World War I he served in the army and for several years after followed a business pursuit. In 1921 he moved to New York, began writing songs, and in the following year launched a long and successful career with the hit song *My Honey's Lovin' Arms,* a collaboration with lyricist Harry Ruby. Isham Jones had a contemporary record that sold well for Brunswick, but the song has become a jazz standard recorded by some of the most famous names in the business, from the Original Memphis Five to more recent discs by Benny Goodman and Duke Ellington. Pee Wee Erwin, who led the jazz band at "Nick's" in Greenwich Village for many years, once confused the announcer who handled their radio broadcasts, John St. Leger, by listing the title as *Mahoney's Eleven Arms*. In 1924 Meyer struck gold again with a song that has never died out, *California, Here I Come*. The words are the work of Buddy DeSylva and Al Jolson, and Jolson had a lot to do with its popularity. First of all, he included it in the stage musical he was touring in, "Bombo," he recorded it for Brunswick, then later he sang it in another stage show, "Big Boy." In later years he reprised the tune in the movie *Rose of Washington Square* (1939), did it again in *The Jolson Story* (1946), and dubbed it on the soundtrack for Larry Parks in *Jolson Sings Again* (1949). It's safe to say the song is identified more with Jolson than Joseph Meyer, who just happened to write the music. But Jolson wasn't alone in featuring the song. Georgie Price recorded it for Victor, and George Jessel sang it in the 1929 movie *Lucky Boy*. The Benny Goodman band played it in the 1937 film *Hollywood Hotel*. Bandleader Abe Lyman used it as the theme song of his band. In the interim, it has been played and sung countless times on radio broadcasts and in live performances.

Buddy DeSylva contributed the lyrics to the 1925 Meyer hit, *If You Knew Susie*. Like *California, Here I Come,* the *Susie* song has developed a life of its own. First offered to Al Jolson, who tried it out in one show and then dropped it, it then went to Eddie Cantor. It became associated with him thereafter. He recorded it for Columbia, featured it in his vaudeville act, and promoted it into a standard. In 1936 Buddy Doyle, impersonating Cantor, sang it in the film *The Great Ziegfeld*; Gene Kelly and Frank Sinatra vocalized it in *Anchors Aweigh* in 1945. Then Eddie Cantor came back as the producer and star of the film *If You Knew Susie* and sang the tune on the soundtrack as the film credits rolled. That was in 1948, but he still wasn't finished. In 1953 he sang it again for *The Eddie Cantor Story,* and his voice was dubbed on the soundtrack for Keefe Braselle, who portrayed him in the film.

The year of 1925 was a busy one for Meyer. Besides *If You Knew Susie,* he had three other successful songs that year, *A Cup of Coffee, A Sandwich, and You; Headin' for Louisville;* and another big one, *Clap Hands, Here Comes Charley*. Billy Rose and Ballard MacDonald wrote the words, and the song was introduced by Johnny Marvin, who recorded it for OKeh. Other records included Fletcher Henderson's Dixie Stompers on Harmony, Eddie Peabody on Banner, and Chick Webb on Decca. Red Norvo waxed it for Brunswick, Count Basie for Vocalion, and Jimmy Dorsey for Columbia.

The next important entry for Meyer was *Blue River,* a collaboration with Alfred Bryan in 1927. Although not a great song, it was lucky enough to be arranged by Bill Challis and recorded by the Jean Goldkette band and by the Frankie Trumbauer unit made up of Goldkette men. In both instances Bix Beiderbecke was present, automatically conferring immortality on the song. *Crazy Rhythm,* which came out in 1928, is usually associated with bandleader Roger Wolfe Kahn, but it should be pointed out that he shared composing credit with Joseph Meyer on this all-time standard. The lyrics were by Irving Caesar. Needless to say, the song has had a highly successful tenure on records, in films, on radio, and is still very much around.

As with so many other tunesmiths, a subtle change takes place in the compositions of Joseph Meyer with the advent of the thirties. The melodies gradually become smoother and more tuneful, and the lyrics more sophisticated. One Meyer title for 1930 was *You're Simply Delish,* with words by Arthur Freed. A good song, it was sung by Cliff Edwards and Fifi D'Orsay in the movie *Those Three French Girls.* Bert Lown's band recorded it for Victor, and Smith Ballew did it for Columbia. The High Steppers made it for Crown. The delightful *Just a Little Closer* had words by Howard Johnson. It was sung by Charles King in the film *Remote Control,* and recorded by Nick Lucas for Brunswick and by Rudy Vallee for Victor. A third number, *Singing a Song to the Stars,* rated a Victor recording by Leo Reisman's Orchestra but created little excitement. E. Y. (Yip) Harburg was the lyricist for the Meyer melody in 1933, *Isn't It Heavenly.* It did very well for an independent offering and was recorded by Morton Downey and the bands of Eddy Duchin, Will Osborne, Bert Lown, and Victor Young.

In the following year Meyer returned to his rhythmic format with the swinging melody line for *I Wish I Were Twins.* Frank Loesser and Eddie DeLange combined to shape the words, and it was the first hit song for DeLange. A happy tune, it fits well into the treatment it got from Fats Waller on Victor and other jazz-oriented sides by Adrian's Ramblers (Rollini) on Brunswick, Red Allen on Perfect, and Coleman Hawkins for Decca. And, as I have mentioned elsewhere, in later years it drew a standing ovation performed by the piano duet of Dick Wellstood and Dick Hyman. Another title for Meyer in 1934, *Junk Man,* was well received. It had lyrics by Frank Loesser and turned out to be his first hit song. The rather sardonic sentiment was recorded by Benny Goodman on Columbia, with the vocal by Mildred Bailey; and Isham Jones made it for Victor, with the impish Eddie Stone reciting the words with gleeful enthusiasm. Jack Teagarden recorded it for Brunswick two years later.

Although he continued to publish as late as 1948, what may be considered Joseph Meyer's last important song, *Hurry Home,* came out in 1938. It was a collaboration with Buddy Bernier and Bob Emmerich, and it was represented on recordings by Bob Crosby, Kay Kyser, Jan Savitt, Al Donahue, and Sammy Kaye. More Meyer compositions include *You're So Sweet; As We Leave the Years Behind; Bamboo Babies; My Sugar Plum; Sweetheart Time; Who Loves You as I Do?; You Came Along; Humpty Dumpty; Imagination; Golden Gate; Sweet So and So; Happy Go Lucky Lane; There's Something in That; I Love You More Than Yesterday; All Aboard; You're Perfect; An Open Book; Buy Buy for Baby; Chirp Chirp; How Long Will It Last; According to the Moonlight; It's an Old Southern Custom; Hunka-*

dola; And Then They Called It Love; Do You Remember Last Night?; Love Lies; Busy as a Bee; Cherry Blossoms on Capitol Hill; Peekaboo to You; Let's Give Love a Chance; But I Did; Passé; and *Scalawwag.*

Irving Mills

A familiar name to record collectors or anyone interested in the background and history of our popular music, Irving Mills was born in New York City on January 16, 1894. He attended local schools and at an early age started out as a song plugger. In 1919 he founded his first music publishing firm with his brother Jack, Mills Music Inc. As a publisher, lyricist, manager, agent, and sometime composer, he had a strong influence on the careers of some very famous people and musical aggregations, and his name is on a long list of songs as a collaborator. During his active career from the early twenties into the forties he was associated with many of our foremost songwriters, including Duke Ellington, Sammy Fain, Will Hudson, Jimmy McHugh, Cliff Friend, and the hot jazz team of Jack Pettis and Al Goering. A partial list of songs he is credited with includes *When My Sugar Walks Down the Street; The Lonesomest Girl in Town; Riverboat Shuffle; Blues in My Heart; Minnie the Moocher; Mood Indigo; It Don't Mean a Thing; Sophisticated Lady; Moonglow; Devil in the Moon; In a Sentimental Mood; Organ Grinder's Swing; You're Not the Kind; Caravan; You're My Desire; Solitude; I Let a Song Go Out of My Heart; If Dreams Come True; If You Were in My Place; Prelude to a Kiss; Straighten Up and Fly Right;* and many more.

Besides Mills Music, Irving Mills was a partner or an executive in the firms of American Academy of Music, Ranger Music, Gotham Music, and Pampa Music. As the boss of Mills Artists & Exclusive Publications, he produced musical movie shorts and radio shows and also organized recording sessions with all-star jazz personnel that resulted in some classic sides. A number of these were released under the name of the Hotsy Totsy Gang, others under Irving Mills's name or pseudonyms. He also assumed credit for promoting the Duke Ellington band in its early years, the Cab Calloway Orchestra, and the one that worked under the name Mills Blue Ribbon Band, fronted by Lucky Millinder. In 1983 Retrieval Records, an English company, released three LPs spanning the Hotsy Totsy Gang sessions from 1928 to 1930 (FJ-122, FJ-123, FJ-127), two LPs of the Jack Pettis records, including several sides on which Mills is credited as cocomposer, and others that were recorded under his auspices (FJ-129, FJ-130).

Sidney D. Mitchell

Lyric writer Sidney D. Mitchell was born in Baltimore, Maryland, on June 15, 1888. He was educated at the Baltimore Polytechnic Institute and Cornell University. He worked as a newspaper reporter in Baltimore for five years and began his songwriting career in 1918, but only became successful ten years later. His first published song was included in the stage show "Ziegfeld Follies of 1918" and reflected the mood of the times with one of the longest titles in songwriting history, *Would You Rather Be a Colonel With an Eagle on Your Shoulder, or a Private With a Chicken on Your Knee?* Eddie Cantor sang it in the show. The song enjoyed a brief revival with the advent of World War II.

Mitchell can be credited with a number of hit songs, as well as some very successful ones after he began writing for the movies in 1929, but more than likely his most enduring title is the standard *Sugar,* which came out in 1928 with music by Maceo Pinkard. A long-time favorite of jazz people, it got off to a good start with recordings by Ethel Waters and by the Paul Whiteman Orchestra in a Bill Challis arrangement featuring Bix Beiderbecke. Four takes were made at the Whiteman session, with take two issued in July 1928, and take one released eight years later in July 1936. The tune has since been recorded dozens of times, by stars such as Bobby Hackett, Louis Armstrong, and Teddy Wilson; and it was featured in the 1955 film *Pete Kelly's Blues,* sung by Peggy Lee backed by Matty Matlock's all-star jazz band. Matlock recorded it for Victor and Columbia as an instrumental; Peggy Lee reprised it as a vocal for Decca.

In 1929 Mitchell teamed with Con Conrad and Archie Gottler, two composers he would work with frequently, and for the movie *Broadway,* they turned out *Hittin' the Ceiling* and *Sing a Little Love Song*. The first title was recorded by Smith Ballew for OKeh and by Paul Specht for Columbia. In that same year the tuneful trio had songs in two other films, *The Fox Movietone Follies of 1929* and *The Cockeyed World.* Songs in the former title were *Big City Blues* (which went the gamut of record labels, with Annette Hanshaw on OKeh, Bert Lown on Harmony, George Olsen on Victor, Arnold Johnson on Columbia, and Lou Gold on Perfect); *Breakaway* (also recorded by Arnold Johnson with Harold Arlen on piano); *Walking with Susie* (recorded by George Olsen on Victor, Milt Shaw on Columbia, and Hal Kemp [Carolina Club Orchestra] on OKeh; and *That's You, Baby,* a production number in the movie. The songs in *The Cock-Eyed World* were unimportant, but an independent title by Mitchell, Conrad, and Gottler, *Look*

What You've Done to Me, is one of those overlooked gems that every now and then get unexpected recognition. Originally, the song received modest treatment, with records by Leo Reisman, Irving Mills, and vocalist Lee Morse; but Nat "King" Cole and his trio waxed the tune for Capitol in the forties.

1936 was a banner year for Sidney Mitchell. Still writing for films, he collaborated with a variety of partners on some very popular songs. For *Captain January,* a Shirley Temple feature, he paired with Lew Pollack for *At the Codfish Ball* and *Early Bird.* The *Codfish* song got jazz treatment from Edythe Wright and Tommy Dorsey's Clambake Seven. And for *Pigskin Parade,* Mitchell and Pollack turned out an entire score, the titles including *It's Love I'm After; You Do the Darndest Things, Baby; You're Slightly Terrific; The Balboa; Texas Tornado; Hold That Bulldog;* and *T.S.U. Alma Mater. Sing, Baby, Sing,* another movie that year, included songs by several composers. Mitchell and Louis Alter had one entry, but a very good one, *You Turned the Tables On Me.* Benny Goodman waxed a classic rendition for Victor with Helen Ward on the vocal, and later on Ella Fitzgerald, the Merry Macs, and Gene Krupa all had sides.

All My Life, another gem, has a melody by Sam H. Stept and was featured by Phil Regan in the movie *Laughing Irish Eyes.* He also recorded it for Brunswick. Other records were made by the Benny Goodman Trio, with Helen Ward; Teddy Wilson, with Ella Fitzgerald; and Putney Dandridge. Teddy Wilson played piano on all three. The song was reprised in the 1943 film *Johnny Doughboy.* Rounding out 1936, Mitchell worked with Louis Alter on two songs for the Fred MacMurray debut film *Trail of the Lonesome Pine. A Melody From the Sky,* sung in the picture by Fuzzy Knight, was nominated for an Academy Award and recorded across the board. *Twilight on the Trail,* also introduced in the movie by Fuzzy Knight, became the title song of a 1941 picture starring William Boyd (the future Hopalong Cassidy). Bing Crosby had the hit recording, which became a favorite of President Franklin D. Roosevelt. The record and a copy of the Mitchell–Alter manuscript, gifts to the president from Mrs. Roosevelt, are in the FDR Museum in Hyde Park, New York. Other Sidney Mitchell titles are *Mammy's Soldier Boy; Now I Lay Me Down to Sleep; So Long; Elenita; So Dear to Me; Crazy Feet; To Whom It May Concern; There's Nothing Else to Do in Na-La-Ka-Mo-Ka-Lu; Big Chief Swing It; Why Talk about Love?; My Secret Love Affair; Overnight; I've Taken a Fancy to You; I'll Never Let You Cry; Moonshine Over Kentucky,* and others.

Sidney Mitchell died in Los Angeles, on February 25, 1942.

Vic Mizzy

Composer, arranger, and writer Vic Mizzy was born in Brooklyn, New York, on January 9, 1916. He was educated at Alexander Hamilton High School and NYU, and started writing for college and variety shows and for awhile he taught the Schillinger system at NYU. During World War II he served in the navy. His songwriting career began after he won a songwriting contest on the Fred Allen show. Primarily an arranger for dance bands and singers, he also is responsible for the background music for many of the top television series, as well as a number of films.

His first hit song, written in collaboration with lyricist Irving Taylor, was *Three Little Sisters,* performed by the Andrews Sisters in the movie *Private Buckeroo* in 1942. He did even better in 1945, this time working with Mann Curtis. The tune was *My Dreams Are Getting Better All the Time,* and it was sung by Marion Hutton in the Abbott and Costello film *In Society.* Les Brown had the best-selling record, with Doris Day; other waxings were released by Johnny Long, the Phil Moore Four, and vocalist Billy Daniels. *The Whole World Is Singing My Song,* again written with Mann Curtis and again recorded by Les Brown with Doris Day, enjoyed some success in 1946; then the pair hit again in 1954 with the brilliant and bouncy *The Jones Boy.* The Mills Brothers had the hit record.

Other songs by Vic Mizzy are *I'll Never Fail You; There's a Faraway Look in Your Eye; I Can't Get You Out of My Mind; Take It Easy; You Grew Up to Be Some Baby; Johnny Get Your Girl; Wedding Invitations; That's What a Rainy Day Is For; Look Out, I'm Romantic; I Had a Little Talk With the Lord; Pretty Kitty Blue Eyes;* and *Choo'n Gum.*

Billy Moll

Lyric writer Billy Moll was born in Madison, Wisconsin, on April 18, 1905. Information on his background is sparse; however, he is credited with collaboration on some important songs. His songwriting career began in 1927 with the hit novelty song *You Scream, I Scream, We All Scream for Ice Cream,* written with Howard Johnson and Robert A. King. Harry Reser and Fred Waring had popular recordings of this timeless classic. But better things were coming.

In 1930 Moll paired with Robert King on *Moonlight on the Colorado,* a dreamy waltz recorded by Nat Shilkret on Victor and by Seger Ellis on Crown, and then worked with Murray Mencher on two songs, the jazz favorite *I Want a Little Girl* and a feature for entertainer Harry Richman (who shared com-

Ben Bernie in the mid-twenties.

The *Stardust* man: Hoagie Carmichael

Benny Carter: Man of many talents.

Buck Clayton: Jazz trumpeter, composer, arranger. *Photo by Nancy Miller Elliott.*

Zez Confrey, composer of *Kitten on the Keys* and *Stumbling*.

Duke Ellington at a recording session for Columbia. *Photo courtesy of Columbia Records*.

Ferdee Grofé.

Bob Haggart.

W. C. Handy.

Master arranger, bandleader, and composer Fletcher Henderson. *Photo courtesy of Columbia Records.*

Claude Hopkins. *Photo courtesy of Jack Bradley.*

Isham Jones, c. 1926.

Composer Peter Mendoza in a publicity portrait made in the early thirties. The only photograph known to exist of the brilliant but neglected English songwriter. *Photo courtesy of Mrs. Maureen Mendoza.*

Rudy Vallee.

The legendary Fats Waller surrounded by admirers in the studio at RCA Victor. *Photo courtesy of RCA Victor.*

Harry Woods (right) in conversation with his friend Diamond Jim Greer. *Photo courtesy of Jim Greer.*

poser credit), *Ro-Ro-Rollin' Along*. The first title, originally recorded by the famous McKinney's Cotton Pickers on Victor, has since been perpetuated by classic waxings by Count Basie, the Kansas City Six, Buck Clayton, and others. It is frequently heard at jazz concerts. *Ro-Ro-Rollin' Along* was featured and recorded by Harry Richman and also by the Crooning Songwriter, Sammy Fain. The Meyer Davis orchestra recorded it for Brunswick.

Most likely Moll's most successful year was 1931. With fellow wordsmith Ted Koehler, he wrote the lyrics to Harry Barris's great song *Wrap Your Troubles in Dreams* and with Harry Woods, the delightful *Hang Out the Stars in Indiana*. Bing Crosby featured and recorded (several times) the Barris song. It has long since become a standard. Ray Noble and the New Mayfair Orchestra gave *Hang Out the Stars in Indiana,* with an Al Bowlly vocal, the usual tasteful treatment on HMV, and the side was issued on Victor in the United States. In 1932 Moll worked with composer Joseph Meyer to turn out *Long About Sundown*. It was recorded by Don Bestor's Orchestra.

Billy Moll died in Stoughton, Wisconsin, on January 17, 1968.

James V. Monaco

Composer James V. Monaco, who wrote the music for many of our most memorable songs, was born in Fornia, Italy, on January 13, 1885. He came to this country when he was six years old, taught himself how to play piano, and by the time he was seventeen was playing piano in New York clubs. During the thirties he led a dance band. His long and brilliant career as a songwriter began in 1911 with a song called *Oh, Mr. Dream Man,* but his first hardy perennial came in the following year as part of the "Ziegfeld Follies of 1912," *Row, Row, Row*. A collaboration with William Jerome, it was introduced in the show by Lillian Lorraine. Ada Jones had a popular contemporary recording. It has popped up repeatedly through the years, including several appearances in movies. Betty Hutton sang it in the 1944 film *Incendiary Blonde;* Eddie Cantor dubbed it for Keefe Brasselle in *The Eddie Cantor Story* (1953); and Bob Hope, with a coterie of kids, sang it in *The Seven Little Foys* in 1955. Dick Robertson recorded it with the house band for Decca in 1940.

With Joseph McCarthy providing the words, Monaco had two successful songs in 1913, *I Miss You Most of All* and *You Made Me Love You*. The second title appealed to Al Jolson. He recorded it for Columbia, the record made a hit, and he incorporated the song into his appearances at the Winter Garden. But he was only the first in a string of entertainers who did well with the song. Judy Garland sang it to a photograph of Clark Gable in the movie

The Broadway Melody of '38, and she recorded it as *Dear Mr. Gable* on a big record for Decca. Then in 1941 Harry James waxed it as an instrumental for Columbia, featuring his own trumpet in a solo heavy on schmaltz, and the Columbia side sold a million copies. Al Jolson came back to sing the tune in *The Jolson Story* (1946), and it was used again in *Jolson Sings Again* in 1949. Doris Day, portraying Ruth Etting, sang it in the 1955 film *Love Me or Leave Me,* and it was also heard in two other movies, *Syncopation* in 1942 and *Private Buckeroo* in 1945. Besides the James record, over the years the tune has been recorded by Louis Armstrong, Jimmy Dorsey, Chick Bullock, and Miff Mole, among others. In 1916 Monaco composed a rollicking tune, and James McCarthy and Howard Johnson came up with words to match. The song is *What Do You Want to Make Those Eyes at Me For?* Once again Ada Jones, along with Billy Murray, had the contemporary hit recording. The song was played in the movie musical *The Merry Monahans,* starring Donald O'Connor and Peggy Ryan, and also in the Texas Guinan bio film *Incendiary Blonde,* with Betty Hutton. Singer-pianist Bob Howard recorded a swinging version for Decca in 1937.

Monaco continued to publish songs every year. In 1922 he did well with *You Know You Belong to Somebody Else,* which had lyrics by Eugene West and was featured and recorded by vaudeville headliner Nora Bayes. And in the following year, *Dirty Hands, Dirty Face,* a collaboration with Edgar Leslie, scored with the public. Al Jolson used the song in the 1927 "talkie" *The Jazz Singer*. The parade of hits goes on. In 1927 it was *Red Lips, Kiss My Blues Away,* with words by Alfred Bryan and Pete Wendling sharing some credit for the melody. In 1928 Edgar Leslie was back, and the song was *Me and the Man in the Moon.* This was a feature for the Boop-boop-a-doop girl, Helen Kane, and was also recorded by Ted Weems, with a vocal by Art Jarrett; Ukulele Ike Edwards; and Arnold Johnson's Orchestra. Joseph McCarthy penned the words to *Through,* one of the better songs published in 1929, and it received prime attention from Glen Gray and the Casa Loma Orchestra, Roger Wolfe Kahn, Leo Reisman, Jimmy Noone, and even Ted Lewis. In Britain it was recorded by vocalists Maurice Elwin and Una Mae Carlisle and by bandleader Philip Lewis.

In 1932 Monaco teamed with Edgar Leslie again and the result was *Crazy People,* a novelty introduced by the Andrews Sisters in *The Big Broadcast of 1932*. It was recorded by Ukulele Ike Edwards, Gene Kardos's band, and Benny Krueger's orchestra. That same year, Edgar Leslie and Cliff Friend shared the lyrics on the catchy *You've Got Me in the Palm of Your Hand,* which enjoyed considerable airtime, although it suffered from the dearth of recordings in that Depression year. *You're Gonna Lose Your Gal,* a 1933 entry with words by Joe Young, was recorded by the Casa Loma Orchestra and by Jan Garber on Brunswick and Victor, respectively. Ozzie Nelson made it for Brunswick. In 1961 Doris Day sang it in the movie *Starlift*.

In 1938 Monaco began an association with lyric writer Johnny Burke, and together they turned out a long series of hit songs for Bing Crosby films. That year they worked on two, *Doctor Rhythm* and *Sing You Sinners*. For the first picture they wrote *On the Sentimental Side; My Heart Is Taking Lessons; This Is My Night to Dream;* and *Doctor Rhythm*. For the second they contributed *I've Got a Pocketful of Dreams; Don't Let That Moon Get Away; Laugh and Call It Love;* and *Where Is Central Park?* In 1939 for the Crosby film *East Side of Heaven* they offered the title song, plus *Hang Your Heart on a Hickory Limb; Sing a Song of Sumbeams;* and *That Sly Old Gentleman*. For *The Star Maker* the songs were *An Apple for the Teacher; Go Fly a Kite; Still the Bluebird Sings;* and *A Man and His Dream*. In 1940 the films were *If I Had My Way, The Road to Singapore,* and *Rhythm on the River*. The collective list of Monoco–Burke titles includes *April Played the Fiddle; I Haven't Time to Be a Millionaire; Meet the Sun Halfway; The Pessimistic Character; I'm Too Romantic; The Sweet Potato Piper; Kaigoon; Rhythm on the River; That's for Me; The Moon over Madison Square;* and *Only Forever*.

For good measure Monaco worked with Charles Newman to produce the big novelty hit *Six Lessons from Madam LaZonga*. Jimmy Dorsey, with vocalist Helen O'Connell, had the big record. Monaco continued to write for films but had no more big hits until 1945, when *I Can't Begin to Tell You,* a collaboration with Mack Gordon in the film *The Dolly Sisters,* became popular, with friend Bing Crosby making it that way with a record for Decca. Tragically, Monaco died on October 16, 1945, in Beverly Hills, California, at the peak of the song's popularity.

The long list of James V. Monaco songs includes *Oh, You Circus Day; Mr. Fortune Tellin' Man; I'm Crying Just for You; Pigeon Walk; If We Can't Be the Same Old Sweethearts; You're a Doggone Dangerous Girl; Caresses; Me and the Boy Friend; I'll Take Her Back if She Wants to Come Back; We're Back Together Again; My Rainbow; I Love a Man in Uniform; Say It With a Solitaire; I'll Take Care of Your Cares; Nesting Time; My Troubles Are Over; Can I Help It?; I'm Telling the World About You; Maybe, Someday; Lonesome Lover; I'm an Unemployed Sweetheart; I'm Yours for Tonight; Over the Weekend; It Might Have Been a Diff'rent Story; It's a Whole New Thing; Ev'ry Night About This time;* and others.

Neil Moret

See Charles Neil Daniels.

Russ Morgan

The popular and versatile bandleader Russ Morgan was born in Scranton, Pennsylvania, on April 29, 1904. Best known for his wah-wah trombone stylings, he was also a capable pianist and arranger and managed to share the credit for some important songs. Most likely his most famous composition is the song he used as the theme for his band for many years, *Does Your Heart Beat for Me*. Mitchell Parish wrote the lyrics, and Arnold Johnson collaborated with Morgan on the melody. The Morgan Orchestra recorded it twice, once for Brunswick in 1936 and again for Decca in 1939. It was sung by Jason Graae in the Mitchell Parish theater musical "Stardust" in 1987.

In 1937 Morgan, Dick Howard, and Bob Ellsworth composed *Somebody Else Is Taking My Place*. It attained fair popularity that year, but in October 1941 the Morgan orchestra recorded it for Decca, and the Benny Goodman band followed through in November for the OKeh label, with Peggy Lee as the vocalist. Both records did well, but the Goodman side was a smash. So the song zoomed to the number one spot on *Your Hit Parade* in 1942. As a result it was interpolated in two films that year, *Strictly in the Groove* and *Call of the Canyon*. Morgan played it in the 1947 movie *Sarge Goes to College*.

Meanwhile, Morgan had two entries for 1940. With Remus Harris and Irving Melcher he wrote *So Long*. As customary, the Morgan orchestra recorded it for Decca, but Gene Krupa's band also made it for Columbia. The vocal group the Charioteers waxed it for Columbia too, and it was revived in 1954 by the Four Aces. The other title was the wistful *Flower of Dawn,* a collaboration with Eddie DeLange and Carl Lamagna. As usual, it was recorded by Morgan, but the Eddy Duchin band also made it for the Vocalion label. Along with the delayed success of *Somebody Else Is Taking My Place,* 1942 was made memorable for Russ Morgan by still another hit, *Sweet Eloise*. On this, the delightful melody was by Russ Morgan, and the words by Mack David. The Morgan orchestra recorded it, but the big record was by the Glenn Miller band, with Ray Eberle and the Modernaires.

Morgan had another super hit in 1944, *You're Nobody 'til Somebody Loves You*. This time the collaboration was with Larry Stock and Jimmy Cavanaugh. Morgan recorded it, of course, and the side was very successful, but the song also enjoyed favor with country and western performers. Then in 1965 Dean Martin pushed the tune to a new high in popularity with a recording for the Reprise label, and it has become a semistandard ever since. *So Tired* made its appearance in 1949. Jack Stuart was Morgan's partner on this one. Morgan sang it on his recording for Decca, and Kay Starr followed suit on one of her early hit records for Capitol. Merv Griffin had a good side with the Freddy Martin band on Victor. Other songs by Russ Morgan include *California Orange Blossom; Don't Cry, Sweetheart; Whisper; Homespun; Tell Me You Love Me; Wise Guy; Goodnight, Little Angel; You Gorgeous Dancing Doll; It Only Takes a Minute;* and *It's All Over But the Crying.*

Russ Morgan died in Las Vegas, Nevada, on August 8, 1969.

Ferdinand (Jelly Roll) Morton

Pioneer jazz pianist, bandleader and composer Ferdinand "Jelly Roll" Morton was born on September 20, 1885. Some sources say New Orleans was where the event took place, but Gulfport, Mississippi, is also mentioned. He started out playing piano in New Orleans sporting houses and developed a highly original piano style. With roots in ragtime, it was more advanced in harmony and permitted improvisational freedom—a jazz approach with a unique and seminal individuality. As a pianist he influenced trends in jazz, and as a bandleader-arranger he made recordings that have become classics. His compositions, although never contenders for hit status in the popular market, have become all-time standards in the jazz catalog. His first published composition, *Jelly Roll Blues,* came out in 1915. He had written it much earlier, but it took years to get it published. He recorded it for Gennett in 1924. Subsequent records were made by Bunny Berigan's orchestra and by the Lawson–Haggart Jazz Band.

Jelly Roll Morton was a prolific composer, but most likely his best-known compositions are *King Porter Stomp, Wolverine Blues,* and *Milenberg Joys.* He usually worked alone, but shared credit with the Spikes Brothers on *Wolverine* and with Paul Mares and Leon Roppolo on *Milenberg. King Porter Stomp* came out in 1924, and Morton recorded it for Gennett the same year. The tune was named after a contemporary pianist, Porter King. Fletcher Henderson was fond of the song and recorded it several times. He also wrote the arrangement for the very popular Benny Goodman record. Other sides were made by Glenn Miller, Harry James, Erskine Hawkins, and Bob Crosby. The song was played in the movie *Hollywood Canteen* in 1944 and featured again in *The Benny Goodman Story,* a 1955 film.

Wolverine Blues and *Milenberg Joys* were both recorded by the New Orleans Rhythm Kings in 1923. Brian Rust lists sixteen other sides for *Wolverine Blues* in his *Jazz Records 1897–1942,* and that's only scratching the surface for this popular instrumental. The same can be said for *Milenberg Joys,* which has undergone respectful treatment on any number of occasions, including early sides by the New Orleans Rhythm Kings, the Casa Loma Orchestra, Tommy

Dorsey, and Bob Crosby. Other Morton titles that are often heard and recorded are *Kansas City Stomp(s); The Chant; Sweet Substitute; Buddy Bolden's Blues;* and *Shoe Shiner's Drag.* Morton also wrote *The Pearls; Grandpa's Spells; Steamboat Stomp; Mr. Jelly Lord; Winin' Boy Blues* (at one time the theme song of the Jim Cullum band from San Antonio); *Frog-i-More Rag; Wild Man Blues; The Crave; Sidewalk Blues; Shreveport Stomp; Big Foot Ham;* and many more.

Jelly Roll Morton died in Los Angeles, on July 10, 1941.

James (Jimmy) Mundy

James (Jimmy) Mundy was born in Cincinnati, Ohio, on June 28, 1907. His education included a B.A. degree from Northwestern University and study with Dr. E. Toch. In the midtwenties and early thirties he played tenor sax in the bands of Erskine Tate and Carroll Dickerson and then joined Earl Hines as a sideman-arranger. He also turned out stock arrangements for general use. In 1935 he submitted material to the Benny Goodman organization and in the following year became a full-time arranger for the band. During this important period in his career he wrote a number of swing instrumentals, including *Mad House, Swingtime in the Rockies, House Hop,* and *Air Mail Special.* All of these were closely identified with Goodman and successful selling records. *Swingtime in the Rockies,* which started out as *Cavernism* when Mundy was with Earl Hines, was an especially big hit.

Mundy also collaborated on several songs for the popular market. In 1939 he worked with Charles Carpenter and Trummy Young on the ballad *A Lover Is Blue,* which Tommy Dorsey recorded for Victor, with Jack Leonard as the vocalist. In 1940 Mundy teamed with Jack Lawrence and Eddie White on the swinging *So Far, So Good.* This one attracted attention on all sides and resulted in records by Bob Crosby, Duke Ellington, Will Bradley, and Count Basie. In 1943 the Mundy entry was *Trav'lin' Light,* with lyrics by Johnny Mercer. Paul Whiteman recorded it for the neophyte Capitol label, with the vocal by "Lady Day," pseudonym for Billie Holiday. It was a very successful record. *Don'cha Go 'Way Mad* came out in 1950. The words were by Al Stillman, and Mundy shared composing credit with Illinois Jacquet. The melody was an adaptation from the Jacquet composition *Black Velvet.* Harry James had a good record on Columbia, and Ella Fitzgerald for Decca.

Other jazz titles by Jimmy Mundy include *Bolero at the Savoy; Solo Flight; Queer Street; Killer Diller; Take It Easy; Mush Mouth; Night in Sudan; Futile Frustration; Fiesta in Blue;* and *Fiesta in Brass.*

Jack (John) Murray

Lyricist Jack (John) Murray was born in New York City and his education included attendance at DeWitt Clinton High School, the City College of New York, Columbia University, and Brooklyn Law School. However, there is no indication that he ever used his law training, because he devoted his efforts to a career as a comedy writer for top stars like Eddie Cantor, Jack Benny, the Marx Brothers, Milton Berle, Ethel Merman, and Jack Albertson. He also wrote scenarios for the movies and contributed sketches to Broadway revues. His credits as a songwriter are not extensive, but he was involved in some quality songs of the thirties. Possibly his earliest effort was a collaboration with Henry and Charles Tobias, the 1929 entry *Hello, Sunshine, Hello.* It was recorded by Sam Lanin with a vocal by Scrappy Lambert but received spirited treatment in England by the New Mayfair Orchestra on HMV. *If I Were You (I'd Fall in Love with Me)* also came out that year, to mild attention. Ben Selvin's orchestra made it for Columbia under the name "the Knickerbockers."

In 1931 Murray teamed with Al Hoffman and Barry Trivers, and they submitted a song that did very well in a year filled with good songs. This was *Oh, What a Thrill (To Hear It From You).* Ben Selvin recorded it for Columbia, and Jack Denny made it for Victor. (When considering the scarcity of recordings for songs during the early thirties, it must be kept in mind that the Depression and the popularity of radio almost ruined the market for records.) That same year, Murray and Barry Trivers fashioned English lyrics to a French song, and the result was *Two Loves Have I.* The song became quite popular and was originally introduced in Paris by Josephine Baker. Frank Munn recorded it, accompanied by Ted Black's Orchestra, and Paul Small made it with Vincent Rose backing him.

A couple of years slipped by, and then Murray, with Ben Oakland composing the music, came up with an excellent song for the 1933 market, *If I Love Again.* It was introduced in the stage musical "Hold Your Horses" by Stanley Smith and Ona Munson. It received excellent airplay, especially by singers of the day, and commanded even greater attention in later years, with records by Artie Shaw, Glen Gray, and Paul Weston. Barbra Streisand sang it in the movie *Funny Lady* in 1975. *Have a Little Dream on Me,* with words by Jack Murray and Billy Rose and music by bandleader Phil Baxter, was a pleasant entry in 1934 and got respectful treatment by Fats Waller for Victor, Anson Weeks on Brunswick, and Joe Reichman on Vocalion.

Ted Murray

See Murray Mencher.

Richard Myers

Composer and producer Richard Myers was born in Philadelphia, Pennsylvania, on March 25, 1901. He was educated at the William Penn Charter School. He began his composing career in 1926, writing music for three stage shows, "The Greenwich Village Follies of 1925–26"; "By the Way"; and "Bubbling Over." None of the songs are important, nor are others for shows in 1927 and 1928, but in 1929 he contributed *Jericho,* a bouncy melody with words by Leo Robin, to the movie *Syncopation,* in which it was introduced by Fred Waring's Pennsylvanians. The tune caught on and enjoyed a brief spell of radio exposure. It surfaced again in 1943, sung by Lena Horne, accompanied by Hazel Scott at the piano, in the Red Skelton movie *I Dood It.*

Myers had another hit song in 1932, this one with lyrics by Edward Heyman. The song was *My Darling,* and it was featured in "Earl Carroll's Vanities of 1932." It did pretty well in a year that was crammed with great songs and was recorded by Don Bestor for Victor and by Frank La Motta for Crown. Myers and Heyman followed through the next year with *Me for You Forever,* another pleasant ballad. It was from the stage show "Murder at the Vanities" and was to be heard on records by Henry King, Leo Reisman, and Glen Gray's Casa Loma Orchestra.

Considerable time elapsed before Myers, who was very busy producing shows himself, had another hit. In 1954 he paired with Jack Lawrence, who wrote the words for *Hold My Hand,* the hit song from the film *Susan Slept Here.* It was nominated for an Academy Award, and Don Cornell, backed by Jerry Carr's orchestra, had a million-seller for Coral. Other songs by Richard Myers include *Go South; Whistle Away Your Blues; I've Found the Bluebird; Looking Around; Bubbling Over; Breezin' Along; I'm a One-Man Girl; True to Two; Say It With a Uke; Where Have You Been All My Life; Pull Yourself Together; Blow Hot and Heavy; Say That You Love Me; I Want the World to Know; Ankle Up the Altar With Me; Whistling for a Kiss; Forsaken Again; Music in My Fingers; It's High Time I Got the Lowdown on You.*

Richard Myers died in Perigueux, France, on March 12, 1977.

Josef Myrow

Composer Josef Myrow was born in Russia on February 10, 1910. He was brought to the United States in 1912. He attended Philadelphia public schools and continued his education at the University of Pennsylvania, the Philadelphia Conservatory of Music, and the Curtis Institute of Music. An accomplished pianist, he played guest concerts with the symphony orchestras of Philadelphia, Cleveland, and other cities. He also conducted for Canadian musicals.

He began his composing career writing for nightclub revues in New York and Florida and had his first published song in 1935, the spectral *Haunting Me*. Eddie DeLange wrote the words, and it was recorded by Hal Kemp's orchestra for Brunswick and by Chick Bullock, with the usual all-star studio group, for the ARC labels. A few years slipped by, and then in 1940 Myrow came up with two winners, *The Fable of the Rose* and *The Five O'Clock Whistle. The Fable of the Rose,* a pleasant ballad with lyrics by Philadelphia's pride and joy, Bickley Reichner, did very well on recordings by Benny Goodman, Glen Gray, Tommy Dorsey with Frank Sinatra, Charlie Barnet, and Buster Bailey. *The Five O'Clock Whistle* was a Glenn Miller bestseller with Marion Hutton vocalizing. Kim Gannon and Gene Irwin shared composing credit with Myrow. Ella Fitzgerald, Duke Ellington, Woody Herman, Will Bradley with Ray McKinley, Erskine Hawkins, and even George Shearing all made records of the novelty.

From the standpoint of musical quality, the two Myrow offerings for 1943 are among his best, the moodily beautiful *Autumn Nocturne,* which Claude Thornhill made into a minor masterpiece on his recording for Columbia, and *Velvet Moon,* which was also an exceptional record by the Harry James band. Kim Gannon wrote the lyrics for *Autumn Nocturne,* and Eddie DeLange those for *Velvet Moon*. In each case the hit records were instrumentals. In 1946 Myrow teamed with Mack Gordon, and they wrote songs for the movie *Three Little Girls in Blue*. The film starred June Haver, Vivian Blaine, Vera-Ellen, and Celeste Holm, and they sang and performed four Myrow hit songs, *You Make Me Feel So Young; On the Boardwalk in Atlantic City; Somewhere in the Night;* and *This Is Always*. Frank Sinatra helped make hits of them all.

Myrow and Gordon repeated their success in 1947 with two songs for the movie *Mother Wore Tights*. The tunes were *You Do* and *Kokomo, Indiana. You Do* was nominated for an Academy Award and resulted in top ten recordings for Dinah Shore, Bing Crosby, Vaughn Monroe, Margaret Whiting, and Vic Damone. Dinah Shore and Vaughn Monroe also had successful sides of *Kokomo, Indiana*. Myrow continued to write for the movies, but as we have often mentioned, the market for good songs was dwindling and hits were rare. However, he and Mack Gordon did pretty well with a 1956 entry, *Lullaby in Blue,* introduced by Debbie Reynolds and Eddie Fisher in the film *Bundle of Joy*.

Other songs by Josef Myrow include *Overheard in a Cocktail Lounge; I Love to Watch the Moonlight; If I'm Lucky; One More Vote; Bottom Dollar;*

Follow the Band; One More Tomorrow; This Is My Favorite City; There's Nothing Like a Song; On a Little Two-Seat Tandem; Rolling Down to Bowling Green; Fare-Thee-Well Dear Alma Mater; By the Way; What Did I Do?; It Happens Every Spring; Everytime I Meet You; Baby, Won't You Say You Love Me?; Wilhelmina Down on Wabash Avenue; Where Did You Learn to Dance?; A Lady Loves to Love; I Know What He'll Look Like; Saturday Afternoon before the Game; Nowhere Guy; You; If I Love You a Mountain; The Girl Next Door; Well, I'll Be Switched; What Is This That I Feel? ; Love Is Eternal; and *Endless Love.*

Sammy Mysels

Pianist, composer, lyricist Sammy Mysels was born in Pittsburgh, Pennsylvania, on November 17, 1906. At age ten he received a scholarship in sculpture to Carnegie Tech. He became an assistant instructor there for several years. He worked as a pianist in vaudeville, nightclubs, and on the radio and then joined the staff of a music publisher. He served in the military during World War II and was wounded, the first member of ASCAP to become a casualty. As a composer-lyricist Mysels worked with a number of collaborators, with the designation "Words and Music By" usually the credit. In 1935, for example, he worked with Nat Simon and Billy Hueston, and together they produced *Throwin' Stones at the Sun,* which received outstanding treatment for a song by relatively unknown writers. It made the rounds of the record labels, with discs by Benny Goodman with Helen Ward on Columbia, Freddy Martin on Brunswick, Joe Haymes on Melotone, Archie Bleyer on Vocalion, Bob Howard on Decca, and Willie Bryant on Victor.

Two years later Mysels and Bob Burke published *A Strange Loneliness.* Artie Shaw made it for Brunswick, but this was before his recording of *Begin the Beguine* made him a household name, so the record had little impact. More time elapsed, and then in 1940 Mysels hit the jackpot. With Dick Robertson and Nelson Gogane he had two hits, one of which, *We Three,* made number one on the charts and *Your Hit Parade.* The other, *Is There Somebody Else?,* sold well for Decca as recorded by Ella Fitzgerald and Again with the Delta Rhythm Boys accompanied by the Gulf Coast Five. *We Three* had two best-selling platters, one by the Tommy Dorsey band with Frank Sinatra, and the other by the Ink Spots. That same year Mysels, Mack David, and Dick Sanford offered *The Singing Hills,* which appealed to singers. Bing Crosby had the big record, followed by Dick Todd, Eddy Howard, and Gene Autry. Then Mysels, Dick Robertson, and James Hanley submitted *You Forgot About Me,* which did well on records by Bob Crosby, Larry Clinton, Artie Shaw, Connee Boswell, and Gene Krupa.

Yesterday's Gardenias was the entry for 1942, another collaboration with Dick Robertson and Nelson Gogane, and it rated a recording by the popular Glenn Miller band, with the vocal by Ray Eberle and the Modernaires. Charlie Spivak's band made it for Columbia.

Uncle Sam kept Mysels busy for a few years, but in 1947 he was back with four titles: *Dreams Are a Dime a Dozen; Mention My Name in Sheboygan; Red Silk Stockings and Green Perfume;* and *His Feet Too Big for de Bed.* Pat McCarthy and Jimmy Cavanaugh were Mysels's partners on *Dreams Are a Dime a Dozen,* which Vaughn Monroe recorded; and Bob Hilliard and Dick Sanford formed the team for *Mention My Name in Sheboygan* (a best seller for the irrepressible Beatrice Kay) and *Red Silk Stockings and Green Perfume,* an unlikely but successful title for Ray McKinley and his new band on Majestic. Sammy Kaye and Tony Pastor also waxed it. Mysels, Sanford, and somebody named Herman Braña were responsible for the pseudo-calypso *His Feet Too Big for de Bed,* another unlikely side for Stan Kenton's orchestra, with the vocal by June Christy. Other Mysels titles are *At Least You Could Say Hello; A Strawberry Moon; Heaven Drops Her Curtain Down; Idaho State Fair; The Horse With the Lavender Eyes; Chocolate Whiskey and Vanilla Gin; Michigan Bank Roll; Time Alone; Somebody Else's Roses; I'm in Love; Never Make a Promise in Vain; The Address Is Still the Same; Them Hillbillies are Mountain Williams Now;* and *I'll Be Hanged if They're Gonna Hang me.*

Sammy Mysels died in Los Angeles, California, on February 5, 1974.

Clayton E. Naset

Composer, lyricist, and musician Clayton E. Naset was born in Stoughton, Wisconsin, on May 7, 1895. After graduating from high school, he began playing saxophone and clarinet in dance bands and in the twenties was a member of the Russo–Fio Rito Orchestra that recorded for Brunswick. He played a number of years on radio with Joseph Gallichio and in the pit for Broadway musicals. As a songwriter, his credits are few but interesting and worthwhile. His most important song is the melodic *Dreamy Melody,* a collaboration with Ted Koehler and Frank Magine that was published in 1922 and recorded in January of the following year by Art Landry and his Call of the North Orchestra on Gennett 5255. It was the band's first record and a runaway best-seller for all concerned; reportedly over a million copies were sold.

In 1924 Naset and Gus Kahn penned a sprightly little tune that had the good fortune to be one of those recorded by Bix Beiderbecke and the Wolverines for Gennett. As a result, *Susie* has been reissued in numerous Beiderbecke collections, revived by jazz bands working in the Beiderbecke tradition, and no doubt will go on to immortality. *Golden Day* was the title of another song by Naset that apparently went nowhere.

Clayton E. Naset died in Chicago, Illinois, on February 19, 1966.

Ogden Nash

Writer-poet (Frederic) Ogden Nash was born in Rye, New York, on August 19, 1902. A graduate of Harvard, he is famous for his clever collections of verse. As a lyric writer he is primarily important for the songs he wrote with composer Kurt Will for the musical "One Touch of Venus." Of these, the most popular was *Speak Low,* an outstanding song in every way. It was introduced in the 1943 stage production by Mary Martin. In the 1948 film version, it was sung by Dick Haymes with Eileen Wilson dubbing for Ava Gardner. Barbra Streisand reprised the song on an album in 1994. Two other songs from the show were introduced by Mary Martin and recorded back-to-back by her for Decca, *Foolish Heart* and *That's Him.* A third, *I'm a Stranger Here Myself,* was performed by Martin, and a fourth, *Westwind,* was sung by John Boles.

Other titles attributed to Nash are *Wooden Wedding; Madly in Love; You're Far from Wonderful; Roundabout;* and *Out of the Clear Blue Sky.*

Ogden Nash died in Baltimore on May 19, 1971.

Al J. (Allen) Neiburg

Lyricist Al J. (Allen) Neiburg, best-known for his collaborations with lyricist Marty Symes and composer Jerry Livingston, was born in St. Albans, Vermont, on November 22, 1902. He was educated at Boston University and early in his career worked for a music publisher. His first published song was written with bandleader Doc Daugherty and Ellis Reynolds in 1930 and has since become a well-known standard, *I'm Confessin' That I Love You.* Helped to early popularity by Rudy Vallee, who recorded it for Victor, it was also inducted into the status of a jazz standard by Louis Armstrong.

In 1933 the team of Neiburg, Marty Symes, and Jerry Livingston was formed and immediately flooded the market with hits, all of them high-quality songs—*When It's Darkness On the Delta; Under a Blanket of Blue; It's the Talk of the Town;* and *When It's Sunday Down in Caroline.* The Glen Gray Casa Loma Orchestra had top-selling records of *Under a Blanket of Blue* and *It's the Talk of the Town*—both with vocals by Kenny Sargent; and Isham Jones, likewise, did well with *When It's Darkness On the Delta* and *When It's Sunday Down in Caroline,* Eddie Stone handling the lyrics. However, the outstanding arrangement of the latter tune was created by the master, Ray Noble, who recorded it with his New Mayfair Orchestra for HMV in England and turned it into a minor classic. Al Bowlly, of course, was the vocalist.

Obviously pleased by the success of the 1933 entries, Glen Gray and his Casa Lomans followed through with records of *Learning* in 1934 and two songs in 1935, *I've Got an Invitation to a Dance* and *Where There's Smoke, There's Fire.* All three are typical offerings for the Golden Age. Also in 1934, the team produced *In Other Words, We're Through,* a rather unhappy thought, and the gently sentimental *Ol' Pappy.* Adrian Rollini waxed *Ol' Pappy* for Banner. Al Bowlly did full justice to *In a Blue and Pensive Mood,* another Neiburg–Symes–Livingston offering in 1935 for Victor. Joe Reichman and his new band recorded *Star Gazing* and *Where There's Smoke, There's Fire,* two more fine songs.

In 1936 Neiburg and Jerry Livingston, without Marty Symes, wrote *Moonrise on the Lowlands,* a sequel of a sort to *When It's Darkness On the Delta.* They also came up with a painfully prophetic ditty, *Whatcha Gonna Do When There Ain't No Swing?* The question was delineated with vim by an all-star group under Frankie Froeba's name on Columbia, with Bunny Berigan and Joe Marsala in the line-up and Midge Williams posing the query. Neiburg went on as a freelancer, and in 1940 he worked with Sammy Tinberg and Winston Sharples to produce *It's a Hap-Hap-Happy Day,* which was featured in the full-length animated cartoon *Gulliver's Travels.* Other titles credited to Neiburg include *When April Comes Again; It's a Lot of Idle Gossip; Topic of the Tropics; A Little Bit Later On; There Goes My Attraction; You're Looking for Romance; I've Got Rain in My Eyes; Moonlight Whispers; The Bluest Word I Know Is "Lonesome"; That's How It Goes;* and *You Intrigue Me.*

Allen J. Neiburg died in New Haven, Connecticut, on July 12, 1978.

Ed G. Nelson

Pianist-composer-bandleader Ed G. Nelson was born in New York City on March 18, 1885. A high school graduate, he studied the piano in private lessons. Early in his career, he played piano in cabarets and nightclubs and for several years led his own orchestra. Still later he began composing material for vaudeville and the movies. Although he is credited with a long list of titles over the years, and no doubt many of his songs made money—especially novelties like *Josephine, Please No Lean On the Bell*—it seems that comparatively few are outstanding either from the musical standpoint or association with performers and recordings. Of course, judging songs this way has to be an arbitrary decision, but I believe those I have selected are representative of Nelson's best work.

Peggy O'Neil, an entry into the popular market of songs with an Irish theme, came out in 1921. Harry Pease, Gilbert Doge, and Nelson were the writers, and the song sold well on piano rolls and sheet music. It did even better in 1947, when it was revived on a hit recording by the Harmonicats. Frankie Carle also recorded it. That same year, 1921, Nelson and Ira Schuster wrote the music, and Harry Pease and Johnny White the words, for *Ten Little Fingers and Ten Little Toes.* It made hit records for Irving Kaufman on Columbia and for the team of Billy Murray and Ed Smalle on Victor and did well on music rolls.

Up Jumped the Devil, a title attributed to Nelson, Harry Pease, and the ubiquitous Irving Mills, is dated 1926 and was recorded that year by Tony Parenti's band for Columbia. However, Merritt Brunies and His Friar's Inn Orchestra recorded it for Autograph in 1924 and again for Okeh in 1926. Earl Hines recorded a Jimmy Nundy arrangement of the tune for Bluebird in 1941. In 1927 Nelson and Harry Pease published *In a Shady Nook,* an enjoyable little song that was recorded by Adrian Schubert for the various Plaza labels and by Johnny Marvin on Victor.

As is evident in the work of many tunesmiths, there was a subtle change in the compositions of Nelson in the early thirties. The songs became more sophisticated harmonically, and the melodies more imaginative. This is illustrated by three songs of that period, the 1931 ballad *I Apologize,* written in collaboration with Al Hoffman and Al Goodhart; *Auf Wiedersehen, My Dear,* a collaboration of the same three plus Milton Ager that came out the following year; and *In a Little Second Hand Store,* a 1933 entry by Nelson, Pease, and Dave Dreyer. *I Apologize* was introduced by Bing Crosby, who recorded it for Brunswick, but it went the rounds of the labels, with other sides by Kate Smith (as Ruth Brown on Harmony). Nat Shilkret, and Phil Spitalny. In 1951 Billy Eckstine revived it with a smash recording for MGM, backed by an orchestra arranged and conducted by Peter Regulo. *Auf Wiedersehen, My Dear* was recorded and popularized by Russ Columbo, but Vincent Rose, Jack Denny, and Phil Spitalny also made it; and it rated considerable airtime on radio. Connee Boswell waxed *In a Little Second Hand Store* for Brunswick, backed by the Dorsey Brothers Orchestra, and Chick Bullock made it for the ARC labels with the usual studio group, this time including Joe Venuti.

Other titles by Nelson are *When Yankee Doodle Learns to Parlez Vous Français; Hang Your Head in Shame; Why Do They Always Say No?; Light a Candle in the Chapel; Pretty Kitty Kelly; All for the Love of Mike; In the Old Town Hall; The Pal That I Loved Stole the Girl That I Loved; I'm Climbing Up a Rainbow; Red Roses for My Blue Baby; That's My Mammy; There'll Never Be Another You; Setting the Woods On Fire; Nobody's Love Is Like Mine; One Little Kiss Did the Trick; Worried Over You;* and *You're Only in My Arms to Cry on My Shoulder*.

Henry Nemo

Composer-lyricist-actor and all-around entertainer Henry Nemo was born in New York City on June 8, 1914. Early in his career he entertained in vaudeville and nightclubs and broke into the songwriting field by adding lyrics to songs by Duke Ellington. In 1938 alone he and the Duke were responsible for nine songs, several of them popular hits. They included *I Let A Song Go Out of My Heart; If You Were in My Place; Swingtime in Honolulu; Carnival in Caroline; Skrontch; I'm Slappin' Seventh Avenue; Born to Swing; Jump Jump's Here;* and *I Haven't Changed a Thing*. The Ellington orchestra recorded most of them, and more often than not, the so-called "Ellington Units," small groups under the nominal leadership of Ellington star sidemen like Johnny Hodges, Barney Bigard, and Rex Stewart, also made them.

In 1939 Nemo began composing on his own and right from the start turned out quality songs. With Mack Gordon writing the words, he submitted *If What You Say Is True*. The Jan Savitt band, with Bon Bon vocalizing, made it for Decca. Then Nemo took the next step, writing both words and music for *Blame It On My Last Affair,* a ballad that was represented on all the major labels—Mildred Bailey on Vocalion, Count Basie on Decca, Harry James on Brunswick, Spud Murphy on Bluebird, and Mitchell Ayres on Vocalion. *You're the Moment in My Life* was another Nemo entry that year, with Mildred Bailey again lending support, along with a record by Jack Teagarden's band.

Nemo had three songs in the running for 1940: *Somebody Told Me; A Bee Gazindt;* and *Be Happy*. They didn't stir up much interest, but as though doing his best to make up for this, he came back the following year with two blockbusters, *Don't Take Your Love From Me* and *'Tis Autumn*. Both are excellent songs and worthy additions to the top echelon of titles from the Golden Age. Contemporary sides of *Don't Take Your Love From Me* were recorded by Mildred Bailey; Artie Shaw—with Lena Horne singing—Alvino Rey's orchestra, vocal by Yvonne King; and Harry James's band with Lynn Richards. Glen Gray recorded the tune in1944. A semistandard, it has been recorded many times since. *'Tis Autumn,* a song that describes the season perfectly, both in words and music, came out in 1941 and was introduced and popularized by Woody Herman on a hit record for Decca. Les Brown and Jan Savitt also had well-received records.

Two more good songs for Nemo came out in 1942. One in particular is on a par with *'Tis Autumn* and *Don't Take Your Love from Me;* a soulful plea, *Please Be There*. Woody Herman, who seems to have had an inside track with Nemo, had a fine record highlighted by his own vocal. *Hip Hip Hooray,* the second title, was written with a collaborator, Milt Ebbons. It did very well on a Bluebird recording by Vaughn Monroe by having the good luck to be coupled with his best-selling version of *When the Lights Go On Again All over the World*. Other sides were made by Johnny "Scat" Davis and by Andy Kirk. Other Henry Nemo songs include *But I Do Mind If Ya Don't; Tell Me How Long's the Train Been Gone; I Was Dancing With Someone;* and *Do You Know Why?*

Charles Newman

Lyricist Charles Newman, who wrote the words to many of my favorite songs, including those composed by Isham Jones, was born in Chicago, Illinois, on February 22, 1901. Details of his personal life are sparse, other than the information that he was educated at Columbia University, but he worked with a number of top-flight composers. It appears he started in 1928. In that year he collaborated with Carmen Lombardo on *Sweethearts On Parade.* It was dutifully recorded and promoted on the radio by brother Guy and all the other loyal and "Royal Canadians" and turned out to be the first hit song for both writers. A semistandard now, it is still frequently played and recorded.

In 1930 Newman began an association of four busy years working with Isham Jones. Together, and with an occasional assist, they produced a number of excellent songs and a respectable score of hits. Of course, it helped a lot that the Isham Jones orchestra was enjoying its peak popularity, with Brunswick and then Victor recording contracts, and frequent airtime. During the first year the title was *What's the Use,* a very pleasant song that lends itself well to jazz interpretation, as proven by Bud Freeman and His Gang on an early Commodore recording for Milt Gabler. This was just the beginning of a highly successful collaboration, and in the following year their output included *I Keep Remembering; I Wouldn't Change You for the World;* and *You're Just a Dream Come True.* Jones recorded them all for Brunswick, and *I Wouldn't Change You for the World* was also waxed by Guy Lombardo and by Gene Kardos. The beautiful *You're Just a Dream Come True* was subsequently fitted with a new arrangement by Gordon Jenkins and became the radio theme of the Isham Jones band.

In that banner year of great songs, 1932, Newman and Isham Jones were top contenders. With bandleader Ben Bernie as a collaborator they offered *I Can't Believe It's True,* a very successful song and, almost simultaneously, a still bigger hit, *If You Were Only Mine.* This great tune was revived in the early forties on recordings by Buddy Clark (Columbia), Don Cornell (Coral), and Dick Haymes with Artie Shaw's orchestra (Decca). But Jones and Newman had still more to offer. That same year they had three more fine songs: *I'll Never Have to Dream Again,* a lovely waltz; *The Wooden Soldier and the China Doll;* and *Let's Try Again.* The novelty, *The Wooden Soldier and the China Doll,* rated unusually heavy attention for a year with a decidedly poor market for records, and it was recorded by Ben Bernie, Nat Shilkret, Rudy Vallee, and Sleepy Hall. *Let's Try Again,* on the other hand, a definitely superior composition, was largely neglected. Bing Crosby made it, backed by the Isham Jones band on Brunswick, coupled with *Sweet Georgia Brown* (a standard even then), but for some reason it was quickly withdrawn. *Sweet Georgia Brown* was then recoupled with *Some of These Days.* Newman even branched out a little that year. With Gus Kahn assisting on the lyrics and Victor Young providing the music, they produced *Was I To Blame? (For Falling in Love With You),* a memorable composition. It was the theme song of Glen Gray's Casa Loma Orchestra before *Smoke Rings,* and still later it was adopted by Richard Himber as the theme of this radio program for Studebaker. He recorded it for Decca in 1940.

The Jones and Newman team was far from finished, however. In 1933 they rang the bell three times, with *You've Got Me Crying Again; Why Can't This Night Go On Forever;* and *Honestly.* All three were typically outstanding Jones melodies, and the first two were big hits. When Bill Borden founded his Monmouth–Evergreen record label, the "Evergreen" part of the name was adapted from his first LP release: *Twelve Isham Jones Evergreens,* played by Rusty Dedrick's orchestra. The foregoing titles were included.

Newman wasn't active in 1934, and when he came back the following year it was with new partners. With Charlie Tobias and Murray Mencher, he wrote *Flowers for Madame;* and with Tobias and Sam H. Stept, produced *Tiny Little Fingerprints* and *I'm Painting the Town Red.* Joe Reichman recorded the first title, a sentimental offering, but jazz musicians took a liking to *I'm Painting the Town Red,* with a number of good records as a result. Teddy Wilson made it for Brunswick with Billie Holiday; Bob Howard turned in a swinger for Decca; the Little Ramblers did the same for Bluebird; and Richard Himber made it for Victor. In 1936 Newman paired with Murray Mencher and Al Sherman for *Take Another Guess* and then with Mencher and Milt Ager for *You Can't Pull the Wool Over My Eyes.* Benny Goodman recorded both titles; the first, with a vocal by Ella Fitzgerald, caused a resulting hassle with Decca (who had Fitzgerald under an exclusive contract) that forced Victor to withdraw the side. Helen Ward sang *You Can't Pull the Wool over My Eyes,* and so did Dolly Dawn, who recorded it with George Hall's band. Another entry from the Newman–Ager–Mencher combination was *It's No Fun.* It did pretty well on discs by Jimmy Dorsey (vocal by Seger Ellis), Wingy Manone, and Gene Kardos, with Bea Wain.

Newman had another big song in 1940, the clever *Six Lessons from Madame La Zonga,* written with James V. Monaco. Jimmy Dorsey had a best-seller with Helen O'Connell's vocal. In 1941 it became the title song for a Lupe Velez movie. *Why Don't We Do This More Often?* was a popular offering in 1941. Eddie Stone, with Freddy Martin's band, had a big seller, and the vocal team of Ginny Simms and Harry Babbitt had one too with Kay Kyser's band. Allie Wrubel was the composer. Ray Noble recorded *It Isn't a Dream Any More* for Columbia in 1942. Newman's lyrics were coupled with a melody by Walter Samuels. Other Newman songs are *That's What Puts the "Sweet" in Home Sweet Home; Dream Train; Moonlight March; Let's Swing It; West Wind; In Your Own Little Way; Summer Souvenirs; The Answer Is Love; It's a Whole New Thing;*

Rancho Pillow; A Boy in Khaki, a Girl in Lace; I Met Her on Monday; Private Buckeroo; There's Nothing the Matter With Me; and *Don't Throw Cold Water On the Flame of Love.*

Charles Newman died in Beverly Hills, California, on January 9, 1978.

Alberta Nichols

Composer Alberta Nichols was born in Lincoln, Illinois, on December 3, 1898. Her education included the Louisville Conservatory and study with Alfred Kalzin and George Copeland. During her career she wrote special material for vaudeville, radio theme songs, and commercial jingles. Nichols's prime collaborator was her husband, Mann Holiner, and together they contrived some excellent songs. Their first hit, *You Can't Stop Me From Loving You,* a 1931 entry, was originally intended for a Billy Rose musical, "Corned Beef and Roses," which never made it to Broadway, so the song was interpolated in a Lew Leslie review, "Rhapsody in Black," starring Ethel Waters and Blue McAllister. Cab Calloway recorded it for the ARC labels, Ethel Waters made it for Columbia, Chick Bullock for Conqueror and allied labels, and the Washboard Rhythm Kings for Victor.

Your Mother's Son-in-Law was the tricky title of a 1933 Nichols–Holiner offering. It was introduced in Lew Leslie's "Blackbirds (1933–1934 Edition)." Benny Goodman recorded it with Billie Holiday. In the following year Nichols and Holiner published one of their best songs, *I Just Couldn't Take It, Baby.* It too was introduced in Lew Leslie's "Blackbirds," and it proved to be a winner. Ethel Waters recorded it for Columbia, backed by Benny Goodman's orchestra; Jack Teagarden made it for Brunswick; and Eddy Duchin for Victor; and they all did well. Still later records of the song were made by Hal Kemp, Lionel Hampton, and Neal Hefti.

Until the Real Thing Comes Along came along in 1936, and for some unknown reason Nichols and Mann Holiner shared composing credit with a "committee," including Sammy Cahn, Saul Chaplin, and L. E. Freeman. Andy Kirk and His Clouds of Joy had the hit record on Decca, with Pha Terrill on the vocal, and it became the band's theme song. Fats Waller also recorded it for Victor, Erskine Hawkins for Vocalion, and Charlie Barnet for Bluebird, among others. Other titles credited to Nichols are *There Never Was a Town Like Paris; Sing a Little Tune; What's Keeping My Prince Charming?; I'm Walking the Chalk Line; A Love Like Ours;* and *Why Shouldn't It Happen to Us?*

Alberta Nichols died in Hollywood, California, February 4, 1957.

Johnny (John Avery) Noble

Composer-writer-orchestra leader Johnny Noble was born in Honolulu, Hawaii, on September 17, 1892. He was educated at St. Louis College. For seventeen years he led orchestras that played the exclusive Moana and Royal Hawaiian hotels in Honolulu, then in 1925 he went to Los Angeles, where he directed Hawaiian musicals and broadcast Hawaiian programs on radio networks. As a songwriter, he was the composer and cocomposer of a number of songs with Hawaiian themes that achieved hit stature. One of his early efforts was the musical discourse in Hawaiian terminology, *My Little Grass Shack in Kealakakua Hawaii,* a 1934 offering written in collaboration with Billy Cogswell and Tom Harrison. Ted Fio Rito recorded it for Brunswick, and Ben Pollack made it for Columbia, The song was accorded a lot of airtime and was very popular.

In 1935 Noble continued the language lesson with *I Want to Learn to Speak Hawaiian,* a well-spoken sentiment on a Decca side by the Orville Knapp orchestra; and then he teamed with Don Diarmid and Leo Wood for the sprightly *Little Brown Gal.* Noble's songwriting career peaked in 1936 with the publication of *Hawaiian War Chant.* Ralph Freed wrote English lyrics to the melody composed by Noble and Prince Leleiohaku, and the song was an instant success. Tommy Dorsey's band had a best-seller in 1939, and Spike Jones made a successful spoof in 1946. In 1942 it was played in the Deanna Durbin film *It's a Date* by Harry Owens and His Royal Hawaiians and again in *Song of the Islands.* It was also played in the 1941 movie *Moonlight in Hawaii* and the 1944 musical "Song of the Open Road." There are reputed to be over a hundred recorded versions. Other successful songs by Noble are *Hilo Hattie; My Tane; King Kamehaneha; Naughty Hula Eyes; Tropic Trade Winds; Island Serenade;* and *Hula Blues.*

Johnny Noble died in Honolulu on January 13, 1944.

Ray Noble

Of the great horde of composers of popular songs who were active during the Golden Age of songwriting, not many topped Ray Noble in the ability to turn out material of consistent quality. His songs are strikingly original in concept, expertly crafted, and most notable for their beautiful melodies. Many attained peak popularity, for the most part without the advantage of being featured in shows or movies. On the other hand, Noble did have one very important plus in the difficult job of creating a market for his tunes, a luxury only a few others have shared—Duke Ellington and Isham Jones, in particular—his own orchestra. This made it automatically possible to showcase his compositions by arranging and recording them to best advantage, and it not only presented an ideal way to promote them, but many times resulted in hit recordings for the Noble band. Furthermore, for the many collectors of Ray Noble's music throughout the world, his recordings now offer the most complete library of his compositions. With only a few exceptions, he recorded them all.

Ray Noble was born in Brighton, England, on December 17, 1903, the son of a prominent London doctor. He began taking piano lessons at age ten and only a few years later was already a professional performer with a strong interest in the dance bands of the day. For several years he carefully studied and analyzed the music he heard on phonograph records, learning all he could about the technique and development of arranging for a dance band. In 1926 he submitted an arrangement in a contest sponsored by *The Melody Maker,* a monthly music publication, and won. In commenting on his work, the judges predicted, "When Ray Noble's arrangement is published, as it will be shortly, it will be seen we have in him a man who will go a long way."

It was a farsighted statement, but at that stage no one could have foretold the brilliant career the young man would eventually have. Nevertheless, winning the contest opened the door of opportunity, and before long Noble was contributing arrangements to Jack Payne's BBC Dance Orchestra and had already published his first song, *Nobody's Fault But Your Own,* which enjoyed a fair success in 1929. Later in the same year it was announced that Carrol Gibbons, the American pianist and bandleader who had been recording director for the Gramophone Company, which produced His Master's Voice records, the British equivalent of American Victor, was returning to the United States; and his place would be filled by Ray Noble. The assignment was only supposed to be temporary, but the way things worked out, all the records turned out by the New Mayfair Orchestra, and later by Ray Noble and His New Mayfair Orchestra or Ray Noble and His Orchestra, from the fall of 1929 until August 20, 1934, were directed by Noble and, for the most part, arranged by Noble. The result was a series of outstanding records that quickly developed a quality that could readily be identified as the Noble touch—expert musicianship, impeccable tempos, and imaginative and tasteful voicings, often featuring solo instruments. The arrangements and records were actually well in advance of their time and still compare favorably with anything made since.

In the meantime, Noble continued to compose. Early in 1931 a New Mayfair session produced six titles, all featuring Al Bowlly as vocalist, including a Noble original, *Goodnight, Sweetheart.* The record and the song were instant successes. Countless are the dance parties that have since ended with the playing of the tune. Long ago it became a standard that everybody knows; most likely it is Noble's most famous composition. But it was only one in a chain of excellent songs. His next published item, *I Found You,* is a beautiful ballad but unusual to the extent that it is one of the few Noble songs that, for some unknown reason, he never recorded. The contemporary Bert Ambrose orchestra gave it a respectable treatment, and the recording was issued in the United States on Victor 22893. This was followed by another Noble big success, *By the Fireside,* a Bowlly–Noble collaboration that still makes great listening. Issued in England in 1932, it did very well but had to wait until 1935 to be introduced to the American public, at which time it was a hit all over again.

Noble was relentless. His next two entries, written for a movie starring his old boss Jack Payne's band, were *Love Is the Sweetest Thing* and *I'll Do My Best to Make You Happy.* In December of 1932 he struck again, with two more written for a movie, *The Little Damozel, What More Can I Ask?* and *Brighter Than the Sun.* The successful chain remained unbroken to that point, but for some strange reason (who can figure these things out?) his next effort, *That's What Life Is Made Of,* didn't click, although it received the usual Bowlly–Noble surefire treatment. The same can be said for *If You'll Say "Yes," Cherie,* a rather nice waltz recorded in 1933. Undaunted, Ray came back strong with *Love Locked Out* and *Happy and Contented* in the latter part of 1933, the first title an especially delightful melody. In the spring of 1934 the Bowlly–Noble collaboration scored again, recording a song that not only included a typically beautiful Noble melody, but lyrics he penned to match. The song is *The Very Thought of You. It's All Forgotten Now,* another composition with both words and music by Noble, was recorded at the last session he did before leaving England for the United States, and although not the great hit created by *The Very Thought of You,* it is a very worthy entry in the panoply of Noble originals.

In 1934 Noble, accompanied by his drummer Bill Harty, who was also his band manager, and vocalist Al Bowlly, the only members of his British recording group that the American musicians' union would permit him to bring with him, took over leadership of the all-star orchestra that Glenn Miller had organized at the instigation of the Rockwell–O'Keefe booking agency. Ensconced at the swank Rainbow Room atop Manhattan's RCA building (Rockefeller Center), the band immediately began recording for RCA–Victor, and Noble continued to write great songs. The band was featured in a segment of the movie *Big Broadcast of 1935,* filmed in the Long Island studio maintained by Paramount. Noble wrote *Why Stars Come Out at Night* for the picture. The band also recorded it for RCA–Victor, the inimitable Al Bowlly doing the vocals in both instances. Again, Noble provided both words and music. He followed through in 1936 with *The Touch of Your Lips,* also recorded for Victor with a Bowlly vocal.

Then Al Bowlly got homesick and went back to England, the Victor contract ran out, and Noble signed with Brunswick, commemorating the new arrangement almost immediately with the superb *I Hadn't Anyone Till You,* again providing both words and music. Tony Martin was the vocalist on the record. A short time later came the first of the Indian Suite, the redoubtable *Cherokee,* recorded as an instrumental arranged by Will Hudson. Then in quick succession two beautiful ballads that never achieved the status they deserved, *You're So Desirable* and *You That I Love,* followed by two instrumentals, *Friday Night at the Hartys* and *Saturday Night at the Nobles.* These concluded the Brunswick period. With the revival of the Columbia label additions to the Indian Suite appeared in fast order, all instrumentals—*Comanche War Dance; Iroquois; Seminole;* and *Sioux Sue*. Another instrumental, the wistfully beautiful *Far Away,* was from this period. Other Noble compositions include *A Little Bit of Blarney; A Grecian Melody;* and *What a Sweet Surprise.*

Ray Noble died of cancer in a London hospital in 1978. He was seventy-one years old. In his obituary, John S. Wilson wrote: "Mr. Noble's recordings had several distinguishing qualities. He wrote beautifully textured ensembles, particularly for the saxophones. He used jazz elements in a popular dance-band context with an ingenuity that anticipated Benny Goodman's band by several years. He employed violins with a validity that no other dance-band arranger had achieved.

"His arrangements sparkled with fascinating blends of sound and subtle shifts and changes. And the band was recorded with a full, rich fidelity that was one of the technical marvels of the day. In addition he had a vocalist, Al Bowlly, a South African with an oddly appealing, slightly nasal voice who had an unerring sense for phrasing and shading a ballad."

Ray Noble approached everything he did—arranging, bandleading, songwriting, acting—without pretense and with quiet but meticulous taste. It is evident in the songs he wrote and in the arrangements he put together with deceptive simplicity but with such superb musicianship that they still hold up well over half a century after they were written. The fine musical groups he assembled during his career as a superior bandleader are still admired as among the best of all time.

Bibliography:

Rust, Brian. Liner notes for the booklet contained in the EMI boxed set *The Ray Noble Orchestra featuring Al Bowlly; The HMV sessions 1930–1934.*
Vaché, Warren W. *This Horn for Hire,* [Pee Wee Erwin biography]. Metuchen, N.J.: Scarecrow Press with Rutgers Institute of Jazz Studies, 1987.

Pierre Norman

See Joseph P. Connor.

George A. Norton

Pianist-songwriter George A. Norton was born in St. Louis, Missouri, on April 16, 1880. He was educated at the Peabody Conservatory and early in his career worked as a pianist in vaudeville and wrote special material. He also became a newspaper reporter and then an advertising executive. As a songwriter he was prolific, but from the standpoint of meriting inclusion in this book, he is best known for three songs: *She Wore a Yellow Ribbon; My Melancholy Baby;* and *Memphis Blues.*

Norton is credited with both words and music for the first title, which was initially published in 1917. Robert Lissauer describes this as "the most popular version of an American folk song." If the time period depicted in the John Wayne movie *She Wore a Yellow Ribbon* (1949) is authentic, then the song is much older. As it is, the Wayne movie revived the tune, and the Andrews Sisters had a hit record with Russ Morgan's orchestra on Decca. Eddie "Piano" Miller recorded it for Rainbow Records. Norton wrote the words to Ernie Burnett's all-time hit standard *My Melancholy Baby* in 1912. It was Burnett's only hit, but it has been recorded hundred of times, played even more, and has been featured in a number of films, including *The Birth of the Blues,* a 1941 picture in which it was sung by Bing Crosby; *A Star Is Born,* with Judy Garland in 1954; and *The Helen Morgan Story,* with Gogi Grant dubbed in for Ann Blyth on the soundtrack (1957).

Memphis Blues was W. C. Handy's first published song. He wrote it in 1912 as an instrumental to help elect Edward H. Crump as mayor of Memphis. It was called *Mr. Crump* and proved to be so popular that Norton added lyrics to it in 1913. Now a standard, played and recorded many times, it was also in the Bing Crosby movie *The Birth of the Blues.* Prior to that it was heard in the 1934 film *Belle of the Nineties* and again in W. C. Handy's biographical film *St. Louis Blues* in 1938.

To do Norton full justice, here is a partial list of other compositions: *Sing Me a Song of the South; Two Little, True Little Eyes; Sweetie, Be King to Me: That's Gratitude; At the Old Square Dances Down in Arkansas; Where Is My Boy Tonight?; The Black Hand Rag; Suicide Blues;* and *Down Georgia Way.*

George A. Norton died in Tucson, Arizona, on September 14, 1923.

Ben Oakland

Pianist-composer-producer Ben Oakland was born in Brooklyn, New York, on September 24, 1907. He was educated at Commercial High School, and at age nine gave a piano concert at Carnegie Hall. He started his show business career in vaudeville playing piano for Helen Morgan and George Jessel. Starting in the early thirties, he began writing songs for Broadway and nightclub revues. During World War II he toured with USO shows. Still later he functioned as writer-director and producer for personal appearances of star performers like Van Johnson, Tony Martin, Jeannette MacDonald, Joe E. Lewis, and others and for two years produced the George Jessel show "Down Tin Pan Alley."

As a composer he wrote the music for a number of hit songs, collaborating with top lyricists. An early success (1933), *If I Love Again,* with words by Jack Murray, was introduced by Ona Munson and Stanley Smith in the stage show "Hold Your Horses." It has since become a semistandard. Barbra Streisand sang it in the 1975 movie *Funny Lady*. Artie Shaw recorded it for Victor in 1941 with his large orchestra with strings, among others. *The Champagne Waltz* was a popular entry for 1934, a collaboration with Con Conrad and Milton Drake. The dance team of Veloz and Yolanda danced to it in the 1937 movie with the same title, *The Champagne Waltz. I'm Counting on You,* another Oakland offering in 1934 with words by Milton Drake, was recorded by the Paul Whiteman orchestra, with Ramona as the vocalist.

Still writing for films, Oakland had moderate successes in 1935 and 1936, but in 1937 he scored big again with *I'll Take Romance,* the title song of a film starring Grace Moore. Oscar Hammerstein II contributed the lyrics. The song went on to other things. In 1948 it was sung by Gloria Jean in the movie *Manhattan Angel,* and it was heard on the soundtracks of *Jolson Sings Again* and *Holiday in Havana,* both in 1949. In 1956 it was played in *The Eddy Duchin Story*. It has been played and recorded many times over the years. *Roses in December,* a pleasant song with words by George Jessel, was heard in the film *Life of the Party* that same year, performed by Harriet Hilliard and Gene Raymond and recorded for Brunswick by Ozzie Nelson with Harriet Hilliard singing. More time went by, and then in 1941 Oakland and Milton Drake struck gold again with *Java Jive,* a novelty that produced a hit record for the Ink Spots on Decca. The King Sisters, with Alvino Rey's orchestra, also had a big seller on Bluebird. Herb Magidson and Oakland worked together on *Beau Night in Hotchkiss Corners,* a tune that was featured in the nightclub George White's Gay White Way, and it did very well. Artie Shaw and Bob Chester had popular records. Raymond Scott made it for Columbia.

In 1947 Ray Noble, with Buddy Clark singing, had a top side on *I'll Dance at Your Wedding,* another Oakland–Magidson entry. It was also recorded by Tony Martin and Peggy Lee. Other songs by Ben Oakland include *Do the New York; Sidewalks of Cuba; I'm a Hundred Percent for You; Valse Moderne; Like a Bolt From the Blue; Twinkle Twinkle Little Star; Where Have You Been All My Life?; Zilch's Hats; I Don't Like Music; My Dreams Have Gone With the Wind; When You're in the Room; That Week in Paris; A Mist Is Over the Moon; Everybody's Laughing; If It's You; A Pink Cocktail for a Blue Lady; Dixieland Rendezvous; You're Not So Easy to Forget; I'll Never Make the Same Mistake Again; We're Not Getting Any Younger, Baby; Johannesburg; The Kissing Song; Happiness; Don't Play That Song; Goodbye, Little Girl; Puppy Love; Summer Vacation; River River; Golden Wedding Waltz; Cool Tango; L'il Abner; Dimples and Cherry Cheeks; Winter Sun.*

Ben Oakland died in Beverly Hills, California, on August 26, 1976.

Charles O'Flynn

Lyric writer and publisher Charles O'Flynn was born in New York City on August 12, 1897. His education included Fordham University and Manhattan College. It would appear that one of his earliest efforts was the novelty classic variously listed as *Hay Hay (Farmer Gray Took Another Load Away)* or *The Farmer Took Another Load Away, Hay Hay*. In any case, this knee-slapper, a collaboration between O' Flynn, Edgar Leslie, and Nat Vincent, was very popular in 1925 and was recorded by Paul Whiteman's orchestra, the comedy team of Billy Jones and Ernie Hare, Nathan Glantz, and in more recent incarnation by the Hoosier Hotshots.

However, five years later O'Flynn was in tune with the new decade and turned out some nice songs. One was a cooperative venture with Al Hoffman and bandleader Will Osborne called *Roses Are Forget-Me-Nots,* which Osborne recorded for Columbia. It had a fair reception. Another was *Good Evenin',* a really good song written with Al Hoffman and Tot Seymour, which Rudy Vallee plugged on the radio and recorded for Victor. Still another was *Jungle Drums,* with Carmen Lombardo and Charles O'Flynn providing English lyrics to a melody by Ernesto Lecuona. Guy Lombardo had a contemporary record, but in 1939 the song enjoyed a revival, with records by Sidney Bechet, Artie Shaw, and Dinah Shore with Xavier Cugat's orchestra. And most likely the biggest hit of the year for O'Flynn was *Swingin' in a Hammock,* with Tot Seymour again helping with the lyrics and the music by Pete Wendling. It was a popular radio tune, and Guy Lombardo and Leo Reisman recorded it.

Still changing partners, O'Flynn worked with Jack Meskill and Max Rich on the 1931 challenge to the Depression blues, *Smile, Darn Ya, Smile,* something not easy when there wasn't much to smile about; but like its counterpart, *Happy Days Are Here Again,* it found favor with the public. In 1932 O' Flynn and J. Fred Coots combined on a worthy contender in the golden year, *Strangers.* An excellent song, it rated full attention, with sides by Sleepy Hall on Melotone, Art Kassel on Columbia, Mildred Bailey for Victor, and Phil Spitalny on Hit of the Week. As with *Jungle Drums, Strangers* enjoyed a brief renascence some years later with recordings by Tommy Dorsey with the vocal by Don Cherry on Decca and by Buddy Morrow on Victor, with Tommy Mercer singing. Other titles by O'Flynn include *When You Walk With the One You Love; Early in the Mornin'; Melodies Bring Memories; Who Threw the Confetti in Angelo's Spaghetti?; Happy Nothing to You; God's Rain; The Angelus;* and *Rosary of Roses.*

Charles O'Flynn died in New York City on April 25, 1964.

Joseph (King) Oliver

Although not in the category of a "popular" songwriter, Joseph "King" Oliver, pioneer jazz cornetist and bandleader, composed a respectable number of instrumental compositions that have become standards in our musical heritage. He was born on May 11, 1885, most likely in New Orleans, where he started his career playing for parades and funerals and then organized his own band. In 1918 he went to Chicago, played with Kid Ory and other bands, then again organized in his own band, joined by Louis Armstrong. They started to make historic recordings in 1923. In that year King Oliver and Louis Armstrong together recorded numerous jazz classics, including several originals by Joe Oliver, *Chimes Blues; Canal St. Blues;* and *Dippermouth Blues* (sometimes called *Sugar Foot Stomp*). King Oliver recorded all of these for Gennett, and they have been perpetuated by countless renderings since.

In 1926 he wrote and recorded *Snag It,* another classic for Brunswick. In 1927 he teamed with Walter Melrose, who wrote the words to *Doctor Jazz,* which was introduced and turned into a best-seller by Jelly Roll Morton's Hot Peppers on a Victor record.

In 1928 Clarence Williams added words to a King Oliver melody, and it became *West End Blues*. They recorded it for Vocalion, but the outstanding side was by Louis Armstrong and His Hot Five for OKeh.

In spite of his successes as a bandleader and a composer—not to mention his talent as a cornetist or his introduction and development of his protege, Louis Armstrong—King Oliver died penniless and practically forgotten on April 8, 1938, in Savannah, Georgia.

Dave Oppenheim

Lyricist Dave Oppenheim was born in Dubuque, Iowa, on September 16, 1889. He attended DeWitt Clinton High School and in his younger years played minor league baseball. Besides writing songs, he wrote material for Broadway nightclub shows and the movies. As so many of his contemporaries did, Oppenheim started his songwriting career in the early thirties, taking advantage of the burgeoning market, and in 1931 he and Abel Baer scored a moderate success with a happy offering, *It's the Girl*. It was a popular radio number and picked up considerable support on recordings, considering the sorry state of the business. Sides were made by Lee Morse for Columbia, Fred Rich for Hit of the Week, Ben Selvin for Harmony and allied labels, Leo Reisman on Victor, and Bob Haring on Perfect. Oppenheim also wrote the words for Cliff Friend's tribute to carefree college life, *Freddy the Freshman.* Dick Robertson extolled its merits on a recording for Crown, and Gene Kardos obliged with one for Victor. The next year Oppenheim and Baer combined on two more songs, *The Night That Love Was Born* and *Thank You, Mr. Moon.* Considering the heavy competition, they did pretty well. Eddy Duchin's orchestra recorded the first title for Columbia, and Ruth Etting made it as a vocal for the same label. Adrian Schubert recorded it for Crown. Russ Carlson (possibly a pseudonym for the same band) made the second song, and other sides came out by Nat Shilkret and Smith Ballew.

In 1933 Oppenheim joined with bandleader Little Jack Little and Ira Schuster to write the popular *Hold Me.* Little Jack Little recorded it, of course, and so did Eddy Duchin, Ted Fio Rito, and Walter Feldkamp. A few years elapsed before Oppenheim had another hit, and this time he worked with Michael Cleary and Jacques Krakeur to produce *When a Lady Meets a Gentleman Down South.* Benny Goodman and Helen Ward turned it into a swinger for Victor, and Ted Weems did likewise for Decca. Lee Wiley reprised it on Coral.

Dave Oppenheim died in New York City on December 5, 1961.

The Original Dixieland Jazz Band

Nick LaRocca
Larry Shields
Henry Ragas
J. Russel Robinson

Those who are familiar with jazz history, prior to the modern era launched by Gillespie, Parker, and Monk, will recognize the above names as belonging to four eminent members of the pioneering Original Dixieland Jazz Band. Nick LaRocca and Larry Shields were New Orleans musicians who hit it big when they organized the ODJB in Chicago in 1916 and went on to bigger things at Reisenweber's Restaurant in New York, highly successful early recordings, and a sensational tour of England. The ODJB played music culled from a variety of sources, many of them obscure and, it is said, based on old classic themes or marches. It has also been claimed that many of the compositions credited to LaRocca—more accurately, to the ODJB, because all of the members contributed to the finished compositions—were not originals but were "borrowed" or "revamped" from other works, and this may be true. It is a fact that the band ran into trouble with its recording of *Livery Stable Blues,* but it's also a fact, as any dixieland musician is well aware, that the ODJB developed the basic library of this musical style. Although there is a tendency to sneer at these grand old stompers as "war horses," the truth is they have more than proven their worth and intrinsic musical merit by outlasting many of the things that have been written long afterward.

Nick LaRocca is credited as the composer of *Ostrich Walk* (a classic as interpreted by Bix Beiderbecke and Frankie Trumbauer a decade later); *Fidgety Feet, Original Dixieland One Step* (affectionately known in the trade as *Rum Dum*); *Tiger Rag* (a plagiarized piece in its own right, so the story goes, but in turn the most plagiarized tune in history); *Skeleton Jangle* (a Bobby Hackett favorite); *Sensation Rag* (better known as just *Sensation*); *Lazy Daddy;* and *At the Jazz Band Ball.* Larry Shields shares credit for *Jazz Band Ball, Fidgety Feet,* and *Lazy Daddy,* but is cocomposer with Emil Christian on another dixieland standard, *Satanic Blues.* Two other members of the ODJB can't be left out either. The original piano player, Henry Ragas, gave us *Blu' in the Blues,* best known for the splendid version by Muggsy Spanier and his Ragtime Band on Bluebird B-10532 and subsequent reissues. Ragas shares credit with Larry Shields for *Clarinet Marmalade.* Sometimes it is difficult to determine who composed what, or to what extent, but perhaps this is as it should be. The important thing to keep in mind is the truly remarkable heritage the ODJB has left us as a collective inheritance.

J. Russel Robinson, who took over the piano chair after Ragas, was born in Indianapolis, Indiana, July 8, 1892, and has to be accorded some special consideration. As the composer of *Margie,* with Con Conrad and Benny Davis, he brought the ODJB into the popular song market with a tremendous hit and in the same year (1920) again teamed with Con Conrad on the music for *Singin' the Blues,* destined for immortality as recorded by Bix Beiderbecke and Frankie Trumbauer on OKeh 40772. Robinson went on to write a number of outstanding songs, among them *Mary Lou; Aggravatin' Papa; Halfway to Heaven; Rhythm King;* and *There's No Other Girl.* (The last title is a classic as performed by Joe Venuti and friends on Columbia 2535-D—also reissued many times.) One of J. Russel Robinson's earliest efforts, *Palesteena,* another with Con Conrad, received a spirited revival in 1938 by the Bob Crosby band on Decca 2011, with a vocal by the irrepressible Nappy Lamare.

J. Russel Robinson died in Palmdale, California, September 29, 1963.

Will Osborne

If you're old enough to have been around in the thirties, you probably remember Will Osborne very well. He started out as a drummer and then fronted a little band molded in the same pattern as Rudy Vallee's Connecticut Yankees, much to Rudy's annoyance, a situation further aggravated by network and recording company rivalries. Vallee recorded for Victor, so Osborne made Columbia records. Rudy was on NBC, so Osborne showed up on CBS. It was fun while it lasted. In the meantime, however, both tried their hands at songwriting, with very creditable results. Vallee's big hit was *Deep Night.* Osborne countered with the beautiful little ballad *Beside an Open Fireplace,* which became so popular that even Vallee recorded it. Osborne also wrote *On a Blue and Moonless Night* and his own theme song, *Just Think of Me Sometime,* along with several other pleasant ballads for the thirties.

In 1940 he entered the swing decade with *Between 18th and 19th on Chestnut Street,* which, you may remember, was well dusted over by both Crosbys,

Bing and brother Bob's Bobcats, and then further burnished by Bob Zurke. Osborne also contributed two more swingers, *Pompton Turnpike* (which New Jerseyans will readily recognize as the old name for Route 23, the thoroughfare that took the faithful to Frank Dailey's famous "Meadowbrook" when it was the home of name bands) and *Missouri Scrambler*. Other compositions were *Dry Bones* and *Wouldst Could I But Kiss Thy Hand, Oh Babe*.

Osborne's real name was Will Oliphant, and he was born in Toronto, Canada, November 25, 1906. His collaborators included Paul Denniker, Al Hoffman, Charles O'Flynn, and Dick Rogers.

Robert (Harry) Owens

Composer and bandleader Harry Owens, who did much to make Hawaii a romantic ingredient of our popular songs, was born in O'Neil, Nebraska, on April 8, 1902. His education included St. Ignatius College and Loyola University in Los Angeles. Although there is a certain amount of disparity in the dates involved, it is fairly certain that Owens met bandleader Vincent Rose while he was still in college, and the result was a collaboration on the 1923 hit song *Linger Awhile*. Owens is credited with the lyrics. Brian Rust, in his *American Dance Band Discography, 1917–1942,* lists Harry Owens on trumpet with Vincent Rose and his Montmartre Orchestra, which recorded some sides for Victor in Oakland, California, on June 9, 1924. This conflicts somewhat with the information that immediately after graduating from Loyola in 1924 Owens organized his own orchestra to tour the western states, but it appears he did organize and lead a successful band. The big event in his career took place in 1934, when he went to Hawaii and organized an orchestra he called the Royal Hawaiians, which featured Hawaiian music. He brought it back to tour the United States and Canada, winding up in Hollywood, where he wrote for films—with the band in some of them—and also instituted a twelve-year stint with his own show on CBS TV.

Nineteen thirty-six was a good year for Owens. He composed and published *To You, Sweetheart, Aloha* and introduced and featured the song with his band, which was playing at the Royal Hawaiian Hotel in Honolulu. Del Courtney, who played there afterwards, recorded the song for Vocalion. Louis Armstrong made it for Decca and Gray Gordon for Victor, but Bing Crosby, who became very partial to Harry Owens songs, had the big selling record. He also recorded another Owens title that year, *Hawaiian Paradise*. Of course, all of this was just a warm-up because in 1937 Bing Crosby starred in the movie *Waikiki Wedding,* in which he sang *Sweet Leilani*. He also recorded it, and the Decca platter sold over one million copies. *Sweet Leilani* won the Academy Award. Other records were made by Ruby Newman, Dick McIntire, and George Hall. *Dancing Under the Stars* was another Owens offering in 1937, with records by the composer's band, along with Nye Mayhew for Vocalion and Jesse Crawford on Bluebird.

Bobby Breen sang *Down Where the Trade Winds Blow,* an Owens song, in the 1938 film *Hawaii Calls,* and the Royal Hawaiians played and sang his composition *Cocoanut Grove* in the movie of the same name. It went on to be recorded by Owens for Decca. Benny Goodman for Columbia, Teddy Wilson for Columbia, and Johnny Long for Decca. Betty Grable and Hilo Hattie introduced and sang *Sing Me a Song of the Islands,* another movie title song. The Owens orchestra was also in the 1942 film, and Owens composed the score, with lyrics by Mack Gordon. *Blue Shadows and White Gardenias* was another successful song from the picture. Eddy Howard had the best recording.

Other Harry Owens compositions include *Hawaii Calls; Let's Go for Broke; Voice of the Tradewinds; Lei Aloha; Maui Girl; Ma-lu-na (Bottoms Up); Princess Poo-pooly Has Plenty Papaya; Hula Breeze; Syncopated Hula Love Song; Palace in Paradise; If Your Aloha Means I Love You; Maunaloa; Take It Easy by Slow; Cool Head Main Thing; Do Unto Others; Little Butch; Timmy; Melinda; Hawaii My Island; Menehene Lullaby; O'Brien Has Gone Hawaiian; Beneath a Banyan Tree; Singing River;* and *My Isle of Love.*

Jack Palmer

Just recently a slightly overloaded gentleman, with more persistence than politeness, kept yelling the same request at a little jazz group, which, just as persistently, pretended they couldn't hear him, although if he had used a different approach they would have been glad to play the tune he was after. *"I've Found a New Baby!"* he kept hollering. "That's a good one!" And he's right. It is a good one, even after some tens of thousands of playings. But, ten to one, if he were asked, our loud friend couldn't tell you who wrote it. And he's not alone. Even most of the musicians who have played the tune countless times and have it engraved in their brains don't know. So for them and all the rest of you who don't know, the composer—elected by his peers to the ASCAP Hall of Fame in 1971—is Jack Palmer. He also wrote *Everybody Loves My Baby,* which was his first published song. But before you get the idea that these two hit standards, which everybody knows and everybody plays, made him rich, you should know that he sold them outright for one hundred dollars apiece and had to wait twenty-eight years before he could renegotiate with the publishers for additional royalties. In the meantime he knew some periods of starvation.

Jack Palmer was born on May 29, 1900, in Memphis, where his father owned a piano store. "I learned to play from the old player pianos that were so popular then. I was always interested in writing songs and my father decided I should have some formal musical education. He sent me to this old German music professor, but after awhile the professor told my father he was wasting his money because I wasn't ever going to learn what he was trying to teach me." In the long run, this may have been the best thing, because Palmer continued to compose his own way. Along with other tunes, he turned out one called *Silver Dollar*. Somehow, without being published, this was picked up and became a big hit on college campuses throughout the country in the twenties. W. C. Handy, then leading his famous band in Memphis, liked Palmer's tunes and often featured them. Freddie Rich, on a visit to Memphis, heard them and encouraged Palmer to go to New York. But the real push came from Damon Runyon, who heard *Silver Dollar* played in Alaska and wrote a column asking if anybody knew the identity of the composer. Palmer identified himself, and Runyon wrote another column about the song and its composer.

So with high hopes, great ambitions, and little else, Palmer headed for New York—and wound up playing piano in a Greenwich Village speakeasy. As usual, New York was unimpressed by the new talent that had arrived. However, Palmer kept playing his songs, and one night *Everybody Loves My Baby* was heard by Tess Cardella, then a well-known entertainer, who performed under the name of Aunt Jemima. She sent Palmer to a music publisher who bought the tune. "I was so thrilled to be able to hold that song in my hands and see my name on the cover that I just carried it around with me all the time, looking at it in disbelief. It was the greatest thrill of my life." Aunt Jemima included the song in her repertoire, and soon it was introduced in the "Ziegfeld Follies" by Ann Pennington. Sophie Tucker sang it in "Earl Carroll's Vanities," and Jane Green further popularized it in "Ed Wynn's Grab Bag." The big hit was quickly followed by *I've Found a New Baby,* and now Palmer had two to his credit. Again he accepted a flat payment of one hundred dollars for the song, which seemed like a fortune to him at the time, only to wind up without a job or an income when the Depression came along and so broke he wound up sleeping on park benches. Finally, he got a job as an elevator operator in a hotel, another as a bell captain, and then shipped out in the merchant marine.

Palmer has 136 songs to his credit, some of which have been published in many languages. He has written in collaboration with Spencer Williams (*Give Me Just a Little Bit of Your Love*), Little Jack Little (*Oh, My Aching Heart*), and wrote the lyrics for Willard Robison's *Pigeon Toed Joad.* His first song, *Silver Dollar,* finally published in 1939, eighteen years after he composed it, became an instant hit and sold over a million copies in 1940. *I've Found a New Baby* was chosen by the French Academy of Music as a typical example of the word "swing" as a musical term in the French dictionary. In addition, through the years a number of famous artists and entertainers have recorded and used his songs to help build their popularity. *Jumpin' Jive* was a big success by Cab Calloway; *9:20 Special,* a swinger for the Count Basie band on OKeh 6244 in a 1941 arrangement by Buster Harding; *Sentimental Baby,* a 1928 entry recorded by Frank Trumbauer on OKeh 41128 and recalled by Bud Freeman many years later; *It All Begins and Ends With You,* delineated by Mildred Bailey with Red Norvo on Brunswick 7732 in 1936. Others included *Boog-It,* a Glenn Miller hit; *I Don't Want to Take a Chance,* by Ella Fitzgerald; *Hep Cat's Ball,* Louis Armstrong; *Love Doesn't Grow on Trees,* Benny Goodman; *Oh, My Aching Heart,* Tony Martin; and *Christmas Spell,* by Peggy Lee.

Jack Palmer died in Waterbury, Connecticut, on March 17, 1976.

Mitchell Parish

Mitchell Parish, who wrote the lyrics to so many great songs that the list reads like an all-time "hit parade," was born in Shreveport, Louisiana, on July 10, 1900, but grew up in New York City. He graduated Phi Beta Kappa from NYU, earned a doctorate of letters at Tusculum College and a DHL at the University of Charleston. Early in his career he went to work as a staff writer for a music publisher. He started to write lyrics for a few songs in the twenties but really hit his stride in the thirties and continued to contribute well into the fifties. Among the composers who were his collaborators through the years are many of the more illustrious names in the business: Hoagy Carmichael, Duke Ellington, Peter DeRose, Frank Perkins, Sammy Fain, Cliff Burwell, Will Hudson, Leroy Anderson, Glenn Miller, Ben Oakland, plus others.

Parish's lyrics were never banal, although sometimes amazing in their simplicity, as illustrated by the words he wrote for *Hands across the Table,* a sixteen-bar song by Jean Delettre in 1934. But he had the gift of creating precise imagery in the listener's mind of romantic scenes, gorgeous girls, and sometimes delicious melancholy that depicted just enough sadness to bring home the point of the song. As a result, songs with lyrics by Parish are often as well remembered for the words as for the melody. Starting with 1928, the year Parish wrote the words to Cliff Burwell's only hit song, the indelible *Sweet Lorraine,* he had at least one successful title every year up to and including 1942. It's a very enviable record, and one not too many people can duplicate. Following is a resume:

1929: *Missouri Moon.*
1930: *Is That Religion?* Music by Maceo Pinkard.
1931: *Star Dust*. Music by Hoagy Carmichael.
1932: *Cabin in the Cotton*. Music by Frank Perkins.
Scat Song. Music by Frank Perkins and Cab Calloway.
Sentimental Gentleman from Georgia. Music by Frank Perkins.
Take Me in Your Arms. Music by Fred Markush.
1933: *Down a Carolina Lane*. Music by Frank Perkins.
Sophisticated Lady. Music by Duke Ellington.
1934: *Christmas Night in Harlem*. Music by Raymond Scott.
Emaline. Music by Frank Perkins.
Evenin'. Music by Harry White.
Hands Across the Table. Music by Jean Delettre.
One Morning in May. Music by Hoagy Carmichael.

Sidewalks of Cuba. Music by Ben Oakland.
Stars Fell on Alabama. Music by Ray Perkins.

1935: *A Blues Serenade*. Music by Frank Signorelli.
Louisiana Fairy Tale. Music by J. Fred Coots.

1936: *Does Your Heart Beat for Me?* Music by Russ Morgan and Arnold Johnson.
Organ Grinder's Swing. Music by Will Hudson.

1937: *Mr. Ghost Goes to Town*. Music by Will Hudson.
Sophisticated Swing. Music by Will Hudson.

1938: *Don't Be That Way*. Music by Edgar Sampson and Benny Goodman.
It's Wonderful. Music by Stuff Smith.
Who Blew Out the Flame? Music by Sammy Fain.

1939: *Deep Purple*. Music by Peter DeRose.
The Lamp Is Low. Music by Peter DeRose and Bert Shefter.
Lilacs in the Rain. Music by Peter DeRose.
Moonlight Serenade. Music by Glenn Miller.
Stairway to the Stars. Music by Matty Malneck and Frank Signorelli.

1940: *Angel*. Music by Peter DeRose.
The Moon Fell in the River. Music by Peter DeRose.
Orchids for Remembrance. Music by Peter DeRose.
Starlit Hour. Music by Peter DeRose.

And if that isn't enough, other songs with lyrics by Mitchell Parish are *Bells of Avalon; Missouri Moon; It Happens to the Best of Friends; I'm in a Happy Frame of Mind; My Window Faces the South; When a Blackbird Is Blue; You're So Different; The Moon Is a Silver Dollar; Orange Blossom Lane; All I Need Is You; Let Me Love You Tonight; The Blue Skirt Waltz; Mademoiselle de Paree; All My Love; Tzena, Tzena, Tzena; Ruby; Dream Dream, Dream; Heart of Paris;* and *Volare*.

Frank Perkins

Frank Perkins didn't write a lot of songs, but he deserves high marks for composing good ones. He was born in Salem, Massachusetts, on April 21, 1908. He was educated at Brown University and also studied composing and conducting privately. He started out arranging for a music publisher then for Waring's Pennsylvanians until 1938, when he went to Hollywood to work for Warner Brothers Pictures as a composer-arranger.

As outlined in the profile of Mitchell Parish, they began to write songs together in 1932, and in that first year had three successful songs: *Cabin in the Cotton; The Scat Song;* and *Sentimental Gentleman from Georgia. Down a Carolina Lane,* a song promoted and recorded by the great Isham Jones band in 1933, was followed the next year by two outstanding tunes, *Emaline* and *Stars Fell on Alabama. Emaline* was quickly adopted by jazz people and recorded by Cab Calloway on Victor, Mildred Bailey singing with a Benny Goodman band on Columbia, Frankie Trumbauer for Brunswick, and Charlie Barnet for Melotone. Art Tatum made it for Decca as a piano solo. In England, Lew Stone's band made an excellent side with a vocal by Louis Armstrong disciple Nat Gonella. In recent years the song has attained the status of a semistandard and is frequently heard at jazz concerts. *Stars Fell on Alabama,* of course, has been a standard for many years. It was a favorite of Jack Teagarden, who recorded it at least twice, and was recorded by practically every other band and artist in the music business, among them Guy Lombardo, Freddy Martin, Benny Goodman, Vincent Rose, Richard Himber, Woody Herman, and Stan Getz.

Frank Perkins continued to compose and arrange for films and television but for some unknown reason produced no other popular song.

Ray Perkins

Ray Perkins, who recorded piano solos for Edison and made piano rolls, was born in Boston, Massachusetts, on August 23, 1896. His education included Columbia University, Juilliard, and Denver University, along with private study. A reserve officer in the United States Army, he was awarded the Bronze Star, serving in both world wars. He began a career in radio in 1924 and in later years performed as a producer and emcee at a Denver radio station and still later as a disc jockey in Florida.

His brief career as a songwriter began in 1924 when he wrote the music to words by Brooke Johns for *Tessie, Stop Teasin' Me.* A catchy ditty, it caught on with jazz groups, particularly with the Adrian Rollini units that recorded under the names of Five Birmingham Babies, the Goofus Five, and the Little Ramblers. Under the three names they waxed the tune on three different labels: Pathe, OKeh, and Columbia. Other contemporary sides were made by Ray Miller, the California Ramblers, Hal Kemp (as the Carolina Club Orchestra); and in Berlin, Germany, Alex Hyde's Original New Yorker Dance Orchestra recorded the tune for Deutsche Grammophon. In 1940 Carl Ravazza revived the tune on a recording for Bluebird.

In 1929 Ray Perskins teamed with lyricist Herman Ruby on *Smiling Irish Eyes,* a song that was introduced by Colleen Moore and James Hall in a film with the same title. But he hit the jackpot the following year, writing both words and music to the engaging ballad *Under a Texas Moon.* A favorite with a lot of people, the song was introduced by Frank Fay as the title song of another movie, and it went on to be recorded across the board. Gene Austin vocalized it on Victor, and Ted Fio Rito's band played it for the same company. Guy Lombardo made it for Columbia, Seger Ellis for OKeh, Lee Sims for Brunswick. Dale Evans reprised it at a much later date for Majestic. Other songs by Perkins include *Bye-Lo; Down the Old Church Aisle; Scandinavia;* and *Stand Up and Sing for Your Father.*

Ray Perkins died in Bradenton, Florida, on January 31, 1969.

Bernice Petkere

Pianist-composer Bernice Petkere was born in Chicago, Illinois, on August 11, 1906. She attended Englewood High School and then the Henshaw Conservatory of Music on scholarships for voice. In the meantime, she taught herself to play the piano and as a child toured in vaudeville. Then, as so many songwriters have done before her and after, she went to work as a pianist for a music publishing firm in New York. Later in her career she wrote the score for M-G-M's "Ice Follies of 1938" and shooting scripts for movies and TV.

Although Petkere may have written songs at an earlier date, judging by the number of titles she had published in the magic year of 1932, she burst upon the scene like an exploding skyrocket. They include *Lullaby of the Leaves; By a Rippling Stream; Close Your Eyes; Starlight; The Lady I Love;* and *Did You Mean What You Said Last Night?* These are all excellent songs, but, of course, the big one is *Lullaby of the Leaves.* Joe Young wrote the words, and even though the record market was at a very low ebb, contemporary platters were turned out by Ben Selvin (Columbia), Phil Spitalny (Hit of the Week), Adrian Schubert (Crown), Connee Boswell (Brunswick), George Olsen (Victor), and Roy Smeck (Melotone). The song has since become a standard, and more recent sides have been released by Art Tatum, Neal Hefti, and Dizzy Gillespie, among others.

Close Your Eyes, a very pretty ballad, received gentle treatment by the Eddy Duchin Orchestra on Victor but drew major attention in England, where it was recorded by Ray Noble for HMV, Lew Stone for Decca, Ambrose for Columbia, and Jack Hylton for Brunswick. Petkere wrote both words and music. Joe Young contributed the lyrics to *Starlight,* another very melodic Petkere entry that year. Bing Crosby crooned it on Brunswick, Jack Denny's band made it for Victor, Casa Loma for Brunswick, and Smith Ballew for Crown. Young also wrote the words to *The Lady I Love,* which was introduced and recorded by Russ Columbo, and for *Did You Mean What You Said Last Night?*, which Eddy Duchin made for Victor. However, Petkere was entirely responsible for *By a Rippling Stream,* a nice song that didn't get much attention. *Stay Out of My Dreams,* a collaboration with Ned Washington, was the Petkere entry for 1933. It drew plenty of airtime on the radio, but recordings were tapering off. Nevertheless, Freddy Martin recorded it on Melotone under the pseudonym of Owen Fallon.

Other titles by Bernice Petkere are *It's All So New to Me; Our Love; A Mile a Minute; Happy Little Farmer; Oh, Moon; Half a Mile Away from Home; That's You Sweetheart; My River Home; Hats Off, Here Comes a Lady; Barcelona Goodbye; Tell the Truth;* and *Dancing Butterfly.*

Jack Pettis & Al Goering

This is one of those instances where two men worked so closely together that it's next to impossible to determine who wrote what. The situation is even more unusual because Pettis and Goering were not a songwriting team in the usual format of composer and lyric writer. For the most part, they collaborated on writing instrumentals in a hot jazz vein for recordings. Both men were accomplished performers. Pettis was a pioneer saxophonist, and Goering an excellent pianist and arranger; and they were members of the very popular and successful Ben Bernie Hotel Roosevelt Orchestra that recorded prolifically for Vocalion and Brunswick in the twenties. The Bernie recordings were mainly straightforward dance band arrangements of tunes aimed at the pop market, but as early as January 1926—most likely with Ben Bernie's permission and encouragement—the band began to make records that were released as Al Goering's Collegians. By the year's end, the first of a series of sides for the Plaza labels—Banner, Domino, Oriole, etc—featuring Jack Pettis and His Band began to appear.

It is mainly through the label credits on these and later recordings that the composing efforts of Pettis and Goering can be traced. Information in the various reference works is scarce and incomplete. For example, the *ASCAP Biographical Dictionary* (Fourth Edition) offers a brief paragraph on Al Goering as a "composer," dosen't even mention that he played piano, lists five collaborators—Ben Bernie, Walter Hirsch, Jack Fulton, Caesar Petrillo, and Raymond Klages—and only credits him with songs for the pop market: *Who's*

Your Little Whosis?; One of Us Was Wrong; Holding My Honey's Hand; Paradise Isle; Face to Face; Looks Like a Cold, Cold Winter; and *Heads You Do (And Tails You Don't).* Conspicuously and strangely absent is any mention of Jack Pettis, and this lack is emphasized by the omission of his name from the *ASCAP dictionary*. Why this is so is hard to understand, but the neglect is consistent. The majority of reference works, while very stingy with information on Pettis, list him as cocomposer, along with Elmer Schoebel and Billy Meyers, of *Bugle Call Rag*. The latter two are in the ASCAP book, and so credited, but Jack Pettis isn't mentioned. It may be that Jack Pettis was never a member of ASCAP, but one of his earliest collaborators was Thomas "Fats" Waller, and together they turned out two titles, both published and recorded, *St. Louis Shuffle* and *Candied Sweets*. Neither song is listed in the Waller bio, nor is Jack Pettis included as a Waller collaborator. The Goering–Pettis combination, therefore, can best be traced through the recordings they made, beginning with the aforementioned *Up and At 'Em,* recorded in January 1926 and published in the same year. *Stockholm Stomp* was another 1926 entry, an early recording under the Jack Pettis name.

Once Over Lightly, recorded in December of 1927, and another original, *Steppin' It Off,* gave composer credits to Al Goering, Bill Moore, and Jack Pettis. Bill Moore was a trumpet player in the Bernie band and played on most of the Pettis records. *Candied Sweets,* the Waller–Pettis composition, was also recorded at this session. On June 20, 1928, Jack Pettis and His Pets, with Pettis and Goering directing things, recorded three originals for the Vocalion label: *Dry Martini; Hot Heels;* and *Broadway Stomp*. They followed through in the very next month with two more for Victor: *Spanish Dream* and *A Bag O' Blues*. The latter title was coupled with *Freshman Hop,* still another Goering–Pettis number on Victor 29793. Both tunes came in for repeated treatment on the OKeh label on February eighth. This time Irving Mills was included in the composer credits. *Sweetest Melody,* a Goering–Pettis ballad turned into a tour de force by young Benny Goodman, was waxed at the same time.

Prior to this, on January tenth, a so-called Whoopie Makers session, although the band was the Pettis group augmented by Jimmy Dorsey and Matty Malneck, made three titles for Vocalion, all attributed to Goering–Mills–Pettis: *Rush Inn Blues; Freshman Hop;* and *I've Never Been Loved by Anyone Like You*. Then shortly after the OKeh date a similar group—with Benny Goodman but apparently without Jack Teagarden—was back in a studio to record *Freshman Hop; Sweetest Melody;* and *Bag O' Blues* for the Pathé and Perfect labels. These were issued under various pseudonyms such as Mills's Musical Clowns, the Ten Freshman, etc. Another session for Victor as Jack Pettis and His Pets took place on May 9,

1929, and resulted in four titles: *Companionate Blues; Campus Crawl; Wild and Woolly Willie;* and *Bugle Call Blues*. Only the last title was released. The first three were only saved for posterity by the preservation of test pressings. More than likely these are Goering–Pettis compositions but this hasn't been confirmed. Another date for Victor on May twenty-third, was released as Irving Mills and His Modernists, with a Pettis tune, *At The Prom*. The ubiquitous Mills is listed as cocomposer.

The Pettis association with Irving Mills carried over to several Hotsy Totsy Gang sessions for Brunswick. Jack is included in the personnel of the first recording group under this name on July 27, 1928. This was followed by the Mills-produced Whoopee Makers session on January 10, 1929, that turned out *Rush Inn Blues; Freshman Hop;* and *I've Never Been Loved by Anyone Like You*. The Mills's Musical Clowns date of February fourteenth (also depending on the label), released as by the Ten Freshmen, Ten Black Diamonds, and Jack Pettis and His Orchestra, gave us two versions of *Freshman Hop,* one for Pathé–Perfect and one for Banner–Cameo. Still another date took place only a week later on the twenty-first, by the Lumberjacks of *I've Never Been Loved by Anyone Like You*. There may be, and most likely are, other sides in this confusing and mostly unsubstantiated list of recording dates, such as Cameo 9207, which offers a Pettis title, *Hot Heels*.

A Hotsy Totsy Gang session on May 23, 1929, which it appears for some reason didn't include Jack Pettis, although Al Goering and most of the Bernie crew were present, nevertheless recorded a Pettis–Mills collaboration, *What a Night*. Almost a year later, March 21, 1930, an all-star group recorded two Pettis compositions, *I Wonder What My Gal is Doin' Now* and *Crazy 'Bout My Gal*. As released on Brunswick 4998, *I Wonder What My Gal Is Doin' Now* was coupled with *What a Night* and received the gratuitous "Mills–Pettis" credit. *Crazy 'Bout My Gal* was released with *Railroad Man* on Brunswick 4998, both titles awarded to Irving Mills as composer. In *B. G. on the Records,* D. Russell Connor attributes *Crazy 'Bout My Gal* to "Jack Pettis–Irving Mills" and *Railroad Man* to "Elmer Schoebel–Billy Meyers–Sid Erdman," the same combination that, along with Jack Pettis, is credited with composing *Bugle Call Rag*. It seems a bit odd that Pettis isn't included here too.

Judging by the compositions discussed so far, it may seem that the Goering–Pettis team only turned out instrumentals on the hot side. To a large extent this is true, but not entirely. Although the jazz element is present in the recordings of *Sweetest Melody* and *I've Never Loved Anyone Like You,* these are melodic pieces of superior construction and imagination. Also, both writers made attempts to crack the popular market. As early as 1925, utilizing the added commercial boost of the boss's name, Ben Bernie, they penned a song called *Dreamy Monterey* and tried again the following year with *Who'll Be the One?*, lyrics credited to Ray Klages. In 1927 they wrote a waltz, *Paradise Isle,* and still another in 1928. This one, *A Kiss to Remember,* did fairly well and was recorded by Rudy Vallee on Victor.

Pettis left the Bernie organization around 1929 to strike out on his own, once again most likely sponsored by Ben Bernie, leading a band on the cruise liner SS *Leviathan* and then directing a group to accompany singer Morton Downey. But Al Goering stayed with Bernie and teamed with the boss on a series of tunes aimed at the popular market. Of these, *Who's Your Little Whozis?* (1931) was the most successful. Other titles were *Holding My Honey's Hand* (1932); *Chicago on Parade* (1933); *Ain't That Marvelous (My Baby Loves Me)* (1933); *An Old Lullaby* (1934); and *A Bowl of Chop Suey and You* (1934). Goering and lyric writer Gus Kahn collaborated on *One of Us Was Wrong,* a 1931 entry, which received respectable treatment by Ted Weems and Elmo Tanner on a Victor recording; and in 1933, he and Gertrude Lincoff combined on the melody of *Huggin' and Kissin' You,* with lyrics by Walter Hirsch. Hirsch is listed along with Goering and Bernie on *After the Dance Was Over,* but it's Al Silverman and Bernie taking credit for the words to the 1934 tender ballad *What Do the Animals Do (When They Wanna Say I Love You?).*

Pettis and Hal Brown combined for a 1929 composition called *Cool Off,* which appeared in an arrangement by Kenn Sisson, another Bernie associate. I know of no recording of this, although in that same year Pettis and Goering were both very busy in the recording studios. In fact, after this frantic period in the Pettis career there is no further recording activity until April 21, 1937, when four sides were cut in Hollywood by a group labeled Jack Pettis and His Orchestra. As notated in Rust's *Jazz Records, 1897–1942,* the pick-up group included Shorty Sherock, Jack Pettis, and Al Goering. Only two of the sides were released, appearing on the short-lived Variety label as number 558. These were *Hawaiian Heat Wave* and *Swing Session in Siberia.* The latter title was published in a stock arrangement by Arthur Birkley, with composer credit going to Pettis and Goering, with lyrics by Desmond O'-Connor. It's possible, even likely, that the other titles—*Going Harlem in Havana; Oh Yeah;* and *Hawaiian Heat Wave*—were Pettis–Goering pieces too, but up to this time this can't be confirmed.

Pettis is recognized as a pioneer in the art of playing "hot" saxophone (C-Melody, alto, and tenor), establishing what Bud Freeman referred to as the "Chicago School" of that instrument. He was born in Danville, Illinois, in 1902. As a youngster he made his way to Chicago, taught himself how to play the C-Melody sax, and began taking jobs around the city, eventually winding up as a member of the New Orleans Rhythm Kings, working at the fabled Friar's Inn. Pettis is on a number of the historic sides the band recorded for Gennett. He also collaborated with pianist Elmer Schoebel and singer Billy Meyers in composing the jazz standard, *Bugle Call Rag*. When he left the band, he formed a group of his own to back the Broadway star Ann Pennington and in 1924 joined the popular Ben Bernie band at the Roosevelt Hotel in New York. Pianist Al Goering was already in the band. In 1926 Jack managed to wangle a recording commitment from the Plaza Record Company, starting a career in the recording studios that continued without interruption until 1929.

Pettis left the Bernie band that year, most likely with the Old Maestro's blessing, and took a job leading the band aboard the Atlantic liner SS *Leviathan*. Still later he fronted a group accompanying singer Morton Downey and then is reported as playing long engagements at the Hotel New Yorker. No records were made during this period. The trail grows dim after this. It is suggested that he went to Pittsburgh and then to Hollywood, fronted bands, and was active into the thirties. Little is known about the recording session of April 21, 1937, and this is the last tangible clue to his whereabouts. Nobody seems to know where or when he died.

Al Goering was born in Chicago, Illinois, December 20, 1898. A talented youngster, he was playing piano with a trio at the Friar's Inn when he was only seventeen. After several years of barnstorming around the country, especially a five-year stint in Florida where he developed and sharpened his arranging skills, he joined the Ben Bernie band in 1922 as a pianist and assistant arranger and stayed until 1938. When the Bernie orchestra, which had been working in California, returned to New York, Goering stayed behind and played in Frank Trumbauer's band. However, he continued to write arrangements for Bernie and other leaders and remained active until the forties. He died in Chicago on April 16, 1963.

As I have attempted to show, the Jack Pettis–Al Goering collaboration was not only unique—to the extent that it has been almost completely ignored—but exceptional in that it was mostly in the form of jazz instrumentals. The result was a long series of hot jazz recordings of outstanding quality and originality and a repertory of music that deserves much greater recognition and appreciation as classic jazz than it has ever received.

For those interested in learning more about Jack Pettis, I recommend:

Roger Kinkles. *The Complete Encyclopedia of Jazz and Popular Music, 1900–1950.*

John Chilton. *Who's Who in Jazz.* Time-Life Special Edition, 1978.

Derek Coller. *More on Jack Pettis. The Mississippi Rag* April 1993.

Kingscross Music, 211 Grays Road, London WC1X 8PX, England, has released a double CD album of Jack Pettis sides, including the Plaza Label material and those made for Victor, OKeh, Vocalion, Pathé, and Perfect. This is the most comprehensive collection of Jack Pettis recordings ever available, and the transfers were engineered by John R. T. Davies with remarkable results. Also, while they are available, there is more Pettis to be heard on the Retrieval CDs *Irving Mills and His Hotsy Totsy Gang*. The three volume set is Numbers FJ-122, FJ-123, and FJ-127, and the informative liner notes are by Dave Carey. These sides were also engineered by John R. T. Davies. The Retrievals may be had, while inventory lasts, from Charlie Crump, 24 Jersey Drive, Petts Wood, Kent BR5 1ER, England.

Sid Phillips

Composer–arranger-bandleader Sid Phillips was born in London, England, on June 14, 1907. An accomplished musician, he played piano, alto sax, baritone sax, and clarinet. When he organized his big band in 1946, he earned the title of England's King of the Clarinet. In 1925 he put his first group together to tour the European continent and two years later reorganized another seven-piece unit that included his three brothers—Harry on trumpet, Ralph on bass, and Woolf on trombone. As the "Melodians," they won the fifth Open London Dance Band Contest and then went on to make a number of records. They continued to play and record until 1932. In the meantime, Sid Phillips had taken a job as staff arranger for the Lawrence Wright Music Publishing Company and decided to break up the band and devote his time to composing and arranging.

He began contributing arrangements and original instrumentals to the fine Ambrose orchestra, and it is generally acknowledged that the band's popularity owed a lot to the Phillips material. For five years he played baritone sax in the band. His arrangements of *Deep Henderson; Hors D'oeuvres; Hide and Seek;* and *Peanut Vendor* were outstanding recordings by the Ambrose band, but even more important were his originals, especially the flamboyantly descriptive *Cotton Pickers Congregation*. This was just one of a series of swinging instrumentals that included *The Night Ride; A Burmese Ballet; Early Morning Blues; Wood and Ivory; Hick Stomp; Message from Mars;* and *B'Wanga,* among others. Also at this time Phillips wrote and arranged the beautiful *Blue Romance,* an opulent ballad that was recorded by Ambrose and then later by Sid Phillips and his orchestra for Columbia.

Sid Phillips continued to compose, arrange, and lead a band until his death. He died in Chertsey, Surrey, England, on May 26, 1973.

Al Piantadosi

Composer, pianist, publisher, and ASCAP charter member (1914), Al Piantadosi was born in New York City on July 18, 1884. A ragtime pianist, he toured Europe and Australia popularizing the music. He also played in nightclubs and vaudeville. Later still, he worked for a New York music publisher; and then became a publisher himself, retiring in 1930. Coincidentally, 1930 was the same year the song I consider his best effort, *Hurt,* was published. Harold Solomon wrote the words, and it was recorded for Columbia by Ben Selvin (disguised as "Mickie Alpert's Orchestra"), for Victor by Leo Reisman, and for Perfect by Lou Gold. Roy Fox gave the tune its best treatment on English Decca.

Hurt, a sentimental ballad very much in the vogue of the new decade, almost seems to be a defiant final effort by Piantadosi, as though he is telling the world, "Big deal! I can write this kind of song if I want to!" Because, successful as he was for many years, his reputation was based on novelties like *My Mariucca Take a Steamboat* and cornball tearjerkers like *Pal of My Cradle Days* and *The Curse of an Aching Heart.* Still, it was to be admitted that the latter 1913 entry, with lyrics by Henry Fink, had a popular appeal that saw it revived in the forties. Eddie Cantor sang it in the movie *Show Business,* and it was featured on radio shows such as *The Gay Nineties.*

Al Piantadosi died in Encino, California, on April 8, 1955.

Maceo Pinkard

Maceo Pinkard occupies a special niche in the annals of American songwriting, because either by accident or on purpose, quite a few of his songs have been turned into jazz classics for the simple reason that they were recorded by exceptional artists in outstanding performances. As you will see, there are several examples of this. That such lucky circumstances may not have been entirely accidental, though, is due to the well-known fact that Pinkard wrote songs that adapted well to jazz treatment—they were rhythmic, and they swung.

He was born in Bluefield, West Virginia, on June 27, 1897, and educated at the Bluefield Institute. Early in his career he toured with his own orchestra and in 1922 wrote the score for the successful all-black revue "Liza." For a time he operated a theatrical agency in Omaha then moved on to New York, where he established a publishing firm, Pinkard Publications. One of his earliest compositions was published in 1919, *Mammy O'Mine.* The lyrics were by William Tracey, a writer Pinkard would work with years later. *Mammy O' Mine* was recorded on a contemporary side by Yerkes Jazarimba Orchestra for Victor. In 1942, twenty-three years later, Milt Gabler, who doted on old songs, had Eddie Condon and His Band—featuring Max Kaminsky and Pee Wee Russell—record a twelve inch platter for his Commodore label.

Pinkard had his first big hit in 1925 with *Sweet Georgia Brown.* Bandleader Ben Bernie shared in the credits, along with pianist Ken Casey. The Bernie orchestra featured the song, recorded it (Vocalion 15002), and also played it on a pioneering sound film sparked by two sizzling choruses by saxman Jack Pettis. A jazz favorite and a standard almost from the start, the song has been recorded countless times since, and still gets played at least once at every jazz festival. To later generations, it is readily recognized as the theme song of the famous Harlem Globetrotters basketball team. The next year, Pinkard collaborated with Roy Turk and Jack Smith (pianist-singer "Whispering Jack Smith") on the novelty ditty *Gimme a Little Kiss, Will Ya, Huh?* Not an especially musical song, it achieved immortality with a recording by the Jean Goldkette band, on which Bix Beiderbecke projects the sound of a loud kiss on his cornet. Whispering Jack Smith recorded the song and promoted it. The Goldkette orchestra also featured the 1927 Pinkard entry *Here Comes the Showboat* (lyrics by Billy Rose). Sultry singer Vaughn DeLeath made it for Edison. In 1929 the song was interpolated in the movie musical *Show Boat.*

Still hitting home runs, Pinkard and Sidney D. Mitchell combined to turn out the melodic *Sugar* in 1928. (Not to be confused with two other songs of the same title, one published in 1927, written by Red Nichols, Jack Yellen, Milton Ager, and Frank Crum; and the other a 1931 tune by Joe Young and George Meyer.) Ethel Waters was one of the first to record the Pinkard *Sugar,* and once again it had the good luck to be arranged for the Paul Whiteman orchestra by Bill Challis on a Victor record that featured Bix Beiderbecke. Thus established as a jazz classic, it has been played and recorded steadily since. In 1940 Lee Wiley, backed by Jess Stacy and Muggsy Spanier, recorded it for Commodore. In 1955 it was featured in the film *Pete Kelly's Blues,* sung by Peggy Lee with Matty Matlock's Dixieland group. They also recorded it.

1930 was a big year for Pinkard, with four good songs in the running. *Congratulations,* one of those "committee" offerings with credits going to Coleman Goetz, Bud Green, and Sam H. Stept along with Maceo Pinkard, was a pleasant ballad, well received and recorded by the Dorsey Brothers on Regal, Smith Ballew for OKeh, Nat Shilkret on Victor, Jack Denny on Brunswick, and Paul Small on Velvetone. Then Pinkard worked with lyricist William Tracey, and they came up with a swinger, *Okay, Baby,* which received appropriate treatment from McKinney's Cotton Pickers on a Victor side and a strange kind of immortality as one of the songs chosen by Ray Noble to occupy a groove on the famous *Puzzle Record #1,* originally made for HMV in England but issued here on Victor. If you have never seen nor heard this unusual recording, here's a brief explanation. On each side of the 78 RPM disc are three songs—all by Ray Noble's New Mayfair Orchestra, but without any credit on the label. The "puzzle" is to find the three songs, and the trick is to put the needle down at a different spot in the starting groove, because the three tracks were recorded separately, each with its own groove on the record.

The third title, *I'll Be a Friend With Pleasure,* is another of the examples I mentioned earlier. With words by William Tracey, it was definitely aimed at the popular market but wound up as one of three songs recorded at the historic session for Victor on September 9, 1930, by Bix Beiderbecke and His Orchestra. As such, it has been reissued many times and has become a semi-standard. The fourth entry for 1930 was *Them There Eyes,* with words by William Tracey and Doris Tauber. A standard for many years, one of the earliest records was cut by the Gus Arnheim orchestra with a vocal by the Rhythm Boys, Bing Crosby, Al Rinker, and Harry Barris. It has since been played and recorded by Louis Armstrong, Billie Holiday, Benny Goodman, Duke Ellington, the Quintent of the Hot Club of France, Bob Crosby, Teddy Wilson—and just about anybody else you might name. Other songs by Pinkard include *Don't Be Like That; At Twilight; Don't Cry, Baby, Don't Cry; Sweet Man; There Must Be Somebody Else; That Wonderful Boy Friend of Mine; Let's Have a Showdown; Wonderful Pal, Dawning; Lila;* and *Is That Religion?*

Maceo Pinkard died in New York City on July 21, 1962.

Lew Pollack

It's quiz time. Are you ready? Who wrote *That's A-Plenty*?

Aw, you peeked at the name at the top of this entry, but you're right. Lew Pollack did write *That's A-Plenty,* but in spite of the title finality of this all-time jazz standard, he wasn't satisfied to stop there. The average man in the street (or anywhere else, for that matter) may admit he has never heard of Pollack, but that same man (unless he's under thirty) will know one or more of his songs.

Like many of his contemporaries, Lew Pollack was a native of New York City, born there on June 16, 1895. He graduated from DeWitt Clinton High School and at age fourteen performed as a boy soprano with the Walter Damrosch Choral Group. Later he sang and played in vaudeville, writing original material for himself and other acts. *That's A-Plenty* was his first published song, a 1914 contender, but wasn't followed by another song until 1919, when a tune called simply *Buddha* appeared. This opus was undoubtedly another entry conceding to the vogue for pseudo-oriental tunes of the time but didn't make a stir compared to hits like *When Buddha Smiles, Japanese Sandman, Oriental Strut,* and others in the idiom.

Possibly Pollack kept writing, but his material wasn't being accepted, so nothing happened again until 1921 when he collaborated with composer Al Goodman on a score for a stage show called "The Whirl of New York" and still another called "Midnight Rounders of 1921," both long forgotten and of little musical excitement. So again a few years went by, during which Pollack most likely was busy working as a singer-pianist in vaudeville, but in 1925 he came back in a big way with two hits back-to-back. One was *Cheatin' On Me,* revived to new life and popularity many years later with the hit record by Jimmie Lunceford's band, and the other *My Yiddishe Momme,* which enjoyed a brief vogue. In 1926 a lukewarm entry came out, *I Wish I Had My Old Girl Back;* but 1927 was the bonanza year, with *Cobblestones; Diane; Charmaine,* and *Miss Annabelle Lee* ringing up sales all over the country. *Cobblestones* made it into posterity via a fine recording by the Ted Weems band, and *Diane* and *Charmaine,* both waltzes, appealed to the postwar nostalgia engendered by movies like *What Price Glory* and were big hits. Both had memorable melodies, but *Diane* was chosen by Jack Teagarden for one of his virtuoso performances on Commodore 505 with Eddie Condon and His Windy City Seven. Both tunes are standards in the catalog of better American waltzes but easily adapt to a four-four tempo. *Miss Annabelle Lee* was another big seller for the Ted Weems band.

Another stage show, "Luckee Girl," made its debut in 1928 but didn't go anywhere, and neither did the two tunes Lew Pollack contributed, *A Flat in Montmartre* and *In Our Little Studio;* but 1929 brought one of his nicest songs, *Some Sweet Day*. This enjoyed a very respectable success but was subsequently forgotten, possibly because nobody with a big name recorded it. Still another time lapse takes place, and it's not until 1934 that Pollack is heard from again. This time he has two successful entries, *Two Cigarettes in the Dark* and *Water Under the Bridge*. Then Hollywood beckoned and a Shirley Temple picture, *Captain January,* in 1936, featured three songs. *At the Codfish Ball* (given a jazz treatment by Tommy Dorsey's Clambake Seven); *The Right Somebody to Love;* and *Early Bird,* followed in the same year by *Pigskin Parade,* with two good tunes in the score, *You Do the Darndest Things, Baby* and *It's Love I'm After*. Two others were featured, *Sing,*

Baby, Sing, the title song, and *Love Will Tell. King of the Burlesque* included a Pollack novelty, *I Love to Ride the Horses on the Merry-Go-Round.* The next two years were busy ones writing for the screen and produced some fairly good tunes, such as *Who's Afraid of Love; Overnight; I've Taken a Fancy to You;* and *I'll Never Let You Cry* (the last two recorded on Decca by Teddy Grace with the house band, which included clarinetist Don Watt and a young Bobby Hackett), and *Moonshine over Kentucky.*

Pollack died in Hollywood in 1946, leaving a very creditable heritage of songs. Remember him the next time you play or hear *That's A-Plenty.*

George Posford

George Posford, an English composer who wrote some excellent songs in the popular vein, two of which competed very favorably with the homegrown variety in this country, was born in Folkestone, England, on March 23, 1906. He was educated at Dawnside and Christ's College, Cambridge, studying law, but music exerted a greater appeal, and he decided to become a professional composer. Early in his career he specialized in material for radio, and one of his best songs was written during this period, the 1932 title, *Lazy Day.* A successful import to this country, the song underwent some modification in the process. The sheet music, as published here, credits four composers: Earl Martin, Gus Kahn, George Posford, and Grace LeBoy Kahn, explaining that Martin and Posford wrote the English lyric and melody, and Gus and Grace Kahn the American version. Actually, there is little difference between the two, and the Kahns merely polished a rough spot here and there. Ray Noble's New Mayfair Orchestra recorded the song for the HMV label in England, with the usual masterful arrangement by Noble, and Bing Crosby recorded it for Brunswick in the United States (also the bands of Jack Denny and Roger Wolfe Kahn), so it's easy to compare the two versions. Both are fine, and the song was a success in both countries.

Posford began to write for the British stage and movies, and in 1932 he had two songs in the Jack Buchanan film *Goodnight Vienna.* In the liner notes by Brian Rust for the boxed set of Ray Noble New Mayfair recordings reissued in England some years ago, he states, "The next session . . . produced a coupling of two numbers from the Jack Buchanan film, *Goodnight, Vienna,* namely the title song, and *Living in Clover.* Although issued in the early summer of 1932, at a season when record sales have been less than impressive from earliest times, this one was a huge success, and it was rushed to America, where, despite the Depression, it was welcomed with open bankbooks."

Ray Noble, who always knew a good song when he came across one, also recorded two more Posford titles the following year, both from the Jessie Matthews movie *The Good Companions*. The titles are *Three Wishes* and *Let Me Give My Happiness to You*. The original Ray Noble HMV sides were issued on Victor, and Jessie Matthews's vocal versions are issued on Columbia. Ted Weems recorded *Let Me Give My Happiness to You,* with a vocal by Elmo Tanner; and Freddy Martin made *Three Wishes* for Brunswick. In 1936 Posford composed *The World is Mine,* with the words contributed by Holt Marvell (Eric Maschwitz). It was introduced by Nino Martini in the film *The Gay Desperado* and recorded in the United States by Tony Martin on Decca and by Richard Himber's orchestra on Victor. Then in 1939 Maschwitz and Posford combined on *At the Balalaika*. It was performed by Nelson Eddy and Ilona Massey with the Russian Cossack Choir in the movie *Ballalaika* and was the only song retained from the English stage show of 1936, which was the basis for the film. Again the song underwent some modification, with Robert Wright and George Forrest credited with the new lyrics for the movie. Posford continued to write for the stage and films well into the forties. In 1942 he wrote *Transatlantic Rhapsody* to celebrate the maiden voyage of the *Queen Mary* and in 1952 composed the rhapsody *Broadcasting House*.

George Posford died in Worplesdon, Surrey, England, on April 24, 1976.

Teddy Powell

Composer and bandleader Teddy Powell was born in Oakland, California, on March 1, 1906. He was educated at the San Francisco Conservatory of Music. He joined the Abe Lyman band in 1926, playing banjo and guitar and singing with a trio, and stayed with Lyman for seventeen years. He began composing in 1935, mainly collaborating with Walter Samuels and Leonard Whitcup, and their first success was the pseudo-cowboy song, *Take Me Back to My Boots and Saddle*. Two other entries for the year did well too, *I Couldn't Believe My Eyes* and *March Winds and April Showers*. The new Tommy Dorsey band had the big record on *Boots and Saddle,* but the Dorsey Brothers were still together when *I Couldn't Believe My Eyes* was recorded on Decca. Wingy Manone made a swinger out of *March Winds and April Showers* for Banner and associated labels. *Cottage by the Moon* was the only offering in 1936, and it didn't attract much attention. Nevertheless, Wingy gave it a treatment on Bluebird.

Powell and Leonard Whitcup worked together to produce the instrumental *Snake Charmer* in 1937. Jerry Blaine's orchestra made it for Bluebird.

Then, with Walter Samuels back again, they published two very pleasant ballads, *Heaven Help This Heart of Mine* and *If My Heart Could Only Talk.* Mildred Bailey, Dick Robertson, and Eddy Duchin all had recordings of the former, and Tommy Dorsey and Billie Holiday the latter. *Bewildered,* by Powell and Whitcup, came out in 1938, and again Tommy Dorsey had the top record. The song was revived in 1949 by Billy Eckstine for M-G-M and by Herb Jeffries on Columbia. Powell and Whitcup did well with *Am I Proud* in 1940, which had good presentation on sides by Tommy Dorsey and Freddy Martin.

A bit of confusion exists concerning the song *Somebody's Thinking of You Tonight.* Brian Rust lists it as first recorded by Dick Robertson's orchestra for Decca on November 10, 1937, but the side was rejected. Made exceptional by the fact that Bobby Hackett and Don Watt were in the band, it was remade on January 14, 1938, and released on Decca 1619. The Teddy Powell band, with ace clarinetist Irving Fazola in the lineup, recorded the song for Bluebird on April 30, 1942.

Other Teddy Powell titles are *Precious Little One; The Lady from Fifth Avenue; Rollin' Plains; Spring Cleaning; Love of My Life; Little Genius; Singin' in the Saddle; If I Could Be the Sweetheart of a Girl Like You; Raindrops; My Love Is Yours; Flea on a Spree; The Sphinx; Teddy Bear Boogie; With Faith in Your Heart; Unsuspecting Heart; Always Look Up; All I Need Is You;* and *April Give Me One More Day.*

Lew Quadling

Pianist-composer-arranger Lew Quadling was born in Cedarville, New Jersey, on June 7, 1908. He was educated in the public schools and at Curtis Institute. An accomplished big band pianist, he worked with many of the biggest names, including Ted Weems, Anson Weeks, Phil Harris, and Dick Jurgens. It was while he was in the Dick Jurgens band that he wrote his biggest hit song, *Careless,* which came out in 1939 with Eddy Howard sharing credit. As recounted by Robert Lissauer in his *Dictionary of Popular Music in America,* the trio of writers—all associated with the Jurgens band—submitted the song to the Irving Berlin publishing company. Berlin overheard Dave Dreyer, the company manager, running over the song and liked the melody but not the lyrics. Fearing that if they turned the song down, the Jurgens band would boycott other Berlin titles, Berlin took the song home and wrote new words for it and gave it the new title, *Careless*. The tune went on to become a number one best-seller and made a lot of money, but Berlin received none of the credit, nor any of the royalties.

Undeterred, Howard and Jurgens were back with Lew Quadling the next year to write the outstanding song *A Million Dreams Ago*. The Jurgens orchestra gave it suitable treatment on the OKeh label, with vocalist Harry Cool, and had the best-selling record of the tune. Glenn Miller waxed the title for Bluebird, with Ray Eberle singing. By this time Eddy Howard, who had been featured with Jurgens for many years, had left to strike out on his own.

In 1941 Quadling worked with lyricist Jack Elliott and again turned out a little gem, *Do You Care?* Dinah Shore had a winner for Bluebird, and Sam Donahue's band made it for the same label. Other sides, all successful, were made by Bob Crosby, Raymond Scott, Les Brown, and Al Donahue. Quadling composed, arranged, and directed all the movies made for the Signal Corps at a Long Island studio during the years 1943 to 1945 and then went on to arrange and conduct record dates for such stars as Dean Martin, Eydie Gorme, Eddy Howard, and the McGuire Sisters. In 1950 he surfaced again with Jack Elliott on the engaging *Sam's Song,* which proved to be a big hit for Decca as performed by a vocal duo billed as "Gary Crosby and

Friend." The "friend," of course, was Bing Crosby, and the record and the song took off.

Other songs by Lew Quadling include *I Do, Do You?; The Lights of Home; It's Snowing in Hawaii; So Long Train Whistle; I Haven't Been Home in Three Whole Nights; I'm Not Good Enough for You; College November; Plenty of Brass; Trumpet Rag;* and *Double Shuffle.*

Ralph Rainger

Ralph Rainger, one of the most prolific composers of the thirties with a long list of hit songs to his credit, was born in New York City on October 7, 1901. He was educated at the Damrosch Institute of Musical Art and Brown University Law School. A graduate lawyer, he turned instead to working as a professional pianist. He worked with Edgar Fairchild as a two-piano team in the stage shows "Queen High" (1926) and "Ziegfeld Follies of 1927," and they co-led the orchestra for "Cross My Heart" in 1928. Rainger contributed two songs to the score of "Queen High" but had his first hit with *Moanin' Low,* a collaboration with Howard Dietz. It was sung by Libby Holman in "The Little Show" and launched her career as well as Rainger's.

He started writing for the movies in 1930, and clicked immediately with *When a Woman Loves a Man,* which was sung by Fanny Brice in *Be Yourself.* Billy Rose wrote the words. Fanny Brice recorded the song for Victor, coupled with another hit from the picture, *Cooking Breakfast for the One I Love.* The Libby Holman and Annette Hanshaw sides for Brunswick and OKeh followed the same pattern. In 1932 Rainger combined with lyricist Leo Robin, and they turned out one successful song after another, especially for Bing Crosby movies. They started with *The Big Broadcast of 1932,* contributing *Please* and *Here Lies Love,* both successful and in the melodic thirties tradition. The team had moderate entries in 1933 and most of 1934, and then came the Bing Crosby film *She Loves Me Not,* in which he and Kitty Carlisle sang *Love in Bloom.* The song was nominated for an Academy Award and was recorded by Crosby (the best-seller, of course), along with Paul Whiteman, Hal Kemp, Claude Hopkins, and Georgie Price. Jack Benny played it in the 1937 movic *College Holiday* and then adopted it as his personal theme.

The Crosby magic continued, and in 1935 Robin and Rainger wrote the score for *Here Is My Heart,* which included *June in January; Here Is My Heart;* and *With Every Breath I Take. I Wished On the Moon,* with words by Dorothy Parker, was introduced by Bing in *The Big Broadcast of 1936,* and like all the other songs in the film, it sold well. But Robin and Rainger, with expert help from Richard Whiting, were responsible for *Why Dream?; Double Trouble;* and the swinging *Miss Brown to You,* all in the same picture.

Ray Noble's orchestra was featured in the film and recorded all the songs for Victor. Among the other sides made of the tunes, probably the Teddy Wilson Brunswick version of *Miss Brown to You,* with the vocal by Billie Holiday, is the most outstanding and has established the song as a jazz classic.

Just as *The Big Broadcast of 1936* was filmed in 1935, so *The Big Broadcast of 1937* was made in 1936. This time Benny Goodman's band was featured, and the Robin and Rainger songs included *Here's Love in Your Eyes; You Came to My Rescue; I'm Talking Through My Heart; Vote for Mr. Rhythm;* and *Night in Manhattan.* Goodman recorded *Here's Love in Your Eyes* on Victor 25351; and a Goodman unit, under Teddy Wilson's name, made *You Came to My Rescue* and *Here's Love in Your Eyes* for Brunswick. Helen Ward was the vocalist on both platters. Robin and Rainger continued to write for films, and in 1937 they again hit the jackpot with a Bing Crosby movie, *Waikiki Wedding,* contributing three quality songs, *Blue Hawaii; In a Little Hula Heaven;* and *Sweet is the Word for You. Blue Hawaii* won the Academy Award for the Best Song and was a best-selling record by Bing Crosby (coupled with *Sweet Leilani,* the Harry Owens hit song from the picture). In that same year, Robin and Rainger had the title song in the movie *Blossoms on Broadway* and again for the film *Ebb Tide.* Then, just to balance things off, they penned *Easy Living* as a freelance offering, which Teddy Wilson and Billie Holiday once more turned into a jazz classic.

It's easy to imagine a conference of movie producers discussing what picture to make next and then predictably deciding that it was time for another *Big Broadcast.* And so there was *The Big Broadcast of 1938.* This one starred Bob Hope and Shirley Ross, with Shep Fields's orchestra, and the Robin and Rainger hits were *Thanks for the Memory; You Took the Words Right Out of My Heart;* and *Mama, That Moon Is Here Again.* All the songs were popular, but *Thanks for the Memory* won another Academy Award for the team of Robin and Rainger, and Bob Hope and Shirley Ross had a best-selling record. Hope made *Thanks for the Memory* his theme song, and it has become a standard. Benny Goodman had a successful coupling of *What Goes On Here in My Heart?* and *A Little Kiss at Twilight,* two excellent songs from the movie *Give Me a Sailor,* which starred Bob Hope and Betty Grable. Martha Tilton was the vocalist on the 1938 recording. Then the urbane maker of hits, Bing Crosby, was back in a film called *Paris Honeymoon,* and the songs were *I Have Eyes; The Funny Old Hills; You're a Sweet Little Headache;* and *Joobalai.* Crosby recorded them all, with the usual results.

Robin and Rainger wrote for the movies on a nonstop basis well into the forties, although no more outstanding hits were scored. And then came the tragic ending. Ralph Rainger was killed when the New York–bound plane he was on collided in midair with an army bomber near Palm Springs on October 23, 1942. Rainger was on his way to a conference with his partner Leo Robin and song publisher Jack Robbins to discuss plans for the songs they had written for an upcoming movie, *Coney Island.* The movie and the songs were released in 1943. The team of Robin and Rainger was one of the longest-lasting collaborations in the history of the business. They worked together for twelve years.

Other songs by Ralph Rainger are *I'm Afraid of You; Seems to Me; Brother, Just Laugh it Off; I'll Take an Option On You; Give Me Liberty or Give Me Love; In the Park in Paree; Look What I've Got; Thank Heaven for You; She Was a China Teacup, and He Was Just a Mug; I'm a Black Sheep Who Is Blue; Low Down Lullaby; Laugh, You Son-of-a-Gun; Take a Lesson From the Lark; Hills of Old Wyomin'; I Don't Want to Make History; Will I Ever Know; Where Is My Heart?; Long Ago and Far Away; Swing Tap; Little Rose of the Rancho; If I Should Lose You; Thunder over Paradise; A Rhyme for Love; So What?; If It Isn't Pain, Then It Isn't Love; You're Lovely, Madame; What Have You Got That Gets Me?; The Waltz Lives On; This Little Ripple Had Rhythm;* and many more.

Don Raye (Donald McCrae Wilhoite)

Songwriter Don Raye, who composed both words and music, was born Donald MacCrae Wilhoite Jr., on March 16, 1908, in Washington, D.C. A talented youngster, in 1924 he won the Virginia state dancing championship. After that, he sang and danced in vaudeville, touring all over the United States and parts of Europe. In the thirties he performed in nightclubs, went to work as a staff writer for a music publisher, and still found time to attend NYU. In 1935 he began writing songs and collaborated with Sammy Cahn on the lyrics to music composed by Jimmie Lunceford and Saul Chapman. The song was *Rhythm in My Nursery Rhymes.* Lunceford recorded it for Decca, and other jazz-oriented sides were made by Tommy Dorsey's Clambake Seven (Victor); Wingy Manone (Vocalion); Teddy Wilson (Brunswick); and Joe Haymes for ARC.

Other moderate successes followed—*Yodelin' Jive; Well, All Right!; Casbah Blues*—with the inevitable result that Raye started to write for movies. In the film *Down Argentina Way,* the Andrews Sisters sang the Don Raye–Hughie Prince collaboration *Rhumboogie,* and they also recorded it for Decca in a best-selling record. Will Bradley's Orchestra, featuring Ray McKinley on drums and vocals, also had a successful side—the beginning of many by this band for Raye. It was followed by another tune from the same movie and the same writers, *Beat Me Daddy, Eight to the Bar*. The Bradley band recorded it in two parts for a big hit on Columbia. The Andrews Sisters also made it for Decca. In quick order that same year came *Scrub Me Mama With a Boogie Beat,* a solo effort by Raye again accorded hit records by Will Bradley and the Andrews Sisters, and the clever *Down the Road A-Piece,* with both words and music by Raye. The Bradley organization made the most of the lyrics by featuring a small unit playing the song, with a conversation between drummer Ray McKinley and pianist Freddie Slack. Other titles that year were *This Is My Country; I Love You Much Too Much;* and *Your Red Wagon.*

The close association with the Andrews Sister continued the next year, with Raye and Hughie Prince providing the music for the Abbott and Costello movie *Buck Privates,* which also starred the Andrew Sisters. *Boogie Woogie Bugle Boy* was the hit song for all concerned. Two more Abbott and Costello films came along in quick succession, *In the Navy,* from which came *Starlight, Starbright;* and *Keep 'Em Flying* with songs by Raye and Gene DePaul—*You Don't Know What Love Is* and *Pig Foot Pete,* among others. Carol Bruce introduced the first title in the picture, and Martha Raye the second. Martha Raye also recorded it for Decca, and the song was nominated for an Academy Award. That same year Raye got together with bandleader Harry James, putting words to *Music Makers*. James recorded it as a hit instrumental, and so did Count Basie, but Tommy Dorsey's Victor recording featured Raye's lyrics sung by the Pied Pipers.

Raye had a busy year in 1942. With Patricia Johnston he shared credit for the words to the beautiful Gene DePaul tune *I'll Remember April,* introduced by Dick Foran in the film *Ride 'em Cowboy*. Woody Herman recorded it for Decca, and Charlie Barnet for Bluebird, but the song was off to a slow start. It came to be more appreciated in later years and can now be considered a standard. From another movie, *Behind the Eight Ball,* starring the Ritz Brothers, came the Raye–DePaul song *Mr. Five by Five*. The tune became associated with Count Basie's vocalist, Jimmy Rushing, who recorded it for Columbia. A popular novelty, it was sung by Jane Frazee in still another film that year, *Almost Married,* and the Andrews Sisters recorded it for Decca and then performed it in the 1943 film *Always a Bridesmaid*. Freddie Slack had a good recording on Capitol, and Harry James had the best-seller on Columbia. James also had a popular side on *He's My Guy,* a freelance offering by Raye and DePaul. Other sides were made by the bands of Tommy Dorsey, Dick Stabile, and Freddie Slack and vocalist Dinah Shore. In 1943 the tune was used in two films, *Hi Ya, Chum* and *Follow the Band.*

Star Eyes, another outstanding ballad by the team, was introduced by Jimmy Dorsey's orchestra with the vocal by Helen O'Connell and Bob

Eberle in the 1943 Red Skelton movie *I Dood It.* Jimmy also had the best-selling record on Decca, but it was sung by Kitty Kallen. O'Connell left the band after the completion of the film. *Cow Cow Boogie,* a hit recording by Ella Mae Morse with Freddie Slack's band on Capitol in 1943, was actually published a year earlier and was sung by Ella Fitzgerald in the movie *Ride 'em Cowboy,* but for some reason was deleted before the picture was released. After the successful Capitol record, Ella Mae Morse and the Slack band repeated the performance in the film *Reveille With Beverly.* The song was credited to Don Raye, Gene DePaul, and Benny Carter. It was an adaptation of pianist Cow Cow Davenport's *Cow Cow Blues,* and this led to litigation when *Cow Cow Boogie* was first released, possibly the reason it was withdrawn from *Ride 'em Cowboy.* A settlement was made with Charles Davenport, who sold his rights to the song to the writers of *Cow Cow Boogie.*

Raye wrote words to the Artie Shaw–Charlie Shavers composition originally called *Pastel Blue,* and recorded in 1939 by both the John Kirby group and the Artie Shaw band, and it became *Why Begin Again.* Under the new title, Artie Shaw recorded it, Tommy Dorsey made it, and so did singer Dick Todd—all for Victor.

Other songs by Don Raye include *Amigo, We Go Riding Tonight; Oh, He Loves Me!; Rock-a-bye the Boogie; Bounce Me, Brother, With a Solid Four; You're a Lucky Fellow, Mr. Smith; I Wish You Were Here; When Private Brown Becomes a Captain; We're in the Navy; Let's Keep 'em Flying; The Boy With the Wistful Eyes; Rockin' and Reelin'; Give Me My Saddle; Beside the Rio Tonto; You Were There; Ain't That Just Like a Man?; Milkman, Keep Those Bottles Quiet; The House of Blue Lights; A Song Is Born;* and numerous others.

Andy Razaf

One of the most prolific lyricists of the twenties and thirties, Andy Razaf was born in Washington, D.C., on December 16, 1895. The son of a Malagasy nobleman, he was also the nephew of Queen Ranavalona III of Madagascar and was a grand duke. His real name was Andrea Paul Razafkeriffo, or Andreamenentania Paul Razafinkeriefo. He attended public schools but also studied privately. Razaf wrote for many nightclub shows, and in 1928 he collaborated with Thomas "Fats" Waller on the song *Willow Tree,* which was used in the stage musical "Keep Shufflin'." A classic recording of the song was made for Victor by the Louisiana Sugar Babes, a group that included Jabbo Smith on cornet, Garvin Bushell on reeds, James P. Johnson on piano, and Fats Waller on the organ. In that same year Razaf worked on two songs with James P. Johnson, *Dusky Stevedore* and *Take Your Tomorrow*. These were also turned into jazz classics on recordings by Frankie Trumbauer's orchestra featuring Bix Beiderbecke. Then, with an assist from Bob Schafer on the lyrics, Razaf and James P. Johnson added two other songs that are in the category of immortal performances: *Louisiana,* as recorded by Paul Whiteman's orchestra with Bix and the vocal by Bing Crosby and a quartet, in an arrangement by Bill Challis; and *When,* which received similar treatment minus Crosby, as arranged by Tom Satterfield. Bix Beiderbecke and His Gang also recorded *Louisiana* for the OKeh label. It has become a standard, played and recorded many times since.

Razaf and Fats Waller collaborated on four outstanding songs in 1929: *Honeysuckle Rose; Ain't Misbehavin'; Black and Blue;* and *My Fate Is in Your Hands. Honeysuckle Rose* was introduced in the revue "Load of Coal" at the famed nightclub Connie's Inn. *Ain't Misbehavin'* and *Black and Blue* were in the stage musical "Hot Chocolates," and *My Fate Is in Your Hands* was a popular freelance effort. All have taken their place as well-known items in the Fats Waller song book.

However, Razaf was busy in other pastures that year. With Paul Denniker supplying the music, he penned *S'posin'*, which was given a handy boost toward immortality by Rudy Vallee; and then with Don Redman he wrote *Gee, Baby, Ain't I Good to You,* which also received a hearty send-off on a recording by McKinney's Cotton Pickers under the direction of Don Redman. He teamed with still another partner in 1929, Eubie Blake, and together they turned out a fine score for Lew Leslie's "Blackbirds of 1932," a theater musical. Included were the unforgettable *Memories of You; You're Lucky to Me; That Lindy Hop; Baby Mine;* and *Green Pastures*. Then—maybe just to prove he could do it—Razaf wrote both words and music for *On Revival Day*. The song was introduced by Bessie Smith and recorded by the rampaging Rube Bloom and His Bayou Boys for Columbia, Ford Leary for Bluebird, Johnny Johnson for Victor, and Bob Howard on Decca. And not to be overlooked in that fruitful year, Razaf and Fats Waller got together again for the magnificent *Blue, Turning Grey over You.*

In contrast, the output for 1931 was sparse, consisting of the Razaf–Waller tune *Concentratin' (On You)*. Waller introduced and featured it, and it enjoyed fair success, with other sides by Mildred Bailey, the California Ramblers, and Blanche Calloway. But more titles with Waller came along in 1932, especially the delightfully swinging *Keepin' Out of Mischief Now* and the wistfully blue *Lonesome Me*. The equally excellent *Ain'tcha Glad?* kicked off 1933, and then Razaf went "a-wanderin'" again. Working with pianist Earl Hines and English composer Reginald Foresythe, he produced *Deep Forest* and, with Forsythe alone, *Mississippi Basin.* Hines introduced *Deep Forest* and adopted it as his band's theme. *Mississippi Basin,* although well represented on records by Louis Armstrong, Glen Gray, Bert Lown, and others, never quite made it in the popular market. Back with Fats Waller in 1934, Razaf put the words to another gem, *How Can You Face Me?,* which got appropriate treatment from Fats on a recording in which he identifies the protagonist as "you dog." Razaf also reunited with James P. Johnson on the infectious *A Porter's Love Song to a Chambermaid.*

For some reason, Razaf didn't work in 1935, but he more than made up for the slack in the next year by collaborating with a variety of composers. With Fernando Arbello he wrote *Big Chief DeSota.* With Leon Berry it was *Christopher Columbus.* With Paul Denniker he penned *Make Believe Ballroom,* the theme song of disc jockey Martin Block's long-lasting radio program. With Denniker and Joe Davis he authored *The Milkman's Matinee,* another radio theme, this time for the late-night program run by personality Art Ford. Another reunion with Fats Waller produced *Stealin' Apples,* and then Razaf was part of the committee (Edgar Sampson, Chick Webb, and Benny Goodman) that shared credit for *Stompin' at the Savoy.*

I Can't Break the Habit of You was the only quiet entry for 1937. Nothing happened in 1938, but Razaf and Joe Garland hit paydirt in 1939 with *In the Mood.* Razaf repeated in 1940, working with Frankie Carle and Larry Wagner on *A Lover's Lullaby,* a popular entry. Razaf and Fats Waller combined on a typical Waller romp, *The Joint Is Jumpin'.* Pianist Luckey Roberts provided the melody for the 1942 song *Massachusetts,* which made successful records for Gene Krupa and Johnny Long; and Phil Harris fell in love with *That's What I Like About the South,* another tune that Razaf composed by himself. Harris recorded it three or more times, performed it on stage and on Jack Benny's radio program, and, to all intents, adopted it as his personal property.

Andy Razaf was cited by the Treasury Department for writing songs to promote the bond drives during World War II. He continued to write well into the forties and in the early fifties took up residence in California. A severe stroke incapacitated him, and he spent many years in a wheelchair. He died in North Hollywood, California, on February 3, 1973.

Don Redman

One of the most underrated and neglected giants in the history of jazz and American popular music is the little man of many talents, Don Redman. He was born in Piedmont, West Virginia, on July 29, 1900. A musical prodigy, at the age of six he was playing saxophone professionally and at fourteen was admitted to Storer's College. This was followed by study at the Boston Conservatory. As an arranger, Redman played a big part in pioneering the development of big bands, performing this role with Fletcher Henderson's band and then with McKinney's Cotton Pickers. As a bandleader, he organized one of the finest units of the thirties, well remembered for a long stint at the famous Connie's Inn and its exceptional theme song, *Chant of the Weed.*

Chant of the Weed was an original composition by Redman, and in the liner notes for the RCA Vintage *Don Redman, Master of the Big Band* (LPV 520), Duke Ellington is quoted this way:

"He was a great writer and arranger, a forerunner whose ideas have been copied and have reappeared in various guises right down the line. When he got his own band he became a competitor, and I didn't appreciate the fact at all, because he was so tough. Nor did I appreciate his laying that *Chant of the Weed* on us either, but more than twenty years later I asked him to do the arrangement for us to record. We play it from time to time, and it still sounds good!"

Of course, Duke Ellington had nothing to fear from Redman as a competing composer, but the Duke recognized quality when he heard it. Although Redman's output was not even close to the Ellington proliferation, the quality is evident. Many of his songs are still favorites in the more jazz-oriented contemporary groups, such as *Gee, Baby, Ain't I Good to You* and *I Want a Little Girl.* (These were both standards in the repertoire of the late Doc Cheatham.) *Save It Pretty Mama* was a song the late, great trombonist Vic Dickenson liked to sing; and then there is the perennial that sometimes gets confused with another old standard, *Coquette*—the melodic swinger, *Cherry,* recorded many times, but given exceptional treatment by the Harry James band on a record for Columbia in 1942.

But Redman's talents weren't limited to composing and arranging. He had another that is often overlooked, that of a semi-vocalist. I use the word "semi," because Don didn't really sing. He recited lyrics with an impish, tongue-in cheek humor that was infectious. He was at his best performing his own compositions, making them individual classics. They include *Try Getting a Good Night's Sleep; The Way I Feel Today; Miss Hannah; Shakin' the African; About Rip Van Winkle;* and *I Got Ya.* Other titles by Don Redman are *My Girl Friday; How'm I Doin'; How Can I Hi De Hi?; If It Ain't Love; Down, Down, Down; If It's True; The Flight of the Jitterbug; You Ain't Nowhere; Carrie Mae Blues; Who Wants to Sing My Love Song;* and *Frantic Atlantic.*

Don Redman died in New York City on November 30, 1964.

Bickley (Bix) Reichner

According to the obituary in the *Philadelphia Inquirer* for Wednesday, April 12, 1989, lyricist Bickley "Bix" Reichner died the previous Sunday at age eighty-four. It went on to say that he was a resident of West Chester and had also lived for many years in Paoli. These are suburbs of Philadelphia, where he was born on April 6, 1905. Although writing lyrics for popular songs eventually became a full-time occupation for Reichner, his first love was working as a newspaperman, and he even passed up a lucrative offer from Hollywood to write songs for the movies in order to stay on the job as a reporter and in Philadelphia near his family. In the meantime, he looked on songwriting as a part-time hobby. He knew that it could become much more profitable if he moved to New York, as his publishers kept urging him to do, but he passed that up too.

Nevertheless, Reichner was active in songwriting right up to the end, and his later activities included writing lyrics for such potboilers as *Papa Loves Mambo,* the Perry Como hit, and Elvis Presley's *I Need Your Love Tonight.* He also wrote for the country and western TV show *Hee Haw.* With bandleader Elliott Lawrence, he worked on *The Ballad of Valley Forge,* a symphony performed at Valley Forge in celebration of the 1976 Bicentennial. But most likely Reichner will be remembered for the excellent songs he and Clay Boland turned out for the Mask and Wig productions at the University of Pennsylvania. By happy coincidence this was the period when the big bands were at their peak, so we have a number of outstanding recordings of the Reichner–Boland compositions. For example, the Tommy Dorsey Orchestra coupled two of them back-to-back on Victor 26030—*Ya Got Me* and *There's No Place Like Your Arms*—and also recorded the hit tune *Stop Beatin' Around the Mulberry Bush* (Victor 26012).

When I Go A-Dreamin' got the full treatment. It received an outstanding rendition by the Benny Goodman band, with the vocal by Martha Tilton, on Victor 26021; another by Kay Kyser, with Harry Babbitt, on Brunswick 8215; still another by Jan Savitt, with "Bon Bon" Tunnell on Bluebird 9186; and a vocal version by Dick Todd on Victor 26057. If you don't think that was an impressive start, check out these titles, which illustrate what the competition was like in the songwriting world of 1938: *A-Tiskit, A-Taskit; By Myself; Change Partners; Don't Be That Way; Flat Foot Floogie; Get Out of Town; Heart and Soul; I Hadn't Anyone Till You; Jeepers Creepers; Kinda Lonesome; Love Walked In; Moments Like This*—Well, you get the idea. They were writing them fast and writing them well that year, and all of the big guns were still firing.

The obituary goes on to tell a cute story about the way Reichner's newspaper career was terminated. Bix had been a "leg man" for the *Philadelphia Bulletin* for twenty-five years, respected by his colleagues, the police, the firemen, and all those with whom he had contact. Then a new editor pulled him away from his West Philadelphia beat and assigned him to the city room writing picture captions. Bix wasn't happy with the change. One day he came across a photo of a puppy sitting in an overturned derby, and he captioned it "In Your Hat!" The picture appeared in one edition of the paper, then it and Bix Reichner departed.

Other songs by Bickley Reichner are *You Better Go Now; Midnight On the Trail; Stop It's Wonderful; The Red We Want Is the Red We've Got (In the Old Red, White and Blue); If You Know the Lord; Don't Wait for the Hearse to Take You to Church; Cathedral of Peace; The Fable of the Rose; Mambo Rock; Teenage Prayer; Nightfall; Heart to Heart:* and *Dixie Danny.*

Leon T. Rene & Otis J. Rene Jr.

Leon T. Rene was born in Covington, Louisiana, on February 6, 1902. His education included study at Xavier University, Southern University, and Wilberforce University. He moved to Los Angeles in 1922 and for a time worked as a bricklayer. Later on, he led his own orchestra and eventually became a music publisher and owner of a record company. Otis J. Rene Jr. was born in New Orleans, Louisiana, on October 2, 1898. He also attended Wilberforce University but earned his B.S. in pharmacy at the University of Illinois. He owned and operated a drugstore in Los Angeles for ten years.

Leon and Otis wrote songs together, collaborating on material for films, and became partners in song publishing and as owners of a record company. Their songwriting careers were so closely intermingled that their composing efforts are identical. Probably the best-known song by the Renes is the 1931 entry *When It's Sleepy Time Down South,* forever identified with Louis Armstrong who recorded it and then adopted it as his theme song. It was composed in collaboration with a gentleman named Clarence Muse, who managed to get his name on the copyright, and it appears to be the first hit by the team. It has since been played and recorded hundreds of times and is one of the all-time standards. Armstrong also recorded *That's My Home* in 1932, another Rene title that was also waxed by Leon Rene and his orchestra on Victor, but was't released. Nat Gonella, the English Armstrong emulator, made it a couple of times on British labels. It's a good song that deserved better exposure than it got.

Dusty Road was a descriptive ballad that was recorded in 1936 by Nelson Eddy. He liked it so much that he sang it again in the 1938 film *Let Freedom Ring*. Leon Rene scored big in 1940, writing both words and music for *When the Swallows Come Back to Capistrano*. A pleasant ballad with an unusual title, the song was recorded across-the-board on every label, with platters by the Ink Spots (Decca); Glenn Miller (Bluebird); Gene Autry (OKeh); Xavier Cugat with a vocal by Dinah Shore (Victor); Gene Krupa (Columbia); Guy Lombardo (Decca); Ray Herbeck (Vocalion); and Billy May (Capitol). Obviously, with all that exposure the song could hardly miss.

Leon and Otis Rene had two good entries in 1941. *If Money Grew On Trees,* a wistful ballad of wishful thinking, received appropriately pensive treatment by Eddie "Rochester" Anderson on a Columbia record, and Erskine Butterfield made it for Decca. But the hit tune was *Someone's Rocking My Dream Boat*. The Ink Spots had a big record, but the best musical version was the Benny Goodman side for OKeh, with Art Lund. Artie Shaw recorded the song for Victor, Woody Herman made it for Decca, and Erskine Hawkins did it for Bluebird. A good song, it was also heard frequently on radio broadcasts. Emerson Scott shared composing credit.

The inimitable composer-entertainer-singer Johnny Mercer, who founded Capitol Records in the forties and then proceeded to make hit records for the label, turned in a minor classic with his rendition of *I Lost My Sugar in Salt Lake City,* a Rene composition with overtones of jazz and the blues combined with a nice melody and clever lyrics. Mercer enhanced the material with a "Chamber-of-Commerce" recitation extolling the merits of Salt Lake City and the surrounding countryside, all done in perfect meter and with a tinge of pathos that has to be heard to be appreciated.

Other compositions by Leon and Otis Rene include *Sweet Lucy Brown; I Sold My Heart to the Junkman; When It's Sleeptime in Hawaii; I Woke Up With a Teardrop in My Eye; I'm Lost; I Never Had a Dream; Chapel in the Valley;* and others.

Harry Revel

Although they eventually parted and collaborated with other composers, one of the most prolific and successful songwriting teams of the thirties was made up of lyricist Mack Gordon and composer Harry Revel. Revel, who had a fertile and tuneful imagination, was born in London, England, on December 21, 1905. He attended the Guildhall of Music in London but was mainly a self-taught pianist. Nevertheless, when only fifteen years old he was already touring Europe with an orchestra. His composing career also started early. He wrote for musical presentations in all of Europe's capitals and acquired an enviable reputation in the process. Based on this, he decided to try his luck in the United States and made the trip in 1929, only to discover that his reputation hadn't preceded him. He found it rough going until he met Mack Gordon, and they decided to work as a team.

Even then they took awhile to get started, writing songs for unsuccessful or mediocre Broadway shows, along with some freelance tunes for the popular market, but eventually they claimed shares in a singing gold mine named Bing Crosby, writing songs that he immediately turned into hits. Ironically, however, the first movie featuring Gordon and Revel songs starred Crosby's competitor Russ Columbo. This was *Broadway Through a Keyhole,* and the songs were *Doin' the Uptown Lowdown,* a tune that jazz musicians are fond of, and *You're My Past, Present and Future,* which was recorded by the Isham Jones band. Gordon and Revel had several other good songs published in 1933, notably *A Tree Was a Tree* (again an Isham Jones feature); *An Orchid to You;* and *It Was a Night in June*.

Picking up speed, the team had a banner year in 1934, holding up well against the heavy competition. They started it off with the score for the film *Sitting Pretty,* which starred Jack Oakie, Ginger Rogers, Jack Haley, Art Jarrett, and Thelma Todd and included *Have You Ever Seen a Dream Walking; You're Such a Comfort to Me; Good Morning, Glory;* and *Many Moons Ago*. Then in quick succession came *We're Not Dressing,* with Bing Crosby surrounded by a typical cast of the period, Carole Lombard, Leon Erroll, Ethel Merman, Burns & Allen, and Ray Milland; then *She Loves Me Not.* (And in this one Bing had to put up with Kitty Carlisle, Miriam Hopkins, Edward Nugent, and Lynne Overman.) *Shoot the Works,* another Jack Haley romp, with Alison Skipworth, Roscoe Karns, Arline Judge, and William Frawley, all backed by Ben Bernie's orchestra was next. *College Rhythm* starred comedian Joe Penner, with Jack Oakie, Lyda Roberti, and Lanny Ross; and Gorden and Revel contributed two songs to the Fred Astaire film *The Gay Divorcée.*

Without mentioning every song in every picture, here's another sampling of their output: *May I?; Love Thy Neighbor; She Reminds Me of You; Goodnight, Lovely Little Lady; Once in a Blue Moon; With My Eyes Wide Open I'm Dreaming; Don't Let it Bother You; Stay as Sweet as You Are.* And the magic continued. In 1935 Gordon and Revel wrote songs for *Love in Bloom,* a film featuring the future Mrs. Bing Crosby, Dixie Lee; and then for Bing's film *Two for Tonight* we heard *Here Comes Cookie; Got Me Doin' Things; My Heart Is an Open Book; Without a Word of Warning; Takes Two to Make a Bargain,* plus others.

The next year started off with another Joe Penner–Jack Oakie comedy, including singer Frances Langford, Betty Grable, and Ned Sparks. Langford recorded the two Gordon and Revel songs from the film, *You Hit the Spot* and *I Feel Like a Feather in the Breeze*. Next came *Poor Little Rich Girl,* a Shirley Temple film, and then still another, *Stowaway*. The two films combined produced *When I'm With You; But Definitely; Goodnight, My Love;* and *A Star Fell Out of Heaven.*

Gordon and Revel turned out an excellent score for the movie *Wake Up and Live,* the 1937 film starring Alice Faye, Jack Haley, Patsy Kelly, Ben Bernie, and Walter Winchell. The tunes were *Wake Up and Live; Never in a Million Years; There's a Lull in My Life; It's Swell of You;* and *Bubbling Over*. They also wrote songs for *Thin Ice, You Can't Have Everything, Head Over Heels in Love,* and *Ali Baba Goes to Town,* all productions of that year with a combined list of hits that includes: *Afraid to Dream; The Loveliness of You; May I Have the Next Romance with You?; Looking Around Corners for You; There's That Look in Your Eyes Again;* and *I've Got My Heart Set on You*. Incidentally, all Gordon and Revel songs were accorded very respectable treatment on both radio and recordings.

They continued as a team through 1938 and 1939 and turned out some outstanding songs: *Sweet as a Song; I've Got a Date With a Dream; Thanks for Everything;* and *Sweet Someone*. But with the advent of the forties, they parted. Both men continued to write, collaborating with other composers, and Harry Revel kept working well into the fifties with moderate success. He died in New York City on November 3, 1958.

Max Rich

Composer Max Rich was born in Brooklyn, New York, on August 22, 1897. He was educated at Boys High School and, like so many of his contemporaries, got an early start on a musical career by playing piano for silent movies and for music publishers. This led to a stint as an accompanist in vaudeville and then to managing a music publishing firm. In the twenties he went to Hollywood to write songs for the movies and founded a music publishing company with Mack Gordon, Gordon and Rich. He continued to write special material for nightclub shows and revues and collaborated with several of the top lyricists in the business, including Pete Wendling, Ned Washington, Henry Creamer, and Al Hoffman.

Although the list of Max Rich songs isn't very long, compared to other writers of the period, and none of them were sensational hits, all of them are typical of the early thirties in offering pleasant and imaginative melodies that make nice listening. Rich usually composed the music, but oddly enough, one of his earliest ventures into songwriting was a collaboration with Jack Meskill on the lyrics to a song by Pete Wendling, *Wonderful You,* which came out in 1929. The following year he began writing the music himself and combined on three very nice songs. One of these was *I Don't Mind Walkin' in the Rain (When I'm Walkin' in the Rain with You),* a soggy sentiment put to words by Al Hoffman but immortalized by Bix Beiderbecke's orchestra of all-stars in a recording session for Victor. Coincidentally, it was one side of bandleader Ozzie Nelson's first record for Brunswick. Another tune had lyrics by Henry Creamer and was called *My Bluebird Was Caught in the Rain.* In spite of all the heavy dew, both songs were successful, and the latter title was one of Rudy Vallee's hits on Victor. The third entry for the year was a collaboration with Mack Gordon, *Ain'tcha,* which was sung and introduced by the Boop-boop-a-doop Girl, Helen Kane, in the movie *Pointed Heels.* She also recorded it. Kate Smith, enjoying a meteroric rise to radio stardom, managed to get her name included with others in the committee credited with composing the 1931 hit *Making Faces at the Man in the Moon.* No doubt this was in trade for her agreeing to record the song as a backing for her theme, *When the Moon Comes over the Mountain.* The others in the committee were Rich, Al Hoffman, and Ned Washington.

While radio and talking pictures were gold mines to many of those in the entertainment business, the average man was having a hard time just trying to survive in the dark year of 1931, so the prevailing mood was one of deep gloom. This inspired lyricists Jack Meskill and Charles O'Flynn to pen *Smile, Darn Ya, Smile* to a melody by Rich, all in the forcefully optimistic vein of *Happy Days Are Here Again,* the Milton Ager–Jack Yellen song that made such a hit the year before. The inspirational themes made the songs popular but did little to change the realities of daily life. *The Girl in the Little Green Hat* was Rich's contribution to the popular market of 1932. The song was recorded by George Olsen's orchestra on Victor and with more zest by Joel Shaw's band on Crown. The lyrics were provided by Jack Scholl and Bradford Brown. Radio personality Brad Brown was a multitalented gentleman who carved a niche in immortality by conceiving and producing a network radio program called *The Nitwit Hour.*

Other songs by Max Rich are *Wake Up, Sleepy Moon; I'll Smile Again; Hold Me Closer; Couldn't You Fall for Me?; Somewhere Beyond the Sunset; In the Wink of an Eye; An Ol' Tin Cup; I Behold You;* and *Shake Hands With a Millionaire.*

Harry Richman

The definitive song-and-dance man of stage and screen, part-time composer, and pioneering airman Harry Richman was born in Cincinnati, Ohio, on August 10, 1895. He began his extensive career as a youngster performing in blackface. Then, working in small vaudeville houses as a pianist-singer, he gradually made his way to New York, where he worked as an accompanist to Nora Bayes, Mae West, and the Dolly Sisters. Meanwhile, he perfected his own act, moving into top vaudeville locations, including the famed Palace Theater. He used props to project the image of a dapper man-about-town, sometimes a cane and top hat or a straw hat, and sang in the gusty style originated by Al Jolson. He starred in Broadway musicals in the twenties and thirties and then moved on to movies, radio, and nightclubs. As a part-time pilot he set a world altitude record in 1935 for a single motor amphibious plane (19,000 feet), and in the next year, with copilot Dick Merrill, made the first transoceanic roundtrip flight in history.

His songwriting career began in 1926 with the publication of three songs he was associated with in composing: *I Found a Roundabout Way to Heaven; (I Don't Believe It But) Say It Again;* and the hit *Muddy Water;* the latter a collaboration with Peter DeRose and Jo Trent, who provided the lyrics. Richman introduced and popularized the songs in his act and on records. He scored again in 1927, working with Lew Pollack and Sidney Clare on the popular *Miss Annabelle Lee.* A hit in the States, it received still more attention on records in Europe than it did here. Nevertheless, it was featured in vaudeville by James Barton; was revived in a movie, *Gentlemen Marry Brunettes,* in 1955; and sung again by Dick Shawn in the stage musical "A Musical Jubilee" in 1975.

In 1930 Harry Richman again had three songs in the running. Two of them, *Singin' a Vagabond Song* and *Ro-Ro-Rolling Along,* became associated with him. The third, *There's Danger in Your Eyes, Cherie,* was a collaboration with Pete Wendling and Jack Meskill and became a popular ballad offering. *Singin' a Vagabond Song,* with words and music by Val Burton, Richman, and Sam Messenheimer, was introduced by Richman in the film *Puttin' on the Ritz,* and he recorded it for Brunswick. *Ro-Ro-Rollin' Along* was the work of Murray Mencher, Richman, and Billy Moll. Again it was introduced and recorded by Richman. Both songs were in the semimilitary, swaggering tradition.

(There Oughhta Be a) Moonlight Saving Time was a pleasant entry in 1931, Harry Richman working with Irving Kahal. Without fail, it was introduced

by Richman but also recorded by Guy Lombardo, Maurice Chevalier, Annette Hanshaw, and Dick Robertson. Richman was also cowriter of *One Little Raindrop* and *Help Yourself to Happiness,* two other titles that year. Other songs by Harry Richman include *C'est Vous (It's You); Life Begins When You're in Love; She Came Rolling Down the Mountain; You Don't Need Glasses to See;* and *I Think You're Wonderful.*

Harry Richman died in California on November 3, 1972.

Dave Ringle

Pianist, composer, and lyricist Dave Ringle was born in Brooklyn, New York, on November 20, 1893. He was educated at Commercial High School. During the First World War he served as first sergeant in the 3RD Machine Gun Battalion. After the war, he played piano in dance bands and worked as a contract writer for various music publishers. Later he organized and toured with his own orchestra, appeared in vaudeville, and worked in radio, the movies, and eventually TV. In 1932 he became a music publisher and then a partner in a record firm, Selva-Ringle Record Co.

Ringle rates inclusion in this book primarily for taking part in the composition of three songs, *Wabash Blues; Roll On, Mississippi, Roll On;* and *Sailin' on the Robert E. Lee. Wabash Blues,* probably his first published song, came out in 1921. He wrote the words, and Fred Meinken the music. Two hit records resulted, one by the Isham Jones orchestra on Brunswick, the other by the Benson Orchestra of Chicago on Victor. Not really a blues, the tune has a blues tonality that made it popular and something of a semi-standard. It still gets played.

Roll On, Mississippi, Roll On, a 1931 entry, and *Sailin' On the Robert E. Lee,* which was published in 1933, are both collaborations between Ringle, Eugene West, and James McCaffrey, and so similar in design that it's clear the second title was aimed at repeating the success of the first. They also share in the good luck of having being recorded by Ray Noble and the New Mayfair Orchestra in England, and thus have been reissued a number of times. Other compositions credited to Dave Ringle include *Blue Eyes; Ragging the Scales; After All Is Said and Done; Changes; Memory Lane; Any Old Time at All;* and *Down in Sleepy Hollow Lane*. It seems only fair to point out, though, that this *Ragging the Scales* is not the *Ragging the Scale* written by Edward B. Claypoole in 1915, and this *Changes* is not the famous Walter Donaldson song of 1927.

Dave Ringle died in Brooksville, Florida, on July 20, 1965.

Allan Roberts

Pianist-composer Allan Roberts was born in Brooklyn, New York, on March 12, 1905. He was educated in the public schools and trained as a bookkeeper. But he had other ambitions, and began writing special material for burlesque acts and nightclub skits, eventually attaining a close association with producer Mike Todd. This lasted for several years. Gravitating to Hollywood, Roberts was contracted to Columbia. He wrote special material for Sid Caesar, Red Buttons, Eddie Cantor, Bea Lillie, and Herb Shriner. As a songwriter he collaborated with such well-known writers as Jay Livingston, Al Hoffman, Al Goodhart, and others, but his most successful work was done with Doris Fisher.

Nevertheless, most likely the song that was his earliest hit was the 1937 entry, *Me, Myself, and I,* written with Al Kaufman and Irving Gordon. It enjoyed considerable airplay and was recorded by Billie Holiday, Joe Haymes, and, in England, Nat Gonella. The collaboration with Doris Fisher took place in the forties and resulted in a number of hit titles. The team had a banner year in 1944. They had three very respectable offerings, *Invitation to the Blues* (on which they were aided by Arthur Gershwin); *You Always Hurt the One You Love;* and *Into Each Life Some Rain Must Fall. Invitation to the Blues* was a successful side by Ella Mae Morse on Capitol; *You Always Hurt the One You Love* was a million seller by the Mills Brothers on Decca; and *Into Each Life Some Rain Must Fall* was a number one recording by Ella Fitzgerald with the Ink Spots for Decca.

In the following year they came up with *Tampico,* another million-seller by Stan Kenton's band with a vocal by June Christy on Capitol, and in 1946 they followed through with *Put The Blame on Mame*. This was introduced by Anita Ellis, whose voice was dubbed on the soundtrack for Rita Hayworth in the film *Gilda*. The song was also used that same year in another movie, *Betty Coed*. Archie Bleyer recorded it for Columbia with a vocal by Jannette Davis. Two more hits by Roberts and Fisher came out in 1947, *Tired,* which got a definitive performance by Pearl Bailey in the movie *Variety Girl,* also on record; and *You Can't See the Sun When You're Crying*. The Ink Spots and Vaughn Monroe had hit records on this one.

In 1948 Buddy Clark, enjoying a short-lived spot at the top of his career, which was cut short by his tragic death in a plane crash, recorded several hit records for Columbia accompanied by Ray Noble's orchestra. One of these was *I Wish I Knew the Name (Of the Girl in My Dreams)*. A clever and catchy ballad by Roberts and lyricist Lester Lee. In 1952 Roberts worked with Perry Como's pianist and arranger, Robert Allen, to compose *To Know You Is to Love You,* which Perry obligingly made into a hit record.

Other titles by Allan Roberts are *You Opened My Eyes; Every Single Little Tingle of My Heart; Teacher's Pet; Chatterbox; That Wonderful Worrisome Feeling; What's the Good Word, Mr. Bluebird; A Tender Word Will Mend It All; Saltin' Away My Sweet Dreams; Angelina; Jodie Man; Good, Good, Good; Benny's Coming Home on Saturday; Either It's Love or It Isn't; A Man Is a Brother to a Mule; They Can't Convince Me; Let's Stay Young Forever; People Have More Fun Than Anyone; That's Good Enough for Me; I'm Sorry I Didn't Say I'm Sorry; Please Don't Kiss Me; My Heart's in the Middle of May; The River Seine; Dreamer With a Penny; Nobody's Tears Are Falling but Mine; I Wish Somebody Knew I Was Lonesome; Find Me; Sweethearts Holiday; Noodlin' Rag; Neither Am I;* and *Someone Loves Someone.*

Allan Roberts died in Hollywood, Florida, on January 14, 1966.

Luckeyth (Lucky) Roberts

The legendary Harlem pianist Luckeyth (Lucky) Roberts was born in Philadelphia, Pennsylvania, on August 7, 1893. He was educated by private tutors and studied music with Eloise Smith and Melville Charlton. At the tender age of five he was already appearing in vaudeville as a singer, dancer, and pianist. A short time later, he toured Europe several times. During his long career he owned a restaurant, taught music, had his own orchestra, performed as an actor, and in the heyday of radio played piano on a number of programs, including the popular *Moran & Mack.*

Although he wrote scores for Broadway shows and composed a number of instrumental and piano pieces, his contributions to the popular market are limited. However, he did have one outstanding hit in the 1942 song *Moonlight Cocktail.* The melody was adapted by Roberts from an old ragtime piece he had composed called *Ripples on the Nile.* With lyrics by Kim Gannon it became a number one recording by Glenn Miller's band on Bluebird. That same year Roberts teamed with Andy Razaf on another song that did very well, *Massachusetts.* The bands of Gene Krupa and Johnny Long had big-selling records.

Other compositions by Luckeyth Roberts are *Railroad Blues; Helter Skelter; Elder Eatmore Sermons; Pork and Beans; Music Box Rag;* and *Shy and Sly.*

Dick Robertson

Singer Dick Robertson was born in Brooklyn, New York, on July 3, 1903. He began his career as a freelance vocalist at an early age and performed in theaters and nightclubs throughout the United States, Canada, England, and

France. In addition, he was one of the most prolific studio vocalists of all time, recording with studio groups, name bands, and quite often under his own name. Anybody who bought popular records during the thirties and forties would be familiar with his voice. Besides performing as a vocalist, Robertson also doubled as a songwriter, collaborating on a number of very respectable entries in the popular field. His biggest hit was the wistful ballad *We Three (My Echo, My Shadow, and Me),* a 1940 offering that made number one on the charts and the Hit Parade. Frank Sinatra made it with Tommy Dorsey's band on Victor, and the Ink Spots had a best-seller on Decca. Working with Robertson on the tune were Sammy Mysels and Nelson Cogane.

Most likely Robertson's first published songs were two that appeared in 1939—*At Least You Could Say Hello,* written with Sammy Mysels and Charles McCarthy, and *Out of Port,* a collaboration with Ira Schuster and Paul Cunningham. The first title rated good records by Larry Clinton and Jack Teagarden, and Eddy Duchin made the second one for Brunswick. Robertson, Sammy Mysels, and Nelson Cogane had another good song in 1940, *Is There Somebody Else,* which received the usual excellent treatment by Ella Fitzgerald on Decca. The Delta Rhythm Boys also made it for the same label. Then Robertson and Mysels teamed with James F. Hanley to turn out *You Forgot About Me*. This one made the rounds of the record labels, with sides by Connee Boswell, Bob Crosby, Larry Clinton, Artie Shaw, and Gene Krupa.

But it was Robertson, Mysels, and Cogane back together again in 1942 for *Yesterday's Gardenias,* which resulted in platters by Gene Krupa and Charlie Spivak. However, by 1944, when Robertson was involved with another successful tune, *A Little On the Lonely Side,* he was working with Frank Weldon and James Cavanaugh. A good song, it was recorded by Frankie Carle, Guy Lombardo, and the Phil Moore Four. Russ Morgan recorded another tune that year, *Goodnight Wherever You Are,* credited to Robertson, Weldon, and Al Hoffman. The following year Robertson, Weldon, and James Cavanaugh penned the wishful *I'd Do It All Over Again,* and it was recorded by Hal McIntyre's Orchestra and Frankie Carle's.

Other songs by Dick Robertson are *Dearest Darling; You Can Cry on Somebody Else's Shoulder; My Old Gal;* and *If You Cared.*

Leo Robin

One of the most prolific lyricists who ever put words to a melody, Leo Robin was born in Pittsburgh, Pennsylvania, on April 6, 1900. His education included attendance at the University of Pittsburgh Law School and Carnegie Tech Drama School. Perversely, his first job was working as a newspaper reporter, followed by a stint as a press agent. Then he started writing songs. Although he had a long and successful association with composer Ralph Rainger, Robin collaborated with a number of other writers, including many of the most famous in the profession—Jerome Kern, Richard A. Whiting, Harry Warren, Dana Suesse, David Rose, Lewis E. Gensler, Vincent Youmans, Sam Coslow, Clarence Gaskill, Russ Columbo—just to mention the more obvious. As a result, besides the many hit songs he turned out working with Ralph Rainger, his name is on a lot of others, many of them standards.

He began writing for stage shows in 1926, but it wasn't until the following year that he had his first big hit, *Hallelujah!* With music by Vincent Youmans and lyrics by Robin and Clifford Grey, it was included in the Broadway production of "Hit the Deck" and turned out to be a showstopper. It has since become a standard. The show "Hit the Deck" has been recreated in two movies, with the song revived in each one. More shows and more songs came after, but Robin had to wait until 1929 before making an impact. This time the songs were from movies: *True Blue Lou,* a tune with very clever lyrics and a collaboration with Sam Coslow and Richard A. Whiting, which was introduced by Hal Skelly in the film *Dance of Life;* and *Jericho,* written with Richard Myers for the movie musical *Syncopation,* in which it was played by Fred Waring's Pennsylvanians. This could be a real swinger, as demonstrated by Bob Haggart's band many years later on a recording for M-G-M. But probably the most important of all, this was the year that Maurice Chevalier sang a song in the film *Innocents of Paris* that not only became an all-time standard, it was always identified with him. The song was *Louise,* by Robin and Richard A. Whiting. Chevalier recorded it, but so did Paul Whiteman's "Rhythm Boys," Crosby–Rinker, Barris (on a contemporary side), and many others since.

Robin and Richard Whiting, aided by Franke W. Harling, struck it big again in 1930. This time the song was *Beyond the Blue Horizon,* from the film *Monte Carlo.* It was sung and introduced by Jeannette MacDonald in the movie, and she apparently liked it so much she repeated the performance in the 1944 film *Follow the Boys.* She recorded it, too, but so have a lot of other people, including Artie Shaw, who gave it a good workout in 1941. Maurice Chevalier was back that year, also, in another movie, *Playboy of Paris,* and he sang *My Ideal.* Dick Whiting and Newell Chase combined on the deceptively simple but beautiful melody. It was an immediate favorite with radio bands and singers and has become a standard.

In 1931 Robin supplied the words to another hardy perennial, the Russ Colombo–Clarence Gaskill *Prisoner of Love.* Columbo introduced it and recorded it, and the song was a success—only to top itself in 1944, when the

Victor record by Perry Como proved to be a best-seller. The song was on the Hit Parade for fifteen weeks. The ritual was repeated in 1963, with the King recording by James Brown included in the top twenty on the charts. The following year Robin began his association with Ralph Rainger that would result in a long string of hits, but he continued to work with Richard Whiting and others. For instance, with Whiting, he turned out *(I'd Love to Spend) One Hour With You.* The cards were stacked on this one, and it was introduced by Jeannette MacDonald, Maurice Chevalier, Genevieve Tobin, Charlie Ruggles, and Donald Novis in the film *One Hour with You.* On records it got the full treatment, with MacDonald and Novis having individual singles, as well as Morton Downey, Jimmie Grier, and Andy Sannella. To top this off, Eddie Cantor adopted the tune as the closing theme for his Chase and Sanborn radio broadcast. You might say, the song could hardly miss.

By now Robin's partnership with Ralph Rainger was in full swing, but he still found time for outside work. In 1931 he and Dana Suesse combined on *Have You Forgotten (the Thrill)?,* one of those Golden Age sleepers that are so typical of the era. Ruth Etting recorded it for Perfect, Ben Selvin made it for the Columbia subsidiary labels, and Henry Busse's orchestra waxed it for Victor. In 1933 Robin, Buddy DeSylva, and Richard Whiting got together, and the result was the catchy and witty *Be Careful.* Don Bestor's Orchestra made the most of it on a recording for Victor. In 1935 Robin and Lewis E. Gensler came up with *Love Is Just Around the Corner,* a home run in anybody's ballgame. Introduced by Bing Crosby in the movie *Here Is My Heart,* it was later recorded by him for Decca. It has long since become a favorite of jazz musicians and is frequently heard at jazz festivals.

Covering all bets, it would seem, Robin, Ralph Rainger, and Richard A. Whiting teamed together and contributed three songs to *The Big Broadcast of 1936,* another movie. The tunes were *Why Dream?; Double Trouble;* and *Miss Brown to You.* The film, actually released in 1935, featured one of those fabled casts that seem so impossible now and were commonplace then, Bing Crosby, Lyda Roberti, Ethel Merman, Ina Ray Hutton, Jack Oakie, Ray Noble's orchestra, Bill Robinson, Burns & Allen, Amos & Andy, Mary Boland, Charlie Ruggles, Wendy Barrie, and Henry Wadsworth. *Why Dream?* was introduced in the film by Henry Wadsworth. Ray Noble's orchestra recorded it for Victor in an arrangement by Glenn Miller and with a vocal by Al Bowlly, Jack Oakie made the tune for Melotone, and Little Jack Little did it for Columbia. *Double Trouble* got the same treatment from the Noble aggregation and was also recorded by Red McKenzie, Frank Dailey, and Babs and Her Brothers. *Miss Brown to You,* featured in the movie by Ray Noble's band with the Nicholas Brothers and Bill Robinson, achieved immortality in a swinging version by Teddy Wilson's band on Brunswick, with Billie Holiday. Robin and Whiting had still another song in a Bing Crosby picture, *I Can't Escape From You,* which was featured in *Rhythm on the Range*. Bing recorded it, or course, and so did Jimmie Lunceford for Decca and Shep Fields and His Rippling Rhythm. The year was 1936.

Ralph Rainger was killed in a plane crash in 1942, bringing to an end one of the longest songwriting partnerships of all time, but Leo Robin continued to write songs well into the fifties. In 1943 he worked with Harry Warren to produce *No Love, No Nothin',* and in 1946 with Jerome Kern for *In Love in Vain,* Kern's last song, written just before a fatal heart attack.

Other songs in the long list credited to Leo Robin include *Looking Around; I've Found the Bluebird; Bubbling Over; Breezin' Along; I'm a One-Man Girl; True to Two; Say It with a Uke; My Cutey's Due at Two to Two Today; Where Have You Been All My Life?; Pull Yourself Together; Blow Hot and Heavy; Give Trouble the Air; Why, Oh Why?; Harbor of My Heart; Join the Navy; Judy, Who D'Ya Love?; Poor Cinderella; Looking for a Thrill; Wear Your Sunday Smile; Pretty Little Stranger; You Came Along; Humpty Dumpty; Paree!; Say That You Love Me; I Want the World to Know; I Wanna Go Places and Do Things; I'm All A-Twitter; The Flippity Flop; Wait Till You See Ma Cherie; It's a Habit of Mine; On Top of the World Alone; Always in All Ways; Give Me a Moment Please; She'll Love Me and Like It; All I Want Is Just One; It's a Great Life; I Have to Have You; If I Were King; What Would You Do?; Three Times a Day; Please; Here Lies Love; We Will Always Be Sweethearts; I'll Take an Option on You; Gather Lip Rouge While You May; How Do I Look?; Give Me Liberty or Give Me Love; In the Park in Paree; Look What I've Got; Thank Heavens for You; She Was a China Teacup and He Was Just a Mug; My Bluebird's Singin' the Blues; I'm a Black Sheep Who Is Blue; Low Down Lullaby; Laugh, You Son-of-a-Gun; Take a Lesson From the Lark; Love in Bloom; Song of the Crusades; Here Is My Heart; June in January; With Every Breath I Take; My Heart and I; Here's Love in Your Eye; You Came to My Rescue; I'm Talking Through My Heart; Vote for Mr. Rhythm; Night in Manhattan; Hills of Old Wyomin'; I Don't Want to Make History; Will I Ever Know?; Where Is My Heart?; Long Ago and Far Away; If I Should Lose You; Thunder over Paradise; The House Jack Built for Jill; Drink It Down; Make Way for Tomorrow; Moonlight and Shadows; Whispers in the Dark; I Adore You; A Rhyme for Love; So What?; If It Isn't Pain, Then It Isn't Love; Blue Hawaii; In a Little Hula Heaven; Sweet Is the Word for You; Blossoms on Broadway; Ebb Tide; Kinda Lonesome; You're Lovely, Madame; What Have You Got That Gets Me; Do the Buckaroo; Thanks for the Memory; You Took the*

Words Right Out of My Heart; Mama, That Moon Is Here Again; The Waltz Lived On; This Little Ripple Had Rhythm; A Little Kiss at Twilight; What Goes on Here in My Heart; The U.S.A. and You; I Have Eyes; You're a Sweet Little Headache; The Funny Old Hills; Joobalai; Havin' Myself a Time; The Lamp on the Corner; Silver on the Sage; Love with a Capital "You"; The Wind at My Window; I Was Afraid of That; I Shoulda Stood in Bed; Faithful Forever; Bluebirds in the Moonlight; We're All Together Now; All's Well; I Hear a Dream; Loveliness and Love; You Started Something; I've Got You All to Myself; Hurrah for Today; Is That Good?; I Want to Be the Guy; I'm Making a Play for You; Wishful Thinking; Hello, Ma! I Done It Again; Here You Are; Oh, the Pity of It All; On the Gay White Way; Midnight at the Masquerade; Me and My Fella and a Big Umbrella; I'm Still Crazy for You; I'll Be Marching to a Love Song; I Heard the Birdies Sing; Are You Kidding Me?; Except with You; Beautiful Coney Island; Take It From There; Miss Lulu from Louisville; Get the Money; There's Danger in a Dance; Old Demon Rum; You're the Rainbow; Whistling in the Light; I'm the Secretary to the Sultan; Later Tonight; I Like It Here; Dancing in the Dawn; I'm All A-Twitter over You; We Always Get Our Girl; Wintertime; Paducah; Minnie's in the Money; A Journey to a Star; The Lady in the Tutti-Fruitti Hat; The Polka-Dot Polka; You Discover You're in New York; Pickin' on Your Mama; Sleepy Moon; Silent Senorita; So-o-o-o-o in Love; and others.

Leo Robin died in 1984.

J. Russel Robinson

Pioneer jazz pianist, songwriter, and publisher J. Russel Robinson was born in Indianapolis, Indiana, on July 8, 1892. His education included graduating from Shortridge High School and private music study. Early in his career he and his brother, John C. Robinson, toured silent movie theaters as a piano and drum combination called the Robinson Brothers. Later on he worked in vaudeville as a single. His first published song, *Sapho Rag,* came out in 1909. An accomplished pianist, he cut hundreds of piano rolls for the famous QRS Company, and in 1919 he joined the Original Dixieland Jazz Band as a replacement for Henry Ragas, who had died. Still later, he worked as a vocal coach on radio. He is reputed to have composed over six hundred songs, and his material is on file in the Traditional Music section of the University of Indiana. He was honored by the Indiana State House of Representatives for his contributions to music and entertainment.

Although Robinson had a number of popular song hits to his credit during his long career—probably the most notable being the 1920 super hit *Margie*—a number of his compositions have achieved the enviable status of all-time standards due to their longevity as jazz classics. This is especially true of his early works. Even *Margie* lends itself to jazz treatment, and the first recording of it was made by the Original Dixieland Jazz Band, as were two other Robinson titles in 1920, *Singin' the Blues (Till My Daddy Comes Home)* and *Palesteena.* Before these, however, he is listed in one of those "committee" credits favored by the members of the ODJB, for *Original Dixieland One-Step,* along with Nick LaRocca and Joe Jordan in 1918, although, like so many titles associated with the ODJB, this is open to question.

Singin' the Blues, which went on to an illustrious life of its own, was introduced as something of an afterthought on the ODJB's Victor record of *Margie.* On the recording, only Con Conrad and "J. R. Robinson" are listed as composers, but Benny Davis wrote the words to *Margie,* and Sam M. Lewis and Joe Young were the lyricists for *Singin' the Blues. Palesteena,* this time correctly attributed to Conrad and Robinson, was the flip side of the record, recorded as an instrumental, so you had to buy the sheet music or a piano roll to get the clever lyrics the composer added. All three songs long ago became standards, *Margie* as a nostalgic gem of "The Good Old Days," *Singin' the Blues* as a jazz classic, and *Palesteena* as an all-time novelty. *Margie* has been recorded, played, and sung countless times. *Singin' the Blues* was immortalized by Bix Beiderbecke and Frank Trumbauer on their famous recording for the original OKeh company. *Palesteena*'s lyrics got off to an early start on a record by Frank Crumit on Columbia but received a definitive treatment by Bob Crosby's Bob Cats on a Decca recording in 1938. The irrepressible Nappy Lamare recited the words.

Sweet Man O' Mine was a 1921 entry by Robinson and Roy Turk. It was made on contemporary sides by the popular band of Benny Kreuger, Lavinia Turner and her jazz band, and a few others. Then, a ballad in the same vein, *Aggravatin' Papa (Don't You Try to Two-Time Me),* another collaboration with Roy Turk, plus Addy Britt, made its debut in 1922. This one found favor with Bessie Smith, Marion Harris, and Sophie Tucker, all of whom recorded it. *Mary Lou,* a rather innocuous but harmless ditty with words by bandleader Abe Lyman and George Waggner, came out in 1926. Naturally, it was introduced and recorded by Abe Lyman, and it enjoyed moderate success.

Robinson returned to jazz in 1928 with *Rhythm King,* a tune with descriptive lyrics by Jo Trent. It was recorded by Bix Beiderbecke "and His Gang," on OKeh; Ben Bernie's Hotel Roosevelt Orchestra, with Jack Pettis in the line-up, on Brunswick; and the Coon-Sanders band on Victor. The tune has been rediscovered in recent years and is enjoying a revival. Another novelty, *Is I in Love? I Is,* made a brief stir in 1932, words by Mercer Cook; and then a few years slid by before Robinson had anything significant to offer. By then swing was the thing, and he acknowledged this with *Swing, Mr. Charlie,* written with Harry Brooks. Bunny Berigan recorded it for Vocalion, and Louis "King" Garcia did the same for Bluebird.

In 1947 Robinson teamed with Arthur Tucker and Harry Pyle, who wrote the words for *Meet Me at No Special Place (And I'll Be There at No Particular Time).* The sarcastically sentimental lyrics were appropriately interpreted by Nat "King" Cole on Capitol and by Joe Mooney with his quartet on Decca. Nat "King" Cole had a best-seller in 1948 with *A Portrait of Jennie.* The Gordon Burge lyric was inspired by the Robert Nathan book and the movie, and the melody was composed by Robinson. Harry Babbitt also had a successful record. Other songs by Robinson include *Yeah Man; Beale Street Mama; On the Eight O' Clock Train; Blue Eyed Sally; Let Me Be the First to Kiss You Good Morning; When Dixie Stars Are Playing Peek-a-boo; Hello, Sweetheart, Hello; I Won't Believe It; St. Louis Gal; Rampart Street Blues; Ringtail Blues;* and many others.

J. Russel Robinson died in Palmsdale, California, on September 30, 1963.

Willard Robison

Perhaps not many people will remember the name or the accomplishments of Willard Robison, but to those who do, his songs place him in the select category of men with exceptional talent who wrote material of timeless quality. An excellent pianist as well as a composer, Robison organized a dance band as early as 1917, and under the name of the Deep River Orchestra it toured the Midwest and Southwest for a number of years in the early twenties, earning a reputation for excellence and playing in many of the prestigious locations. Among the musicians who worked with him during this period was Pee Wee Russell, the distinguished jazz clarinetist, who told me this story.

The Deep River Orchestra was hired to play a dance in one of the many small towns in the Midwest. As was often the case in those days, the venue was an open-air pavilion, surrounded by farmland and within walking distance of the railroad station. The band arrived by train, carried its equipment and instruments to the pavilion and went about the business of setting up. Leader Willard Robison was also the pianist, and with some amusement he called the band's attention to the piano he was to work on, an old nickel-in-the-slot mechanical monster. It even had a music roll ready to run, a waltz, the ever-popular *Let Me Call You Sweetheart.* The locale, the people, even the weather were all satisfactory, but there was a fly in the pie that had the musicians a trifle nervous. They were booked to play until midnight, and the last train out of town came through at 11:00 P.M. If they missed it, they might have to wind up sleeping on the floor of the pavilion. As eleven o'clock drew near the men started to exchange anxious glances, but Willard had been doing some heavy thinking; he had a plan. It was a customary feature to have a "moonlight waltz" take place around eleven o'clock. This meant the lights were dimmed or turned off, and the dancers romantically maneuvered by the light of the moon.

"Here's what we're going to do," Willard told the men. "When the lights go out we'll start to play a waltz set. Each man will take two choruses. When you finish pack up quietly, sneak out the back and run like hell to the station. Each guy has to take part of the drum equipment, 'cause he can't carry it all by himself. I'll be the last one to leave, and when I hear the train whistle in the distance I'll slip a coin in the slot of the piano and play *Let Me Call You Sweetheart.* If I'm lucky it should take a minute or two for the crowd to catch on, which will give me just enough time to beat them to the station. If things work out right we'll be on the train before they get there." Following instructions, under the cover of darkness each musician played his two choruses, packed up, and slipped out the back way. Finally Willard was the only one left. He played a chorus of *Let Me Call You Sweetheart* in the same key as the music roll on the piano, and then dropped a nickel in the coin slot. In the distance he heard the train whistle as it approached the station. The music roll started to play, and Willard made his escape. The ruse worked long enough for him to get a headstart across the fields, but then the dancers caught on and began to chase him. Nobody will ever know what they would have done if they caught up with him, but the timing was perfect. The train pulled in just as he reached the station, the band hurriedly boarded, and the frustrated crowd arrived just in time to see them pull out of the station.

In later years, long after both were well established in the pantheon of immortal songwriters, Robison and Harry Woods became a pair of friends in the category fondly referred to as "drinking buddies." Together they made the rounds of night spots that featured jazz and others that featured well-stocked bars. One location was more or less a regular stop, "Nick's," in Greenwich Village. Pee Wee Erwin recalled seeing them frequently during his long tenure as bandleader in the place, and pianist Johnny Varro remembered them vividly.

"Every Friday night Harry Woods would come in to Nick's with Willard Robison—they were good buddies. They'd come in and when we started work at nine o'clock these two guys were already deep in their cups, feeling no pain. Then, around eleven o'clock they would have ordered their dinner—two of Nick's nice juicy steaks—and they'd both be fast asleep, so the steaks would just sit there. Now, don't forget, these two guys were legends in the songwriting business. Nobody was about to wake them up or tell them to get out. They'd just leave them alone and the steaks would get cold. Finally, at the end of the night, one of us would wrap a steak up and take it 'home for the dog.' I enjoyed several. One evening they stayed pretty sober, so Phil Napoleon decided to invite Willard up to the bandstand to sing and play a couple of his tunes. And I should point out that this was pretty unusual in itself, because the format at Nick's was pretty cut-and-dried and hardly ever varied. However, Willard came up and did his *Old Folks,* and a couple of other songs, which was fine, but when he finished Phil was practically obligated to call on Harry Woods. I tried to warn him not to, because I knew that Harry was missing his left hand. He only had a stump, with a little button on it, but Phil went ahead and announced, 'We have another famous composer in the house, Harry Woods.' And Harry stood up eagerly, climbed on the bandstand and sat down at the piano. 'This, I gotta see,' I said to myself, but he played. He played in G♭ so he could hit the black keys with that little nub. And he did quite well."*

The Robison musical legacy is a collection of superior songs, many of them recognized gems of the songwriting craft. They were never "written down" for the sake of commercial success. Instead they are prime examples of the highest standards of originality, imagination, and melodic invention. He was a genius at creating a mood germane to the story told by the lyrics. And Robison songs almost always tell a story, sometimes humorous, sometimes gently nostalgic, but frequently with a serious undercurrent of loneliness and heartbreak. Most likely his biggest hit, and the one best remembered, is *A Cottage for Sale,* a haunting tune with a melody perfectly suited to the Larry Conley lyrics, which paint a graphic picture of loneliness and loss.

Lonely Acres is another title that evokes the same tinge of sadness and despair. It was a famous radio theme in the thirties when Paul Tremaine's band was at the height of its popularity, and it is still a favorite of musicians who love its beautiful melody and advanced chord changes. An outstanding treatment of the song was recorded by Frank DeVol's orchestra and chorus for Capitol Records in the fifties. The title of the song is descriptive enough in itself, but it's hard to imagine anyone listening to the stark loneliness de-

*Warren Vaché Sr., "A Visit with Johnny Varro." *Jazz Gentry* (Lanham, Md.: Scarecrow Press, 1999).

picted in the lyrics without an instinctive shiver. Just the opening line, "Lonely acres in the west . . ." is enough to chill the mind with a drab picture of miles and miles of vacant land in some far-off and lonely place. Unlike the innocuous words to most popular songs, those of a Robison tune pack the punch of grim reality and the human experience.

Two other Robison classics, *Old Folks* and *Pigeon-Toed Joad,* describe two lovable old characters who are sure to remind us of someone we know, or would like to know. Both songs depart from the format of conventional songwriting by pointing out the inevitability of old age and death, yet the stories are told with such gentle humor and understanding, that the results are almost classic in their simplicity and universal appeal. Each composition is so completely a Robison creation that it almost bears a trademark. Mildred Bailey knew and worked with Robison early in her career and had a great admiration for his songs. Her Vocalion recording of *Old Folks* delineates the saga.

Joad was a longtime favorite of the master trombonist Jack Teagarden, and his drawling delivery of the lyrics was ideally suited for adding the right touch of lazy nostalgia. Nevertheless, as with all Robison's songs, although the lyrics were perfectly attuned, *Joad* can stand on its own melodically, as Dick Cathcart proved by recording it as a very soulful trumpet solo a few years ago.

Teagarden was a big fan of Robison's music, and he paid tribute to the composer by recording an album of his songs in 1962 entitled *Think Well of Me,* which is also the title of one of the numbers in the album. The collection was issued on the Verve label as V/V6-8465 and includes ten Robison compositions. The great trombonist played in Robison's Deep River Orchestra in the twenties, recorded with him in later years, and had a deep affinity for the moods projected by the Robison songs. A prior Teagarden album for Verve, *Misery and the Blues,* offered several Robison titles, leading to the wider treatment on *Think Well of Me.* Aided and abetted by trumpeter Don Goldie, Teagarden plays and sings *A Cottage for Sale; I Guess I'll Go Back Home This Summer; I'm a Fool About my Mama; Don't Smoke in Bed; In a Little Waterfront Café; Think Well of Me; Old Folks; Country Boy Blues; 'Tain't So, Honey, 'Tain't So;* and *'Round the Old Deserted Farm.*

Of historical as well as musical interest is a ten-inch LP issued on the Coral label, *Willard Robison and His Deep River Music.* From the historical standpoint it offers a high-fidelity recording of the Robison singing voice; and musically it is a satisfying tribute to his talent as both performer and composer. The Robison voice is ideally in tune with the songs he wrote and just as unique. There is no false pretense in his delivery, and he presents the lyrics with sharp clarity and meticulous timing. At the same time, there is an appealing quality to his singing, and a timbre that is entirely individualistic. The songs he chose for the album offer several examples of the two sides of the Robison outlook, humor and pathos, and four of the titles he wrote completely, both music and lyrics: *Revolvin' Jones; Moonlight Mississippi (A Whistle Stop); Book at My Bedside;* and *Heard a Mocking Bird Sing (In California).* Of the other selections in the album, *Old Folks* was written with Dedette Lee Hill; *Run for the Roundhouse, Nellie,* with Jack Palmer; and *I Guess I'll Go Back Home Next Summer* and *Sharecroppin' Blues* in collaboration with Ray Mayer. Willard sings them all with impartial sincerity.

Willard Robison was born in Shelbina, Missouri, September 18, 1894. His musical talent was evident at a very early age, and he was composing music by the time he was fourteen years old. His Deep River Orchestra toured the midwest until 1925, and then he moved to New York City and immediately published a large selection of his compositions. He was a pioneer on radio with his orchestra and started a long recording career with a series of original compositions he numbered as part of his *American Suite.* These are very rare collector's items today. They were issued on the Pathé and Perfect labels.

	New York c. October 1, 1926
107125	*After Hours* ("American Suite #1") PA 365407, Per 14728
	October 22, 1926
E-2569-A	*Piano Tuner's Dream* ("American Suite #2") PA 36562, 11329, Per 14743
E-2570-C	*Darby Hicks (Gotta Lotta Hot Licks)* ("American Suite #3") PA 36563, 11329, Per 14744
E-2571-B-C	*Mobile Mud* ("American Suite #6") PA 36575, 11349, Per 14756
	New York, November 22, 1926
E-2597-B	*Deep River* ("American Suite #7") PA 36593, Per 14774
E-2598-C	*The Music of a Mountain Stream* ("American Suite #4") PA 36574, 11383, Per 14755
E-2599-B	*Tampico* ("American Suite #5") PA 36574, 11349, Per 14755
	New York c. April 20, 1927
	Harlem Blues ("American Suite #8") PA 36640, Per 14821

Robison continued to write and record continuously with his Deep River Orchestra until late 1928 (see Brian Rust—*The American Dance Band Discography 1917–1942,* Arlington House, 1975). He died in Peekskill, New York, June 24, 1968. Besides the aforementioned compositions, his contributions to the great American heritage of superior songs include *Peaceful Valley; A Woman Alone with the Blues; Six Studies in Modern Syncopation; Rural Revelations; Wake Up, Chillun, Wake Up; What's This World A-Comin' To.* In addition, he penned a twenty-two-minute musical biography of Will Rogers called "Will Rogers, American" and a tribute to the "Band Upstairs," which he visualized as including Bix Beiderbecke, Bunny Berigan, Fats Waller, and other great musicians who have passed on.

Dick Rogers

Pianist, composer, and bandleader Dick Rogers was born in New York City on September 23, 1912. His education included attendance at Fordham Prep, following which he became a vaudeville entertainer, touring the United States and England for a number of years. In 1938 he joined Jack Hylton's band and toured Europe. As a writer of special material, he worked for Joe E. Lewis, Sophie Tucker, Jerry Lewis, Ted Lewis, Buddy Lester, and others.

Around 1936 he joined the Will Osborne orchestra on piano, and in 1940 he and Will Osborne collaborated on writing a few songs that were successful and worthwhile efforts. Probably the most important, from the standpoint of recordings, is *Between 18th and 19th on Chestnut Street,* a reference to a mythical jazz location in Philadelphia. The Will Osborne orchestra recorded the tune, but so did Bing Crosby with Connee Boswell, Bob Zurke, Charlie Barnet, and Bob Crosby. The lyrics of the song laud the efforts of a boogie-woogie piano player named Stacy Trent—which is the name of a hotel in Trenton, New Jersey.

This preoccupation with geography shows up again in *Pompton Turnpike,* another Rogers–Osborne entry that year. This one proved to be a hit record for Charlie Barnet, with Billy May featured on the trumpet. Pompton Turnpike, also known as Route 23 in Cedar Grove, is where the Frank Dailey "Meadowbrook" was located, a nationally famous venue for name bands in New Jersey. Other bands also paid tribute to their stints at the place. The Al Donahue orchestra called theirs *Route 23,* and the Jan Savitt band recorded *Meadowbrook Shuffle*. Rogers and Osborne had two other songs in the running, the novelty *Dry Bones* and the coyly titled *Wouldst Could I But Kiss Thy Hand, Oh Babe*. Everybody had fun with *Dry Bones,* including Fats Waller, Bing Crosby, Tommy Dorsey, and the Merry Macs. Will Osborne and the Glen Gray band recorded the second title.

Dick Rogers died in New York City on September 13, 1970, just ten days before his birthday.

Sigmund Romberg

Sigmund Romberg was born in Nagy Kaniza, Hungary, on July 29, 1887. Although a prolific composer of Broadway musicals in the operetta vein—many of them very successful—and with hundreds of songs to his credit, his contributions to the catalog of popular songs are comparatively few, but important. He began his musical career in Hungary, studying composition, conducting, and arranging and mastering several musical instruments. He served two years with the Hungarian army and in 1909 immigrated to the United States. Three years later, he became a citizen. He worked as a pianist in cafes and nightclubs and led an orchestra in New York's Bustanoby's Restaurant. After he succeeded in getting several compositions published, he was hired by the Schuberts to write the music for the 1914 show "The Whirl of the World." From that point forward he wrote scores for Broadway shows until his death in 1954. In between, he wrote for early sound movies, conducted orchestras on the radio, and in the forties toured with a stage show, "An Evening with Sigmund Romberg." Through the years his collaborators included Otto Harbach, Oscar Hammerstein II, Dorothy Fields, Gus Kahn, and Leo Robin, among others.

Despite all the songs written for shows from 1914 on, it isn't until 1922 that one of any significance to the popular market came along. This is the delightful *When Hearts Are Young*. Cyrus Wood was the lyricist, and Al Goodman helped with the melody. It was sung by Wilda Bennett in the stage show "The Lady in Ermine," with contemporary recordings by the Paul Whiteman and Joseph C. Smith orchestras. It has since become a standard. We then jump to 1926 and the successful Broadway production "The Desert Song." Otto Harbach and Oscar Hammerstein II shared credit for the lyrics. The score was reprised in movie versions in 1929, 1943, and 1952, with four of the songs becoming well known: *The Desert Song; One Alone; The Riff Song;* and *Romance*. For the most part they were favored by vocalists.

"The New Moon," staged in 1928, again with lyrics by Oscar Hammerstein II, introduced several of Sigmund Romberg's most enduring songs, *Lover, Come Back to Me; Softly, As in a Morning Sunrise; Wanting You; One Kiss; Marianne;* and *Stout Hearted Men*. The first two in particular, although written as ballads, have taken on a new character as jazz standards. The others, as with most of Romberg's work, appeal to vocalists. "The New Moon" also went through two movie adaptations, and *Lover, Come Back to Me* was sung in the Romberg biographical film *Deep in My Heart* (1954).

Nineteen hundred thirty-five was a good year for Sigmund Romberg and Oscar Hammerstein II. In the movie *The Night Is Young,* they had two hit songs, *The Night Is Young* and the perennial *When I Grow too Old to Dream.* The highly successful "May Wine" also opened on Broadway. Two numbers enjoyed a brief popularity, *Somebody Ought to Be Told* and *I Built a Dream One Day*. Dorothy Fields provided the words for *Close As Pages in a Book,* which was featured in the stage musical "Up in Central Park" in 1945. Unlike so many of Romberg's earlier works, this one fit well in a dance band format, and Benny Goodman had a good record of the tune. It became quite popular and was reprised in the movie of *Up in Central Park* in 1948.

Sigmund Romberg died in New York City on November 9, 1951.

Billy Rose (William Samuel Rosenberg)

Billy Rose was born in New York City on September 6, 1899. He was educated at the High School of Commerce, where he studied Gregg shorthand and became so highly proficient that he won a speed dictation contest at age sixteen. The following year he went on to become the shorthand reporter for the War Industries Board. He started writing song lyrics in the early twenties and had his first hit song in collaboration with Cliff Friend, *You Tell Her, I Stutter* in 1922. The novelty tune was a favorite of the popular song teams Van and Schenk and Billy Jones and Ernie Hare, and they recorded it.

Still milking the novelty cow, Rose teamed with composer Con Conrad in 1923 to honor a popular cartoon character, *Barney Google*. Eddie Cantor featured the song in vaudeville, and again Jones and Hare recorded it. Rose and Conrad had another hit with *You've Got to See Mamma Ev'ry Night (Or You Can't See Mamma at All)*. Sophie Tucker plugged the tune and recorded it for OKeh. Years later, it was revived by Kay Starr on Capitol and Carol Channing on Command. That same year Rose started a policy that he followed throughout his career. He began sharing lyric credit with other lyric writers, and since his collaborators are highly regarded professionals, such as Mort Dixon, Al Dubin, Lew Brown, Ballard MacDonald, Dave Dreyer, and Ira Gershwin, it seems reasonable to wonder how much Rose contributed to the compositions.

In 1923 the song was *That Old Gang of Mine,* and the lyrics are credited to Rose and Mort Dixon; music by Ray Henderson. Rose, Dixon, and Henderson followed through in 1924 with *Follow the Swallow,* a hit for Al Jolson; but Rose, ever the opportunist, shared the words for that glowing tribute to the American pastime of chewing gum, *Does the Spearmint Lose Its Flavor on the Bedpost Overnight?* with Marty Bloom. Ernest Breuer wrote the music. Harry Richman featured the novelty song, and Jones and Hare recorded it.

Judging by the number of times his name crops up on song titles, 1925 was a banner year for Rose. With Al Dubin he wrote the words for the Joseph Meyer hit *A Cup of Coffee, A Sandwich, and You.* Then he generously shared honors with Lew Brown on the Ray Henderson ditty *Don't Bring Lulu;* with Ballard MacDonald on another Joseph Meyer success, *Clap Hands, Here Comes Charley;* and rejoined his buddies Mort Dixon and Ray Henderson on *If I Had a Girl Like You.* As though to dispel any lingering doubts concerning the legitimacy of all those credits in 1925, Rose went on his own in 1926, and with composer Lee David produced the very successful *Tonight You Belong To Me.* A hit when it was first introduced, it enjoyed a great revival in 1956. But Rose wasn't content with only one hit. With Harry Woods penning the melody, he contributed the words to *Poor Papa (He's Got Nuthin' at All).*

The following year he worked with Maceo Pinkard, and they wrote *Here Comes the Showboat.* Vocalist Vaughn DeLeath plugged it on radio and on an Edison record, and the Jean Goldkette band made it for Victor. In 1929 it was added to the score of the movie musical *Show Boat.* But now Rose reverts to sharing again, and with Dave Dreyer and Al Jolson he came up with *Four Walls* (featured by Jolson) and *Me and My Shadow.* The second title, a hardy perennial, became identified with Ted Lewis, who performed it in the 1941 movie *Hold That Ghost.* Donald O'Connor reprised it in the film *Feudin' Fussin' and A-fightin',* and it made another appearance in the Fanny Brice story *Funny Lady.* In 1962 Frank Sinatra and Sammy Davis Jr. recorded it in a duet.

Rose, Dreyer, and Jolson scored again in 1928 with *Back in Your Own Backyard,* which proved to be a bonanza for Jolson, who sang it in three movies. But with 1929 Rose moved on again, and next is found with Edward Eliscu as a collaborator on the lyrics for two songs by Vincent Youmans, *More Than You Know* and *Without a Song,* both well-known and respected standards. But no more so than the Fats Waller classic *I've Got a Feeling I'm Falling,* with words by Billy Rose. In 1930 Rose assisted Ira Gershwin on the lyrics to the Harry Warren hit *Cheerful Little Earful* and then did the same with Mort Dixon for Warren's *Would You Like to Take a Walk?* and with Charlotte Kent for Louie Alter's *Overnight.* However, he worked alone on the lyrics to Ralph Rainger's *When a Woman Loves a Man* and Mabel Wayne's *It Happened in Monterey.* Altogether, 1930 was a good year.

And Rose continued to help. In 1931 he helped Mort Dixon pen the words to Harry Warren's *I Found a Million Dollar Baby;* in 1933 he did the same for E. Y. Harburg, who needed help with Harold Arlen's *It's Only a Paper Moon;* and he aided Edward Heyman, who was struggling with the Johnny Green effort *I Wanna Be Loved.* In 1934 Rose and Basil Adlam composed

The House Is Haunted (By the Echo of Your Last Goodbye), and then Billy teamed with Paul Francis Webster on John Jacob Loeb's *Got the Jitters.* In 1935 he worked with Irving Kahal on the Dana Suesse gem *The Night Is Young and You're So Beautiful,* which coincidentally was first performed at Billy Rose's Casa Manana, in Fort Worth, Texas, part of the Frontier Days Fair.

Besides writing songs, Rose doubled as a show producer, a nightclub owner, and a radio commentator. For awhile he was married to Fanny Brice and later to swimmer Eleanor Holm.

Billy Rose died in Jamaica, West Indies, on February 10, 1966.

Fred Rose

Pianist, composer, and vocalist Fred Rose was born in Evansville, Indiana, on August 24, 1897. He grew up in St. Louis and was educated in the public schools. When he was only fifteen he was already singing and playing the piano in Chicago honky-tonks and clubs and in the late twenties recorded a number of records for Brunswick as a singer-pianist. For awhile he worked with Paul Whiteman then teamed with Elmo Tanner on Chicago radio. Still later, he had his own show. Early in his career he wrote songs for the popular market, some of them in the jazz vein. In the thirties he started to write for the profitable country and western field, but our interest is in his earlier efforts.

In 1922 Rose succeeded in publishing a song called *Doo Dah Blues,* but most likely his first success was a collaboration with Leo Wood, who contributed the words to *Honest and Truly,* which was published in 1924. It was recorded that year by the Jean Goldkette orchestra on Victor, but it went on to a varied history on records. Rose and Henry Burr were among the early artists, but in later years the song was waxed by the swing bands of Jimmie Lunceford, Ralph Flanagan, and Billy May. This open-mindedness also pertained to another 1924 entry, *Red Hot Mama,* a collaboration with Gilbert Wells and Bud Cooper and a tune that had an early association with Sophie Tucker, who recorded it for OKeh. Joining in from time to time were such varied personages as the Coon–Sanders orchestra (Victor), Jimmy O'Bryant (Paramount), Freddie "Schnickelfritz" Fisher (Decca), and Beatrice Kay (Columbia).

Nothing of note took place in 1925, but in 1926, with Walter Hirsch along to write the words, Rose penned one of the all-time jazz standards, *'Deed I Do.* Characteristically, it went the gamut, from Johnny Marvin on an early Victor to later platters by Jack Teagarden, Ruth Etting, Tommy Dorsey, Bunny Berigan, Lena Horne, Ben Pollack, Charlie Barnet, and many others. A favorite of jazz musicians, it is still heard frequently at festivals and concerts. *Deep Henderson* was the second Rose title that year, and it has received a number of treatments as an instrumental, especially in the year it was published. Among the early recording are sides by King Oliver, the Indiana Five, the Buffalodians, Joe Candullo, Sam Lanin, Mike Markel, the Pebbles, Charlie Skeete, Charlie Straight, and Julie Wintz. Overseas it was recorded in Germany by John Fuhs and in England by Don Parker. The Ambrose band revived the tune in 1937 on English Decca, as arranged by Sid Phillips. *Flamin' Mamie* was a hot title, to say the least, and was unique to the extent that Paul Whiteman shared composer credit with Rose. The Whiteman orchestra recorded it, and so did Coon–Sanders and Mike Markel.

No doubt Fred Rose kept writing, but quite some time went by before anything of significance came along—1936, to be exact, and that year he had two good songs, *Love Came Out of the Night,* recorded by Eddy Duchin's orchestra and those of George Hall and Jan Garber, and *Moon Rose*. Fats Waller and Red McKenzie had good sides on the latter song. Around this time Rose turned to writing country–western songs, teaming quite often with movie star Gene Autry.

Fred Rose died in Nashville, Tennessee, on December 1, 1954.

Vincent Rose

Composer-bandleader Vincent Rose was born in Palermo, Italy, on June 13, 1880. He studied music in his native land at a very early age and came to the United States in 1897, settling in Chicago. He worked with various orchestras as a pianist and/or violinist for a time and then moved on to Los Angeles to become musical director for a chain of hotels. He organized his first orchestra in 1904 and went on to front it until his death. The list of Rose's compositions isn't very long, and most of them you probably have never heard of, but how would you like to lay claim to the following? *Whispering; Avalon; Linger Awhile; Pardon Me, Pretty Baby; Were You Sincere; The Umbrella Man;* and *Blueberry Hill.* My personal favorite is a tune accorded the customary exceptional treatment by Ray Noble and Al Bowlly on a recording for HMV, *Love Tales,* one of the bumper crop of musical jewels published in 1933.

The Vincent Rose orchestra was always melodic and listenable, but in the music business where irony is more often the rule than the exception, the most famous recording under his name will probably be Melotone 13158, a coupling of *Stars Fell on Alabama* and *Learning,* two fine songs. The problem is they aren't played by the Vincent Rose orchestra. These things are never easy to understand, but for some strange reason the record producers decided to use Vincent Rose's name as a pseudonym for Benny Goodman. Also by way of coincidence, the vocals on the record are by Tony Sacco, another songwriter, composer of *The Breeze (That's Bringin' My Honey Back to Me)*. Other songs by Rose are *May Time; Tonight or Never;* and *Kiss by Kiss*. Lyricists collaborating with him are Larry Stock, James Cavanaugh, Jack Meskill, Raymond Klages, Al Lewis, Buddy DeSylva, Richard Coburn, and John Schonberger.

Vincent Rose died in Rockville Center, New York, on May 20, 1944.

Harry Ruby

Songwriter Harry Ruby was born in New York City on January 27, 1895. He was educated in the public schools and early in his career worked as a pianist and song-plugger for music publishers, including the firms of Gus Edwards and Harry Von Tilzer. Then he toured in vaudeville as a pianist accompanying the Messenger Boys Trio and the Bootblack Trio. In a career writing songs that began in 1918, Ruby collaborated with a number of lyricists, but his most outstanding successes were written with Bert Kalmar. The team started writing songs for Broadway shows, with moderate success until 1923 when they had a hand in composing one of our all-time standards, *Who's Sorry Now*. The odd part of this is that Kalmar and Ruby wrote the song's words, with Ted Snyder composing the music. The song has had a life of its own. Popular in 1923, it was featured by Van and Schenk in vaudeville and recorded by Marion Harris and by the band of Isham Jones, and it never quite died out. But in 1950 Gloria DeHaven sang it in the Kalmar–Ruby biographical movie *Three Little Words,* which starred Fred Astaire and Red Skelton as the songwriting team. In 1958 singer Connie Francis revived it on a record for M-G-M. The platter was so popular that *Who's Sorry Now* was on the popular *Your Hit Parade* program for six weeks. The song was heard on the soundtrack of another film in 1979, *All That Jazz*. More important to the longevity of the tune, it has become a favorite of jazz musicians, is frequently heard and played in concerts and jazz festivals, and has been recorded numerous times.

Kalmar and Ruby had another hit in 1927, written for the show "Five O'-Clock Girl." The song was *Thinking of You,* and this time Ruby wrote the melody. Fred Astaire and Vera Ellen performed it in the film *Three Little Words,* leading to a spurt of new recordings by Eddie Fisher (his first "chart" record), Don Cherry, and Sarah Vaughn. In 1928 Kalmar wrote the lyrics and Ruby teamed with Herbert Stothart on the melody for *I Wanna Be Loved by You,* which was introduced and sung by Helen Kane in the stage show "Good Boy." Helen Kane gave the song her personal trademark ending for each eight-bar phrase, "Boop-boop-a-doop," and her Victor record was a big hit. In *Three Little Words,* Helen Kane was dubbed on the soundtrack for Debby Reynolds, singing with Carlton Carpenter. In 1955 it was sung by Jane Russell, Rudy Vallee, and Anita Ellis, whose voice was dubbed in for Jeanne Crain, in the film *Gentlemen Marry Brunettes.* Marilyn Monroe sang it in *Some Like it Hot* in 1955, and in 1975 it was reprised in the stage show "A Musical Jubilee" by Patrice Munsel, Tammy Grimes, and Lillian Gish. The Helen Kane version also spawned the cartoon character "Betty Boop."

With these hits under their belts, Kalmar and Ruby headed for Hollywood and in 1930 managed to have several hit songs, especially one written for the Amos & Andy movie *Check and Double Check, Three Little Words.* This all-time standard was almost instantly frozen for immortality on a Victor recording by the Duke Ellington orchestra, with a vocal by the Rhythm Boys (Bing Crosby, Harry Barris, and Al Rinker). Fred Astaire, portraying Bert Kalmar, sang it in *Three Little Words. I Love You So Much* was featured in the Wheeler and Woolsey comedy *The Cuckoos.* Contemporary records were made by the Ohman–Arden orchestra, Smith Balleaw, Bob Haring, and Eddie Walters. Most important during that period, it was a very popular item on the radio. And in that same year, Kalmar and Ruby made the acquaintance of the Marx Brothers, resulting in the film version of the stage show "Animal Crackers," with *Watching the Clouds Roll By,* a popular offering and a tune that became a theme song for Groucho Marx, *Hooray for Captain Spaulding.* "Top Speed," both a stage show and a movie, featured two Kalmar and Ruby songs, *What Would I Care?* and *Keep Your Undershirt On.* The latter morsel of sentiment became a jazz classic as recorded by the Ben Pollack orchestra, with Benny Goodman, Jack Teagarden, and Jimmy McPartland in the band.

In 1931 Kalmar and Ruby authored two freelance songs, *I'm So Afraid of You,* which got nice treatment on Victor from the Bert Lown orchestra, and *Nevertheless.* Now a standard, *Nevertheless* did well on contemporary sides by the bands of Rudy Vallee and Jack Denny and by vocalist Seger Ellis. Like so many of the writers' hits, it was included in the biographical *Three Little Words,* sung by Fred Astaire, Red Skelton, and Anita Ellis (dubbed in for Vera Ellen). The film engendered a rash of new recordings, and the song became a top hit all over again. Among the many sides were those by the Mills Brothers, Paul Weston, Ray Anthony, Ralph Flanagan, Frank Sinatra, and Frankie Laine.

The team went on to produce a number of fine songs in the ensuing years—*Look What You've Done; What a Perfect Combination; Keep on Doin' What You're Doin'; In the Moonlight*—but Bert Kalmar died in 1947. Although he worked with other lyricists, Harry Ruby went into semiretirement. In 1945 he reversed his usual role and wrote the words to a song composed by Rube Bloom, *Give Me the Simple Life,* and did it again in 1949, penning the lyrics for Johnnie Scott's melody *Maybe It's Because.* In 1935 Kalmar and Ruby had written a song they called *Moonlight On the Meadow.* Rewritten with a new lyric and title by Kalmar and Oscar Hammerstein II, it was intended for the Marx Brothers movie *A Night at the Opera,* but it wasn't used. In 1951 it was finally performed by Kay Brown and Louis Armstrong in a film called *The Strip,* and then Armstrong recorded it. The recording, *A Kiss to Build a Dream On.* was a sensational success, and it and the song have become classics.

Other Harry Ruby songs include *What a Girl Can Do; Come On, Papa; The Dixieland Volunteers; Daddy Long Legs; We've Got the Stage Door Blues; I'm a Vamp From East Broadway; Timbuctu; So Long, Oolong; My Sunny Tennessee; She's Mine, All Mine; Beautiful Girls; I Gave You Up Just Before You Threw Me Down; I Like a Big Town/Happy Ending; It Was Meant to Be; All Alone Monday; Alma Mater; Just One Kiss; Any Little Tune; You Smiled at Me; Sweeter Than You; Whistle; Up in the Clouds; Happy Go Lucky; Dancing the Devil Away; Sweet Someone; Wherever You Are; Why Am I So Romantic?; Everyone Says "I Love You"; Tired of It All; One Little Kiss; What a Beautiful Night; When You Dream About Hawaii; Goodnight Kisses; Only When You're in My Arms; You're On My Mind; Time to Sing; I Wish I Could Tell You; Do You Love Me; Another Night Like This;* and others.

Harry Ruby died in Los Angeles, California, on February 23, 1974.

Herman Ruby

Lyricist Herman Ruby was born in New York City on March 15, 1891. Although the list of songs his name is connected with isn't long, it is still impressive. He collaborated with a number of the top composers, including Harry Ruby, Harry Woods, Sam Stept, Harry Akst, Con Conrad, and Joseph Meyer. In 1921 Ruby teamed with Bert Kalmar and Harry Ruby, and the result was *My Sunny Tennessee,* a song featured by Eddie Cantor in the theater musical "The Midnight Rounders." In 1950 Fred Astaire and Red Skelton sang it in the Kalmar–Ruby biographical film *Three Little Words.*

In the next year Ruby and Joseph Meyer worked together to produce a favorite standard in the jazz category, and Meyer's first hit song, *My Honey's Lovin' Arms.* Isham Jones had a contemporary hit recording, but through the years it has been recorded by many of the biggest names in the business—Red Nichols, Benny Goodman, Duke Ellington, just to name a few—and it is frequently heard in concerts. In 1925 composer Dave Dreyer provided the melody for Ruby's words to the engaging novelty *Cecilia.* It was featured on radio and records by the popular Whispering Jack Smith and sold extremely well on sheet music and piano rolls. Lee Morse also had a contemporary platter, and in later years it has been revived from time to time on records by Dick Jurgens, Bob Crosby, and Neal Hefti.

Flower of Love was a 1928 entry, with Dave Dreyer, David Mendoza, William Axt, and Ruby all sharing the credit. The bands of Ted Weems and Bob Haring recorded it. But 1929 was another big year for Ruby. He and Bud Green penned the words to Sam H. Stept's big hit *I'll Always Be in Love With You.* It was introduced by Morton Downey in the movie *Syncopation,* and he recorded it for Victor. So did Waring's Pennsylvanians, who were also in the film. Written as a waltz, the song is often played in four-four and has become a standard. Other songs by Herman Ruby are *Since I Found You; Stolen Kisses; The Egg and I; In a Boat for Two; Pals Just Pals;* and *My Sunday Girl.*

He died in Los Angeles, California, on July 31, 1959.

Charles Ellsworth (Pee Wee) Russell

Jazz clarinetist, recording artist, and part-time composer Pee Wee Russell was born in St. Louis, Missouri, on March 27, 1906. His education included the Western Military Academy and the University of Missouri, but he devoted a lifetime to working as a reedman in jazz and dance bands. Along the way he played with many of the most famous musicians in the history of American music and established an enviable reputation as a soloist with a highly individual style on the clarinet. Not to be taken at face value is the following quote from his biographical profile in the *ASCAP Biographical Dictionary* (4th edition): "Clarinetist with Tex Beiderbecke, Frank Trumbauer, Eddie Condon & Buddy Hackett, in nightclubs 30's & 40's. . . ."

Although Pee Wee Russell didn't compose for the popular market, the jazz catalog of instrumental compositions was enhanced by some of his work, particularly the plaintively lovely *Pee Wee's Song* and the equally delightful *Pee Wee's Blues. Cutie Pie* is another swinger. The foregoing titles plus *Oh No!; I Got 'Em Again; What's the Pitch; Midnight Blue; Twenty-eighth and Eighth; Muscogee Blue; Are You Here?;* and *Missy*—all Pee

Wee Russell compositions—can be heard to advantage on an Arbors compact disc (ARCD 19130), *Pee Wee's Song—The Music of Pee Wee Russell,* as played by clarinetist Bobby Gordon backed by an all-star recording group that includes Jon-Eric Kellso, trumpet; Dan Barrett, trombone; Rick Fay, tenor sax; Johnny Varro, piano; Marty Grosz, guitar; Bob Haggart, bass; and Gene Estes, drums. Other compositions by Pee Wee Russell are *Englewood; Mama's in the Groove; D. A. Blues; Pee Wee Squawks; You're There in a Dream; Write Me a Love Song, Baby;* and *This Is It.*

Pee Wee Russell died in New York City on February 14, 1969.

Readers interested in a complete biography and discography of Pee Wee Russell are referred to *Pee Wee Russell, The Life of a Jazzman,* by Robert Hilbert, Oxford University Press, New York, 1993 and *Pee Wee Speaks,* by Robert Hilbert in collaboration with David Niven, Scarecrow Press (with the Rutgers Institute of Jazz Studies), Studies in Jazz #13, Metuchen, NJ, 1992.

Luis Russell

Pianist, composer, bandleader Luis Russell was born in Careening Cay, Panama, on August 6, 1902. His father was a pianist, organist, and music teacher. Luis took lessons from him and also studied the guitar and violin. As a youngster he started out playing for silent movies in Panama theaters and then worked in a nightclub. In 1919 he won three thousand dollars in a lottery, and this enabled him to move with his mother and sister to New Orleans.

In 1923 he joined the band led by Albert Nicholas and took over as leader when Nicholas left. The following year he moved on to Chicago, where he played with Doc Cooke and King Oliver. He was with Oliver when the band hit New York but left to join the band playing at The Nest, a short time later taking over as leader. The band played the best spots in New York, such as the Savoy Ballroom, the Saratoga Club, and Connie's Inn, with plenty of airtime and recordings. In the fall of 1935 Louis Armstrong took over the band, with Russell staying on as pianist, arranger, and rehearsal leader. Then almost ten years later Russell reorganized another band and kept it active until he retired from music in 1948.

As a composer Russell is credited with a number of jazz instrumentals, several of which are well known in that category, and most were recorded by his band. These include *Jersey Lightning; Feeling the Spirit; Song of the Swanee; Saratoga Shout; Sweet Mumtaz; Call of the Freaks; Dolly Mine; Savoy Shout; The Ghost of the Freaks; Hocus Pocus; Muggin' Lightly; Louisiana Swing; Higgenbotham Blues;* and *Doctor Blues.* Oddly enough, probably his best-known composition, a collaboration with drummer Paul Barbarin, *Come Back, Sweet Papa,* owes its popularity to the Bob Crosby band recording and to subsequent remakes by the musicians who were in the Crosby orchestra. It has became a standard.

Luis Russell died in New York City on December 11, 1963.

Sidney Keith (Bob) Russell

Lyric writer Sidney Keith (Bob) Russell was born in Passaic, New Jersey, on April 15, 1914. His education included a scholarship at Washington University, St. Louis. He started out as an advertising copywriter and then began to write special material for films. His entry into the songwriting field began in 1940, when he and Ray Charles combined to write English words to the Mexican song *Frenesi*. The original Spanish lyrics were by the composer of the melody, Alberto Dominguez. Artie Shaw imported the tune and recorded it for Victor as an instrumental. The record was number one for thirteen weeks and in the top ten for thirty weeks. The song was on the Hit Parade for nineteen weeks, three times as number one. It was also recorded by Woody Herman, Xavier Cugat, and Glenn Miller.

Recognizing a good thing, Russell followed through in the next year, writing English lyrics to another Mexican song, *Maria Elena*. Composed by Lorenzo Barcelata as a tribute to the wife of the president of Mexico, the song was first heard as background music in the Paul Muni film *Bordertown*. Lawrence Welk's orchestra had the first recording of the English version, but the hit record was by the Jimmy Dorsey band with Bob Eberly on the vocal. The song was on the Hit Parade for twenty-two weeks. Jimmy Dorsey, with Bob Eberly and Helen O'Connell, made the top ten list again that same year with *Time Was,* another Russell Mexican adaptation, with music by Miguel Prado. Originally called *Duerme,* the Spanish words were by Gabriel Luna.

Since it worked so well with Mexican tunes, S. K. Russell (as he was listed on this early work) joined with Fred Wise and Milton Leeds on composing words in English for a song with words and music by a Greek, N. Roubanis. The song was *Miserlou*. Harry James had a hit instrumental. Carol Bruce recorded it as a vocal, and it did very well. Still riding a winning horse, Russell composed English lyrics for the Cuban song *Tabu,* as it was named and written by the composer, Margarita Lecuona, and it became *Taboo*. Not exactly a new song, it was first recorded as an instrumental in this country by Vic Berton's orchestra on Vocalion in 1935 and again by

Enric Madriguera in 1939. Sammy Kaye introduced the English lyric on a Victor record with a vocal by Tommy Ryan in 1942. Others followed, especially one by Desi Arnaz, who became identified with it. Written by the same composer, Margarita Lecuona, in 1939, *Babalu* got the Russell treatment in 1942 and was featured by Xavier Cugat's Orchestra in the 1944 film *Two Girls and a Sailor*. In 1945 it was sung by Miquelito Valdez in another movie, *Pan-Americana,* and the song has since been identified with him.

In spite of the popularity of the foregoing, most likely the more enduring of Russell's works are the lyrics he wrote to melodies by Duke Ellington, which were primarily written as instrumentals. The first of these, *Don't Get Around Much Anymore,* evolved from *Never No Lament*. Ellington recorded the new version on Columbia with a vocal by Al Hibbler. Adding to the song's popularity on radio and records were platters by the Ink Spots and Glen Gray's Casa Loma Orchestra. It has since become a standard. The second Russell–Ellington collaboration took place the following year of 1943. This time the instrumental, *Concerto for Cootie,* written as a feature for trumpeter Cootie Williams, became *Do Nothin' Till You Hear From Me*. Stan Kenton and Woody Herman had successful records, among others, and the song was a popular hit.

But Russell was still intrigued by songs with foreign roots, and that same year he put English words to the Portuguese samba written by Ary Barroso, which the composer had called *Aquarela do Brasil,* and it became simply *Brazil*. It was first introduced in a feature cartoon film, *Saludos Amigos,* by Eddy Duchin's orchestra. Of all the Russell adaptations, this one went on to the greatest success. Xavier Cugat and Jimmy Dorsey had contemporary hit records. Carmen Miranda sang the tune in the movie musical *The Gang's All Here* (1943); Nan Wynn did the same in *Jam Session* (1944); it was the title song of another movie in 1944, *Brazil;* it was played in *The Road to Rio* in 1948; and in *The Eddy Duchin Story* in 1956. Guitarist Les Paul paired it with *Lover* on his first hit record using his technique of overdubbing sound tracks.

In 1944 Russell returned to the Ellington goldmine, and this time *Sentimental Lady* was fitted with a new dress and became *I Didn't Know About You*. It went the rounds. Ellington recorded it for Victor, with Joya Sherril singing; Count Basie made it for Columbia with a vocal by Thelma Carpenter; Boyd Raeburn, with Don Darcy, made it for Guild; and vocal versions were waxed by Lena Horne on Victor and Jo Stafford for Capitol. Like the other Ellington titles, this one has become a standard. Russell, busy writing scores for movies, nevertheless continued to contribute words to hit songs. In 1947 it was *Ballerina,* with Carl Sigman. In 1948 came *You Came a Long Way From St. Louis,* with John Benson Brooks (and a hit record for the new Ray McKinley band). In 1949, another effort with Carl Sigman, *Crazy, He Calls Me,* became a Billie Holiday hit. In 1950 the melody was by Paul Weston, and the Russell title was *No Other Love*. In 1952 Russell converted the Sir Charles Thompson–Illinois Jacquet instrumental *Robbins Nest* into *Just When We're Falling in Love,* and Les Brown had a successful record. Still working, in 1967 Russell added lyrics to the Quincy Jones music and came up with *The Eyes of Love*. Other songs by Bob Russell include *Busy as a Bee; Time Was; At the Crossroads; Matinee; May I Still Hold You; It's a Quiet Town; Circus; The Story of My Life; Would I Love You; Dear! Dear! Dear!; Lady Love; Once; Mambo on My Mind; Trinidad; Lady, I've Been Kissed Before; I Didn't Want to Love You; I Have One Gift; I Know, I Know, I Know; It's the Beast in Me; The Matador; Interlude; The Color of Love; A Lonesome Cup of Coffee; Bugle Blues; The Sandman Cometh; I Happen to Love You; Dreamer's Cloth; Darlene; He Never Looked Better in His Life:* and *I Fear Nothing*.

Bob Russell died in Beverly Hills, California, on February 18, 1970.

Edgar Sampson

Multitalented musician-composer-arranger Edgar Sampson was born in New York City on August 31, 1907. He started his long career in music as a violinist in 1924, working in nightclubs. Then he switched to playing alto sax and in 1927 worked with Duke Ellington and Arthur Gibbs. He was with the famous bands of Charlie Johnson and Rex Stewart, then Fletcher Henderson, and still later Chick Webb. While working with these bands, Sampson was perfecting his arranging technique, and composing, and when both efforts became profitable he quit playing to concentrate on them. His resultant work in the mid to late thirties produced some of the most famous instrumentals of the swing period.

One of his earliest compositions was *Blue Lou,* a hard-swinging but melodic instrumental published in 1933. Irving Mills added lyrics, but as a favorite of jazz and swing bands it has been recorded by many of the top names: Benny Goodman, Benny Carter, Chick Webb, Wingy Manone, Bunny Berigan, Fletcher Henderson, Neal Hefti, Eddie Heywood, and the All-Star Band in 1939 on Victor. A perennial, it is still being played and recorded. *Stompin' at the Savoy,* possibly the most famous instrumental of the swing era, was first recorded by the Chick Webb Band on Columbia in 1934 in an arrangement by Sampson. Two years later, he arranged it for the Benny Goodman orchestra, and the resulting Victor record was a smash hit. Along the way, the composing staff of Sampson and Andy Razaf was expanded to include Chick Webb and Benny Goodman. The Goodman Quartet made another recording of it in 1937, and it made the complete rounds of the record labels with sides by Teddy Wilson, Jimmy Dorsey, Ben Pollack, Woody Herman, and Jonah Jones, among many others.

Benny Goodman and Irving Mills were along to share the credit for *If Dreams Come True,* a 1938 Sampson tune that manages to successfully bridge the invisible gap between a popular song and a jazz instrumental. Goodman had a hit record arranged by Sampson, and so did Andy Kirk. Bobby Hackett's band from "Nick's," the Greenwich Village jazz club, gave it exceptional treatment, and Teddy Wilson used Hackett and Pee Wee Russell on his recording for Brunswick. As a standard, it has been played and recorded many times since. Another entry that year was the tricky *Lullaby in Rhythm,* which originated with pianist Clarence Profit, was polished and arranged by Sampson, attained lyrics from Walter Hirsch, and was recorded on a hit record by the Benny Goodman orchestra. All concerned shared composing credits.

Don't Be That Way, the song that rated several clumsy references in the dialogue of the Benny Goodman biographical film *The Benny Goodman Story,* was also a hit in 1938, with Sampson and Goodman listed as composers of the melody and Mitchell Parish author of the words. It was recorded as an instrumental by the Chick Webb band in 1934, with only Sampson as the composer and arranger. Besides the best-selling Goodman recording on Victor, the tune was waxed by Mildred Bailey with Red Norvo's band on Vocalion; Teddy Wilson on Brunswick; Bing Crosby on Decca; and Lionel Hampton on Victor, plus others. Other Edgar Sampson compositions are *Blue Minor; Serenade To A Sleeping Beauty; Sampson Stomp; That Man's Here Again; Don't Try Your Jive on Me; Jumpin' for Joy; March of the Swing Parade; Hoopdee Whodee; Happy and Satisfied; I'll Be Back For More; Cool and Groovy; Dark Rapture; Lucky; The Blues Made Me Feel This Way; Light and Sweet; I'm Not Complainin';* and *The Sweetness of You.*

Edgar Sampson died in Englewood, New Jersey, on January 16, 1973.

Walter Samuels

Walter Gerald Samuels was born in New York City on February 2, 1908. His education included graduation from DeWitt Clinton High School and New York University, where he studied law. His musical education was extensive, including eight years of classical piano with Eugene Bernstein and fifteen years of theory and harmony with Reubin Goldmark. During World War II he represented ASCAP as a composer and entertainer in the South Pacific, for which he received an award from the National Red Cross. His first published song, written in collaboration with Leonard Whitcup, *Fiesta,* came out in 1931. Whitcup and Samuels, with the addition of Teddy Powell, would later form a team that marketed several successful songs, working on both words and music. But in 1933 Samuels worked alone on *Dark Clouds,* which attained moderate popularity and was recorded by Henry "Red" Allen and by Coleman Hawkins.

In 1934 Leonard Whitcup returned, and the pair did well with *Infatuation,* a rather somber vehicle that was recorded by Glen Gray and the Casa Loma Orchestra. However, they offset the gloom with the bright and cheery *True,* which enjoyed much wider acceptance. It was recorded by Paul Whiteman on Victor, Guy Lombardo on Brunswick, Chick Webb on Vocalion, Ted Black on Bluebird, and in the forties was briefly revived by singer Andy

Russell, backed by Paul Weston, on Capitol. Teddy Powell joined the pair in 1935, and immediately production increased and several successful songs resulted, *March Winds and April Showers; (Take Me Back to My) Boots and Saddle;* and *I Couldn't Believe My Eyes.* Ruth Etting, Abe Lyman, and Victor Young were among those recording the first title. Gene Autry had a hit record on the second, but it was also waxed by a diversified collection of artists, including John Charles Thomas (Victor), Red Allen (Vocalion), Victor Young (Decca), Jimmy Ray (Bluebird), and whistler Fred Lowery (Columbia). Freddy Martin and the Dorsey Brothers had good recordings of *I Couldn't Believe My Eyes,* and it was a popular radio selection.

Cottage by the Moon was the only entry for 1936, and a not a very impressive one, but the team made up for it in the following year, producing two quality songs, *Heaven Help This Heart of Mine* and *If My Heart Could Only Talk. Heaven Help This Heart of Mine* received respectable treatment on records by Mildred Bailey, Eddy Duchin, and Dick Robertson; *If My Heart Could Only Talk* was recorded by the Tommy Dorsey Orchestra on Victor, and by Billie Holiday on Vocalion. The writers had three other songs that year, *Spring Cleaning (Getting Ready for Love); Rollin' Plains;* and *The Lady From Fifth Avenue.* Of the three, the pseudo-cowboy song *Rollin' Plains* fared the best. It was the title song of a movie, in which it was sung by Tex Ritter, and Jimmy Ray and Dick Robertson recorded it. *Spring Cleaning* was favored with good records by Dick McDonough and Bob Howard. Tommy Dorsey and Ray Noble each had easy-listening records of *It Isn't A Dream Anymore,* a 1941 composition by Samuels and Charles Newman.

Other songs by Walter Samuels are *Little Genius; The Swiss Bellringer; Lamento Gitano; There's Nothing the Matter with Me; I Gotta Have You; Blue Mist;* and *The Mailman's Got My Letter.*

Joe Sanders

Pianist, composer, singer, and bandleader Joe Sanders was born in Thayer, Kansas, on October 15, 1896. Known as "The Old Left-Hander," he distinguished himself as a baseball player early in his career with the Kansas City Athletic Club, establishing a world record for strikeouts. With drummer Carleton Coon, he organized a dance band in the twenties, the Coon–Sanders Original Nighthawk Orchestra, which pioneered radio broadcasts and attained a worldwide reputation. Although Sanders only had a few songs that reached the popular market—*Beloved,* a 1933 entry with words by Gus Kahn possibly the main exception—his compositions were important to the renown of the orchestra, especially on records, and are still closely associated with the band's jazz-oriented character. Well known to the many fans and collectors of this vintage dance band are the following titles: *High Fever* (1926); *Sluefoot* and *The Wail* (1927); *Blazin; What a Girl, What a Night;* and *Little Orphan Annie* (1928); *Tennessee Lazy* and *Gotta a Great Big Date with a Little Bitta Girl* (1929). Other songs by Sanders are *I'll Never Forget I Love You; I Found a Rose in the Snow;* and *Nighty Night Dear.*

Joe Sanders died in Kansas City, Missouri, on May 14, 1965.

The Santly Brothers (Henry, Joseph H., Lester)

The Santly Brothers were all musicians, songwriters, and eventually partners in their own music publishing firm. The oldest was Joseph H. Santly, who was born in New York City on August 21, 1886. He was educated in the public schools and toured in vaudeville as a boy soprano. Afterwards, he worked as a staff member of a publishing firm but then returned to vaudeville as a partner in an act billed as Santly & Norton for a span of six years. Later he became a manager at Remich and then in 1929 founded his own publishing company in partnership with his brothers.

Joseph Santly started writing songs in the early twenties and managed to compile a fair list of successful ones. In 1920 he collaborated with lyricist Howard Johnson on a novelty item, *At the Moving Picture Ball,* in which the names of the film stars of the era were all mentioned. It was revived on a Decca recording by Freddie "Schnicklefritz" Fisher in 1939 and still later given an ensemble performance in the 1975 stage production "A Musical Jubilee." In 1924 Joseph Santly paired with Cliff Friend on the catchy and tuneful *There's Yes Yes in Your Eyes,* which was well accepted and recorded by the Paul Whiteman orchestra on a contemporary side, and through the years was also waxed by the bands of Guy Lombardo, Art Kahn, Artie Shaw, and Eddy Howard, among others. The song is at least a semistandard.

In 1926 Cliff Friend supplied the words to the Santly melody of *Tamiami Trail,* a song that sold well on sheet music and music rolls, and teamed with Sidney Clare on the words to *Big Butter and Egg Man.* The last named had the good fortune to be recorded by Louis Armstrong on an Okeh side that year, and it was thus established as a standard in the jazz library. Among other famous recordings are those by Muggsy Spanier's Ragtime Band and Wild Bill Davison. The song is frequently played at jazz festivals and concerts. Other titles by Joseph H. Santly include *Hawaiian Butterfly; Before We Say Goodnight; Friends;* and *Mother, Dixie and You.*

Joseph H. Santly died in New York City on August 28, 1962.

Henry Santly, pianist and partner with his brothers in the music publishing firm, was born in New York City on October 23, 1890. During World War I he served in the 51ST Pioneer Infantry Division. As a songwriter his chief collaborator was Pete Wendling. Although Henry had no outstanding hits, he did succeed in having a number of songs published, including *Put Your Arms Around Me Where They Belong; Will You Remember Me?;* and *What Good Is Good Morning.*

Henry Santly died in New York City on February 13, 1934.

Lester Santly was born in New York City, on April 2, 1894. He was educated at DeWitt Clinton High School and studied the violin and piano. Early in his career he worked in dance bands and then became a staff writer for music publishers. In 1929 he joined his brothers in founding Santly Joy Co. His list of published compositions is short, but it includes a song that has achieved standard status, *I'm Nobody's Baby,* which was published in 1921 in collaboration with Benny Davis and Milton Ager. A tune that appeals to female vocalists, it has been recorded by many of them through the years, starting with Marion Harris on a contemporary side. Since then other recordings have been made by Helen Forrest (with Benny Goodman), Connie Haines (with Tommy Dorsey), Betty Hutton (with Nelson Riddle), Marian Mann (with Bob Crosby), and Judy Garland (with Bobby Sherwood). Judy Garland also sang the song in the film *Andy Hardy Meets a Debutante* in 1940, and this—along with the records—promoted the tune to repeat popularity; it made the Hit Parade for eleven weeks. Other Lester Santly titles include *Heart of Wetona; All That I Need Is You; Hi-Lee, Hi-Lo;* and *The Sunrise.*

Jan Savitt

Violinist, bandleader, and composer Jan Savitt was born in Petrograd, Russia, on September 4, 1913. Brought to the United States the following year, he was educated at the Curtis Institute on a scholarship and studied with Carl Flesch, Arthur Rodzinski, and Fritz Reiner. At the tender age of fourteen he was playing with the Philadelphia Orchestra and in 1931 organized a string quartet. In 1934 he became the music director for the Philadelphia radio station WCAU and formed a "house" band that attracted national attention. A successful career in records, radio, and movies followed.

As a composer, his name is associated with two hit songs of 1940 written in collaboration with Harold Adamson, who wrote the lyrics, and arranger Johnny Watson, who shares credit for composing the music. The songs are *It's a Wonderful World* and *720 in the Books.* The Savitt orchestra, known as the Top Hatters, recorded both songs for Decca, and the Charlie Barnet band did the same on Bluebird. All of the recordings sold well. The Savitt sides featuring vocalist Bon Bon Tunnell, were very popular, and were important factors in establishing the Savitt organization as a name band. Other Savitt compositions are *Now and Forever; It's the Tune That Counts; It Must Be Love;* and *Beloved Friend.*

Jan Savitt died in Sacramento, California, on October 4, 1948.

Victor Schertzinger

Multitalented violinist, composer, author, director, and producer Victor Schertzinger was born in Mahanoy City, Pennsylvania, on April 8, 1890. He was educated at Brown Preparatory School in Pennsylvania and the University of Brussels School of Music. At the age of eight he was a featured violin soloist with the Victor Herbert Orchestra, and as a teenager he toured the United States and abroad as a concert artist. For a time he conducted orchestras in Los Angeles and in the pit for Broadway shows and then gravitated to Hollywood and a career writing for the movies. He is credited with a long list of successful songs from 1929 to 1942. However, one of his first published songs dates from 1913. This was *Marcheta,* for which he wrote both words and music. Tommy Dorsey's band recorded it as an instrumental in 1939, and it still surfaces every now and then.

In 1929 Schertzinger and lyricist Clifford Grey wrote the score for the Maurice Chevalier–Jeanette MacDonald film *The Love Parade,* which resulted in three songs that scored well in the popular market, *My Love Parade; Dream Lover;* and *March of the Grenadiers.* All were in the Victor Herbert tradition of light operetta music, and this was also true of the 1934 waltz *One Night of Love,* a collaboration with Gus Kahn written as the title song for the film starring Grace Moore. But by 1936 the tone of the Schertzinger melodies underwent a change, as typified by *Life Begins When You're in Love,* a sprightly ditty with words by Lew Brown and Harry Richman. It was introduced by the song-and-dance man in *The Music Goes 'Round,* and he also recorded it for Decca. Other platters were made by Isham Jones, Teddy Wilson, and Richard Himber. In 1941 Schertzinger worked with Frank Loesser to turn out three songs for *Kiss the Boys Goodbye,* a film that starred Mary Martin and Don Ameche. The titles were *I'll Never Let a Day Pass By; Sand in My Shoes;* and the title song, *Kiss the Boys Goodbye.* Mary Martin had the hit record on the last. Harry James, Charlie Spivak, and Charlie Barnet all had successful sides of *I'll Never Let a Day*

Pass By. Sand in My Shoes, probably the best song of the three, was recorded as a rhumba instrumental by the new band of Sonny Dunham.

Victor Schertzinger died in Hollywood, California, on October 26, 1941, but the songs he wrote with Johnny Mercer for the movie *The Fleet's In* were released posthumously in 1942, with three of the songs making big hits, *Tangerine; Arthur Murray Taught Me Dancing in a Hurry;* and *I Remember You.* The Jimmy Dorsey orchestra was featured in the film and had best-selling records of the first two with Helen O'Connell on the vocals, and *I Remember You* with Bob Eberly.

Other songs by Victor Schertzinger are *My Wonderful Dream Girl; Nobody's Using It Now; If I Knew You Better; Love Me Forever; Follow Your Heart; Magnolias in the Moonlight; Something to Sing About; Out of the Blue; The Moon and the Willow Tree; I Don't Want to Cry Anymore; Not Mine;* and *If You Build a Better Mousetrap.*

Elmer Schoebel

I can see your wrinkled brow right now. "Elmer Schoebel? A great songwriter? I've never heard of him." Well, if you're a student of jazz history, of course you have. And if you're a traditional jazz fan you certainly know Elmer Schoebel's music, if only the indestructible *Nobody's Sweetheart,* which all by itself should qualify a composer as great. To record collectors and anybody familiar with jazz history in the formative twenties, Elmer Schoebel's is a well-known name in the personnel listings for the first recordings made by the pioneering hot band the New Orleans Rhythm Kings under the pseudonym of the Friars Society Orchestra in August of 1922. Schoebel is listed as both pianist and leader of that distinguished group, which also included Paul Mares, George Brunies, Leon Rappolo, Jack Pettis, Lew Black, Arnold Loyacano (who played string bass, contrary to all those who insist only the tuba is "traditional"), and Frank Snyder. Among the eight titles the band recorded on those two famous days in the history of our music are two on which Schoebel is listed as cocomposer, *Farewell Blues* (Rappolo–Schoebel–Mares), and *Discontented Blues* (Rappolo–Schoebel–Mares).

Actually, there is good reason to believe that Schoebel should be credited with three titles, including the most famous one of them all, *Bugle Call Rag.* Although he is generally recognized as the composer of this classic, as is often the case with early copyrights, there is some mystery surrounding the claim. Roger Kinkle, author of the *Encyclopedia of Popular Music and Jazz,* on page eighteen of Volume One of his *Music Year by Year,* unobtrusively lists *Bugle Call Rag* for 1916, and credits J. Hubert Blake (Eubie Blake) and Carey Morgan as the composers. In *Jazz Records 1897–1942,* Brian Rust draws attention to the fact that a *Bugle Call Rag* was published in 1916, but another—the famous one—appeared in 1922 and is sometimes shown as *Bugle Call Blues*. It's important to note that the Rhythm Kings' recording of the tune is under the title of *Bugle Call Blues* (as is the 1929 Jack Pettis recording on Victor V-38106), even though any difference between this and *Bugle Call Rag* is undetectable. Still it has a different title. Furthermore, the composer credits listed on the Riverside reissue go to Snyder, Pettis, and Brunies. Schoebel isn't even mentioned. On subsequent recordings his name always appears, but his cocomposers vary. For example, on the Eddie Lang record the names appear as Pettis—Mills—Schoebel, and on another side by Dicky Wells's Orchestra as Pettis—Schoebel—Myers. Other combinations can probably be found, but the important point is that Kinkle, in his biography of Schoebel, credits him with cocomposing *Bugle Call Rag*. None of this explains why Schoebel was given no composer credit on the original record by the Rhythm Kings. But the odds are that he had a hand in writing the tune, because he went on to establish a fairly successful career as a songwriter and did very well with *Nobody's Sweetheart; Prince of Wails;* and *Hot Aire*. Kinkle also credits him with *House of David Blues; Spanish Shawl; Everybody Step;* and *Ten Little Miles from Town,* but although these enjoyed a modest success in their time, they are hardly among the well-remembered tunes of yesterday.

Schoebel was primarily a jazz pianist and bandleader, and his reputation is mainly based on these pursuits, with his compositions more in the way of supplementing them than a major effort. Nevertheless, many a songwriter with a far more prolific output would be happy to claim the durable standards we've mentioned. Schoebel was born in East St. Louis on September 8, 1896, and got his early experience in music playing piano for silent movies and touring for several years as an accompanist in vaudeville. In 1920 he began to work around Chicago and joined the Rhythm Kings in 1922.

Elmer Schoebel died in December 1970.

Ira Schuster

Pianist and songwriter Ira Schuster was born in New York City on October 13, 1889. He was educated in the public schools. He started out as a staff writer in a publishing firm and later became a publisher himself. He also wrote for films and performed on the radio. As a songwriter he always collaborated with others, including on the song that was most likely his first successful one, *Ten Little Fingers and Ten Little Toes*. On this 1921 entry, lyric writers Harry Pease and Johnny White shared credit, and Schuster and Ed G. Nelson are listed as composers of the melody. Popular records were made by Irving Kaufman on Columbia and Billy Murray and Ed Smalle on Victor.

In 1930 Schuster worked with Joe Young to produce a waltz that enjoyed considerable airtime on radio and sold well on sheet music and music rolls. The song was *I'm Alone Because I Love You*. Then two years later, Schuster and Young teamed with Little Jack Little on a tune that is probably their most famous, *In A Shanty in Old Shanty Town*. The song was a reasonable success in 1932, with records by Ted Lewis, Singin' Sam, and Ted Black and inclusion in the movie *The Crooner,* as sung by Teddy Joyce. But in 1946 Johnny Long and his band made a record for Decca of the song, chanting a parody of the lyrics, and it became a favorite on jukeboxes around the country. The revival made the song a standard.

Still working with a team, in 1933 Schuster combined with Little Jack Little and Dave Oppenheim on *Hold Me*. The title had been used before, but the song was a pleasant offering in a year of many such, and it was recorded by Eddy Duchin, then at the height of his popularity, and Ted Fio Rito. Years later, Peggy Lee revived it on Capitol. Quite a few more years went by, and in 1945 Schuster, with Dave Cavanaugh and Larry Stock, published *Did You Ever Get That Feeling in the Moonlight?* Perry Como posed the question on record, and so did Russ Morgan and His Orchestra. Other compositions by Schuster are *The Navy Took Them Over, and the Navy Will Bring Them Back; I Am an American; Hats Off to MacArthur; Dance of the Paper Dolls;* and *Let's Grow Old Together*.

Ira Schuster died in New York City on October 10, 1945.

Arthur Schwartz

One of our most prolific composers, Arthur Schwartz was born in Brooklyn, New York, on November 25, 1900. His education included B.A. and LL.D. degrees from New York University, and an M.A. from Columbia University, from which he graduated Phi Beta Kappa. In the twenties he taught English in New York high schools and from 1924 to 1928 he practiced law. In the meantime, although he had little formal musical training, he began to compose for Broadway musicals, working with lyric writer Howard Dietz. They were moderately successful, and in 1929 Schwartz began devoting his time to composing. Instant success came with the music he wrote for "The Little Show," especially the hit song *I Guess I'll Have to Change My Plan,* and a brilliant career was off to a great start.

Writing mainly for Broadway shows, with occasional digressions to compose for movies or for the London stage, Schwartz compiled an impressive list of quality songs, many of them hits. His early efforts were mainly collaborations with Howard Dietz, but in later years he also worked with Dorothy Fields, Frank Loesser, Johnny Mercer, Ira Gershwin, Ed Hyman, Leo Robin, Al Stillman, and Oscar Hammerstein II. Although he composed songs well into the sixties, with an occasional hit here and there, it's fairly safe to say that his best-known songs were written in the thirties—most of them with Howard Dietz. Then too, as usually is the case, many of the songs while important in the context of a show or movie, never became popular in the mainstream of public approval. But there is something else to keep in mind. In the thirties, and into the early forties, dance bands and singers leaned heavily on stage and movie musicals for material, so the general public got to hear and appreciate it. With the advent of rock this changed, and the songs no longer got the exposure they once did. Thus a composer like Arthur Schwartz, while still turning out quality songs, went largely ignored. Nevertheless, he contributed a number of outstanding songs to the library of American standards.

The two big songs for Schwartz in 1930 both had English origins. *Something to Remember You By,* with American lyrics by Howard Dietz, started out in a London musical, "Little Tommy Tucker," as *I Have No Words to Say I Love You.* With the new words it was introduced by Libby Holman in the Broadway production of "Three's a Crowd." She sang it to a sailor who sat with his back to the audience during the entire performance. An unknown at the time, the sailor was the future movie star Fred MacMurray, who was doubling as a saxophone player in the "California Collegians," the stage band in the show. Holman recorded the song for Brunswick, and it didn't hurt the tune that it was coupled on the record with *Body and Soul,* the Johnny Green hit from the same show. Leo Reisman's orchestra recorded it for Victor, Jimmie Noone made it for Vocalion, and Sam Lanin made it on Hit-of-the-Week. Ziggy Elman revived it on a Bluebird recording in 1939, and Claude Thornhill played it in a Gil Evans arrangement on a Columbia disc in 1942. The other 1930 title, *She's Such a Comfort to Me,* claimed a quartet of lyric writers, Douglas Furber, Max Lief, Nathaniel Lief, and Donovan Parsons, and was introduced by Jack Hulburt in the English stage production of "The House That Jack Built." Another Jack—Buchanan—introduced it in this country in the show "Wake Up and Dream." It received excellent radio play in that year of dearth in recordings.

Dancing in the Dark is undoubtedly the big Schwartz and Dietz hit of 1931. It was in the stage show "The Band Wagon," sung by John Barker and danced to by Tilly Losch. It surfaced again as the title song of a movie, *Dancing in the Dark,* in1949 as performed in song and dance by Betsy Drake. Fred Astaire and Cyd Charisse danced to it in the movie of *The Band Wagon* in 1953. Artie Shaw's band had a million-selling record in 1941. It has been recorded many times both here and abroad. *I Love Louisa* was also in "The Band Wagon" and followed the same path as *Dancing in the Dark* in subsequent productions. The third hit tune from the show was *High and Low.* It was played as an instrumental in the movie of "The Band Wagon" in 1953.

"Flying Colors," a 1932 stage musical with one of those legendary casts—Clifton Webb, Patsy Kelly, Tamara Geva, Buddy and Vilma Ebson, Imogene Coca, Larry Adler, and Philip Loeb—offered a trio of songs by Schwartz and Dietz, all hits: *Louisiana Hayride; Alone Together;* and *A Shine on Your Shoes.* Artie Shaw had another big record on the Bluebird label in 1939 of *Alone Together. A Shine on Your Shoes* was introduced in "Flying Colors" by the Ebsons, Monette Moore, and Larry Adler. Fred Astaire danced to it in the movie *The Band Wagon.* I recall hearing a radio program with Fred Waring and his Pennsylvanians making a production number out of *Louisiana Hayride.* The song had a "down home" appeal that fit well to such groups.

Trouble in Paradise, which came out in 1933, is something of an oddball in the Schwartz roster of titles. First of all, it was a freelance offering. Secondly, Schwartz shares composing credit with Milton Ager. And third, the words were written by Ned Wever. Nevertheless, it was well received, with records by Ted Weems, Charley Agnew, Freddy Martin, and Walter Feldkamp. One more thing—this was the only song by Schwartz published in 1933. "Revenge With Music," a 1934 Broadway musical, opened on November 28, and ran for 158 performances. The Schwartz and Dietz score included *You and the Night and the Music* and *If There Is Someone Lovelier Than You.* The melody of the first title was first heard as background music for a nighttime radio serial, *The Gibson Family.* Libby Holman and George Metaxa sang it in "Revenge with Music." In the 1953 movie *The Band Wagon,* it was sung by a chorus. Now a standard, it has been played and recorded countless times. *If There Is Someone Lovelier Than You* also began on *The Gibson Family.* George Metaxa sang it in "Revenge with Music."

In 1933, Edward Hyman provided the words to the Schwartz melody for *After All You're All I'm After,* which was sung by John Beal in the play "She Loves Me Not" and by Bing Crosby in the musical movie version in 1934. Ray Noble recorded a sprightly rendition on HMV. *Born to be Kissed,* with lyrics by Howard Dietz and a delightful melody that has been mainly overlooked, was a 1934 entry that was used in the movie *The Girl from Missouri*. Paul Whiteman recorded it with Ramona, and Ben Selvin made it for Columbia. The best recording was by Anthony Trini's Village Barn Orchestra on Bluebird. *Then I'll Be Tired of You,* another freelance offering, had lyrics by E. Y. Harburg. A quality song, it was recorded by the bands of Isham Jones, Freddy Martin, and Ambrose and was frequently heard on radio broadcasts.

Other outstanding songs by Arthur Schwartz are *An Old Flame Never Dies; Love and Learn; I See Your Face Before Me; By Myself; They're Either Too Young or Too Old; Rhode Island is Famous for You;* and *That's Entertainment*. In addition he wrote the music for *Alibi Baby; Brother, Just Laugh It Off; I'm Afraid of You; Little Igloo for Two; Polar Bear Strut; Romany; You're the One; I've Made a Habit of You; Little Old New York; I Need You So; I Love You and I Like You; The Moment I Saw You; Right at the Start of It; Lucky Seven; Sunrise; I'll Never Leave You; New Sun in the Sky; Where Can He Be?; Hoops; White Heat; When You Love Only One; Got a Bran' New Suit; Farewell, My Lovely; Love Is a Dancing Thing; You and I Know; Seal it With a Kiss; Under Your Spell; You Have Everything; This Is It; It's All Yours; Tennessee Fish Fry; Thank Your Lucky Stars; The Dreamer; Sweet Nevada; Oh, But I Do; A Gal in Calico; Make the Man Love Me; Alone too Long; I'd Rather Wake Up By Myself; Waitin' for the Evening Train; Where You Are;* and *Before I Kiss the World Goodbye*.

Arthur Schwartz died in 1984.

Jean Schwartz

Composer-pianist Jean Schwartz was born in Budapest, Hungary, on November 4, 1878. Ten years later his family immigrated to New York, and young Jean learned to play piano from his sister. In 1902 he became an American citizen and started taking odd jobs playing piano in sheet music departments of department stores. For awhile he worked with a band in Coney Island then became a song plugger and demonstrator for Shapiro & Bernstein. Touring in vaudeville, he accompanied the famous Dolly Sisters and also teamed with William Jerome, who became his collaborator on early songs. He married one of the Dolly Sisters, Rosie.

Schwartz and Jerome began writing songs in 1899 and by 1901 were already successful, contributing material to Broadway revues. In 1903 they had their first hit, *Bedelia,* introduced in the stage musical "The Jersey Lily" by Blanche Ring. It was well recorded for the day by the Haydn Quartet on

Victor; Billy Murray, Edison; George T. Gaskin, Columbia; and Arthur Pryor's band, also on Victor. Then in 1906 came the song that is their most famous, and one that has been a standard, especially with jazz and swing bands, for many years, *Chinatown, My Chinatown*. However, the song had to wait until 1910 to become popular, and this took place after it was included in the revue "Up and Down Broadway." Eventually the song was incorporated into several movies: *Bright Lights* (1931), *Is Everybody Happy?* (1943), *Jolson Sings Again* (1949), *The Seven Little Foys* (1955), and *Young Man with a Horn* (1950). As a standard, it has been recorded through the years by dozens of bands and vocalists, including Tommy Dorsey, the Mills Brothers, Fletcher Henderson, and Louis Armstrong. Brian Rust, in his *Jazz Records, 1897–1942,* lists twenty-two records in his index.

A short time later Schwartz began working with a new pair of collaborators, Sam M. Lewis and Joe Young, and they wrote the words for a number of his best songs. In 1917 it was *I'm All Bound 'Round with the Mason–Dixon Line,* which Al Jolson recorded and promoted into a hit. It was revived by Jimmy McPartland's "Squirrels" in 1939 for Decca. In 1918 the team had a popular offering in the timely ballad *Hello, Central, Give Me No Man's Land,* also recorded and featured by Jolson. However, he got the most mileage out of *Rock-A-Bye Your Baby With a Dixie Melody,* which came out that same year and was forever after a part of his repertoire. Years later he sang it in the movie *Rose of Washington Square* (1939), *The Jolson Story* (1946), and again in *Jolson Sings Again* (1949). In the latter two, his voice was dubbed in for Larry Parks, who portrayed him on the screen. The song, however, had a career of its own. It was heard in the film *The Show of Shows* in 1929 and *The Merry Monahans* in 1944. In 1956 Jerry Lewis made it for Decca Records, and it was a best-seller for three months. Moving into the thirties, Schwartz had another new partner, Jack Meskill, who added the lyrics to *Au Revoir, Pleasant Dreams,* which became the closing theme of the popular Ben Bernie orchestra. Then in 1937 it was Milton Ager and Ned Wever with the words for one of the prettiest songs in the Schwartz library, *Trust in Me*. It did well, making the number two spot on the Hit Parade radio program and with popular records by Mildred Bailey, Wayne King, and Abe Lyman, among others. It also enjoyed a revival in 1952 on platters by Eddie Fisher, Chris Connor, Roy Rogers, and Patti Page.

A partial list of the many titles composed by Jean Schwartz is *Dusky Dudes; Rip Van Winkle Was a Lucky Man; I'm Tired; Any Old Place I Hang My Hat is Home Sweet Home to Me; I'm Unlucky; The Story Adam Told to Eve; Hamlet Was a Melancholy Dane; The Ghost That Never Walked; My Irish Daisy; My Lady of Japan; Any Old Time at All; Over the Hill and Far*

Away; The Hat My Father Wore on St. Patricks Day; I'll Make a Ring around Rosy; Upon the Hudson Shore; Sit Down, You're Rocking the Boat; I've Got Everything I Want but You; Hello, Hawaii; Why Do They All Take the Night Boat to Albany?; Lamp of Love; Cherry Blossom Lane; Whisper in My Ear; When There's No One to Love; Lotus Flower;My Rose of Spain; One Sunny Day; One Little Raindrop; If I Didn't Care; and *There's Rain in My Eyes.*

Jean Schwartz died in Sherman Oaks, California, on November 30, 1956.

Johnnie Newhall Scott

Pianist-composer Johnnie Scott was born in Dalles, Oregon, on May 11, 1907. He studied music and was educated at the University of Washington and made his way to San Francisco, where he worked as a musician in numerous locations, including the Mark Hopkins. Still later he performed as staff pianist and accompanist for Fox Studios in Los Angeles for fifteen years. Although his compositions are few in number, he worked with top lyricists Harry Ruby, Sammy Cahn, and bandleader Anson Weeks, and his songs were quality entries and well received.

In 1931 he worked with Anson Weeks and Harry Tobias to produce *I'm Sorry Dear*. It was introduced and recorded by the Anson Weeks orchestra on Columbia, and Bing Crosby sang it on the flip side of his theme song, *Where the Blue of the Night Meets the Gold of the Day*. Other records included a Victor waxing by the Lofner–Harris Orchestra (Carol and Phil), Red McKenzie on Columbia, and Jacques Renard on Brunswick. Quite a few years went by before Scott's next hit, *Maybe It's Because,* a collaboration with Harry Ruby in 1949. Another good song, it appealed to some of the top vocalists of the period. Dick Haymes recorded it for Decca; Eddy Howard and his new orchestra made it for Mercury; Connie Haines waxed it with Roy Ross's orchestra on Coral; and Marian Morgan sang it with Bob Crosby on Columbia. *This May Last Forever* was another of Scott's songs.

Johnnie Scott died in Los Angeles on July 25, 1963.

Raymond Scott (Harry Warnow)

Composer-arranger-conductor Harry Warnow, better known by his professional name of Raymond Scott, was born in Brooklyn, New York, on September 10, 1909. He received his musical education at Juilliard and in the thirties worked as a pianist in the radio orchestras of his brother Mark

Warnow, Freddie Rich, and André Kostelanetz. In 1936 he formed his first "Quintette" (actually a sextet, but Scott didn't like that word) to perform on the popular CBS radio program *The Saturday Night Swing Club*. In the following year they began to record Scott's zany compositions, and *Twilight in Turkey* was a hit and led to further instrumentals along the same line. With the death of Mark Warnow, Scott took over as conductor of the orchestra on the prestigious *Your Hit Parade* program. He also continued to record with a large orchestra, featuring a lot of his own work.

Other titles in the Raymond Scott repertoire include *Minuet in Jazz; The Toy Trumpet; War Dance for Wooden Indians; The Penguin; Egyptian Barn Dance; The Happy Farmer; In an Eighteenth-Century Drawing Room; Boy Scout in Switzerland; Siberian Sleigh Ride; Tobacco Auctioneer; Reckless Night on Board an Ocean Liner; Dinner Music for a Pack of Hungry Cannibals; Bumpy Weather over Newark; Peter Tambourine; Huckleberry Duck; Business Man's Bounce; Yesterthoughts; Pretty Little Petticoat; Copyright 1950; Enchanted Forest;* and *Magic Garden.*

Eddie Seiler

Lyricist Eddie Seiler was born in Iwonicz, Austria, on March 14, 1911. Details of his life are scarce, but when I knew him he operated an army–navy store in Rahway, New Jersey, and wrote songs in his spare time. His collaborators were mainly Sol Marcus, Bennie Benjamin, and Eddie Durham. The team's first successful song was *I Don't Want to Set the World on Fire,* which was first recorded by Harlan Leonard and His Rockets On Bluebird in 1940 but went nowhere until Tommy Tucker's band made it for the OKeh label, with a vocal by Amy Arnell. It was Tucker's biggest recording, and the song became a smash hit, making *Your Hit Parade* for fifteen weeks, four of them in the number one spot. Other successful records were made by the Ink Spots (Decca) and Horace Heidt (Columbia). And just to prove that nobody is infallible, early in the proceedings, when the writers were desperately looking for its promotion, Benny Goodman asked Fletcher Henderson to consider arranging the song for a record and Henderson turned it down as not worthy of the effort.

The success of *I Don't Want to Set the World On Fire* opened the doors of publishing houses to other songs by the team, and in 1942 they came up with the timely war ballad *When the Lights Go On Again (All Over the World).* Vaughn Monroe had a hit record on Victor, and Lucky Millinder's band made it for Decca. In addition the song got heavy radio play. Seiler, Marcus, and Guy Wood came up with another hit in 1944, *Till Then.* This was recorded by the Mills Brothers for Decca, coupled with their sensational home run, *Paper Doll. Paper Doll* sold in the millions. The record was on every jukebox in the country, and the song was on *Your Hit Parade* for twenty-three weeks. The record was so popular that jukebox play wore the *Paper Doll* side white, at which point thrifty jukebox operators turned the record over automatically exposing *Till Then* to the enviable position of being on thousands of jukeboxes sung by the still very popular Mills Brothers. It was a good song and became a hit in its own right. Eddie Seiler, Marcus, and Al Kaufman also did well with the 1947 entry *Ask Anyone Who Knows,* which had popular records by the Ink Spots (Decca), Margaret Whiting (Capitol), and Anita Ellis (Mercury).

Seiler also shared credit for *Strictly Instrumental,* a best-seller for the Harry James band in 1941, along with Marcus, Benjamin, and Edgar Battle. The Columbia platter was on the charts for three months. Other songs by Eddie Seiler include *Cancel the Flowers; Ashes in the Tray; You're Gonna Fall and Break Your Heart; Small World; Fishin' for the Moon; And Then It's Heaven; The Girl from Jones Beach; Because You Love Me; To Remind Me of You; If Every Day Would Be Christmas; It All Begins and Ends With You; You Can't Hide Your Heart;* and *Somehow Days Go By.*

Eddie Seiler died in Linden, New Jersey, on January 1, 1952.

Tot Seymour

Lyricist Tot Seymour, one of the distinguished ladies in the annals of American songwriting, was born in New York City. She was educated at Miss Ely's School and then became a staff writer for a New York publishing firm. She wrote special material for headliners Sophie Tucker, Fannie Brice, Mae West, and Belle Baker. For awhile she was under contract to Paramount Pictures and also wrote scripts and songs for radio. Her career as a lyric writer began in earnest in 1930 and spanned the decade. During that time she collaborated with a bevy of top writers, primarily Vee Lawnhurst, but also J. Fred Coots, Jesse Greer, Pete Wendling, and Jean Schwartz.

Her name was on three good songs in 1930: *I Miss a Little Miss; Swingin' in a Hammock;* and *Good Evenin'*. The first title, written with J. Fred Coots, was a popular radio selection and also rated good coverage on recordings by Ben Selvin (Columbia), Seger Ellis (Columbia), Roy Smeck (Melotone), and Nick Lucas (Brunswick). Of the three, *Swingin' in a Hammock* was the biggest hit. Seymour shared lyric credit with Charles O'Flynn on this one, and Pete Wendling was the composer. The song was heard frequently on radio broadcasts and was recorded by Guy Lombardo's orchestra, Leo Reisman, and Chick Bullock. *Good Evenin'* was a collaboration with Al Hoffman and Charles O'Flynn. A very pretty song, it gained respectful treatment by Rudy Vallee, Guy Lombardo, Freddie Rich, and Ambrose. Only one title came out in 1931, *On the Beach with You,* words by Seymour, music by Jesse Greer. Ozzie Nelson had a good record on Brunswick, and Johnny Hamp made it for Victor. Smith Ballew, under his favorite alias, Buddy Blue, made it for Crown.

In 1935 Seymour shifted into high gear, writing a collection of hit songs with Vee Lawnhurst, all of them successful, and starting a mutually beneficial association. *Accent On Youth,* a quality song, was the title tune of the movie starring Herbert Marshall and Sylvia Sidney. Duke Ellington recorded it, with Johnny Hodges featured in a solo; and the short-lived but influential band of Orville Knapp had a good recording. *And Then Some,* a tune that emphasized Seymour's lyric cleverness, was a hit record for Ozzie Nelson's band on Brunswick. Bob Crosby made it for Decca, and Joe Reichman for ARC.

No Other One, a bouncy ballad, got appropriate treatment by Putney Dandridge on Vocalion, Bob Crosby for Decca, and Little Jack Little on Columbia. *When the Leaves Bid the Trees Goodbye* was recorded by Dick Messner's band, and Victor Young made *An Evening in June* for Decca.

It was an auspicious start for the team, and they continued to turn out hit songs. In 1936, for the "Ziegfeld Follies," they contributed *You Don't Love Right,* and Hal Kemp's band recorded it for Brunswick. Then in quick succession they offered *Cross Patch; Please Keep Me in Your Dreams; Us On a Bus; What's the Name of That Song?; The Day I Let You Get Away;* and *The Bride Comes Home.* Hal Kemp's band made records of the first and last titles. *Cross Patch* was waxed by Louis Prima on Brunswick and by Willie Bryant for Bluebird. The romantic *Please Keep Me in Your Dreams* got nice treatment from Billie Holiday on Vocalion, Al Donahue's orchestra on Decca, and George Hall, with Dolly Dawn on the vocal, for Bluebird. *Us On a Bus* was delineated with glee by Fats Waller for Victor, with more restraint by Rudy Vallee for ARC, and by Shep Fields on Bluebird. *What's the Name of That Song?,* possibly the biggest hit of them all, frequently played on radio broadcasts, was recorded by Ozzie Nelson on Brunswick and Bob Crosby on Decca.

Boyd Bunch shared composing credit with Seymour and Lawnhurst on *The Day I Let You Get Away.* Woody Herman sang it with the Isham Jones band on Decca; Tommy Dorsey's Clambake Seven made it with Edythe Wright on Victor; and Jack Shilkret made it for Brunswick. *Alibi Baby* came out in 1937, with Seymour working with Edward Heyman on the lyric to the music by Vee

Lawnhurst. Dolly Dawn recorded it for Vocalion; Tommy Dorsey's Clambake Seven, with Edythe Wright, for Victor; and Mal Hallett's band, with a vocal by Teddy Grace, for Decca. Other Seymour titles include *A Cabana in Havana; Watchin' the Trains Go By; Pretending You Care; Arlene; I'm Making Hay in the Moonlight;* and *Sunday Go To Meetin' Time.*

Tot Seymour died in New York City on August 31, 1966.

Bob Shafer

Singer, songwriter, and music publisher Bob Shafer was born in New York City on July 24, 1897. He was educated at the Holy Name School. During his career he worked as a staff writer for a music publisher and performed as a singer on radio with his wife. He is credited with a number of songs, but his most important are the 1923 entry *Walk, Jennie, Walk,* written with Henry Creamer and Sam Wooding, and *Louisiana,* a collaboration with Andy Razaf and J. C. Johnson.

Walk, Jennie, Walk, a favorite of jazz bands, was well represented on contemporary recordings by the Original Memphis Five, the Cotton Pickers, and others, but it was elevated to the category of a jazz standard by Horace Henderson's arrangement for the Benny Goodman band in 1936. *Louisiana,* now a standard, got off to a sensational start with the 1928 Paul Whiteman recording that featured Bing Crosby and the Rhythm Boys (Harry Barris and Al Rinker) and Bix Beiderbecke on cornet. Bix recorded it a year later with his Gang on OKeh. A quality song, it has received respectful treatment through the years on records by Toots Mondello, Count Basie, Duke Ellington, Pete Dailey, and Pete Kelly's Big Seven (Matty Matlock), among others. Other titles by Bob Shafer include *Calling Sweetheart for You; Sonya; Tell Me Why You and I Should Be Strangers; Some Other Bird Whistled a Tune;* and *Midnight Moon.*

Bob Shafer died in New York City on September 28, 1943.

Terry Shand

Terry Shand was an accomplished pianist and a better than average vocalist who also wrote songs. He was born in Uvalde, Texas, on October 1, 1904, and started his professional career playing piano in silent movie houses. Later he led his own dance band, which pioneered early radio broadcasts. As a native Texan he was an early associate of Jack Teagarden's when they both played in the band of the legendary pianist Peck Kelley in the twenties. Moving on to New York in the early thirties he had a brief association with Rudy Vallee and then began a long tenure as pianist and vocalist with Freddy Martin's orchestra. He can also be heard playing jazz piano on a series of recordings made for Decca in 1934 under the revived name New Orleans Rhythm Kings and in the company of such stalwarts as Muggsy Spanier, Wingy Manone, Sidney Arodin, George Brunies, Eddie Miller, and Red McKenzie. A few years later he organized his own band, recording a number of sides for Decca from mid-1938 to early in 1942.

Shand wrote a fairly extensive library of songs, two of which became outstanding hits. *My Extraordinary Gal,* one of the better entries in the highly competitive year of 1931, was his first published work and an instant hit. This was followed in 1937 by *I Double Dare You,* also a respectable success. However, although he continued to publish a series of tunes well into the fifties, none were the equal of the first two. He did fairly well with *Cry, Baby, Cry* in 1938 and *Why Doesn't Somebody Tell Me These Things* in the same year, but while all the later entries were good, they met with indifferent acceptance.

His other songs include *I'm Gonna Lock My Heart and Throw Away the Key; Dance With a Dolly; What's the Matter with Me?; If You're Ever Down in Texas Look Me Up; You Don't Have to Be a Baby to Cry;* and *If There's Anybody Here (From Out of Town).*

Shand also wrote the Freddy Martin theme, *Bye-Lo-Bye Lullaby,* and the Al Donahue theme, *Low Down Rhythm in a Top Hat.*

James Royce Shannon

Composer, writer, and producer James Royce Shannon was born in Adrian, Michigan, on April 13, 1881. A multitalented man, he organized his own theatrical company and toured the United States and Europe. Afterwards, he managed a chain of music stores and helped produce weekly shows for the Majestic Theater in Detroit. As if this wasn't enough, he wrote special material for vaudeville acts and dance numbers for Pavlova. He also functioned as a drama critic for the *Detroit Free Press.* As a songwriter his reputation is based on two songs that have become classics in American music, *Too-Ra-Loo-Ra-Loo-Ral (That's an Irish Lullaby)* and *The Missouri Waltz.*

Too-Ra-Loo-Ra-Loo-Ral was published in 1914 with words and music by Shannon and was introduced by Chauncey Olcott. Thirty years later Bing Crosby sang it in the movie *Going My Way,* and his subsequent recording for Decca sold over a million copies. This time it made *Your Hit Parade* and became established as a song that everybody knows. *The Missouri Waltz* was published with lyrics by Shannon in 1916. The melody, composed by Frederick Knight Logan, had been previously published in 1914 as based "on an original melody procured by John Valentine Eppell." It achieved a degree of permanence when it was adopted as the state song of Missouri but moved into still greater prominence as the favorite song of President Harry Truman. Truman often played it on the piano for guests at the White House. Other songs by Shannon are *Aloha Sunset Land; My Dream of Yesterday; Just an Old Sweetheart of Mine; Mary Was a Real Nice Girl; Raise a Little Army of Your Own; There Is a Red Bordered Flag in the Window; Spanish Rose;* and *Climbing the Stairway of Love.*

James Royce Shannon died in Pontiac, Michigan, on May 19, 1946.

Ted Shapiro

Pianist, composer, and publisher Ted Shapiro was born in New York City on October 31, 1899. After graduating from high school, he began a career in vaudeville, accompanying stars like Nora Bayes and Eva Tanquay, and then as arranger and musical conductor for Sophie Tucker, a function he performed from 1921 to 1966. In the meantime, he composed popular songs and opened his own publishing firm in Miami, Florida. Without any question, the best-known song by Ted Shapiro is the all–time favorite standard *If I Had You.* It was originally published in England by Campbell and Connelly (who promptly put their names on it as cowriters), and it became very popular. Imported to the States, it was immediately adopted by Rudy Vallee, who recorded it and plugged it on his radio programs. Musicians liked the song, and it continued to be played over the years and developed into a standard. It had already reached this status when the Benny Goodman Sextet recorded it on October 18, 1941. They made two takes, and the second one was issued on OKeh 6486. It created a mild sensation due to the wonderful piano chorus by Mel Powell. The alternate first take was later issued on an Epic LP.

In 1936 Shapiro teamed with Sammy Lerner and Jack Lawrence on the quirky *Sittin' in the Sand A-Sunnin',* and it rated good recordings by Johnny Johnson, Shep Fields, and Guy Lombardo. Then in 1939 Shapiro and Benny Davis reached an amicable agreement with bandleader Tommy Dorsey, and the result was two hit songs, *To You* and *This Is No Dream.* The Tommy Dorsey orchestra recorded them both for Victor with vocals by Jack Leonard. *To You* was also recorded by Glenn Miller, Paul Whiteman, and

Al Donahue. The Jimmy Dorsey band joined the parade in waxing *This Is No Dream,* and Horace Heidt made it too.

A Handful of Stars, one of the prettiest ballads of the 1940 selections, is credited to Jack Lawrence and Shapiro, and Robert Lissauer, in his *Encylopedia of Popular Music in America,* relates the story of how it came about. As mentioned earlier, Shapiro was the longtime accompanist of Sophie Tucker. He was performing that function for Tucker one night during an appearance at Manhattan's Copacabana when Jack Lawrence was in the audience. His attention was caught by a two-bar melodic strain that Shapiro used as a filler, and with Shapiro's permission he developed the original thirteen notes into a complete song. A popular entry, it made the rounds of the record labels, with platters by Glenn Miller, Artie Shaw, Jimmy Dorsey, and Ina Ray Hutton. *Far Away Island* was a Benny Davis–Ted Shapiro collaboration in 1946. It was recorded by the bands of Claude Thornhill and Skitch Henderson. Other Ted Shapiro songs include *He's Home for a Little While; Winter Weather; Now I'm in Love; You'll Be Reminded of Me; Starlight Souvenirs; Time; Dog on the Piano; Puttin' On the Dog;* and *Ask Anyone in Love.*

Artie Shaw (Arthur Arshawsky)

Clarinetist, composer, bandleader, and author Artie Shaw was born in New York City on May 23, 1910. He grew up in New Haven, Connecticut, studied music, and by the age of fifteen was already playing local jobs in dance bands. An excellent musician and an exceptional clarinetist, he worked with most of the top bands during the twenties and early thirties, including radio and recordings, and learned arranging. In 1937 he organized a swing band that recorded for Bluebird and rose to almost instant popularity with a record of *Begin the Beguine,* arranged by Jerry Gray. Shaw went on to organize and lead several fine bands until his retirement in the fifties. He has written several books, produced shows for stage and screen, and was featured with his band in the 1941 movie *Second Chorus,* which starred Fred Astaire and Burgess Meredith.

Shaw's composing efforts were mainly instrumentals designed to showcase his band, but he is also responsible for some very pretty ballads. *Free Wheeling* and *The Chant* were both written in 1937 and recorded by Shaw's first band for Brunswick. This also applies to *Nightmare,* the band's theme, and *Any Old Time.* Both titles were better sellers on Bluebird after the release of *Begin the Beguine,* and *Any Old Time* became a classic for the Billie Holiday vocal. *Back Bay Shuffle* was another successful instrumental in 1938, and in the following year Shaw collaborated with trumpeter Charlie Shavers on *Pastel Blue,* which Shaw recorded for Bluebird. In 1943 Don Raye added lyrics to the melody, and as *Why Begin Again* it became a popular song. It was recorded by Shaw on Victor and by Tommy Dorsey as well. Dick Todd made it for Victor too.

In 1940, now leading a larger orchestra with strings, Shaw combined with Johnny Mercer on another ballad, *Love of My Life*. It was sung by Fred Astaire in the film *Second Chorus,* and Shaw had a very successful record on Victor, with the vocal by Anita Boyer. The song was nominated for an Academy Award. That same year Shaw composed one of his most swinging titles, *Who's Excited,* another successful recording for his band. In 1944 Shaw wrote still another instrumental, and this was recorded by his "Gramercy Five." The tune was *Summit Ridge Drive,* and the record was well received. It did even better when it was reissued during the recording strike of 1943–1944 and is considered one of the great recordings of all time.

Other compositions by Artie Shaw include *Non-stop Flight; Man From Mars; Prelude in C Major; Scuttlebutt; Mysterioso; The Gentle Grifter; Crumbun; Hop, Skip and Jump; Traffic Jam; One Night Stand; Let's Walk; I Ask the Stars; Sad Sack; Monsoon; Concerto for Clarinet; Comin' On; Easy to Say; Moonray; Whispers in the Night;* and *If It's You.*

Larry Shay

Pianist, composer, arranger Larry Shay was born in Chicago, Illinois, on August 10, 1897. He was educated at the Bush Conservatory of Music. During World War I he organized an orchestra and entertainment unit. Later, he became a musical director for MGM and then a program director for NBC in New York. Although the list of his published songs is not very long, it includes some very popular titles, along with a few that have become standards. All were published in the five-year span between 1925 and 1930.

There were two entries in 1925, *Tie Me to Your Apron String Again* and *I'm Knee Deep in Daisies (And Head Over Heels in Love)*. Joe Goodwin was the lyricist on these. The first title resulted in records by Bailey's Lucky Seven and Jack Chapman's orchestra in 1925 and two more sides in 1926 by the orchestras of Gus Kahn and Jack Linx. *I'm Knee Deep in Daisies* rated treatment by George Olsen and His Music, with the vocal duet by Fran Frey and Bob Rice. In 1935, exactly ten years after it was published, Chick Bullock recorded the *Apron* song for ARC. The next year went by fallow, but there were three Shay songs in 1927, and all did well. *Highways Are Happy Ways* still sounds good as played by the Ted Weems band on a contemporary recording for Victor. The song was a collaboration with Harry Harris and Tommy Malie. The other title did even better. *Everywhere You Go,* written with Joe Goodwin and Mark Fisher, enjoyed some airtime when it was first published but indifferent attention on records. In 1949 it was revived and recorded for Decca by Guy Lombardo, with the maestro's usual Midas touch. Singer Doris Day also had a good record for Columbia. The third title, *Beautiful,* with words by Haven Gillespie, is unique for being the first single recorded by future star Dick Powell.

Charles Tobias and William Jerome wrote the words for the 1928 Shay composition *Get Out and Get under the Moon,* Paul Whiteman had the big record. Helen Kane sang it with Nat Shilkret's orchestra. Both records were for Victor. But the *Moon* song appealed to a lot of people, and other sides were made by the California Ramblers, singers Beth Challis and Annette Hanshaw (she made it twice), Red Nichols, Sam Lanin, and Noble Sissle. *Who Wouldn't Be Jealous of You,* another collaboration with Haven Gillespie, came out in 1929. It was recorded by the bands of Coon–Sanders, Sam Lanin, Ray Miller, and the California Ramblers.

When You're Smiling (The Whole World Smiles with You) is without question the most important song in the Larry Shay collection. It was written with Mark Fisher and Joe Goodwin. However, there is some confusion regarding the publishing date. Roger Kinkle gives it as 1930, Robert Lissauer as 1928. However, the recording that launched the song into immortality, by Louis Armstrong, was issued in September of 1929. King Oliver recorded it on Victor in 1930. Among the host of sides made since are renditions by Teddy Wilson, Cab Calloway, and Clyde McCoy. The tune became the title song for the 1950 film *When You're Smiling,* and Frank Sinatra sang it in the movie *Meet Danny Wilson* in 1952.

Other songs by Larry Shay include *You're in Kentucky, Sure As You're Born; Too Tired; That's Georgia; I'd Love to Call You My Sweetheart; Gee, But I'd Like to Make You Happy; Our Old Home Team; In the Light of the Stars; Don't Cross Your Fingers, Cross Your Heart; Love Me Sweet and Love Me Long; It Takes So Long to Say Goodbye; The Fly Flew Faster Than the Flea;* and *There's a Ranch in the Sky.*

Al Sherman

Songwriter Al Sherman, who wrote both lyrics and music, depending on the need, was born in Kiev, Russia, on September 7, 1897. His education included attendance at the Gymnasium in Prague and private music study. In

1911 he came to the United States and for a time played piano in silent movie houses and for music publishers. From this he moved into writing for Broadway revues and then for Hollywood movies. His first hit song, *Save Your Sorrow (for Tomorrow),* was published in 1925. He composed the music and Buddy DeSylva wrote the words. It was recorded by the popular Ray Miller orchestra and by the pioneer crooner Gene Austin.

Gene Austin had a hit record on another Al Sherman song the following year. The clever lyric for *(Ho, Ho, Ha, Ha) Me Too* was a collaboration between Sherman and Charles Tobia (*his* first hit song), with music by Harry Woods. Paul Whiteman also had a popular recording. In 1927 Sherman and a handful of fellow writers turned out a cluster of titles: *Everything's Made for Love; A Siren Dream; Lindbergh, the Eagle of the U.S.A.;* and *On a Dew-Dew-Dewy Day*. In 1928 he and Al Dubin wrote *I Must Be Dreamin'*. None of these were big hits, but they all enjoyed a brief span of popularity.

In 1929 Sherman began writing for the movies, and with Al Lewis—who would become his most important collaborator—penned the lyrics to a melody by Abner Silver. The song, *He's So Unusual,* was introduced by Helen Kane in the film *Sweetie*. She also recorded it, and so did Annette Hanshaw and Vaughn DeLeath, also the Meyer Davis orchestra. But bigger and better things were still to come. In 1930 the movie was the Maurice Chevalier epic *The Big Pond,* and this time Sherman wrote the music and Al Lewis the words for *Livin' in the Sunlight, Lovin' in the Moonlight*. Chevalier sang it in the picture and also recorded it. Other sides were made by the bands of Ben Bernie and Paul Whiteman. In 1931 the film was Eddie Cantor's *Palmy Days,* which introduced *(Potatoes are Cheaper, Tomatoes are Cheaper) Now's the Time to Fall in Love*. In that gloomy year of the Great Depression it wasn't easy to find something good to say about life, but Sherman and Lewis managed to do it. In 1946 Eddie Cantor sang the song for the soundtrack of *The Eddie Cantor Story,* and his voice was dubbed in for Keefe Brasselle, who portrayed him in the picture.

Writing for the movies didn't stop Sherman from turning out freelance entries, and in this category he and Al Lewis teamed with Con Conrad for *Nine Little Miles from Ten-Ten-Tennessee,* which Duke Ellington recorded; *Ninety-Nine Out of a Hundred (Wanna Be Loved),* introduced and recorded by Rudy Vallee (a Sherman–Lewis tune); and *You Gotta Be a Football Hero*. On the latter, Sherman and Lewis were abetted by Buddy Fields. The bands of Ben Bernie and Harry Reser had fun with it. As the thirties decade moved into high gear, so did Sherman and Lewis. In 1934 they penned the quirky *Over Somebody Else's Shoulder*. Then, reverting to collaborating with a wider field, Sherman teamed with Jack Meskill and Abner Silver on the popular hit *On the Beach at Bali Bali* in 1936 and with Murray Mencher and Charles Newman for *Take Another Guess*. The bands of Chick Webb and Benny Goodman had successful sides on that one. *The Mood That I'm In,* a beautiful ballad with words by Abner Silver and melody by Al Sherman, came along in 1937 and was given deferential treatment by the musical groups of Teddy Wilson, Lionel Hampton, and Dick McDonough, among others.

Sherman continued to write into the forties and fifties and had a successful entry in 1946 with *Pretending,* a collaboration with Marty Symes. Andy Russell had the big record, backed by Paul Weston's orchestra. Other songs by Sherman include *I Must Be Dreaming; Promises; Got the Bench, Got the Park; Isn't It a Shame; No, No, a Thousand Times No; Somebody Cares for You; Every Now and Then; Hypnotized; One Night in Monte Carlo; It's Like Reaching for the Moon; Darling, Not Without You; On a Little Bamboo Bridge; When the Organ Played "Oh Promise Me"; Roses Remind Me of You;* and *Woodland Reverie*.

Al Sherman died in Los Angeles, California, on September 15, 1973.

Manning Sherwin

Composer Manning Sherwin was born in Philadelphia, Pennsylvania, on January 4, 1902. He was educated at Columbia University and then went on to write for musical revues in New York and London. Although the list of his compositions isn't long, it includes some quality and very popular songs. Sherwin wrote the music for *Lovely One* in 1937. Frank Loesser wrote the words, his first song for the movies. It was used as a production number in the 1938 musical "Vogues of '38." Frank Loesser was also the lyricist for a Manning Sherwin–Arthur Altman melody, *I Fall in Love With You Every Day,* featured in the 1938 film *College Swing*. It was introduced in the movie by Florence George and John Payne and was recorded on all the major labels. Larry Clinton made it for Victor, with the vocal by Bea Wayne; Jimmy Dorsey recorded it for Decca, with Bob Eberly singing; the delightful Dolly Dawn waxed it with George Hall's orchestra for Vocalion; the Horace Heidt crew did it for Brunswick; and Abe Lyman obliged for Bluebird.

Sherwin's biggest song came out in 1940, the very popular *A Nightingale Sang in Berkeley Square*. This time the words were by Eric Maschwitz, and the song was featured and introduced in the London production of "New Faces." The Glenn Miller band had the best-selling record, vocal by Ray Eberle; but Guy Lombardo, with brother Carmen singing, was close behind.

The most musical recording was by Ray Noble on Columbia, with Larry Stewart. Sammy Kaye also recorded the song, with Tommy Ryan for Victor. Other songs by Sherwin are *Who's Taking You Home Tonight?; Music for Romance; The Moment I Saw You; Wrap Yourself in Cotton Wool; His Servant;* and *She Came Rolling Down the Mountain.*

Manning Sherwin died in Los Angeles, California, on July 26, 1974.

Ren Shields

Pioneering songwriter Ren Shields was born in Chicago, Illinois, on February 22, 1868. As a very young man he performed as a song-and-dance man in minstrel shows. Later on he sang with the Empire City Quartet in vaudeville. After four years of this, he teamed with Max Million in a vaudeville act and toured with it from 1894 to 1897. During this time he wrote material for other acts.

In 1900 Shields went to New York City and began to write songs, several of them with George "Honey Boy" Evans. Probably the most famous of these was published in 1902, *In the Good Old Summertime*. It was introduced by Blanche Ring in the theater musical "The Defender," and in its initial go-round sold over a million copies of sheet music. Many years later it became the title song of a Judy Garland–Van Johnson movie, *In the Good Old Summertime*. Shields and Evans tried to repeat their success in the following year and came close with *In the Merry Month of June*. Shields introduced the song himself in vaudeville.

In 1906 Shields reversed his role and composed the music for the hit *Waltz Me Around Again, Willie ('Round, 'Round, 'Round).* Will D. Cobb wrote the words. Blanche Ring introduced the tune in the stage musical "His Honor, the Mayor." Billy Murray and the Haydn Quartet had the hit record on Victor. Shields was back writing lyrics in 1908, and with Kerry Mills produced another popular vaudeville favorite, *The Longest Way 'Round Is The Shortest Way Home*. If the logic here seems vague, it may help to know the song was about "spooning" in that new-fangled invention, the automobile. Shields explored another mode of transportation in that same year, collaborating with Percy Wenrich on *Up in a Balloon*. Apparently both songs were successful, because two years later Shields and the Leighton Brothers, a vaudeville team made up of brothers Bert and Frank, combined on *Steamboat Bill*. Like *In the Good Old Summertime,* this one will most likely always be with us.

Ren Shields died in Massapequa, New York, on October 23, 1913.

Nat Shilkret

Nat Shilkret, conductor, composer, and classical clarinetist, is a personage well known to anybody even slightly interested in the history of popular music, phonograph records, and radio. He was born in New York City on December 25, 1895, educated at Bethany College, and studied privately with Henius, Hambitzer, and Floridia. At age thirteen he was already playing clarinet in symphony orchestras, including the Russian Symphony, the New York Philharmonic, and the orchestra of the Metropolitan Opera House. In between he played with the concert bands of John Philip Sousa, Arthur Pryor, and Edwin Franko Goldman. In the twenties he became the music director for Victor Records and made numerous records conducting superior studio orchestras. Active in radio, he is said to have played three thousand broadcasts by the end of 1938. In 1935 he went to Hollywood, performing as an arranger, conductor, and musical director and was active in West Coast radio.

Primarily a composer of so-called "serious" music, Shilkret also wrote some popular songs of merit. One of his earliest successes was the waltz *Jeannine, I Dream of Lilac Time,* written as the theme song of the 1928 movie *Lilac Time,* which starred Colleen Moore and Gary Cooper. The lyrics were by L. Wolfe Gilbert. Shilkret had one of the most popular records of the song, and it was also waxed by Gene Austin, and John McCormack. Austin, popular singer of the twenties, also teamed with Shilkret in revising and popularizing *The Lonesome Road,* which was based on an old spiritual. Austin wrote the words. The song was dubbed onto the sound track of the first filmed version of *Show Boat* in 1929. It was also made on several successful recordings—Gene Austin and Ted Lewis, among the contemporary sides, Bing Crosby in 1935.

That same year (1929) Shilkret composed the music for *Some Sweet Day,* one of those delightful "sleepers" that never got the recognition it deserved. Lew Pollack was the lyricist, and the song was used as the theme of another non-musical movie, *Children of the Ritz,* starring Dorothy Mackail. It didn't get much attention, but Shilkret recorded it for Victor. In 1930 Shilkret wrote another waltz, *Down the River of Golden Dreams,* with John Klenner providing the lyrics, which received some nice radio play. In 1937 he and Allie Wrubel came up with *The First Time I Saw You,* which was introduced in the movie *The Toast of New York,* sung by Frances Farmer. The song did very well and rated top airplay and recording attention by the bands of Charlie Barnet, Bunny Berigan, Jimmie Lunceford, and Emery Deutsch.

Maurice Sigler

Lyricist Maurice Sigler was born in New York City on November 30, 1901. However, it appears that at a very early age he moved to Birmingham, Alabama, and was educated in the Birmingham public schools. He learned to play the banjo and worked with local dance bands, then organized his own. For three years he wrote and produced radio shows there and originated the *Uncle Remus* radio series. In 1933 he collaborated with composer Michael Cleary on *Here It Is Monday, and I've Still Got a Dollar,* probably Sigler's first published song. Rudy Vallee plugged it on his radio show and also recorded it for Columbia. Fred Waring made it for Victor.

In 1934 Sigler went to England for a three-year stay, working with Al Goodhart and Al Hoffman on British stage shows and movies. In that first year they produced half-a-dozen songs, and four of them were successful—*I Saw Stars; The Prize Waltz; Why Don't You Practice What You Preach?;* and *Little Man, You've Had a Busy Day. I Saw Stars,* a pretty song, was recorded by the bands of Paul Whiteman, Joe Haymes, and Freddy Martin. The Boswell Sisters had the hit record of *Why Don't You Practice What You Preach?* for Brunswick. Isham Jones recorded *Little Man, You've Had a Busy Day.* On the latter song Sigler and Hoffman were responsible for the words to a melody by Mabel Wayne. The title was suggested by a best-selling book by Hans Fallada, *Little Man, What Now?* Other sides were made by the Pickens Sisters, Frank Luther, and Emil Coleman. The two other titles were *Jimmy Had a Nickel* and *Your Guess Is Just As Good As Mine*.

Black Coffee was the only Sigler title in 1935, but in the following year the team of Sigler, Goodhart, and Hoffman made up for it. For the English stage show "This'll Make You Whistle," they wrote *Crazy with Love; I'm in a Dancing Mood; There Isn't Any Limit to My Love;* and *My Red Letter Day*. Jack Buchanan starred in the show and in the film remake and introduced and recorded *I'm in a Dancing Mood* and *There Isn't Any Limit to My Love*. The English bandleader Bert Ambrose had a good record of the first title, which was released in the United States, and the Gene Kardos band made *There Isn't Any Limit to My Love* for Melotone, with a vocal by Bea Wayne, one of her earliest recordings.

The team quickly followed through, and for the English movie *She Shall Have Music,* they wrote the title song and *My First Thrill*. Jack Hylton recorded *She Shall Have Music* for Victor, and Rudy Vallee made it for Melotone. Charlie Barnet waxed *My First Thrill* for the ARC labels. For the Jessie Matthews movie *First a Girl,* they contributed *Everything's in Rhythm With My Heart; Say the Word and It's Yours;* and *I Can Wiggle My*

Ears. For the film *Jack of All Trades,* they wrote *Where There's You, There's Me* and for *Come Out of the Pantry, Everything Stops for Tea*. Other Sigler songs are *There's Always a Happy Ending; If You Ever Change Your Mind; I'll Wait for You Forever; Tell Me a Story.*

Maurice Sigler died in Flushing, New York, on February 6, 1961.

Carl Sigman (Jessie Barnes, Craig Lee, Lee Burke)

Songwriter Carl Sigman was born in Brooklyn, New York, on September 24, 1909. His education included a law degree from New York University. He started writing songs, both words and sometimes the music, in the late thirties. During his career, which spanned the forties, fifties, and into the sixties, he collaborated with a number of composers and lyricists and has an impressive list of successful songs to his credit in almost every category—ballads, novelties, rumbas, polkas, and foreign adaptations. During World War II he was in the 82ND Airborne Division and earned the Bronze Star and six Combat Stars. He wrote *The All-American Soldier,* the official marching song of the 82ND Airborne.

Sigman started off big in 1940. Among others he collaborated on that year was the fine Duke Ellington composition *All Too Soon*. Originally introduced and recorded by the Ellington orchestra, it has been recorded many times since and like most of Ellington's music is now a standard. That same year, Sigman worked with composer-arranger Jerry Gray, and the result was the sensational Glenn Miller orchestra hit *Pennsylvania 6-5000,* a song based on the telephone number of the Hotel Pennsylvania where the band was playing. Recorded on Bluebird, the song sold over a million and is still identified with the Miller legend. And as if that wasn't enough, Sigman and Ralph Freed dreamed up the words to *Love Lies,* a ballad by Joseph Meyer, and it went the rounds of the record labels. Tommy Dorsey made it for Victor, with Frank Sinatra singing; Larry Clinton, with the vocal by Terry Allen, did it for Bluebird; the OKeh version was by Gene Krupa's band with Howard Dulany; the Mills Brothers were on the Decca entry, along with one by Frances Langford; and Sammy Kaye, with Tommy Ryan, recorded it for the new label, Varsity.

Oddly enough, no hits resulted for the next couple of years, and then Sigman decided to become a soldier. But he was back in 1946, teaming with Eddie DeLange and Joseph Meyer on *Passé,* which was recorded by Tex Beneke and Ray McKinley and their new orchestras and also as a vocal by Margaret Whiting. Then, with Peter DeRose, he wrote *Put That Kiss Back Where You Found It,* picked by Benny Goodman as a vehicle for one of his rare vocals. Neither tune made any great stir, but Sigman did better by adding lyrics to an instrumental composed by harpist Robert Maxwell and violinist-bandleader Matty Malneck. Originally recorded by its composers as a concerto in two parts for Columbia in 1946, the year of publication, it received Sigman's words in 1964 and became the hit song *Shangri-La.* It was then recorded by several vocal groups. Sarah Vaughn recorded *If You Could See Me Now,* another entry for 1946. Tad Dameron wrote the music.

In 1947, for the stage show "Angel in the Wings," Sigman and Bob Hilliard composed four successful songs: *The Big Brass Band from Brazil; Civilization (Bongo, Bongo, Bongo, I Don't Want to Leave the Congo); The Thousand Islands Song (I Left My Love on One of the Thousand Islands);* and *Once Around the Moon. The Big Brass Band from Brazil* was introduced by the company in the revue and was recorded by Jack Smith with Frank DeVol's orchestra for Capitol. The Art Mooney Orchestra made it for the M-G-M label, and it sold very well because it was coupled with *I'm Looking Over a Four-Leaf Clover,* the old Harry Woods perennial that was enjoying a revival. Arthur Godfrey got a lot of mileage out of *The Thousand Islands Song,* both on his radio program and his recording for Columbia. Johnny Mercer made it for Capitol. Peggy Lee waxed *Once Around the Moon,* also for Capitol. But *Civilization,* the clever and satiric jab at modern living, drew the most attention. Danny Kaye had a big-selling record on Decca with the Andrews Sisters, closely followed by the RCA–Victor side by Louis Prima's orchestra. It was also recorded by Ray McKinley, Woody Herman, and Jack Smith with Frank DeVol. The collaboration between Hilliard and Sigman was unusual to the extent that Sigman wrote the music, Hilliard the lyrics. This also pertained to *Careless Hands,* the popular entry for 1948, which resulted in chart records for Mel Tormé (with Sonny Burke's orchestra on Capitol), Sammy Kaye with Don Cornell on RCA-Victor, and Bing Crosby on Decca.

Sigman scored big a number of times as the years went by. In 1950 he had four big sellers: *Enjoy Yourself (It's Later Than You Think),* words by Herb Magidson, music by Sigman, and a hit for the Guy Lombardo orchestra with a vocal by Kenny Gardner; *It's a Marshmallow World,* as interpreted by Bing Crosby; *My Heart Cries for You;* and *Crazy She Calls Me.* Sigman changed horses again, writing the lyrics to *It's a Marshmallow World,* with the melody by Peter DeRose, and working both sides of the action for *My Heart Cries for You,* with Percy Faith. The latter was a million-seller for Guy Mitchell with Mitch Miller's orchestra on Columbia and apparently the first time DeRose attempted an adaptation. The melody was a reworking of an old French folk song, *Chanson de Marie Antoinette.* Dinah Shore and Vic Damone also had big records. The fourth title, *Crazy She Calls Me,* with lyrics by Bob Russell and a Sigman melody, was a hit for Billie Holiday on Decca.

It's All in the Game, published in 1951, featured words by Sigman to an old song called *Melody,* written in 1912 by future vice president Charles Dawes. Tommy Edwards recorded it in 1951 and rerecorded it in 1958. The second time around made the big strike, and the song was the number one hit of the year. *Ebb Tide,* a hit in 1953, was another song that began life as an instrumental by harpist Robert Maxwell. It was recorded by an assortment of people. In England, Frank Chacksfield's British orchestra made it for London, Vic Damone for Mercury, and Roy Hamilton for Epic. In 1960 the Platters recorded it for Mercury, and the Righteous Brothers had a top ten record in 1966. *Dream Along With Me (I'm On My Way To a Star)* was not only Perry Como's theme song, it was a Sigman composition in its entirety, both words and music. Needless to say, Perry Como had the best record.

Other songs by Carl Sigman are *Please Come Out of Your Dream; Busy as a Bee; Cherry Blossoms on Capitol Hill; Peekaboo to You; Let's Give Love a Chance; Matinee; My Fair Lady; If it Were Easy to Do; The Blossoms on the Bough; Hop Scotch Polka; Sarong; Twenty-Four Hours of Sunshine; The Story of My Life; River of Smoke; The Breeze Is My Sweetheart; If You Turn Me Down; The Chesapeake & Ohio; No One But You; Beautiful Music to Love By; There's Always My Heart; Did Anyone Call;* and *Why Does It Have to Be Me?*

Frank Signorelli

Pianist, composer, and bandleader Frank Signorelli was born in New York City on May 24, 1901. He attended public schools and studied music with his cousin Pasquale Signorelli. Early in his career he was a member of the pioneering Original Dixieland Jazz Band, following which he organized the Original Memphis Five, which went on to make numerous recordings, not only under that name, but also as Ladd's Black Aces, the Cotton Pickers, etc. Considered one of the finest exponents of the new music called jazz, Signorelli was much in demand, recording with many of the stars of the twenties, including Bix Beiderbecke and Joe Venuti. In the late thirties he recorded with Paul Whiteman's "Swing Wing."

Signorelli's composing efforts were often tinged with a jazz feeling, and as such they appealed to jazz musicians. Two of his earliest compositions were recorded into jazz history by the Dorsey brothers, Jimmy and Tommy, as individual solo efforts. In 1929 Tommy Dorsey made a record for the original OKeh label under the name of Tom Dorsey and His Novelty Orchestra. The others in the little studio unit were Frank Signorelli, Eddie Lang, and Stan King. They recorded two songs, one of which, *You Can't Cheat a Cheater,* was a Signorelli composition. Tommy Dorsey played it as a trumpet solo. A group still using the name of the Original Memphis Five, with Signorelli and both Dorseys, recorded *Anything* for Columbia in 1931, featuring Jimmy Dorsey on the alto saxophone.

Signorelli also maintained a close relationship with the jazz violinist Joe Venuti, recording a number of records with Venuti's Blue Four. On June 10, 1931 they recorded a composition called *Little Buttercup,* a collaboration between Matty Malneck and Signorelli, as an instrumental. With lyrics added by Gus Kahn, it was published in 1932 as *I'll Never Be the Same,* one of the many fine songs that came out that year. Mildred Bailey sang it on the Paul Whiteman record for Victor, and the side was also released on an experimental long-playing record. Other contemporary sides were made by Adelaide Hall on Brunswick, Guy Lombardo on Brunswick, and Adrian Schubert on Crown. The song has seen increased appreciation through the years and is now a standard. More recent recordings have been made by Artie Shaw, Teddy Wilson, Ziggy Elman, Phil Napoleon, and Paul Weston. In that same year Matty Malneck and Signorelli combined on another excellent song, *So at Last It's Come to This,* with Gus Kahn again contributing the words. The Whiteman band recorded it, with Matty Malneck directing and the vocal by Irene Taylor. So many good songs came out that year, this one seemed to get lost in the crowd.

Signorelli, trombonist Vincent Grande, and clarinetist Jimmy Lytell all took credit for the melody published in 1935 as *A Blues Serenade*. Mitchell Parish wrote the words. Another outstanding song, it was adopted as a theme song in 1937 by Henry King and His Orchestra, and they also recorded it for Decca. Other records were made by Bing Crosby, backed by Matty Malneck's Orchestra; Duke Ellington; and Johnny Hodges; all made in 1938. Matty Malneck and Signorelli composed an instrumental suite they called *Park Avenue Fantasy,* and the Malneck orchestra recorded it in two parts for Columbia. Mitchell Parish added words, and as *Stairway to the Stars* it became one of the top songs of 1939, with twelve weeks on *Your Hit Parade,* four of them in the number one spot. In this it was assisted with records by Glenn Miller, Sammy Kaye, Kay Kyser, and Al Donahue, plus sides by Martha Raye and Kenny Baker. Since then it has been recorded many times.

Other songs by Frank Signorelli include *Gypsy; And Then Your Lips Met Mine; Fool That I Am; Big Town; Love; Sioux City Sue; Midnight Reflec-*

tions; A Lover's Fantasy; A Serenade to You; Goin' Nowhere Fast; Waltzing With a Dream; Bonnie's Boogie; and *Rockin' the Bass.*

Abner Silver

Abner Silver was a native New Yorker, born in Manhattan on December 28, 1899, and began his songwriting career in 1920. He was a graduate of NYU Law School, became a dance band pianist, and then—as so many songwriters did—went to work for a song publisher, ultimately becoming one himself. He had a fairly good hit with Harry Woods in the 1921 stage show "Bombo," which starred Al Jolson, a tune called *I'm Goin' South;* and in the following year did even better with *Angel Child,* composing the melody for lyrics by Georgie Price and Benny Davis, which was featured in another show, "Spice of 1922." (If you are a fan of the Glenn Miller band, you may remember this as one of Glenn's early recordings for Bluebird, B–107967.)

Silver did fairly well in 1923 with a tune called *Bebe,* with words by Sam Coslow, dedicated to silent film star Bebe Daniels, and in succeeding years achieved enough recognition to have his songs recorded by some of the best dance bands in the country. *Barbara* was recorded by Ted Weems, and *Bashful Baby* is one of the classic Ben Pollack sides with Goodman, Teagarden, and McPartland. The Isham Jones band was one of many to record *I Hate Myself,* a 1931 song, and Bert Ambrose's orchestra had a hit side with the 1932 entry, *Pu-leeze, Mr. Hemingway! Farewell to Arms* was the title song of a very successful movie in 1933, and in that golden period of the thirties when superior songs were the rule rather than the exception, Silver contributed some very good ones: *Isn't It a Shame; There Goes My Heart; Every Now and Then; Hypnotized;* and *Chasing Shadows.* As the decade passed the midway point, he had two respectable hits, *For Sentimental Reasons* and *On the Beach at Bali Bali.* He continued to write prolifically until 1960, including songs for three Elvis Presley movies, but most likely he will be remembered for his earlier compositions.

Abner Silver died in New York City on November 24, 1966.

Nat Simon

Nat Simon—composer, pianist, bandleader—was born in Newburgh, New York, on August 6, 1900. After high school he led his own orchestra, playing local dates, and then went to New York City, where he went to work as a pianist for publishing firms and as an accompanist to singers. In 1938 he went to London to write for British films. He began writing songs in the midthirties and had a successful song in 1935 in collaboration with Sammy Mysels and Billy Hueston, *Throwin' Stones at the Sun.* It rated considerable attention on recordings from the orchestras of Joe Haymes (Melotone), Benny Goodman, with the vocal by Helen Ward (Columbia), Freddy Martin (Brunswick), Willie Bryant (Victor), Archie Bleyer (Vocalion), and Bob Howard (Decca).

In 1938 Simon teamed with Ray Bloch and Al Stillman for *In My Little Red Book,* which was recorded by Dick Powell, by the Ted Weems band with Perry Como, and by the Original Dixieland Jazz Band. And in that same year he worked with Charles Tobias to produce *Is That the Way to Treat a Sweetheart.* Amy Arnell, singing with the Tommy Tucker Orchestra, had a good record. Simon had two good songs in 1940. *Crosstown* was written with Jimmy Cavanaugh and John Redmond and was recorded by the bands of Glenn Miller, on Bluebird, and Dick Jurgens, on OKeh. Only Jimmy Cavanaugh helped with *Goody Goodbye,* a swinging little ditty that appealed to Dolly Dawn, who recorded it for Vocalion, and Perry Como, who sang it with Ted Weems for Decca. The Smoothies did the same for Bluebird, backed by a Hal Kemp unit; and the Gray Gordon orchestra recorded it for Victor. In 1943 Buddy Bernier wrote English lyrics to the Simon melody of *Poinciana (Song of the Tree).* Featured as an instrumental by the David Rose Orchestra on Victor, it resulted in a best-selling record, followed closely by another by Benny Carter's band and a vocal version by Bing Crosby. Others to record it were George Shearing, Steve Lawrence, the Four Freshmen, and Tex Beneke.

Other titles by Nat Simon include *A Million Miles Away; I'm in Love; Every Single Little Tingle of My Heart; And Still No Luck With You; There's a Platinum Star in Heaven Tonight (Jean Harlow); Little Lady Make Believe; Among Those Sailing; The Shabby Old Cabby; The Gaucho Serenade; Little Curly Hair in a High Chair; Don't Make Me Laugh; Wait for Me, Mary; There's a Lot of Moonlight Being Wasted; No Can Do; The Old Lamplighter; And Mimi; Sweet Heartaches;* and *Her Bathing Suit Never Got Wet.*

Nat Simon died in New York City on September 5, 1979.

Seymour R. Simons

If you're old enough to remember the thirties and were an avid radio listener and dance band fan in those days (as most people of excellent taste but moderate means were), you may remember hearing broadcasts from the Midwest by Seymour Simons and His Orchestra. Simons always managed to organize very listenable and musical groups and enjoyed a fine reputation in the areas around Chicago and Detroit. But bandleading was only one of the talents of Simons, who was a genuine triple-threat man in the music business. He was also a prolific songwriter, with many all-time and prestigious hits to his credit, and in his later years became a booking agent and record company executive.

Simons was born in Detroit on January 14, 1896, and died there on February 12, 1949, but in between those dates he had a very productive career and made a number of high quality contributions to the American song treasury. One of these is his famous collaboration with Gerald Marks, *All Of Me;* another is one of practically everybody's favorites, *Honey,* written with Haven Gillespie aiding on the lyrics and music by Richard Whiting. In addition is the standard *Breezin' Along With the Breeze,* with the same writers, and one of my favorites, *Tie a Little String Around Your Finger*. Like many other songwriters, he took advantage of the fantastic market for quality songs that opened up with the advent of the thirties. He had a respectable hit in *Sweetheart of My Student Days,* with lyrics by Gus Kahn, which got a considerable lift from the hit-maker of those years, Rudy Vallee. Hal Kemp's band, with the inimitable Skinnay Ennis, made a poignant cry out of *Sweet Misery of Love* in 1936 (BR 7711). Not as well known as the foregoing, but enjoying considerable success when they were published, are *The One I Love Can't Be Bothered With Me; Wasn't It Nice; Now That Summer Is Gone;* and *It's the Little Things That Count.*

Simons started his career early in the century, collaborating with the stage star Nora Bayes on two songs for her Broadway musical in 1918, "Ladies First." Three years later he wrote the score for another one of her shows, "Her Family Tree." In the early twenties he wrote material for variety shows in London and Paris, following which he came back to the United States and organized his first dance band. In 1928 he disbanded and became a booking agent but reorganized another band in 1931 and continued to work with it until 1937. Unfortunately, like many fine bands of the Depression years, when radio had temporarily ruined the record market and record companies were going broke in quick succession, it never recorded. Nevertheless, Seymour Simons succeeded in leaving behind a legacy that will assure him of a respectable niche in the musical hall of fame—some very beautiful and enduring songs.

Louis C. Singer

Composer–arranger Louis Singer was born in New York City on February 26, 1912. His education included Columbia University, New York University, and Juilliard. During his career he performed as an arranger on CBS staff, and for publishing houses, including Chappel and Schirmer.

His work as a composer is memorable for two outstanding songs, *One Meat Ball* and *Sleepy Serenade. One Meat Ball,* with lyrics by Hy Zaret, was published in 1945, and was based on an old song, *One Fish Ball.* It was introduced and recorded by folk artist Josh White. It was also recorded by the Andrews Sisters, coupled with *Rum and Coca Cola,* and the pair sold in the millions.

Sleepy Serenade, a gently moving ballad, had lyrics by Mort Greene but was played and recorded as an instrumental by the orchestras of Claude Thornhill (Columbia), and Woody Herman (Decca). The Andrews Sisters sang it in the movie *Hold That Ghost,* accompanied by Ted Lewis and his band, and they also recorded it for Decca.

Among other titles by Louis Singer are *The Lass With the Delicate Air; If I Had a Ribbon Bow; Night Whispers;* and *Strange Interval.*

Louis Singer died in Forest Hills, New York, on December 10, 1966.

Noble Sissle

Bandleader–lyricist Noble Sissle was born in Indianapolis, Indiana, on July 10, 1889. He was educated at Butler College and in his early years toured with the Thomas Jubilee Singers. For two years he paired with Eubie Blake as a vaudeville team and then joined Jim Europe's band, the Hell Fighters, during World War I. After Jim Europe's death he took over as leader. Later on he organized his own band and toured Europe and the United States. His credits as a lyric writer are primarily tied to his association with composer Eubie Blake, especially the songs they wrote for the 1921 stage musical "Shuffle Along." Of these, the biggest hit was *I'm Just Wild About Harry,* which was sung by the chorus. In 1939 the song was used in two movies, *Babes in Arms,* with Mickey Rooney and Judy Garland, and *Rose of Washington Square,* which starred Alice Faye, with Louis Prima and his band. Still later it was included in the films *Broadway* (1942), *Is Everybody Happy?* (1943), and *Jolson Sings Again* (1949). In 1975 Tammy Grimes performed it in the stage musical "A Musical Jubilee." When Harry Truman was running for president, it was adopted as his campaign song.

Other songs from the show "Shuffle Along" include the title song; *Love Will Find a Way;* and *Bandana Days.* Eubie Blake recorded the last title for Victor in 1921. Sissle didn't get around to it until 1937, when he waxed it for the short-lived Variety label. Other titles by Noble Sissle are *Gypsy Blues; Hello, Sweetheart, Hello; Goodnight, Angeline; Slave of Love; Low-down Blues; Characteristic Blues; Yeah, Man;* and *Okey Doke.*

Sunny Skylar (Selig, Sydney, Shaftel)

Singer and songwriter Sunny Skylar was born in Brooklyn, New York, on October 11, 1913. He attended public schools and graduated from Madison High School. He started writing songs in 1935 and from 1937 to 1945 was active as a band vocalist with Abe Lyman, Ben Bernie, Paul Whiteman, Ted Lewis, and Vicent Lopez. After that he performed as a single in nightclubs. Skylar enjoyed his primary success in the forties. In 1941 he published *Just a Little Bit South of North Carolina,* sharing credit with Bette Cannon and Arthur Shaftel. Gene Krupa's band had the best record, made for OKeh. Then in 1942 he worked with arranger George Williams and pianist Chummy MacGregor, both members of the Glenn Miller band, and they turned out the classic *It Must Be Jelly 'Cause Jam Don't Shake Like That*. The Miller band recorded the tune, but it wasn't released by RCA–Victor until the following year.

That same year Skylar wrote his first lyric to a Mexican song, *Besame Mucho,* written by Consuelo Velasquez, who also wrote the original Spanish words. The song became a hit. Jimmy Dorsey had the big record, with the vocal by Kitty Kallen and Bob Eberle on Decca. Andy Russell made it for Capitol, and Abe Lyman for Hit. In 1944 the tune was included in the film *Follow the Boys*. Recognizing a good thing, Skylar again turned out the English lyric for another Mexican song, *Amor,* in 1944. Ricardo Lopez Mendez wrote the Spanish version, and the music was composed by Gabriel Ruiz. It was introduced by Ginny Simms in the movie *Broadway Rhythm* and was another bestseller for Bing Crosby on Decca. Other sides were made by Andy Russell (Capitol) and Xavier Cugat (Columbia). In 1946 it was heard in still another movie, *Swing in the Saddle*.

Gotta Be This or That, with both words and music by Skylar, came out in 1945 and is unique for being chosen by Benny Goodman for one of his rare attempts to vocalize. In spite of that, he had the best-selling record. Sammy Kaye made it for Victor, and Glen Gray waxed it for Decca, with Billy Daniels singing. Then, in that same year, Skylar and the popular disc jockey Martin Block combined on *Waitin' for the Train to Come In*. Peggy Lee made it for Capitol as her first recording as a single; and the bands of Harry James and Johnny Long also had sides. Skylar wrote both words and music for *I'd Be Lost Without You,* in 1946. It rated good records by the bands of Frankie Carle and Guy Lombardo.

In 1952 Skylar returned to Mexico, penning English words for a melody by Maria Teresa Lara. Originally called *Noche De Ronda,* it became *Be Mine Tonight*. Les Baxter had the best-selling record for Capitol. Bill Farrell made it for M-G-M.

Other songs by Sunny Skylar include *Hair of Gold, Eyes of Blue; It's All Over Now; Don't Wait Too Long; You'll Always Be the One I Love;* and *Love Me With All Your Heart.*

Chris Smith

Pianist-composer Chris Smith was born in Charleston, South Carolina, on October 12, 1879. He was a member of a vaudeville and nightclub act with Edgar Bowman and wrote special material for other acts as well as his own. His best-known composition is the standard *Ballin' the Jack,* with words by Jim Burris. The 1913 song was introduced by the vaudeville song and dance team of Billy Kent and Jeannette Warner. Prince's orchestra had a contemporary recording on Columbia. In 1914 it was featured in the touring company of the stage musical "The Girl from Utah." In more recent incarnations it was performed by Gene Kelly and Judy Garland in the film *For Me and My Gal* (1942), by Danny Kaye in *On the Riviera* (1951), and by Dean Martin in *That's My Boy* (1952). In 1938 Eddie Condon and His Band recorded *Ballin' the Jack* as a jazz instrumental for Milt Gabler's Commodore label, and it has since become a jazz standard, often heard at jazz concerts and festivals and recorded many times since.

Smith had two other songs that were very successful in their time. *Down Among the Sugar Cane,* with lyrics by Avery and Hart and Cecil Mack sharing credit for the music, was published in 1908; that same year Cecil Mack penned the words to Smith's melody for one of Bert Williams's famous orations, *You're in the Right Church, But the Wrong Pew.* Other titles by Smith are *Good Morning, Clarrie; He's a Cousin of Mine; Constantly; Never Let the Same Bee Sting You Twice; All In Down and Out; Beans, Beans, Beans; Down in Honky Tonk Town;* and *Come After Breakfast.*

Chris Smith died in New York City on October 4, 1949.

Ezekial L. G. Smith

See Stuff Smith.

Harry Bache Smith

Lyricist-librettist Harry Bache Smith was born in Buffalo, New York, on December 28, 1860. He was educated in both public and private schools in Chicago. Early in his career he worked as a reporter for the *Chicago Daily News* and then as a music critic. For the *Chicago Tribune,* he was a drama critic. He started writing for shows in 1887 and collaborated with many of the most famous composers, among them Reginald DeKoven, Victor Herbert, Jerome Kern, Raymond Hubbell, Robin Hood Bowers, Ted Snyder, and Sigmund Romberg. His output through the years until 1932 was prolific. Besides writing lyrics and librettos, he also wrote fiction, magazine articles, and adaptations of foreign operettas. Not many of the songs he wrote are well known, although they were important in the productions they were written for. Nevertheless, a number of them are familiar standards.

Smith was associated with two hit songs in 1921. *Bright Eyes,* a sprightly melody by Otto Motzan and M. K. Jerome with lyrics by Smith, was popular that year but was recorded as an instrumental by Paul Whiteman and Leo Reisman. Then Smith and Francis Wheeler combined on the words to Ted Snyder's classic *The Sheik of Araby,* inspired by the Rudolph Valentino movie *The Sheik.* A song favored by jazz musicians, it has never quite died out and is still heard frequently. In 1922 Eddie Cantor sang it in the stage musical "Make It Snappy," and in 1942 it was revived in the film *Tin Pan Alley.*

Dancing Fool, by the same composing team, came out in 1922. It was recorded on a contemporary side by the Club Royal Orchestra on Victor. This was another title rescued from oblivion by Eddie Condon, who recorded it in 1940 for Milt Gabler's Commodore label. It is now considered part of the jazz repertoire. In 1926 Smith wrote the libretto for the Broadway production of the Viennese operetta "Countess Maritza," which included the song *Play Gypsies, Dance Gypsies,* with music by Emmerich Kallman. The hit song of the show, it was recorded for Victor by Paul Whiteman in a "Countess Maritza Medley."

In 1931 Smith wrote an English lyric to the Franz Lehar song *Yours Is My Heart Alone.* Imported from Austria, the song was originally called *Dein ist Mein Ganzes Herz,* with words by Ludwig Herzer and Fritz Lohner. It was introduced by Richard Tauber in Germany. In the United States it was featured and recorded by James Melton, Frank Munn, and the Jack Hylton orchestra. Later records were made by Glenn Miller, Jan August, and Everett Marshall. Other songs by Smith include *Brown October Ale; Gypsy Love Song; Romany Life; Strollers We; The Kissing Bug; The Queen of Bohemia; De Cake Walk Queen; There Once Was an Owl;* and *You Belong to Me.*

Harry Bache Smith died in Atlantic City, New Jersey, on January 1, 1936.

Richard B. (Dick) Smith

Richard B. Smith was born in Honesdale, Pennsylvania, on September 29, 1901. He was educated at Penn State University, where he was editor in chief of the college newspaper, *Pennsylvania State Froth*. He wrote all the lyrics for the college theater productions. As a songwriter his reputation is mainly based on the words he wrote, or cowrote, for three well-known songs, *Winter Wonderland; The Breeze (That's Bringing My Honey Back to Me);* and *When a Gypsy Makes His Violin Cry*.

Winter Wonderland, published in 1934 with words by Smith and music by Felix Bernard, is one of those lucky songs that is revived every Christmas season and has become a perennial. Contemporary recordings of it were made by Ted Weems, Archie Bleyer, and Richard Himber, but it also received considerable radio promotion. It was also played in the 1944 film *Lake Placid Serenade*. Still later, Guy Lombardo and the Andrews Sisters had a hit record for Decca in 1950. In the meantime, it has been performed and recorded by every singer and bandleader who ever played a Christmas show. In that same year, Smith, Tony Sacco, and Al Lewis published the catchiest song they ever wrote, *The Breeze (That's Bringing My Honey Back to Me)*. Well played on the radio, where the most important exposure came in 1934, it was also recorded by the Dorsey Brothers, Anson Weeks, and Henry King. Anthony Trini's orchestra had a good record for Bluebird.

The third title, *When a Gypsy Makes His Violin Cry,* is another one of those "committee" songs, with Smith, bandleader Frank Winegar, and Jimmy Rogan sharing credits for the words to a melody by another bandleader, Emery Deutsch. Emery Deutsch recorded the song and also used it as the theme for his orchestra, helping to popularize it. Enric Madriquera recorded it for Victor and the Pickens Sisters for Columbia. Other titles by Richard B. Smith include *Slumbertime along the Suwanee; I Thrill When They Mention Your Name; Early to Bed; Me and My Wonderful One; Windmill Willie; The Bluebirds are Singing a Blues Song; Campus Moon; Under a Ceiling of Stars;* and *Half a Mile to Honeysuckle Lane*.

Richard B. Smith died in New York City on September 28, 1935, just one day before his thirty-fourth birthday.

Stuff Smith (Ezekial Leroy Gordon Smith)

Violinist-composer-bandleader Stuff Smith was born in Portsmouth, Ohio, on August 14, 1909. He took violin lessons from his father, who taught him in an unorthodox manner. He went on to perfect a style of playing that featured a strong, vibrant tone and a swinging sense of time, a highly original approach to the instrument unlike any other. During the twenties, Smith toured with the Aunt Jemima revue then joined the Alphonse Trent orchestra. After two years with Trent he worked briefly in New York with Jelly Roll Morton then organized an entertainment combo of his own. With trumpeter Jonah Jones in the lineup, they opened at the Onyx Club on New York's 52nd Street in 1936 and were an immediate success.

During this period Smith and Jones composed and featured the novelty *I'se a Muggin'*. Through the thirties Smith continued to play top locations. In 1938 he composed the music for the popular ballad *It's Wonderful.* Mitchell Parish contributed the lyrics, and the song won favor with many of the top recording artists of the era, including Louis Armstrong, who made it for Decca; Red Norvo, with a telling vocal by Mildred Bailey on Brunswick; Benny Goodman with Martha Tilton for Victor; Maxine Sullivan for Vocalion; Bob Crosby on Decca; and Shep Fields for Bluebird. A quality song, it has survived and is still being heard and played. Not as well known but musically outstanding is the surprisingly introspective and beautiful *My Thoughts,* an original that Smith recorded for Varsity in 1939. It was then picked up and issued on Commodore by Milt Gabler. Other titles by Smith are *You's a Viper; Desert Sands; Skip It; Time and Again; Midway; Stop, Look; Would You Object?; Blues for Jane; I Wrote My Song;* and *Blow, Blow, Blow.*

Stuff Smith continued to tour and perform until his death. He died in Germany on September 25, 1965.

Ted Snyder

It's a safe bet that most people are well acquainted with the old jazz standards *Who's Sorry Now* and *The Sheik of Araby,* but it would be a real long shot to bet they could also name the man who wrote them. Ted Snyder is the man's name, and he was one of the pioneers of Tin Pan Alley in the early years of the twentieth century. Snyder was born in Freeport, Illinois, August 15, 1881. He started out as a club pianist in Chicago then migrated to New York, where he started writing songs. He established his own publishing firm, the Ted Snyder Publishing Company, in 1908. He is credited with being the man who gave Irving Berlin his start. He hired Berlin as staff pianist for his publishing company and then went on to collaborate with him on writing songs. Eventually, Berlin became a partner in the company.

Most of Snyder's compositions are only familiar to collectors of very early recordings, but at least one other, besides the two standards we've mentioned, has achieved immortality. This is *Dancing Fool,* a 1922 composition resurrected by that connoisseur of long-forgotten melodies, Milt Gabler, for a Commodore recording by Eddie Condon and His Band. This particular Condon gang included Marty Marsala, Pee Wee Russell, George Brunis, Artie Shapiro, and George Wettling but is most notable for the presence of the piano player, a gentleman listed on the label as "Maurice" but, as most everybody knows, was Fats Waller. As rendered by Fats and the other Condon redoubtables, *Dancing Fool* is a gem.

Ted Snyder died in Woodland Hills, California, on July 16, 1965.

Harold Spina

Composer Harold Spina was born in New York City on June 21, 1906. He attended Public School 45 and taught himself to read and write music. At the age of ten he was already writing songs and at fifteen was organizing a neighborhood band. In 1924 he went to work as a staff writer for publishing houses, also working as a pianist, arranger, vocalist, and writer of special material, and by the age of twenty-three was a professional songwriter.

Annie Doesn't Live Here Anymore, with a lyrical story line by Joe Young and Johnny Burke, made its debut in 1933, and the interesting words and catchy melody were a hit, both on radio and on records. For Johnny Burke and Spina it was the first big success. It was recorded by Guy Lombardo, Art Kahn, and Ramona with Roy Bargy's orchestra. In England, *Annie's* sad saga was rendered with befitting pathos by trumpeter Nat Gonella, vocalizing with Lew Stone's orchestra. In the same year the team of Young, Burke, and Spina scored reasonably well with *Shadows on the Swanee*. It received kind treatment by Isham Jones on Victor, Irving Aaronson on Vocalion, the Allen–Hawkins combination on Perfect, Paul Ash for Columbia, and Hal Kemp on Brunswick. Vocalists Irene Taylor and Ethel Waters also recorded it. All in all a very respectable representation in that Depression year.

In 1934 Spina, now working with Johnny Burke as the lone lyric writer, had three good songs: *Beat O' My Heart; It's Dark On Observatory Hill;* and *I've Got a Warm Spot in My Heart for You*. The first title drew the most attention. Ray Noble recorded it for HMV in England, and the side was released on Victor in the United States. In addition, sides were turned out by Leo Reisman for Brunswick, Smith Ballew for Melotone, Ben Pollack for Columbia, and the Pickins Sisters for Victor. Ozzie Nelson recorded *It's*

Dark On Observatory Hill, a pleasant ballad that really deserved more recognition, and Isham Jones did the usual fine job on *I've Got a Warm Spot in My Heart for You.*

My Very Good Friend, the Milkman was the Spina–Burke hit for 1935. The Dorsey Brothers orchestra made it for Decca; George Hall, with Dolly Dawn and Sonny Schuyler (also known as Sunny Skylar); and Anson Weeks for Brunswick. The song got a lot of radio play. Disc jockey Martin Block favored it.

Spina and Burke presented two very fine ballads in 1936, *So This Is Heaven* and *Too Much Imagination.* The first title was recorded by Freddy Martin and also by Richard Himber. The second got nice treatment from the bands of Al Donahue, Johnny Johnson, and Freddy Martin. Possibly both ballads may have made a greater impression at another time, but this was the year that swing was sweeping the popular field.

Around this time Spina made the customary successful songwriter's trek to Hollywood to write for the movies. In 1937, for the film *Fifty-Second Street,* he wrote five songs, all with lyrics by Walter Bullock: *I Still Love to Kiss You Goodnight; Don't Save Your Love; I'd Like to See Samoa of Samoa; Nothing Can Stop Me Now;* and *Sing, and Let Your Hair Down.* All good songs, they made little impression. The same holds true for the following year. Spina and Bullock contributed songs to several movie musicals, including two Shirley Temple pictures, but although they were entertaining features in the films, they failed to make a splash in the popular market.

It appears that Spina was busy with other endeavors for a number of years, but he was back in 1950, and with Jack Elliott writing the words, provided a hit record for Dinah Shore, *It's So Nice to Have a Man Around the House.* Then, as though not wanting to appear they were playing favorites, they did the same for Mindy Carson, and for June Hutton, both of whom did well with recordings of *Be Mine.* Spina continued to write well into the sixties. Though published, there's no doubt his songs suffered from the change in the public's musical taste.

Other songs by Harold Spina include *Irresistible; Love Dropped in for Tea; You're So Darn Charming; Now You've Got Me Doing it; The State of My Heart; You Appeal to Me; I Love to Walk in the Rain; Brass Buttons and Epaulets; How Can I Thank You?; Sing Me an Old Fashioned Song; Half Moon on the Hudson; Would I Love You?; Don't Tempt Me; Let Me Kiss Your Tears Away; The Velvet Glove; Argentine Fire Brigade; Ask Me; Till All the Stars Fall into the Ocean; The Day That the Circus Left Town;* and *I Love You (And You Love Me).*

David Stamper

Composer David Stamper was born in New York City on November 10, 1883. In his early years he worked as a pianist in a Coney Island dance hall and in music publishing houses and for several years was the accompanist for the vaudeville headliners Nora Bayes and Jack Norworth. Although he wrote prolifically for Broadway shows, mainly the Ziegfeld "Follies," only a few of his songs reached the popular market. On the other hand, a few won favor with jazz bands. For the "Follies" of 1921, Stamper and Gene Buck collaborated on *Sally, Won't You Come Back,* which was introduced in the show by Joe Schenck. It rated contemporary recordings by Ted Lewis, Nathan Glantz, and Sam Lanin and was also waxed by Joe Schenck. In later years Red Nichols revived it (1929), and so did Earl Hines (1941).

Gene Buck was again the lyric writer for the songs Stamper contributed to the "Ziegfeld Follies of 1923," a show with a fabulous cast that included Fanny Brice, Eddie Cantor, Ann Pennington, and the Paul Whiteman orchestra. Two of the songs were recorded by jazz bands of the period. *Shake Your Feet* was waxed by the Memphis Five, Fletcher Henderson, the Georgians, the California Ramblers, and by Paul Whiteman. *Swanee River Blues* was also made by Fletcher Henderson, the Georgians, and Paul Whiteman. In 1931 the New Mayfair Orchestra, directed by Ray Noble, recorded an excellent song, *Moonlight and Shadows,* with Stamper receiving sole composing credit on the HMV side. Other Stamper songs include *Jealous Moon; Beautiful Garden of Girls; My Arabian Maid; Hello, My Dearie; Some Boy; Daddy Has a Sweetheart and Mother Is Her Name; Everything Is Different Nowadays; Tulip Time; Lonely Little Melody; Lovely Lady;* and *Too Wonderful for Words.*

David Stamper died in Poughkeepsie, New York, on September 18, 1963.

Sam H. Stept

Composer Sam H. Stept was born in Odessa, Russia, on September 18, 1897, but came to this country in 1900 and grew up in Pittsburgh, Pennsylvania. He started out as a staff pianist for a local music publisher and then toured in vaudeville, accompanying stars like Jack Norworth and Mae West. From 1925 until 1930 he led a dance band at the Cleremont Cafe in Cleveland; then he organized a singing group, the Record Boys, for radio work. He began writing songs in the twenties and at the end of the decade went to Hollywood to write for the movies.

A prolific producer, Stept has three blockbuster hits to his credit—*That's My Weakness Now; I'll Always Be in Love with You;* and *Please Don't Talk About Me When I'm Gone. That's My Weakness Now* may not be among your favorite songs, but it was a smash hit in 1928 and launched the composer's career. He followed it up quickly with three good songs in 1929—*I'll Always Be in Love With You; Do Something;* and *Good Little Bad Little You,* the latter made into a minor classic by Cliff Edwards on a recording with Venuti and Lang, Columbia 1705–D. The next year he did well with a song called *Congratulations,* but better still in 1931 with the perennial *Please Don't Talk About Me When I'm Gone. Swingy Little Thingy* was recorded by Don Bestor's popular band in 1933—well before swing took the country by storm. Stept contributed two more fine titles in 1934: *London On a Rainy Night* and *I'm Painting the Town Red.* Rather appropriately, Bert Ambrose's English band had the top record on *London On a Rainy Night,* and Teddy Wilson, with Billie Holiday, assured *Painting the Town Red* a permanent niche in the classic library of recorded jazz.

Two titles from 1936 are memorable as part of the Benny Goodman output of that year, *All My Life* (a vocal by Helen Ward with the trio) and *Breakin' In a Pair of Shoes,* a feature for the full band. In 1937 the Stept entry was *Sweet Heartache,* and in 1937 it was *My First Impression of You,* providing another tour de force for Teddy Wilson and Billie Holiday. In 1942 Stept had his last big hit, *Don't Sit Under the Apple Tree,* performed by the Andrews Sisters in the film *Private Buckaroo* and recorded by them for Decca. Glenn Miller also had a big seller on Bluebird. He continued to write until 1953, but interest in good songs was tapering off by then, and they drew little attention.

Other titles by Sam Stept include *I Came Here to Talk to Joe; This Is Worth Fighting For; Comes Love; When They Ask About You; I Fall in Love With You Ev'ry Day; If You Should Love Me; On Accounta I Love You; Every Minute of the Hour; Seems Like Yesterday;* and *Prairie Fairy Tale.* His collaborators included lyricists Bud Green, Charles Tobias, Herman Ruby, Herb Magidson, Sidney Mitchell, Ned Washington, Lew Brown, Sidney Clare, and Charles Newman.

Sam H. Stept died in Los Angeles, California, on December 2, 1964.

Andrew B. Sterling

Lyricist Andrew B. Sterling was born in New York City on August 26, 1874. He began his career writing parodies for vaudeville acts and started writing songs around 1898. Most of his work was done with composer Harry Von

Tilzer, but one of his earliest songs—and one of his best known—*Meet Me in St. Louis,* was composed by Kerry Mills and published in 1905. This popular song was written in the year of the Louisiana Purchase Exposition in St. Louis. As a result it was performed by a number of vaudeville headliners. In 1944 it was revived in the Judy Garland movie *Meet Me in St. Louis* and again in the 1989 stage version of "Meet Me in St. Louis."

Sterling's association with Harry Von Tilzer began even earlier. In 1899 they collaborated on *Where the Sweet Magnolias Grow,* and in 1905 they combined on *Wait Till the Sun Shines, Nellie*. This big hit of the early 1900s has proved to be a perennial. It received a big boost in that direction in 1941, when Bing Crosby and Mary Martin sang it in the film *Birth of the Blues*. The duet was subsequently released on Decca. In the next year it was used again in the Gale Storm film *Rhythm Parade*. Then in 1952 it was the title song of another movie starring David Wayne and Jean Peters. In 1910 Sterling and Von Tilzer had another popular entry, *Under the Yum Yum Tree*. In 1912 they turned out that favorite of barbershop quartets *In the Evening by the Moonlight*. They hit twice the next year, with *On the Old Fall River Line,* Sterling sharing lyric credit with William Jerome, and *Goodbye Boys*. This time William Dillon helped with the words.

Oddly enough, the biggest hit for Sterling wasn't a Harry Von Tilzer song. This was *When My Baby Smiles at Me,* with a melody by Bill Munro. It was introduced by Ted Lewis and his band in the theater musical "Greenwich Village Follies of 1919." Lewis took credit with Sterling for the lyrics. It is recording of the song for Columbia broke sales records for the year. It became a Ted Lewis trademark, he adopted it as his theme song, and he performed it countless times for the rest of his career. The Ritz Brothers sang it in the film *Sing, Sing, Sing* (1936), and it was the title song of the film *When My Baby Smiles at Me* in 1949, as sung by Dan Dailey. In 1941 it was heard in the Abbott and Costello movie *Hold That Ghost* and again in the following year in the movie musical *Behind the Eight Ball.*

Other songs by Andrew B. Sterling include *Sleepy Valley; That's No Dream; I Wonder If She's Waiting; Strike Up the Band, Here Comes a Sailor; Down Where the Cotton Blossoms Grow; All Aboard for Dreamland; Hannah, Won't You Open That Door?; What You Goin' to Do When the Rent Comes 'Round?; All Aboard for Blanket Bay; Last Night was the End of the World; You'll Always Be the Same Sweet Girl;* and *We're Going Over*.

Andrew B. Sterling died in Stamford, Connecticut, on August 11, 1955.

Jack Stern

Composer Jack Stern was born in New York City on March 6, 1896. He attended DeWitt Clinton High School and then went to work as a song plugger and pianist for Waterson, Berlin & Snyder Music Publishers. He also worked as an accompanist in vaudeville and in a number of motion pictures, from 1925 to 1935. After 1935 he became a vocal coach. As a composer of popular songs he was most active in the thirties.

In 1934 Stern teamed with Russ Columbo and Bernie Grossman to write songs for the last movie Columbo was ever to make, *Wake Up and Dream.* The result was two lovely ballads, *Let's Pretend There's a Moon* and *Too Beautiful for Words. I Was Lucky,* a collaboration with lyricist Jack Meskill, was featured in the 1935 movie *Follies Bergere* and was introduced by Maurice Chevalier and Ann Sothern. The Dorsey Brothers Orchestra recorded it for Decca, with a vocal by Bob Crosby; Benny Goodman made it for Columbia with Helen Ward singing. *Rhythm of the Rain* was from the same picture and was recorded by the Dorsey Brothers, Vincent Rose, and Abe Lyman. Another title for 1935 was *Singing a Happy Song,* written with Jack Meskill and recorded by the mystery band of Todd Rollins.

Other songs by Jack Stern include *Au Revoir, L'Amour; When You're in Love; I'm Not Ashamed of You, Molly; When I Come Back to You; Tonight, Lover, Tonight; You Can't Lose Me; There's a Hole in the Old Oaken Bucket.*

Mel Stitzel

Pianist, composer, arranger Mel Stitzel was born in Chicago, Illinois, on January 9, 1902. He was educated in the public schools and early in his career toured the Orpheum vaudeville circuit as an accompanist. In 1923 he was a member of the famous New Orleans Rhythm Kings, the pioneering Chicago jazz band, and as such shares composing credit with the other musicians for the jazz standard *Tin Roof Blues.* In 1964 *Tin Roof Blues* was watered down and republished as *Make Love to Me,* with lyrics added by Bill Norvas and Allan Copeland. In this crippled state it became a million-record seller for vocalist Jo Stafford on Columbia. However, long before this momentous event took place, the song had become a standard and a favorite of jazz bands. In the twenties it was recorded by the New Orleans Rhythm Kings, the Memphis Five, and the Original Indiana Five, with dozens of sides made since. In the hey-day of "Nick's," the jazz club in Greenwich Village, it was used as the sign-off tune between sets. When the club had two jazz bands working, the one finishing up a set would play *Tin Roof Blues,* and the musicians starting the next set would pick up the melody as they stepped up on the bandstand and would continue it until they were all seated.

In 1924 Stitzel teamed with bandleader Art Kassel to write the popular hit *Doodle Doo-Doo,* which Kassel then adopted as his theme song. In later renditions it was recorded by Joe "Fingers" Carr on Capitol, Tiny Hill on Vocalion, and Clyde McCoy for Decca. Stitzel turned out two jazz classics in 1926. He gets sole credit for *The Chant,* which achieved immortality as recorded by Jelly Roll Morton and His Red Hot Peppers on Victor. Fletcher Henderson recorded it for Columbia, with Fats Waller in the band. That same year Stitzel collaborated again with Art Kassel, and another jazz classic was the result. This was *Jackass Blues,* which made such an impression on the contemporary jazz scene that it was recorded by practically every hot group of the time. Fletcher Henderson made it twice, once as the Dixe Stompers for Harmony and once under his own name for Columbia. Other sides were turned out by the Original Indiana Five, King Oliver, Joe Candullo, Clarence Williams, and Thomas Morris and His Seven Hot Babies.

In 1935 an all-star group under the heading of Paul Mares and His Friars Society Orchestra—a revival of the name first used by the New Orleans Rhythm Kings—recorded four titles for the original OKeh label in Chicago on January 26, a remake of a prior session from which no takes were issued. One of the titles was *The Land of Dreams,* a Stitzel composition. Other songs by Stitzel include *I'm Goin' Home* and *Bittersweet Rag.*

Mel Stitzel died in Chicago on December 31, 1952.

Larry Stock

Songwriter and music publisher Lawrence Stock was born in New York City on December 4, 1896. He was educated at Townsend Harris Hall and at Juilliard. He studied piano with Clarence Adler and composition with Percy Goetschius. Early in his career he played in dance bands and appeared in concerts. During the First World War he took part in Liberty Bond drives and then enlisted in the navy at age eighteen. As a songwriter, his output was prolific, and he collaborated with other top composers; but the list of well-known songs to his credit is short.

Blueberry Hill, written with Al Lewis and Vincent Rose, is probably his biggest hit song. It was published in 1940 and recorded by Glenn Miller, Connee Boswell, and Sammy Kaye. The song was on the Hit Parade for fourteen weeks and in the top ten on the charts. The following year Gene

Autry sang it in his movie *The Singing Hills,* and in 1949 Louis Armstrong waxed it for Decca, backed by Gordon Jenkins's orchestra. Then in 1956 Fats Domino had a million seller, the tune was again in the top ten, and Decca reissued the Louis Armstrong side, which soared to the top seller list and has since become a classic in the Armstrong library.

In 1944 Stock teamed with bandleader Russ Morgan and Jimmy Cavanaugh on *You're Nobody 'Til Somebody Loves You.* Russ Morgan recorded it for Decca, but the surprising thing was the song's popularity with country and western performers. Dean Martin gave it a second shot in 1965 with a good selling record on Reprise. *Did You Ever Get That Feeling in the Moonlight?* was the Stock entry in 1945, written with Jimmy Cavanaugh and Ira Schuster and recorded by Perry Como and the ever-faithful Russ Morgan. And this was followed early in 1946 by *You Won't Be Satisfied Until You Break My Heart.* Only Teddy Powell collaborated on this song, and it resulted in a number of successful recordings, by Les Brown, with Doris Day, on Columbia; Ella Fitzgerald and Louis Armstrong on Decca; and Perry Como on Victor. From the musical standpoint, an outstanding record was made in Denmark by the Sven Asmussin group.

Other titles by Larry Stock are *Moon at Sea; The Umbrella Man; Navajo Nocturne; If Wishes Were Kisses; Dreams of Old Hawaii; Raindrop Serenade; Tell Me a Story; I Don't Wanna See You Cryin'; With All My Heart and Soul; On the Little Big Horn;* and *Pretty Little Busybody.*

Axel Stordahl

Arranger, conductor, and composer Axel Stordahl was born in Staten Island, New York, on August 8, 1913. He was educated in the public schools and took trumpet lessons and studied arranging. In 1934 he joined the excellent Bert Block orchestra as a sideman arranger. Vocalist Jack Leonard was also in the band, which benefited from frequent radio broadcasts and a great theme song, *Moonglow.* All this came to the attention of Tommy Dorsey, who made one of his famous raids and acquired Stordahl and Leonard for his own band. Stordahl became a key arranger for Dorsey and was with him until 1943, when he left to arrange and conduct for Frank Sinatra. He performed this function for ten years and subsequently went on to do the same thing for other stars.

As a songwriter, Stordahl's contributions are not extensive, but in collaboration with Sammy Cahn and fellow arranger-conductor Paul Weston, he can claim credit for two excellent songs. In 1945 they wrote *I Should Care,* which was introduced by Robert Allen in the movie musical *Thrill of a Romance*. Frank Sinatra had a big record for Columbia, and other popular sides were made by Martha Tilton, Tommy Dorsey, and Jimmy Dorsey. In a second go-round Ralph Flanagan had a chart record in 1952, and Jeff Chandler another in 1954.

In 1946 the team of Stordahl, Cahn, and Weston repeated their success with *Day by Day,* a hit record for Sinatra and Stordahl on Columbia, closely followed by a Capitol side by Jo Stafford with Paul Weston's orchestra. Doris Day did well with the Les Brown band and also for Columbia, and Bing Crosby, with Mel Tormé and the Meltones, made it for Decca. Other titles associated with Stordahl are *Ain'cha Ever Comin' Back?; Talking to Myself About You; Night after Night; Recollections; Return to the Magic Islands; Ride Off;* and *Jasmine and Jade*.

Axel Stordahl died in Encino, California, on August 30, 1963.

Herbert Stothart

Composer Herbert Stothart was born in Milwaukee, Wisconsin, on September 11, 1885. He was educated at the Milwaukee Teachers College and the University of Wisconsin. He studied music in Europe. On his return he became a teacher in the Milwaukee schools and then at the University of Wisconsin. Although not a household name, Herbert Stothart had the good fortune or misfortune—depending on how you look at it—of collaborating with many of the most famous names in American music, including fellow composers Rudolf Friml, George Gershwin, Vincent Youmans, Harry Ruby, and George Posford. In the process, he also worked with lyric writers Otto Harbach, Oscar Hammerstein II, Clifford Grey, Bert Kalmar, Bob Wright, Chet Forrest, and Gus Kahn. Stothart's name is on some very important songs, but in almost every instance it is overshadowed by his collaborators. While he probably enjoyed the prestige of his associations, both artistically and financially, his reputation as a composer came in second best.

He started composing in 1920, writing for the Broadway stage. And in 1923,working with Vincent Youmans, Oscar Hammerstein II, and Otto Harbach, he had a hit show in "Wildflower," which included three successful songs, *Wildflower; Bambelina;* and *April Blossoms*. The title song was introduced in the show by Guy Robertson. The Ben Bernie band recorded it on Vocalion as an instrumental. The Paul Whiteman Orchestra had a big-selling record on *Bambelina*.

"Rose-Marie," starring Dennis King, was the hit stage production of 1924 and again Otto Harbach and Oscar Hammerstein II wrote the book and lyrics. Stothart shared credit for the musical score with Rudolf Friml. Included were the hit songs *Rose-Marie; Indian Love Call; The Song of the Mounties;* and *The Door of My Dreams.* The production was reincarnated twice in the movies, once in 1936 and again in 1954. The most durable song has been *Indian Love Call.* In the original stage show it was sung by Dennis King and Mary Ellis. In the 1936 movie *Rose Marie* (without the hyphen), it was a duet by Jeanette MacDonald and Nelson Eddy, and their Victor recording with Nat Shilkret's orchestra sold a million copies. In the 1954 remake, it was sung by Fernando Lamas and Ann Blyth. In 1938 it had the good luck to be coupled with *Begin the Beguine* on the sensational record by Artie Shaw's band, and in 1952 it topped sales figures again as a country and western entry by Slim Whitman.

Harbach and Hammerstein were still writing books and lyrics, and in 1926 it was for the theater musical "Song of the Flame." This time the music was by George Gershwin and Stothart. Contemporary sides of the title song were recorded by the Ipana Troubadors (Sam Lanin), Vincent Lopez, and—believe it or not—the Victor Light Opera Company. In 1928 Stothart and Harry Ruby wrote the music for the hit song *I Wanna Be Loved By You,* featured in the theater musical "Good Boy" and sung by Helen Kane, the Boop-boop-a-doop Girl. She recorded it on a hit record for Victor. In the forties, Rose Murphy, the Chee-Chee Girl, made it with her own brand of sounds. However, Helen Kane wasn't finished, and in 1950 her voice was dubbed on the soundtrack for Debbie Reynolds in the film biography of Kalmar and Ruby, *Three Little Words.* More films followed. In 1955 it was sung by Jane Russell, Rudy Vallee, and Anita Ellis in *Gentlemen Marry Brunettes*—Ellis's voice dubbed for Jeanne Crain. In 1959 Marilyn Monroe sang it in *Some Like It Hot,* and in 1975 Patrice Munsel, Lillian Gish, and Tammy Grimes yodeled it as a trio in "A Musical Jubilee."

In 1933 Stothart wrote the melody for one of the very few songs not identified with a stage production or a movie, and he did it by himself, with Gus Kahn writing the words. The song is *Sweetheart Darlin',* and it rated nice representation on records by the bands of Jack Hylton, Ted Fio Rito, and Adrian Schubert and vocalists Annette Hanshaw and Morton Downey. *The Donkey Serenade,* the 1937 big song as interpreted by Allan Jones in the movie *The Firefly,* is credited to lyricists Robert Wright and George Forrest, with music by Rudolf Friml and Stothart. It started out as a solo piano piece entitled *Chanson.* Then in 1927 words were added by Dailey Paskman, Sigmund Spaeth, and Irving Caesar, and it became *Chansonette.* With a few more modifications plus a new title and lyrics, it was introduced in the 1937 film as *The Donkey Serenade.* It has been recorded many times since and has made several reappearances in films. Stothart is also credited with the following titles: *Always You; Syncopated Heart; Baby Dreams; Cute Little Two by Four; I'll Build a Bungalow; You're Never Too Old to Learn; Look Around; Totem Tom-tom; Jungle Shadows; If He Cared; Shepherd's Serenade; Cuban Love Song; At the Balalaika;* and *Toreador Song.*

Herbert Stothart died in Los Angeles, California, on February 1, 1949.

Billy Strayhorn

Arranger, composer, and Duke Ellington's alter ego, Billy Strayhorn was born in Dayton, Ohio, on November 29, 1915. He was educated in Pittsburgh, where he studied arranging and composition. His talents in these categories were so similar to Duke Ellington's that it's sometimes difficult to tell them apart. Like Ellington's, Strayhorn's compositions were often instrumental pieces designed to showcase the Ellington orchestra, or a musician, rather than specifically written as popular songs. For the most part, they are more complicated and imaginative than the average popular song, with advanced chord changes and highly original melodic lines. Since Strayhorn worked so closely with Duke Ellington and the Ellington organization, the association is almost inseparable, and in the main, the definitive recordings of Strayhorn's work are by the Ellington orchestra or the Ellington "units" that were under the nominal leadership of Johnny Hodges, Rex Stewart, Barney Bigard, et al.

Strayhorn joined the Ellington organization in 1939 as a sometime pianist, arranger, composer, and assistant director. At first he collaborated with Ellington on pieces like *Barney Goin' Easy; Grievin';* and *I'm Checkin' Out, Go-om Bye,* and they continued to write together as time went on. Strayhorn also began to build an impressive list of original compositions. Probably the best known, because it became the band's theme song, is *Take the "A" Train,* which has been frequently recorded and played. *Satin Doll,* another Ellington–Strayhorn effort, with lyrics by Johnny Mercer, is probably next. It started out as a typical Ellington instrumental and with Mercer's lyrics went on to become a popular hit and a standard. *Lush Life,* an intricate song with both melody and lyrics by Strayhorn, is an exception to the foregoing. A very difficult song to sing, it was accorded the decisive rendition by Nat "King" Cole on a Capitol record in 1949.

Aside from these, it is obvious that Strayhorn was not too interested in writing for the popular market. His many compositions more closely resemble tone poems, the ever-shifting chords and harmonies evoking emotional moods in a way few popular songs can. With his mentor, Duke Ellington, Billy Strayhorn succeeded in creating a library of American music that is timeless. Among his other compositions are *Chelsea Bridge; Something to Live For; Passion Flower; Day Dream; Raincheck; Johnny Come Lately; Just A-Settin' and A-Rockin'; Midriff; A Flower Is a Lovesome Thing; Lotus Blossom; Blood Count;* and the wonderful *Isfahan.*

Billy Strayhorn died in New York City on May 31, 1967.

Harry Stride

Composer Harry Stride was born in Isleworth, England, on May 31, 1903. He was educated in Montreal, Canada, and then immigrated to the United States. He wrote special material for nightclub acts and during World War II toured with a USO unit. Although his composing credits are comparatively few and without any heavy hits, during the midthirties he collaborated on some quality songs that fared well in spite of the tremendous competition.

Please Handle With Care, a collaboration with F. B. Ballard, was published in that year of many great songs, 1932, and managed to get reasonable representation on records by Isham Jones, Charles "Buddy" Rogers, and Enric Madriquera. But Stride made some big ones in 1933. *Lonely Park,* a rather sad ballad, was recorded by Ted Weems. *Heaven Only Knows,* with words by Milton Drake, was waxed by Don Bestor's Orchestra and also by Will Osborne. *Bless Your Heart,* probably the most successful of the three 1933 songs, with a very catchy melody, was recorded by George Olsen on Columbia and Ernie Holst on Bluebird. Cocomposing credits went to Milton Drake and Duke Enton. In 1935 Stride offered *Me and My Wonderful One*. It didn't attract much attention, but Cleo Brown recorded it for Decca.

Other titles by Harry Stride include *A-Hunting We Will Go* and *More Than Anything in the World.*

Jule Styne

One of the most prolific and successful songwriters working in the three decades from the forties through the seventies, Jule Styne has a long series of hit shows, hit movies, and hit songs to his credit. So many, in fact, that it wouldn't be practical to review them all here, so I have selected an outstanding song or two for each year as representative of his contributions for that time and as an example of the excellent quality and craftsmanship of his music. Styne was born in London, England, on December 31, 1905. He came to the United States when he was eight years old and lived in Chicago, where he quickly attracted attention as a child prodigy on the piano. At age nine he was performing as a soloist with the Chicago Symphony. His education included the Chicago School of Music and a scholarship to Northwestern University.

In the thirties he began working with dance bands and for awhile led one himself, writing his own arrangements. In 1935 he became pianist-arranger for the Art Jarrett band in New York. Next, he tried his hand as a vocal coach and then started writing background music for movies. In the forties he began writing songs for movies and eventually stage shows, scoring successes in both. *In the Cool of the Evening* was one of Styne's earliest songs. It was introduced by Frances Langford in the film *Hit Parade of 1941* and also recorded by her for Decca. It was also heard in the movie *Is Everybody Happy* in 1943.

Styne's first big hit came in 1942. The song was *I Don't Want to Walk Without You,* and the words by Frank Loesser struck a timely note in that year when the military was taking so many men. It was introduced by Johnny Johnson in the movie *Sweater Girl.* The Harry James band had an outstanding arrangement on Columbia with the vocal by Helen Forrest, and it soared to number one on the charts. Right behind it were sides by Bing Crosby on Decca and Dinah Shore on Bluebird. The song made a second appearance in the film *You Can't Ration Love* in 1944. Twenty years later Phyllis McGuire had a hit record on Reprise; and in 1980 Barry Manilow had a successful revival on Arista.

In 1943 lyric writer Sammy Cahn started what was to become a long association with Styne on the production of a number of outstanding hits, starting off with *I've Heard That Song Before*. The song was introduced by Bob Crosby and his band in the film *Youth on Parade,* but again the outstanding record was made by Harry James with Helen Forrest on Columbia. It was a million-seller, on the charts for thirteen weeks and on *Your Hit Parade* for fifteen weeks, four of them in the number one spot. It was also nominated for an Academy Award in 1942 but lost out to *White Christmas*. In 1944 Styne and Cahn had two winners, *There Goes That Song Again* and *I'll Walk Alone*. Although both titles continued the themes established by *I Don't Want to Walk Without You* and *I've Heard That Song Before,* they were equally successful. *There Goes That Song Again* was introduced in the movie *Carolina Blues* by Kay Kyser's Orchestra, with Georgia Carroll singing, and they had a good selling record on Columbia. Other top sides were made by Russ Morgan (Decca), Sammy Kaye (Victor), and Kate Smith (Columbia). The outstanding record was by Margaret Whiting with Billy Butterfield's orchestra, since the tune was coupled with another million-seller, *Moonlight in Vermont.*

I'll Walk Alone, another nomination for an Academy Award, was introduced by Dinah Shore in the film *Follow the Boys*. She also had the number one record for Victor. Other sides, all selling well, were made by Martha Tilton on Capitol and Mary Martin for Decca. The song enjoyed a substantial revival in 1952, when it was included in the Jane Froman biographical film *With a Song in My Heart,* her voice dubbed on the soundtrack for Susan Hayward, who portrayed her in the picture. Froman recorded it for Capitol, and other records were made by Don Cornell, Richard Hayes, and Margaret Whiting.

The year was an exceptionally good one for Styne and Cahn. Joining in on the trend for songs glorifying the states, they came up with one of the best, *Poor Little Rhode Island*. It was sung by Ann Miller in *Carolina Blues*. Guy Lombardo had the best record. Then, still working the topic of separation, they penned *Saturday Night Is the Loneliest Night of the Week*. Frank Sinatra had the best seller on Columbia, backed by Axel Stordahl's orchestra. Other records were made by Sammy Kaye for Victor, Frankie Carle for Columbia, Woody Herman for Decca, and the King Sisters for Victor.

Frank Sinatra was a big factor in promoting more songs for Styne and Cahn in 1945. He introduced two of them in the movie *Anchors Aweigh, The Charm of You* and *I Fall in Love Too Easily*. The latter title won another Academy Award nomination. Still maintaining a close affinity for the national sentiment, Styne and Cahn put words and music to the happy return of servicemen after long years of separation and worry. The song was *It's Been A Long, Long Time,* and it quickly soared to the top. It was on *Your Hit Parade* for fourteen weeks, five of them in the top spot, and it provided top selling records for Bing Crosby with Les Paul's Trio on Decca and the Harry James band, with the vocal by Kitty Kallen, on Columbia, and has since attained the status of a semistandard. In 1950 it was heard in the film *I'll Get By,* a remake of *Tin Pan Alley*.

Having songs on *Your Hit Parade,* was becoming routine for Styne and Cahn, and in 1946 they did it again. This time the song was *Let It Snow! Let It Snow! Let It Snow!* It made number one on *Your Hit Parade* and then went on to become a hardy perennial that is played and heard every winter and Christmas season. Vaughn Monroe had the original big record on Victor, with other successful sides by Woody Herman for Columbia and Connee Boswell, with Russ Morgan's band, on Decca. Harry James had a swinging arrangement on Columbia of the 1947 Styne and Cahn entry *I Still Get Jealous*. The song was introduced by Nanette Fabray and Jack McCauley in the theater musical "High Button Shoes," and their rendition was released as a single on RCA–Victor. Other records were made by the Three Suns (RCA–Victor), Gordon MacRae (Capitol), Guy Lombardo (Decca), and Jimmy Dorsey (M-G-M).

Monotonous as it may seem, Styne and Cahn had another Academy Award nominee in 1947, *It's Magic*. The song was performed by Doris Day in her first picture, *Romance on the High Seas,* and her subsequent recording for Columbia was a million-seller. By this time the big bands had been supplanted by the vocalists, and other singers cashed in on the bonanza, including Dick Haymes, Gordon MacRae, Tony Martin, Sarah Vaughn, and Vic Damone. In 1962 the tune was revived by the Platters singing group on the Mercury label. Doris Day was also responsible for another hit in 1948, introduced in *Romance on the High Seas*. This was the whimsical *Put 'Em in a Box, Tie 'Em With a Ribbon, and Throw 'Em in the Deep Blue Sea*. She sang it in the movie accompanied by the Page Cavanaugh Trio and then recorded it for Columbia. Again she had a best-seller, closely followed with sides by Eddy Howard on Majestic and Nat "King" Cole on Capitol. In 1949 the long collaboration with Sammy Cahn came to an end, and Leo Robin wrote the words to *Bye Bye Baby,* introduced by Carol Channing and Jack McCauley in the stage production of "Gentlemen Prefer Blondes." Marilyn Monroe sang it in the movie version in 1953 and recorded it for M-G-M. Channing and Peter Palmer revived it in the Broadway show "Lorelie" in 1974.

Styne leaned heavily toward stage productions in the fifties and sixties. Working with Betty Comden and Adolph Green, he had two fine songs in the fifties, *Just in Time* and *The Party's Over*. Both songs were from the stage musical "Bells Are Ringing" and were repeated in the film version in 1960. In 1957 Styne and Stephen Sondheim combined on the hit song from "Gypsy," *Everything's Coming Up Roses*. In the stage production it was sung by Ethel Merman. In the 1962 movie it was performed by Rosalind Russell. The song was a reworking of a prior collaboration with Sammy Cahn called *Betwixt and Between,* meant for the musical "High Button Shoes" but rejected. Styne continued to write scores for Broadway shows through the sixties and into the seventies, sometimes with moderate successes in the popular market like *Make Someone Happy* and *Don't Rain on My Parade,* but by this time show tunes were no longer a factor in the marketplace.

The list of songs by Jule Styne is very long, but among them are *Who Am I?; Forever and Ever; Barrelhouse Bessie From Basin Street; Harlem Sandman; You're So Good to Me; Three Dreams Are One Too Many; Out of This World; As Long As There's Music; And Then You Kissed Me; Some Other Time; You Make Me Dream Too Much; I Begged Her; Guess I'll Hang My*

Tears Out to Dry; Five Minutes More; I Love an Old Fashioned Song; I'm Glad I Waited for You; The Things We Did Last Summer; You're My Girl; Papa, Won't You Dance with Me?; Time after Time; What Am I Gonna Do About You?; I Don't Care If It Rains All Night; It's You or No One; Diamonds Are a Girl's Best Friend; and *Blame My Absent Minded Heart.*

Jule Styne died in New York City on September 29, 1994.

Dana Suesse

Composer and author Dana Suesse (rhyme it with keys) was born in Kansas City, Missouri, on December 3, 1909. Her early education included attending the Sacred Heart Convent school through elementary and high school grades and intensive training as a concert pianist. At age eight she gave her first piano recital. In 1932 she performed her own *Jazz Concerto* with the Paul Whiteman orchestra at Carnegie Hall. Unsuccessful at marketing her classical compositions, she started writing for the popular market and turned out a respectable number of fine songs, especially in the thirties.

In 1931 Suesse had three hit songs: *Have You Forgotten (The Thrill)?; Ho-Hum;* and *Whistling in the Dark. Have You Forgotten,* a pleasant ballad with words by Leo Robin, was recorded by the bands of Henry Busse on Victor and Ben Selvin (as Lloyd Keating) for the Columbia subsidiary labels (Harmony, Clarion, Velvet Tone, et al). Ruth Etting made a vocal side for Perfect. *Ho-Hum* rated a classic rendition by the Gus Arnheim band on Victor, made notable by a Bing Crosby vocal. The lyric was by Edward Heyman. *Whistling in the Dark,* with words by Allen Boretz, got the usual special treatment by the Guy Lombardo orchestra on Columbia and by Rudy Vallee on Victor. All three songs were recorded on the Crown label, that faithful barometer of the best of Tin Pan Alley's output. Smith Ballew, disguised as Buddy Blue, made *Have You Forgotten* and *Whistling in the Dark,* and the Lou Gold orchestra made *Ho-Hum.*

It was an auspicious beginning for the young songwriter, but only a prelude. In the following year she reworked a segment of her instrumental *Jazz Nocturne,* and with a lyric by Edward Heyman it became *My Silent Love,* which, in spite of the heavy competition of fine songs in the popular market, was an instant hit. Contemporary records were made by Isham Jones on Brunswick, Roger Wolfe Kahn on Columbia, Ruby Newman for Victor, and, oddly enough, the Washboard Rhythm Kings—also on Victor. Adrian Schubert, the man who made all musical decisions for Crown, recorded it with a studio crew for that label. But this was only the beginning. Over the years the song became a favorite standard, played and recorded frequently. Among others of later date it has been recorded by Carmen Cavallaro on Decca, Dick Jurgens for OKeh, Luis Russell on Apollo, Paul Weston for Columbia, and by vocalists Anita Boyer (on V-Disc) and Fran Warren (Victor).

In 1934 Suesse worked solo on a contribution to the Ziegfeld "Follies," *Moon About Town.* It was recorded by Emil Coleman's Orchestra on Columbia, and Freddy Martin made it for Brunswick; but as moon songs go, it didn't attract much attention. Fortunately for Suesse, another song in the "Follies," sung by Jane Froman and with lyrics by Ed Heyman, was a hit on radio and records and is still to be heard now and then. The song is *You Oughta Be in Pictures.* It went the rounds of the record labels—Guy Lombardo on Melotone, George Hall for Bluebird, Little Jack Little on Columbia, and the Boswell Sisters on Brunswick. In England Ray Noble was still cutting exceptional sides for HMV. Al Bowlly had fun with the vocal. In 1951 Doris Day and Gordon MacRae sang the song in the movie musical *Starlift.* It has since become a semistandard.

Taking her own advice, Suesse, with Ed Heyman, had three songs in a 1935 film, *Sweet Surrender.* They were *Love Makes the World Go 'Round; Take This Ring;* and *I'm So Happy I Could Cry.* No hits resulted. But in 1936 she wrote the melody for the beautiful waltz *The Night Is Young and You're So Beautiful,* which was introduced at Billy Rose's Casa Mañana, in Fort Worth, Texas, part of the "Frontier Days Fair." The words were by Irving Kahal and Billy Rose. The song was a popular radio selection. Wayne King recorded it.

Dana Suesse continued to write for the rest of the thirties and into the forties, without any other outstanding successes. Nevertheless, the list is impressive: *Gone With the Dawn; A Table in a Corner; Blue Moonlight; Yours for a Song; This Changing World; American Nocturne; Concerto in Rhythm; Two Irish Fairy Tales; Afternoon of a Black Faun; Free; Missouri Misery; Blue Melody; You Have to Live a Little; He's the Man I Adore; It Happened in Chicago;* and *The Girl Without a Name.* She also wrote longer works: *Jazz Concerto; Concertino; Concerto in A for Piano and Orchestra; Symphonic Waltzes; Young Man with a Harp* (suite dedicated to harpist Casper Reardon); and *Three Cities.*

Einar Aaron Swan

Composer, writer, and arranger Einar Swan was born in Fitchburg, Massachusetts, on March 20, 1904. Details are scarce about his life, but it is known that he was educated both in the United States and in Europe. In 1927 he is listed playing trumpet with the Vincent Lopez orchestra but apparently ultimately decided on a career of arranging for radio and concert engagements. In 1931 Swan wrote both the music and the words for one of the most beautiful songs in the library of American popular music, *When Your Lover Has Gone*. In spite of the fact that the competition that year was fierce, with all the top composers turning out excellent material, and even though the recording industry was struggling to stay alive while being smothered in the twin grip of the Depression and radio, the song was an instant hit; and it drew attention from those recording artists lucky enough to still be working and who appreciated a quality song. Thus it was made for OKeh by Louis Armstrong. Bert Lown's band, at its peak at the time, recorded it for Victor. Ben Selvin, with an all-star group including Benny Goodman, waxed it for Columbia. Eubie Blake and his orchestra made it for Crown, Bob Haring for the Plaza labels, and Ben Bernie on Brunswick. Harry Richman sang it on Brunswick. Through the years it has never really died out, and every so often another recording of it is made. Among later sides are renditions by Frank Sinatra, Roy Eldridge, Stan Kenton, and George Shearing.

In spite of his success, from all indications Swan made no attempt to cash in on it with a flurry of other compositions. As it is, his only other effort of any note was published in 1938. Al Stillman wrote the words, and the song is *A Room With a View,* not to be confused with the tune with the same title by Noël Coward published in 1928. It was recorded by Helen Forrest on Bluebird and Seger Ellis for Brunswick. Other titles by Swan are few, and not very well known. They include *The Trail of Dreams; In the Middle of a Kiss; Swan's Serenade;* and *The Spirit of St. Louis.*

Einar Swan died in Greenwood Lake, New York, on August 8, 1940.

Arthur Swanstrom

Lyricist Arthur Swanstrom was born in Brooklyn, New York, on August 4, 1888. He started his professional career as a dancer in vaudeville and nightclubs. In 1919, 1920, and 1921, he teamed with John Murray Anderson on writing the book and lyrics for the "Greenwich Village Follies" for those years. In 1927 he worked with Eugene Ford and Carey Morgan on the words and music for the hit song *Rain*. Popular recordings were made by Sam Lanin's orchestra on Banner and Arnold Frank's Rogers' Cafe Orchestra on OKeh. Don Voorhees made it for Columbia.

Swanstrom coproduced the 1929 Broadway musical "Sons O' Guns," which starred Lili Damita and Jack Donahue, with William Frawley, and collaborated with Benny Davis on the lyrics to several songs in the show composed by J. Fred Coots. The titles are *Why?; Cross Your Fingers; It's You I Love; May I Say "I Love You?";* and *Red Hot and Blue Rhythm.* The orchestras of Vincent Lopez and Ohman and Arden recorded the first title. Nat Shilkret made *Cross Your Fingers* for Victor. The other songs, while important in the show, attracted little attention. Swanstrom and Louis Alter penned a nice ballad in 1933, *Morning, Noon, and Night,* just one more of the many quality songs in that year. It was recorded by Freddy Martin's band and by Guy Lombardo. Elmer Feldkamp made it for Crown.

The 1935 entry by Swanstrom and James F. Hanley was *Twenty-four Hours a Day.* Sung by Frank Parker in the movie *Sweet Surrender,* it was recorded by Teddy Wilson for Brunswick, Chick Bullock for the ARC labels, Jan Garber on Bluebird, and Al Donahue on Decca.

Ten O'Clock Town, with a melody by Michael F. Cleary, was the Swanstrom song in 1937. Nat Shilkret recorded it on Victor.

Arthur Swanstrom died in Scarsdale, New York, on October 4, 1940.

Kay Swift

Composer Kay Swift didn't write many popular songs, but one of them is a favorite of mine, *Can't We Be Friends.* More about it later. Swift was born in New York City on April 19, 1905. Her extensive education included a scholarship to the Juilliard School of Music and attendance at the New England Conservatory, where she studied with Bertha Tapper, Gebbard, and Arthur Johnstone and Loeffler. Among her many other credits, she toured as an accompanist to concert artists, was a staff composer for two years at Radio City Music Hall, pioneered as a radio columnist in magazines, wrote scripts for radio programs, and performed as solo pianist with the New York Philharmonic at Lewisohn Stadium.

In 1929 she collaborated with lyricst Paul James (a pseudonym for James Warburg) on *Can't We Be Friends,* which was introduced by Libby Holman in the first edition of the theater musical "The Little Show." In 1952 it was heard in the movie *Young Man with a Horn,* with Harry James playing trumpet on the soundtrack for Kirk Douglas. The song, a favorite of musicians, served as theme song for the Johnny Messner orchestra in the thirties. It has been recorded many times, with outstanding sides by the Benny Goodman band on Victor and by Jess Stacy in a solo performance for Capitol.

In the following year Swift wrote the score for the show "Fine and Dandy," including the title song and *Can This Be Love,* again in collaboration with

Paul James. Other songs by Kay Swift are *Calliope: Up Among the Chimney Pots; Forever and a Day; A Moonlight Memory; Once You Find Your Guy; I Gotta Take Off My Hat to You; In Between Age;* and *Sagebrush Lullaby.*

Marty Symes

Lyricist Marty Symes was born in Brooklyn, New York, on April 30, 1904. He was educated at Erasmus High School. During the mid-thirties he collaborated with Al Neiburg on the words and with Jerry Levinson (Livingston), who composed the music, to produce a number of outstanding songs. In 1935 the titles were *Under a Blanket of Blue; (When It's) Darkness on the Delta; It's the Talk of the Town;* and *It's Sunday Down in Caroline.* All four songs were favorites on radio broadcasts by dance bands and typified the high quality of material being turned out in the Golden Era, not only by those writing for the stage and screen, but by independent songsmiths. Glen Gray and the Casa Loma Orchestra had best-selling records of *Under a Blanket of Blue* and *It's the Talk of the Town,* with Kenny Sargent as the vocalist. *Darkness on the Delta* rated fine treatment by the great Isham Jones band and was also recorded by Ted Fio Rito, Del Lampe, and Chuck Bullock. *It's Sunday Down in Caroline* was recorded by Isham Jones on Victor, but by far the best interpretation was the HMV recording made in England by Ray Noble with Al Bowlly, who somehow managed to convey the impression they knew all about Sunday in Carolina.

Symes, Neiburg, and Livingston offered four more nice tunes in 1934: *Learning; Ol' Pappy; I've Got an Invitation to a Dance;* and *In Other Words We're Through.* Will Osborne was the lucky recipient of the dance invitation and bragged about it on the ARC labels. Kenny Sargent got one too, along with Glen Gray. *Learning* was a good seller for Glen Gray. Isham Jones recorded it on a transcription but not on a commercial side. The nostalgic *Ol' Pappy,* riding along on the fad for songs with southern motif, was recorded by Mildred Bailey with the Benny Goodman band on Columbia; and Benny Goodman and His Music Hall Orchestra cut it for the ARC label. Jack Teagarden waxed it for Brunswick.

In 1935 the team came up with three more excellent songs: *In a Blue and Pensive Mood; Stargazing;* and *Where There's Smoke There's Fire.* Al Bowlly recorded the first title as a solo effort on Victor. Pianist Joe Reichman made *Stargazing* for Melotone with former Isham Jones vocalist Joe Martin. Kay Kyser's band recorded the song on Brunswick. Freddy Martin, who had the pick of all the best songs and seldom passed up the opportunity, recorded *Where There's Smoke There's Fire,* with Elmer Feldkamp vocalizing.

In 1936 Symes wrote material for a revue called "Hollywood Revels," but none of the songs are memorable. He made up for it by penning the words to the Isham Jones melody for *There Is No Greater Love,* which Jones recorded with Woody Herman vocalizing. It has since become a standard.

The next year Symes paired off with Milton Ager, and they came up with one of the big hits of 1937, *You Can Tell She Comes From Dixie.* Benny Goodman had a swinging version on Victor with the vocal by Margaret McRae. They got the jump on everybody by recording the song late in December of 1936. Other sides were made by Artie Shaw for Brunswick, Anson Weeks for Decca, and Phil Harris for Vocalion.

Symes continued to have reasonable successes through the forties and in 1947 wrote the words to an adaptation by Johnny Farrow of an Italian song, *O Marinariello.* As *I Have but One Heart,* it was a best-seller by singers Vic Damone, Frank Sinatra, Monica Lewis, and Bob Allen with Carmen Cavallaro's orchestra. Other songs by Symes are *When April Comes Again; It's a Lot of Idle Gossip; Mary Had a Little Lamb; You're Giving Me a Song and a Dance; It's All So New to Me; Let's Give Love a Chance; By the River of the Roses; How Many Hearts Have You Broken?; I Don't Want to Be Loved; Pretending; Why Did It Have to End So Soon?; You Dreamer You;* and *Music by the Angels.*

Marty Symes died in Forest Hills, New York, on June 19, 1953.

Doris Tauber

Pianist, composer, and vocalist Doris Tauber was born in New York City, on September 13, 1908. She was educated in the New York public schools and started her musical training at an early age. As a youngster she played concerts at Town Hall. For thirteen years she worked as musical secretary for Irving Berlin. She sang and played on her own radio program and also accompanied and wrote vocal arrangements for stars of radio and the stage. As a composer, she contributed scores to nightclub revues and musicals.

In the popular field her contributions are scarce, the best-known song her collaboration with Maceo Pinkard and William Tracey, *Them There Eyes.* This 1930 hit was first recorded by Gus Arnheim's Orchestra on Victor, featuring a vocal by the Rhythm Boys, Bing Crosby, Harry Barris, and Al Rinker. This treatment may have established at an early stage the tune's adaptability to jazz renditions, and through the years it has been a favorite of jazz musicians and jazz bands. Louis Armstrong recorded it for OKeh in 1931, and Billie Holiday made it for Vocalion in 1939. The song is frequently heard at jazz concerts and is a standard.

I Was Made to Love You, another Tauber entry in 1930, was recorded by the Duke Ellington orchestra for Victor and by Cornell (Smelser) and an all-star combination on OKeh. In 1955 Tauber worked with lyricist Mann Curtis to produce the song *Fooled,* which Perry Como recorded for RCA–Victor. Other Tauber songs include *Drinking Again; Who's Afraid; Why Remind Me; Living Dangerously; Compromise; I Don't Get It;* and *Spinner.*

Harlan Thompson

Lyricist, writer, producer Harlan Thompson was born in Hannibal, Missouri, on September 24, 1890. He was educated at the University of Kansas, where he studied engineering. However, he went on to become a newspaper reporter, then drama critic, and finally editor of the *Kansas City Star.* During World War I he was a member and commanding officer of the 267th Aero Squadron. After the war he became a reporter and feature writer for the *New York World.* He wrote and produced films, and during the Second

World War was in charge of producing training films for the Signal Corps. Later he became head of CBS West Coast film production.

As a lyricist he contributed words to some well-known songs. Of these, probably the most popular is *I Love You,* written with composer Harry Archer for the hit show of 1923, "Little Jessie James." It was sung in the show by Nan Halperin and Jay Velie. The Paul Whiteman Orchestra was in the pit for the show and had the hit recording on Victor. Other successful contemporary sides were made by Ohman & Arden, Carl Fenton, Ben Selvin, Joseph P. Samuels, and Vincent Lopez. In 1939 it was recorded by the bands of Jimmie Lunceford and Ozzie Nelson and still later, in 1948, by Kay Kyser's band. The song was featured in the movie *Stalag 17,* in an on-the-spot improvisation by the camp prisoners.

In 1925 Thompson again teamed with bandleader Harry Archer, and they wrote *It Must Be Love* for the stage show "Merry Merry." The Harry Archer Orchestra recorded the song on Vocalion, and other sides were made by Sam Lanin and Harry Reser, among others. *Dance Away the Night* was a collaboration with composer Dave Stamper in 1929 for the movie musical *Married in Hollywood.* It was introduced in the film by J. Harold Murray and Norma Terris. Leo Reisman and Ben Selvin recorded it. *Melody in Spring* was a movie musical in 1934, starring Ann Sothern, Lanny Ross, and Charlie Ruggles. Thompson and Lewis Gensler wrote the title tune, *Melody in Spring,* and *Ending with a Kiss,* which Lanny Ross sang in the movie. Henry King's Orchestra had a nice record. In 1935 Thompson and Gensler wrote *Fatal Fascination* for the film *Ship Cafe,* in which it was sung by Carl Brisson.

Other songs by Harlan Thompson include *Suppose I Had Never Met You; Open Road;* and *A Man and A Maid.*

Harry Austin Tierney

Pianist-composer Harry Tierney was born in Perth Amboy, New Jersey, on May 21, 1890. His education included attendance at the Virgil Conservatory in New York City. He also studied classical piano with his mother and Nicholas Morrissey. He toured the United States as a concert pianist. In England he worked as a staff composer then as a music publisher in London. Back in the States, he went to work for Remick in New York. As a composer, he went the usual route of writing for stage musicals and then went to RKO under contract in 1931 to write for films.

Tierney's first hit song was a musical spelling lesson, *M-I-S-S-I-S-S-I-P-P-I.* Introduced in Ziegfeld's "Midnight Revue" in 1916, the song had lyrics by Bert

Hanlon and Benny Ryan and was introduced by Frances White. In the following year it was sung by Grace LaRue in the stage musical, "Hitchey-Koo of '17." In succeeding years there's no doubt it helped a lot of kids remember how to spell the tricky word. In 1919 Tierney collaborated with lyricist Joseph McCarthy to write songs for the Broadway musical "Irene." Along with the popular title song, they contributed *Castle of Dreams* and one of the most popular waltzes ever written, *Alice Blue Gown.* The song's title referred to the light blue color that was favored by Alice Roosevelt Longworth, Theodore Roosevelt's daughter. Edith Day sang it in the original show, Anna Neagle in the 1940 movie *Irene,* and Debbie Reynolds had the honor in the Broadway revival of the show in 1973. The tune has been recorded and played on radio and in concerts on a steady basis through the years.

Tierney and McCarthy also had a song in the "Ziegfeld's Follies of 1919," *My Baby's Arms.* Contemporary recordings were made by the Green Brothers orchestra, George Hamilton and Joe Green, and Art Hickman. In 1921 they had another independent entry, *Saw Mill River Road,* which also drew recorded interest by Ben Selvin, Nathan Glantz, and the Great White Way Orchestra, among others. The careers of both men peaked in 1927 with the score for the hit show "Rio Rita." Along with the title song, this included *You're Always in My Arms; Sweetheart, We Need Each Other; The Ranger's Song; Following the Sun Around; If You're in Love You'll Waltz;* and *The Kinkerjou. Rio Rita,* coupled with *The Kinkerjou,* was recorded by the Knickerbockers (Ben Selvin) on Columbia, Sam Lanin for OKeh, and Nat Shilkret on Victor. Carl Fenton backed *Rio Rita* with *Following the Sun Around* on Brunswick.

Tierney continued to write for stage and movies but no more important songs resulted. Other titles he is credited with include *Just for Tonight; If You Can't Get a Girl in the Summertime; It's a Cute Little Way of My Own; Cleopatra: I Found the End of the Rainbow; Journey's End; If Your Heart's in the Game;* and *Someone Loves You After All.*

Harry Tierney died in New York City on March 22, 1965.

Peter Tinturin

It's very possible the name Peter Tinturin means little or nothing to you, although he has composed some very respectable songs in the American treasury of popular music. Most likely the main reason for this is that even though some of his songs were moderately successful, he seems to have missed a blockbuster hit—the kind that brings instant fame. Nevertheless, the tunes he wrote—primarily during the thirties and forties—are well constructed, listenable, and hold up well in comparison to others produced during the Golden Era. Tinturin was born in Ekaterinoslav (now Dneprodzerzhinsk), Russia, on June 1, 1910, and quickly developed into a child prodigy on the piano. He was educated at the Vienna Conservatory and the University of Vienna and made his concert debut at the tender age of nine. This was followed by concert tours all over Europe. He began composing at fifteen—at least his first published song appeared at that time—and he went on to compose music for shows in Vienna and Paris. In 1929 he immigrated to the United States, and in 1932 his first song written for the American market was published, *It's About Time*. The lyrics were by another aspiring young songsmith, Johnny Mercer. It was a moderate success and was recorded for Victor by the Joe Haymes band.

Five years later, Tinturin and Jack Lawrence, who would become his primary collaborator, contributed a song to the score of a movie musical, *Manhattan Merry-Go-Round.* This was *Have You Ever Been in Heaven,* a good tune that was recorded by the bands of Bunny Berigan for Victor and Ben Pollack for Decca. It was the start of a profitable year for the team, and they went on to publish *Big Boy Blue* (recorded by Mal Hallett's orchestra and by Ella Fitzgerald with the Mills Brothers, both on Decca); *What Will I Tell My Heart,* a popular side by Bing Crosby; and *Foolin' Myself* (turned into a classic on Brunswick by Teddy Wilson and Billie Holiday in the company of Lester Young, Buster Bailey, Buck Clayton, Jo Jones, Freddie Green, and Artie Bernstein). Two other titles, *All Over Nothing at All* and *Deep in the Heart of the South,* were recorded by Ella Fitzgerald and her Savoy Eight and issued back-to-back on Decca 1339.

The 1938 film *Outside of Paradise* included several Tinturin compositions, the title song among them, but no hits resulted. In 1939 Tinturin and Al Jacobs penned *I'm a Lucky Devil (To Find an Angel Like You),* which did fairly well against the terrific competition that year. Dick Robertson's recording of the song on Decca made out with his usual success on the jukeboxes. During World War II Tinturin served in the Signal Corps and organized, wrote, and directed musical shows for the military.

Other songs by Peter Tinturin are *I'll Close My Eyes to Everyone Else; You or No One; When the Lights Are Soft and Low; Take Me Away; The Song Is the Thing; The Monkey and the Organ Grinder; May the Good Lord Take a Liking to You; A New Star Is Shining in Heaven; Saga of the Signal Corps; I'm Sorry; Shenanigans; A Sweet Irish Sweetheart of Mine; I'm Glad for Your Sake; I'm Away From It All; Twilight Interlude; The Funny Thing Called Love; Your Wish Is My Command; Inner Sanctum; Mother Prairie; Hasta Mañana; Debutante Waltz; Don't Gamble with Romance;* and *Legend of the Roses.*

Juan Tizol

Valve trombonist and composer Juan Tizol was born in San Juan, Puerto Rico, on January 22, 1900. He studied music with his uncle, Manuel Tizol, and played trombone in orchestras and groups in San Juan. He came to the United States in 1920 and went to work in the pit band at the Howard Theatre in Washington, D.C. Still in the early twenties, he played with Bobby Lee's Cotton Pickers but gave up music for several years until he joined the Duke Ellington orchestra in 1929. Although he also played in the Harry James band and worked with Nelson Riddle, Nat "King" Cole, and others, he is best known for his association with Ellington and composed many of his songs in collaboration with the Duke.

His most famous composition is the 1937 all-time standard *Caravan*. Irving Mills and Duke Ellington share composer credit on this title, but it is generally taken for granted that Tizol wrote the tune. It has been recorded by the Ellington orchestra several times, as well as by other bands, and has become a favorite solo vehicle for drummers. In 1938 Tizol worked with Duke Ellington, Lou Singer, and Irving Mills to turn out the moody melody *Lost in Meditation,* which was recorded by the Ellington orchestra and also by an Ellington unit under the direction of Johnny Hodges. In 1940 Tizol and Ellington collaborated on *Conga Bravo,* also recorded by the Ellington orchestra.

Perdido, another big song for Tizol, was published in 1941, and he is listed as sole composer. Of course, the Ellington orchestra played it, recorded it, and was largely responsible for its popularity. Like *Caravan,* it has become a standard and is often heard as a framework for improvisation in jam sessions. *Bakif,* an exotic musical offering, was also published in 1941, with Tizol as sole composer. The Ellington orchestra recorded it several times and featured it in concerts. Other titles credited to Tizol include *We May Never Meet Again; Azure; A Gypsy Without a Song; Moonlight Fiesta; Sphinx; Admiration; Keb-lah;* and *Sans-Souci.*

Juan Tizol died in 1984.

Charles Tobias

One of the most prolific songwriters of the twenties and thirties, Charles Tobias was born in New York City on August 15, 1898. He was educated in the public schools of Worcester, Massachusetts. As a youngster, he sang in vaudeville and then went to work as a staff writer for a music publishing firm. In 1923 he founded his own publishing business. Primarily a lyric writer, he sometimes also wrote the music.

In 1926 Tobias collaborated with Al Sherman to write the words to the Harry Woods hit *(Ho, Ho, Ha, Ha) Me Too*. It was Tobias's first successful song. Paul Whiteman had the best-selling record, but Gene Austin had a pleasant side on Victor. Other records of the song were made by the California Ramblers, Sam Lanin, Harry Reser as the "Seven Little Polar Bears," and Ernie Golden's orchestra. Once started, Tobias proceeded to be associated with a long string of successful songs. In 1927 he teamed with composer Roy Turk to write *Just Another Day Wasted Away,* which made a good record for Waring's Pennsylvanians, and with Al Lewis and Howard Johnson produced *On a Dew Dew Dewy Day*. Vocalists Vaughn DeLeath and Ruth Etting both had good records, and Bob Haring also recorded it. In the following year the big song was *Get Out and Get Under the Moon*. William Jerome helped with the lyrics; Larry Shay wrote the music. Paul Whiteman, with Helen Kane as the vocalist, had the best-selling record.

But in 1929 all the Tobiases—Charles, Harry, and Henry—combined on one of the biggest hits of the year, *Miss You*. Rudy Vallee, at the crest of his surge of popularity, featured it on his broadcasts and recorded it for Victor. In 1942 the song was played and sung in the movie *Strictly in the Groove,* which starred Donald O'Connor and Ozzie Nelson's band. New recordings were made by Eddy Howard, Harry Sosnick, and Freddy Martin, and the revival sent the tune to hit status again. It was on *Your Hit Parade* for eleven weeks. In spite of their great success as collaborators, the brothers went back to independent activity, and in 1930 Charles worked with Peter DeRose to compose the popular waltz *When Your Hair Has Turned to Silver*. They repeated in 1931 with *You'll Be Mine in Apple Blossom Time*.

Brother Henry came back to join Charles and Haven Gillespie in composing *Along Came Love* for "Earl Carroll's Vanities of 1932." Don Bestor's Orchestra recorded it for Victor featuring a vocal conversation between the bandleader and singer Neil Buckley. At this point (1933), Charles Tobias shifted into high gear, collaborating on four titles: *Goodnight Little Girl of My Dreams; In the Valley of the Moon; Sing a Little Lowdown Tune;* and *Two Tickets to Georgia*. The last named was a joint undertaking with Joe Young and J. Fred Coots. The Ben Pollack band made it on Victor. Victor Young's orchestra did the same for Brunswick.

In 1934 Charles Tobias and Jack Scholl wrote the words to a melody by Murray Mencher—one of those wistful and nostalgically sad little ballads that typified the thirties—*Throw Another Log on the Fire*. Freddy Martin's band, working as the house band for Brunswick and allied labels, recorded it as "Albert Taylor and his Orchestra," on Perfect, with an anonymous vocal by Russ

Morgan, whose voice is readily recognizable. Other titles for the year are *Alice in Wonderland* and *An Old Water Mill.* The next year was a busy one. Charles Tobias contributed to three songs for "Earl Carrolls's Sketch Book of 1935"—*Let's Swing It; Moonlight and Violins;* and *Silhouettes Under the Stars;* plus four more as freelance offerings: *Flowers for Madame; Tiny Little Fingerprints; Dancing On the Moon;* and *I'm Painting the Town Red.* The last title proved to be the most memorable as recorded by a Teddy Wilson all-star group for Brunswick and a vocal by Billie Holiday. Other sides were made by Richard Himber for Victor, Bob Howard for Decca, and the Little Ramblers on Bluebird. The song was a collaboration between Charles Tobias and Charles Newman on the words, with music by Sam H. Stept.

In 1936 Charles Tobias paired with Sammy Fain for *Am I Gonna Have Trouble With You?* and with Cliff Friend and Boyd Bunch for *That Never-to-Be-Forgotten Night.* Then with Carmen Lombardo and Cliff Friend, he wrote *Wake Up and Sing.* All were moderately successful. This can also be said for the steady output of songs by Charles Tobias into the sixties. Of these the following are the most outstanding: *Gee, But You're Swell* (melody by Able Baer); *My First Impression of You* (melody by Sam H. Stept); *Is That the Way to Treat a Sweetheart?* (melody by Nat Simon); *Let's Make Memories Tonight* (melody by Sam H. Stept); *Time Waits for No One* (music by Cliff Friend); and *For the First Time (I've Fallen in Love)* (music by Dave Kapp). Other songs by Charles Tobias include *After My Laughter Came Tears; Everything's Made for Love; Don't Be Like That; Song of the Moonbeams; Fascinating You; Got a Great Big Date With a Little Bitta Girl; Somewhere in Old Wyoming; I'm Just a Dancing Sweetheart; Sweet Varsity Sue; I'm Hatin' This Waitin' Around; Love Marches On; I Want You for Christmas; It's Time to Say Aloha; Fuddle Dee Duddle; Little Lady Make Believe; What Are You Doing the Rest of Your Life?; Comes Love; I Can't Afford to Dream; A Boy Named Lem; A Prairie Fairy Tale; It's the Last Time I'll Fall in Love; Trade Winds; Rose O'Day; Below the Equator; We Did It Before; Don't Sit under the Apple Tree; Moon on My Pillow; I Came Here to Talk for Joe; The Old Lamplighter; That's Where I Came In; A Million Miles Away;* and *Those Lazy-Hazy-Crazy Days of Summer.*

Charles Tobias died in New York City on July 7, 1970.

Harry Tobias

Harry Tobias was born in New York City on September 11, 1895. He was educated in the public schools of Worcester, Massachusetts. He started writing songs as a youngster and had his first one published in 1911. Although primarily a lyricist, in 1916 he wrote the music for two successful songs with

Will Dillon, *Take Me to My Alabam'* and *That Girl of Mine*. After serving in the army during WW I, he was active in Florida real estate but returned to New York and to writing songs in 1929. He was just in time to join his brothers, Charles and Henry, in composing *Miss You,* one of the few songs they worked on together as a team. That same year, Harry Tobias wrote material for the stage show "Earl Carroll's Sketch Book."

Moving to the West Coast to write for films, he apparently made friends with bandleader-composer Gus Arnheim and other members of his orchestra at the time, Harry Barris and Bing Crosby. The result was a collaboration with Harry Barris on two songs, *At Your Command* and *What Is It?* Bing Crosby shared credit on the lyric for the first tune and made a major production of it on a recording for Brunswick. Smith Ballew had a nice record of *What Is It?* on Columbia. With Gus Arnheim and Jules Lemare, Harry Tobias wrote two other successful songs in that fruitful year (1931). *Sweet and Lovely* became the Arnheim theme song and then went on to be a major hit and is now a standard. (Tenor Donald Novis sang it on the Arnheim record for Victor. Bing Crosby recorded it for Brunswick.) *I'm Gonna Get You,* sung by Crosby on the Arnheim record, was the other hit.

Then, as though demonstrating his independence, Harry Tobias worked with another West Coast bandleader, Anson Weeks, and Johnnie Scott, to write *I'm Sorry Dear*. Once again, Bing Crosby helped popularize the song by recording it for Brunswick; Mildred Bailey sang it in a medley by the Paul Whiteman orchestra released on one of Victor's experimental long-play records. But Harry Tobias wasn't finished with 1931. With composer Charles Kisco he wrote *It's a Lonesome Old Town,* which bandleader Ben Bernie recorded for Brunswick, backed by *Au Revoir, Pleasant Dreams,* and then promoted both songs into popularity by adopting them as theme songs for his radio broadcasts.

Harry Tobias took a rest, it would appear, after all this activity, and it isn't until 1934 that he again surfaces. This is with another beautiful tune, *Wild Honey*. On this he shared lyric credit with George Hamilton. The melody was by Neil Moret. The song launched the recording career of the Dick Jurgens band, which recorded it for Decca. The Joe Haymes band made it for the ARC labels. In 1936 Tobias worked with former bandleader-vocalist Roy Ingraham to produce another quality song, *No Regrets*. This one went the rounds of all the record labels—Tommy Dorsey on Victor, Wingy Manone for Bluebird, Joe Haymes on Melotone, Billie Holiday on Vocalion, and Artie Shaw for Brunswick. Frances Faye made it for Decca.

Other songs by Harry Tobias are *In God We Trust; The Daughter of Peggy O'Neill; Brother; Thy Will Be Done; The Bowling Song; I Want You to Want*

Me; Oh, Bella Mia; So Divine; Take Me Back to Those Wide Open Spaces; When It's Harvest Time; A Letter From Home; Rolleo Rolling Along; It Ain't All Roses; Song of the Moonbeams; Fascinating You; Sail Along Silv'ry Moon; Lovely Debutante; The Trouble with Me Is You; Love Is All; If It Wasn't for the Moon; I'll Keep the Lovelight Burning; and *Wait for Me, Mary.*

Henry Tobias

Henry Tobias, the youngest of the three song-writing brothers, was born in Worcester, Massachusetts, on April 23, 1905. He attended the Worcester public schools and then Morris High School in New York. In a varied career he performed as a pianist in vaudeville, wrote special material for stars of stage and radio, and for nightclubs and theaters. As a songwriter he often wrote the music to others' lyrics. This is true of his first published song, *Katinka,* written with Bennee Russell in 1926.

In 1929 Tobias collaborated with his brothers on *Miss You* and *Got a Great Big Date With a Little Bitta Girl.* But in 1930 he wrote the music for *Cooking Breakfast for the One I Love,* which was featured in "Earl Carroll's Vanities of 1932." The lyrics were by Billy Rose. He repeated the effort for "Earl Carroll's Sketchbook of 1935," collaborating with brother Charles and Al Lewis on *At Last,* a pleasant song that was recorded by Eddy Duchin on Victor. In 1939 he worked with Moe Jaffe and Larry Vincent on *If I Had My Life to Live Over.*

Other titles for Henry Tobias include *What Are You Doing the Rest of Your Life?; Moon on My Pillow; I Used to Be Her One and Only; No Longer; I Remember Mama; The Bowling Song; Let's Go Skiing; Easter Sunday With You Brother;* and *The Old Square Dance Is Back Again.*

Clarence E. Todd

Pianist-composer and singer Clarence Todd was born in New Orleans, Louisiana, on February 23, 1897. He was educated in the public schools and studied piano with his sister. He went on to play piano and sing with a number of the famous New Orleans bandleaders of the day, including Kid Ory, Sidney Bechet, and Buddy Petit. He saw service in the First World War. In 1921 he moved to New York, where he put in time as staff pianist for a music publisher, performed on the radio, and worked as a member of the Clarence Williams Trio. In the years that followed he worked in vaudeville, nightclubs, and Broadway musicals.

As a songwriter his list of credits isn't long, but it includes some notable titles. Probably his first published song, written in cooperation with Clarence Williams and Spencer Williams, is *Papa-de-da-da*. This 1925 entry won early favor with jazz groups and singers. Contemporary recordings were made by Buster Bailey, Clarence Williams, King Oliver, the Birmingham Serenaders, The St. Louis Rhythm Kings, and singers Bessie Brown, Virginia Liston, and Eva Tayor and Lil Armstrong in a duet.

Todd wrote the words, and Carmen Lombardo the melody, for the 1936 hit *Oooh! Looka There Ain't She Pretty*. Of course, the Guy Lombardo band recorded it, but so did Fats Waller, Larry Clinton, Clarence Williams, and the Charioteers. *Love Grows on the White Oak Tree* was a solo effort by Todd in 1939, and the song rated records by three of the top bands of the day, Hal Kemp, Charlie Barnet, and Glen Gray. *Chilly and Cold,* a collaboration with George Immerman, came out in 1940. It received nice treatment by the Bob Chester band on Bluebird. It was a good song that should have gotten better recognition. Another Clarence Todd title is *Sweet and Tender*.

Truman (Pinky) Tomlin

Composer-singer-bandleader Pinky Tomlin was born in Eureka Springs, Arkansas, on September 9, 1908. He grew up in Durant, Oklahoma, working on farms and tending a dairy route, and at the same time managed to master several stringed instruments. He attended the University of Oklahoma for three-and-a-half years, studying music, geology, and law, and played in local dance bands. In 1934 he collaborated with bandleader Jimmie Grier and lyricist Coy Poe on the hit song *The Object of My Affection*. He recorded it, backed by the Jimmie Grier orchestra on Brunswick, and the highly successful song and recording launched him on a starring career as a songwriter, vocalist, and entertainer. Other records of the tune were made by the Boswell Sisters, Jimmy Dorsey, Paul Pendarvis, Jan Garber, Archie Bleyer, and Joe Reichman. In 1937 the song and Tomlin were featured in the movie *Times Square Lady,* and the Lionel Hampton orchestra recorded it for Victor. Then years later it surfaced again in the film *The Fabulous Dorseys* and was played by their orchestra. A semistandard, the song is still heard on occasion.

In 1935 Earl Hatch joined the team of Tomlin, Poe, and Grier, and the result was *What's the Reason I'm Not Pleasin' You*. This was also sung by Pinky Tomlin in *Times Square Lady,* and he recorded it with the Grier orchestra for Brunswick. Other sides were made by Guy Lombardo, Fats Waller, the Mills Brothers, Jimmy Dorsey, and Red McKenzie. That same year Tomlin was also featured in the film *King Solomon of Broadway,* in which he introduced another Tomlin–Poe–Grier song, *That's What You Think.* Still on a successful roll, he also recorded it with the Grier orchestra. Other sides were made by Red McKenzie and Will Osborne. Gene Krupa revived it in 1942. *Don't Be Afraid to Tell Your Mother* was also an entry for 1935. The Grier Orchestra, with Tomlin, made the customary side for Brunswick. Other records were issued by the Mills Brothers, Little Jack Little, and Charlie Barnet.

In 1937, working alone, Tomlin wrote both words and music for the hit song *The Love Bug Will Bite You (If You Don't Watch Out).* Again, he had the top recording with the Jimmie Grier band, but the very popular song sold well on records by the Mills Brothers, Jimmy Dorsey, Louis Prima, Guy Lombardo, and George Hall. In 1938 Tomlin found a new partner in Harry Tobias, and they collaborated on *Lost and Found.* Only a moderate hit, the song was still well represented on platters by Pinky Tomlin, Kay Kyser, Dick Stabile, and Jimmy Dorsey. The association continued, and in 1940 they penned *If It Wasn't for the Moon* and *Love Is All.* The latter title was introduced by Deanna Durbin in her movie *It's a Date,* and she also recorded it.

Other songs by Pinky Tomlin are *I'm Just a Country Boy at Heart; The Trouble With Me Is You; In Ole Oklahoma; Everything Will Be All Right; I Did It and I'm Glad; Changing My Ambitions; What Are You Doin' Tonight?; I'm in Love; My! My! Ain't That Somethin';* and *Let's Dream Awhile.*

Mel Tormé

Multitalented musician, vocalist, arranger, and songwriter Mel Tormé was born in Chicago, Illinois, on September 13, 1925. His career as an entertainer began at a very early age and included vaudeville and roles in soap operas on Chicago radio. In 1941, only fifteen years old, he published his first song, *Lament to Love,* providing both words and music. It was recorded as an instrumental by the bands of Harry James and Sonny Dunham; Les Brown made it with a vocal by Betty Bonney on OKeh. Vocalist Lanny Ross recorded it for Victor. In 1945 he repeated the solo effort with *Stranger in Town,* a melancholy but appealing composition, which he recorded with his vocal group, The Meltones, for Decca. He also recorded it for Capitol.

In the following year he partnered with lyricist Robert Wells, and their first effort produced an all-time favorite Christmas song, which is called exactly that, *The Christmas Song.* Tormé recorded and introduced it, but the hit was the Capitol record by Nat "King" Cole, which sold in the millions. Doris Day also had a nice recording with the Les Brown band, and, of course, it has been played and recorded hundreds of times since. Nat "King" Cole recorded it again with Nelson Riddle's orchestra in 1954 for Capitol. The song is a perennial and is revived and played every Christmas season.

In the "I Like to be Sad" mood that Tormé favored, he and Robert Wells turned out *Born to Be Blue* in 1947. He recorded it for the Musicraft label (which he once described as the "record with the built-in surface noise"), backed by the Sonny Burke orchestra. The song continued in the original and musically sophisticated vein of his other work. More songs by Mel Tormé are *Willow Road; Country Fair; Magic Town; Ain't Gonna Be Like That; Welcome to the Club; There Isn't Any Special Reason; A Stranger Called the Blues; Whisper Not; Four Months, Three Weeks, Two Days, One Hour Blues; The Jet Set;* and *Got the Gate on the Golden Gate.*

Mel Tormé died in Los Angeles, California, on June 6, 1999.

William G. Tracey

Lyricist William G. Tracey was born in New York City on July 19, 1893. He attended the public schools and then went to work as a staff writer for music publishers. He was a charter member of ASCAP. As with most early composers in the Tin Pan Alley tradition, his reputation is largely based on the songs he wrote that have survived the test of time. In this instance the Tracey name is credited with three songs that qualify: *Gee, But It's Great to Meet a Friend From Your Home Town,* a collaboration with composer James McGavish in 1910, revived for posterity by Bunny Berigan and His Orchestra on a Victor recording in 1937; *Mammy O' Mine,* written with Maceo Pinkard in 1919 and immortalized by Eddie Condon and His Band on Commodore 1509 in 1942; and *Them There Eyes,* another work with Maceo Pinkard, plus Doris Tauber, in 1930. Needless to say, the latter title is the best known and can be considered a standard. Other titles by William G. Tracey are *Bring Back My Daddy to Me; He's Had No Lovin' for a Long, Long Time; Dixie Is Dixie Once More; Give a Little Credit to Your Dad;* and *Is My Baby Blue Tonight?*

William G. Tracey died in New York City on September 5, 1957.

Jo Trent

Lyricist Jo Trent was born in Chicago, Illinois, on May 31, 1892. Educated at the University of Pennsylvania and City College of New York, Trent went on to a varied career as a manager and staff writer for music publishers and film companies, also functioning as a coach and tutor. Mainly active in the twenties and thirties, Trent is credited with a number of hit songs in those years. An early entry (1926) was *Muddy Water,* a collaboration with Peter DeRose and Harry Richman. Richman introduced and recorded it, and so did the Ben Bernie orchestra; but the song picked up greater popularity in the following year as recorded by the Paul Whiteman orchestra, with the vocal by Bing Crosby. Jack Pettis and His Band made it for the Plaza labels, with hot improvisations by Joe Venuti and Eddie Lang.

In 1928 Trent, still working with Peter DeRose, penned the words to *I Just Roll Along (Havin' My Ups and Downs),* in the trend established by Harry Woods with *Side by Side*. It received fine treatment from the All Star Orchestra on Victor and Willard Robison on Pathé and Perfect. Ray Starita waxed it in London. That same year, Trent got together with J. Russel Robinson to write *Rhythm King,* a jazz-oriented number that was first recorded by Bix Beiderbecke and His Gang for OKeh. Other sides were made by Ben Bernie and the Coon–Sanders crew. Possibly by way of returning a favor, Trent provided the lyrics to Willard Robison's *Wake Up, Chillun, Wake Up,* one of the better entries in 1929, recorded by Nat Shilkret for Victor.

Gotta Feelin' for You, with music by Louis Alter and words by Trent, was introduced by Joan Crawford and Paul Gibbons and the Baltimore Trio in the movie musical *Hollywood Revue of 1929*. The song made a second appearance a year later in another film, *Chasing Rainbows*. But the most successful of the Trent–Alter collaborations was *My Kinda Love*. Bing Crosby recorded it as a vocal for Brunswick; Ben Pollack's band made it for Victor; and Claude Hopkins revived it on Decca in 1937. It has since become a semistandard. In 1933 Trent joined with Harry Tobias and Neil Moret for *Here You Come With Love*. It attracted surprising attention on recordings in that gloomy year of the Great Depression, and sides were made by Leo Reisman, Bert Lown, and Freddy Martin. Other songs by Trent include *Because I Feel Low Down; Ploddin' Along; Maybe I'm Wrong Again;* and *I Want It Sweet Like You.*

Jo Trent died in Barcelona, Spain, on November 19, 1954.

Roy Turk

Lyricist Roy Turk was born in New York City on September 20, 1892. He was educated at City College of New York and served in the navy during WW I. Early in his career he wrote special material for vaudeville stars like Sophie Tucker and Nora Bayes and then worked as a staff writer for a music publisher. During his rather brief career he collaborated with top composers and can be credited with writing the words to a number of outstanding songs. One of his early efforts was *Aggravatin' Papa (Don't You Try to Two-Time Me),* written with J. Russel Robinson and Addy Britt. It won approval from female blues singers. Marion Harris recorded it for Brunswick, Aileen Stanley for OKeh, Bessie Smith for Columbia, Alberta Hunter for Paramount, Lucille Hegamin for Cameo, Esther Bigeou for OKeh, Lizzie Miles for Emerson, and Inez Wallace for Black Swan. But impressive as that list is, it isn't complete. Other sides were recorded by the Memphis Five, the Georgians, the Synco Jazz Band, Isham Jones, Ladd's Black Aces, Vincent Lopez, and the Virginians. Not many songs rated that much attention, especially in 1922.

But Roy Turk was just beginning. In 1923 he teamed with Lou Handman on *My Sweetie Went Away (But She Didn't Say Where, When, or Why).* Billy Murray and Ed Smalle recorded it as a hit duet on Victor; Ben Bernie made it for Vocalion; Dolly Kay waxed it for Columbia; and Aileen Stanley recorded it for Victor. The song also did well on music rolls. Still picking winners, in 1924 Turk worked with Grant Clarke, George W. Meyer, and Arthur Johnston, and the team came up with *Mandy, Make Up Your Mind.* It was introduced by Florence Mills in the stage musical "Dixie to Broadway" and was recorded by Paul Whiteman, Clarence Williams, and Fletcher Henderson. In 1939 it was revived by Muggsy Spanier and His Ragtime Band on Bluebird. Tommy Dorsey followed through with a record on Victor, and the song has since become a standard in the jazz repertoire.

Gimmie a Little Kiss (Will Ya, Huh?) came out in 1926, a collaboration between Turk, Maceo Pinkard, and "Whispering" Jack Smith. Smith featured and recorded it, but the song was immortalized by the Jean Goldkette recording for Victor, which features Bix Beiderbecke simulating the sound of kisses with his trumpet. Latter-day recordings were made by Gene Krupa and by Jerry and Patti Lewis. Deanna Durbin sang the song in her 1945 film *Lady On a Train.*

In 1927 Turk and Charles Tobias turned out *Just Another Day Wasted Away (Waiting for You).* Waring's Pennsylvanians had a successful record. But it was nothing compared to the entry for 1928, a collaboration with Fred A. Ahlert and the first in a series of hits, *I'll Get By.* This all-time standard did well on contemporary sides by Gus Arnheim's band, the Ipana Troubadors, and the Original Wolverines, and it has gone on to be played, sung, and recorded by practically every band and vocalist you can name. Among these are Harry James, Andy Kirk, Teddy Wilson, Jack Jenney (of the pre-LP era), and dozens more since. In the meantime, it has been featured in a series of movies. Harry Richman did it in the 1930 film *Puttin' on the Ritz.* In 1943

Irene Dunne sang it in *A Guy Named Joe*. In the following year, Dinah Shore sang it in *Follow the Boys*. This, along with a hit record of the tune by Harry James with vocalist Dick Haymes, pushed the song to *Your Hit Parade* status for twenty-two weeks. And more movies followed. In 1948 Dan Dailey sang it in *You Were Meant for Me*. It was the title song and theme of the 1950 picture *I'll Get By,* with June Haver singing it. Judy Garland did the same in *A Star Is Born* in 1954, and Gogi Grant's voice was dubbed in for Ann Blyth in *The Helen Morgan Story*.

Needless to say, the team of Roy Turk and Fred Ahlert was hot, and just to prove that *I'll Get By* was no accident, they followed with another smash, *Mean to Me*. Introduced and recorded by Ruth Etting, the song became identified with her, and in 1955 Doris Day, as Etting in the biographical movie *Love Me or Leave Me,* reprised the tune. Then in 1972 Diana Ross, as Billie Holiday, sang it in *Lady Sings the Blues*. Nell Carter sang it in the stage production of "Ain't Misbehavin'" in 1978. Like *I'll Get By,* the song has long been a standard. Another successful song for Turk and Ahlert in 1929 was *The One That I Love Loves Me,* featured and recorded by the hit-maker Rudy Vallee.

Walkin' My Baby Back Home was still another big song for Turk and Ahlert. It was introduced by Harry Richman in 1931. Nick Lucas recorded it, and other contemporary sides were made by Louis Armstrong, Maurice Chevalier, and Parker Gibbs with the Ted Weems band. In 1952 crybaby Johnny Ray revived it on a Columbia record, and the tune made number one on *Your Hit Parade*. Dean Martin and Nat "King" Cole also had big selling records. To cap things off, Donald O'Connor sang it as the title song of his movie *Walkin' My Baby Back Home* in 1953. *I Don't Know Why,* a title that has been plagiarized a couple of times since, was another Turk–Ahlert standard from 1931. Russ Columbo had the big record and is identified with the song, but it has been played and recorded many times to the present day. *Can't You See,* an excellent song by Turk and Ahlert that same year, was recorded by Paul Whiteman, with Mildred Bailey singing, on Victor. Ben Selvin made it for the Columbia subsidiary labels (as Lloyd Keating and His Orchestra); and Phil Spitalny waxed it for Perfect.

Where the Blue of the Night Meets the Gold of the Day, published in 1932, includes Bing Crosby in the credits for the lyrics with Turk. Crosby introduced the song in the film *The Big Broadcast,* recorded it, and then adopted it as his theme song on radio broadcasts. The Bob Crosby band recorded it for Decca in 1940. Other songs with lyrics by Roy Turk include *I'm Still Without a Sweetheart, With Summer Coming On; Dixie Dreams; I'm a Little Blackbird Looking for a Bluebird; Are You Lonesome Tonight?; After My*

Laughter Came Tears: From One 'Til Two; Just Because You're You; Beale Street Mama; and *O How I Laugh When I Think How I Cried About You.*

Roy Turk died in Hollywood, California, on November 30, 1934.

Rudy Vallee

Hubert Prior (Rudy) Vallee was born in Island Pond, Vermont, on July 28, 1901. He grew up in Westport, Maine. He attended the University of Maine for a year, then transferred to Yale. As a musician he was a self-taught saxophonist of considerable merit, playing with English dance bands for a year and then, after graduating from Yale in 1927, touring in vaudeville with a band called the Yale Collegians. In 1928 he landed a job at the Heigh-Ho Club in New York, and subsequent radio broadcasts made him an overnight sensation. The following year he started a weekly broadcast on NBC sponsored by Fleischman's Yeast that became one of the top shows of the thirties. A shrewd judge of song material suited to his presentation and singing voice, Vallee became one of the hit-makers of the era. At the same time, although not usually thought of as a songwriter, he is credited with a number of good songs, either as a cocomposer or as lyricist.

One of the earliest of these is *Deep Night.* With a melody by Charles Henderson and words by Vallee, this 1929 entry was the first song recorded by the Connecticut Yankees on Victor and immediately became identified with Vallee. A quality song, it has endured and been revived on recordings in recent years. In 1957 it was featured in the movie musical *The Helen Morgan Story,* with Gogi Grant's voice dubbed on the soundtrack for actress Ann Blyth. Vallee also collaborated on the song that became the theme of his first movie, *The Vagabond Lover.* The song, *I'm Just a Vagabond Lover,* was a collaboration with Leon Zimmerman. Vallee recorded it for Victor and featured it on radio broadcasts. In the following year he and the Connecticut Yankees performed it in another movie, *Glorifying the American Girl.* Meanwhile, still in 1929, Vallee and composer John Klenner produced *I'm Still Caring,* another song the bandleader recorded and featured and which became identified with him. Still another was the Argentine Tango, *Mé Querés (Do You Love Me?),* for which he provided the English lyrics. In 1930 Vallee teamed with J. Paul Fogarty on the novelty *Betty Coed,* in the format of a college marching song. It enjoyed the usual Vallee success. In 1947 it saw new life as the title song for the movie *Betty Coed.*

As time went on, Vallee developed a talent for restyling and revising old songs into new and very successful material. One such was *The Maine Stein*

Song from the University of Maine, which he featured and promoted into becoming the most famous drinking song of all time. Another was Yale's *Whiffenpoof Song*. In 1937 he made a hit out of the French–Italian song, *Vieni, Vieni,* giving it English lyrics, recording it, and featuring it on radio. Still later he struck gold with such novelties as *The Old Sow Song; With Her Head Tucked Underneath Her Arm;* and *Mad Dogs and Englishmen*. Other Vallee titles are *Two Little Blue Little Eyes; Oh! Ma-Ma;* and *My Cigarette Lady*.

Rudy Vallee died in California on July 3, 1986.

Egbert Van Alstyne

Tin Pan Alley pioneer Egbert Van Alstyne was born in Chicago, Illinois, on March 5, 1882. He was educated at the Chicago Musical College and Cornell College in Iowa. Like so many of his contemporaries, he toured in vaudeville as a youngster and then went to work for a song publisher in New York, inevitably starting to write songs himself. After some success as a freelancer, he began writing scores for Broadway musicals. Three of Van Alstyne's early major hits were written with lyricist Harry H. Williams. They include *In the Shade of the Old Apple Tree* (1905); *Won't You Come Over to My House?* (1906); and *What's the Matter With Father?* (1910). All three have been revived from time to time, and the old ballad *In the Shade of the Old Apple Tree* has undergone numerous arrangements—especially in the thirties—as a jazz and swing composition. As such it has been recorded by Louis Armstrong, Artie Shaw, Claude Hopkins, Gene Kardos, Midge Williams, and others.

In 1915 Van Alstyne wrote the waltz that lyricist Gus Kahn called *Memories*. A top-seller in sheet music and recordings that year, it went on to become a standard, evoked whenever memories or a nostalgic subject is presented. It served as background music in the movie *Tin Pan Alley* (1940) and was played by Ted Lewis and his band in *Is Everybody Happy?* (1943). In the biographical film of Gus Kahn, *I'll See You in My Dreams,* it was featured twice (1951). Van Alstyne collaborated with Tony Jackson on the music for *Pretty Baby,* with words by Gus Kahn. Written in 1915 and introduced in the stage show "A World of Pleasure," it was interpolated in the hit show "The Passing Show of 1916" by Dolly Hackett. That was just the beginning, and when movie musicals became the vogue it went through a series of reincarnations. In 1939 Al Jolson sang it in *Rose of Washington Square*. It was heard in the Ted Lewis story, *Is Everybody Happy?* in 1943, and Charles Winninger and Gloria DeHaven sang it as a duet in *Broadway*

Rhythm that same year. Al Jolson did it again in *Jolson Sings Again* (1949), and Danny Thomas, as Gus Kahn, sang it in *I'll See You in My Dreams* (1951). Not to be outdone, Eddie Cantor, dubbed in on the soundtrack for Keefe Brasselle, was heard in *The Eddie Cantor Story* (1953). *Your Eyes Have Told Me So* was another winner with Gus Kahn in 1919, and like the others it went on to a strong afterlife. James Melton sang it in the 1936 movie *Sing Me a Love Song*. It was background music in *I'll See You in My Dreams* in 1951, and Gordon MacRae and Doris Day sang it in *By the Light of the Silvery Moon* in 1952.

Van Alstyne continued to write, and in 1925 he worked with a team composed of Haven Gillespie (lyrics) and Erwin R. Schmidt and Loyal Curtis, who shared composing credit for the melody, on *Drifting and Dreaming*. It was Gillespie's first hit. George Olsen's orchestra had the best-selling contemporary recording, but Les Brown's band had a bigger seller in 1950. In the meantime, bandleader Orrin Tucker used the song as his theme. Van Alstyne worked with Gillespie again on the 1931 song *Beautiful Love*. Victor Young and Wayne King shared credit for the music. It was Van Alstyne's last hit. It was introduced by Wayne King, James Melton recorded it for Columbia, and Lewis James waxed it for Victor. In 1934 Victor Young's orchestra recorded the song for Decca, with a vocal by Donald Novis. Art Tatum made two takes of the tune for the same label on solo piano that year. Among other titles by Egbert Van Alstyne are *Navajo; Back, Back, Back to Baltimore; Seminole; My Dreamy China Lady; I'm Afraid to Come Home in the Dark; There Never Was a Girl Like You; Love Makes the World Go 'Round; Who Are You With Tonight?; Goodnight Ladies; That Old Girl of Mine; Sailin' Away on the Henry Clay;* and *Kentucky's Way of Saying Good Morning*.

Egbert Van Alstyne died in his hometown of Chicago, Illinois, on July 9, 1951.

Jimmy Van Heusen

Another giant in the annals of American music, Jimmy Van Heusen was born Edward Chester Babcock in Syracuse, New York, on January 26, 1913. Like a lot of people he didn't like his name, so he borrowed that of the famous shirt company for his professional nom de guerre. As it is, anyone familiar with the career of Bing Crosby and the many great songs he sang will readily recognize the work of Jimmy Van Heusen, because so many of Bing's hits—both in the movies and on recordings—were Van Heusen songs. And the list is quite long, so here are the highlights:

From *The Road to Zanzibar—It's Always You; You Lucky People You; Birds of a Feather; You're Dangerous; The Road to Zanzibar; African Etude.*

From *The Road to Morocco—Moonlight Becomes You; Constantly; Ain't Got a Dream to My Name; Aladdin's Daughter.*

From *Dixie—Sunday, Monday, or Always; If You Please; She's from Missouri; A Horse That Knows His Way Home.*

From *Going My Way—Going My Way; Swingin' on a Star; The Day After Forever.*

From *The Road to Rio—But Beautiful; You Don't Have to Know the Language; Apilachicola, Florida; For What?*

From *The Bells of St. Mary's—Aren't You Glad You're You?*

From *The Road to Utopia—Welcome to My Dreams; Personality; It's Anybody's Spring; Put It There, Pal.*

From *The Road to Bali—Chicago Style; Hoot Mon.*

The list goes on, but after you finish with the Crosby titles, you can continue with a whole string of Frank Sinatra hits—*The Tender Trap; Love and Marriage; All the Way; Come Fly with Me; High Hopes; The Second Time Around; Call Me Irresponsible; My Kind of Town;* plus others. He started out writing for college musicals and then made his way to New York, where like many another budding songwriter he took a job in a publishing house. His first tunes were published in 1938—almost at the end of the Golden Decade—but he had no less than five hits that year—*It's the Dreamer in Me; So Help Me; This Is Madness; When a Prince of a Fella Meets a Cinderella;* and *Deep in a Dream.* Encouraged by such a fantastic start, the next year Van Heusen opened his own publishing firm. One of his earliest enterprises was the music for "Swingin' a Dream," the unsuccessful stage show that starred Benny Goodman's Sextet. It still resulted in a hit song, *Darn That Dream,* and Van Heusen kept it company with another string of hits—*All I Remember Is You; Blue Rain; Can I Help It?; Heaven Can Wait; Oh You Crazy Moon; Good for Nothin' but Love;* and *I Thought about You.*

And thus it continued throughout the years. In 1940, for instance, a prolific output included *All This and Heaven Too; Imagination; Polka Dots and Moonbeams;* and *Shake Down the Stars.* Van Heusen took it easy the following year, content with the score for *The Road to Zanzibar,* establishing a pattern for the Crosby films that lasted until 1952, when *The Road to Bali* was presented. In 1953 Van Heusen tried another unsuccessful stage show, "Carnival in Flanders," which nevertheless produced a hit song, *Here's That Rainy Day.* Shortly after came the string of Frank Sinatra films and hits.

Jimmy Van Heusen's collaborators included Eddie DeLange, Johnny Burke, and Sammy Cahn. He died in California on February 7, 1990.

Peter Venning

See Peter Hygham Mendoza.

Joe Venuti

Jazz violinist, bandleader, and composer Joe Venuti was born on September 1, 1904. It has been reported the event took place at sea while his parents were coming to the United States as immigrants, but Joe claimed he was born in Philadelphia. At any rate, he grew up in that city and attended the public schools. In the process he met and became firm friends with a schoolmate named Salvatore Massaro—later to become famous as Eddie Lang—who played guitar. The rest is jazz history, and Venuti and Lang went on to create a good portion of it, both as a pioneering and highly original duo and as individual artists.

As a composer, Venuti is credited with an impressive list of instrumental pieces, many of them stemming from his early recordings with Eddie Lang, such as *Doin' Things; Goin' Places; Cheese and Crackers; Beatin' the Dog; Kickin' the Cat;* and *The Wild Dog*. With Eddie Lang listed as cocomposer, other tunes are *Wild Cat; Penn Beach Blues;* and *Stringin' the Blues*. Other Venuti compositions include *Satan's Holiday* and several titles that appear to be on-the-spot improvisations for record sessions that also reflect Venuti's oddball sense of humor, such as Decca 2312. One side of the record is called *Something,* the other *Nothing*. Clark Galehouse is listed as the co-conspirator in these antics. He plays tenor sax on the sides, as he does on the companion Decca record 2313, which features two more intriguing titles, *Flip* and *Flop*. Venuti claims full credit for these.

It has to be pointed out that Venuti's composing efforts were strictly personal for the most part and not intended for the popular mass market. Of course, there's always the exception, and this time it's a very pleasant tune as sung by Bing Crosby on Decca 24476, accompanied by Venuti and His Orchestra, *Ain't Doin' Bad Doin' Nothin'*. It appears the lyric was written by Lee Jarvis. It requires a big book to cover Joe Venuti's long and varied career, and one is presently under preparation by lifelong Venuti fan Robert Mohr. I suggest you watch for it.

Joe Venuti died in Seattle, Washington, on August 14, 1978.

Joe Verges

Songwriter Joe Verges was a native of New Orleans. He was born there on October 26, 1902, and died there on August 12, 1964. He became a member of ASCAP in 1928 and apparently was briefly active in writing songs in the midtwenties. No other information is available. Verges was not associated with any big hits, but his name is included as a collaborator on several good songs with respected writers. One of these is *When I First Met Mary,* published in 1926 and written with Little Jack Little and Larry Shay. It received excellent coverage on records by Sam Lanin, Ben Pollack, Irwin Abrams, and Ben Selvin.

In 1928 Verges paired with Tom Malie, and they wrote *Our Bungalow of Dreams*. This also was well represented, with recordings by Sam Lanin, Harry Reser, Freddie Rich, and Frankie Masters; but the side that will carry the song into immortality was made by Frankie Trumbauer and His Orchestra for OKeh, featuring Bix Beiderbecke in the lineup. That same year Verges got together with Walter Hirsch and Bennie Krueger, and they turned out *Oh Look at That Baby*. Johnny Hamp's band recorded it, among others, as it did still another Verges title, *The Waltz of Love,* a collaboration with Ted Koehler.

Nat Vincent

Songwriter-singer Nat Vincent was born in Kansas City, Missouri, on November 6, 1889. He was educated at Betts Mill Academy in Stamford, Connecticut. Early in his career he worked as a sheet music demonstrator in New York department stores. He also managed music publishing companies. In vaudeville, he performed as a member of the team Tracey and Vincent, and later, Franklyn and Vincent. When radio came along he worked with Fred Howard as "the Happy Chappies." Meanwhile, he wrote material for Broadway shows and revues, and also English stage productions. In the process, he collaborated with many of the top composers of the time, including Maceo Pinkard, James Kendis, and Russ Morgan.

Although Vincent is credited with a long list of titles, without any question his greatest claim to lasting fame is sharing recognition on the composition of the tremendous hit of 1919, *I'm Forever Blowing Bubbles*. Due to contractual obligations and a dispute over the song's earnings, the lyrics were attributed to a "Jean Kenbrovin," which was a name derived from a combination of James Kendis, James Brockman, and Nat Vincent. The music was written by John W. Killette, and even less is known about him. He was not an ASCAP member. Ben Selvin's Novelty Orchestra recorded the tune on Victor, but considering the tons of sheet music that were sold, the representation on records was nil. Most likely it did much better on piano rolls. In later reincarnations, the song was used in two movies, the 1941 film

The Great American Broadcast and *On Moonlight Bay* in 1951. It long ago became a favorite of sing-alongs.

Vincent teamed with composer John Alden in 1920, and the result was one of the most delightful songs of the era, *La Veeda.* A popular song that year, it was recorded by the bands of Isham Jones, Art Hickman, and the Columbia Saxophone Sextette. However, it remained for Nat Brandwynne's band to give it passing notice in the Decca album of *Songs of Our Times* for 1920. Brandwynne combined it in a medley with two other well-known titles of the year, *A Young Man's Fancy* and *Look for the Silver Lining.*

In 1931 Vincent wrote the words to the western-styled song, *When the Bloom Is on the Sage.* The music was composed by Fred Howard Wright, and it became the theme song of the radio series *Tom Mix and His Straight Shooters.* Other titles credited to Nat Vincent include *My Old Man; Pretty Little Cinderella; The Strawberry Roan; I Know What It Means to Be Lonesome; Give a Little Credit to Your Dad; Little Girl Dressed in Blue; Pucker Up and Whistle;* and *That Railroad Rag.*

Nat Vincent died in Burbank, California, on June 6, 1979.

Albert Von Tilzer (Albert Gumm)

Albert Von Tilzer was born in Indianapolis, Indiana, on March 29, 1878. A younger brother of composer Harry Von Tilzer, his family name, like Harry's, was Gumm. Harry (Harold) adopted Von Tilzer as a name for songwriting and made it so famous that all his brothers, including Albert, took the name. Albert had a high school education, toured for awhile in vaudeville, and worked as a shoe buyer for a Brooklyn department store. After a stint on the staff of his brother's publishing house in Chicago, he went on to establish his own firm with brother Jack in 1903.

Albert Von Tilzer wrote songs from the turn of the century well into the fifties, but for the most part it is his earlier work that has proved to be the most memorable. In many instances, these songs are such familiar items in the American heritage of popular songs that they almost approach the status of folk songs—tunes everybody knows and takes for granted were always around. The most outstanding example of this is probably *Take Me Out to the Ballgame,* published in 1908, with words by stage star Jack Norworth. It would be impossible to say how many times this song has been played and sung since, but long ago it became synonymous with baseball and will probably be around as long as the game is. Norworth and Von Tilzer combined on another standard that same year. Although it will never equal the ballgame song, *Smarty* was introduced and popularized by Jack Norworth, was recorded by the team of Ada Jones and Billy Murray on Victor, and pops up every now and then as a novelty.

Put Your Arms Around Me, Honey came out in 1910 with words by Junie McCree. It was introduced in vaudeville by Blossom Seeley, and in the following year Arthur Collins and Byron G. Harlan made the first hit record on Victor. But that was just the beginning. It was used in the stage show "Madame Sherry" by Elizabeth Murray. Betty Grable sang it in the 1943 movie musical *Coney Island,* and that same year it served as background music for the John Wayne epic *In Old Oklahoma.* Judy Canova performed it in another film musical, *Louisiana Hayride,* in 1944; and Judy Garland sang it in the 1949 production of *In the Good Old Summertime.* She also recorded it with Georgie Stoll's orchestra for MGM.

In 1912 Albert Von Tilzer began a collaboration with lyricist Lew Brown that was to continue for a number of years. One of their earliest efforts was *I'm the Lonesomest Gal in Town.* A hit the first time around, it was revived with telling effect by Kay Starr on a Capitol record in 1950. It was also heard in two movies, *Make Believe Ballroom* in 1949 and *South Sea Sinner* in 1950. *Oh! By Jingo! Oh, by Gee! (You're the Only Girl for Me),* by Brown and Von Tilzer, was the hit of the 1919 stage production of "Linger Longer Letty," introduced by Charlotte Greenwood. Betty Hutton sang it in the role of Texas Guinan in the 1945 movie *Incendiary Blonde,* and it showed up again as interpreted by Vivian Blaine in the move musical *Skirts Ahoy* in 1952. The tune was recorded by Yerkes Dance Orchestra on Vocalion and has made return waxings every so often. In 1933 a trio calling themselves "the Three Keys" and featuring Bon Bon Tunnell recorded it for Brunswick. In 1937 the Gene Kardos band made it for the ARC labels, and in 1940 Ella Logan, backed by the Perry Botkin band, recorded it for Columbia.

I Used to Love You (But It's All Over Now) was the vengeful sentiment expressed by Brown and Von Tilzer in 1920 and recorded by Frank Crumit for Columbia and the Peerless Quartet for Victor. As most of Albert Von Tilzer's melodies do, it adapted well to jazz treatment, and trombonist Georg Brunis demonstrated this on a Commodore record in 1946. Also in 1920, Von Tilzer collaborated with lyric writer Neville Fleeson to compose *I'll Be With You in Apple Blossom Time.* It was featured by Nora Bayes, recorded by Jones and Hare on Brunswick, and made by Charles Harrison for Victor. It was revived with a bang in 1941 by the Andrews Sisters, who featured it in their movie *Buck Privates* and then recorded it as a best-seller for Decca. In 1959 it was again pushed to the top by Tab Hunter on a record for Warner Brothers, and again in 1959 by Wayne Newton, who had a "chart" record for Capitol.

Other titles by Albert Von Tilzer are

Good Morning, Carrie; I Take Things Easy; Teasing; Tell Me With Your Eyes; Honey Boy; Good Evening, Caroline; Kentucky Sue; Please Don't Take My Lovin' Man Away; My Little Girl; I May Be Gone for a Long, Long Time; Give Me the Moonlight, Give Me the Girl; Dear Old Daddy Long-legs; Chili Bean; Dapper Dan; As Long As I Have You; My Cutey's Due at Two to Two Today; Roll Along Prairie Moon, and many others.

Albert Von Tilzer died in Los Angeles, California, on October 1, 1956.

Harry Von Tilzer (Harold Gumm)

Composer Harry Von Tilzer was born in Detroit, Michigan, on July 8, 1872. He grew up in Indianapolis and learned to play the piano. At age fourteen he was touring with a circus and still later was with a road show as a man-of-all-trades, filling in as a pianist, actor, singer, and composer. In 1892 he made it to New York and began writing special material for the stars of stage and vaudeville. Five years later he published his first song, *Jack, How I Envy You,* and in the following year had his first hit, *My Old New Hampshire Home,* with lyrics by Andrew B. Sterling. Thus established, he went on to a long career as a composer, producer, and song publisher. Many of his songs have become standards, and some of them are often used as background music typical of the early years of the twentieth century. One is *A Bird in a Gilded Cage*. In the "tearjerker" tradition of the time, this was one of the most successful songs of the 1900s, selling millions of sheet music copies. Revivals took place in 1941 when the song was used in the Ann Sothern film *Ringside Mamie* and again in 1943, in the film *Coney Island.* Singer Beatrice Kay, who featured songs of the "Gay Nineties" and the turn of the century, recorded it for Columbia, and Virginia O'Brien, the lady with the dead-pan expression, made it for Decca.

In 1902 Vincent P. Bryan and Harry Von Tilzer wrote *Down Where the Wurzburger Flows,* a touching ballad that was introduced by Nora Bayes at New York's Orpheum Theater. The song was a big hit, and Bayes was from then on often referred to as the Wurzburger Girl. In the meantime, the song was a big boost for Wurzburger beer—not to mention the Von Tilzer reputation and pocketbook. Bryan and Von Tilzer also had another popular song that year, *In the Sweet Bye and Bye,* and then the composer teamed with another lyric writer, J. Tim Brymn, on the novelty *Please Go 'Way and Let Me Sleep,* introduced and made into a hit by minstrel-man Arthur Deming in vaudeville.

Still recognizing a good thing, Von Tilzer and Andrew B. Sterling wrote another beer song, this one called *Under the Anheuser Bush.* A hit in vaudeville, it was recorded for Victor by Arthur Collins and Byron Harlan, and Billy Murray made it for Columbia. The tune was well liked in London, too, but the English changed the title to *Down at the Old Bull and Bush.*

In 1905 Sterling and Von Tilzer combined on a song that is most likely their biggest hit, *Wait Till the Sun Shines, Nellie.* Byron Harlan had two hit records of the day, one for Columbia and one for Edison. The song underwent a tremendous revival in 1941, as the result of a duet between Bing Crosby and Mary Martin in the film *Birth of the Blues.* They recorded it for Decca, and the Harry James band made a swinging version on Columbia. It went on to be featured in the 1942 film *Rhythm Parade,* starring Gale Storm and then to become the title song for the David Wayne–Jean Peters movie *Wait Till the Sun Shines, Nellie* in 1952.

I Want a Girl (Just Like the Girl That Married Dear Old Dad), with words by William Dillon, came along in 1911. Like many of the Von Tilzer titles, this one pops up every now and then. In 1938 vocalist Chick Bullock revived it on the Vocalion label, and in 1940 Dick Robertson did the same for Decca. Then in 1944 it was performed by George Murphy, Constance Moore, Eddie Cantor, and Joan Davis in the film *Show Business.* It made another appearance two years later in the film *The Jolson Story,* as presented by Al Jolson and minstrels. Andrew Sterling and Von Tilzer were back together in 1912, and they turned out what would become a favorite of barbershop quartets, *In the Evening by the Moonlight.*

Although his output became scarce, Harry Von Tilzer continued to write well into the twenties, and in 1925, with lyricist Dolph Singer, had one more hit, *Just Around the Corner.* The contemporary singing group the Revelers had a popular record. It was also recorded by the bands of Lou Gold (Cameo), Art Landry (Victor), and Jack Linx (OKeh). The Harry Von Tilzer list of titles is long. Following is a partial listing.

> *That's No Dream; I've Just Received a Telegram from Baby; I'd Leave My Happy Home for You; Her Name is Rose; When the Harvest Days Are Over, Jennie Dear; Down Where the Cotton Blossoms Grow; Down on the Farm; All Aboard for Dreamland; What You Goin' to Do When the Rent Comes 'Round?; Where the Morning Glories Twine 'Round the Door; Take Me Back to New York Town; Where the Sweet Magnolias Grow; Under the Yum Yum Tree; Knock Wood; And the Green Grass Grew All Around; On the Old Fall River Line; That Old Irish Mother of Mine;* and *Under a Wurzburger Tree.*

Harry Von Tilzer died in New York City on January 10, 1946.

Larry Wagner

Composer-arranger Larry Wagner was born in Ashland, Oregon, on September 15, 1907. He was educated at the University of Oregon and studied the Schillinger System. In 1938 he became the staff arranger for Glen Gray and the Casa Loma Orchestra and performed that function until 1942, when he left to join the marines and served during the Second World War. Wagner's most famous composition is an instrumental, *No Name Jive,* which he composed and arranged in 1940, and was recorded in two parts by Glen Gray and the Casa Loma Orchestra for Decca. It proved to be one of the band's biggest hits and a rare instance of a two-part instrumental making it into a top ten rating on the charts. The band played it in the movie musical *Jam Session* in 1944. Gene Krupa recorded a condensed rendition on Columbia, and Charlie Barnet's band played a two-part session for Bluebird.

That same year, Wagner worked with pianist Frankie Carle on the melody of *A Lover's Lullaby*. Andy Razaf wrote the words. The popular song was recorded by Glen Gray, the Frankie Carle band, and Frankie Masters. In 1941 Wagner and Bert Stevens composed the music for *Whistler's Mother-in-Law,* with Jimmy Eaton providing the lyric. Bing Crosby recorded the clever song, backed by Woody Herman's orchestra. It was also waxed by the British band of Johnny Claes and His Clay Pigeons for Columbia. Ten years later Jimmy Eaton again provided the words to a Wagner melody, composed in collaboration with Con Hammond, *Turn Back the Hands of Time*. It was introduced and popularized by Eddie Fisher on an RCA–Victor record with Hugo Winterhalter's orchestra.

Other compositions by Larry Wagner include *Over the Rhythm of Raindrops; Hearts Without Flowers; Penguin at the Waldorf; Flamenco Love; Billy and I; One to Remember; You'll Never be Lonely;* and *Speak Well of Me*.

Oliver Wallace

Organist-composer-conductor Oliver Wallace was born in London, England, on August 6, 1887. He attended London public schools and studied music privately. In 1906 he immigrated to the United States and by 1914 had become a citizen. One of his earliest accomplishments was accompanying silent movies with a pipe organ. In 1930 he went to Hollywood, going to work in the Disney studios as a composer and conductor. In this capacity he composed the music for many cartoon shorts, along with animated Disney full-length features.

As a popular songwriter his output wasn't extensive, but it includes two important contributions. The first is the well-known standard *Hindustan,* which was published in 1918 with words by Harold Weeks. Big band arrangers have developed an affinity for this tune over the years, beginning with the first recording by the Joseph C. Smith orchestra in 1918. In 1928 the Ben Bernie band recorded it on Brunswick. In 1939 the Bob Crosby crew made it for Decca, followed by Alvino Rey's orchestra in 1941 on Bluebird and Artie Shaw's in the next year for Victor. It has been played and featured numerous other times in between and is now a favorite of small jazz bands.

Wallace is responsible for both words and music to his other major hit, *Der Fuehrer's Face.* This 1942 salute to Hitler was hilariously performed by Spike Jones and His City Slickers on a smash record for Bluebird and has since assumed the status of a novelty classic. Other titles by Wallace include *When I See An Elephant Fly; Indiana Moon; Rainbow of My Dreams; Other Lips;* and *Last Night I Had That Dream Again.*

Oliver Wallace died in Hollywood, California, on September 16, 1963.

Thomas (Fats) Waller

The British trombonist George Chisholm recorded a tune many years ago called *All Is Not Gold That Glitters,* a title that might aptly apply to the Golden Age of songwriting, because the songwriting business, a very profitable one, has developed a few peculiar characteristics. One of these results in credit for composing song hits going to some who had nothing to do with writing them. Stories are common about songs that became big moneymakers that were sold for ridiculous prices by composers who were desperate for a few ready dollars, and many a big-name bandleader or established songwriter got his name listed as a cocomposer in return for his ability to get a tune published or help promote it into a hit. Some publishers, especially in the early years, accepted tunes for publication and then copyrighted them under their own names, sometimes changing the title in order to do a thorough job of cheating the composers of their rights.

Still another aspect confuses the issue. No one will ever know how many songs were written by prolific composers to be sold outright for ready cash, or simply given away because the writer was capable of turning out songs on an unlimited basis. Here the name of Thomas "Fats" Waller, the great entertainer and pianist, comes to mind. He could compose superior songs so easily and quickly that it seems he could turn out original melodies on demand and in a matter of minutes. While at this stage there is no way of proving it, more than likely he is responsible for many more songs than those he is credited with—especially in the early days of his career. As it is, he is known to have written dozens, and many of these have become classics in the American library of standards.

Waller's approach to songwriting was that of a jazz musician. His work exemplifies material written from a jazz-oriented base, as opposed to that of other writers who wrote from non-jazz backgrounds. In all of his songs there is a strong leaning toward blues progressions and a natural swing to the melody lines that has made them favorites of jazz musicians. A Waller composition seems to form a complete pattern, so perfectly fitting and proper that the first impression is one of utter simplicity, followed by the logical question, "This is so right, how come nobody else ever thought of it?" Under more careful analysis the impression of simplicity is quickly dispelled. Fats was not only capable of beautiful melodic conception, he coupled it with a tricky and original use of chord changes to turn out songs that on first hearing immediately appeal to the listener, yet are of such quality that they have lasting value. Of course, like all songwriters Waller also wrote tunes that have become obscure or are completely forgotten—though sometimes they don't deserve to be—but a sufficient number of his compositions have survived the years to attest to his genius. It's even a pretty safe bet that on any given night of the year, somewhere, some place, somebody is playing a Fats Waller song.

Thomas "Fats" Waller was born in New York City on May 21, 1904. A musical prodigy, he was playing piano at a very early age, before he took lessons. He then went on to playing the organ in church. Later on he took lessons from the master of stride piano, James P. Johnson, taking the style to new dimensions and popularity. His apprenticeship included playing piano for rent parties and in nightclubs, working as an organist in New York's Lincoln Theater, and playing for silent movies in a Washington, D.C. theater. His first published song, *Squeeze Me,* was written in 1925, with words by Clarence Williams, and it set the pattern for a brilliant career. To this day, *Squeeze Me* is a favorite of jazz bands and jazz singers and is frequently heard wherever a jazz festival is taking place. Still, it was three years later before Waller struck again, this time contributing two songs to the stage show "Keep Shufflin'," the title song and *Willow Tree.* The latter received outstanding treatment at a recording session in 1935 for Decca featuring Mildred Bailey and Her Alley Cats, along with two other Waller titles,

Squeeze Me and *Honeysuckle Rose*. Mildred's "Alley Cats" were Bunny Berigan, Teddy Wilson, Johnny Hodges, and Grachan Moncur.

The next year, 1929, disastrous for most, was a bonanza for Waller. Besides having four songs—two of them big hits—in the stage show "Hot Chocolates," *Ain't Misbehavin'; Black and Blue; Song of the Cotton Fields;* and *Sweet Savannah Sue;* he struck gold with *Honeysuckle Rose; My Fate Is in Your Hands;* and *I've Got a Feeling I'm Falling*. And the landslide continued for the next five years, with at least one Waller tune a solid hit for each year. In 1930 it was *Blue, Turning Gray over You,* backed by the moderate success, *Rollin' Down the River*. In 1931 there were three entries: *I'm Crazy 'Bout My Baby; Concentratin';* and *Take It from Me*. Another big one kicked off 1932, *Keepin' Out of Mischief Now,* along with a delightful little gem, *My Heart's at Ease. Lonesome Me,* which has enjoyed some renewed recognition in recent years, was another contender that year, along with *Sheltered by the Stars, Cradled by the Moon.*

Ain'tcha Glad was the solitary Waller title published in 1933, but it was a memorable one that still gets play. There were three in 1934, the formidable *How Can You Face Me?,* the title punctuated in typical Waller dialog on his recording of the tune with "You dog!" The others were *If It Ain't Love*—one of the tunes mentioned earlier that deserves to be revived—and *Rhythm Man.*

For some reason no popular ballads were added to the Waller string in the next two years, but maybe he was saving them up, because in 1937 five songs made it to the market—*Our Love Was Meant to Be; The Joint Is Jumpin; How Can I?; What Will I Do in the Morning?;* and *How Ya, Baby. What Will I Do in the Morning?* deserved a better reception than it got and was the best of the offerings. Fats gave it appropriate treatment with His Rhythm on Victor 25712, coupled with *How Ya, Baby*. Waller continued to write and publish for the pop market up to 1943, the year of his death (on board a train, December 15), but had no more hits.

In addition to songs for the popular market he composed an extensive list of pieces for the piano: *Minor Drag; Harlem Fuss; A Handful of Keys; Viper's Drag; Numb Fumblin'; Alligator Crawl; The Jitterbug Waltz; Clothes Lines Ballet; Fractious Fingering; African Ripples;* and *Smashing Thirds*. He also composed a number of jazz instrumentals, including *Zonky; Stealin' Apples;* and *Yacht Club Swing*. With bandleader-composer Jack Pettis, he collaborated on *St. Louis Shuffle* and *Candied Sweets,* early efforts for both men. During a visit to England in 1939 Waller composed and rerecorded a tone poem entitled *The London Suite,* inspired by the various districts in the city—*Soho, Chelsea, Piccadilly, Limehouse, Whitechapel,* and *Bond Street*. In the book *Ain't Misbehavin', The Story of Fats Waller* (Dodd,

Mead, 1966), Ed Kirkeby relates that due to circumstances brought about by the London blitz, the records that Waller made of his compositions were not released until twelve years later.

Fats Waller died tragically young. Although he left us a priceless heritage of songs that will be appreciated by generations to come, we will never know how much greater that heritage might have been if he had lived longer.

Charles B. Ward

Composer-singer-vaudevillian Charles B. Ward was born in London, England, on August 21, 1865. He came to the United States as a youngster and toured in vaudeville as a singer-entertainer under the title of "the Original Bowery Boy." As part of his presentation, he wrote his own songs. One of these was published in 1895, with words by John E. Palmer, *The Band Plays On*. Ward introduced it himself at Hammerstein's Harlem Opera House, and it was an early hit record by Dan Quinn on Columbia. The song enjoyed even greater popularity in 1941, when it was featured in the James Cagney–Rita Hayworth film *The Strawberry Blonde*. Guy Lombardo's band had the hit record. The song popped up again ten years later in the movie *Cattle Town,* sung by Dennis Morgan.

In 1900 Ward wrote another ballad that was popular in its day, and then went on to a strong revival, *Strike Up the Band, Here Comes a Sailor*. With words by Andrew B. Sterling, it was a hit in vaudeville. More than four decades later (1943) it was revived by Jack Oakie with a female chorus in *Hello, Frisco, Hello*. It also was heard in the 1946 movie *In Old Sacramento*. Other songs by Ward are *How the Irish Beat the Band; In Your Own Town; Maisey, Maisey, Fine and Daisey; While the Band Is Playing Dixie;* and *The Kissing Trust*.

Charles Ward died in New York City on March 21, 1917.

Harry Warnow

See Raymond Scott.

Harry Warren

One of the last of the songwriting greats, Harry Warren died in Hollywood, California, on September 11, 1987, and with the news of his passing it seemed as though a huge, ponderous door had slammed shut on the most wonderful era in our musical history. There were many giants in those days, but time is relentlessly taking its toll, and with Harry Warren we lost one of the tallest. Salvatore Guaragnce, better known as Harry Warren, was born in Brooklyn, New York, on December 24, 1893, and although it's certain nobody suspected it at the time, the world was being blessed with a marvelous Christmas present. Throughout his long and prolific career, Warren did his best to make this a great world to be in by writing hundreds of songs. All kinds of songs—novelties, ballads, love songs, funny songs, tragic songs, sad songs, happy songs, torch songs, and jazz. Jazz musicians have always had a fondness for many of Warren's tunes, and they are mainly responsible for the longevity of perennials like *Rose of the Rio Grande; Lulu's Back in Town; September in the Rain; With Plenty of Money and You* (the latter sometimes disguised, as it is on the Lionel Hampton Victor recording, *House of Morgan*). But the real backbone of Warren's long and successful career was the almost endless stream of popular hits of the day, quality songs that many of us identify with places and events in our lives.

A self-taught musician, he learned to play piano and the accordion and in the tradition of so many songwriters served his apprenticeship playing for silent movies and then working as a songplugger for Shapiro–Bernstein, and Remick Music. His first hit song, *Rose of the Rio Grande,* published in 1922, was a collaboration with lyricist Edgar Leslie and pianist Ross Gorman. It was introduced by Paul Whiteman but has long since become a standard. The incomparable Bobby Hackett turned it into a tour de force on a 78 RPM platter for the short-lived Melrose label. He backed it with another classic, *Pennies From Heaven.* And whoever printed the label reversed the composer credits. *Rose of the Rio Grande* is attributed to Burke-Johnston, and *Pennies From Heaven* to Warren, Gorman, and Leslie. This more or less proves you can't always trust record labels.

Warren was reasonably successful in the twenties, and he had enough hits to establish himself as a consistent winner—*I Love My Baby, My Baby Loves Me; Where Do You Work-a, John; Nagasaki*—but with the advent of the thirties he really hit his stride. No better example can be had than his output for 1930 alone, every song a success—*Cheerful Little Earful; Would You Like to Take a Walk; Have a Little Faith in Me; Crying for the Carolines; Absence Makes the Heart Grow Fonder; Reminiscing; I Remember You From Somewhere; Telling It to the Daisies;* and *He's Not Worth Your Tears.* A good many songsmiths would be satisfied to claim any one of these, but Warren produced song hits in clusters. His collaborators made up a distinguished crew, all lucky to share in the credits—Sam M. Lewis, Joe Young, Ira Gershwin, Billy Rose, Mort Dixon, and Edgar Leslie.

Warren did it again in 1931. Just hitting the highlights, we have *You're My Everything; Ooh! That Kiss; I Found a Million Dollar Baby In a Five-and-Ten Cent Store;* and *By the River Sainte Marie*. In 1932 he formed a fairly permanent partnership with lyricist Al Dubin, and they proceeded to turn out hit scores for one Hollywood film after another, racking up prime titles like *Forty-Second Street; Shuffle Off to Buffalo; You're Getting To Be a Habit with Me; We're in the Money; Pettin' in the Park; Why Do I Dream Those Dreams; Boulevard of Broken Dreams; I'll String Along With You; I Only Have Eyes for You*—and again I'm only hitting the high spots.

Still, as so often is the case, it's the lesser-known titles that seem to linger with the sweetest nostalgia, and among these are such gems as *You Can Be Kissed; I'd Rather Listen to Your Eyes; I'll Sing You a Thousand Love Songs;* and *Something Tells Me*. The association with Al Dubin lasted until 1939. After that Warren began to work with other noted lyricists, including Johnny Mercer, Ira Gershwin, and Mack Gordon.

Even a partial list of the fantastic output of Harry Warren compositions beginning in the thirties and lasting into the fifties has to include some of everybody's favorites. Here are a few samples: *Sweet Music; Where Am I; Remember Me; Love Is Where You Find It; Jeepers Creepers; Say It With a Kiss; You Must Have Been a Beautiful Baby; Chattanooga Choo Choo; It Happened in Sun Valley; I Had the Craziest Dream; Kalamazoo; This Heart of Mine; On the Atcheson, Topeka, and Santa Fe; You Wonderful You; That's Amore;* and so on, and so on.

Yes, indeed! In those days there were musical giants in the land.

Joe ("Country") Washburne

Joe "Country" Washburne, composer-singer-bandleader and virtuoso of the brass bass, was born in Houston, Texas, on December 28, 1904. In 1929 he joined the Ted Weems band playing brass bass, doubling on string bass and as a vocalist, and during the long tenure as such, he collaborated with Weems on *Oh! Mona*, a novelty in the jazz vein in 1931. The tune was a hit record for the Weems organization on Victor in 1931, and they recorded it again ten years later for Decca. Other contemporary sides in the year of publication were made by Joel Shaw (Gene Kardos) on Crown and British bandleader Billy Cotton on English Columbia. Latter-day records were made by the Dinning Sisters (Capitol) and Pee Wee King (Capitol).

In 1942 Washburne and Roger Lewis shared credit for the lyrics to a melody that was the result of a collaboration between Dick Jurgens and Walter Donovan. The tune was *One Dozen Roses,* and the committee of composers benefitted substantially from the song's fourteen weeks on *Your Hit Parade,* twice in the number one spot. Dick Jurgens had a hit recording, and so did Harry James, followed closely by vocalist Dinah Shore and Glen Gray and the Casa Loma Orchestra.

Other Country Washburne compositions include *You Don't Know What Lonesome Is; Everybody Calls It Swing; I Saw Esau; At Last I'm First With You;* and *We'll Sing the Old Songs.*

Ned Washington

Lyricist Ned Washington was born in Scranton, Pennsylvania, on August 15, 1901. His education included technical high school and the Charles Sumner School. Early in his career he performed as a master of ceremony in vaudeville and as an agent, also writing special material. This led him into writing lyrics for songs, including work for many hit shows and later on the movies. One of the most prolific writers in the business, he collaborated with top composers and is credited with a number of outstanding songs.

In 1928 Washington contributed two songs to the Earl Carroll's "Vanities" of that year, a stage show, working with composer Michael Cleary. The songs, *My Arms Are Wide Open* and *Getting the Beautiful Girls,* were not especially important, but they opened the door to Washington's career. The following year he worked with Herb Magidson, and between them they wrote the lyrics to a tune by Michael Cleary that proved to be the big hit from the prestigious movie *Show of Shows.* This was *Singin' in the Bathtub,* sung by Winnie Lightner in the picture. Then to cap things off for the year, the three writers turned out *Hello, Baby* (also called *H'lo, Baby* in some instances), which did well on recordings by Bert Lown, Waring's Pennsylvanians, and Phil Spitalny's Orchestra in the domestic market. The Rhythmic Eight recorded it on Zonophone in England.

The next two years offer nothing important, but in 1932 Washington more than made up for the lapse. With composer Victor Young he wrote two excellent songs, *Can't We Talk It Over?* and *My Love.* Both received top treatment from Bing Crosby on Brunswick, and Bing was also listed as a co-composer of a third song, *Waltzing in a Dream.* Then Washington contributed the words to two more songs that were destined to become famous theme songs. With George Bassman it was *I'm Getting Sentimental Over*

You, which wound up as Tommy Dorsey's theme; and with Gene Gifford, guitarist-arranger for the Casa Loma Orchestra, it was *Smoke Rings,* Glen Gray's haunting theme. For good measure, Washington teamed with Edgar Hayes and Irving Mills on *Someone Stole Gabriel's Horn,* also known as *Somebody Stole etc.* This title stirred up a lot of action on recordings. Bing Crosby made it for Brunswick, backed by the Dorsey Brothers orchestra, with Bunny Berigan in the lineup, and then the Dorsey Brothers orchestra made it under their own name for Brunswick. Jack Teagarden's band recorded it for Columbia, as did the trio known as the Three Keys; and the Washboard Rhythm Kings waxed it for Victor. Jack Bland and the Rhythmakers took care of Banner and related labels, and in England Nat Gonella and Spike Hughes recorded it for Parlophone and Decca respectively.

This would seem to be sufficient to satisfy any song spinner, but Ned Washington was just warming up. In 1933 he again paired with the estimable Victor Young, and for the movie *Murder at the Vanities,* contributed the beautiful *Sweet Madness.* Two other excellent songs also resulted, *I'd Be Telling a Lie* and *Love Is the Thing.* Bing Crosby stepped in again to share the glory for *Ghost of a Chance,* but made it a good deal by recording and promoting the song into a hit and then a standard. Like Gus Kahn, Washington seemed willing to work with any composer who came along with a good song, so with Bernice Petkere he penned the words to *Stay Out of My Dreams,* a nice tune that got the usual respect from Freddy Martin; and with Allie Wrubel he wrote the words to *I'll Be Faithful.* Adrian Rollini liked this so much he recorded it twice for Banner and associated labels; it was also made by Ozzie Nelson and Jan Garber.

Nevertheless, Washington was back working with Victor Young in 1934, and some more great songs resulted. One has since become a standard, helped considerably in that direction by Jack Teagarden, who not only recorded it, but favored it as a vocal offering. The song is *A Hundred Years From Today.* It was introduced by Kathryn Perry in Lew Leslie's "Blackbirds," which opened in 1933, and was also featured in the film *Girl from Missouri* in 1934. Among the contemporary recordings were Ethel Waters with the Benny Goodman orchestra on Columbia, Eddy Duchin on Victor, Glen Gray and the Casa Loma orchestra on Brunswick with the vocal by Lee Wiley, and the aforementioned Jack Teagarden on Brunswick. It has been recorded many times since.

Jack Teagarden was also among those who recorded *Love Me,* another title by Young and Washington. Don Bestor made it on Victor. Subsequent sides were waxed by Woody Herman on Decca, Billy Eckstine on MGM, and Dean Martin, backed by Dick Stabile's orchestra, on Capitol. *Give Me a*

Heart to Sing To, a third title, was introduced in the movie *Frankie and Johnny,* which was filmed in 1934 but was held up by censorship problems until 1936. Helen Morgan recorded the song, as did Guy Lombardo and Henry King. Playing the field again, Washington teamed with Walter Gross on *Your Love,* recorded by Freddy Martin, and with Sam Stept for *London on a Rainy Night.* Appropriately, Bert Ambrose's English band had the best recording.

From this point on, Washington became heavily involved with songs for movies. In 1940 he worked with Leigh Harline on music for the full-length Disney cartoon *Pinocchio* and the hit song *When You Wish Upon a Star,* sung on the soundtrack by Cliff Edwards as the voice of Jiminy Cricket. The song was given an Academy Award. That same year he and Hoagy Carmichael produced another standard, *The Nearness of You.* This one went the full round of the contemporary recording labels—Glenn Miller and Dinah Shore on Bluebird, Guy Lombardo and Connee Boswell for Decca, Larry Clinton on Victor, Ray Herbeck on Vocalion, and Eddy Howard on Columbia. Again, it has been recorded many times since.

In 1946 Washington reunited with Victor Young to provide the lyric to a revamping of the theme from a 1934 movie, *The Uninvited.* The result was another standard, *Stella by Starlight.* Victor Young and His Orchestra were the first to record it, but it has since gone on to dozens of renditions. *On Green Dolphin Street* was another adaptation of a movie theme, this time from *Green Dolphin Street.* The music is by Bronislaw Kaper. The Jimmy Dorsey orchestra recorded it for Decca, and Ralph Martiere debuted with a big band for Mercury on the new material for pressing records, vinyl. The ballad went on to become a favorite vehicle for bop musicians, who changed the meter, the melody, and sometimes the chords.

Ned Washington continued to write for films well into the sixties, often providing lyrics to the title songs. Among these are *Take the High Ground; The High and the Mighty; The Man from Laramie; Gunfight at the OK Corral; Fire Down Below; The Roots of Heaven; Town Without Pity;* and *Ship of Fools.*

Johnny Watson

See Johnny Kluczko.

Grady Watts

Multitalented Grady Watts—a virtuoso of the trumpet, composer, and writer—was born in Texarkana, Texas, on June 30, 1908. He was educated at the Allen Military Academy in Texas and the University of Oklahoma. In the early thirties he joined the Casa Loma Orchestra, under the direction of Glen Gray, and was a member of the brass team for twelve years. Following that he worked as an artist's representative and then as an executive for a chemical company.

His composing efforts took place while he was with Casa Loma, and the band recorded most of them. One of his earliest titles was *Rhythm Man,* a 1932 release, recorded by Casa Loma with a vocal by Pee Wee Hunt. In 1934 the band recorded another Watts tune, *You Ain't Been Livin' Right,* a collaboration with Winston Tharp, and still another in 1937, *I Remember,* a ballad sung by Kenny Sargent. *Daddy's Boy,* with words and music by Watts, came out in 1938, and Casa Loma recorded it for Brunswick with a Kenny Sargent vocal. In the following year he collaborated with Maurice Sigler and Bud Green to write *If You Ever Change Your Mind.* This one rated the usual treatment by Casa Loma, plus a Bluebird recording by Artie Shaw, with Helen Forrest vocalizing, and another by Tommy Dorsey, with Edythe Wright, on Victor. *Blue Champagne,* another superior ballad, made its appearance in 1941, with composer credits to Watts, Frank Ryerson, and Jimmy Eaton. Jimmy Dorsey's band recorded it for Decca, with the vocal by Bob Eberle; Freddy Martin gave it svelte treatment on Bluebird as an instrumental. Another song by Grady Watts is *Touch and Go.*

Mabel Wayne

Pianist-singer-composer Mabel Wayne was born in Brooklyn, New York, on July 16, 1904. Her education included private music studies in Switzerland, followed by further study at the New York School of Music. Her career included performing as a concert singer and pianist both in the United States and abroad. She started to concentrate on writing popular songs in the midtwenties. In 1925 she teamed with lyricists L. Wolfe Gilbert and Abel Baer, and the result was, *Don't Wake Me Up, Let Me Dream,* which enjoyed reasonable popularity that year and was recorded by the bands of Vincent Lopez and Howard Lanin.

She did even better the following year, this time working with veterans Sam Lewis and Joe Young. They produced *In a Little Spanish Town.* As a waltz in its original form, the tune was a hit and was a popular recording by Paul Whiteman's orchestra on Victor and also by the singing group, the Reverlers, on the same label. It was also Wayne's first big hit. However, the melody is very adaptable and through the years has been recorded as a fox-trot as well as a jazz tune. In the latter category it was arranged and recorded by Glenn Miller with a studio group for Columbia in 1935 and in 1940 as a piano solo by Joe Bushkin on Commodore. Bing Crosby recorded the song on Decca, and in 1943 it was sung by a trio consisting of Virginia O'Brien, June Allyson, and Glorida DeHaven in the movie *Thousands Cheer*. Shedding its format as a waltz many years ago, the song is now a standard.

Still partial to waltzes, Wayne and L. Wolfe Gilbert penned another hit in 1927, *Ramona*. This time the composition involved a gimmick. The song was deliberately aimed at promoting the silent movie *Ramona,* and the intention was to have it played to accompany the film. The operation was a great success; the tune was a hit even before the picture was released. With a big publicity buildup, Dolores Del Rio, who was the star in the movie, sang the song in a coast-to-coast radio hookup from Hollywood, accompanied by Paul Whiteman's orchestra in New York. Whiteman also recorded the tune as did singer Gene Austin. Both records were a hit. Unlike *In a Little Spanish Town, Ramona* never made the transition to four beats to a measure.

Not the same for *It Happened in Monterey,* however, which was featured in the Paul Whitman film *King of Jazz* in 1930. Once again a waltz to begin with, it carried on the Wayne infatuation with things Spanish in a lyric by Billy Rose. John Boles sang it in the movie, and the Paul Whiteman Orchestra recorded it on Columbia, with a vocal by Jack Fulton. It has since been played and recorded many times—as a fox-trot. In that same year, Wayne collaborated with Edgar Leslie on *When Kentucky Bids the World "Good Morning."* Red Nichols had the best record.

In 1934 Wayne worked with Maurice Sigler and Al Hoffman, writing *Little Man, You've Had a Busy Day*. The title was suggested by the best-selling book *Little Man, What Now?* by Hans Fallada and was definitely aimed at the sentimental market. It was well represented on recordings by Isham Jones (Victor), Emil Coleman (Columbia), the Pickens Sisters (Victor), and Frank Luther (Melotone). Years later, Jerry Lewis and his wife Patti revived it on a recording for Capitol.

I Understand, a 1940 collaboration with Kim Gannon and one of Wayne's nicest ballads, was a very successful entry as recorded by Jimmy Dorsey's band, with Bob Eberle on the vocal. The song also rated considerable airplay. The pair scored again nine years later with *A Dreamer's Holiday*. By this time the singers had taken over the popular market, so Perry Como had the hit record for Victor and Buddy Clark for Columbia. The bands of Gordon Jenkins (Decca) and Ray Anthony (Capitol) also made it. In 1950 Wayne worked with veteran lyricist Lew Brown, and they came up with *On the Outgoing Tide,* another successful record for Perry Como on RCA–Victor, backed by the Mitchell Ayres Orchestra.

Other songs by Mable Wayne are *Chiquita; Indian Cradle Song; Do Ya Love Me?; At a Cabana in Havana; Be Fair; It Happened in Hawaii; Why Don't You Fall in Love With Me?; South Wind; Under a Strawberry Moon; When the Sandman Rides the Trail; The Language of Love; The Right Kind of Love; So Madly in Love; I'm Wond'rin'; Guessing; His Majesty the Baby; Rose Ann of Charing Cross; If I Didn't Already Love You, Baby; Music for Madame; Little Rag Doll; The Crazy Things You Do When You're in Love; Betwixt and Between;* and *Tiny Tim.*

Paul Francis Webster

Lyricist Paul Francis Webster was born in New York City on December 20, 1907. He was educated at Cornell University and NYU and then served a hitch as an able-bodied seaman. After that he became a dancing instructor in New York. After being associated with several hit songs in the early thirties, he went to Hollywood in 1935 under contract with 20th Century Fox to write material for Shirley Temple. When this was up he began to freelance and in the ensuing years collaborated with a number of the foremost composers.

In 1928 Webster collaborated with another three-name songwriter, John Jacob Loeb, in writing a song they called *Masquerade,* which was the first hit for both of them. A waltz, Ted Black's orchestra recorded it for Victor and Morton Gould for Columbia. It was also made by Arthur Tracy, the "Street Singer," on Brunswick and by organist Jesse Crawford for Victor. Rudy Vallee claimed a share of the lyrics on *Two Little Blue Little Eyes,* another Loeb–Webster song in 1931, and he recorded it and promoted it to popularity on radio broadcasts. He also helped in this regard with the 1933 song *My Moonlight Madonna.* Another waltz, the melody was adapted by bandleader William Scotti from a composition called *Poeme* by Zdenko Fibich. Webster added the words. The tune was recorded by Paul Whiteman, Rudy Vallee, and Victor Young. Singers Conrad Thibault and Jack Fulton also waxed it. Loeb and Webster, still working together, also had a delightful entry that same year, *Reflections in the Water.* It received considerable radio play and was recorded by Arthur Tracy on Brunswick. Many years later David Rose arranged and reprised the song on an LP album for MGM called *Reflections in the Water* (E3603).

Billy Rose shared credit with Webster on the 1934 melody by John Jacob Loeb, *Got the Jitters,* with descriptive lyrics depicting life in the fast lane.

Eddie Stone did them justice on a recording by Isham Jones for Victor. It was introduced by Ben Pollack's band at the Casino de Paris in Manhattan, and he recorded it for Columbia. Don Redman made it for Melotone, and so did Adrian Rollini. But that year Webster found a new partner in Lew Pollack, and together they wrote two songs, *Two Cigarettes in the Dark* and *Water Under the Bridge*. The first title was introduced by Gloria Grafton in a movie called *Kill That Story*. Records were made by the orchestras of Glen Gray and Johnny Green and also by Morton Downey and Joe Morrison. It has been revived several times on recordings. *Water under the Bridge* was recorded by Will Osborne's band for the ARC labels and by Lanny Ross for Brunswick. In 1936 Webster and composer Louis Alter wrote three songs for the movie *Rainbow on the River,* starring young Bobby Breen, the title song; *A Thousand Dreams of You;* and *You Only Live Once*.

For the next few years Webster was busy in the movie studios, and although writing a lot of songs, had nothing spectacular until 1941. In that year he had the good fortune to work with Duke Ellington on two songs that were introduced in the West Coast revue "Jump for Joy." Again, this included the title song, plus *I Got It Bad, and That Ain't Good*. The Ellington orchestra recorded them both. *I Got It Bad* was also recorded by the Benny Goodman band with the vocal by Peggy Lee. All of the records sold well, and the tune has gone on to become a much-recorded standard.

In 1942 Webster had his first pairing with Hoagy Carmichael on *The Lamplighter's Serenade*. Not the best work for either one, the song nevertheless was given first-rate attention by the Glenn Miller band on Bluebird and by Bing Crosby on Decca. Frank Sinatra made it as a single shortly after leaving the Tommy Dorsey band. Webster and Ted Fio Rito also provided another hit record for Bing, in a duet with Mary Martin, on *Lily of Laguna*. Carmichael and Webster reunited in 1945 for two songs. *Memphis in June* was introduced by Hoagy in the film *Johnny Angel*. He recorded it for ARA. Harry James made it on Columbia, Johnny Mercer on Capitol, and Betty Bonney on Victor. The other title, *Baltimore Oriole,* got the typical Carmichael rendition in the movie *To Have and Have Not*. The Carmichael connection continued for the 1946 movie *The Stork Club* and collaboration on *Doctor, Lawyer, Indian Chief*. Best-selling domestic sides were made by Betty Hutton, who starred in the film, Hoagy Carmichael, and Les Brown's band. Overseas, an outstanding recording was made by violinist Svend Asmussen on the Danish Odeon label.

In 1948 Webster began writing with Sonny Burke, and one of their first titles was *Black Coffee,* a rather gloomy song accorded fine treatment by Peggy Lee on Capitol, Ella Fitzgerald on Decca, and Sarah Vaughn on Columbia. The association continued with the hit record for Buddy Clark with Doris Day on Columbia, *You Was*. Freddy Martin's band recorded it for RCA–Victor. And in 1949 they wrote *How It Lies, How It Lies, How It Lies!*—a sentiment Kay Starr found favorable on Capitol and Connie Haines on Coral.

Sammy Fain was the cocomposer of *Secret Love,* the big hit for Doris Day from the movie *Calamity Jane*. The song won an Academy Award, and Doris Day's recording on Columbia was the biggest hit of her career. Still turning out music for films at a prolific rate, Webster struck paydirt again in 1965 working with composer Johnny Mandel. The song was *The Shadow of Your Smile,* introduced in the movie *The Sandpiper,* by a chorus under the final credits of the film. Tony Bennett had the best-selling record, and the tune won a Grammy as the Song of the Year.

Other titles by Paul Francis Webster include *Make a Wish; Music in My Heart; Put Your Heart in a Song; The Sunny Side of Things; Happy As a Lark; Goodbye, My Dreams, Goodbye; Blue Italian Waters; I'd Like to Set You to Music; Happiness Bound; Remember Me to Carolina; Things Have Changed; The Three Rivers; Follow the Swallow to Hide-away Hollow; The Loveliest Night of the Year; Watermelon Weather; I Speak to the Stars; April Love; The Green Leaves of Summer; The Mood I'm In; Somewhere My Love;* and *A Time for Love*.

Kurt Weill

Composer-conductor Kurt Weill was born in Dessau, Germany, on March 2, 1900. His musical education included study with Albert Bing, Humperdinck, Krasselt, and Busoni. At age fifteen he was already the choral director and opera company accompanist in Dessau. A short time later he became the musical conductor for the Ludenscheid, Westphalia, opera company. In Berlin he continued his studies and began composing for ballet and opera. In 1928 he composed the opera, *Die Dreigroschenoper (The Threepenny Opera)* and in the succeeding five years toured Europe presenting it in thousands of performances. The lyrics by Bertolt Brecht portrayed the German Left's attitude toward the country's deteriorating condition, rendered in beer hall style. Kurt Weill married the leading lady in the show, Lotte Lenya. His last German opera, *The Lake of Silver* in 1933, was set for a long run, but the increasing unrest created by the Nazi movement made him decide to take his wife and leave Germany. Their first stop was Paris, where Weill wrote for the French theater, and then in 1935 the pair sailed for the United States.

In the following year Weill presented his first Broadway musical, "Johnny Johnson." It ran for sixty-eight performances. *To Love You and to Lose You,* with words by Edward Heyman, was the popularized version of *Listen to My Song (Johnny's Song),* which was sung in the show by Russell Collins, with a lyric by Paul Green. Ray Noble's orchestra recorded the tune for Victor early in 1937. "Knickerbocker Holiday," a 1938 musical starring Walter Huston, with book and lyrics by Maxwell Anderson, was an outstanding success. The hardy perennial *September Song,* sung by Huston in the show and recorded by him for Brunswick, was the hit song. Charles Coburn sang it in the movie *Knickerbocker Holiday* in 1944. For the film *A September Affair* in 1951, the Huston recording was played as a background theme on the soundtrack. In 1960 Maurice Chevalier reprised the song in the movie *Pepe.* It has been recorded numerous times, including versions by Frank Sinatra, Jimmy Durante, the bands of Eddy Duchin and Artie Shaw, and the Red Norvo Trio. *My Ship,* with words by Ira Gershwin, was sung by Gertrude Lawrence in the 1941 Kurt Weill production of "Lady in the Dark." She recorded it for Victor, and Danny Kaye—who was in the show, but didn't sing the song—recorded it on Columbia. So did Eddy Duchin.

In 1943 Ogden Nash was the lyricist for *Speak Low,* the beautiful Weill melody that was sung by Mary Martin and then again with Kenny Baker in "One Touch of Venus." In the 1948 movie version, it was reprised by Dick Haymes and Eileen Wilson (dubbed in on the soundtrack for Ava Gardner). Guy Lombardo recorded it for Decca. Then in 1948 Alan Jay Lerner penned the words for *Here I'll Stay,* introduced by Nanette Fabray and Ray Middleton in "Love Life." Jo Stafford had a good record on Capitol. Maxwell Anderson was back to write the words for *Lost in the Stars* in 1949, the title song for the Weill stage show of that year. It was introduced by Todd Duncan. In the 1974 movie version it was sung by Brock Peters.

And now we come to *Mack the Knife.* This originated as *Moritat* in the 1928 German production of the *Threepenny Opera.* The German lyrics were by Bertolt Brecht; the English by Marc Blitzstein. It had a varied recording history over the years, but the first big hit record was by Louis Armstrong for Columbia in 1956. This was followed by another smash, made by Bobby Darin in 1959, which won a Grammy Award for Record of the Year, and then Ella Fitzgerald had still another in 1960. Melodically the song is not in the class of other Weill compositions, and its success is primarily due to outstanding presentations.

Other Kurt Weill compositions are *On the Rio Grande; Heart of Love; It Never Was You; There's Nowhere to Go but Up; Spring Again; The Right*

Guy for Me; Jenny; This Is New; One Life to Live; How Much I Love You; I'm a Stranger Here Myself; All at Once; If Love Remains; Moon-Faced and Starry Eyed; Remember That I Care; Green-up Time; and *Bilbao Song.*

Kurt Weill died in New York City on April 3, 1950.

Frank Weldon

Composer Frank Weldon was born in Lawrence, Massachusetts. He was educated at the New England Conservatory of Music. Early in his career he toured in vaudeville as a writer and musical director. Later, he led dance bands in the New England area. He started writing popular songs in the midthirties, and while his output isn't great, it includes some quality songs and some very successful ones.

In 1933 he started things off with the sprightly *I Like Mountain Music,* with words by Jimmy Cavanaugh that extolled "a hillbilly band" but wasn't in the hillbilly idiom. Ted Weems had a good record with Elmo Tanner. George Olsen also made it with Ethel Shutta. More importantly in that era, it enjoyed good radio time. Charles O'Flynn collaborated with Jimmy Cavanaugh to write the words to the 1934 Weldon entry *Neighbors.* Eddie Stone did it full justice on a Victor record with the Isham Jones band. In 1939 John Redmond worked with Cavanaugh, and the song was *The Man with the Mandolin.* Although not up to the merit of *Neighbors,* it had the advantage of a better market. Glenn Miller had a best-seller on Bluebird, with the vocal by Marion Hutton, closely followed by Horace Heidt on a Brunswick side. The tune made the number two spot on *Your Hit Parade* and was on the program for ten weeks.

Sidewalk Serenade was another Weldon–Cavanaugh–Redmond song in 1940. Sammy Kaye recorded it. In 1944 Dick Robertson joined the team of Weldon and Cavanaugh for *A Little On the Lonely Side.* A very pleasant ballad, this drew serious attention from Frankie Carle on Columbia, Guy Lombardo on Decca, and the Phil Moore Four on Victor. Robertson–Weldon–Cavanaugh repeated the next year with *I'd Do It All Over Again.* This one was recorded by Hal McIntyre's band and Frankie Carle's. Other songs by Frank Weldon are *Why Have a Falling Out?; On a Simmery Summery Day; Goodnight Wherever You Are; Why Did It Have to End So Soon?; A Lovely Rainy Afternoon; Dancing On a Rooftop; Rural Rhythm; Christmas in Killarney; What Do You See in Her?; Dearest Darling; Laughing Sailor; Grand Central Station;* and *I Came, I Saw, I Conga'd.*

Frank Weldon died in Jackson Heights, New York, on January 19, 1970.

Pete Wendling

Back in the days when my friend Henry Pilch reminisced about his younger years in his monthly column in *Jersey Jazz,* called Notes for Nostalgia, he repeatedly mentioned a song that impressed him as typifying the new jazz age, *All the Quakers Are Shoulder Shakers (Down in Quaker Town).* While it probably had very little appeal to the Quakers, this little ditty helped establish its composer as a hit songwriter. He was Pete Wendling, a jazz-minded gentleman and gifted pianist who was born in New York City on June 6, 1888, and at the age of eighteen won a contest for ragtime piano playing. He went on to become a welcome guest in countless American homes during the twenties and thirties where player pianos played the dozens of music rolls he made.

In spite of Henry's fondness for *All the Quakers Are Shoulder Shakers,* the tune was only a minor composition, and Wendling's reputation is really based on a solid foundation of excellent songs. One of his earliest hits was *Yaaka Hula Hickey Dula.* It was published in 1916 but became part of jazz history when Red Nichols and His Five Pennies recorded it for Brunswick in 1931. Another was *Take Your Girlie to the Movies,* a timely suggestion for 1919, when both the movies and writing popular songs were about to graduate into the big time.

In 1920 Pete Wendling wrote *What-cha Gonna Do When There Ain't No Jazz?*—a chilling prophecy even more poignant now than when it was first made. In 1928 he scored big with *Bright Eyes,* and then as the twenties blended into the Golden Age of songwriting, his contributions increased. In 1930 for the movie *Puttin' on the Ritz,* he composed *There's Danger in Your Eyes, Cherie,* plus the freelance offerings *Swingin' in a Hammock; Crying Myself to Sleep; I'll Be Blue Just Thinking of You;* and *I'm Tickled Pink With a Blue-Eyed Baby.* In the fruitful year of 1931 came *Thanks to You* (an early Bing Crosby classic with Gus Arnheim's band on Victor) and *You're Twice as Nice as the Girl in My Dreams* (an Al Bowlly gem with Ray Noble on HMV). *I Believe in Miracles* (immortalized by Fats Waller for Victor) was published in 1935, along with another good song, *I'm Growing Fonder of You.*

Wendling worked with an illustrious list of collaborators, including Sam M. Lewis, Joe Young, Bert Kalmar, Edgar Leslie, Harry Richman, John Klenner, Charles O'Flynn, Jack Meskill, and composer George W. Meyer. He died in his native New York City on April 7, 1974, at the ripe old age of eighty-six, but his niche of immortality in our musical heritage is assured on three counts—his piano rolls, carefully preserved by many collectors; his songs, pleasantly melodic and deceptive in their seeming simplicity; and by the title of one of his enduring hits, *Take Me to the Land of Jazz,* which aptly sums up the jazz buff's idea of Heaven.

Percy Wenrich

Composer Percy Wenrich was born in Joplin, Missouri, on January 25, 1887. He attended the Chicago Musical College and then went to work as a staff writer for a Chicago publishing house. For fifteen years he toured with his wife Dolly Connelly in vaudeville. A charter member of ASCAP, Wenrich started publishing popular songs in 1908. That year he had two songs on the market, *It's Moonlight All the Time On Broadway* and *Up in a Balloon.* The lyrics for both songs were by Ren Shields. The first title glorified the lights on Broadway, and the second the growing interest in air travel. In the following year he composed the first of an amazing number of all-time standards, *Put On Your Old Gray Bonnet.* Stanley Murphy wrote the words to this old favorite, which has been played, sung, and recorded countless times since. Ozzie Nelson made a feature number out of it in 1933 and recorded it for Vocalion.

Wenrich scored heavily again in 1912 with *Moonlight Bay,* a favorite sing-along tune through the years going back as far as the days of the bouncing ball in theaters. The words were written by Edward Madden. A popular song when it first came out, it rated a recording for Victor by the American Quartet, who then turned around and recorded it again for Edison as the Premier Quartet. Barbershop quartets have loved the tune ever since. What's more, it has gone on to bigger and better things. In 1940 it was sung by Alice Faye in the film *Tin Pan Alley,* and in 1943 it was used in another movie musical *Is Everybody Happy?* It was the title song of the Doris Day film *On Moonlight Bay* in 1951, and she sang it in the picture. Bing Crosby recorded it with son Gary for Decca and made the top twenty listing that same year.

Nothing happened in 1913, but among other songs by Wenrich published in 1914 was *When You Wore a Tulip (And I Wore a Big Red Rose).* Jack Mahoney was the lyricist for this big hit, which was an immediate success in vaudeville and was again recorded by the American Quartet for Victor. Gene Kelly and Judy Garland sang it in the 1942 movie *For Me and My Gal,* and the recording they made for Decca was one of the biggest sellers of the year. The song was also used in *Hello, Frisco, Hello* in 1943, *The Merry Monahans* in 1944, and *Has Anybody Seen My Gal?* in 1952. *Sweet Cider Time When You Were Mine,* with words by Joseph McCarthy, was another

Wenrich offering in the early years. A spirited rendering of the venerable ballad was recorded on Decca for an album called *Jazz Band Ball* by Eddie Condon and His Orchestra, with the vocal by Jimmy Atkins (DL 5196).

Still writing well into the thirties, Wenrich had another big hit in 1937, *Sail Along Silv'ry Moon.* Harry Tobias collaborated on this one, the last successful song by Wenrich after three decades of turning out hits. It had good records by Red McKenzie and Gene Autry—both for Vocalion—and by Horace Heidt on Brunswick. In 1953 it was revived as an instrumental by Billy Vaughn and His Orchestra on Dot and made the top ten rating. Other songs by Wenrich include *Silver Bells; Sugar Moon; Kentucky Days; Where Do We Go From Here?; A Girl in Your Arms; Look for the Girl; All Muddled Up; Lantern of Love; Baby; Love Rules the World; Nobody but You; Make My Bed Down in Dixieland; When the Moon Hangs High; Red Rose Rag;* and *A Rainbow From the U.S.A.*

Percy Wenrich died in New York City on March 17, 1952.

Eugene West

Lyricist Eugene West was born in Louisiana on August 27, 1883. He was educated in the public schools and like many of his contemporaries got his early experience touring in vaudeville as a singer and pianist. Eventually reaching New York City he went to work as a staff writer for a music publishing firm and provided material for the "Passing Shows" and the "Ziegfeld Follies." In 1920 he collaborated with composers Martin Freed and Otis Spencer on *Broadway Rose,* a tune that drew considerable attention from the recording companies of the day. It was waxed by the Original Dixieland Jazz Band on Victor, and the Peerless Quartet made it for the same label. The bands of Art Hickman and Ted Lewis made it for Columbia, and Harry Raderman recorded it on Lyric.

You Know You Belong to Somebody Else (So Why Don't You Leave Me Alone?), with words by West and music by James V. Monaco, was introduced, featured, and recorded (Columbia) by Nora Bayes in 1922. Bennie Krueger recorded it for Brunswick and the Virginians for Victor. And in the following year West paired with Ira Schuster on the popular novelty *Hi-Lee Hi-Lo,* which resulted in a big record for the team of Billy Murray and Ed Smalle on Victor, plus sides by the Joseph P. Samuels orchestra on the Plaza labels, Bob Haring on Cameo, Nathan Glantz for Pathe, and the Broadway Dance Orchestra on Edison. In 1931 West worked with James McCaffrey and Dave Ringle on *Roll On, Mississippi, Roll On,* a brightly optimistic tune in that year of Depression gloom. It was a popular radio feature and was recorded by the Boswell Sisters on Brunswick. Noble Sissle's orchestra made it for the same company, but the best-selling record was the Victor by Ray Noble's New Mayfair Orchestra, originally recorded in England on HMV and released in this country on the exchange agreement between the two companies. The success of the Mississippi song was most likely the inspiration for the same team to follow up with a similar offering the following year, *Sailin' On the Robert E. Lee.* Again Ray Noble had the best-selling record.

Hallelujah, Things Look Rosy Now was a collaboration with Ira Schuster in 1936, and it received special attention by the irrepressible Fats Waller, who recorded it twice for Victor, with a vocal and without. The hot group of Tempo King and His Kings of Tempo also made it for Bluebird. Other songs with lyrics by West include *When You're Alone; Everybody Shimmies Now; Please Come Back to Me; Don't Say You're Sorry Again; Looks Like a Beautiful Day; My Dream of the South; The Scissors Grinder's Song; Te Amo; Stud Polka; Need I Say?; He's a Carousel Cowboy;* and *Arizeh.*

Eugene West died in New York City on May 26, 1949.

Paul Weston (Paul Wetstein)

Arranger-conductor-composer Paul Weston was born in Springfield, Massachusetts, on March 12, 1912. He graduated from Dartmouth College with a B.A. degree in 1933. While a student there he organized and led a dance band, playing piano. In New York City later on, he worked as a freelance arranger, contributing charts to Rudy Vallee, Phil Harris, and Joe Haymes. When Tommy Dorsey took over the Haymes band, Weston became the staff arranger and filled that spot for the rest of the thirties. In 1940 he worked for Bob Crosby and freelanced, providing material for singers, bands, and the movies. Then in 1943 he joined the new Capitol Recording Company as arranger-conductor and in the next year took over as A & R director. Around this time he began recording albums of standards with all-star studio orchestras, showcasing the songs with impeccable arrangements and excellent musicianship. The series began in the forties and continued well into the fifties with the development of the LP record.

As a composer he entered the field with a top entry written in collaboration with Axel Stordahl and Sammy Cahn in 1945, *I Should Care.* It was introduced by Robert Allen in the movie musical *Thrill of a Romance,* and it went the circuit of the record labels. Frank Sinatra had the best-selling record on Columbia, followed closely by Martha Tilton on Capitol, Tommy Dorsey on Victor, and Jimmy Dorsey for Decca. It came back again with a chart record by Ralph Flanagan in 1952 and again two years later with a recording for Decca by Jeff Chandler. The team repeated in 1946 with another superior ballad, *Day by Day*. Frank Sinatra recorded it with Axel Stordahl's orchestra on Columbia, and Jo Stafford made it with husband Paul Weston's orchestra for Capitol. Doris Day—no doubt fascinated by the title—made it with Les Brown's band on Columbia, and Bing Crosby and Mel Tormé intoned it with the Meltones for Decca.

Weston and Joel Benton shared the credit for *This Time,* published in 1946 and not to be confused with several others of the same title that came along later. It was tastefully recorded by the bands of Tommy Dorsey and Claude Thornhill. Weston rejoined Axel Stordahl in 1947 in writing the plaintive *Ain'tcha Ever Comin' Back?,* delineated by Frank Sinatra and the Pied Pipers with Stordahl's orchestra on Columbia. *Congratulations* were in order in 1949, as composed by Weston and Sid Robin. Jo Stafford recorded the song with Weston's orchestra, and Frankie Carle also made it. In 1951 Weston and Paul Mason Howard combined on the biggest hit—and least musical—of Weston's career, *Shrimp Boats*. He recorded it, featuring wife Jo Stafford with the Paul Luboff Choir, and the record sold over a million for Capitol.

Other songs by Paul Weston are *Talking to Myself About You; Gandy Dancers' Ball; Indiscretion; Autumn in Rome; No Other Love; Hasegawa General Store;* and *When April Comes Again.*

Paul Wetstein

See Paul Weston.

Ned Wever

Lyricist Ned Wever was born in New York City on April 27, 1899. His education included the Pawling School and Princeton University. In his senior year at Princeton he wrote the book and lyrics for the Triangle Club Show. He also appeared in several Broadway plays. In 1932 he began what would become a frequent collaboration with Milton Ager. The tune was *Sing a New Song,* and it was recorded by the bands of Art Kassel, Bennie Krueger, and Coon–Sanders. It was followed by *Trouble in Paradise* the next year, with Arthur Schwartz working with Ager on the melody. It did very well in that highly competitive year in the popular song market and was neatly represented on records by Ted Weems (Bluebird), Charley Agnew (Columbia), and Freddy Martin (Melotone).

The trio of Wever, Ager, and Schwartz published one of their best songs in 1937, *Trust in Me*. It was featured and recorded (on Vocalion) by Mildred Bailey, Bobby Hayes and His Orchestra on the ARC labels, Wayne King on Victor, and Abe Lyman on Decca. The song soared to the number two spot on *Your Hit Parade*. In a series of revivals, it made the charts with records by Eddie Fisher (Victor) and Roy Rogers (Decca) in 1952, Chris Connor (Atlantic) in 1957, Patti Page (Mercury) in 1959, and Etta James (Argo) in 1961. With Jerry Livingston replacing Arthur Schwartz on the team, Wever and Ager had another winner in 1938. This was *Sweet Stranger*. Glenn Miller recorded it for Brunswick; Al Bowlly made it in a solo effort on Bluebird; and Reggie Childs's orchestra waxed it for Decca. That same year Wever wrote the words to a melody by Paul Mann, *I Simply Adore You*. The Bob Crosby crew recorded it for Decca, and George Hall did the same for Vocalion. Walter Donaldson wrote the music for *I Can't Resist You,* a 1940 ballad that Helen Forrest sang on a Benny Goodman record for Columbia that year. Hal Kemp's band made it for Victor, Van Alexander for Varsity, and Jimmy Dorsey for Decca.

Other titles by Ned Wever are *An Orchid for the Lady* and *I've Never Had a Sweetheart Like You.*

Leonard Whitcup

Composer-lyricist-publisher Leonard Whitcup was born in New York City on October 12, 1903. He was educated at NYU and studied music with David Sapeton and Orville Mayhood. During his career, he performed on the radio, writing his own material, and also played in a trio, the Playboys. He wrote special material for vaudeville acts, revues, and for the film *Sweet Moments.* As a writer of popular songs he was mainly active in the thirties, working in a team with Teddy Powell and Walter G. Samuels or alone with Powell. The team shared credit for composing both words and music.

Fiesta, an early effort, was published in 1931. Henry Busse recorded it for Victor, and it rated considerable airplay as a popular rumba. Then in 1934 the team scored with a very good song, *True*. Contemporary sides were made by Paul Whiteman (Victor), Guy Lombardo (Brunswick), Ted Black (Bluebird), and Chick Webb (Vocalion). It was revived in 1940 by Andy Russell backed by Paul Weston's orchestra on a good selling record for Capitol. Still doing well, the team marketed *March Winds and April*

Showers in 1935, recorded by the popular singing star Ruth Etting, Abe Lyman's orchestra, and Victor Young's. They also published a second entry, *I Couldn't Believe My Eyes*. The Dorsey Brothers Orchestra recorded it for Decca. Both songs were popular radio selections. But the heavy hitter of the year was a pseudo-western song, *Take Me Back to My Boots and Saddle*. It's not surprising that Gene Autry introduced the song and had a popular record on Vocalion, but the variety of artists who also recorded it for other labels is worth a raised eyebrow—John Charles Thomas for Victor, Red Allen for Vocalion, Victor Young on Decca, Jimmy Ray on Bluebird, and whistler Fred Lowery on Columbia. For good measure, other sides were made by Tommy Dorsey on Victor, Chick Bullock for ARC, Joe Haymes's orchestra, and Art Tatum, the latter two on transcriptions.

Cottage by the Moon was the 1936 entry. A nice tune, it was recorded by jazzman Wingy Manone. Two more fine ballads came out in the next year, *If My Heart Could Only Talk* and *Heaven Help This Heart of Mine*. Billie Holiday recorded the first title for Vocalion, and Tommy Dorsey's Orchestra, with the vocal by Jack Leonard, made it for Victor. Mildred Bailey, Dick Robertson, and Eddy Duchin all had records on the second one. That same year Whitcup and Teddy Powell came up with something a little different from the team's usual work. This was *Snake Charmer*, a descriptive offering that was recorded by Larry Clinton's orchestra on Victor and Jerry Blaine's on Bluebird.

Bewildered was the team's entry for 1938. Tommy Dorsey had the best selling record. Billy Eckstine reprised the tune in 1949 on a record for MGM, and Herb Jeffries did the same for Columbia. Teddy Powell and Whitcup worked as a pair again in 1940 on *Am I Proud?* It got swinging treatment by the Tommy Dorsey band, with the vocal by Anita Boyer, on Victor, and a more sedate but still musical rendering by Eddie Stone with Freddy Martin's orchestra on Bluebird. Other songs by Whitcup include *Precious Little One; The Lady From Fifth Avenue; Rollin' Plains; Spring Cleaning; Little Genius; Singin' in the Saddle; I Am an American; From the Vine Came the Grape; Kissin' on the Phone; The Song of the Victory Fleet; Tears in My Heart; People to People; The "A" Team;* and *An Empty Glass*.

Leonard Whitcup died in New York City on April 6, 1979.

George Whiting

Lyricist George Whiting was born in Chicago, Illinois, on August 16, 1884. He was educated in the public schools and as a singer toured in vaudeville and entertained in cafes. As a songwriter he collaborated with a number of the best early composers—Abel Baer, Ernest Ball, Henry Von Tilzer, Fred Fisher, Joe Burke, Irving Berlin, etc. One of Whiting's earliest efforts was *Saloon,* a wryly sentimental ballad written with Ernest Ball. Another was *My Wife's Gone to the Country (Hurrah! Hurrah!),* on which he shared lyric credit with Irving Berlin to the music by Ted Snyder.

Without any question, the most famous song of Whiting's career is *My Blue Heaven,* written with Walter Donaldson. It was published and made popular in 1927 but was introduced by Whiting in vaudeville two years earlier. However, it wasn't a hit until Eddie Cantor sang it in the "Ziegfeld Follies of 1927." The Victor recording by Gene Austin sold over five million copies, setting a record that wasn't broken until Bing Crosby made *White Christmas. My Blue Heaven* has been a standard ever since, played and recorded countless times.

Still writing into the thirties, Whiting worked with Nat Schwartz on the words to *Believe It Beloved* and *Don't Let Your Love Go Wrong* in 1934. The music for both tunes was by J. C. Johnson. Fats Waller had a popular record of the first title on Victor, and other sides were made by Isham Jones, with the inimitable Eddie Stone singing, on Decca, and by Red Allen on Perfect. In the early fifties vocalist Al Hibbler revived the tune on a Mercury recording, backed by Johnny Hodges's orchestra. *Don't Let Your Love Go Wrong,* a rumba, was also recorded by Isham Jones and Eddie Stone and by Red Allen. The Boswell Sisters made it for Brunswick, and Gene Kardos for Vocalion. Other songs with lyrics by Whiting are *Strolling Through the Park One Day; I Picked a Flower the Color of Your Eyes; West of the Great Divide; Beautiful Eyes; Oh What I'd Do for a Girl Like You; Little Black Boy;* and *Who Told You I Cared?*

George Whiting died in the Bronx, New York, on December 18, 1943.

Richard Whiting

One of the most eminent names in the pantheon of song-writing geniuses is that of Richard Whiting, who was born in Peoria, Illinois, on November 12, 1891, and only forty-six short years later died in Beverly Hills, California, on February 10, 1938. During his comparatively short career the quality and quantity of the songs he wrote are constant reminders of the great loss this was to our musical heritage, the more so because this prolific genius was cut off in the middle of his most productive period. Had he lived, the world may well have benefited from another decade of superior songs from his fertile mind. As it is, we have some excellent musical gems from this master craftsman, worthy contributions to the wonderful heritage the great songwriters have left to America and to the world.

He was educated at the Harvard Military school in Los Angeles. As a pianist and composer he was mainly self-taught. He started writing songs for music publishers and became the manager of one at the age of twenty-one. He wrote scores for Broadway shows and a number of the movie musicals of the thirties, and many of his contributions to these are memorable. But first and foremost he was a songwriter with an inborn talent for original melodies. This was evident early in his career, and the proof is in the fact that two of his earliest songs have endured in the standard library, *The Japanese Sandman* and *Till We Meet Again.*

Like all writers, Whiting wrote a lot of songs that have been forgotten, even though they enjoyed popularity in their time, but those that have become standards make up an impressive list. These include *Sleepy Time Gal; Ain't We Got Fun; Breezin' Along with the Breeze; True Blue Lou; Honey; Louise; She's Funny That Way; Beyond the Blue Horizon; It Seems to Be Spring; My Ideal; My Future Just Passed; Guilty; Miss Brown to You;* and *Too Marvelous for Words*. There are others that enter the sphere of personal favorites for a lot of people, including me, and among these are delightful "sleepers" like *You're An Old Smoothie; When Did You Leave Heaven?; Not That I Care; Be Careful;* and *Just a Quiet Evening*. It's even slightly ironic that Whiting wrote a sadly prophetic song in 1934 called *Rock and Roll.* As mentioned above, Richard Whiting was at the peak of his career when he died and conceivably could have added more excellent songs to the list.

Some of his tunes were important factors in advancing the careers of many top names in show business, particularly Maurice Chevalier *(Louise),* Shirley Temple *(On the Good Ship Lollipop),* and Bing Crosby *(I Can't Escape from You; Too Marvelous for Words; Sentimental and Melancholy; Just a Quiet Evening).* Collaborating with him at times were Johnny Mercer, Gus Kahn, Buddy DeSylva, Sidney Clare, Leo Robin, Haven Gillespie, Raymond Egan, Arthur Jackson, George Marion Jr., and Walter Bullock.

Richard Whiting had two daughters. Margaret became a star vocalist in the forties and fifties and often featured her father's music. Barbara, the younger, did well as a singer and actress.

Joan Whitney

See Zoe Parenteau Kramer.

Alec Wilder

Composer-arranger-author Alec Wilder was born in Rochester, New York, on February 17, 1907. He was educated at the Eastman School of Music and first attracted attention with his unusual mode of composing and arranging in the thirties, recording many of his compositions with a woodwind octet. Not designed for the popular market, they were still indicative of Wilder's superior musicianship and talent. As a songwriter of popular ballads, Wilder's reputation is based on a cluster of songs he produced in the forties, usually writing both words and music.

One of these was the outstandingly descriptive and melodic *It's So Peaceful in the Country,* a 1941 entry that received a respectful and restrained treatment by Mildred Bailey, supported by an all-star rhythm section and the Delta Rhythm Boys Quartet on Decca. Jan Savitt and Harry James also had good records. Another was *Soft As Spring,* published that same year and featured on a Columbia record by Benny Goodman's band with a vocal by Peggy Lee and arrangement by Eddie Sauter. The delicately plaintive *Who Can I Turn To?,* with a lyric by Bill Engvick, was one of the better ballads of 1942. It rated first-class waxings on all labels of the day, with the exceptions of Decca and Capitol. Tommy Dorsey, with Jo Stafford singing, made it on Victor; Will Bradley, with Terry Allen, on Columbia; Gene Krupa, with Howard DuLany on OKeh; and Shep Fields and His New Music on Bluebird.

Wilder wrote both words and music for the 1943 ballad *I'll Be Around.* A better-than-average song in its own right, it had the good luck to be coupled on Decca's recording by the Mills Brothers' *Paper Doll,* the smash hit of the year. As with other songs fortunate enough to back a hit, its success was almost assured due to a peculiarity of the jukebox business. When a hit recording in a jukebox got so many plays that it was worn out, the operator, instead of replacing it, usually turned it over to the other side. With hundreds of the hit record on boxes all over the country, this practically guaranteed that the exposure would promote the second side into another hit. But *I'll Be Around* wasn't the only Wilder hit that year. In a rare collaboration, he composed the music with Mort Palitz for *When We're Young.* Bill Engvick was again the lyricist. Mabel Mercer is credited with introducing the song in clubs, but it also was featured on popular recordings by Tony Bennett, Georgia Gibbs, Peggy Lee, and Meredith Willson.

In 1946 Wilder joined with Eddie Sauter and Ray Gilbert on *All the Cats Join In,* which was featured in the Walt Disney cartoon, *Make Mine Music.* The Benny Goodman orchestra and quartet played it in the film and years later their work was released on a Capitol EP called *Two for the Record.*

Other Wilder songs include *All the King's Horses; Lonely Night; Milwaukee; J. P. Dolley III; Moon and Sand; Goodbye, John; Good for Nothin'; Give Me Time; Sing Our Song of Love; Kalamazoo to Timbukto; Crazy in the Heart;* and *Stop That Dancin' Up There: At the Swing Shift Ball.*

Alec Wilder died on December 24, 1980.

Donald McCrae Wilhoite

See Don Raye.

Clarence Williams

Pianist-composer-publisher-bandleader Clarence Williams was born in Plaquemin, Louisiana, on October 6, 1893, but he grew up in New Orleans. When he was twelve years old he ran away from home to join a minstrel show. Still later he toured in vaudeville as dancer, singer, and pianist, played piano in local bands, and tried his hand at composing and publishing. For awhile he owned a music store in Chicago, then he moved to New York and established a music publishing company. From 1923 to 1928 he was musical director for OKeh's race records, and during this period he recorded prolifically with his own jazz groups and accompanying blues singers. In the process he hired and recorded many of the foremost names in the business. In 1921 he married blues singer Eva Taylor and during the twenties and thirties worked with her on radio and recordings. As a composer, Williams is responsible for some of the greatest jazz standards, songs that have been played and recorded countless times over the years. In most cases he is credited with words and music.

One of his earliest tunes was published under the title *(You're Some) Pretty Doll* in 1917. In 1939 Eddie Condon resurrected the tune for a Commodore record session, with trombonist Georg Brunis in the band. Subsequently, Brunis composed a new title and words to the song and frequently sang it as a member of the band at Nick's, the jazz club in Greenwich Village. In 1943, on another recording date for Commodore, the Georg Brunis Jazz Band waxed *Ugly Chile,* the antithesis of *Pretty Doll,* but with the same Williams melody. At the same session Brunis recorded another Williams standard, written with Spencer Williams, *Royal Garden Blues*. This originated in 1921, and among the contemporary sides were records by the Original Dixieland Jazz Band (Victor), Mamie Smith and Her Jazz Hounds (OKeh), and Ethel Waters and Her Jazz Masters on Black Swan. Bix Beiderbecke also recorded it with the Wolverines in 1924, and again for OKeh in 1927, and the subsequent list is long and illustrious, including Duke Ellington, Benny Goodman, Count Basie, Bob Crosby, Glen Gray, and numerous jazz bands.

The two Williams boys, Clarence and Spencer, also scored big in 1919 with *I Ain't Gonna Give Nobody None o' This Jelly Roll.* The selfish sentiment was expressed on early discs by Sidney Bechet and Wilbur Sweatmen but, like almost all of the Clarence Williams standards, has gone on to countless recordings, along with immeasurable renditions at jazz concerts and festivals. Clarence Williams had a very busy 1923 and the standards he produced are still around to prove it. They include *T'Ain't Nobody's Bizness if I Do,* a collaboration with Porter Grainger and Graham Prince made notable by Bessie Smith's rendition on Columbia; *Gulf Coast Blues,* also recorded by Bessie Smith, accompanied by Williams on the piano; and *Sugar Blues,* with words by Lucy Fletcher, but mainly remembered for the 1935 Decca recording by Clyde McCoy and His Orchestra. Helped to popularity by disc jockey Martin Block, who used it as a theme for his *Make Believe Ballroom* program on WNEW radio in New York, the record was a smash hit, and the song has been identified with McCoy ever since. Probably the most popular song in the Clarence Williams songbook is *Baby, Won't You Please Come Home,* another from 1923, with words by Charles Warfield. Williams recorded it a couple of times himself, and it received attention on contemporary sides by Bessie Smith and Eva Taylor, but this was just the start. Through the years it has been recorded almost steadily, with records by McKinney's Cotton Pickers, Don Redman, Pee Wee Russell, Sidney Bechet, Cab Calloway, Bob Haggart, Frank Trumbauer—and it still goes on.

In 1928 Clarence Williams turned lyricist, writing the words to *Squeeze Me,* Fats Waller's first hit song, and now another standard in the hot jazz repertory. With Joe "King" Oliver, Williams wrote *West End Blues.* He recorded it on Vocalion with an all-star group that included King Oliver, but it was Louis Armstrong's rendition for OKeh that assured the song immortality. Other Williams compositions are *Shout, Sister, Shout; West Indies Blues;* and *Organ Grinder Blues.*

Clarence Williams died in New York City on November 6, 1965.

Harry Williams

Harry Williams was a pioneer toiler in the thickets of Tin Pan Alley. He was born in Faribault, Minnesota, on August 29, 1879. As a boy he attended both public and military schools. With Egbert Van Alstyne he joined the circus, and they toured in vaudeville as a team, also composing songs. In 1902 Williams went to work as a staff writer for a New York music publisher and then went on to open his own firm. As a lyric writer he enjoyed considerable success in partnership with Van Alstyne, but he also wrote the words to notable songs by Neil Moret, Art Hickman, and others.

In 1903 he collaborated with Van Alstyne on *Navajo,* which enjoyed some success and was followed up in 1904 by *Seminole* and in 1906 by *Cheyenne (Shy Ann).* That was the same year they wrote the hit *Won't You Come Over to My House?,* reprised three decades later by Dick Robertson on a Decca record with jazz stars Bobby Hackett and Don Watt. But before composing that immortal work, they produced the one that everybody knows, *In the Shade of the Old Apple Tree.* Even in those early years of the recording industry the song rated sides by Arthur Pryor's band on Victor, the Haydn Quartette, also on Victor, Henry Burr for Edison, and Albert Campbell for Columbia. Since then, of course, it has appeared on a long string of recordings, including the parody by Georg Brunis and His Jazz Band on Commodore.

In 1907 the partners wrote another song as a follow-up to their Indian titles, *San Antonio,* and in 1910 asked the pertinent question, *What's the Matter With Father?* The answer, as Williams wrote it, was an emphatic, "He's all right!" *Goodnight, Ladies,* the perennial closer that served for many years as a gentle hint that the festivities were over, until eventually replaced by Ray Noble's *Goodnight, Sweetheart,* came out in 1911. In 1912 Williams took a new partner, and with Jack Judge wrote the popular hit *It's a Long Way to Tipperary.* It was interpolated into the theater musical "Chin Chin," and in 1914 Al Jolson sang it in "Dancing Around," another stage show. Contemporary recordings were made by John McCormack and by the American Quartet, both for Victor. In later reincarnations it was used as background music in the movie *The Story of Vernon and Irene Castle* in 1939, sung by Judy Garland in *For Me and My Gal* in 1942, and performed by Julie Andrews in *Darling Lili* in 1970. In the meantime, as a song associated with the First World War, it was revived quite a bit for the second one.

Still freelancing, in 1918 Williams wrote the words to Art Hickman's great classic, *Rose Room,* and then teamed with Neil Moret on *Mickey.* The tune was unique as one of the earliest attempts for a song to serve as background music for a silent movie. The film was *Mickey,* starring Mabel Normand. It was also revived by Dick Robertson on a Decca recording in 1940. Other titles by Williams are *Back, Back, Back, to Baltimore; Camp Meetin' Time; I'm Afraid to Come Home in the Dark; There Never Was a Girl Like You; Rebecca; A Little China Doll; Love Makes the World Go 'Round; Alabama; Signs of a Honeymoon; We'll All Go Home; Who Are You With Tonight?; Up in My Aeroplane; Lovelight; Honolulu Rag; Ring Me Up in the Morning; That's Good; Down in the Old Meadow Lane; Oh, You Cutie!;* and *Peggy.*

Harry Williams died in Oakland, California, on May 14, 1922.

Hugh Williams

See Wilhelm Grosz.

Mary Lou Williams

Pianist-arranger-composer Mary Lou Williams was born Mary Elfrieda Winn in Pittsburgh, Pennsylvania, on May 8, 1910. She was educated in high school but studied music privately with B. Sterzio, A. Alexander, Ray Lev, and Don Redman. In later life she was awarded seven honorable degrees. As a teenager Mary Lou toured with a road show as Mary Lou Burleigh (her stepfather's name) and then joined saxophonist John Williams's band, which toured in vaudeville in 1925 and 1926. Mary Lou married Williams. In 1927 he left to take a job with the Terrence Holder band, and Mary Lou took over the band. Later she joined the Holder band too, and both were with it when Andy Kirk took over as leader in 1929.

An accomplished pianist with a light, deft, swinging style, Mary Lou became the star of the Andy Kirk orchestra, billed as "Andy Kirk and His Twelve Clouds of Joy." She also began to compose and arrange for the band, adding much to its originality and individuality and was known as "The Lady Who Swings the Band." After she left Kirk in 1942, having divorced Williams, she married trumpeter Harold Baker and for awhile they led a combo. Then Baker was asked to join Duke Ellington, and Mary Lou went along as an arranger. From the midforties until well into the seventies, Mary Lou Williams worked as a single, playing in clubs and making lengthy stays in France and England, composing and arranging for bands like those of Benny Goodman, Louis Armstrong, Tommy Dorsey, Earl Hines, Glen Gray, and so on.

Although her compositions are often melodic—such as *Lonely Moments* and *What's Your Story, Mornin' Glory?*—primarily Mary Lou Williams wrote instrumentals, and a number of them resulted in big-selling records, such as *Camel Hop* and *Roll 'Em,* which she wrote and arranged for the Goodman band. Other titles by Williams include *Foggy Bottom; Mary's Idea; Walkin' and Swingin'; Scratchin' the Gravel; Little Joe from Chicago; Night Life; Overhand;* and *Whistle Blues.*

Mary Lou Williams died in Durham, North Carolina, on May 28, 1981.

Spencer Williams

Having a name like Williams has its advantages and disadvantages. The big advantage is that everybody can pronounce and spell it. The disadvantage is that the name is so common—especially in sports and the music world—one particular individual tends to be overlooked. This is especially true of songwriters, where composer credits are often confined to last names only. When you consider that Clarence Williams, Bert Williams, Mary Lou Williams, Cootie Williams, Hank Williams, and Harry Williams all wrote published songs, you can readily see what I mean. So it is that you may not be familiar with all of the great songs that Spencer Williams either wrote or collaborated on, and he started out very early.

Williams was born in New Orleans, Louisiana, on October 14, 1889. He was educated at St. Charles University in New Orleans and while still a youngster went to Chicago to earn a living as a pianist and entertainer. Still later he made his way to New York. In 1925 he collaborated with Claude Hopkins in writing material for the "Revue Negre," which toured Europe and starred Josephine Baker. Many years later he accompanied Fats Waller to Paris and wound up living there for a long time before returning to the States.

A list of Spencer Williams compositions includes a number of jazz standards, and some are all-time favorites of just about everybody. Quite a few are bound to be yours. Take your pick: *I Ain't Got Nobody; I Ain't Gonna Give Nobody None of My Jelly Roll; Everybody Loves My Baby; I've Found a New Baby* (the latter two in partnership with Jack Palmer); *Basin St. Blues; Royal Garden Blues; Shim-Me-Sha-Wabble; Tishomingo Blues; Mahogany Hall Stomp; Snake Hips; Arkansas Blues; When Lights Are Low; Church St. Sobbin' Blues; Papa De-Da-Da*—and that's just a sampling.

Besides bandleader Claude Hopkins and composer Jack Palmer, Williams worked with some of the most famous and respected names in jazz history. An early entry, *Arkansas Blues* (1921), was written with Anton Lada. In the same year, the hardy perennial *Royal Garden Blues* was a cooperative effort with Clarence Williams. In later years he teamed frequently with Fats Waller, and the Benny Carter composition *When Lights Are Low* has lyrics by Williams. He can also take solo credit for composing *Tishomingo Blues* and *Shim-Me-Sha-Wabble*. In 1931 he picked up an unexpected assist on his 1928 song *Basin St. Blues* when Glenn Miller and Jack Teagarden put together a verse to the tune for a Charleston Chasers recording (Columbia 2415-D). In case you've forgotten, this starts off with "Won't You Come Along With Me . . . ."

Spencer Williams died in Flushing, New York, on July 14, 1965.

Meredith Willson

Composer-writer-musician Meredith Willson was born in Mason City, Iowa, on May 18, 1902. He was educated in the public schools, attended the Damrosch Institute of Musical Arts, and studied privately with George Barrere, Henry Hadley, Mortimer Wilson, Bernard Waggenaar, and Julius Gold. From 1921 to 1923 he was first flute in the John Philip Sousa band; from 1924 to 1929 he was with the New York Philharmonic. During World War II he was a major in the Armed Forces Radio Service. Willson composed several symphonies and wrote scores for a number of movies. He conducted orchestras on radio and television and acquired a respected reputation as a composer and a personality. As a writer of popular songs he composed both words and music for a number of high quality hits, some as freelance offerings and others as part of the scores for two hit shows, "The Music Man" and "The Unsinkable Molly Brown."

In 1941 he had his first big success with the delightful *You and I.* It went the rounds of the record labels, recorded by top names—Glenn Miller on Bluebird, Bing Crosby on Decca, Dick Jurgens for OKeh, and Tommy Dorsey on Victor, with the vocal by Frank Sinatra. *It's Beginning to Look a Lot Like Christmas,* one of the better songs for the holiday, was a Willson entry in 1952, but as so often is the situation with successful Christmas songs, it is heard every holiday season and has become a perennial. Perry Como had the big record.

In 1957 Willson composed both score and libretto for the hit Broadway show "The Music Man," starring Robert Preston, and from it came several good songs, notably *Seventy-Six Trombones* and *Till There Was You.* The trombone song was a solo feature for Preston, and he sang a duet with Barbara Cook on *Till There Was You.* In the movie made in 1962, he sang it with Shirley Jones. Both songs enjoyed frequent radio play and resultant popularity. *Lida Rose,* another good song from the show, was introduced and sung in both productions by the vocal group the Buffalo Bills. *I Ain't Down Yet* was the most popular song from "The Unsinkable Molly Brown" in 1960, another hit stage show, made into a movie in 1964. Another was *Belly Up to the Bar, Boys,* but many of Willson's songs, while important in the context of the shows and usually ideal for singers, were not easily adapted to dance music, and therefore not too successful in the popular market. Other titles by Willson include *Never Feel Too Weary to Pray; Two in Love; May the Good Lord Bless and Keep You; Here Comes the Springtime and There Goes My Heart; It's Easter Time; I See the Moon; Trouble; Goodnight, My Someone; Gary, Indiana; Marian the Librarian; Colorado Is My Home; I'll*

Never Say No; He's My Friend; Here's Love; My Wish; My State, My Kansas, My Home; Love, Come Take Me Again; and *Pine Cones and Holly Berries.*

Meredith Willson died on June 15, 1984.

P. G. Wodehouse (Pelham Grenville Wodehouse)

Author-lyricist-librettist P. G. Wodehouse was born in Guildford, Surrey, England, on October 15, 1881. He was educated at Dulwich College and Oxford University. He started his writing career turning out a column for the *London Globe* from 1903 to 1909 and providing material for the London stage. One of his early collaborators was Jerome Kern, with whom he later wrote Broadway shows. After making visits to the United States he decided to stay and began writing for Broadway shows around 1915. He also began a prolific output of humorous novels that established his reputation.

Although as a librettist and lyricist he collaborated on a host of songs for shows and worked with top names like Kern, Gershwin, Romberg, and Friml, the majority of them never became popular. However, he did succeed in chalking up a few hit standards. In this regard, 1917 was a big year. With Jerome Kern composing the music, Wodehouse provided the words to *Have a Heart,* for the musical of the same name. This presented the unusual situation of a composer writing two songs with the same title, because Kern had collaborated with Gene Buck the year before on a song named *Have a Heart* for the "Ziegfeld Follies of 1916." Kern and Wodehouse also wrote *The Siren's Song,* which was sung by Edith Hallor in the show "Leave It to Jane," and then Wodehouse teamed with Guy Bolton on the words to *Till the Clouds Roll By,* for still another 1917 production, "Oh! Boy!" All three of these songs have survived to the present.

In 1928 Wodehouse and Oscar Hammerstein II provided the lyrics for *Bill,* another Jerome Kern composition. As some songs do, this one has developed a history. Wodehouse had written an early version in 1918 for the show "Oh, Lady! Lady!", but it was dropped. Later still, Marilyn Miller rejected the song for another show, and it was finally included in the score for "Show Boat." Introduced by Helen Morgan, who also recorded it for Victor, it became an all-time hit. She sang it again in the first movie version of "Show Boat" in 1929 and in the remake of 1936. In the third version, in 1951, Annette Warren sang it on the soundtrack, dubbed in for Ava Gardner; and in 1957 Gogi Grant was dubbed in for Ann Blyth in the title role of

The Helen Morgan Story. That same year Wodehouse worked with Ira Gershwin, and they came up with *How Long Has This Been Going On,* the great Gershwin standard that was featured in "Rosalie." Actually, they had written the tune the previous year for a show called "Funny Face," but it was dropped. However, it did make it for the movie version of "Funny Face," in which it was sung by Audrey Hepburn in 1957. It has been recorded a number of times.

P. G. Wodehouse continued to turn out books for many years, his last one published just before his ninety-second birthday. He died in Southampton, New York, on February 14, 1975.

Harry Woods

It's typical of the small ironies of the songwriting business that most people, if asked to name the composers who wrote our standard library of songs, will remember Berlin, Gershwin, Porter, Rodgers, possibly Ellington, and maybe one or two of the more recent writers, but hardly any will mention Harry Woods, even though they are almost always familiar with his music. Why is this so? Well, since it is well known that the situation isn't confined to Harry Woods, but applies to the majority of our great songwriters, one reason might be that they were not fortunate enough to write scores for successful Broadway shows or, to a lesser extent, movie musicals. Those writers got the most publicity, and their names and reputations grew in proportion. In contrast, even in the heyday of the songwriting craft, freelancers never got much recognition for their work. At best, their names were listed at the top of the sheet music or mentioned in very little type under the title of the song on a phonograph record (which nobody bothered to read). Most of the time the performing artists got the top billing, with their pictures splashed all over the sheet music covers. This was especially true if their reputations were big enough to help the sale of the song.

So it isn't surprising, if you happen to be the enterprising kind, that you might be able to win a lot of bets in the City of Brotherly Love just by wagering the guy on the next barstool he can't name the composer of *I'm Looking Over a Four Leaf Clover,* which has been adopted as the unofficial anthem of the Philadelphia string bands in the annual Mummer's Day Parade. Then again, if you're the lazy type and would rather not travel, just turn to your spouse and ask who wrote her favorite romantic called *Try a Little Tenderness,* as soulfully intoned by none other than Frank Sinatra. In my column The Unsung Songwriters, one sentence sums up what I consider to be an honest appraisal of his composing efforts in the twenties: "There is nothing phony or pretentious about Harry Woods's music, but there is an underlying sincerity in all of it, and most of his songs have a happy, rhythmic lift that is infectious." To coin a phrase, "That ain't easy!" Although some of his songs seem so simple and logical that anybody—your Uncle Joe, for instance—could have composed them, the truth is just the opposite. It takes a special gift to compose a melody that is easy to play, easy to remember, and above all, original. Harry Woods did it over and over again. Woods is entitled to much more credit than he ever gets, and his contributions to our American song heritage—as both composer and lyricist—are considerable. Yet even Alec Wilder ignored him completely in his book *American Popular Song,* and the chances are better than good that musicians who play his songs never heard of him.

Harry MacGregor Woods was born in North Chelmsford, Massachusetts, on November 4, 1886. Biographical material is very slim, brief, and hard to come by, so there is no information to be had about his father, which suggests he may have died while Harry was very young. It is his mother, Edith MacGregor Woods, a concert singer of some reputation, who is credited with passing on her musical talent to her son; she also trained him at the keyboard. The most remarkable thing abut this, and a definite indication of Harry Woods's determination, is that he had no fingers on his left hand, yet he learned to play so proficiently that in later years he paid for his education at Harvard by thumping a piano in clubs and singing in church choirs.

His first published song was a good one, *I'm Goin' South,* which was featured by Al Jolson in the 1921 stage show "Bombo." Jolson also recorded it for Brunswick, backed by the very popular Isham Jones band of the period. Like the majority of tunes Woods would write during his prolific career, *I'm Goin' South* is an optimistic ditty subscribing to the idea that things may be tough but they're due to get better, and it flows along with a natural lift to the melody line that reflects jazz inspiration. It enjoyed a pretty fair sale, so the part-time songwriter who was definitely more inclined to a physical mode of making a living, like farming on Cape Cod (which he tried for awhile) or fishing off Nantucket (which he often did, and continued to do whenever the mood struck him), was off to a pretty good start.

I'm Goin' South was recorded on practically all of the major record labels of the day by groups leaning toward hot dance or jazz—Bailey's Lucky Seven on Gennett, Ray Miller on Brunswick, Paul Specht on Columbia, the Virginians on Victor—a quite respectable showing for a first song, but for some reason these recordings were not made until the end of 1923 or early 1924. Most likely, the publisher of the tune didn't think it was worthwhile to push it. But in the meantime, Woods came up with an offering that immediately appealed to jazz bands, was widely recorded by many of them (Ladd's Black Aces, the St. Louis Syncopators, Albert Short's Tivoli Syncopators, Bennie Krueger, etc.), and even made it as suitable material for three prominent blues singers of the day, Ethel Waters, Hannah Sylvester, and Viola McCoy. This was *Long Lost Mama,* which made a stir in 1923 and very possibly moved the publisher of *I'm Goin' South* into taking greater interest in it.

In the light of such a promising beginning, you might expect that the next year would be filled with Woods compositions, but instead only a rather pale entry, *Oh, How I Love My Darling,* appeared in 1924. Maybe Woods was preoccupied with his fishing. But, whatever the reason, in 1925 he came back strong with a number of tunes written in collaboration with others—*What's a Fellow Gonna Do?; Where Is My Old Girl Tonight?;* and *Spread a Little Happiness As You Go*—none of which created much excitement. But then the popular vaudeville and recording star Ukulele Ike, Cliff Edwards, was persuaded to feature one of Woods's novelty tunes, *Paddlin' Madeline Home,* and the dam broke. From that point on, Woods never had to worry about getting a tune published or about where his next meal was coming from.

It's a well-known fact that many songwriters have one big hit and are never able to repeat the magic formula. But for Woods, the sensation made by *Paddlin' Madeline Home* merely convinced him that songwriting could be more profitable—if not as enjoyable—than farming or fishing, and he began to regard it as a full-time career. He continued to collaborate and in 1926 turned out *Poor Papa (He Ain't Got Nothin' at All),* the lyrics by Billy Rose; *Tenting Down in Tennessee,* with Dick Howard; *Who'd Be Blue,* with Mort Dixon; *Take in the Sun, Hang Out the Moon,* with Sam Lewis and Joe Young; and *(Ho Ho, Ha Ha), Me Too,* with Al Sherman and Charles Tobias. All were moderately successful, especially *Poor Papa* and *Me Too*. (The latter title accounted for two hit records, one by popular singing star of the twenties Gene Austin and the other by Paul Whiteman's orchestra.) But Woods struck pure gold on his own with one of the hardy perennials to come out of the twenties, *When the Red, Red Robin Comes Bob-Bob Bobbin' Along*. To the casual observer, it might seem that these songs, unpretentious and obviously written to make money, were merely commercial potboilers with little musical merit, because the melody lines seem to flow with very little effort. Actually, although he would later on write songs of much greater sophistication, these early efforts set the pattern for his entire songwriting career—a happy, light-hearted approach that seems to carry the trademark of the composer's impish, tongue-in-cheek outlook on life. And therein lies the genius of Harry Woods—simplicity and honesty, combined with a frankly romantic, homespun sincerity—qualities that permeate his works and offer a basic appeal to the better side of humanity.

I'm Looking Over a Four-Leaf Clover, with lyrics by Mort Dixon, was published in 1927, and although it has become associated with cornball renditions in more recent times, it achieved early immortality with the Jean Goldkette recording featuring Bix Beiderbecke. Pretty much the same can be said for the other Woods home run of the same year, *Side by Side*. There have been countless versions played and recorded right up to the present time, but the standard was set by the contemporary Paul Whiteman record featuring Bing Crosby and the Rhythm Boys, along with some marvelous Red Nichols cornet. Other Woods ditties in 1927 included the wistful hit *Just Like a Butterfly That's Caught in the Rain,* with Mort Dixon lyrics; *Since I Found You,* with lyrics by Sidney Clare; and two more with Dixon, *Moonbeam, Kiss Her for Me* and *You're So Easy to Remember*. All succeeded quite nicely, and there was no longer any question in Tin Pan Alley as to whether Harry Woods had the necessary talent and staying power to become a consistent writer of hits. The big guy with the wrestler's grip, the sportsman's physique, and love for the outdoors, the sea, and the soil, had finally convinced everybody he had the heart and soul of a musical genius.

What's more, the lure of big money to be made with ballads and novelties couldn't entirely subvert the jazz influence, nor suppress the Woods off-the-wall humor. Both had to have their innings, so the former crops up in three tunes that have become classics in the hot jazz collectors' libraries: *She's a Great, Great Girl,* forever frozen into an artistic gem by Jack Teagarden's solo on the Roger Wolfe Kahn recording; *What a Day!,* a typically happy romp by Parker Gibbs and the Ted Weems band; and *The Man from the South,* written in collaboration with pianist Rube Bloom and riotously rendered by Rube Bloom and His Bayou Boys—Manny Klein, Benny Goodman, Tommy Dorsey, and Adrian Rollini among them—on a record that must have wrecked the studio. Then a few years later, *Pink Elephants* emerged as a Woods–Dixon salute to the many Prohibition imbibers of bathtub gin and the attendant results.

However, the rambunctious twenties were waning, and with their departure—accented by the thunderous boom of the crashing stock market—went much of that happy, live-for-today, tomorrow-will-take-care-of-itself attitude that had bubbled over into the songs of the era. Now, stimulated by the overnight success of a slant-eyed bandleader named Rudy Vallee, who slowed the bouncy dance tempos down to accommodate his crooning vocal style, the romantic, more melodic approach became the vogue. Some found it hard to adjust, but not Woods, who made the transition as easily as crossing the street from one side to the other, providing the crooning Rudy with a brand-new theme song for his band, *Heigh Ho, Everybody, Heigh Ho,* and a nice little bonus ballad, *A Little Kiss Each Morning*. Both tunes were featured in the Vallee movie *The Vagabond Lover*.

As the thirties progressed—unquestionably the Golden Decade for songwriters—a subtle change can be noticed in the Woods compositions as he kept pace with public taste. They became more melodic, more sophisticated in structure, and more romantic. The market for such songs was almost insatiable, fed by the increasing popularity of radio, dance bands, singing bandleaders, the movie musicals, and stage shows, as the Depression deepened. Faced with the everyday gloom of reality, the public turned to the artificial glitter of entertainment as desperately as a drowning man grabbing for a life preserver. The songwriters rushed to fill the demand. Early Harry Woods contributions to the trend included *You Darlin'*, recorded for Victor by that villain among bandleaders, Blue Steele (1930); *Hang Out the Stars in Indiana,* a Ray Noble cameo performance on HMV (1931); *Lovable,* recorded by Red McKenzie on Columbia when Red had hopes of becoming a big singing star on radio (1932) and in England by Al Bowlly with Roy Fox's band; and the superfine *We Just Couldn't Say Goodbye*. In 1931 he also wrote *River, Stay 'Way from My Door,* a song with wide topical appeal in that gloomy year made more miserable by floods along the Mississippi.

But for Woods the gloom was lined with gold, and he struck it again with another theme song—this time with something new for him, a waltz—*When the Moon Comes Over the Mountain,* which quickly sprinted to top popularity with Kate Smith. And still another Woods hit in 1932, *Just an Echo in the Valley,* received very respectable treatment on Brunswick by Bing Crosby—and most disrespectful treatment by the irrepressible Joe Venuti on a bootleg recording on an LP (Broadway BR-108) offering a collection of vintage items featuring "The Titan of the Tuba," Joe Tarto. The cut is attributed to "The New Yorkers," and besides the two Joes, includes Bunny Berigan, Manny Klein, Jimmy Dorsey, Carl Kress, and other luminaries. *Just an Echo in the Valley* established a relationship between Woods and the English songwriting team of Reginald Connelly and Jimmy Campbell, who collaborated on writing the tune, and they may have been responsible in paving the way for his sojourn in England writing for the British market, a period that was to prove very rewarding. From the standpoint of melodic composition, at the very least, it was Woods's most productive and resulted in a number of highly superior songs, starting almost immediately with *Try a Little Tenderness*. Campbell and Connelly collaborated again, and like so many of the tunes of this era of Woods's career, it was arranged for an exceptionally fine record by the master of good taste, Ray Noble, at that time recording director for the prestigious HMV label. (The side was reissued in England on a World Records LP, *Notable Noble.*) Since then, of course, *Try a Little Tenderness* has been recorded countless times and is probably one of the best-known tunes in the Harry Woods legacy. Ray Noble also did full justice to *Hustlin' and Bustlin' for Baby,* another of those bouncy tunes that Woods seemed to enjoy writing and which lent themselves so readily to jazz-oriented renditions. One such is the Adrian Rollini disc cut for the American Record Company, with Jimmy and Tommy Dorsey, Eddie Lang, and Manny Klein.

Meanwhile, Woods began to write for English movies and in the process turned out a series of outstanding songs. Unfortunately, many of them never received much recognition in the United States, but they did in England, and our musical heritage and the Woods legacy is the richer for the excellent recorded interpretations by the fine British dance bands of the day—Lew Stone, Roy Fox, Ray Noble, Jack Hylton, and Bert Ambrose, to mention those best known here—which were much enhanced by the superior technical quality of English recordings. Most of these have been reissued in recent years. Woods wrote two songs for a Gaumont–British film starring the English dancer Jessie Mathews. One is a prime example of the songwriter's art at its finest, *When You've Got a Little Springtime in Your Heart.* With the companion tune, *Over My Shoulder,* it proved the Woods optimism was undimmed. (The original Ray Noble recordings have been reissued several times—in this country first on a Capitol LP, and then on Monmouth Evergreen, both produced by Bill Borden, and more recently by World Records in England.) Then, for another British production, *Aunt Sally,* he wrote a typically whimsical score including *We'll All Go Riding On a Rainbow* (a foretaste in style of the later *What a Little Moonlight Can Do); My Wild Oat; The Wind in the West;* and the one that scored on both sides of the ocean, *You Ought to See Sally on Sunday.*

Ray Noble seems to have had a strong empathy for a Harry Woods melody, and the New Mayfair recording of *Midnight, the Stars, and You,* written in collaboration with Campbell and Connelly, must be considered a classic example of an arrangement fitting the song to perfection. It's probably a left-handed compliment to both composer and arranger that this side was used as background music for the phantom ballroom scene in the Jack Nicholson film *The Shining,* but the producers of the movie didn't see fit to give either one of them credit for their artistry. Meanwhile, on the freelance market, which had always been very good to Woods, 1935 was notable for five solid hits. *Wouldn't I Be a Wonder?* was recorded with appropriate amazement by Red McKenzie on Decca; *I'll Never Say "Never Again"* was promised by Ozzie Nelson on Brunswick; *What a Little Moonlight Can Do* was explored on a steamy sizzler by Teddy Wilson and Billie Holiday, also for Brunswick; *When Somebody Thinks You're Wonderful* was delineated with carefree abandon by kindred spirit Fats Waller for Victor; and *A Little Door, a Little Lock, a Little Key* was inventoried by vocalist Chick Bullock for ARC in front of a swinging studio group sparked by the horn of Bunny Berigan. Another Gaumont–British production, *It's Love Again,* starred Jessie Mathews and Robert Young, and this time the Woods contribution was another standout, *I Nearly Let Love Go Slipping Through My Fingers.* Just a tinge of unhappiness here, but everything turns out all right—just as Woods knew it would.

In 1937 Harry Woods wrote his last published song. It is called *So Many Memories,* and the title evokes the impression that at last the perennial optimist was feeling a bit tired and ready to quit. Then again, maybe he sensed, even at this early stage, that the golden days were over and the market for a well-written tune was disappearing. Whatever his reasons, he decided to retire from songwriting. But, robust character that he was, he continued to live life to the fullest. Pee Wee Erwin led his jazz band at Nick's in Greenwich Village for many years and recalled Woods as a frequent patron. "He used to come in all the time with Willard Robison. I guess they enjoyed sitting at the bar comparing stories about their songs. No question, they both wrote great ones. And I know they both loved jazz." Still later, Woods gave up the cold and damp of the East and moved to Arizona, and this is where Jim Greer found him in 1964.

"I went to Phoenix, Arizona, for two months to recuperate from a severe bout with pneumonia. One night I drove down to the 'Carefree Inn,' located about seventeen miles out in the desert from Phoenix, which was a posh hotel newly opened. I was on my own, so I had dinner in the main dining room, and then afterwards at the bar got chatting with the bartender. He told me that after the 'kids' in the dining room who had waited on me got through around nine p.m., they and he would change into their jeans and meet at a 'crazy bar' just down the street. He asked if I would like to join them, and I was delighted. Over the bar was a picture of Jack Dempsey, easily recognized, but I had to ask who was the chap he was pictured with.

" 'Oh, that's Harry Woods,' was the easy reply.

" 'You mean *the* Harry Woods, the songwriter?'

"I remarked that I had been a fan of Harry Woods for many years and would like to meet him someday. They told me I stood a good chance of meeting him right there in the 'crazy bar' because he often came in to play the old-time piano, but if I wanted to be sure to meet him, I could call him at his home, and they gave me his address and telephone number. I was hesitant about calling him, so I wrote him a letter instead, and the very next day Harry Woods called me at my apartment in Phoenix and said he would be delighted to meet me. We set a date for lunch at the Executive House in Scottsdale, and I brought along as many copies of his sheet music as I could lay my hands on, to have him autograph them for me. He very graciously signed them all!

"Right after the luncheon I left for Grand Canyon, but Harry insisted I call him upon my return and come to his home on Missouri Avenue for dinner and to meet his wife Barbara (he always referred to her as 'The Queen'). So I did, and a dinner date was set at his home. I went to a department store, bought a vase to give to his wife, and when I looked for a presentation card to go with it, was delighted to find one which started off with the words, 'Oh, we ain't got a barrel of money,' which, of course, is the opening line of *Side by Side*.

"When I arrived at their front door, Barbara (very petite) welcomed me, but when she saw the card she threw her arms around me and swore she would cherish it forever.

"Harry had a beautiful home with a swimming pool, a guest house, and a couple of riding horses. After dinner that night, he sat down at his studio piano and played and sang many of his great compositions. One I taped was *When the Red, Red Robin,* and when I got home in the spring of 1964 I got together with our local good-music station, and we prepared an hour's program on the life and music of Harry MacGregor Woods. I sent Harry a copy of the show, and when he received it he called me long distance, and said he was so pleased he was having copies made for each of his three sons.

"In 1967 I made an 11,000 mile motoring trip through your Deep South (New Orleans, Florida, etc.) and then headed for Los Angeles where Harry happened to be attending a composers' convention for one particular reason, to extend royalty rights beyond the period whereby songs become part of the 'public domain.' He was very keen on that. He canceled his flight home to Phoenix and drove with me all the way back from L.A., during which I learned much of his life story. We stopped for lunch with friends of mine in Fontana, California, and they were delighted when he sat down and played several of his compositions on their piano. Then we had dinner in Yuma, Arizona, and when the waitress found out who he was, she dashed for her autograph book.

"We arrived at his home around ten o'clock that night. He and I shared the guest house for a couple of nights, because Harry liked to visit the various nightspots. Everyone knew and loved him, and when he walked into a place they insisted he sit down and play. He always obliged, so we usually didn't get back to his home until pretty late, and in order not to disturb his wife we stayed in the guest house.

"After a few nights as their guest, I was on my way, and I still have a picture taken in front of their home of Harry and Barbara waving goodbye to me. How was I to know it was for the last time? In January of 1970 he was struck by a car in front of his house and killed. I lost a great friend, and the world a great composer. I can tell you, he was a superb human being, a gentleman in every sense of the word, and a composer who wrote with sincere feeling. But perhaps one of his most impressive assets was his modesty."

Allie Wrubel

Although he was born on January 15, 1905, Allie Wrubel didn't start composing until the thirties and forties. He was born in Middletown, Connecticut, attended Wesleyan and Columbia, and then went on to play sax in various dance bands. For awhile, it is said, he was in the Paul Whiteman organization. He also led a band that toured England. For several years he was a theater manager. His first song was published in 1931, a nice tune called *Now You're in My Arms,* with words by Morton Downey. It was introduced by Downey on his radio show and recorded by Bert Lown's orchestra on Victor 22689, with Elmer Feldkamp as the vocalist, and enjoyed moderate success.

It was followed in 1932 by one of those songs that seem to typify the high quality of writing in the Golden Decade, *As You Desire Me,* with both words and music by Wrubel and the big-seller for Russ Columbo on Victor 24076. The next year, however, saw Wrubel slipping into high gear with a cluster of hits—*And So Goodbye; Emperor Jones; I'll Be Faithful; Farewell to Arms;* and *Gypsy Fiddles. I'll Be Faithful* was written with Ned Washington doing the lyrics, and *Farewell to Arms* featured words by Abner Silver. Wrubel worked alone again on *And So Goodbye* and *Gypsy Fiddles,* both tunes receiving the famous Ray Noble treatment by his New Mayfair Orchestra in England.

Wrubel began writing for the movies, especially Warner Brothers, and later Walt Disney, and from this point on most of his production was slanted to this market. Two Dick Powell movies featured Wrubel songs in 1934, *Happiness Ahead,* which included the title song, and *Pop! Goes Your Heart.* For the big hit, *Flirtation Walk,* he again wrote the title tune, plus *Mr. and*

Mrs. Is the Name. In 1935 the movies were *I Live for Love,* with the title song and a superior balled, *Mine Alone;* and *In Caliente,* which included the hit rumba, *The Lady in Red.* The Rudy Vallee feature *Sweet Music* offered two Wrubel songs, *Fair Thee Well, Annabelle* and *I See Two Lovers.* Mort Dixon collaborated on *Mine Alone.*

Still holding his own in the highly competitive market of the decade, Wrubel did very well in 1937. For the movie *The Toast of New York,* he contributed *The First Time I Saw You,* and for *Life of The Party, Let's Have Another Cigarette.* But the year will be mainly remembered by Wrubel fans and song connoisseurs for *Gone With the Wind,* which, in spite of the title, had nothing to do with the movie of the same name. He had several entries in 1938, mainly in movies, but his big song of the year was *Music, Maestro, Please,* an independent entry with lyrics by Herb Magidson. This super hit is reported to be the biggest sheet music seller of 1938; it made the Hit Parade as number one for twelve solid weeks and was recorded by Tommy Dorsey (Victor 25866) and Kay Kyser (Brunswick 8149).

In the following year there are two more Wrubel titles, *The Masquerade Is Over* and *How Long Has This Been Going On.* Although the Golden Decade was ending, he continued on into the next, writing songs of superior quality, many of them memorable—*I'm Stepping Out With a Memory Tonight; Where Do I Go From You?; There Goes That Song Again; Why Don't We Do This More Often?; I'll Buy That Dream; Zip-a-Dee-Doo-Dah; I Walk Alone;* and many more. Wrubel stopped writing for a few years after 1949 and didn't pick up again until 1952, when he had one song, *Please, My Love.* Then again he stopped until 1959, when he contributed two titles to the movie *Never Steal Anything Small,* including the title song and *It Takes Love to Make a Home.* He wrote only sporadically in the sixties.

The world lost a great talent when Allie Wrubel died of a heart attack December 13, 1973, in Twenty-nine Palms, California.

Jack Yellen

Lyricist Jack Yellen was born in Poland on July 6, 1893. He was the son of a pawnbroker who immigrated to the United States in 1897. The young man attended the University of Michigan and then for awhile worked as a reporter for a Buffalo newspaper. But by 1913 Yellen was in New York City, writing the words to songs composed by such stalwarts as Harold Arlen, Ray Henderson, Lew Pollack, and Sammy Fain. He got off to a fast start that year with a song he wrote with George L. Cobb, *All Aboard for Dixie Land,* and two years later they had back-to-back hits with *Alabama Jubilee* and *Are You From Dixie,* both very familiar titles.

In 1920 Yellen teamed up with Milton Ager to write for Broadway musicals, the earliest of which, "What's in a Name," included the all-time standard *A Young Man's Fancy.* Ager and Yellen were a natural pair, complementing each other perfectly, and they were just getting warmed up. In 1922 they had two successes, *Who Cares?,* featured by Al Jolson in "Bombo," and *Lovin' Sam (the Sheik of Alabam),* introduced by Grace Hayes in the stage show "The Bunch and Judy." In the 1950 movie *Young Man with a Horn,* it was performed as a duet by Kirk Douglas and Hoagy Carmichael.

The following year Ager and Yellen came up with the Flapper's Declaration of Independence, *Mama Goes Where Papa Goes (Or Papa Don't Go Out Tonight).* It was introduced by Sophie Tucker and vigorously reinterpreted by Kay Starr on a Capitol recording in the fifties. The team had a trio of hits in 1924. *Baghdad* was introduced in vaudeville by Fred Waring's Pennsylvanians, and Paul Specht's band had a best-selling record as an instrumental on Columbia. *Hard-Hearted Hannah (the Vamp of Savannah)* was a popular vaudeville selection, and both Belle Baker and Lucille Hegamin had contemporary sides. In later years it was revived with successful records by Ray McKinley, Ray Charles, and Peggy Lee. Ella Fitzgerald sang it in the 1955 film *Pete Kelly's Blues* and also recorded it for Decca. The third title, the sentimental *I Wonder What's Become of Sally,* was introduced by Van and Schenck at the prestigious Palace Theater in New York and also got prime treatment on records by Ted Lewis, Al Jolson, and Bennie Krueger's orchestra. *Cheatin' on Me,* a song that became a super hit for the

Jimmie Lunceford band over a decade later, was a Yellen collaboration with Lew Pollack in 1925. It was introduced by Sophie Tucker. Ben Bernie's orchestra had the best-selling record on Vocalion. Pollack and Yellen also wrote *My Yiddishe Momme,* another successful vaudeville item for Al Jolson, Willie Howard, and Sophie Tucker.

In 1927 Yellen and Milton Ager put together one of those songs that have come to epitomize the Roaring Twenties, *Ain't She Sweet.* It has subsequently survived as a standard even to being recorded by the Beatles in 1964. In the interim, it was an immediate hit on records by Paul Whiteman's Rhythm Boys (Bing Crosby, Al Rinker, and Harry Barris) on Victor, Ben Bernie on Brunswick, Gene Austin on Victor, Harry Richman on Brunswick, and the Dixie Stompers (Fletcher Henderson) on Harmony. In 1939 the Jimmie Lunceford band had a hit recording on the arrangement by Sy Oliver. The song has also had a movie career. In 1946 it was played in the movie *Margie* and two years later in *You Were Meant for Me,* as sung by Dan Dailey, Jeanne Crain, and Barbara Lawrence. Pianist Carmen Cavallaro played it for the soundtrack of *The Eddy Duchin Story,* and it was dubbed in for Tyrone Power.

For Ager and Yellen it was just the beginning. That same year they followed through with *Crazy Words—Crazy Tune; Forgive Me; Is She My Girl Friend; Ain't That a Grand and Glorious Feeling;* and *Vo-Do-Do-De-O Blues.* Then just for good measure, Yellen wrote *Dream Kisses* with M. K. Jerome. In 1928 Ager and Yellen wrote the score for the Broadway musical "Rain or Shine," turning in some good songs—*Rain or Shine; Falling Star; Forever and Ever*—but in one of those ironic twists often encountered in the songwriting game, the song that has survived from the show was written by an unknown composer, Owen Murphy. A long-term favorite of jazz musicians, the tune is *Oh, Baby.*

Yellen wrote special material for many of the big stars of the era, especially Sophie Tucker, for whom he contributed *Mr. Segal, You Gotta Make It Legal* and *I'm the Last of the Red-Hot Mamas.* He continued to write steadily well into the forties and in the process compiled a long list of hits and standards. Here are a few high spots: *Glad Rag Doll; Happy Feet; Happy Days Are Here Again* (Franklin D. Roosevelt's first campaign song); *You Said It; Sweet and Hot; Learn to Croon; Nasty Man; Hold My Hand; According to the Moonlight.*

Jack Yellen was one of the earliest members of ASCAP and served on its board of directors from 1951 to 1969. In 1976 he was elected to the Songwriters Hall of Fame. In the forties he retired to a farm near Springfield, New York, where he died on April 17, 1991, at the age of ninety-eight.

Vincent Youmans

Pianist-composer Vincent Youmans was born in New York City on September 27, 1898. He was educated at Trinity School, in Mamaroneck, New York, and Heathcote Hall, in Rye, New York. For awhile he worked in a Wall Street firm and then joined the navy during World War I, helping to produce musicals at the Great Lakes Naval Training Station. After the war he went to work as a pianist and song plugger for Harms Music and as rehearsal pianist for Victor Herbert. This eventually led to his writing for the stage, and in 1921 he scored a moderate success with the music for "Two Little Girls in Blue," with lyrics by Ira Gershwin under the pseudonym of Arthur Francis. Two years later he teamed with Herbert Stothart on the music and Otto Harbach and Oscar Hammerstein II on the lyrics for the Broadway musical "Wildflower." It ran for almost five hundred performances, and two of the songs were very popular, *Wildflower* and *Bambalina.* Although Stothart's name appeared on all the music for the show, indications are that Youmans wrote these two songs. Ben Bernie's band had the top recording on Vocalion of *Wildflower,* and Paul Whiteman, for Victor on *Bambalina,* had one of the best-sellers of the year.

No big songs resulted from 1924, but in 1925 Youmans composed the music for "No, No, Nanette," with Otto Harbach and Irving Caesar writing the words, and from this show came two all-time hit songs, *Tea for Two* and *I Want to Be Happy. Tea for Two* has been played and recorded countless times in a variety of styles. The society bands bounced it, jazz bands have swung it, and it was even adapted as a cha-cha. Just about the same things can be said of *I Want to Be Happy,* including the cha-cha bit. *I Know That You Know* was the hit song from the 1926 musical "Oh, Please!" The lyrics were by Anne Caldwell. Again, the song has been played and recorded hundreds of times, as well as making appearances in other shows and movies, but one special aspect has been its function as a tour de force for clarinet players, including outstanding records by Jimmie Noone and Benny Goodman.

In 1927 Youmans produced the musical "Hit the Deck" and also wrote the music. With Irving Caesar he wrote the show's biggest hit, *Sometimes I'm Happy*. The other hit song, *Hallelujah,* had words by Leo Robin and Clifford Grey. Youmans composed the music for this song years before, while stationed at the Great Lakes Naval Training Station. At the time the navy band played it, and later it was performed by the band of John Philip Sousa. For "Hit the Deck," words were added and the song became a showstopper and eventually a standard. It was included in the 1930 film version of the show and in the remake of 1955. As late as 1975 it provided the finale in the musical "A Musical Jubilee," as sung by John Raitt and the show's company.

Youmans also produced the 1929 Broadway show "Great Day." It only ran for thirty-six performances, but from it came three more standard songs—the outstanding *More Than You Know; Great Day;* and *Without a Song*. Billy Rose and Edward Eliscu provided the lyrics. The beautiful *More Than You Know* has become a favorite of singers, and they have made the records to prove it. *Without a Song* was recorded by Lawrence Tibbett for Victor, and he also sang it in the movie *The Prodigal.* The song thereafter became a favorite of strong-voiced singers. Nevertheless, Bing Crosby was the vocalist on the contemporary hit recording by Paul Whiteman, and in later renditions it was sung by Frank Sinatra, with Tommy Dorsey, and by Perry Como. Other sides were made by Nelson Eddy, Jan Peerce, and the bands of Ray McKinley, Eddie Heywood, and Rex Stewart. *Great Day* was coupled with *Without a Song* on the best-selling Whiteman record, and Bing Crosby was the vocalist on both sides.

The all-time favorite *Time On My Hands,* with words by Harold Adamson and Mack Gordon, was introduced in the show "Smiles" in 1930. Paul Gregory sang it to the star of the show, Marilyn Miller, who refused to sing it. In the biographical film *Look for the Silver Lining,* June Haver, portraying Marilyn Miller, did sing it. The song, of course, is a perennial favorite and has been played, sung, and recorded countless times. *Keepin' Myself for You,* with words by Sidney Clare, was a new song incorporated into the movie version of "Hit the Deck" in 1930. It was sung by Jack Oakie and Polly Walker. Popular recordings were made by the bands of Bert Lown and Paul Specht. Later sides were made by Artie Shaw and His Gramercy Five and by Mel Tormé. Tony Martin sang the tune in the 1955 remake of *Hit the Deck.*

In 1933 Youmans wrote music for the film *Flying Down to Rio* and, with Gus Kahn and Edward Eliscu supplying the words, had two more hit songs, *Orchids in the Moonlight* and *The Carioca.* Shortly afterwards, he contracted tuberculosis, had to enter a sanitarium, and although he was finally able to leave, his musical activity was considerably curtailed. His illness continued, and after a stay in a New York hospital, he had to return to the sanitarium in Denver. He died at the early age of forty-eight, on April 5, 1946.

Other songs by Vincent Youmans include *Oh Me, Oh My, Oh You; Dolly; April Blossoms; Toodle-oo; You're Never Too Old to Learn; Look Around; Deep in My Heart; Take a Little One-Step; Tie a String Around Your Finger; Too Many Rings Around Rosie; I've Confessed to the Breeze; Where Has My Hubby Gone Blues; Waiting for You; You Can Dance With Any Girl at All;*

Like He Loves Me; I'm Waiting for a Wonderful Girl; Why, Oh Why; Harbor of My Heart; Join the Navy; Nothing Could be Sweeter; If He'll Come Back to Me; The One Girl; I Like You As You Are; West Wind; Love Is Like a Song; Say "Oui" Cherie; You're the One; Drums in My Heart; Oh, How I Long to Belong to You; So Do I; Rise 'n' Shine; and *Should I Be Sweet?*

Joe Young

Lyricist Joe Young was born on July 4, 1889, in New York City. He was educated in the public schools and early in his career was a professional singer for music publishing firms. During World War I he toured as an entertainer for the troops. The list of composers he collaborated with reads like a Who's Who of songwriters. In 1926 he became a director of ASCAP, a post he held until 1939. Young started writing lyrics in 1911 and was fairly successful. In 1915 he collaborated with Bert Grant on *Along the Rocky Road to Dublin.* It was recorded by the American Quartette on Victor. In the following year with E. Roy Goetz he wrote the words for an early Pete Wendling hit, *Yaaka Hula Hickey Dula.* The Avon Comedy Four made this for Victor, and so did Arthur Collins and Byron G. Harlan. Al Jolson made it for Columbia.

In 1916 Young teamed with fellow lyricist Sam H. Lewis, and the partnership lasted until 1930. In the interim they worked with many of the most respected composers in Tin Pan Alley, including Walter Donaldson, Harry Warren, Fred Ahlert, Jean Schwartz, Ray Henderson, Harry Akst, George W. Meyer, Little Jack Little, Milton Ager, Bernice Petkere, Carmen Lombardo, and Ted Fio Rito. Hitting the highlights of a tremendously prolific output through the years, we start off in 1916 with *Where Did Robinson Crusoe Go With Friday on a Saturday Night?* George W. Meyer contributed the music to this intriguing question, and Al Jolson posed it on a Columbia record.

In the next year there were two popular titles, *Huckleberry Finn* and *I'm All Bound 'Round with the Mason Dixon Line.* Cliff Hess was the composer of the first; Jean Schwartz the second. Van & Schenck told the story of *Huckleberry Finn* on Victor; Jolson, again, was *All Bound 'Round* on Columbia. In 1936, not quite twenty years later, Jimmy McPartland's Squirrels turned it into a vehicle for Chicago jazz interpretation on a recording for Decca. The ubiquitous Al Jolson was much in evidence in 1918, recording several Young–Lewis titles, including *Rock-a-bye Your Baby With a Dixie Melody* (composed by Jean Schwartz); *My Mammy* (Walter Donaldson); and *Hello, Central, Give Me No Man's Land* (also by Jean Schwartz). Still asking questions, Young and Lewis wanted to know in 1919, *How Ya Gonna Keep 'Em*

Down on the Farm? Walter Donaldson provided the melody, and Nora Bayes obligingly recorded it for Columbia.

In 1920 Young and Lewis joined another team, Con Conrad and J. Russel Robinson, who composed the music for a song that was destined to become a jazz classic, *Singin' the Blues ('Till My Daddy Comes Home).* Halfheartedly introduced, as though an afterthought, on the Original Dixieland Jazz Band's recording of *Margie,* the tune was off to a slow start, but it got a tremendous boost in 1927 when Frank Trumbauer and Bix Beiderbecke recorded it for OKeh, each playing masterful improvised solos based on the melody. It was recorded many times since, and Adrian Rollini had an outstanding side on Decca in 1938. George W. Meyer penned the 1921 entry *Tuck Me to Sleep in My Old Kentucky Home.* Contemporary sides were made by the Benson Orchestra of Chicago on Victor and the Columbians, appropriately enough, on Columbia. Billy Jones made it for OKeh. Years later it was revived by "The Melody Masters." *Lovey Came Back,* a Lou Handman composition, was the 1922 offering. Frank Guarente and the Georgians made it for Columbia.

The next year was a big one for Young and Lewis, and they had three big hits: *Dinah,* a collaboration with Harry Akst; *I'm Sitting on Top of the World;* and *Five Foot Two, Eyes of Blue,* both with Ray Henderson. Over the years the first and third titles have held on to become standards, recorded and played many, many times, but *I'm Sitting on Top of the World* rated first-class treatment in 1925, with platters by Al Jolson, Roger Wolfe Kahn, and Freddie Rich, among others. And the hits continued to roll. In 1926 Young and Lewis worked with Mabel Wayne, and the result was *In a Little Spanish Town.* Paul Whiteman had the big record on that one. And with Harry Woods, they wrote *Take In the Sun, Hang Out the Moon.* The Arkansaw Travelers made it for OKeh, and Paul Ash did the same for Columbia.

After a few years with no outstanding titles, Young and Lewis collaborated with a newcomer, Ralph Erwin, on *I Kiss Your Hand, Madame.* The 1929 song did pretty well in the heavy competition of that year, with a good record by Bing Crosby on Columbia, among others. Another successful title was the Ted Fio Rito tune *Then You've Never Been Blue.* Kay Starr revived it on a great record for Capitol years later. As might be expected, Ted Fio Rito had the contemporary side for Columbia. *I Used to Love Her in the Moonlight* was another good song by Ted Fio Rito, with lyrics by Young and Lewis. The Ipana Troubadors recorded it for Columbia, but the song didn't get the attention it deserved.

In 1930, the last year of their partnership, Young and Lewis had three great songs in collaboration with Harry Warren—*Absence Makes the Heart Grow*

Fonder; Have a Little Faith in Me; and *Cryin' for the Carolines*. Singer Gene Austin recorded the first title for Victor, and so did Bernie Cummins and His Orchestra. Art Gillham made it for Columbia backed by *Have a Little Faith In Me*. Like all big songs of the period, they were frequently heard on the radio, and recordings were secondary. Nevertheless, *Cryin' for the Carolines* drew a lot of attention on wax. Among the band recordings were those by Artie Schutt (OKeh), Ben Pollack (Hit-of-the-Week), Jimmie Noone (Vocalion), Sam Lanin (Harmony), Chick Bullock (Vocalion), and in England, Ambrose (HMV) and Phil Green (Parlophone). Other sides were made by James P. Johnson as a piano solo and by overseas groups.

Young and Sam M. Lewis parted that year, but writing as a single Young had two other important songs. One was another ballad by Harry Warren, *Telling It to the Daisies;* the other was a collaboration with Ira Schuster, writing under the name of John Siras, a waltz that Young called *I'm Alone Because I Love You*. Among those who made records of *Telling It to the Daisies* were Gene Austin, Annette Hanshaw, and the California Ramblers. The waltz was a popular radio selection, and in 1941 the redoubtable Dick Robertson recorded it for Decca.

Young's career continued without interruption, and in the following year he had four important songs. On two of them he paired with Mort Dixon on the lyrics to music by Harry Warren, *You're My Everything* and *Ooh! That Kiss*. Russ Columbo had the big record on *You're My Everything,* and it became identified with him; but the song also was a radio favorite. The same can be said for *Ooh! That Kiss*. The Dorsey Brothers recorded it for Columbia, and Ben Selvin took care of the subsidiary labels. Young wrote English lyrics for a German waltz that was the title song of the film *Zwei Herzen im Dreivierteltakt*. It became *Two Hearts in Three-Quarter Time* and was very popular. The composer was Robert Stolz. The fourth title was a song by Harry Akst, of *Dinah* fame, *I Can't Get Mississippi Off My Mind*. The bands of Bert Lown and Paul Tremaine recorded it and plugged it on radio broadcasts.

So far Young had already compiled an enviable record of hit songs, but he was just getting warmed up, because 1932 was a banner year. Taking the titles in alphabetical order, we start with *In a Shanty in Old Shanty Town,* a hit destined for even bigger things as revived by Johnny Long's band in 1942. Little Jack Little and Ira Schuster wrote the music. Next we have *Lullaby of the Leaves,* a rather mournful ballad by Bernice Petkere. Contemporary sides were dutifully recorded by Ben Selvin, George Olsen, and Connee Boswell, among others, but the song enjoyed a resurgence of popularity with the advent of the bop musicians who gave it their modern treatment on records. Among these are sides by Dizzy Gillespie, Gerry Mulligan, and Cal Tjader.

My Heart's at Ease is a delightful little song by Fats Waller with lyrics by Young. Unfortunately it is overlooked, even by Waller fans, but it rated nice records by Chick Bullock, Ruby Newman, and Russ Carlson and enjoyed good radio time. *Snuggled on Your Shoulder,* a composition by Carmen Lombardo, was a popular item in 1932, helped considerably by the Guy Lombardo orchestra's frequent broadcasts. Oddly enough, it didn't record the song, but other bands did, including those of Smith Ballew, Eddy Duchin, and Jack Denny. Vocal sides were made by Morton Downey and Sylvia Froos. *Starlight,* a beautiful song by Bernice Petkere, was recorded by Glen Gray on Brunswick and Ted Wallace on Columbia, but deserved more attention. Young also worked with Sammy Fain that year, and they produced *Was That the Human Thing to Do?,* a plaintive ditty that was waxed by Ben Selvin and Rudy Vallee.

Young had no smash hits in 1933, but he was associated with four good songs. *Shadows on the Swanee,* with music by Harold Spina, had Young sharing lyric credit with Johnny Burke. The Isham Jones band did it justice on Victor; Ethel Waters sang it for Brunswick. *Two Tickets to Georgia,* with a melody by J. Fred Coots, was again a split credit between Young and Charles Tobias. Ben Pollack had the best record for Victor. Victor Young made it for Brunswick. One of Carmen Lombardo's nicest songs also came out that year, and Young added suitable words, *You're Beautiful Tonight, My Dear.* A sleeper, it was largely overlooked, but Will Osborne had a nice record on the ARC labels. Finally, Young contributed the lyrics to the 1933 James V. Monaco song *You're Gonna Lose Your Gal.* A light bit of fluff, it still rated records by Jan Garber and Glen Gray.

I Hate Myself (For Being So Mean to You), with music by Milton Ager and again a split between Young and Benny Davis on the words, was the only important title in 1934. Eddie Stone delineated the idea with Isham Jones on a Victor record. George W. Meyer and Pete Wendling were responsible for the melodic *I'm Growing Fonder of You* in 1935. Freddy Martin had a good record on Brunswick. Another sprightly offering was *You're a Heavenly Thing,* composed by Little Jack Little. It received contrasting treatment on records by Benny Goodman (Victor) and Orville Knapp (Decca). Fred Ahlert and Young collaborated on *Life Is a Song (Let's Sing It Together),* and it was recorded by Connee Boswell and also by Joe Haymes. All compositions from that point forward seem to indicate that Ahlert and Young took the song title to heart, because in the next two years they were a firm partnership.

In 1936 they had a succession of successful songs—*I'm Gonna Sit Right Down and Write Myself a Letter* (a classic as recorded by Fats Waller); *Sing an Old-Fashioned Song (To a Young Sophisticated Lady)* a formula recommended by Red McKenzie, Chick Bullock, and Jack Shilkret; *Take My Heart,* recorded by Nat Brandwynne for Brunswick and Eddy Duchin for Victor; *There's Two Sides to Every Story,* a fact testified by Dick Powell on Decca; and *You Dropped Me Like a Red Hot Penny,* a bouncy item by Chick Bullock and His Levee Loungers on Melotone.

This routine continued for 1937, although Harry Reser managed to squeeze in for credit with Fred Ahlert on the first title, *The Goona Goo.* Bunny Berigan did the best he could with it for Brunswick. The rest are all well-constructed songs, well played by the artists involved, but obviously not promoted to any great extent. *There's Frost on the Moon,* a very good song, was nicely recorded by Dick McDonough's all-star group. Bunny Berigan made another good one, *The Image of You,* and Nat Brandwynne played *To a Sweet Pretty Thing. I've Got a New Lease on Love,* a tune not quite up to the quality of the others, was still adequately waxed by Isham Jones; and Teddy Hill, Bunny Berigan, and Gus Arnheim were unanimous in declaring, *I'm Happy, Darling, Dancing with You.*

Joe Young died in New York City on April 21, 1939.

Victor Young

Victor Young was one of those uniquely talented men who can be extremely successful in almost any career they undertake, exert a tremendous influence in their field of activity, and yet do it all so easily and quietly as to go almost unnoticed. A native Chicagoan, he was born there on August 8, 1900, and died too soon on November 11, 1956, in Palm Springs, California. But he packed those fifty-six years with back-to-back musical activities, any one of which would have satisfied most men. He started out as a violinist playing classical music and apparently was very good at it, studying at the Warsaw Conservatory and then going on to play in the Warsaw Philharmonic and touring Europe. When the First World War broke out he returned to the States and went on a tour as a concert violinist, followed by jobs as concert master in theaters. Eventually, however, he turned to popular music and composing and for awhile worked as a violinist and arranger with Ted Fio Rito's band. Incidentally, he played the violin solo on the hit recording of *Stardust* by the Isham Jones orchestra on Brunswick 4886 in 1930.

From these it was only a short step to leading his own orchestra, which he did on Chicago radio for several years before moving to New York to conduct on network radio, where he backed such personages as Al Jolson and Don Ameche, as well as being featured on his own show. In the meantime, just to keep busy, he was composing some rather successful popular songs, starting out with *Sweet Sue* in 1928, followed by *Beautiful Love* in 1931, and a whole cluster of hits in 1932—the wonderful *Can't We Talk It Over?; My Love; Lawd You Made the Night Too Long; Was I to Blame?; The Old Man of the Mountain;* and *Got the South in My Soul.* He also became a recording director for Decca Records, making a number of sides under his own name and with his own orchestra but also supervising records by the great stable of stars under contract to the company in the thirties.

In 1933 he contributed songs to a couple of stage shows. *A Hundred Years from Today* was featured in "Blackbirds of 1933," and *Sweet Madness* was the hit of "Murder at the Vanities." Then for good measure, Young went on to turn out *A Ghost of a Chance; Street of Dreams; I'd Be Telling a Lie;* and *Any Time, Any Place, Anywhere,* in collaboration with vocalist Lee Wiley. *One Hundred Years from Today* proved to be a bigger hit in 1934 than it had been in 1933, but just to make sure that things would continue to run smoothly, Young added the entreaty *Love Me* and backed it up with *Give Me a Heart to Sing To,* both of which did very well in the marketplace that year.

Now the decade was at midpoint and in high gear, Hollywood beckoned Victor Young, as it did all the great songwriters of the period, and he settled on the West Coast, devoting his time to arranging and composing background music for Paramount. This kept him pretty occupied for the rest of the thirties, but in the forties he again began contributing songs to movies. In 1946 he wrote *Love Letters* for the picture of the same title, then did quite well with a beautiful tune that has become a favorite standard, *Stella by Starlight.* Other movie songs in succeeding years include *Golden Earrings* (1947); *Song of Surrender* (1949); and *My Foolish Heart* (1950).

Altogether, Victor Young composed and arranged music for over 350 movies. He received an Academy Award posthumously for his score for *Around the World in Eighty Days.* It was a futile award, but one that was long overdue for a man who made such a giant contribution to the industry. Personally, I prefer to remember him for *Can't We Talk It Over; Ghost of a Chance; Street of Dreams;* and *Was I to Blame,* a fistful that rate among the finest songs in the great American standard library. Lyricists collaborating with Young through the years include Ned Washington, Ed Heyman, Joe Young, Will Harris, and Jack Osterman.

Other titles by Victor Young include *Waltzing in a Dream; Love Is the Thing; Does The Moon Shine Through the Tall Pine?; Born to Love; A Love Like This; You're Wonderful; Song of Delilah; Pardon Our French; A Face in the Crowd; My Foolish Heart; When I Fall in Love; Alone at Last; A Weaver of Dreams; An Angel Kissed Me Last Night; Where Can I Go Without You?;* and *The World Is Mine.*

Hy Zaret

Lyricist Hy Zaret was born in New York City on August 21, 1907. His education included West Virginia University and Brooklyn Law School. He practiced law in New York for several years. In World War II he was attached to the Special Services section in the army. Active as a writer in radio and TV, he received numerous awards for public service. As a songwriter he is best remembered for the lyrics of a collection of hit songs beginning in the late thirties and into the forties. His first successful entry, *Dedicated to You,* was published in 1937 and was a collaboration with Sammy Cahn and Saul Chaplin. It rated quality recordings by Ella Fitzgerald and Her Savoy Eight (Decca); Tommy Dorsey, with Jack Leonard singing (Victor); and Andy Kirk, with the vocal by Pha Terrell (Decca).

In 1940 Zaret teamed with Irving Weiser on *There I Go,* which turned out to be a big hit for the new band of singing bandleader Vaughn Monroe on Bluebird. The song was also well represented on all the record labels—Tommy Tucker on OKeh, Woody Herman for Decca, Will Bradley on Columbia, and Kenny Baker on Victor. That same year Zaret worked with Joan Whitney and Alex Kramer on *So You're the One,* a tune that enjoyed some popularity and was recorded by the bands of Vaughn Monroe, Hal Kemp, and Eddy Duchin. The three writers would go on to produce a number of hits. In 1941 they had two outstanding titles, *It All Comes Back to Me Now* and *My Sister and I.* The first title made the top five popularity rating, and good records were released by Hal Kemp (Victor); Ted Weems, with Perry Como singing (Decca); Gene Krupa (OKeh); and Eddy Duchin (Columbia). *My Sister and I,* inspired by the book of the same title by the victim of Nazi persecution Dirk van der Heide, made number one on *Your Hit Parade* and resulted in top-selling records by Jimmy Dorsey (Decca); Bea Wain (Victor); Benny Goodman, with a Helen Forrest vocal (Columbia); Bob Chester, Bill Darnell singing (Bluebird); and others.

In 1945 Zaret and Lou Singer reworked an old ballad from the midnineteenth century called *The One Fish Ball,* and it became a tragic little story told by folk-singer Josh White, who introduced it on the first hit recording as *One Meat Ball.* Coupled on a Decca record with *Rum and Coca Cola* by the Andrews Sisters, it went on to sell in the millions.

Other songs by Hy Zaret are *My Lily and My Rose; You'll Never Get Away; To Be Loved by You; Unchained Melody; You Can't Hold a Memory in Your Arms; Be Brave, Beloved; Young and Warm and Wonderful; Train of Love; No Other Arms, No Other Lips; I Woke Up Crying; What More Do You Want?; Counting the Days;* and *The Lass with the Delicate Air.*

Bibliography

ASCAP Biographical Dictionary. 4th ed. New York: R. R. Bowker, 1980.

Berger, Morrow, Ed Berger, and James Patrick. *Benny Carter, A Life in American Music*. Vol. I and II. Metuchen, N.J.: Scarecrow Press and the Rutgers Institute of Jazz Studies, 1982.

Brahms, Caryl, and Ned Sherrin. *Song by Song*. [fourteen great lyricists] Egerton, Bolton, England: Ross Anderson Publications, 1984.

Brunn, H. O. *The Story of the Original Dixieland Jazz Band*. Baton Rouge, La.: Louisiana State University Press, 1960.

Clayton, Peter, and Peter Gammond, ed. *The Guinness Jazz A–Z*. Middlesex, Enfield, England: Guinness Superlatives, 1986.

Jacobs, Dick. *Who Wrote That Song?* Whitehall, Va.: Betterway Publications, 1988.

Kimball, Robert, ed. *Cole: A Biographical Essay by Brendan Gill*. New York: Holt, Rinehard & Winston, 1971.

Kimball, Robert, and Alfred Simon. *The Gershwins*. New York: Atheneum, 1973.

Kinkle, Roger D. *The Complete Encyclopedia of Popular Music and Jazz 1900–1950*. New Rochelle, N.Y.: Arlington House, 1974.

Kirkeby, Ed. "*Ain't Misbehavin':*" *The Story of Fats Waller*. New York: Da Capo Press, 1975.

Lissauer, Robert. *Lissauer's Encyclopedia of Popular Music in America,* revised edition. New York: Facts on File, 1996.

Rust, Brian. *The American Dance Band Discography 1917–1942*. New Rochelle, N.Y.: Arlington House, 1975.

———. *Jazz Records 1897–1941*. New Rochelle, N.Y.: Arlington House, 1978.

Ulanov, Barry. *Duke Ellington*. New York: Da Capo Press, 1972.

APPENDIX

I. Melodies by Those Who Played Them

As anyone can discover merely by checking the composer credits on recordings or browsing through reference books on the subject, quite a number of our favorite and standard songs were not composed by the men with the big names—Berlin, Gershwin, Rodgers, Porter, Kern, et al. In fact, our heritage of songs has been enriched through the years by relatively small contributions—sometimes as little as one or two songs—that comprise the entire output of a bandleader or a sideman musician. A number of examples to illustrate this come quickly to mind. The all-time standard and favorite of both sweet bands and jazz bands, *I'm Confessin' That I Love You,* was composed by Philadelphia bandleader Doc Daugherty. Another standard, *Sweet and Lovely,* was the product of bandleader Gus Arnheim, who also wrote *I Cried for You,* in collaboration with still another baton waver, Abe Lyman.

Three more bandleaders—all with names that begin with the letter B—are responsible for very memorable songs. Phil Baxter, leader of the Texas Tommies, wrote *I'm a Ding Dong Daddy, A Faded Summer Love;* and *Piccolo Pete*. Ben Bernie, the Old Maestro, is credited with co-writing *Sweet Georgia Brown* and the hauntingly beautiful *Strange Interlude*. Earl Burtnett, a bandleader who died in 1936 and is now almost forgotten, was cut short in a very promising career that had already produced *Do You Ever Think of Me; Canadian Capers; 'Leven Thirty Saturday Night;* and *Have You Forgotten?* The aforementioned Abe Lyman has his name on three other important titles, *After I Say I'm Sorry; Mary Lou;* and *Did You Mean It?*

New Jersey native (born in Newark on December 20, 1900) Ted Fio Rito combined a successful songwriting career with leading a band and turned out a number of superior compositions throughout his long career. Those best remembered include *Toot, Toot, Tootsie, Goodbye; Charlie, My Boy; I Never Knew; Then You've Never Been Blue; Now That You're Gone;* and *Three on a Match.* Pioneering bandleader Art Hickman gave us the perennial *Rose Room,* which also enjoys longevity in its alter ego, *In a Mellotone,* composed by Duke Ellington. Bert Lown, who led a very popular band in New York in the early thirties, is credited as a co-composer of *Bye Bye Blues* (the band's theme song, which featured trombonist Al Philburn); *You're the One I Care For;* and *By My Side*. Jazz clarinetist and bandleader Joe Marsala usually wrote instrumentals for his band, but he also turned out a superior ballad in *Don't Cry, Joe* and made much more money with one of the sentimental hits of 1919, *Little Sir Echo.*

Two of the most prolific sidemen to turn out material featured by the bands they played with, and very likely contributed greatly to the success of those bands, were Joe Bishop and Gene Gifford. Bishop, who played brass bass and flugelhorn with the fine Isham Jones band of the early thirties and still later was a member of the Woody Herman band, wrote the great hit *Blue Prelude,* followed by *Blue Lament,* while still with Jones. He was responsible for most of the original material played by Woody Herman's "Band That Plays the Blues," including the theme, *Woodchopper's Ball; Bishop's Blues, Bessie's Blues, Blue Evening, Blues Upstairs,* and *Blue Flame,* Woody's theme during the forties. He also collaborated with Gene Gifford on another hit of the thirties, the futuristic *Out of Space,* which at the time was considered very advanced in its chord structure and harmonies.

Gene Gifford was the guitarist with Glen Gray and the Casa Loma Orchestra and its chief arranger. His ballad style of composing is most likely best represented by the band's theme, *Smoke Rings,* which featured Clarence Hutchenrider on the soulful clarinet solo. His instrumentals were mainly responsible for establishing the band's reputation as a hot group long before the advent of swing. Among the better known of these are *Casa Loma Stomp, Maniac's Ball; Black Jazz; White Jazz;* and *Dance of the Lame Duck.* Special mention is merited by Cliff Burwell, who played piano with Rudy Vallee's Connecticut Yankees in the twenties and early thirties and composed one of the outstanding songs of the era, *Sweet Lorraine*. Published in 1928 with lyrics by Mitchell Parish, it was an instant hit, became an all-time favorite of musicians and singers, and has been recorded countless times since. Tony Maramarco of Simsbury, Connecticut, has attempted to collect every recording made of the song and estimates he now has well over five hundred. Oddly enough, although Rudy Vallee helped Burwell introduce the song, the Vallee orchestra never recorded it.

Coincidentally, almost twenty years later (1946) another pianist who played with Vallee, Walter Gross, contributed another hardy perennial, *Tenderly*. And while we're on the subject of piano-playing composers who have left us with priceless examples of their talent, let's not forget Paul Mertz, who played with Jean Goldkette in the twenties and gave us the 1942 outstanding entry *I'm Glad There Is You.* One of Paul's most cherished possessions was a letter from Cole Porter praising this song as his favorite and mildly complaining because Mertz had published the song under his middle name, Madeira, making it a bit difficult for Porter to track him down so he could express his appreciation.

We can only scratch the surface at this point in mentioning bandleader and sidemen composers, but no discussion of this kind can go without calling attention to the work of a recent inductee into the Jazz Hall of Fame, Bob Haggart. Bob was an outstanding member of the Bob Crosby band, and his compositions and arrangements were important factors in its popularity. His originals are well known: *What's New?; Rampart Street Parade; Big Noise from Winnetka; I'm Prayin' Humble; Dogtown Blues; Dixieland Shuffle;* and *My Inspiration.* For that matter, how can we ignore such contributions as Lil Armstrong's *Struttin' with Some Barbecue* and the delightful *Just for a Thrill;* gems such as Fletcher Henderson's *Down South Camp Meetin'* and *Wrappin' It Up;* or Earl Hine's *Rosetta* and *Monday Date;* Terry Shand's *My Extraordinary Gal;* Claude Hopkins's *I Would Do Anything for You;* Gene Austin's *How Come You Do Me Like You Do; When My Sugar Walks Down the Street;* and *Lonesome Road;* Charlie Shavers's *Undecided;* and so on.

Through the years the American treasury of popular songs has been considerably enriched by the contributions of bandleaders. In the instances of geniuses like Duke Ellington, Ray Noble, Isham Jones, Victor Young, Johnny Green, and Fats Waller, of course, these contributions have been extensive, but even a partial list of leaders and their compositions is impressive and offers quite a few surprises because many of these tunes have long ago become standards, and it's a pretty fair guess that few people know who wrote them—let alone think of these leaders as composers. More than likely the following list is very incomplete, and we have forgotten some worthy candidates. Also, for the sake of brevity, we have only listed one composition for each name, although very often the writer composed a long string of songs.

Van Alexander	*A Tiskit, a Taskit*
Louis Armstrong	*Swing That Music*
Gus Arnheim	*Sweet and Lovely*
Phil Baxter	*I'm a Ding Dong Daddy*
Ben Bernie	*Sweet Georgia Brown*
Don Bestor	*Contented*
Earl Burtnett	*Do You Ever Think of Me*

Henry Busse	*Wang Wang Blues*
Frankie Carle	*Sunrise Serenade*
Benny Carter	*Blue Interlude*
Larry Clinton	*Study in Brown*
Eddie Condon	*Wherever There's Love*
Zez Confrey	*Kitten on the Keys*
Doc Daugherty	*Confessin'*
Jimmy Dorsey	*John Silver*
Duke Ellington	*Mood Indigo*
Ted Fio Rito	*I Never Knew*
Benny Goodman	*Don't Be That Way*
Johnny Green	*Body and Soul*
Bobby Hackett	*Michelle*
Lionel Hampton	*Flying Home*
Edgar Hayes	*If Dreams Come True*
Neal Hefti	*Li'l Darlin'*
Fletcher Henderson	*Wrappin' It Up*
Woody Herman	*Woodchopper's Ball*
Art Hickman	*Rose Room*
Earl Hines	*Rosetta*
Claude Hopkins	*I Would Do Anything for You*
Eddy Howard	*If I Knew Then*
Will Hudson	*Moonglow*
Roy Ingraham	*In the Hush of the Night*
Harry James	*I'm Beginning to See the Light*
Isham Jones	*It Had to Be You*
Roger Wolfe Kahn	*Crazy Rhythm*
Art Kassel	*Sobbin' Blues*
Nick LaRocca	*Fidgety Feet*
Bert Lown	*Bye Bye Blues*
Abe Lyman	*I Cried for You*
Enric Madriguera	*Adios*
Matty Malneck	*I'll Never Be the Same*
Matty Matlock	*March of the Bobcats*
Russ Morgan	*Does Your Heart Beat for Me*
Ray Noble	*Goodnight, Sweetheart*
King Oliver	*Dippermouth Blues*
Sy Oliver	*'Tain't What You Do*
Will Osborne	*Beside an Open Fireplace*
Jack Pettis	*Bugle Call Rag*

Don Redman	*Cherry*
Willard Robison	*A Cottage for Sale*
Joe Sanders	*The Wail*
Raymond Scott	*Twilight in Turkey*
Terry Shand	*My Extraordinary Gal*
Artie Shaw	*Back Bay Shuffle*
Harold Stern	*I'm All Dressed Up with a Broken Heart*
Claude Thornhill	*Snowfall*
Rudy Vallee	*Deep Night*
Peter Van Steeden	*Home*
Fats Waller	*Ain't Misbehavin'*
Victor Young	*Ghost of a Chance*

Collectively this adds up to some great music and individually a worthwhile legacy from each and every composer.

II. One Hitters

Here we pay tribute to the composers who may or may not have written other songs during their careers but only succeeded in having one big hit. Their contributions, nevertheless, are worthwhile and deserving of respect.

Fabian Andre/Wilbur Schwandt	*Dream a Little Dream of Me*
George Bassman	*I'm Getting Sentimental over You*
Felix Bernard/Johnny Black	*Dardenella*
Johnny Black	*Paper Doll*
James Blake/Charles Lawlor	*The Sidewalks of New York*
Nat Bonx	*Collegiate*
Ernie Burnett	*My Melancholy Baby*
Cliff Burwell	*Sweet Lorraine*
N. J. Clesi	*I'm Sorry I Made You Cry*
Will Marion Cook	*I'm Coming Virginia*
George C. Cory Jr.	*I Left My Heart in San Francisco*
Francis Craig	*Near You*
Jimmy Dale	*At a Georgia Camp Meeting*
Julian Dash	*Tuxedo Junction*
Doc Daugherty/Ellis Reynolds	*I'm Confessin' That I Love You*
Charles Davis	*Copenhagen*
Tom Delaney	*Jazz Me Blues*
John DeVries	*Oh! Look at Me Now*
Earl Foxe/Lynn Cowan	*Dream House*
Don Gardner	*All I Want for Christmas Is My Two Front Teeth*
Joe Garland	*In the Mood*
Erroll Garner	*Misty*
Arthur Harrington Gibbs	*Runnin' Wild*
Walter Gross	*Tenderly*
Earle Hagen	*Harlem Nocturne*
Wendell Hall	*It Ain't Gonna Rain No Mo'*
Art Hickman	*Rose Room*
Claude Hopkins	*I Would Do Anything for You*
Raymond Hubbel	*Poor Butterfly*
Roger Wolfe Kahn	*Crazy Rhythm*
Marcy Kauber/Harry Stoddard	*I Get the Blues When It Rains*
John W. Kellette	*I'm Forever Blowing Bubbles*
Charles Kisco	*It's a Lonesome Old Town*

Lou Klein	*If I Had My Way*
Ned Lehac	*You Forgot Your Gloves*
Eddie Leonard/Eddie Munson	*Ida! Sweet As Apple Cider*
Eugene Lockhart/Ernest Seitz	*The World Is Waiting for the Sunrise*
Ange Lorenzo	*Sleepy Time Gal*
Carroll Loveday	*That's My Desire*
Ruth Lowe	*I'll Never Smile Again*
Clarence Lucas/Harold Vicars	*Song of Songs*
Paul Madeira (Mertz)	*I'm Glad There Is You*
Enric Madriguera	*Adios*
William Mayhew	*It's a Sin to Tell a Lie*
Lindsay McPhail	*San*
Dudley Mecum	*Angry*
Jack Norworth/Nora Bayes	*Shine on Harvest Moon*
Tom Pills	*I Never Knew (I Could Love Anybody)*
Louis Prima	*Sing, Sing, Sing*
David Raksin	*Laura*
Ram Ramirez	*Lover Man*
Lee Robert	*Smiles*
Julian Robledo	*Three O'Clock in the Morning*
Ann Runell	*Willow Weep for Me*
Harry Ruskin/Henry Sullivan	*I May Be Wrong (But I Think You're Wonderful)*
Tony Sacco	*The Breeze (That's Bringing My Honey Back to Me)*
Milton Samuels	*Jim (Doesn't Ever Bring Me Pretty Flowers)*
John Schonberger	*Whispering*
John Schraubstader	*Last Night on the Back Porch*
Bill Scotti	*My Moonlight Madonna*
Bruce Seiver/Ord Hamilton	*You're Blasé*
Jack Sharpe/Jerry Herst	*So Rare*
Charlie Shavers	*Undecided*
Frank Silver	*Yes, We Have No Bananas*
Howard Simon	*Gonna Getta Girl*
Stuff Smith	*It's Wonderful*
Harold Solomon	*Hurt*

Anna Sosenko	*Darling, Je Vous Aime, Beaucoup*
Harry Sosnik	*Lazy Rhapsody*
Spikes Brothers (John & Benjamin)	*Someday, Sweetheart*
Mischer Spoliansky	*The Hour of Parting*
Harold Stern	*I'm All Dressed Up with a Broken Heart*
Byron D. Stokes/F. Dudley Vernor	*The Sweetheart of Sigma Chi*
Charlie Straight	*Funny, Dear, What Love Can Do*
Karl Suessdorf	*Moonlight in Vermont*
Einar Swan	*When Your Lover Has Gone*
Sam Theard	*I'll Be Glad When You're Dead, You Rascal You*
Peter Van Steeden	*Home*
Sarah Vimmerstedt	*I Wanna Be Around* (Vimmerstedt, a housewife, sent Johnny Mercer the title and idea for this song. He wrote it and shared the credit and royalties with her.)
Frank Warshauer	*It Isn't Fair*
Anson Weeks	*I'm Sorry Dear*
Harold Weeks	*Hindustan*
Dick Winfree	*China Boy*
Leo Wood	*Somebody Stole My Gal*

III. Clever or Unusual Titles

Chicken Today, Feathers Tomorrow
Johnny Marks
The Coat and Pants Do All the Work, but the Vest Gets All the Gravy
Bert Hanlon
Eve Cost Adam Just One Bone
Charles A. Bayha
The Fly Outflew the Flea
Larry Shay
Going Baroque and All That Jazz
Connie Atkinson
He Holds the Lantern While His Mother Chops the Wood
Lanny Grey
How Could You Believe Me When I Say I Love You When You Know I've Been a Liar All My Life?
Alan Jay Lerner, Burton Lane
How Much Wood Would a Woodchuck Chuck (If a Woodchuck Could Chuck Wood)
Denes Agay
I Can Spell Banana (But I Never Know When to Stop)
Geoffrey Clarkson
I Never Harmed an Onion, so Why Should They Make Me Cry?
Lanny Grey
I Would If I Could but I Can't
Bing Crosby, Lanny Grey, Mitchell Parish
I'd Love to Be a Cowboy, but I'm Afraid of Cows
Bobby Gregory
I'll Putcha Pitcha in the Papers
Nathaniel Lief
I'm a Lonely Little Petunia in an Onion Patch
William Faber
I'm Looking for a Guy Who Plays Alto and Baritone, Doubles on the Clarinet, and Wears a Size 37 Suit
Ozzie Nelson
I'm Pickin' Fights for Christmas (So Presents I Won't Have to Buy)
Art Wight
I've Got Tears in My Ears (From Lyin' on My Back in My Bed While I Cry Over You)
Harold Barlow

If You Talk in Your Sleep, Don't Mention My Name
A. Seymour Brown
It Isn't, It Wasn't, and It Ain't Never Gonna Be
Albert Hammond, Diane Warren
It's Hard to Tell the Depth of the Well from the Length of the Handle on the Pump
Buddy Fields, Sam Lerner
Maggie Get the Hammer There's a Fly on Baby's Head
Catherine Gregory
My Dreamboat Sailed Without Me
Denver Darling
She Fell in the Fall of the Year
Madeline Hyde
She Was a China Teacup, and He Was Just a Mug
Ralph Rainger, Leo Robin
There's No Man with Endurance Like the Man Who Sells Insurance
Benjamin Hapgood Burt, Frank Crumit
They're Burning Down the House I Was Brung Up In
Lee David
Three Nuts in Search of a Nat
Philip Moody
Today Will Be Yesterday Tomorrow
Dan Shapiro
Tyrone Shapiro (the Bronx Caballero)
Dan Shapiro
Whose Izzy Is He, Is He Yours or Is He Mine?
Murray Sturm
Wry on the Rocks
Steve Allen
You Stole My Wife, You Horse Thief
Harry Sims

IV. The Musicmakers: Songwriters Born between 1890 and 1920

A

Stanley Adams	1907
Harold Adamson	1906
Milton Ager	1893
Fred E. Ahlert	1892
Harry Akst	1894
John W. Alden	1895
Van Alexander	1915
Arthur Altman	1912
Edmund Anderson	1912
LeRoy Anderson	1908
Harold Arlen	1905
Lil Armstrong	1902
Louis Armstrong	1900
Gus Arnheim	1897
Paul Ash	1891
Gene Austin	1900
Ray Austin	1915

B

Chester Babcock (Jimmy Van Heusen)	1913
Abel Baer	1893
Phil Baker	1896
Pat Ballard	1899
Dave Barbour	1912
Harold Barlow	1915
Harry Barris	1905
Count Basie	1906
George Bassman	1914
Edgar Battle	1907
Ray Bauduc	1906
Phil Baxter	1896
Bennie Benjamin	1907
Ben Bernie	1891
Buddy Bernier	1910
Joe Bishop	1907
Burke Bivens	1903
Ray Bloch	1902
Rube Bloom	1902
Clay Boland	1903
Phil Boutelje	1895
Brooks Bowman	1913
Jerome Brainin	1916
Harry Brooks	1895
Harvey Brooks	1899
Jack Brooks	1912
John Benson Brooks	1917
Les Brown	1912
Lew Brown	1893
Lou Brown	1912
Nacio Herb Brown	1896
Walter Bullock	1907
Johnny Burke	1908
Sonny Burke	1914
Earl Burtnett	1896
Nat Burton	1901
Val Burton	1900
Cliff Burwell	1898
Joe Bushkin	1916
Henry Busse	1894
Richard Byron	1908

C

Irving Caesar	1895
Sammy Cahn	1913
Cab Calloway	1907
Tutti Camarata	1913
Frankie Carle	1903

Robert L. Carleton	1896
Hoagy Carmichael	1899
Charles Carpenter	1912
Harry Carroll	1892
Ken Casey	1895
Saul Chaplin	1912
Newell Chase	1904
Bob Chester	1908
George Chichester (Chet Forrest)	1915
Frank Churchhill	1901
Sunny Clapp	1899
Sidney Clare	1892
Grant Clarke	1891
Buck Clayton	1911
Michael Cleary	1902
Gordon Clifford	1902
Larry Clinton	1909
Nelson Cogane	1902
Nat "King" Cole	1919
Betty Comden	1919
Zez Confrey	1895
Larry Conley	1895
Joseph P. Connor	1895
J. Fred Coots	1897
Leo Corday	1902
Charles Cornell	1902
Sam Coslow	1902
Rubey Cowan	1891
Bing Crosby	1904

D

Doc Daugherty	1897
Mack David	1898
Benny Davis	1895
Joseph M. Davis	1896
Sylvia Dee	1914
Edgar DeLange	1904
Robert DeLeon	1904
Paul Denniker	1897
Matt Dennis	1914
Gene DePaul	1919
Peter DeRose	1900
Buddy DeSylva	1895
Emery Deutsch	1907
Howard Dietz	1896
Mort Dixon	1892
Robert Emmett Dolan	1906
Walter Donaldson	1893
Jimmy Dorsey	1904
Bert Douglas	1900
Saxie Dowell	1904
Walter Doyle	1899
Dave Dreyer	1894
Al Dubin	1891
Vernon Duke	1903
Jimmy Dupre	1906
Eddie Durham	1909

E

Eddie Edwards	1891
Ray Egan	1890
Duke Ellington	1899
Jack Elliott	1914
Seger Ellis	1904
Robert Ellsworth	1895
Bob Emmerich	1904
Ray Evans	1915
Redd Evans	1912

F

William Faber	1902
Sammy Fain	1902
Edgar Fairchild	1898
Percy Faith	1908
Ed Farley	1904
Walter Farrar	1918
Johnny Farrow	1912

Ted Fetter	1906	Slim Gaillard	1916
Buddy Feyne	1912	Lee Gaines	1914
Dorothy Fields	1905	Sammy Gallop	1915
Lupin Fien	1908	Kim Gannon	1900
Dick Finch	1898	Donald Gardner	1913
Rich Finch	1906	Joe Garland	1903
Edwin Finckel	1917	Clarence Gaskill	1892
Billy Finegan	1917	Charles Gaynor	1909
Henry Fink	1893	Lewis Gensler	1896
Ted Fio Rito	1900	Don George	1909
Carl Fischer	1912	Alex Gerber	1895
Mark Fisher	1895	Arthur Gershwin	1900
Marve Fisher	1905	George Gershwin	1898
Marvin Fisher	1916	Ira Gershwin	1896
Ella Fitzgerald	1918	Arthur Gibbs	1895
Ludwig Flato	1911	Albert Gibson	1913
Brick Fleagle	1906	Gene Gifford	1908
Charles Fleck	1916	Ray Gilbert	1912
Archie Fletcher	1890	Tyree Glenn	1912
Frank Flynn	1900	Kermit Goell	1915
Paul Fogarty	1893	Al Goering	1898
Lou Forbes	1902	Al Goodhart	1905
Hank Fort	1914	Alfred Goodman	1890
Johnny Fortis	1913	Benny Goodman	1909
Larry Fotine	1911	Ben Gordon	1912
Al Frazzini	1890	Irving Gordon	1915
Arthur Freed	1894	Mack Gordon	1904
Ralph Freed	1907	Jay Gorney	1896
Max Freedman	1898	Archie Gottler	1896
Bud Freeman	1906	Morton Gould	1913
Tucker Freeman	1911	Vincent Grande	1902
Henry Friedman	1897	Chauncey Gray	1904
Cliff Friend	1893	Abel Green	1900
Albert Frisch	1916	Adolph Green	1915
Lorenzo Fuller	1919	Bud Green	1897
John Fulton	1903	Harold Green	1913
		Johnny Green	1908
G		Joseph Green	1915
		Mort Greene	1912
Milt Gabler	1911	Jesse Greer	1896

Elliott Grennard	1907
Lanny Grey	1909
Jimmy Grier	1902
Ferde Grofe	1892
Phil Grogan	1909
Walter Gross	1909
Wilhelm Grosz (Hugh Williams)	1894
Ted Grouya	1910
Arthur Grover	1918
John Guarnieri	1917
Meyer Gusman	1894
Howard Gustafson (Bart Howard)	1915

H

Thomas M. Hadley	1905
Bob Haggart	1914
William Haid	1901
Fred Hall	1897
Wendell Hall	1896
George S. Hamilton	1901
Nancy Hamilton	1908
Oscar Hammerstein II	1895
Lou Handman	1894
James Hanley	1892
E. Y. (Yip) Harburg	1896
Leigh Harline	1907
Robert Harrington	1912
Vicki Harrington	1915
Anthony Harris	1916
Harry Harris	1901
Thomas J. Harris	1908
Will J. Harris	1900
Lorenz Hart	1895
Erskine Hawkins	1914
Billy Hayes	1906
Edgar Hayes	1905
Peter Lind Hayes	1915
Lennie Hayton	1908
Walter Heath	1890
Ray Heindorf	1908
Charles Henderson	1907
Fletcher Henderson	1897
Horace Henderson	1914
Ray Henderson	1896
Francis Henry	1905
Frederick Herbert	1909
Jean Herbert	1905
Pinky Herman	1905
Ralph J. Herman	1914
Woody Herman	1913
Joel Herron	1916
Lou Herscher	1894
Cliff Hess	1894
Edward Heyman	1904
Ray Hibbeler	1892
Irene Higgenbotham	1918
Alex Hill	1906
Billy Hill	1899
Dedette Hill	1900
Fred Hillebrand	1893
Bob Hilliard	1918
Richard Himber	1907
Earl Hines	1905
Milt Hinton	1910
Walter Hirsch	1891
Johnny Hodges	1907
Al Hoffman	1902
Mann Holiner	1897
LeRoy Holmes	1913
Ben Homer	1917
Claude Hopkins	1906
George Horton	1911
Eddy Howard	1914
Paul Howard	1909
Richard Howard	1890
George Warren Howe	1909
Will Hudson	1908
Billy Hueston (Bruce Morgan)	1896

Langston Hughes	1902
George P. Hulten	1891
Helen Humes	1913
Ralph Hunsecker	1914
Alberta Hunter	1897
Herman Hupfeld	1894
Danuel Hurd	1918
Alex Hyde	1898
Madeline Hyde	1907

I

Ramiz Idriess	1911
Mary Ijames	1894
Roy Ingraham	1895
George Irwin	1916
William C. K. Irwin	1907
Claude Isaacs	1901
Burl Ives	1909

J

Al Jacobs	1903
Moe Jaffe	1901
Billy James	1895
Harry James	1916
Inez James	1919
Will Jason	1910
Gordon Jenkins	1910
Harry Jentes	1897
Henry Jerome	1917
Jerome Jerome	1906
M. K. Jerome	1893
George Jessel	1898
Anne Johnson	1916
Arnold Johnson	1893
Buddy Johnson	1915
Charles L. Johnson	1910
Edward Johnson	1910
George J. Johnson	1913
J. C. Johnson	1896
James P. Johnson	1891
Paul Johnson	1917
Pete Johnson	1904
William Johnson	1912
Arthur Johnston	1898
Isham Jones	1894
Richard M. Jones	1892
Stan Jones	1914
Roy Jordan	1916
Leonard Joy	1894
Dick Jurgens	1910
Walter Jurman	1903

K

Irving Kahal	1903
Donald Kahn	1918
Grace Kahn	1890
Bronislaw Kaper	1902
Art Kassel	1896
Whitey Kaufman	1899
Julian Kay	1910
Buddy Kaye	1918
Kahn Keene	1909
Ronald Kemper	1912
Charles Kenny	1898
Nick Kenny	1895
Walter Kent	1911
Stan Kenton	1912
Walter Kerr	1913
Mack Key	1917
Baron Keyes	1898
Wayne King	1901
Andy Kirk	1898
Charles Kisco	1896
Marcy Klauber	1896
John Klenner	1899
John Kluczko (Johnny Watson)	1912
Vick Knight	1908
Edwin H. Knopf	1899

Leonard Kobrick	1912
Ted Koehler	1894
Alfred Koppell	1898
Max Kortlander	1890
Alex Kramer	1903
Zoe Kramer (Joan Whitney)	1914
Carl Kress	1907
Richard Krieg (Dick Charles)	1919
Benny Krueger	1899
Lee Kuhn	1912
Manny Kurtz (Mann Curtis)	1911

L

Anton Lada	1890
Charles La Freniere	1914
Frankie Laine	1913
Nappy LaMare	1910
Rene LaMarre	1907
Richard LaMarre	1912
Robert LaMarre	1917
Dave Lambert	1917
Edward Lambert	1897
Frank LaMotta	1904
Carl Lampl	1898
Burton Lane	1912
Eastwood Lane	1897
Edward Lane	1915
Nan Lane	1914
Luther Laney	1916
Eddie Lang	1902
Philip Lang	1911
Henry Lange	1895
Johnny Lange	1909
Dwight Latham	1903
John LaTouche	1917
William Lava	1911
Paul Lavalle	1908
Raymond Laveen	1893
Vee Lawnhurst	1905
Harold Lawrence	1906
Jack Lawrence	1912
Jerome Lawrence	1915
Lou Lawrence	1913
Lester Lee	1905
Milton Leeds	1909
Ned Lehac	1899
Robert Duke Leonard	1901
Walter Leonard	1890
Al Lerner	1919
Samuel Lerner	1903
Albert Lester	1917
Oscar Levant	1906
Abner Leven	1914
Herbert Leventhal	1914
Harold Levey	1898
Robert Levinson	1897
Hal Levy	1918
Richard Lewine	1910
David LeWinter	1908
Al Lewis	1901
Edward Lewis	1909
Meade Lux Lewis	1905
Morgan Lewis	1906
Max Liebman	1902
Nathaniel Lief	1896
Joe Liggens	1916
Enoch Light	1907
Joseph Lilley	1914
Dorothy Link (Dorothy Dick)	1900
Harry Link	1896
Ray Linn	1914
Robert Lissauer	1917
Norman Litman	1917
George Little	1890
Little Jack Little	1900
Alan Livingston	1917
Fud Livingston	1906

Jay Livingston	1915	Shelly Mann	1920
William Livingston	1911	Sy Mann	1920
Gene Lockhart	1891	Maxine Manners	1920
John Jacob Loeb	1910	Zeke Manners	1911
Frank Loesser	1910	Dick Manning	1912
Frederick Loewe	1901	Richard Manning	1914
Benjamin Loewy	1915	Tony Manno	1912
Jules Loman	1910	Wingy Manone	1900
Carmen Lombardo	1903	Jack Manus	1909
Vincent Lopez	1898	Hector Marchese	1901
Ange Lorenzo	1894	Sano Marco	1898
Carroll Loveday	1898	Sol Marcus	1912
Ruth Lowe	1914	Paul Mares	1900
Bert Lown	1903	Charles Margulis	1903
Jimmie Lunceford	1903	George Marion	1899
Nellie Lutcher	1915	Charles Marks	1890
Abe Lyman	1897	Franklyn Marks	1911
Jimmy Lytell	1904	Gerald Marks	1900
		Johnny Marks	1909
M		Adele Girard Marsala	1913
		Joe Marsala	1907
Arthur Mace	1913	Peggy Marshall	1916
Jerry Macell	1899	Ann Marsters	1918
Chummy MacGregor	1903	Paul Martell	1905
Scotty MacGregor	1915	Billy Martin	1908
Herb Magidson	1906	David Martin	1907
Charles Magnante	1905	Hugh Martin	1914
Curley Mahr	1901	Sam Martin	1908
Alexander Maister	1903	Johnny Marvin	1897
Matty Malneck	1903	Jack Mason	1906
Albert Malotte	1895	Curt Massey	1910
Richard Maltby	1914	Frankie Masters	1904
Bernard Maltin	1907	Carmen Mastren	1913
Mana-Zucca	1894	Matty Matlock	1907
Kenny Manges	1913	Jack Matthias	1915
Mary Manion	1907	LeRoy Maule	1904
Charles Mank	1902	Eddie Maxwell	1912
David Mann	1916	Arthur Mayer	1918
Kal Mann	1917	Leonard McCall	1910
Paul Mann	1910	Clarence McCarron	1891
Robert Mann	1902	Pat McCarthy	1903

Joe McCarty	1905
George McConnell	1894
Paul McGrane	1902
Fulton McGrath	1907
Jimmy McHugh	1894
Lani McIntire	1904
Ray McKinley	1910
James McLeod	1912
Lindsay McPhail	1895
Teddy McRae	1908
Jay McShann	1916
Dudley Mecum	1896
Irving Melsher	1906
Murray Mencher	1904
David Mendoza	1894
Peter Mendoza	1902
Johnny Mercer	1909
O. O. Meritt	1919
Benny Meroff	1901
Blanche Merrill	1895
Paul Mertz	1904
Jack Meskill	1897
Johnny Messner	1909
Don Meyer	1919
Joseph Meyer	1894
Sol Meyer	1913
Billy Meyers	1894
Theodore Meyn	1901
Robert Michael	1901
Walter Michels	1895
Charles Midgley	1899
Richard Miles	1916
Bob Miller	1895
Ed Miller	1899
Eddie Miller	1911
Glenn Miller	1904
Harry S. Miller	1895
Herb Miller	1915
Irving Miller	1907
Taps Miller	1915
Sy Miller	1908
Sidney Miller	1916
Carley Mills	1897
Irving Mills	1894
William Mills	1894
Jay Milton	1910
Charles Minelli	1914
Billy Moll	1905
Vaughn Monroe	1911
Harold Mooney	1917
George Moore	1918
McElbert Moore	1892
Thomas Moore	1911
Noro Morales	1911
James Morehead	1906
Larry Morey	1905
Dorinda Morgan	1909
Freddy Morgan	1910
Robert Morgan	1896
Russ Morgan	1904
Jerome Moross	1913
Gene Morra	1906
Charles Morris	1913
Lee Morris	1912
Dolly Morse	1890
Ted Mossman	1914
Tony Mottola	1918
Jimmy Mundy	1907
Owen Murphy	1893
Spud Murphy	1908
Richard Myers	1901
Stanley Myers	1908
Josef Myrow	1912
Sammy Mysels	1906

N

James Nabbie	1920
Phil Napoleon	1901
Clayton Naset	1895
Ogden Nash	1902
John Nedrow	1912

Al Neiburg	1902
Steve Nelson	1907
Henry Nemo	1914
Albert Newman	1900
Alfred Newman	1901
Charles Newman	1901
Alberta Nichols	1898
Red Nichols	1905
Harry Noble	1912
Johnny Noble	1892
Ray Noble	1903
Fred Norman	1910
Alex North	1910
Red Norvo	1908
Eugene Novelo	1912

O

Ben Oakland	1907
Edward Ocnoff	1906
Louis O'Connell	1895
Charles O'Flynn	1897
Phil Ohman	1896
James O'Keefe	1892
Lester O'Keefe	1896
Walter O'Keefe	1900
Henry Olson	1913
Alfred Opler	1897
David Ormont	1898
Will Osborne	1906
Edna Osser	1919
Glenn Osser	1914
Harry Owens	1902
Jack Owens	1912

P

Jack Palmer	1900
Frank Paparelli	1917
Mitchell Parish	1900
Dorothy Parker	1893
Svery Parrish	1917
Milton Pascal	1908
Dailey Paskman	1897
Stephen Pasternacki	1891
Lee Pearl	1901
Bert Pellish	1914
Frank Perkins	1908
Ray Perkins	1896
William Peters	1985
Betty Peterson	1918
Bernice Petkere	1906
Frank Petty	1916
Leo Peusner	1906
Fred Phillips	1890
Howard Phillips	1909
Maceo Pinkard	1897
Neely Plumb	1912
Coy Poe	1907
Edward Pola	1907
Ben Pollack	1903
Lew Pollack	1895
Cole Porter	1891
George Posford	1906
Teddy Powell	1906
Jacques Press	1903
George E. Price	1900
Louis Prima	1911
Hughie Prince	1906
Joseph Priolo	1918

Q

Lew Quadling	1908
Arthur Quenzer	1905

R

Ralph Rainger	1900
David Raksin	1912
Buck Ram	1907
Roger Ramirez	1913

Curtis Ramsay	1916	Carson Robinson	1890
Eugene Ramsay	1918	J. Russel Robinson	1892
Erno Rapee	1891	Willard Robison	1894
Ted Raph	1905	Henry Rocquemore	1909
Raymond Rasch	1919	Richard Rodgers	1902
Eugene Raskin	1909	Joseph Rodney	1917
William Raskin	1896	Vincent Rodomister	1918
George Raymond	1903	Ada Roeter	1906
Andy Razaf	1895	James Rogan	1908
Charles Reade	1911	Dick Rogers	1912
Don Redman	1900	Jack Rollins	1906
John Redman	1906	Tony Romano	1915
Bickley Reichner	1909	Harold Rome	1908
Joyce Reid	1903	Billy Rose	1899
Violet Reiser	1915	David Rose	1919
Bert Reisfeld	1906	Fred Rose	1897
Leon Rene	1902	Harry Rose	1893
Otis Rene	1898	Louis Rosenstein	1908
Harry Revel	1905	Charles Rosoff	1898
Jack Reynolds	1904	Benny Ross	1912
John Ricca	1900	Helen Ross	1912
Louis Ricca	1909	Lanny Ross	1906
Joseph Ricciardello	1911	Walter Rossi	1914
Freddie Rich	1898	Bob Rothberg	1901
Max Rich	1897	Glenn Rowell	1899
Stephen Richards	1908	James Rowles	1918
Arthur Richardson	1899	Hugo Rubens	1905
Harry Richman	1895	Maurie Rubens	1893
Clyde Ridge	1914	Harry Ruby	1895
Mike Riley	1904	Herman Ruby	1891
David Ringle	1893	Jimmy Rushing	1902
Al Rinker	1907	Paul Rusincky	1903
Charles Rinker	1911	Harry Ruskin	1894
Charity Ritter	1917	Bob Russell	1914
Allan Roberts	1905	George Russell	1919
Gene Roberts	1918	Luis Russell	1902
Luckey Roberts	1893	Pee Wee Russell	1906
Dick Robertson	1903	Renee Russell	1902
Leo Robin	1900	Babe Russin	1911
Sydney Robin	1912	Ben Ryan	1892

Frank Ryerson	1905	Ted Sears	1900
		Harley Secrist	1890
S		Sholom Secunda	1894
		Jerry Seelen	1912
John Sacco	1905	Scott Seely	1911
Tony Sacco	1908	Jack Segal	1918
Edgar Sampson	1907	Bernardo Segall	1911
Milton Samuels	1904	Eddie Seiler	1911
Walter Samuels	1908	Charles Seitter	1892
Joe Sanders	1896	Peter Selby	1914
Vin Sandry	1902	Victor Selsman	1908
Dick Sanford	1896	Murray Semos	1913
Herb Sanford	1905	Boyd Senter	1898
Hank Sanicola	1914	Arthur Shaftel	1916
Henry Santly	1890	Terry Shand	1904
Lester Santly	1894	Wayne Shanklin	1916
Paul Santoro	1915	Dan Shapiro	1910
Eddie Sauter	1914	Maurice Shapiro	1906
Jan Savitt	1913	Ted Shapiro	1899
Paul Sawtell	1906	Del Sharbutt	1912
David Saxon	1919	John Sharpe	1909
Tony Scalzi	1918	Winston Sharples	1909
Mary Schaeffer	1893	Charlie Shavers	1917
Bob Shafer	1897	Artie Shaw	1910
Victor Schertzinger	1890	Barnett Shaw	1914
Erwin Schmidt	1890	Charles Shaw	1906
Elmer Schoebel	1896	Cliff Shaw	1911
Vic Schoen	1916	Nelson Shawn	1898
Jack Scholl	1903	Larry Shay	1897
Paul Scholz	1894	Larry Shayne	1909
John Schonberger	1892	Bert Shefter	1904
Carl Schraubstader	1902	Sidney Sheldon	1917
Budd Schulberg	1914	James Shelton	1912
Walter Schuman	1913	Buddy Sheppard	1903
Joseph Schuster	1896	Al Sherman	1897
Wilbur Schwandt	1904	Manning Sherwin	1902
Edward Scott	1919	Jack Shilkret	1896
Johnnie Scott	1907	Nat Shilkret	1895
William Scott	1985	Jimmy Shirl	1909
William Seaman	1910	Francis Shuman	1908

Al Siegel	1898
Paul Siegel	1914
Maurice Sigler	1901
Carl Sigman	1909
Frank Signorelli	1901
Abner Silver	1899
Frank Silver	1896
Phil Silvers	1911
Sid Silvers	1907
Herman Silverstein	1908
George Simon	1912
Howard Simon	1901
Nat Simon	1900
Ted Simonetti	1904
Seymour Simons	1896
Harry Sims	1908
Lee Sims	1898
Frank Sinatra	1915
Ray Sinatra	1904
Arthur Singer	1919
Dolph Singer	1900
Louis Singer	1912
George Siravo	1916
Arthur Sizemore	1891
Red Skelton	1913
Sunny Skylar	1913
Freddy Slack	1910
Beasley Smith	1901
Davis Smith	1915
Richard Smith	1901
Willie "The Lion" Smith	1897
Harold Solomon	1903
Joseph Solomon	1897
Anna Sorenko	1910
Harry Sosnik	1906
Tony Spargo	1897
Larry Spier	1901
Harold Spina	1906
Maurice Spitalny	1893
Phil Spitalny	1890
Ted Steele	1917
Bill Stegmeyer	1916
Jimmy Steiger	1896
Sam Stept	1897
Jack Stern	1896
Cliff Steward	1916
Slam Stewart	1914
Rex Stewart	1907
William Grant Still	1895
Al Stillman	1906
Mel Stitzel	1902
Lawrence Stock	1896
Howard Stocksdale	1905
Harry Stoddard	1892
Morris Stoloff	1898
Kirby Stone	1918
Mickey Stoner	1911
Alex Stordahl	1913
Charley Straight	1891
Billy Strayhorn	1915
Harry Stride	1903
Murray Sturm	1899
Jule Styne	1905
Dana Suesse	1909
Joe Sullivan	1906
Einar Swan	1904
Kay Swift	1905
Marty Symes	1904

T

Joe Tarto	1902
Doris Tauber	1908
Irving Taylor	1914
Sid Tepper	1918
Arthur Terker	1899
Winston Tharp	1905
Sam Theard	1904
Harlan Thompson	1890
Kay Thompson	1913

Claude Thornhill	1908
George Thow	1908
Jane Thurston	1915
Harry Tierney	1890
Burr Tillstrom	1917
Sammy Timberg	1903
Peter Tinturin	1910
Juan Tizol	1890
Charles Tobias	1898
Harry Tobias	1895
Henry Tobias	1905
Lew Tobin	1904
Clarence Todd	1897
Pinky Tomlin	1908
Brigham Townsend	1907
Ben Trace	1897
William Tracey	1893
Jo Trent	1892
Barry Trivers	1912
John Scott Trotter	1908
Bobby Troup	1918
Henry Troy	1908
Frank Trumbauer	1901
John Tucker	1896
Orrin Tucker	1911
Tommy Tucker	1908
Roy Turk	1892
John Turner	1896
Kathleen Twomey	1914

U

Richard Uhl	1918
William Uhr	1907
Steller Unger	1905
Alfred Urbano	1911

V

Rudy Vallee	1901
Bert Van Cleve	1899
Albert Van Dam	1920
Art Van Damme	1920
Paul Vandervoort II	1903
Bob Van Eps	1909
George Van Eps	1913
Katy Van Forst	1904
Paul Van Loan	1892
Al Vann	1899
Esther Van Sciver	1907
Peter Van Steeden	1904
Ted Varnick	1913
Henry Vars	1902
Billy Vaughn	1919
Joseph Velezdy	1912
Mary Velezdy	1912
Anthony Velona	1920
Joe Venuti	1903
Joe Verges	1892
Dud Vernor	1892
Pinky Vidacovich	1904
Manuel Villa	1917
Bob Vincent	1918
John Vincent	1902
Larry Vincent	1901

W

Maybelle Wade	1914
Larry Wagner	1907
Don Walker	1907
Emett Wallace	1909
John Wallace	1914
Fats Waller	1904
Serge Walter	1896
Sam Ward	1906
Leonard Ware	1909
Fred Waring	1900
Tom Waring	1902
Sarah Warner	1898

Buck Warnick	1915
Harry Warnow (Raymond Scott)	1909
Edward Warren	1906
Harry Warren	1893
Frank Warshauer	1893
Ivan Washbaugh	1912
Country Washburne	1904
Ned Washington	1901
Gilbert Watson	1897
Douglas Watt	1914
Grady Watts	1908
Jack Waverly	1896
Mabel Wayne	1904
Ben Webster	1909
Paul Francis Webster	1907
Anson Weeks	1896
Harold Weeks	1893
Willima Weeks	1901
Ed Weems	1901
Kurt Weill	1900
Paul Weirick	1906
Irving Weiser	1913
George Weiss	1913
Stephen Weiss	1899
John Weithaus	1902
Ted Weitz (Ted White)	1907
Lawrence Welk	1903
Charles Wendell	1910
Kay Werner	1918
Sue Werner	1918
Alvy West	1815
Ray West	1904
Paul Weston	1912
Melvin Wettergreen	1909
Ned Wever	1899
Carlton Weyand	1916
Leonard Whitcup	1903
William White	1894
Richard Whiting	1891
Ray Whitley	1901
Art Wight	1911
Donald Wilhoite (Don Raye)	1909
Clarence Williams	1893
Cootie Williams	1908
Joe Williams	1906
Mary Lou Williams	1910
Meredith Willson	1902
Al Wilson	1906
Teddy Wilson	1912
Frank Winegar	1901
Dick Winfree	1898
Hugo Winterhalter	1909
William Wirges	1894
Fred Wise	1915
Andy Wiswell	1905
William Woode	1909
Harry Woods	1896
Marvin Wright	1911
Robert Wright	1914
Allie Wrubel	1905
George Wyle	1916

Y

Jack Yellen	1892
Larry Yoell	1998
Harold Yorke	1893
Vincent Youmans	1898
Lester Young	1909
Trummy Young	1912
Victor Young	1900

V. Nuggets from the Golden Era

Year	Title	Composer(s)	Lyricist(s)
1902	Bill Bailey, Won't You Please Come Home	Hughie Cannon, Will Handy (J. Rosamund Johnson)	
	Oh, Didn't He Ramble		Bob Cole
1903	Ida (Sweet As Apple Cider)	Eddie Leonard	Eddie Munson
1905	My Gal Sal	Paul Dresser	
1907	Vilia	Franz Lehar	
1908	Shine on Harvest Moon	Norah Bayes, Jack Norworth	
1909	By the Light of the Silvery Moon	Gus Edwards	Edward Madden
	Meet Me Tonight in Dreamland	Leo Friedman	Beth Slater Whitson
1910	Chinatown, My Chinatown	Jean Schwartz	William Jerome
	Some of These Days	Shelton Brooks	
	Washington & Lee Swing	Thornton Allen, M. W. Sheafe	C. A. Robbins
1911	Alexander's Ragtime Band	Irving Berlin	
	I Want a Girl (Just Like the Girl That Married Dear Old Dad)	Harry Von Tilzer	William Dillon
1912	My Melancholy Baby	Ernie Burnett	George A. Norton
	Sweetheart of Sigma Chi	F. Dudleigh Vernor	Byron D. Stokes
1913	Ballin' the Jack	Chris Smith	Jim Burris
	Memphis Blues	W. C. Handy	George A. Norton
	Peg O' My Heart	Fred Fisher	Alfred Bryan
	The Trail of the Lonesome Pine	Harry Carroll	Ballard MacDonald
1914	St. Louis Blues	W. C. Handy	

	Song of Songs	Maurice Veaucaire	(English): Clarence Lucas (French): Harold Vicars
	That's A-Plenty	Lew Pollack	
	They Didn't Believe Me	Jerome Kern	M. E. Rourke
1915	Down Among the Sheltering Palms	Abe Olman	James Brockman
	On the Beach at Waikiki	Henry Kailimai	G. H. Stover
	Song of the Islands	Charles E. King	
1916	Allah's Holiday	Rudolph Friml	Otto Harbach
	I Ain't Got Nobody	Spencer Williams	Roger Graham, Dave Peyton
	Poor Butterfly	Raymond Hubbell	John Golden
	Roses of Picardy	Haydn Wood	Frederick E. Weatherly
	What Do You Want to Make Those Eyes at Me For?	James V. Monaco	Joseph McCarthy, Howard Johnson
1917	Beale St. Blues	W. C. Handy	
	Darktown Strutters Ball	Shelton Brooks	
	(Back Home Again in) Indiana	James F. Hanley	Ballard MacDonald
	The Siren's Song	Jerome Kern	P. G. Wodehouse
	(You're Some) Pretty Doll	Clarence Williams	
1918	After You've Gone	Turner Layton	Henry Creamer
	Dallas Blues	Hart A. Wand	Lloyd Garrett
	A Good Man Is Hard to Find	Eddie Green	
	Hindustan	Harold Weeks	Oliver G. Wallace
	I Hate to Lose You	Archie Gottler	Grant Clarke
	Ja-Da	Bob Carleton	
	Smiles	Lee Roberts	J. Will Callahan
	Somebody Stole My Gal	Leo Wood	
	Till We Meet Again	Richard Whiting	Raymond Egan
1919	Baby, Won't You Please Come Home	Charles Warfield, Clarence Williams	
	Dardanella	Felix Bernard, Johnny S. Black, Fred Fisher	

	I Ain't Gonna Give Nobody None o' This Jelly Roll	Clarence Williams	Spencer Williams
	I'm Forever Blowing Bubbles	Jean Kenbrovin	John W. Kellette
	Indian Summer	Victor Herbert	Al Dubin [lyrics written 1939]
	Mammy O' Mine	Maceo Pinkard	William Tracey
	Mandy	Irving Berlin	
	Nobody Knows (and Nobody Seems to Care)	Irving Berlin	
	On Miami Shore	Victor Jacobi	William Le Baron
	A Pretty Girl Is Like a Melody	Irving Berlin	
	Rose of Washington Square	James F. Hanley	Ballard MacDonald
	Rose Room	Art Hickman	Harry Williams
	Someday Sweetheart	John and Benjamin Spikes	
	When My Baby Smiles at Me	Bill Munro	Andrew B. Sterling, Ted Lewis, Gene Lockhart
	The World Is Waiting for the Sunrise	Ernest Seitz	
1920	Avalon	Vincent Rose	Buddy DeSylva, Al Jolson
	Bright Eyes	Otto Motzan, M. K. Jerome	Harry B. Smith
	Do You Ever Think of Me?	Earl Burtnett	John Cooper, Harry D. Kerr
	I Never Knew (I Could Love Anybody)	Tom Pitts	Raymond Egan, Roy K. Marsh
	I Used to Love You (But It's All Over Now)	Albert Von Tilzer	Lew Brown
	Japanese Sandman	Richard Whiting	Raymond Egan
	La Veeda	John Alden	Nat Vincent
	The Love Nest	Louis A. Hirsch	Otto Harbach
	Margie	Con Conrad, J. Russel Robinson	Benny Davis
	Palesteena	Con Conrad, J. Russel Robinson	
	San	Lindsay McPhail, Walter Michels	
	Singin' the Blues (Till My Daddy Comes Home)	Con Conrad, J. Russel Robinson	Sam M. Lewis, Joe Young
	Whispering	Vincent Rose, Richard Coburn	John Schonberger
	A Young Man's Fancy	Milton Ager	John Murray Anderson, Jack Yellen
1921	Ain't We Got Fun	Richard Whiting	Gus Kahn, Raymond Egan
	All by Myself	Irving Berlin	

Year	Song	Composer	Lyricist
	Dear Old Southland	Turner Layton	Henry Creamer
	I'm Goin' South	Harry Woods, Abner Silver	
	I'm Just Wild About Harry	Eubie Blake	Noble Sissle
	I'm Nobody's Baby	Lester Santly, Milton Ager	Benny Davis
	Loveless Love	W. C. Handy	
	Ma! (He's Making Eyes at Me)	Con Conrad	Sidney Clare
	Say It With Music	Irving Berlin	
	The Sheik of Araby	Ted Snyder	Harry B. Smith, Francis Wheeler
	Strut Miss Lizzie	Turner Layton	Henry Creamer
	When Buddha Smiles	Nacio Herb Brown, King Zany	Arthur Freed
1922	Angel Child	Abner Silver	Benny Davis, Georgie Price
	Blue (And Brokenhearted)	Lou Handman	Grant Clarke, Edgar Leslie
	Carolina in the Morning	Walter Donaldson	Gus Kahn
	Chicago	Fred Fisher	
	China Boy	Dick Winfree, Phil Boutelje	
	I Wish I Could Shimmy Like My Sister Kate	Armand Piron	
	Lady of the Evening	Irving Berlin	
	Lovin' Sam (The Sheik of Alabam)	Milton Ager	Jack Yellen
	My Buddy	Walter Donaldson	Gus Kahn
	My Honey's Lovin' Arms	Joseph Meyer	Herman Ruby
	On the Alamo	Isham Jones	Gus Kahn
	Rose of the Rio Grande	Harry Warren, Ross Gorman	Edgar Leslie
	Runnin' Wild	A. Harrington Gibbs	Joe Grey, Leo Wood
	Stumbling	Zez Confrey	
	That Da Da Strain	Edgar Dowell	Mamie Medina
	Toot Toot Tootsie, Goodbye	Ted Fio Rito, Robert A. King	Gus Kahn, Ernie Erdman
	Way Down Yonder in New Orleans	Turner Layton	Henry Creamer
	When Hearts Are Young	Sigmund Romberg, Al Goodman	Cyrus Wood
1923	Bugle Call Rag	Jack Pettis, Elmer Schoebel, Billy Meyers	
	Charleston	James P. Johnson	Cecil Mack

Year	Song	Composer	Lyricist
	Dearest You're the Nearest to My Heart	Harry Akst	Benny Davis
	Farewell Blues	Elmer Schoebel, Paul Mares	Leon Rappolo
	I Cried for You	Gus Arnheim, Abe Lyman	Arthur Freed
	Last Night on the Back Porch	Carl Schraubstader	Lew Brown
	Linger Awhile	Vincent Rose	Harry Owens
	Louisville Lou	Milton Ager	Jack Yellen
	Mama Goes Where Papa Goes (or Papa Don't Go Out Tonight)	Milton Ager	Jack Yellen
	My Sweetie Went Away	Lou Handman	Roy Turk
	Nobody Knows You When You're Down and Out	Jimmie Cox	
	Old Fashioned Love	James P. Johnson	Cecil Mack
	A Smile Will Go a Long, Long Way	Harry Akst	Benny Davis
	Swingin' Down the Lane	Isham Jones	Gus Kahn
	Who's Sorry Now?	Ted Snyder	Harry Ruby, Bert Kalmar
1924	Alabamy Bound	Ray Henderson	Buddy DeSylva, Bud Green
	All Alone	Irving Berlin	
	Big Boy	Milton Ager	
	California, Here I Come	Joseph Meyer, Al Jolson	Buddy DeSylva
	Charley, My Boy	Ted Fio Rito	Gus Kahn
	Copenhagen	Charlie Davis, Walter Melrose	
	Everybody Loves My Baby	Jack Palmer, Spencer Williams	
	Fascinating Rhythm	George Gershwin	Ira Gershwin
	Hard-Hearted Hannah (The Vamp of Savannah)	Milton Ager	Jack Yellen, Bob Bigelow, Charles Bates
	How Come You Do Me Like You Do	Gene Austin	Roy Bergere
	I'll See You in My Dreams	Isham Jones	Gus Kahn
	It Had to Be You	Isham Jones	Gus Kahn
	Jealous	Jack Little	Tommie Mali, Dick Finch
	June Night	Cliff Friend, Abel Baer	
	Limehouse Blues	Philip Braham	Douglas Furber
	The Man I Love	George Gershwin	Ira Gershwin

Year	Song	Composer	Lyricist
	Mandy, Make Up Your Mind	George W. Meyer, Arthur Johnston	Grant Clark, Roy Turk
	My Best Girl	Walter Donaldson	
	Nobody's Sweetheart	Elmer Schoebel, Ernie Erdman, Billy Myers, Gus Kahn	
	Oh, Baby	Walter Donaldson	Buddy DeSylva
	Oh, Lady Be Good	George Gershwin	Ira Gershwin
	The One I Love (Belongs to Somebody Else)	Isham Jones	Gus Kahn
	Shine	Ford Dabney	Cecil Mack, Lew Brown
	Somebody Loves Me	George Gershwin	Ballard MacDonald, Buddy DeSylva
	Spain	Isham Jones	Gus Kahn
	There'll Be Some Changes Made	W. B. Overstreet	Billy Higgins
	There's Yes Yes in Your Eyes	Joseph Santly	Cliff Friend
	When My Sugar Walks Down the Street	Jimmy McHugh, Gene Austin, Irving Mills	
	Why Couldn't It Be Poor Little Me	Isham Jones	Gus Kahn
1925	Always	Irving Berlin	
	Angry	Harry Brunies, Jules Cassar	Dudley Mecum
	Brown Eyes (Why Are You Blue)	George W. Meyer	Alfred Bryan
	Cheatin' on Me	Lew Pollack	Jack Yellen
	Dinah	Harry Akst	Sam M. Lewis, Joe Young
	Five Foot Two, Eyes of Blue	Ray Henderson	Lew Brown
	Here in My Arms	Richard Rodgers	Lorenz Hart
	I Love My Baby (My Baby Loves Me)	Harry Warren	Bud Green
	I Never Knew	Ted Fio Rito	Gus Kahn
	I Want to Be Happy	Vincent Youmans	Irving Caesar
	I Wonder Where My Baby Is Tonight	Walter Donaldson	Gus Kahn
	I'm Sitting on Top of the World	Ray Henderson	Sam M. Lewis, Joe Young
	If I Had a Girl Like You	Ray Henderson	Billy Rose, Mort Dixon
	If You Knew Susie (Like I Know Susie)	Joseph Meyer	Buddy DeSylva
	Jalousie (Jealousy)	Jacob Gade, Vera Bloom	
	Manhattan	Richard Rodgers	Lorenz Hart
	Paddlin' Madeline Home	Harry Woods	
	Poor Little Rich Girl	Noël Coward	
	Remember	Irving Berlin	

Year	Song	Composer	Lyricist
	Riverboat Shuffle	Hoagy Carmichael, Dick Voynow, Irving Mills, Mitchell Parish	
	Sleepy Time Gal	Ange Lorenzo	Richard Whiting, Joseph Alden, Ray Egan
	Sweet Georgia Brown	Ben Bernie, Maceo Pinkard Ken Casey	
	Tea for Two	Vincent Youmans	Irving Caesar
	Washboard Blues	Hoagy Carmichael	Mitchell Parish, Fred Callahan
	Who?	Jerome Kern	Otto Harbach, Oscar Hammerstein
	Yes, Sir, That's My Baby	Walter Donaldson	Gus Kahn
1926	After I Say I'm Sorry	Walter Donaldson	Abe Lyman
	Baby Face	Harry Akst	Benny Davis
	Birth of the Blues	Ray Henderson	Buddy DeSylva, Lew Brown
	The Blue Room	Richard Rodgers	Lorenz Hart
	Breezin' Along With the Breeze	Richard Whiting	Haven Gillespie, Seymour Simons
	Bye-Bye Blackbird	Ray Henderson	Mort Dixon
	'Deed I Do	Fred Rose	Walter Hirsch
	How Many Times	Irving Berlin	
	I Know That You Know	Vincent Youmans	Anne Caldwell
	I Want a Big Butter and Egg Man	Louis Armstrong, Percy Venable	
	I've Found a New Baby	Jack Palmer, Spencer Williams	
	In a Little Spanish Town	Mabel Wayne	Sam M. Lewis, Joe Young
	Me Too	Harry Woods	Charles Tobias, Al Sherman
	Moonlight on the Ganges	Sherman Myers	Chester Wallace
	Mountain Greenery	Richard Rodgers	Lorenz Hart
	Muskrat Ramble	Kid Ory	Ray Gilbert
	Someone to Watch over Me	George Gershwin	Ira Gershwin
	Song of the Wanderer	Neil Moret	
	Sunday	J. Fred Coots	Clifford Grey
	Trouble in Mind	Richard M. Jones	
	When Day Is Done	Robert Katcher	Buddy DeSylva

Year	Song	Composer	Lyricist
	When the Red, Red Robin Comes Bob-Bob Bobbin Along	Harry Woods	
1927	Ain't She Sweet	Milton Ager	Jack Yellen
	Among My Souvenirs	Horatio Nicholls	Edgar Leslie
	At Sundown	Walter Donaldson	
	The Best Things in Life Are Free	Ray Henderson	Buddy DeSylva, Lew Brown
	Blue Skies	Irving Berlin	
	Broken Hearted	Ray Henderson	Buddy DeSylva, Lew Brown
	Changes	Walter Donaldson	
	Chlo-e	Neil Moret	Gus Kahn
	Girl of My Dreams	Sunny Clapp	
	Gonna Get a Girl	Howard Simon	Al Lewis
	I Can't Believe That You're in Love with Me	Jimmy McHugh	Clarence Gaskill
	I'm Coming Virginia	Donald Heywood	Will Marion Cook
	I'm Gonna Meet My Sweetie Now	Jesse Greer	Benny Davis
	I'm Looking Over a Four-leaf Clover	Harry Woods	Mort Dixon
	In a Mist	Bix Beiderbecke	
	It All Depends on You	Ray Henderson	Buddy DeSylva, Lew Brown
	My Blue Heaven	Walter Donaldson	George Whiting
	My Heart Stood Still	Richard Rodgers	Lorenz Hart
	My One and Only	George Gershwin	Ira Gershwin
	Rain	Eugene Ford, Carey Morgan, Arthur Swanstrom	
	Russian Lullaby	Irving Berlin	
	's Wonderful	George Gershwin	Ira Gershwin
	The Same Old Moon	Harry Ruby	Bert Kalmar, Otto Harbach
	A Shady Tree	Walter Donaldson	
	Side by Side	Harry Woods	
	So Blue	Ray Henderson	Buddy DeSylva, Lew Brown
	Sometimes I'm Happy	Vincent Youmans	Irving Caesar
	The Song Is Ended	Irving Berlin	
	Thou Swell	Richard Rodgers	Lorenz Hart

1928	Baby	Jimmy McHugh	Dorothy Fields
	Back in Your Own Backyard	Dave Dreyer, Al Jolson, Billy Rose	
	Because My Baby Don't Mean Maybe Now	Walter Donaldson	
	Bill	Jerome Kern	P. G. Wodehouse, Oscar Hammerstein II
	Blue Shadows	Louis Alter	Raymond Klages
	Cherry	Don Redman	
	Coquette	Carmen Lombardo, Johnny Green	Gus Kahn
	Crazy Rhythm	Roger Wolfe Kahn, Joseph Meyer	Irving Caesar
	Diga Diga Doo	Jimmy McHugh	Dorothy Fields
	Doin' the New Low Down	Jimmy McHugh	Dorothy Fields
	Dream House	Lynn Cowan	Earle Foxe
	From Monday On	Harry Barris	Bing Crosby
	How Long Has This Been Going On	George Gershwin	Ira Gershwin, P. G. Wodehouse
	I Can't Give You Anything but Love	Jimmy McHugh	Dorothy Fields
	I Must Have That Man	Jimmy McHugh	Dorothy Fields
	I Wanna Be Loved by You	Harry Ruby, Herbert Stothart	Bert Kalmar
	I'll Get By	Fred E. Ahlert	Roy Turk
	Let a Smile Be Your Umbrella	Sammy Fain	Irving Kahal, Francis Wheeler
	Let's Do It!	Cole Porter	
	Let's Misbehave	Cole Porter	
	Lonely Melody	Hal Dyson	Benny Meroff, Sam Coslow
	Love Me or Leave Me	Walter Donaldson	Gus Kahn
	Lover, Come Back to Me	Sigmund Romberg	Oscar Hammerstein II
	Louisiana	J. P. Johnson	Bob Schafer, Andy Razaf
	Make Believe	Jerome Kern	Oscar Hammerstein II
	Makin' Whoopie	Walter Donaldson	Gus Kahn
	Manhattan Serenade	Louis Alter	Harold Adamson
	Marie	Irving Berlin	
	Mississippi Mud	Harry Barris, James Cavanaugh	
	A Monday Date	Earl Hines	
	My Baby Just Cares for Me	Walter Donaldson	Gus Kahn
	Nagasaki	Harry Warren	Mort Dixon

	Ready for the River	Neil Moret	Gus Kahn
	A Room with a View	Noël Coward	
	She's Funny That Way	Richard Whiting, Neil Moret	
	She's a Great Great Girl	Harry Woods	
	Softly, As In a Morning Sunrise	Sigmund Romberg	Oscar Hammerstein II
	Sugar	Maceo Pinkard, Sidney D. Mitchell	
	Sunshine	Irving Berlin	
	Sweet Lorraine	Cliff Burwell	Mitchell Parish
	Sweet Sue (Just You)	Victor Young	Will J. Harris
	'Tain't So, Honey, 'Tain't So	Willard Robison	
	That's My Weakness Now	Sam H. Stept	Bud Green
	Why Do I Love You	Jerome Kern	Oscar Hammerstein II
	Who Wouldn't Be Blue	Joe Burke	Benny Davis
	You Took Advantage of Me	Richard Rodgers	Lorenz Hart
	You're the Cream in My Coffee	Ray Henderson	Buddy DeSylva, Lew Brown
1929	Ain't Misbehavin'	Fats Waller, Harry Brooks	Andy Razaf
	Am I Blue?	Harry Akst	Grant Clarke
	Baby—Oh Where Can You Be?	Frank Magine	Ted Koehler
	Birmingham Bertha	Harry Akst	Grant Clarke
	Black and Blue	Fats Waller, Harry Brooks	Andy Razaf
	Button Up Your Overcoat	Ray Henderson	Buddy DeSylva, Lew Brown
	Can't We Be Friends?	Kay Swift	Paul James
	Deep Night	Charles Henderson	Rudy Vallee
	Do Something	Sam H. Stept	Bud Green
	Do What You Do	George Gershwin	Ira Gershwin
	Don't Ever Leave Me	Jerome Kern	Oscar Hammerstein II
	Glad Rag Doll	Dan Dougherty	Milton Ager, Jack Yellen
	Good Little Bad Little You	Sam H. Stept	Bud Green
	Honey	Richard Whiting	Seymour Simons, Haven Gillespie
	Honeysuckle Rose	Fats Waller	Andy Razaf
	How Am I to Know?	Jack King	Dorothy Parker

I Get the Blues When It Rains	Harry Stoddard	Marcy Klauber
I Guess I'll Have to Change My Plan	Arthur Schwartz	Howard Dietz
I Kiss Your Hand, Madame	Ralph Erwin	Sam M. Lewis, Joe Young
I May Be Wrong	Henry Sullivan	Harry Ruskin
I'm a Dreamer—Aren't We All	Ray Henderson	Buddy DeSylva, Lew Brown
I've Got a Feeling I'm Falling	Fats Waller, Harry Link	Billy Rose
If I Had You	Ted Shapiro, James Campbell, Reg Connelly	
Just You, Just Me	Jesse Greer	Raymond Klages
Liza	George Gershwin	Ira Gershwin, Gus Kahn
The Lonesome Road	Nat Shilkret	Gene Austin
Look What You've Done to Me	Con Conrad	Sidney D. Mitchell
Louise	Richard Whiting	Leo Robin
Mean to Me	Fred H. Ahlert	Roy Turk
Miss You	Henry, Charles, and Harry Tobias	
Moanin' Low	Ralph Rainger	Howard Dietz
More Than You Know	Vincent Youmans	Billy Rose, Edward Eliscu
My Fate Is in Your Hands	Fats Waller	Andy Razaf
My Kinda Love	Louis Alter	Jo Trent
My Sin	Ray Henderson	Buddy DeSylva, Lew Brown
Same Old Moon (Same Old June, But Not the Same Old You)	Cliff Friend	
Singin in the Rain	Nacio Herb Brown	Arthur Freed
Some Sweet Day	Nat Shilkret	Lew Pollack
Song of the Islands	Charles King	
S'posin'	Paul Denniker	Andy Razaf
Then You've Never Been Blue	Ted Fio Rito	Sam M. Lewis, Joe Young
Through	James V. Monaco	Joseph McCarthy
True Blue Lou	Richard Whiting	Sam Coslow, Lew Robin
Wake Up, Chillun, Wake Up	Willard Robison	Jo Trent
Why Was I Born?	Jerome Kern	Oscar Hammerstein II
With a Song in My Heart	Richard Rodgers	Lorenz Hart
You Do Something to Me	Cole Porter	

	You Were Meant for Me	Nacio Herb Brown	Arthur Freed
	Yours Sincerely	Richard Rodgers	Lorenz Hart
	You've Got That Thing	Cole Porter	
	Zigeuner	Noël Coward	
1930	Absence Makes the Heart Grow Fonder	Harry Warren	Sam M. Lewis, Joe Young
	Beyond the Blue Horizon	Richard Whiting, Frank W. Harling	Leo Robin
	Bidin' My Time	George Gershwin	Ira Gershwin
	Blue Again	Jimmy McHugh	Dorothy Fields
	Blue, Turning Grey over You	Fats Waller	Andy Razaf
	Body and Soul	Johnny Green	Ed Heyman, Robert Sour, Frank Eyton
	But Not for Me	George Gershwin	Ira Gershwin
	Bye Bye Blues	Chauncey Gray, Bert Lown, Fred Hamm, Dave Bennett	
	Cheerful Little Earful	Harry Warren	Ira Gershwin, Billy Rose
	Congratulations	Maceo Pinkard, Sam M. Stept	Coleman Goetz, Bud Green
	A Cottage for Sale	Willard Robison	Larry Conley
	Embraceable You	George Gershwin	Ira Gershwin
	Exactly Like You	Jimmy McHugh	Dorothy Fields
	Fine and Dandy	Kay Swift	Paul James
	Funny, Dear, What Love Can Do	Charlie Straight, Joe Bennett, George Little	
	Get Happy	Harold Arlen	Ted Koehler
	Happy Feet	Milton Ager	Jack Yellen
	Have a Little Faith in Me	Harry Warren	Sam M. Lewis, Joe Young
	Hurt	Al Piantadosi	Harold Soloman
	I Don't Mind Walkin' in the Rain	Max Rich	Al Hoffman
	I Got Rhythm	George Gershwin	Ira Gershwin
	I Love You So Much	Harry Ruby	Bert Kalmar
	I Never Dreamt	Vivian Ellis, Donovan Parsons	
	I Remember You From Somewhere	Harry Warren	Edgar Leslie

I Still Get a Thrill (Thinking of You)	J. Fred Coots	Benny Davis
I Want a Little Girl	Murray Mencher	Billy Moll
I'm Confessin' (That I Love You)	Doc Daugherty, Ellis Reynolds	Al Neiburg
I've Got a Crush on You	George Gershwin	Ira Gershwin
If I Could Be With You One Hour Tonight	James P. Johnson	Henry Creamer
I'll Be Blue Just Thinking of You	Pete Wendling	George Whiting
I'm a Ding Dong Daddy From Dumas	Phil Baxter	
I'm in the Market for You	James F. Hanley	Joseph McCarthy
I'm Yours	Johnny Green	E. Y. Harburg
It Must Be True	Harry Barris	Gus Arnheim, Gordon Clifford
Just a Little Closer	Joseph Meyer	Howard Johnson
Keepin' Myself For You	George Gershwin	Ira Gershwin
'Leven Thirty Saturday Night	Jess Kirkpatrick, Earl Burtnett, Bill Grantham	
The Little Things in Life	Irving Berlin	
Little White Lies	Walter Donaldson	
Lonesome Lover	James V. Monaco	Alfred Bryan
Looking At You	Cole Porter	
Love For Sale	Cole Porter	
Memories of You	Eubie Blake	Andy Razaf
The Moon Is Low	Nacio Herb Brown	Arthur Freed
My Future Just Passed	Richard Whiting	George Marion Jr.
My Ideal	Richard Whiting, Newell Chase	Leo Robin
Okay, Baby	Maceo Pinkard	William Tracey
On the Sunny Side of the Street	Jimmy McHugh	Dorothy Fields
Overnight	Louis Alter	Billy Rose, Charlotte Kent
Reminiscing	Harry Warren	Edgar Leslie
Rockin' Chair	Hoagy Carmichael	
She's Such a Comfort to Me	Arthur Schwartz	Douglas Furber, Donovan Parsons
Should I?	Nacio Herb Brown	Arthur Freed
So Beats My Heart for You	Pat Ballard	Charles Henderson, Tom Waring
Something to Remember You By	Arthur Schwartz	Howard Dietz
Soon	George Gershwin	Ira Gershwin
Swingin' in a Hammock	Pete Wendling	Tot Seymour, Charles O'Flynn

Year	Song	Composer	Lyricist
	Them There Eyes	Maceo Pinkard	William Tracey, Doris Tauber
	Three Little Words	Harry Ruby	Bert Kalmer
	Time on My Hands	Vincent Youmans	Harold Adamson, Mack Gordon
	Trav'lin' All Alone	J. C. Johnson	
	Under a Texas Moon	Ray Perkins	
	What Is This Thing Called Love?	Cole Porter	
	What's the Use?	Isham Jones	Charles Newman
	When a Woman Loves a Man	Ralph Rainger	Billy Rose
	When You're Smiling (The Whole World Smiles with You)	Larry Shay	Joe Goodwin, Mark Fisher
	Where Have You Been?	Cole Porter	
	Would You Like to Take a Walk?	Harry Warren	Mort Dixon, Billy Rose
	You Brought a New Kind of Love to Me	Sammy Fain, Pierre Norman	Irving Kahal
	You Darlin'	Harry Woods	
	You're Driving Me Crazy	Walter Donaldson	
	You're Lucky to Me	Eubie Blake	Andy Razaf
1931	All of Me	Gerald Marks, Seymour Simons	
	As Time Goes By	Herman Hupfeld	
	Between the Devil and the Deep Blue Sea	Harold Arlen	Ted Koehler
	Blues In My Heart	Benny Carter	Irving Mills
	By My Side	Chauncey Gray, Bert Lown, Harry Link, Dorothy Dick	
	By the River Sainte Marie	Harry Warren	Edgar Leslie
	By the Sycamore Tree	Pete Wendling	Haven Gillespie
	Can't You See	Fred E. Ahlert	Roy Turk
	Concentratin' (On You)	Fats Waller	Andy Razaf
	Dancing in the Dark	Arthur Schwartz	Howard Dietz
	Delishious	George Gershwin	Ira Gershwin
	Dream a Little Dream of Me	Fabian Andre, Wilbur Schwandt	Gus Kahn
	An Evening in Caroline	Walter Donaldson	
	A Faded Summer Love	Phil Baxter	
	For You	Joe Burke	Al Dubin

Song	Composer	Lyricist
Georgia on My Mind	Hoagy Carmichael	Stuart Gorrell
Give Me Your Affection, Honey	Pete Wendling, Carmen Lombardo	Alfred Bryan
Goodnight, Moon	Walter Donaldson	
Goodnight, Sweetheart	Ray Noble, James Campbell, Reg Connelly	
Guilty	Richard Whiting, Harry Akst	Gus Kahn
Hang Out the Stars in Indiana	Harry Woods	Billy Moll
Have You Forgotten (The Thrill)?	Dana Suesse	Leo Robin
Heartaches	Al Hoffman	John Klenner
Hello, Beautiful	Walter Donaldson	
Home	Peter Van Steeden, Harry Clarkson, Jeff Clarkson	
The Hour of Parting	Mischa Spoliansky	Gus Kahn
I Apologize	Al Hoffman, Al Goodhart, Ed Nelson	
I Don't Know Why	Fred E. Ahlert	Roy Turk
I Found a Million Dollar Baby	Harry Warren	Billy Rose, Mort Dixon
I Found You	Ray Noble	
I Heard	Don Redman	
I Keep Remembering	Isham Jones	Charles Newman
I Surrender Dear	Harry Barris	Gordon Clifford
I Wouldn't Change You for the World	Isham Jones	Charles Newman
I'm Crazy 'Bout My Baby (And My Baby's Crazy 'Bout Me)	Fats Waller	Alex Hill
I'm So Afraid of You	Harry Ruby	Bert Kalmar
I'm Sorry Dear	Anson Weeks, Harry Tobias, Johnnie Scott	
I'm Thru With Love	Matty Malneck, Fud Livingston	Gus Kahn
If I Didn't Have You	Milton Ager	E. Y. Harburg
It's a Lonesome Old Town	Charles Kisco	Harry Tobias
It's the Darndest Thing	Jimmy McHugh	Dorothy Fields
It's the Girl	Abel Baer	Dave Oppenheim
Just a Gigolo	Leonello Cassucci	Irving Caesar
Just Friends	John Klenner	Sam M. Lewis
Just One More Chance	Arthur Johnston	Sam Coslow

Lazy River	Sidney Arodin	Hoagy Carmichael
Lies	Harry Barris	George Springer
Life Is Just a Bowl of Cherries	Ray Henderson	Lew Brown
Little Girl	Francis Henry	Madeline Hyde
Love Letters in the Sand	J. Fred Coots	Nick & Charles Kenny
Mood Indigo	Duke Ellington, Barney Bigard	Irving Mills
My Extraordinary Gal	Terry Shand	
My Song	Ray Henderson	Lew Brown
Nevertheless	Harry Ruby	Bert Kalmer
The Night Was Made for Love	Jerome Kern	Otto Harbach
No Wonder I'm Blue	Louis Alter	Oscar Hammerstein II
Now That You're Gone	Ted Fio Rito	Gus Kahn
Old Playmate	Matty Malneck	Gus Kahn
On the Beach With You	Jesse Greer	Tot Seymour
One More Time	Ray Henderson	Buddy DeSylva, Lew Brown
Ooh! That Kiss	Harry Warren	Mort Dixon, Joe Young
Out of Nowhere	Johnny Green	Ed Heyman
Pardon Me, Pretty Baby	Vincent Rose	Raymond Klages, Jack Meskill
Please Don't Talk About Me When I'm Gone	Sam H. Stept	Sidney Clare
Prisoner of Love	Russ Columbo, Clarence Gaskill	Leo Robin
River, Stay 'Way from My Door	Harry Woods	Mort Dixon
Say a Little Prayer for Me	Horatio Nicholls, Joseph Gilbert	
She Didn't Say "Yes"	Jerome Kern	Otto Harbach
Stardust	Hoagy Carmichael	Mitchell Parish
Sweet and Lovely	Gus Arnheim, Harry Tobias, Jules Lemare	
Thanks to You	Pete Wendling	Grant Clarke
That's My Desire	Helmy Kresa	Carroll Loveday
The Thrill Is Gone	Ray Henderson	Lew Brown
Tie a Little String Around Your Finger	Seymour Simons	
Too Late	Victor Young	Sam M. Lewis
Try to Forget	Jerome Kern	Otto Harbach
Walkin' My Baby Back Home	Fred E. Ahlert	Roy Turk

Year	Song	Composer	Lyricist
	When I Take My Sugar to Tea	Sammy Fain	Pierre Norman, Irving Kahal
	When It's Sleepy Time Down South	Leon & Otis Rene, Clarence Muse	
	When Your Lover Has Gone	Einar A. Swan	
	The Wind in the Willows	Vivian Ellis, Desmond Carter	
	Without That Gal	Walter Donaldson	
	Wrap Your Troubles in Dreams	Harry Barris	Ted Koehler, Billy Moll
	You Call It Madness	Russ Columbo, Con Conrad	Gladys DuBois, Paul Gregory
	You Didn't Know the Music	Sam Coslow	
	You Forgot Your Gloves	Ned Lehak	Edward Eliscu
	You Try Somebody Else	Ray Henderson	Buddy DeSylva, Lew Brown
	You're Just a Dream Come True	Isham Jones	Charles Newman
	You're My Everything	Harry Warren	Mort Dixon, Joe Young
1932	All of a Sudden	Harry Woods	
	Alone Together	Arthur Schwartz	Howard Dietz
	April in Paris	Vernon Duke	E. Y. Harburg
	As You Desire Me	Allie Wrubel	
	By the Fireside	Ray Noble, James Campbell, Reg Connelly	
	Can't We Talk It Over?	Victor Young	Ned Washington
	Close Your Eyes	Bernice Petkere	
	Contented	Don Bestor	Roy Turk
	Dancing on the Ceiling	Richard Rodgers	Lorenz Hart
	Fit as a Fiddle	Al Goodhart, Arthur Freed, Al Hoffman	
	Goodbye Blues	Jimmy McHugh	Arthur Johnson, Dorothy Fields
	Here Lies Love	Ralph Rainger	Leo Robin
	Here's Hoping	J. Fred Coots	Harold Adamson
	How Deep Is the Ocean	Irving Berlin	
	I Can't Believe It's True	Isham Jones	Ben Bernie, Charles Newman
	I Gotta Right to Sing the Blues	Harold Arlen	Ted Koehler
	(I Would Do) Anything for You	Claude Hopkins, Alex Hill, Bob Williams	

I'll Follow You	Fred E. Ahlert	Roy Turk
I'll Never Be the Same	Matty Malneck, Frank Signorelli	Gus Kahn
I'll Never Have to Dream Again	Isham Jones	Charles Newman
I'm Getting Sentimental Over You	George Bassman	Ned Washington
I'm Sure of Everything but You	Pete Wendling, George W. Meyer	Charles O'Flynn
I've Told Every Little Star	Jerome Kern	Oscar Hammerstein II
If It Ain't Love	Val Burton, Will Jason	
If You Were Only Mine	Isham Jones	Charles Newman
In a Shanty in Old Shanty Town	Jack Little, John Siras	Joe Young
Isn't It Romantic	Richard Rodgers	Lorenz Hart
It Don't Mean a Thing	Duke Ellington	Irving Mills
It Was So Beautiful	Harry Barris	Arthur Freed
Just Because You're You	Cliff Friend	
Keepin' Out of Mischief Now	Fats Waller	Andy Razaf
Lazy Day	George Potsford	
Let's Put Out the Lights	Herman Hupfeld	
Let's Try Again	Isham Jones	Charles Newman
Living in Dreams	Johnny Green	
Lonesome Me	Fats Waller, Con Conrad	Andy Razaf
Look What You've Done	Harry Ruby, Harry Akst	Bert Kalmer, Irving Caesar
Louisiana Hayride	Arthur Schwartz	Howard Dietz
Lovable	Harry Woods	Gus Kahn
Love Me Tonight	Richard Rodgers	Lorenz Hart
Love, You Funny Thing	Fred E. Ahlert	Roy Turk
Lover	Richard Rodgers	Lorenz Hart
Lullaby of the Leaves	Bernice Petkere	Joe Young
Moon	Miles Caleo	
Music, Music, Everywhere	Harold Arlen	Ted Koehler
My Love	Victor Young	Ned Washington
My Silent Love	Dana Suesse	Ed Heyman
Night and Day	Cole Porter	
Nightfall	Peter DeRose	Harold Lewis
Please	Ralph Rainger	Leo Robin

	Say It Isn't So	Irving Berlin	
	Smoke Rings	Gene Gifford	Ned Washington
	Snuggled On Your Shoulder	Carmen Lombardo	Joe Young
	So at Last It's Come to This	Matty Malneck, Frank Signorelli	Gus Kahn
	Soft Lights and Sweet Music	Irving Berlin	
	Somebody Loves You	Peter DeRose	Charles Tobias
	The Song Is You	Jerome Kern	Oscar Hammerstein II
	Strange Interlude	Phil Baker, Ben Bernie	Walter Hirsch
	Strangers	J. Fred Coots	Charles O'Flynn
	Three on a Match	Ted Fio Rito	Raymond B. Egan
	Too Many Tears	Harry Warren	Al Dubin
	Was I to Blame? (For Falling in Love with You)	Victor Young	Charles Newman, Gus Kahn
	Was That the Human Thing to Do?	Sammy Fain	Joe Young
	We Just Couldn't Say Goodbye	Harry Woods	
	When We're Alone (Penthouse Serenade)	Val Burton, Will Jason	
	Who Cares?	George Gershwin	Ira Gershwin
	Willow Weep for Me	Ann Ronell	
	You Can Depend on Me	Earl Hines, Charles Carpenter,	
		Luis Dunlap	
	You're an Old Smoothie	Nacio Herb Brown, Richard Whiting	Buddy DeSylva
	You're Blasé	Ord Hamilton	Bruce Sievier
	You've Got Me in the Palm of Your Hand	James V. Monaco	Cliff Friend, Edgar Leslie
1933	Ah! But Is It Love?	Jay Gorney	E. Y. Harburg
	Ain'tcha Glad	Fats Waller	Andy Razaf
	And So Goodbye	Allie Wrubel	
	Beautiful Girl	Nacio Herb Brown	Arthur Freed
	Black Moonlight	Arthur Johnston	Sam Coslow
	Blue Interlude	Benny Carter	Manny Kurtz, Irving Mills
	Cabin in the Pines There's a	Billy Hill	
	Darkness on the Delta	Jerry Levinson	Marty Symes, Al Neiburg
	The Day You Came Along	Arthur Johnston	Sam Coslow
	Dinner at Eight	Jimmy McHugh	Dorothy Fields

Doin' the Uptown Lowdown	Harry Revel	Mack Gordon
Don't Blame Me	Jimmy McHugh	Dorothy Fields
Everything I Have Is Yours	Burton Lane	Harold Adamson
Experiment	Cole Porter	
Farewell to Arms	Abner Silver	Allie Wrubel
Ghost of a Chance	Victor Young	Ned Washington, Bing Crosby
Have You Ever Been Lonely	Peter DeRose	George Brown
Hold Me	Jack Little, Dave Oppenheim, Ira Schuster	
How Could We Be Wrong?	Cole Porter	
Hustlin' and Bustlin' for Baby	Harry Woods	
I Can't Remember	Irving Berlin	
I Couldn't Tell Them What to Do	Vee Lawnhurst	Roy Turk
I Cover the Waterfront	Johnny Green	Ed Heyman
I Guess It Had to Be That Way	Arthur Johnston	Sam Coslow
I've Got the World On a String	Harold Arlen	Ted Koehler
I Wanna Be Loved	Johnny Green	Ed Heyman, Billy Rose
I Want to Ring Bells	J. Fred Coots	Maurice Sigler
I Want You—I Need You	Harvey Brooks	Ben Ellison
I'd Be Telling a Lie	Victor Young	Ned Washington
I'll Be Faithful	Allie Wrubel	Ned Washington
I'm Playing With Fire	Irving Berlin	
If I Love Again	Ben Oakland	Jack Murray
Isn't This a Night for Love	Val Burton, Will Jason	
It Isn't Fair	Richard Himber, Frank Warshauer, Sylvester Sprigato	
It Might Have Been a Different Story	James V. Monaco	Raymond Klages, Johnny Mercer
It Was a Night in June	Harry Revel	Mack Gordon
It's Only a Paper Moon	Harold Arlen	E. Y. Harburg, Billy Rose
It's Sunday Down in Caroline	Jerry Livingston	Marty Symes, Al Neiburg
It's the Talk of the Town	Jerry Levinson	Marty Symes, Al Neiburg
Lazybones	Hoagy Carmichael	Johnny Mercer
Learn to Croon	Arthur Johnston	Sam Coslow

Love Is the Sweetest thing	Ray Noble	
Lyin' in the Hay	Roberts, Pepper, Mireille	
Mine	George Gershwin	Ira Gershwin
Moon Song	Arthur Johnston	Sam Coslow
Moonstruck	Arthur Johnston	Sam Coslow
Night Owl	Herman Hupfeld	
No More Love	Harry Warren	Al Dubin
Pardon My Love	Oscar Levant	Milton Drake
Reflections in the Water	John Jacob Loeb	Paul Francis Webster
Roll Up the Carpet	Al Hoffman, Al Goodhart	Raymond Klages
Rosetta	Earl Hines, Henri Woode	
Smoke Gets in Your Eyes	Jerome Kern	Otto Harbach
Snowball	Hoagy Carmichael	
Sophisticated Lady	Duke Elllngton	Mitchell Parish
Stormy Weather	Harold Arlen	Ted Koehler
Street of Dreams	Victor Young	Sam M. Lewis
Strike Me Pink	Ray Henderson	Lew Brown
Supper Time	Irving Berlin	
Sweet Madness	Victor Young	Ned Washington
Temptation	Nacio Herb Brown	Arthur Freed
Thanks	Arthur Johnston	Sam Coslow
This Is Romance	Vernon Duke	Ed Heyman
This Time It's Love	J. Fred Coots	Sam M. Lewis
Three Wishes	George Posford, Douglas Furber	
The Touch of Your Hand	Jerome Kern	Otto Harbach
A Tree Was a Tree	Harry Revel	Mack Gordon
Try a Little Tenderness	Harry Woods, James Campbell, Reg Connelly	
Under a Blanket of Blue	Jerry Levinson	Marty Symes, Al Neiburg
We Were the Best of Friends	George W. Meyer, Pete Wendling	Sam M. Lewis
Weep No More My Baby	Johnny Green	Ed Heyman
What More Can I Ask?	Ray Noble	A. E. Wilkins
Why Can't This Night Go On Forever	Isham Jones	Charles Newman

	Yesterdays	Jerome Kern	Otto Harbach
	You Are Too Beautiful	Richard Rodgers	Lorenz Hart
	You're Beautiful Tonight, My Dear	Carmen Lombardo	Joe Young
	You're Devastating	Jerome Kern	Otto Harbach
	You're Getting to Be a Habit With Me	Harry Warren	Al Dubin
	You're Mine, You	Johnny Green	Ed Heyman
	You've Got Everything	Walter Donaldson	Gus Kahn
	You've Got Me Crying Again	Isham Jones	Charles Newman
1934	All I Do Is Dream of You	Nacio Herb Brown	Arthur Freed
	All Through the Night	Cole Porter	
	And I Still Do	Fred E. Ahlert	Edgar Leslie
	Anything Goes	Cole Porter	
	As Long As I Live	Harold Arlen	Ted Koehler
	Believe It, Beloved	J. C. Johnson	George Whiting, Nat Schwartz
	Born to Be Kissed	Arthur Schwartz	Howard Dietz
	Boulevard of Broken Dreams	Harry Warren	Al Dubin
	The Breeze (That's Bringing My Honey Back to Me)	Al Lewis, Richard B. Smith, Tony Sacco	
	Cocktails for Two	Arthur Johnston	Sam Coslow
	Delta Bound	Alex Hill	
	Did You Ever See a Dream Walking?	Harry Revel	Mack Gordon
	Dream of You	Sy Oliver, Jimmie Lunceford, E. P. Moran	
	Emaline	Frank Perkins	Mitchell Parish
	Ending with a Kiss	Lewis E. Gensler	Harlan Thompson
	For All We Know	J. Fred Coots	Sam M. Lewis
	From Now On	Nacio Herb Brown	Arthur Freed
	Hands across the Table	Jean Delettre	Mitchell Parish
	Here Come the British	Bernie Hanighen	Johnny Mercer
	The House Is Haunted (By the Echo of Your Last Goodbye)	Buzz Adlam	Billy Rose
	How Can You Face Me?	Fats Waller	Andy Razaf

A Hundred Years From Today	Victor Young	Ned Washington
I Ain't Lazy—I'm Just Dreamin'	Dave Franklin	
I Couldn't Be Mean to You	Jesse Greer	Stanley Adams
I Get a Kick Out of You	Cole Porter	
I Just Couldn't Take It, Baby	Alberta Nichols	Mann Holiner
I Like the Likes of You	Vernon Duke	E.Y. Harburg
I Never Had a Chance	Irving Berlin	
I Only Have Eyes for You	Harry Warren	Al Dubin
I Saw Stars	Al Goodhart, Maurice Sigler	Al Hoffman
I Wish I Were Twins	Joseph Meyer	Frank Loesser, Eddie DeLange
I'll Follow My Secret Heart	Noël Coward	
I'll String Along with You	Harry Warren	Al Dubin
I've Had My Moments	Walter Donaldson	Gus Kahn
If I Had a Million Dollars	Matty Malneck	Johnny Mercer
It's All Forgotten Now	Ray Noble	
It's Funny to Everyone but Me	Isham Jones	Dave Franklin
Judy	Hoagy Carmichael	Sammy Lerner
Let's Fall in Love	Harold Arlen	Ted Koehler
Live and Love Tonight	Arthur Johnston	Sam Coslow
London On a Rainy Night	Sam H. Stept	Ned Washington
Lost in a Fog	Jimmy McHugh	Dorothy Fields
Love in Bloom	Ralph Rainger	Leo Robin
Love Locked Out	Ray Noble	Max Kester
Love Me	Victor Young	Ned Washington
Love Thy Neighbor	Harry Revel	Mack Gordon
May I?	Harry Revel	Mack Gordon
Melody in Spring	Lewis E. Gensler	Harlan Thompson
Miss Otis Regrets	Cole Porter	
Moon About Town	Dana Suesse	
Moon Country	Hoagy Carmichael	Johnny Mercer
The Moon Was Yellow	Fred E. Ahlert	Edgar Leslie
Moonglow	Will Hudson	Eddie DeLange, Irving Mills

My Little Grass Shack	Bill Cogswell, Tom Harrison, Johnny Noble	
My Old Flame	Arthur Johnston	Sam Coslow
Neighbors	Frank Weldon	Charles O'Flynn, James Cavanaugh
Not Bad	Johnny Green	James Dyrenforth
The Object of My Affection	Pinky Tomlin	Jimmy Grier, Coy Poe
Okay, Toots	Walter Donaldson	Gus Kahn
Ol' Pappy	Jerry Livingston	Marty Symes, Al Neiburg
One Morning in May	Hoagy Carmichael	Mitchell Parish
Out in the Cold Again	Rube Bloom	Ted Koehler
Over Somebody Else's Shoulder	Al Lewis, Al Sherman	
Pardon My Southern Accent	Matty Malneck	Johnny Mercer
P.S. I Love You	Gordon Jenkins	Johnny Mercer
Rain	Peter DeRose	Billy Hill
Santa Claus Is Coming to Town	J. Fred Coots	Haven Gillespie
Say It!	Buzz Adlam	Nat Burton
She Reminds Me of You	Harry Revel	Mack Gordon
Sittin' on a Log (Pettin' My Dog)	Zez Confrey	Byron Gay
Sleepy Head	Walter Donaldson	Gus Kahn
So Help Me	Irving Berlin	
Song of Surrender	Harry Warren	Al Dubin
Stars Fell On Alabama	Frank Perkins	Mitchell Parish
Stay As Sweet As You Are	Harry Revel	Mack Gordon
Sweetie Pie	John Jacob Loeb	
Thank You for a Lovely Evening	Jimmy McHugh	Dorothy Fields
Then I'll Be Tired of You	Arthur Schwartz	E. Y. Harburg
There Goes My Heart	Abner Silver	Benny Davis
A Thousand Goodnights	Walter Donaldson	
Throw Another Log On the Fire	Murray Mencher	Jack Scholl, Charles Tobias
Tired of It All	Harry Ruby	Bert Kalmar
The World Is Mine	Johnny Green	E. Y. Harburg
Yes to You	Richard Whiting	Sidney Clare

Year	Song	Composer	Lyricist
	You and the Night and the Music	Arthur Schwartz	Howard Dietz
	You Have Taken My Heart	Gordon Jenkins	Johnny Mercer
	You Oughta Be in Pictures	Dana Suesse	Ed Heyman
	You're a Builder-upper	Harold Arlen	Ira Gershwin, E. Y. Harburg
	You're My Thrill	Jay Gorney	Sidney Clare
	You're Such a Comfort to Me	Harry Revel	Mack Gordon
	You're the Top	Cole Porter	
1935	Accent on Youth	Vee Lawnhurst	Tot Seymour
	Alone	Nacio Herb Brown	Arthur Freed
	And Then Some	Vee Lawnhurst	Tot Seymour
	Autumn in New York	Vernon Duke	
	Ballad in Blue	Hoagy Carmichael	Irving Kahal
	Begin the Beguine	Cole Porter	
	Blue Moon	Richard Rodgers	Lorenz Hart
	A Blues Serenade	Frank Signorelli, Jimmy Lytel, Vincent Grande, Mitchell Parish	
	Chasing Shadows	Abner Silver	Benny Davis
	Cheek to Cheek	Irving Berlin	
	Clouds	Walter Donaldson	Gus Kahn
	Dancing with My Shadow	Harry Woods	
	Darling, Je Vous Aime Beaucoup	Anna Sosenko	
	Devil in the Moon	Alex Hill, Manny Kurtz, Irving Mills	
	The Dixieland Band	Bernie Hanighen	Johnny Mercer
	Down by the River	Richard Rodgers	Lorenz Hart
	East of the Sun	Brooks Bowman	
	Eeny Meeny Miney Mo	Matty Malneck	Johnny Mercer
	Every Little Moment	Jimmy McHugh	Dorothy Fields
	Every Now and Then	Abner Silver	Al Lewis, Al Sherman
	Everything's Been Done Before	Jack King, Edwin H. Knopf, Harold Adamson	
	Ev'ry Day	Sammy Fain	Irving Kahal

The Gentleman Obviously Doesn't Believe	Michael Carr, Edward Pola	
Goodbye	Gordon Jenkins	
Got Me Doin' Things	Harry Revel	Mack Gordon
Here Comes Cookie	Harry Revel	Mack Gordon
Here Is My Heart	Ralph Rainger	Leo Robin
How Do I Rate with You	Richard Whiting	Sam Coslow
Hypnotized	Abner Silver	Al Lewis, Al Sherman
I Believe in Miracles	George W. Meyer, Pete Wendling	Sam M. Lewis
I Couldn't Believe My Eyes	Teddy Powell, Walter Samuels, Leonard Whitcup	
I Dream Too Much	Jerome Kern	Dorothy Fields
I Got Pleny O' Nuttin'	George Gershwin	Ira Gershwin
I Live for Love	Allie Wrubel	Mort Dixon
I Wished on the Moon	Ralph Rainger	Dorothy Parker
I Woke Up Too Soon	Dave Franklin	
I Won't Dance	Jerome Kern	Jimmy McHugh, Dorothy Fields
I'd Love to Take Orders From You	Harry Warren	Al Dubin
I'd Rather Listen to Your Eyes	Harry Warren	Al Dubin
I'll Never Say "Never Again"	Harry Woods	
I'm Growing Fonder of You	George W. Meyer, Pete Wendling	Joe Young
I'm in Love All Over Again	Jimmy McHugh	Dorothy fields
I'm in the Mood for Love	Jimmy McHugh	Dorothy Fields
I've Got a Feelin' You're Foolin'	Nacio Herb Brown	Arthur Freed
In a Blue and Pensive Mood	Jerry Levinson	Marty Symes, Al Neibrug
In the Middle of a Kiss	Sam Coslow	
Isn't This a Lovely Day?	Irving Berlin	
It Never Dawned on Me	J. Fred Coots	Sam M. Lewis
It's Easy to Remember	Richard Rodgers	Lorenz Hart
If the Moon Turns Green	Bernie Hanighen	Paul Coates
If You Were Mine	Matty Malneck	Johnny Mercer
June in January	Ralph Rainger	Leo Robin
Just One of Those Things	Cole Porter	

A Little Bit Independent	Joe Burke	Edgar Leslie
Little Girl Blue	Richard Rodgers	Lorenz Hart
Louisiana Fairy Tale	J. Fred Coots	Haven Gillespie, Mitchell Parish
Love and a Dime	Brooks Bowman	
Love Is Just Around the Corner	Lewis E. Gensler	Leo Robin
Lovely to Look At	Jerome Kern	Jimmy McHugh, Dorothy Fields
Lulu's Back in Town	Harry Warren	Al Dubin
Mine Alone	Allie Wrubel	Mort Dixon
Miss Brown to You	Ralph Rainger, Richard Whiting	Leo Robin
Moon Over Miami	Joe Burke	Edgar Leslie
The Most Beautiful Girl in the World	Richard Rodgers	Lorenz Hart
My Romance	Richard Rodgers	Lorenz Hart
The Night Is Young	Sigmund Romberg	Oscar Hammerstein II
No Other One	Vee Lawnhurst	Tot Seymour
No Strings	Irving Berlin	
Now You've Got Me Doin' It!	Harold Spina	Johnny Burke
Outside of You	Harry Warren	Al Dubin
Over My Shoulder	Harry Woods	
A Picture of Me Without You	Cole Porter	
Red Sails in the Sunset	Hugh Williams	Jimmy Kennedy
Rhythm and Romance	J. C. Johnson	George Whiting, Nat Schwartz
Rhythm Is Our Business	Jimmie Lunceford, Saul Chaplin	Sammy Cahn
Sandman	Bonnie Lake	Ralph Freed
Seein' Is Believin'	Milton Ager	Stanley Adams
Solitude	Duke Ellington	Eddie DeLange, Irving Mills
Soon	Richard Rodgers	Lorenz Hart
Stargazing	Jerry Levinson	Marty Symes, Al Neiburg
Summertime	George Gershwin	DuBose Heywood
Sweet Music	Harry Warren	Al Dubin
Tender Is the Night	Walter Donaldson	Harold Adamson
Thanks a Million	Arthur Johnston	Gus Kahn
Thrilled	Harry Barris	Mort Greene
What a Little Moonlight Can Do	Harry Woods	

	When You've Got a Little Springtime in Your Heart	Harry Woods	
	Where Am I?	Harry Warren	Al Dubin
	Where There's Smoke There's Fire	Jerry Levinson	Marty Symes, Al Neiburg
	Whose Honey Are You?	J. Fred Coots	Haven Gillespie
	Why Dream?	Ralph Rainger, Richard Whiting	Leo Robin
	Why Shouldn't I?	Cole Porter	
	Why Stars Come Out at Night	Ray Noble	
	Will Love Find a Way?	Brooks Bowman	K. B. Alexander
	With All My Heart and Soul	Will Hudson	
	With Every Breath I Take	Ralph Rainger	Leo Robin
	Without a Word of Warning	Harry Revel	Mack Gordon
	You Took My Breath Away	Richard Whiting	Sam Coslow
	You're a Heavenly Thing	Jack Little	Joe Young
	Zing! Went the Strings of My Heart	James F. Hanley	
1936	All My Life	Sam H. Stept	Sidney Mitchell
	But Where Are You?	Irving Berlin	
	Christopher Columbus	Leon Berry	Andy Razaf
	Cling to Me	Joe Burke	Edgar Leslie
	Close to Me	Peter DeRose	Sam M. Lewis
	Did I Remember?	Walter Donaldson	Harold Adamson
	Did You Mean It?	Jesse Greer	Mort Dixon
	Dinner for One, Please, James	Michael Carr	
	Does Your Heart Beat for Me?	Russ Morgan, Arnold Johnson	Mitchell Parish
	Dream Awhile	Phil Ohman	Johnny Mercer
	Easy to Love	Cole Porter	
	Every Once in Awhile	Ray Henderson	Mort Dixon
	A Fine Romance	Jerome Kern	Dorothy Fields
	For Sentimental Reasons	Abner Silver	Ed Heyman, Al Sherman
	Goodnight, My Love	Harry Revel	Mack Gordon
	Goody-Goody	Matty Malneck	Johnny Mercer
	Guess Who?	Burton Lane	Ralph Freed

Hawaiian War Chant	Johnny Noble, Leleiohako	Ralph Freed
Here's Love in Your Eyes	Ralph Rainger	Leo Robin
I Can't Escape From You	Richard Whiting	Leo Robin
I Can't Get Started	Vernon Duke	Ira Gershwin
I Nearly Let Love Go Slipping Through My Fingers	Harry Woods	Sam Coslow
I'll Sing You a Thousand Love Songs	Harry Warren	Al Dubin
I'm an Old Cowhand	Johnny Mercer	
I'm Building Up to an Awful Letdown	Fed Astaire	Johnny Mercer
I'm Gonna Sit Right Down and Write Myself a Letter	Fred E. Ahlert	Joe Young
I'm Grateful to You	J. Fred Coots	Benny Davis
I'm Putting All My Eggs in One Basket	Irving Berlin	
I've Got You Under My Skin	Cole Porter	
If I Should Lose You	Ralph Rainger	Leo Robin
If You Love Me	Ray Noble	
In a Sentimental Mood	Duke Ellington	Manny Kurtz, Irving Mills
In My Estimation of You	J. Fred Coots, Carmen Lombardo	Benny Davis
Is It True What They Say about Dixie?	Gerald Marks	Irving Caesar, Sammy Lerner
Isn't Love the Strangest Thing?	J. Fred Coots	Benny Davis
It's Been So Long	Walter Donaldson	Harold Adamson
It's De Lovely	Cole Porter	
It's Got to Be Love	Richard Rodgers	Lorenz Hart
It's Love I'm After	Lew Pollack	Sidney D. Mitchell
Last Night When We Were Young	Harold Arlen	E. Y. Harburg
Let's Call a Heart a Heart	Arthur Johnston	Johnny Burke
Let's Face the Music and Dance	Irving Berlin	
Lost	Phil Ohman	Johnny Mercer, Macy O. Teetor
Midnight Blue	Joe Burke	Edgar Leslie
Moonburn	Hoagy Carmichael	Ed Heyman
The More I Know You	J. Fred Coots	Benny Davis
The Night Is Young and You're So Beautiful	Dana Suesse	Billy Rose, Irving Kahal
No Greater Love	Isham Jones	Marty Symes
No Regrets	Roy Ingraham	Harry Tobias

Song	Composer	Lyricist
Oooh! Looka There Ain't She Pretty	Carmen Lombardo	Clarence Todd
Organ Grinder's Swing	Will Hudson	Mitchell Parish, Irving Mills
Pennies From Heaven	Arthur Johnston	Johnny Burke
Robins and Roses	Joe Burke	Edgar Leslie
Shoe Shine Boy	Saul Chaplin	Sammy Cahn
So This Is Heaven	Harold Spina	Johnny Burke
Stars in My Eyes	Fritz Kreisler	Dorothy Fields
Stealin' Apples	Fats Waller	Andy Razaf
Stompin' at the Savoy	Edgar Sampson, Benny Goodman, Chick Webb	Andy Razaf
Summer Holiday	Johnny Marks	Larry Conley
Swamp Fire	Harold Mooney	
Take Another Guess	Murray Mencher	Charles Newman, Al Sherman
Take My Heart	Fred E. Ahlert	Joe Young
There's a Small Hotel	Richard Rodgers	Lorenz Hart
These Foolish Things	Jack Strachey, Harry Link	Holt Marvell
A Thousand Dreams of You	Louis Alter	Paul Francis Webster
Too Much Imagination	Harold Spina	Johnny Burke
Tormented	Will Hudson	
The Touch of Your Lips	Ray Noble	
Until the Real Thing Comes Along	Saul Chaplin, Alberta Nichols	Sammy Cahn, Mann Holiner, L. E. Freeman
The Way You Look Tonight	Jerome Kern	Dorothy Fields
Welcome Stranger	Johnny Mercer	
What's the Name of That Song	Vee Lawnhurst	Tot Seymour
When a Lady Meets a Gentleman Down South	Michael Cleary, Jacques Krakeur, David Oppenheim	
When Did You Leave Heaven?	Richard Whiting	Walter Bullock
When I'm With You	Harry Revel	Mack Gordon
When My Dreamboat Comes Home	Dave Franklin, Cliff Friend	
Where the Lazy River Goes By	Jimmy McHugh	Harold Adamson
Why Do I Lie to Myself About You?	J. Fred Coots	Benny Davis
Will I Ever Know?	Ralph Rainger	Leo Robin

	With All My Heart	Jimmy McHugh	Gus Kahn
	You	Walter Donaldson	Harold Adamson
	You Came to My Rescue	Ralph Rainger	Leo Robin
	You Can't Pull the Wool Over My Eyes	Murray Mencher, Milton Ager	Charles Newman
	You Do the Darndest Things, Baby	Lew Pollack	Sidney D. Mitchell
	You Hit the Spot	Harry Revel	Mack Gordon
	You Never Looked So Beautiful	Walter Donaldson	Harold Adamson
	You Started Me Dreaming	J. Fred Coots	Benny Davis
	You Turned the Tables On Me	Louis Alter	Sidney D. Mitchell
	You Were There	Noël Coward	
	You're Not the Kind	Will Hudson	Irving Mills
	You're Too Good to Be True	Jesse Greer	Bud Green
	Yours Truly Is Truly Yours	J. Fred Coots, Ted Fio Rito	Benny Davis
1937	Afraid to Dream	Harry Revel	Mack Gordon
	Blue Hawaii	Ralph Rainger	Leo Robin
	Bob White	Bernie Hanighen	Johnny Mercer
	Caravan	Duke Ellington, Juan Tizol	Irving Mills
	'Cause My Baby Says It's So	Harry Warren	Al Dubin
	Dedicated to You	Saul Chaplin	Sammy Cahn, Hy Zaret
	The Dipsy Doodle	Larry Clinton	
	Don't Ever Change	Lou Handman	Walter Hirsch
	Don't You Know or Don't You Care?	Sammy Fain	Irving Kahal
	Easy Living	Ralph Rainger	Leo Robin
	Everything You Said Came True	Dave Franklin, Cliff Friend	
	The First Time I Saw You	Allie Wrubel	Nat Shilkret
	A Foggy Day	George Gershwin	Ira Gershwin
	Foolin' Myself	Peter Tinturin	Jack Lawrence
	Gee, but You're Swell	Abel Baer	Charles Tobias
	Gone With the Wind	Allie Wrubel	Herb Magidson
	Have You Got Any Castles, Baby?	Richard Whiting	Johnny Mercer
	Have You Met Miss Jones?	Richard Rodgers	Lorenz Hart
	I Can't Lose That Longing for You	Jesse Greer	Mort Dixon

I Double Dare You	Terry Shand	Jimmy Eaton
I Know Now	Harry Warren	Al Dubin
I Wish I Were in Love Again	Richard Rodgers	Lorenz Hart
I've Got My Love to Keep Me Warm	Irving Berlin	
If It's the Last Thing I Do	Saul Chaplin	Sammy Cahn
If My Heart Could Only Talk	Teddy Powell, Walter Samuels, Leonard Whitcup	
If You Ever Should Leave	Saul Chaplin	Sammy Cahn
The Image of You	Fred E. Ahlert	Joe Young
In the Still of the Night	Cole Porter	
It's Swell of You	Harry Revel	Mack Gordon
Josephine	Wayne King, Burke Bivens	Gus Kahn
Just a Quiet Evening	Richard Whiting	Johnny Mercer
The Lady Is a Tramp	Richard Rodgers	Lorenz Hart
Let's Call the Whole Thing Off	George Gershwin	Ira Gershwin
Let's Give Love Another Chance	Jimmy McHugh	Harold Adamson
The Love Bug Will Bite You (If You Don't Watch Out)	Pinky Tomlin	
The Loveliness of You	Harry Revel	Mack Gordon
Me, Myself and I	Irving Gordon, Allan Roberts	Al Kaufman
The Mood That I'm In	Abner Silver	Al Sherman
Moonlight and Shadows	Fred Hollander	Leo Robin
My Cabin of Dreams	Nat Madison, Al Frazzini	
My Funny Valentine	Richard Rodgers	Lorenz Hart
Never in a Million Years	Harry Revel	Mack Gordon
Never Should Have Told You	Dave Franklin, Cliff Friend	
Nice Work If You Can Get It	George Gershwin	Ira Gershwin
Once in Awhile	Michael Edwards	Bud Green
One O'Clock Jump	Count Basie	
Our Love Was Meant to Be	Fats Waller, Alex Hill	Joe Davis
Peckin'	Ben Pollack, Harry James	
Remember Me?	Harry Warren	Al Dubin
Rosalie	Cole Porter	

A Sailboat in the Moonlight	Carmen Lombardo, John Jacob Loeb	
Satan Takes a Holiday	Larry Clinton	
Sentimental and Melancholy	Richard Whiting	Johnny Mercer
September in the Rain	Harry Warren	Al Dubin
Smoke Dreams	Nacio Herb Brown	Arthur Freed
So Rare	Jerry Herst	Jack Sharpe
Somebody Else Is Taking My Place	Russ Morgan, Dick Howard, Bob Ellsworth	
Sophisticated Swing	Will Hudson	Mitchell Parish
A Study in Brown	Larry Clinton	
Sweet Heartache	Sam H. Stept	Ned Washington
Sweet Leilani	Harry Owens	
Tea on the Terrace	Sam Coslow	
Thanks for Everything	Isham Jones	Eddie Stone
That Old Feeling	Sammy Fain	Lew Brown
There's a Lull in My Life	Harry Revel	Mack Gordon
There's Frost on the Moon	Fred E. Ahlert	Joe Young
They All Laughed	George Gershwin	Ira Gershwin
They Can't Take That Away From Me	George Gershwin	Ira Gershwin
This Never Happened Before	Jimmy McHugh	Harold Adamson
This Year's Kisses	Irving Berlin	
To a Sweet Pretty Thing	Fred E. Ahlert	Joe Young
Too Marvelous for Words	Richard Whiting	Johnny Mercer
True Confession	Fred Hollander	Sam Coslow
Trust in Me	Milton Ager, Jean Schwartz	Ned Wever
Vienna Dreams	Rudolf Sieczynski	Irving Caesar
What Will I Tell My Heart?	Peter Tinturin	Irving Gordon
Where Are You?	Jimmy McHugh	Harold Adamson
Where or When	Richard Rodgers	Lorenz Hart
Who Knows?	Cole Porter	
With Plenty of Money and You	Harry Warren	Al Dubin
You Can Tell She Comes From Dixie	Milton Ager	Marty Symes

	You Can't Run Away From Love Tonight	Harry Warren	Al Dubin
	You Can't Stop Me from Dreaming	Dave Franklin, Cliff Friend	
	You Showed Me the Way	Chick Webb, Teddy McRae, Ella Fitzgerald, Bud Green	Harold Adamson
	You're a Sweetheart	Jimmy McHugh	
	You're Laughing at Me	Irving Berlin	
	You're My Desire	Will Hudson	Irving Mills
	Yours and Mine	Nacio Herb Brown	Arthur Freed
	You've Got Something There	Richard Whiting	Johnny Mercer
1938	Any Old Time	Artie Shaw	
	At a Perfume Counter	Joe Burke	Edgar Leslie
	At Long Last Love	Cole Porter	
	By Myself	Arthur Schwartz	Howard Dietz
	Deep in a Dream	Jimmy Van Heusen	Eddie DeLange
	Don't Be That Way	Edgar Sampson, Benny Goodman	Mitchell Parrish
	Don't Let That Moon Get Away	James V. Monaco	Johnny Burke
	Every Day's a Holiday	Sam Coslow	Barry Trivers
	Feelin' High and Happy	Rube Bloom	Ted Koehler
	From Now On	Cole Porter	
	Garden of the Moon	Harry Warren	Al Dubin, Johnny Mercer
	Goodnight Angel	Allie Wrubel	Herb Magidson
	Half Moon on the Hudson	Harold Spina	Walter Bullock
	Have You Forgotten So Soon?	Abner Silver	Sam Coslow, Ed Heyman
	Heart and Soul	Hoagy Carmichael	Frank Loesser
	Hurray for Hollywood	Richard Whiting	Johnny Mercer
	I Can Dream, Can't I?	Sammy Fain	Irving Kahal
	I Go for That	Matty Malneck	Frank Loesser
	I Hadn't Anyone Till You	Ray Noble	
	I Have Eyes	Ralph Rainger	Leo Robin
	I Let a Song Go Out of My Heart	Duke Ellington	Henry Nemo, Irving Mills
	I Live the Life I Love	Clay Boland	
	I Married an Angel	Richard Rodgers	Lorenz Hart
	I See Your Face before Me	Arthur Schwartz	Howard Dietz

I Used to Be Color Blind	Irving Berlin	
I Was Doing All Right	George Gershwin	Ira Gershwin
I'll Be Seeing You	Sammy Fain	Irving Kahal
I'll Dream Tonight	Richard Whiting	Johnny Mercer
I've Got a Date With a Dream	Harry Revel	Mack Gordon
I've Hitched My Wagon to a Star	Richard Whiting	Johnny Mercer
If Dreams Come True	Edgar Sampson, Benny Goodman	Irving Mills
If You Were in My Place	Duke Ellington	Henry Nemo, Irving Mills
It's the Dreamer in Me	Jimmy Dorsey	Jimmy Van Heusen
It's Wonderful	Stuff Smith	Mitchell Parish
Jeepers Creepers	Harry Warren	Johnny Mercer
Jubilee	Hoagy Carmichael	Stanley Adams
Just Let Me Look at You	Jerome Kern	Dorothy Fields
Kinda Lonesome	Hoagy Carmichael	Sam Coslow, Leo Robin
A Little Kiss at Twilight	Ralph Rainger	Leo Robin
Love Is Here to Stay	George Gershwin	Ira Gershwin
Love Is Where You Find It	Harry Warren	Al Dubin, Johnny Mercer
Love Walked In	George Gershwin	Ira Gershwin
Lullaby in Rhythm	Clarence Profit, Edgar Sampson, Benny Goodman	
Moments Like This	Burton Lane	Frank Loesser, Walter Hirsh
More Than Ever	Isham Jones	Bud Green
Music, Maestro, Please	Allie Wrubel	Herb Magidson
The Night Is Filled With Music	Irving Berlin	
Now It Can Be Told	Irving Berlin	
Old Folks	Willard Robison	Dedette L. Hill
On the Sentimental Side	James V. Monaco	Johnny Burke
Please Be Kind	Saul Chaplin	Sammy Cahn
Prelude to a Kiss	Duke Ellington	Irving Mills, Irving Gordon
A Room with a View	Einar A. Swan	Al Stillman
'Round the Old Deserted Farm	Willard Robison	
Saving Myself for You	Saul Chaplin	Sammy Cahn
Say It With a Kiss	Harry Warren	Johnny Mercer

	Says My Heart	Burton Lane	Frank Loesser
	September Song	Kurt Weill	Maxwell Anderson
	Silhouetted in the Moonlight	Richard Whiting	Johnny Mercer
	Small Fry	Hoagy Carmichael	Frank Loesser
	Something Tells Me	Harry Warren	Johnny Mercer
	Spring Is Here	Richard Rodgers	Lorenz Hart
	Sweet Someone	Harry Revel	Mack Gordon
	Thanks for the Memory	Ralph Rainger	Leo Robin
	There's Honey On the Moon Tonight	J. Fred Coots	Haven Gillespie, Mack David
	They Say	Paul Mann, Stephen Weiss	Ed Heyman
	This Can't Be Love	Richard Rodgers	Lorenz Hart
	This Time It's Real	Shivers, Buddie Bernier, Bob Emmerich	
	Two Sleepy People	Hoagy Carmichael	Frank Loesser
	The Weekend of a Private Secretary	Bernie Hanighen	Johnny Mercer
	What Goes on Here in My Heart?	Ralph Rainger	Leo Robin
	When I Go A-Dreamin'	Clay Boland	Bickley Reichner
	Who Blew Out the Flame?	Sammy Fain	Mitchell Parish
	Why Doesn't Somebody Tell Me These Things	Terry Shand	Jimmy Eaton
	Why'd Ya Make Me Fall in Love?	Walter Donaldson	
	You Couldn't Be Cuter	Jerome Kern	Dorothy Fields
	You Go to My Head	J. Fred Coots	Haven Gillespie
	You Leave Me Breathless	Fred Hollander	Ralph Freed
	You Must Have Been a Beautiful Baby	Harry Warren	Johnny Mercer
	You're a Sweet Little Headache	Ralph Rainger	Leo Robin
1939	All I Remember Is You	Jimmy Van Heusen	Eddie DeLange
	All in Fun	Jerome Kern	Oscar Hammerstein II
	All the Things You Are	Jerome Kern	Oscar Hammerstein II
	And the Angels Sing	Ziggy Elman	Johnny Mercer
	Baby Me	Archie Gottler, Lou Handman	Harry Harris

Blue Evening	Gordon Jenkins, Joe Bishop	
Blue Orchids	Hoagy Carmichael	
Careless	Dick Jurgens, Eddy Howard, Lew Quadling	
Cuckoo in the Clock	Walter Donaldson	Johnny Mercer
Darn That Dream	Jimmy Van Heusen	Eddie DeLange
Day In—Day Out	Rube Bloom	Johnny Mercer
Deep Purple	Peter DeRose	Mitchell Parish
Do I Love You?	Cole Porter	
Don't Worry 'Bout Me	Rube Bloom	Ted Koehler
East Side of Heaven	James V. Monaco	Johnny Burke
Gotta Get Some Shut-eye	Walter Donaldson	Johnny Mercer
Happy Birthday to Love	Dave Franklin	
Heaven Can Wait	Jimmy Van Heusen	Eddie DeLange
Honolulu	Harry Warren	Gus Kahn
I Didn't Know What Time It Was	Richard Rodgers	Lorenz Hart
I Get Along Without You Very Well	Hoagy Carmichael	
I Never Knew Heaven Could Speak	Harry Revel	Mack Gordon
I Thought about You	Jimmy Van Heusen	Johnny Mercer
If I Didn't Care	Jack Lawrence	
If I Knew Then	Dick Jurgens, Eddy Howard	
It's Easy to Blame the Weather	Saul Chaplin	Sammy Cahn
It's My Turn Now	Saul Chaplin	Sammy Cahn
It's Never Too Late	Carmen Lombardo, John Jacob Loeb	
The Lady's in Love With You	Burton Lane	Frank Loesser
The Lamp Is Low	Peter DeRose, Bert Shefter	Mitchell Parish
The Last Two Weeks in July	Abel Baer	Sam M. Lewis
Lilacs in the Rain	Peter DeRose	Mitchell Parish
Many Dreams Ago	Fred E. Ahlert	Al Stillman
Melancholy Lullaby	Benny Carter	Ed Heyman
Melancholy Mood	Vick Knight	
Moonlight Serenade	Glenn Miller	Mitchell Parish

	Moonray	Artie Shaw, Paul Madison, Arthur Quenzer	
	My Last Goodbye	Eddy Howard	
	Octoroon	Harry Warren	
	Oh, You Crazy Moon	Jimmy Van Heusen	Johnny Burke
	Over the Rainbow	Harold Arlen	E. Y. Harburg
	Rendezvous Time in Paree	Jimmy McHugh	Al Dubin
	Running Through My Mind	Charles & Nick Kenny	
	Shadows	Frankie Carle	
	Snug as a Bug in a Rug	Matty Malneck	Frank Loesser
	So Many Times	Jimmy Dorsey	Don DeVito
	Some Other Spring	Irene Kitchings	Arthur Herzog Jr.
	Stairway to the Stars	Matty Malneck, Frank Signorelli	Mitchell Parish
	Sunrise Serenade	Frankie Carle	Jack Lawrence
	A Table in a Corner	Dana Suesse	Sam Coslow
	'Tain't What You Do	Trummy Young, Sy Oliver	
	This Is No Dream	Ted Shapiro, Tommy Dorsey	Benny Davis
	To You	Ted Shapiro, Tommy Dorsey	Benny Davis
	Undecided	Charlie Shavers	Sid Robin
	Vagabond Dreams	Hoagy Carmichael	Jack Lawrence
	What's New?	Bob Haggart	Johnny Burke
	The Wind at My Window	Ralph Rainger	Leo Robin
	Wishing	Buddy DeSylva	
	You and Your Love	Johnny Green	Johnny Mercer
	You Taught Me to Love Again	Tommy Dorsey, Henri Woode	Charlie Carpenter
	You That I Loved	Ray Noble	
	You're So Desirable	Ray Noble	
	You're the Moment in My Life	Henry Nemo	
1940	All Too Soon	Duke Ellington	Carl Sigman
	Along the Santa Fe Trail	Will Grosz	Al Dubin, Edwina Coolidge
	Because of You	Dudley Wilkenson	Arthur Hammerstein
	Between 18th and 19th On Chestnut Street	Will Osborne, Dale Rogers	

Cabin in the Sky	Vernon Duke	John Latouche
Can't Get Indiana off My Mind	Hoagy Carmichael	Robert DeLeon
Clear Out of This World	Jimmy McHugh	Al Dubin
Day Dreams Come True at Night	Dick Jurgens	
Dreaming Out Loud	Sam Coslow	
Falling Leaves	Frankie Carle	Mack David
Fools Rush In	Rube Bloom	Johnny Mercer
From Another World	Richard Rodgers	Lorenz Hart
Goody Goodbye	Nat Simon	Jimmy Cavanaugh
A Handful of Stars	Ted Shapiro	Jack Lawrence
Harlem Nocture	Earle Hagen	
How High the Moon	Morgan Lewis	Nancy Hamilton
I Can't Love You Anymore	Allie Wrubel	Herb Magidson
I Can't Remember to Forget	George W. Duning	Bill Hampton
I Can't Resist You	Walter Donaldson	Ned Wever
I Concentrate on You	Cole Porter	
I Could Make You Care	Saul Chaplin	Sammy Cahn
I Should Have Known You Years Ago	Hoagy Carmichael	
I Understand	Mabel Wayne	Kim Gannon
I Walk with Music	Hoagy Carmichael	Johnny Mercer
I'd Know You Anywhere	Jimmy McHugh	Johnny Mercer
I'll Never Smile Again	Ruth Lowe	
I'm Nobody's Baby	Milton Ager, Lester Santley, Benny Davis (Revival)	
I'm Stepping Out With a Memory Tonight	Allie Wrubel	Herb Magidson
I'm Too Romantic	James V. Monaco	Johnny Burke
I've Got My Eyes On You	Cole Porter	
Imagination	Jimmy Van Heusen	Johnny Burke
In the Cool of the Evening	Jule Styne	Walter Bullock
It Never Entered My Mind	Richard Rodgers	Lorenz Hart
It's a Blue World	Bob Wright	Chet Forrest
It's a Wonderful World	Jan Savitt, Johnny Watson, Harold Adamson	

Let's Be Buddies	Cole Porter	
A Lover's Lullaby	Frankie Carle, Larry Wagner	Andy Razaf
A Million Dreams Ago	Dick Jurgens, Eddy Howard, Lew Quadling	
The Moon Fell in the River	Peter DeRose	Mitchell Parish
The Nearness of You	Hoagy Carmichael	Ned Washington
A Nightingale Sang in Berkeley Square	Manning Sherwin	Eric Maschwitz
No Name Jive	Larry Wagner	
Now We Know	Willard Robison	Ray Mayer
Ooh, What You Said	Hoagy Carmichael	Johnny Mercer
Our Love Affair	Roger Edens	Arthur Freed
Polka Dots and Moonbeams	Jimmy Van Heusen	Johnny Burke
Say It	Jimmy McHugh	Frank Loesser
720 in the Books	Jan Savitt, Johnny Watson, Harold Adamson	
Shake Down the Stars	Jimmy Van Heusen	Eddie DeLange
So Far, So Good	Jimmy Mundy, Eddie White, Jack Lawrence	
Taking a Chance on Love	Vernon Duke	John Latouche
That's for Me	James V. Monaco	Johnny Burke
There I Go	Irving Weiser	Hy Zaret
This Is the Beginning of the End	Mack Gordon	
Wait Till I Catch You in My Dreams	J. Fred Coots	Lew Brown
We Three	Sammy Mysels, Dick Robertson, Nelson Cogane	
What's the Matter With Me?	Terry Shand	Al Lewis
When the Swallows Come Back to Capistrano	Leon Rene	
Where Do I Go from You?	Allie Wrubel	Walter Bullock
Whispers in the Night	Artie Shaw	Jack Owens
With the Wind and the Rain in Your Hair	Clara Edwards	Jack Lawrence
You Forgot about Me	James F. Hanley, Sammy Mysels, Dick Robertson	
You Say the Sweetest Things, Baby	Harry Warren	Mack Gordon

Year	Song	Composer	Lyricist
	You Walk By	Bernie Wayne	Ben Raleigh
	You've Got Me This Way	Jimmy McHugh	Johnny Mercer
1941	Blue Champagne	Grady Watts, Frank Ryerson	
	Blues in the Night	Harold Arlen	Johnny Mercer
	Day Dreaming	Jerome Kern	Gus Kahn
	Do You Care?	Lew Quadling	Jack Elliott
	Dolores	Louis Alter	Frank Loesser
	Don't Take Your Love From Me	Henry Nemo	
	Easy Street	Alan Rankin Jones	
	Elmer's Tune	Elmer Albrecht, Sammy Gallop, Dick Jurgens	
	Everything Happens to Me	Matt Dennis	Tom Adair
	Ev'ry Time	Hugh Martin	Ralph Blane
	Ev'rything I Love	Cole Porter	
	Heavenly, Isn't It?	Harry Revel	Mort Greene
	How About You	Burton Lane	Ralph Freed
	I Could Write a Book	Richard Rodgers	Lorenz Hart
	I Don't Want to Set the World On Fire	Eddie Seiler, Sol Marcus, Bennie Benjamin, Eddie Durham	
	I Got It Bad, and That Ain't Good	Duke Ellington	Paul Francis Webster
	I Guess I'll Have to Dream the Rest	Harold Green	Mickey Stoner, Martin Block
	I Know Why	Harry Warren	Mack Gordon
	I Went Out of My Way	Helen Bliss	
	It All Comes Back to Me Now	Alex Kramer, Joan Whitney, Hy Zaret	
	It Happened in Sun Valley	Harry Warren	Mack Gordon
	It's Always You	Jimmy Van Heusen	Johnny Burke
	It's So Peaceful in the Country	Alec Wilder	
	It's You Again	Joe McKiernan	Art Wilson
	Let's Get Away from It All	Matt Dennis	Tom Adair
	Love of My Life	Artie Shaw	Johnny Mercer
	Make Love to Me	Paul Mann, Stephan Weiss	Kim Gannon
	Music Makers	Harry James, Don Raye	

	Oh Look at Me Now	Joe Bushkin	John DeVries
	Sand in My Shoes	Victor Schertzinger	Frank Loesser
	Snowfall	Claude Thornhill	
	A String of Pearls	Jerry Gray	Eddie DeLange
	There Goes That Song Again	Allie Wrubel	
	'Tis Autumn	Henry Nemo	
	Too Beautiful to Last	Ruth Lowe	Marty Symes
	Violets for Your Furs	Matt Dennis	Tom Adair
	Why Don't We Do This More Often?	Allie Wrubel	Charles Newman
	Will You Still Be Mine?	Matt Dennis	Tom Adair
	Winter Weather	Ted Shapiro	
	Yes Indeed	Sy Oliver	
	You and I	Meredith Willson	
	You Stepped Out of a Dream	Nacio Herb Brown	Gus Kahn
	You've Changed	Carl Fischer	William Carey
1942	At Last	Harry Warren	Mack Gordon
	Autumn Nocturne	Josef Myrow	Kim Gannon
	Be Careful, It's My Heart	Irving Berlin	
	Constantly	Jimmy Van Heusen	Johnny Burke
	Daybreak	Ferde Grofé	Harold Adamson
	Dearly Beloved	Jerome Kern	Johnny Mercer
	Don't Get Around Much Any More	Duke Ellington	Bob Russell
	I Don't Want to Walk Without You	Jule Styne	Frank Loesser
	I Had the Craziest Dream	Harry Warren	Mack Gordon
	I Remember You	Victor Schertzinger	Johnny Mercer
	I'll Never Forget	Leo M. Cherne	
	I'll Remember April	Gene DePaul	Don Raye, Pat Johnston
	I'm Glad There Is You	Paul Medeira Mertz	
	In the Blue of Evening	D'Artega	Tom Adair
	It Started All Over Again	Carl Fischer	William Carey
	Moonlight Cocktail	Lucky Roberts	Kim Gannon
	Moonlight Mood	Peter DeRose	Harold Adamson

	The Night We Called It a Day	Matt Dennis	Tom Adair
	Please Be There	Henry Nemo	
	Poor You	Burton Lane	E. Y. Harburg
	Serenade in Blue	Harry Warren	Mack Gordon
	Skylark	Hoagy Carmichael	Johnny Mercer
	Sleepy Lagoon	Eric Coates	Jack Lawrence
	Sweet Eloise	Russ Morgan	Mack David
	Tangerine	Victor Schertzinger	Johnny Mercer
	There Are Such Things	George W. Meyer, Abel Baer, Stanley Adams	
	Things Ain't What They Used to Be	Duke Ellington	
	We'll Meet Again	Albert R. Parker	Hugh Charles
	When the Lights Go On Again All Over the World	Eddie Seiler, Sol Marcus, Bennie Benjamin	
	White Christmas	Irving Berlin	
	Who Can I Turn To?	Alec Wilder	Bill Engvick
	Who Wouldn't Love You?	Carl Fischer	William Carey
	You Were Never Lovelier	Jerome Kern	Johnny Mercer
1943	Can't Get Out of This Mood	Jimmy McHugh	Frank Loesser
	Do Nothin' Till You Hear From Me	Duke Ellington	Bob Russell
	For the First Time	David Kapp	Charles Tobias
	Holiday for Strings	David Rose	Sammy Gallop
	I'll Be Around	Alec Wilder	
	I'll Be Home for Christmas	Walter Kent, Buck Ram	Kim Gannon
	I've Heard That Song Before	Jule Styne	Sammy Cahn
	Let's Get Lost	Jimmy McHugh	Frank Loesser
	No Love, No Nothin'	Harry Warren	Leo Robin
	One for My Baby	Harold Arlen	Johnny Mercer
	People Will Say We're in Love	Richard Rodgers	Oscar Hammerstein II
	Poinciana (Song of the Tree)	Nat Simon	Buddy Bernier
	Speak Low	Kurt Weill	Ogden Nash
	Star Eyes	Gene DePaul	Don Raye

Year	Song	Composer	Lyricist
	You'd Be So Nice to Come Home To	Cole Porter	
	You'll Never Know	Harry Warren	Mack Gordon
1944	Accent-tchu-ate the Positive	Harold Arlen	Johnny Mercer
	Candy	Alex Kramer, Joan Whitney, Mack David	
	Don't Fence Me In	Cole Porter	
	Don't You Know I Care?	Duke Ellington	Mack David
	Ev'ry Time We Say Goodbye	Cole Porter	
	G.I. Jive	Johnny Mercer	
	I Couldn't Sleep a Wink Last Night	Jimmy McHugh	Harold Adamson
	I Didn't Know About You	Duke Ellington	Bob Russell
	I Love You	Cole Porter	
	I Promise You	Harold Arlen	Johnny Mercer
	I'll Be Seeing You	Sammy Fain	Irving Kahal [revival]
	I'll Walk Alone	Jule Styne	Sammy Cahn
	I'm Beginning to See the Light	Duke Ellington, Johnny Hodges, Harry James, Don George	
	I'm Making Believe	James V. Monaco	Mack Gordon
	Into Each Life Some Rain Must Fall	Allan Roberts, Doris Fisher	
	It Could Happen to You	Jimmy Van Heusen	Johnny Burke
	Let Me Love You Tonight	Rene Touzet	Mitchell Parish
	Let's Take the Long Way Home	Harold Arlen	Johnny Mercer
	Like Someone in Love	Jimmy Van Heusen	Johnny Burke
	A Little On the Lonely Side	Dick Robertson, James Cavanaugh, Frank Weldon	
	Long Ago and Far Away	Jerome Kern	Ira Gershwin
	The Love I Long For	Vernon Duke	Howard Dietz
	A Lovely Way to Spend an Evening	Jimmy McHugh	Harold Adamson
	Moonlight in Vermont	Karl Suessedorf	John Blackburn
	Only Another Boy and Girl	Cole Porter	
	Poor Little Rhode Island	Jule Styne	Sammy Cahn
	Sentimental Journey	Ben Homer, Les Brown	Bud Green

	Sleigh Ride in July	Jimmy Van Heusen	Johnny Burke
	Spring Will Be a Little Late This Year	Frank Loesser	
	Swinging On a Star	Jimmy Van Heusen	Johnny Burke
	That's What I Like About the South	Andy Razaf	
	There Goes That Song Again	Jule Styne	Sammy Cahn
	Till Then	Sol Marcus, Eddie Seiler, Guy Wood	
	Time Waits for No One	Cliff Friend	Charles Tobias
	You're Nobody 'Till Somebody Loves You	Russ Morgan, Larry Stock	Jimmy Cavanaugh
1945	Aren't You Glad You're You	Jimmy Van Heusen	Johnny Burke
	Autumn Serenade	Peter DeRose	Sammy Gallop
	Close as Pages in a Book	Sigmund Romberg	Dorothy Fields
	Dream	Johnny Mercer	
	Give Me the Simple Life	Rube Bloom	Harry Ruby
	Gotta Be This or That	Sunny Skylar	
	I Can't Begin to Tell You	James V. Monaco	Mack Gordon
	I Don't Care Who Knows It	Jimmy McHugh	Harold Adamson
	I Should Care	Paul Weston, Axel Stordahl	Sammy Cahn
	I Walked In	Jimmy McHugh	Harold Adamson
	I Wish I Knew	Harry Warren	Mack Gordon
	It Might As Well Be Spring	Richard Rodgers	Oscar Hammerstein II
	It's Been a Long, Long Time	Jule Styne	Sammy Cahn
	Just a Little Fond Affection	Lewis Ilda, Elton Box, Desmond Cox	
	Laura	David Raksin	Johnny Mercer
	The More I See You	Harry Warren	Mack Gordon
	My Dreams Are Getting Better All the Time	Vic Mizzy	Mann Curtis
	Nancy	Jimmy Van Heusen	Phil Silvers
	Nevada	Walter Donaldson	Mort Greene
	Seems Like Old Times	Carmen Lombardo, John Jacob Loeb	
	S-o-o-o-o in Love	David Rose	Leo Robin
	Stranger in Town	Mel Tormé	
	There, I've Said It Again	Redd Evans, Dave Mann	
	There Must Be a Way	Sammy Gallop	David Saxon

	Tippin' In	Bobby Smith	
1946	The Christmas Song	Mel Tormé	Robert Wells
	The Coffee Song	Dick Miles	Bob Hilliard
	Everybody Knew but Me	Irving Berlin	
	Gotta Get Me Somebody to Love	Allie Wrubel	
	The Gypsy	Billy Reid	
	I Don't Know Enough About You	Peggy Lee, Dave Barbour	
	I'd Be Lost Without You	Sunny Skylar	
	I'll Close My Eyes	Billy Reid	Buddy Kaye
	I'm Glad I Waited for You	Jule Styne	Sammy Cahn
	It's a Pity to Say Goodnight	Billy Reid	
	Let It Snow! Let It Snow! Let It Snow!	Jule Styne	Sammy Cahn
	Linger in My Arms a Little Longer, Baby	Herb Magidson	
	Love Letters	Victor Young	Ed Heyman
	Personality	Jimmy Van Heusen	Johnny Burke
	Route 66	Bobby Troup	
	Stella by Starlight	Victor Young	Ned Washington
	That's the Beginning of the End	Alex Kramer	Joan Whitney
	They Say It's Wonderful	Irving Berlin	
	You Make Me Feel So Young	Josef Myrow	Mack Gordon
	You Won't Be Satisfied Until You Break My Heart	Teddy Powell	Larry Stock
1947	Across the Alley from the Alamo	Joe Greene	
	Almost Like Being in Love	Frederick Loewe	Alan Jay Lerner
	Aren't You Kind of Glad We Did	George Gershwin	Ira Gershwin
	But Beautiful	Jimmy Van Heusen	Johnny Burke
	Do You Know What It Means to Miss New Orleans	Louis Alter	Eddie DeLange
	For You, For Me, Forevermore	George Gershwin	Ira Gershwin
	I Still Get Jealous	Jule Styne	Sammy Cahn
	I'll Dance at Your Wedding	Ben Oakland	Herb Magidson
	If This Isn't Love	Burton Lane	E. Y. Harburg

Year	Song	Composer	Lyricist
	Ivy	Hoagy Carmichael	
	Linda	Jack Lawrence	
	Mam'selle	Edmund Goulding	Mack Gordon
	Manana	Peggy Lee, Dave Barbour	
	Maybe You'll Be There	Rube Bloom	Sammy Gallop
	Midnight Sun	Sunny Burke, Lionel Hampton	Johnny Mercer
	On Green Dolphin Street	Bronislaw Kaper	Ned Washington
	Roses in the Rain	Frankie Carle	Al Frisch, Fred Wise
	Smoke Dreams	Lloyd Shaffer, John Klenner, Ted Steele	
	Tenderly	Walter Gross	Jack Lawrence
	Time After Time	Jule Styne	Sammy Cahn
	Tomorrow	Gordon Jenkins	
	What Are You Doing New Year's Eve	Frank Loesser	
	When I'm Not Near the Girl I Love	Burton Lane	E. Y. Harburg
	You Do	Josef Myrow	Mack Gordon
	You Don't Have to Know the Language	Jimmy Van Heusen	Johnny Burke
	You're My Girl	Jule Styne	Sammy Cahn
1948	Again	Lionel Newman	Dorcas Cochran
	Be a Clown	Cole Porter	
	Better Luck Next Time	Irving Berlin	
	Here I'll Stay	Kurt Weill	Alan Jay Lerner
	I Love You So Much It Hurts	Floyd Tillman	
	I'm a Fool to Care	Ted Daffan	
	Love Is Where You Find It	Nacio Herb Brown	Earl K. Brent
	My Darling, My Darling	Frank Loesser	
	On a Slow Boat to China	Frank Loesser	
	You Say the Nicest Things, Baby	Jimmy McHugh	Harold Adamson
1949	Baby, It's Cold Outside	Frank Loesser	
	Bye Bye Baby	Jule Styne	Leo Robin
	Congratulations	Paul Weston	Sid Robin
	Don't Cry, Joe	Joe Marsala	

	A Dreamer's Holiday	Mabel Wayne	Kim Gannon
	Far Away Places	Alex Kramer	Joan Whitney
	I Don't See Me in Your Eyes Anymore	Bennie Benjamin, George Weiss	
	Lost in a Dream	Rube Bloom	Edgar Leslie
	Maybe It's Because	Johnnie Scott	Harry Rube
	No Moon at All	Redd Evans	Dave Mann
	So in Love	Cole Porter	
	This Nearly Was Mine	Richard Rodgers	Oscar Hammerstein II
	Why Can't You Behave	Cole Porter	
	Younger Than Springtime	Richard Rodgers	Oscar Hammerstein II
1950	Be Mine	Harold Spina	Jack Elliott
	The Best Thing for You	Irving Berlin	
	Beyond the Reef	Jack Pitman	
	Enjoy Yourself (It's Later Than You Think)	Carl Sigman	Herb Magidson
	From This Moment On	Cole Porter	
	I'll Know	Frank Loesser	
	If I Were a Bell	Frank Loesser	
	It's So Nice to Have a Man Around the House	Harold Spina	Jack Elliott
	Melancholy Rhapsody	Ray Heindorf	Sammy Cahn
	Sam's Song	Lew Quadling	Jack Elliott
	The Thing	Charles R. Green	
	You Wonderful You	Harry Warren	Jack Brooks, Saul Chaplin
	You're Just in Love	Irving Berlin	

Song Title Index

57 Varieties 202
58th Street Blues 209
720 in the Books 3, 247, 433
9:20 Special 364

The "A" Team 540
Aba Daba Honeymoon 124
About a Quarter to Nine 107
About Rip Van Winkle 392
Absence Makes the Heart Grow Fonder 265, 522, 566, 567
Accent on Youth 255, 445
Accent-chu-ate the Positive 14, 316
According to the Moonlight 289, 324, 562
Actions Speak Louder Than Words 219
The Address Is Still the Same 339
Address Unknown 303
Adios, My Madonna 319
Admiration 495
Adorable 301
Afraid (Of Losing You) 293
Afraid to Dream 155, 397
African Etude 510
African Ripples 520
After All Is Said and Done 400
After All You're All I'm After 439
After Hours 413
After I Say I'm Sorry 96, 283
After I've Called You Sweetheart 269
After My Laughter Came Tears 497, 505, 506
After Sundown 135
After the Ball 182, 183
After the Dance Was Over 29, 372
After the Rain 200
After Tonight 101
After You 73
After You've Gone 75, 257
Afternoon of a Black Faun 486
Aggravatin' Papa (Don't You Try to Two-Time Me) 360, 408, 504
Ah! But Is It Love? 181, 156
Ah! But It Happened 242
Ah! Sweet Mystery of Life 190
A-Hunting We Will Go 481
Ain' Cha? 153
Ain'cha Ever Comin' Back? 478, 538
Ain't Doin' Bad Doin' Nothin' 511
Ain't Gonna Be Like That 502
Ain't Got a Dream to My Name 510
Ain't Misbehavin' 36, 37, 390, 520
Ain't Nobody Here but Us Chickens 251
Ain't She Sweet 5, 562
Ain't That a Grand and Glorious Feeling 562
Ain't That Just Like a Man? 389
Ain't That Marvelous (My Baby Loves Me) 29, 372
Ain't We Got Fun 113, 234, 542
Ain'tcha Glad 520
Air Mail Special 151
The Air-Minded Executive 178
Alabama 546

Alabama Barbecue 72, 83
Alabama Jubilee 64, 561
Alabama Stamp 76
Alabama Stomp 224
Alabamy Bound 90, 92, 160, 188
Aladdin's Daughter 510
Alibi Baby 440, 445
Alice Blue Gown 305, 493
Alice in Wonderland 310, 497
All Aboard 324
All Aboard for Blanket Bay 474
All Aboard for Dixie Land 64, 561
Aboard for Dreamland 474, 516
All Alone Monday 422
All American Girl 264
The All American Swing 155
All Ashore 198
All at Once 533
All By My Ownsome 106
All for the Love of Mike 344
All God's Chillun Got Rhythm 235, 238
All I Do Is Dream of You 40, 135
All I Know Is You're in My Arms 243
All I Need Is You 83, 366, 381
All I Remember Is You 84, 510
All I Want Is Just One 406
All In, Down and Out 287, 466
All in Fun 100
All Is Not Gold That Glitters 518
All I've Got Is Me 102
All Mine—Almost 230
All Muddled Up 536
All My Life 327, 473
All My Love 228, 366
All Night Long 38, 309
All of Me 125, 301, 302, 463
All or Nothing at All 12, 256
All Over Nothing at All 494
All That I Need Is You 433
All That I'm Asking Is Sympathy 83
All the Cats Join In 543
All the King's Horses 544
All the Quakers Are Shoulder Shakers (Down in Quaker Town) 534
All the Things You Are 173
All the Time 272
All the Way 50, 510
All the World Is Mine 267
All This and Heaven Too 84, 510
All Too Soon 116, 457
All You Want to Do Is Dance 227
Allah's Holiday 137, 457
The All-American Soldier 180
Alligator Crawl 520
All's Well 407
Alma Mater 422
Almost in Your Arms 271, 272
Almost Like Being in Love 259, 279
Aloha Sunset Land 448
Alone 135
Alone at a Table for Two 197
Alone at Last 571
Alone in a Corner 101
Alone in My Dreams 13
Alone in the Rain 101
Alone Together 94, 439
Alone Too Long 440
Along Came Love 496
Along Came Sweetness 106
Along the Navajo Trail 84
Along the Rocky Road to Dublin 565
Along the Santa Fe Trail 107
Always in All Ways 181, 406
Always in My Heart 142
Always in the Way 183
Always Look Up 381
Always You 480
Am I Asking Too Much? 200
Am I Blue? 8, 9, 62
Am I Gonna Have Trouble with You? 123, 497
Am I Proud? 381, 540
Am I Wasting My Time on You? 223
America, I Love You 157, 261
American Beauty Rose 12, 122

American Nocturne 486
American Serenade 11
The American Way 119
Amigo, We Go Riding Tonight 389
Among My Souvenirs 261
Among Those Sailing 462
Amor 465
And a Little Bit More 132
And I Still Do 261
And Mimi 462
And So Do I 84, 297
And So Goodbye 559
And So to Bed 153
And Still No Luck With You 462
And the Angels Sing 316
And the Band Played On 132
And the Green Grass Grew All Around 222, 516
And Then It's Heaven 299, 444
And Then Some 255, 445
And Then They Called It Love 325
And Then You Kissed Me 484
And Then Your Lips Met Mine 290, 460
Anema e Core (With All My Heart and Soul) 9, 252
Angel 366
Angel Child 81, 461
Angel Eyes 87
Angel in Disguise 142, 297
An Angel Kissed Me Last Night 571
Angelina 402
Angels with Dirty Faces 132
Angeltown 272
The Angelus 357
Animal Crackers in My Soup 49, 188
Anitra's Boogie 166
Ankle Up the Altar With Me 336
Ann 202
Annabelle 244
Annie Doesn't Live Here Any More 45, 470
The Anniversary Song 60, 227
The Anniversary Waltz 134
Another Night Like This 422
Another Perfect Day Has Passed Away 143
The Answer Is Love 347
Any Little Fish 75
Any Little Girl That's a Nice Little Girl Is the Right Little Girl for Me 130
Any Little Tune 422
Any Old Place I Hang My Hat Is Home Sweet Home to Me 316, 441
Any Old Time 449
Any Old Time at All 400, 441
Any Time, Any Place, Anywhere, 570
Any Time's the Time to Fall in Love, 243
Anybody's Love Song 297
Anything 460
Anything Can Happen 188
Anything Your Heart Desires 13
Apalachichola, Fla 45
Apilachicola, Florida 510
An Apple a Day 34, 219
Apple Blossoms and Chapel Bells 252
An Apple for the Teacher 45, 331
Apple Honey 185
The Apple Valley Waltz 52
Apply Honey 191
April Blossoms 478, 564
April Give Me One More Day 381
April in Paris 108, 181
April Love 123, 531
April Played the Fiddle 331
April Showers 90, 228
Aquarela do Brasil 426
Are You from Dixie ('Cause I'm from Dixie Too) 64, 561
Are You Havin' Any Fun 124
Are You Here? 423
Are You Kidding Me? 407
Are You Livin', Old Man 122
Are You Lonesome Tonight? 174, 505

Are You Prepared (To Be True) 315
Are You Sorry? 83
Aren't You Glad You're You? 45, 510
Argentine Fire Brigade 471
Arizeh 537
Arkansas Blues 548
Arlene 446
Armful O' Sweetness 195
Around the Corner 235, 239
Around the World 3
Arrah Go On, I'm Gonna Go Back to Oregon 265
Arthur Murray Taught Me Dancing in a Hurry 316, 435
As Long As I Have You 515
As Long As I Live 14, 249
As Long As There's Music 484
As Time Goes By 214, 215, 254
As We Leave the Years Behind 324
As You Desire Me 559
Ashes in the Tray 444
Ask Anyone in Love 449
Ask Anyone Who Knows 299, 444
Ask Me 471
Ask Your Heart 315
At a Cabana in Havana 529
At a Perfume Counter 44, 261
At Last 499
At Last I'm First With You 524
At Last I'm in Love 95
At Least You Could Say Hello 339, 403
At Sundown 96
At the Balalaika 380, 480
At the Codfish Ball 327, 378
At the Cotton Picker's Ball 1
At the Crossroads 427
At the End of the Road 179, 286
At the Jazz Band Ball 359
At the Moving Picture Ball 432
At the Old Square Dances Down in Arkansas 354
At the Prom 371
At the Swing Shift Ball 544
At the Woodchopper's Ball 190
At Twilight 377
At Your Beck and Call 84
At Your Command 21, 22, 498
A-Tiskit, A-Taskit 393
Atlanta Blues 176
Au Revoir, L'Amour 318, 475
Au Revoir, Pleasant Dreams 318, 441, 498
Auf Wiedersehen, My Dear 6, 149, 205, 344
Aunt Hagar's Blues 176
Aunt Sally 556
Auntie Skinner's Chicken Dinner 124
Autumn in New York 108, 109
Autumn in Rome 538
Autumn Leaves 316
Autumn Nocturne 141, 142, 337
Autumn Serenade 89
Avalon 90, 227, 419
Away Down South in Heaven 160
Awful Sad 116
Azure 116, 495

Babalu 426
Baby 83, 127, 234, 307, 536
Baby Doll 178
Baby Dreams 480
Baby Elephant Walk 294
Baby Face 8, 9, 81, 82
Baby Me 158, 175
Baby Mine 390
Baby Shoes 244
Baby, It's Cold Outside 279
Baby, Just for Me 129
Baby—Oh Where Can You Be? 248
Baby, Take a Bow 157
Baby, Won't You Please Come Home 545
Bachelor in Paradise 80
Back, Back, Back to Baltimore 509, 546
Back Bay Shuffle 308, 449

Back Home Again in Indiana 178, 285
Back in Your Own Backyard 105, 227, 417
The Bad Humor Man 308, 316
A Bag O' Blues 370
Baghdad 561
Bakif 495
The Balboa 327
Ballad in Blue 54, 55, 233
Ballade New Yorkaise 170
Ballerina 426
Ballin' the Jack 466
Baltimore Oriole 55, 530
Bam, Bam, Bamy Shore 94
Bambalina 180, 478, 563
Bamboo 30
Bamboo Babies 179, 324
The Band Played On and On 153
The Band Plays On 521
Bandana Babies 127, 307
Bandana Days 464
Bang Your Box 309
Barbara 461
Barbaric 54
Barcelona 235
Barcelona Goodbye 369
Barney Goin' Easy 480
Barney Google (With the Goo Goo Googly Eyes) 70, 416
Barrelhouse Bessie From Basin Street 484
Basement Blues 176
Bashful Baby 136, 461
Basie Boogie 23
Basin St. Blues 548
Be Anything (But Be Mine) 152
Be Brave, Beloved 574
Be Careful 405, 542
Be Fair 142, 529
Be Happy 345
Be Mine 117, 471
Be Mine Tonight 465
Be My Life's Companion 85, 199
Be My Love 50
Beale St. Blues 176
Beale Street Mama 409, 506
Beans, Beans, Beans 466
Beat Me Daddy, Eight to the Bar 388
Beat O' My Heart 45, 470
Beat the Band 162
Beatin' the Dog 511
Beau Night in Hotchkiss Corners 290, 356
Beautiful 451
Beautiful Anna Bell Lee 322
The Beautiful Blond from Bashful Bend 145
Beautiful Coney Island 407
Beautiful Eyes 541
Beautiful Garden of Girls 472
Beautiful Girl 40, 135
Beautiful Girls 422
A Beautiful Lady in Blue 265
Beautiful Love 148, 243, 509, 570
Beautiful Music to Love By 459
Beautiful Ohio 285
Beautiful One 239
Bebe 73, 441
Be-Bop Spoken Here 85
Because I Feel Low Down 503
Because My Baby Don't Mean Maybe Now 96
Because of Once upon a Time 293
Because You Love Me 299, 444
Bedelia 222, 440
A Bee Gazindt 345
A Bee in Your Boudoir 301
Beebe 98
Be-Bop Spoken Here 85
Before I Kiss the World Goodbye 440
Before I Loved You 251
Before the Dawn 13
Before We Say Goodnight 432
Begin the Beguine 194, 449, 479
Behave Yourself 251
Bei Mir Bist Du Schoen 60
Believe It, Beloved 47, 225, 541

Believing 119
Bell, Book and Candle 10
Bells of Avalon 366
Belly Up to the Bar, Boys 549
Beloved 235, 431
Beloved Friend 434
Below the Equator 497
Bend Down Sister 286
Beneath a Banyan Tree 362
Benny's Coming Home on Saturday 402
Besame Mucho 465
Beside a Babble Brook 96, 235
Beside a Moonlit Stream 209
Beside an Open Fireplace 86, 360
Beside the Rio Tonto 389
Bess, You Is My Woman Now 193
Bessie's Blues 191
The Best Is Yet To Come 259
The Best Things in Life 183
The Best Things in Life Are Free 92, 189
The Best Time of the Day 221
Better Than Gold 183
Betty Coed 507
Between 18th and 19th on Chestnut Street 360, 414
Between the Devil and the Deep Blue Sea 13, 248
Betwixt and Between 484, 529
Bewildered 381, 540
Beyond the Blue Horizon 181, 404, 542
Beyond the Purple Hills 240, 241
Beyond the Shadow of a Doubt 253
Bibbidi Bobbidi Boo 206, 273, 274
The Big Apple 30, 119
The Big Bad Wolf Is Dead 48, 220
Big Boy 5
Big Boy Blue 256, 494
The Big Brass Band from Brazil 199, 458
Big Butter and Egg Man 137, 432
Big Chief DeSota 391
Big Chief Swing It 327
Big City Blues 70, 157, 326
The Big Crash from China 25
Big Foot Ham 334
Big Movie Show in the Sky 95
The Big Noise from Winnetka 24, 171
Big Spender 128
Big Tom 25
Big Town 460
Bigger and Better Than Ever 137
Bilbao Song 533
Bill 173, 550
Billy (For When I Walk) 151
Billy and I 517
A Bird in a Gilded Cage 515
Bird on the Wing 170
A Bird's Eye View of My Old Kentucky Home 235
Birds of a Feather 510
Birmingham Bertha 9
Birmingham Breakdown 116
Birmingham Jailhouse 122
Birth of the Blues 39, 92, 189
Bittersweet Rag 476
Bixology 26
Black and Blue 36, 390, 520
Black and Tan Fantasy 116
Black Bottom 39, 92, 189
Black, Brown and Beige 116
Black Coffee 456, 530
The Black Hand Rag 354
Black Jazz 146
Black Lace 129
Black Moonlight 73
Black Velvet 334
Black-Eyed Susan Brown 206
Blame It On a Dream 209
Blame It On My Last Affair 345
Blame It On My Youth 191, 193, 262
Blame My Absent Minded Heart 485
Blazin' 432
Bless Your Heart 103, 481
Blondy 135

Blood Count 481
Blossoms on Broadway 406
The Blossoms on the Bough 459
Blow, Blow, Blow 469
Blow Hot and Heavy 336, 406
Blowin' Up a Storm 185
Blue (And Broken Hearted) 62, 174, 261
Blue Again 127
Blue and Sentimental 23, 79, 273
The Blue Angel 260
Blue Champagne 527
Blue Danube Waltz 136
Blue Evening 221
Blue Eyed Sally 409
Blue Eyes 400
Blue Fantasy 52
Blue Fool 178
Blue Hawaii 386, 406
Blue Hoosier Blues 137
Blue Hours 244
Blue Interlude 57
Blue Italian Waters 531
Blue Jazz 146
Blue Lament 190
Blue Lou 429
Blue Lovebird 235
Blue Melody 486
Blue Minor 430
Blue Mist 431
Blue Moon in the Sky 312, 315
Blue Moonlight 486
Blue Orchids 55
Blue Prelude 190, 220
Blue Rain 510
Blue River 41, 323
Blue Romance 374
Blue Serge 117
Blue Shadows 10, 244, 245
Blue Shadows and White Gardenias 362
The Blue Skirt Waltz 366
Blue Sky Avenue 71, 290
Blue, Turning Grey over You 390, 520
Blueberry Hill 419, 476
Bluebird of Happiness 191
The Bluebirds Are Singing a Blues Song 468
Bluebirds in the Moonlight 407
Blues Are Brewin' 11
The Blues Country Style 274
Blues for Jane 469
Blues in My Heart 57, 325
Blues in the Night 14, 316
Blues in Thirds 202
Blues Is the Night 131
The Blues Made Me Feel This Way 430
Blues on Parade 190
A Blues Serenade 366, 460
The Bluest Word I Know Is "Lonesome" 343
Bluin' the Blues 360
Bob White 177, 316
Body and Soul 161, 162, 191, 192, 438
Bojangles of Harlem 127
Bolero at the Savoy 334
Bon Voyage (To Your Ship of Dreams) 166
Boneyard Shuffle 55
Bonnie's Boogie 461
Boo Hoo 191, 274, 275, 280
Boogie Woogie Bugle Boy 388
Boog-It 364
Book at My Bedside 413
Boots and Saddle 380, 431
Born to Be Blue 502
Born to Be Kissed 94, 439
Born to Love 571
Born to Swing 344
Bottom Dollar 337
Boulevard of Broken Dreams 107, 523
Boulevard of Memories 275

Bounce Me, Brother, With a Solid Four 389
A Bowl of Chop Suey and Youey 29, 372
The Bowling Song 498, 499
A Boy and a Girl Were Dancing 153
The Boy Friend 40
A Boy in Khaki, a Girl in Lace 348
A Boy Named Lem 497
The Boy Next Door 32, 304
Boy Scout in Switzerland 443
The Boy With the Wistful Eyes 389
Boys Will Be Boys 144
Brass Buttons and Epaulets 471
Brave Man 272
Brazil 26
Break the News to Mother 183
Breakaway 70, 326
Breakin' In a Pair of Shoes 473
Breeze (Blow My Baby Back to Me) 151, 178
The Breeze (That's Bringin' My Honey Back to Me) 264, 420, 468
The Breeze Is My Sweetheart 459
Breezin' Along 336, 406
Breezin' Along with the Breeze 148, 463, 542
The Bride Comes Home 255, 445
Bright Eyes 180, 221, 467, 534
Brighter Than the Sun 351
Bring Back My Daddy to Me 322, 502
Broadcasting House 380
Broadway 309
Broadway Melody 40
Broadway Rose 536
Broadway Stomp 370
Broken Hearted 92, 189
The Broken Record 136
Brother 498
Brother, Can You Spare a Dime? 156, 181
Brother, Just Laugh It Off 387, 440
Brown Eyes 173, 180
Brown Eyes (Why Are You Blue?) 41, 320
Brown Gal 15
Brown October Ale 467
Brussels Hustle 202
Bubbles 275
Bubbles in the Wine 277
Bubbling Over 336, 397, 406
Buckle Down 32
Buckle Down Winsocki 304
Buddha 378
Buddy Bolden's Blues 334
Buds Won't Bud 14
Buenos Noches Mi Amor 319
Buffoon 68
Bugle Blues 427
Bugle Call Blues 371, 436
Bugle Call Rag 371, 373, 435, 436
Build a Little Home 106
Bumble Bee Stomp 187
Bumpy Weather over Newark 443
A Bundle of Beats 99
Bundle of Blue 239
A Burmese Ballet 374
Burning Sands 319
Business Man's Bounce 443
Busy as a Bee 325, 427, 459
Busy Doin' Nothing 45
But Beautiful 45, 510
But Definitely 154, 397
But I Did 325
But I Do Mind If Ya Don't 345
But It Didn't Mean a Thing 274
Buttercup 185
Button, Button 34
Button Up Your Overcoat 92, 189
Buttons and Bows 121, 271
Buy a Kiss 220
Buy Buy for Baby 324
B'Wanga 374
By a Campfire 126
By a Rippling Stream 368, 369
By a Waterfall 233
By a Wishing Well 155

By Jupiter 162
By My Side 158, 159, 266, 267, 282
By Myself 94, 393, 440
By the Beautiful Sea 56
By the Fireside 351
By the Light of the Silvery Moon 112, 288
By the River of the Roses 44, 490
By the River Sainte Marie 261, 523
By the Sign of the Rose 126, 260
By the Sweat of My Brow 287
By the Way 338
Bye Bye Baby 484
Bye Bye Blackbird 94
Bye Bye Blues 158, 159, 281
Bye Bye, Pretty Baby 172
Bye-Bye 272
Bye-Bye Blackbird 188
Bye-Lo 368
Bye-Lo-Bye Lullaby 447

A Cabana in Havana 446
Cabin in the Cotton 365, 367
Cabin in the Sky 254
California, Here I Come 90, 91, 227, 322, 323
California Orange Blossom 333
Call It a Day 312, 315
Call Me Darling 266
Call Me Irresponsible 50, 510
Call of the Canyon 198, 332
Call of the Freaks 424
Calling Sweetheart for You 446
Calliope 489
Calm After the Storm 315
Calypso Blues 145
Camel Hop 547
The Camel Walk 287
Camp Meetin' Time 546
The Campbells Are Swinging 64
Campus Crawl 371
Campus Moon 468
Can I Help It? 84, 331, 510
Can This Be Love 488
Canadian Capers 46
Canadian Sunset 194
Canal St. Blues 357
Cancel the Flowers 298, 444
Candied Sweets 370, 520
Candlelights 26
Candy 80, 251
Cane Bottom Chair 303
Cannery Walk 202
Can't Get Indiana off My Mind 55
Can't Get Mississippi off My Mind 9
Can't Get Out of This Mood 278, 308
Can't Help Lovin' That Man 173
Can't We Be Friends 488
Can't We Talk It Over? 524, 570
Can't Write the Words 302
Can't You See 7, 505
Captains of the Clouds 14
Caravan 325, 495
Carefree 186
Careless 211, 231, 383
Careless Hands 199, 458
Careless Love 176
Carelessly 240, 241
Caresses 331
Carioca 115, 235, 564
Carle's Boogie 52
Carnegie Hall 304
Carnival in Caroline 344
Carolina In the Morning 96, 234
Carolina Moon 44, 83
Carolina Shout 226
Carrie Mae Blues 392
Casa Loma Stomp 146
Casbah Blues 387
Castle of Dreams 305, 493
The Cat and the Canary 271
Cat Ballou 80
Cathedral of Peace 394
Cavernism 201, 334
Cecilia 105, 423
C'est Vous (It's You) 400
Chain Gang 172
The Champ 99

The Champagne Waltz 71, 103, 355
Change Partners 393
Changes 96, 400
Changing My Ambitions 501
Chanson 138, 479
Chanson de Marie Antoinette 458
Chansonette 139, 479
The Chant 334, 449, 476
Chant of the Jungle 40, 135
Chant of the Swamp 239
Chant of the Weed 392
Chantez Les Bas (Sing 'Em Low) 176
Chapel in the Valley 395
Characteristic Blues 464
Charade 294
Charleston 226, 287
Charlestown Chuckles 68
Charley, My Boy 235
The Charm of You 483
Charmaine 378
Chasing Shadows 83, 461
Chattanooga Choo Choo 523
Chatterbox 402
Cheatin' On Me 378, 561
Cheer Up and Smile 319
Cheerful Little Earful 417, 522
Cheese and Crackers 511
Chelsea Bridge 481
Cherie 30
Cherokee 213, 352
Cherry 392
Cherry Blossom Lane 442
Cherry Blossoms on Capitol Hill 325, 459
Cherry Pink and Apple Blossom White 80
Cherry Point 185
The Chesapeake & Ohio 459
Cheyenne (Shy Ann) 546
Chi-Baba Chi-Baba 80, 206, 273
Chicago 131
Chicago on Parade 372
Chicago Style 45, 510
Chili Bean 38, 515
Chilly and Cold 500
Chimes Blues 357
Chinatown, My Chinatown 222, 441
Chinnin' and Chattin' with May 125
Chiquita 147, 529
Chirp Chirp 32
Chloe 77, 235
Chocolate Whiskey and Vanilla Gin 339
Choo'n Gum 328
Christmas Eve 35
Christmas in Killarney 533
Christmas Night in Harlem 365
The Christmas Song 501
Christmas Spell 364
Christopher Columbus 391
Chu Chin Chow 212
Church St. Sobbin' Blues 548
Cigarette 188
Cincinnati 309
Cincinnati Dancing Pig 264
Cinderella 273
The Cinderella Work Song 206, 273
Circus 427
The Circus Is Coming to Town 163
Civilization (Bongo, Bongo, Bongo) 198, 458
Clamback for Saxes 99
Clap Hands! Here Comes Charley! 286, 323, 417
Clarinet Marmalade 360
Clear Out of This World 107
Cleopatra 493
Climbing the Stairway of Love 448
Climbing up the Ladder of Love 245
Cling to Me 44, 261
Close As Pages in a Book 128, 416
Close Enough for Love 295
Close to Me 89, 265
Close to You 206
Close Your Eyes 368
Clothes Lines Ballet 520
Clouds 97

Coal Dust on the Fiddle 145
Cobblestones 378
Cocktails for Two 73, 227
Cocoanut Grove 362
Coffee in the Morning 107
The Coffee Song (They've Got an Awful Lot of Coffee in Brazil) 198
College November 384
Collegiate 219
Collegiate Love 102
The Color of Love 427
Colorado Is My Home 549
Comanche War Dance 352
Come After Breakfast 466
Come Back, Sweet Papa 425
Come Back to Georgia 195
Come Back to Me 254
Come Dance with Me 50
Come Easy Go Easy Love 55
Come Fly with Me 50, 510
Come, Josephine, in My Flying Machine 41, 130
Come On and Make Whoopie 208
Come On, Papa 422
Come Rain or Come Shine 15, 316
Come Up and See Me Sometime 11
Come West, Little Girl, Come West 96
Comes Love 473, 497
Comin' On 450
Comme Ci, Comme Ca 251
Companionate Blues 371
Compromise 491
Concentratin' 520
Concentratin' (On You) 390
Concert in the Park 134
Concerto for Clarinet 450
Concerto for Cootie 116, 426
Concerto in Rhythm 486
Confidentially 107, 316
Conga Bravo 495
Congratulations 376, 473, 538
Connecticut 304
Constantly 466, 510
The Continental 71, 289
Contrasts 98
The Convict and the Bird 104
Cooking Breakfast for the One I Love 385, 499
Cool and Groovy 430
Cool Head Main Thing 362
Cool Tango 356
Copenhagen 309
Copper Colored Gal 83
Copyright 1950 443
Coquette 235, 280, 392
Coral Reef 185
Coral Sea 40
Corn Silk 244
The Corps 181
Cosi-Cosa 238
Cottage by the Moon 380, 431, 540
A Cottage for Sale 68, 411, 412
Cotton Pickers Congregation 374
Could Ja 129
Could You Pass in Love? 155
Couldn't You Fall for Me? 398
Count Off 209
Count Your Blessings 167
Counting the Days 574
Country Boy Blues 412
Country Fair 502
Country Style 45
Cover Me Up with Sunshine 94, 188
Cover Me Up With the Sunshine of Virginia 265, 322
Cow Cow Boogie 57, 88, 389
The Crave 334
Crazy 'Bout My Gal 371
Crazy Feet 327
Crazy Fingers 209
Crazy, He Calls Me 427
Crazy in the Heart 544
Crazy People 261, 330
Crazy Rhythm 49, 323
Crazy She Calls Me 458, 459
The Crazy Things You Do When You're in Love 529

Crazy with Love 149, 456
Crazy Words—Crazy Tune 5, 562
Creepy Weepy 168
Creole Love Call 116
Crew Cut 160
Crosby, Columbo and Vallee 106
Cross over the Bridge 27
Cross Patch 255, 445
Cross Your Fingers 83, 488
Cross Your Heart 144, 303
Crosstown 58, 462
Crumbun 450
Cry Baby Blues 265, 322
Cry, Baby, Cry 447
Cryin' for the Carolines 265, 522, 567
Crying for the Moon 69
Crying My Heart Out for You 209, 225
Crying Myself to Sleep 246, 534
Cuban Love Song 480
Cuckoo in the Clock 97, 316
Cuddle Up a Little Closer 179, 180, 210
A Cup of Coffee a Sandwich and You 106, 323, 417
Curiosity 251
Curly Top 188
The Curse of an Aching Heart 375
Cute 185
The Cute Little Things You Do 179
Cute Little Two by Four 480
Cutie Pie 423

D.A. Blues 424
Daddy 309
Daddy Has a Sweetheart and Mother Is Her Name 472
Daddy Long Legs 422
Daddy, You've Been a Mother to Me 132
Daddy's Boy 527
Daddy's Little Girl 287
Damn the Torpedoes 115, 157
Dance Away the Night 492
Dance Hall Doll 101
Dance Little Lady 74
Dance of the Lame Duck 146
Dance of the Paper Dolls 437
Dance With a Dolly 447
Dance Your Way to Paradise 157
Dancing Butterfly 369
Dancing Fool 467, 470
Dancing in the Dark 94, 439
Dancing in the Dawn 407
Dancing on a Dime 277
Dancing On a Rooftop 533
Dancing On the Moon 497
Dancing the Devil Away 422
Dancing to the Hop 209
Dancing Under the Stars 362
Dancing with Tears in My Eyes 44, 106
Danger, Love at Work 155
Dangerous Nan McGrew 149
Dapper Dan 38, 515
Darby Hicks (Gotta Lotta Hot Licks) 413
Dardanella 27, 131
Dark Clouds 430
Dark Rapture 430
Darkness 201
Darkness on the Delta 272, 273, 489
Darktown Strutters Ball 37
Darlene 427
Darling 119
Darling, Not Without You 453
Darn that Dream 84, 510
The Daughter of Peggy O'Neill 498
Davenport Blues 26
Dawn 274
Day after Day 161, 200
The Day After Forever 510
Day By Day 50, 65, 478, 538
Day Dream 481
Day Dreaming 65, 235, 316
Day Dreams Come True at Night 230

The Day I Let You Get Away 255, 445
Day In Day Out 33
The Day Isn't Long Enough 51
The Day That the Circus Left Town 471
The Day You Came Along 73, 227
The Day You Said Goodbye to Old Hawaii 319
Daybreak 3, 167
The Days of Wine and Roses 294, 316
De Cake Walk Queen 467
Dear! Dear! Dear! 427
Dear Heart 294
Dear Hearts and Gentle People 199
Dear Mr. Gable 305, 330
Dear Old Daddy Long-legs 515
Dear Old Rose 322
Dear Old Southland 75, 257
Dear One 133
Dearest (You're the Nearest to My Heart) 8, 9, 81
Dearest Darling 403, 533
Dearie 199
Dearie (You're Much Older Than I) 296
Death Valley Suite 168
Debutante Waltz 494
Dedicated to You 60, 573
'Deed I Do 203, 418
Deep Dawn 209
Deep Forest 202, 391
Deep Henderson 374, 419
Deep in a Dream 84, 510
Deep in My Heart 564
Deep in the Arms of Love 217
Deep in the Blue 62
Deep in the Heart of the South 494
Deep Night 186, 360, 507
Deep Purple 89, 366
Deep River 75, 413
Dein ist Mein Ganzes Herz 467
Delicado 257
Delightful Delirium 35
Delta Bound 195
Delta Serenade 116
Der Fuehrer's Face 518
Desert Sands 469
The Desert Song 173, 180, 415
Devil in the Moon 196, 325
Diamonds Are a Girl's Best Friend 485
Diane 378
Did Anyone Call 459
Did I Remember? 3, 97
Did 'Ja Ever 252
Did My Heart Beat, Did I Fall in Love? 322
Did You Ever Get That Feeling in the Moonlight? 437, 477
Did You Ever See a Dream Walking? 154
Did You Mean It? 94, 164, 283
Did You Mean What You Said Last Night? 368, 369
Die Parade der Holzsoldaten 286
Diga Diga Doo 127, 307
Dilly Dally 48, 220
Dim the Harbor Lights 69
A Dime and a Dollar! 272
Dimples and Cherry Cheeks 356
Dinah 8, 265, 566, 567
Ding Dong the Witch is Dead 14
Ding-Dong Boogie 309
Dinner at Eight 127, 307
Dinner Music for a Pack of Hungry Cannibals 443
Dip Your Brush in the Sunshine 225
Dipper Mouth Blues 309, 357
The Dipsy Doodle 63
The Dirty Dozen 80
Dirty Hands, Dirty Face 330
Discontented Blues 435
Dixie Danny 394
Dixie Dreams 505
Dixie Highway 234
Dixie Is Dixie Once More 502

Dixie Lee 195
Dixie Vagabond 96, 293
The Dixieland Band 177
Dixieland Detour 99
Dixieland Rendezvous 356
Dixieland Shuffle 171
The Dixieland Volunteers 422
Dizzy Fingers 67
Dizzy Spells 151
Do It Again 90
Do Nothin' Till You Hear from Me 116, 426
Do Something 161, 473
Do the Buckaroo 406
Do the New York 356
Do Unto Others 362
Do Ya Love Me? 529
Do You Believe in Fairy Tales? 80, 256
Do You Care? 117, 383
Do You Ever Think of Me? 46
Do You Know the Way to San Jose 79
Do You Know What It Means to Miss New Orleans? 11, 84
Do You Know Why? 45, 345
Do You Love Me 422
Do You Remember Last Night? 325
Doctor Blues 424
Doctor Jazz 358
Doctor, Lawyer and Indian Chief 55, 530
Doctor Rhythm 331
Dodging the Dean 64
Does the Moon Shine Through the Tall Pine? 571
Does the Spearmint Lose Its Flavor on the Bedpost Overnight? 416
Does Your Heart Beat for Me? 332, 366
Dog on the Piano 449
Dogtown Blues 171
Doin' the New Low Down 127, 307
Doin' the Raccoon 72, 244
Doin' the Susie-Q 83
Doin' the Uptown Lowdown 153, 396
Doin' Things 511
Doll Dance 40
Dolly 564
Dolly Mine 424
The Dolly Sisters 56
Dolores 11, 277
Don'cha Go 'Way Mad 334
The Donkey Serenade 139, 479, 480
Don't Be Afraid to Tell Your Mother 166, 501
Don't Be Late In the Morning 311, 313, 314
Don't Be Like That 377, 497
Don't Be Mean to Me, Baby 258
Don't Be So Mean, Baby 20
Don't Be That Way 150, 366, 393, 430
Don't Blame Me 127, 307
Don't Break the Heart That Loves You 310
Don't Bring Lulu 39, 188, 417
Don't Count Your Kisses 293
Don't Cross Your Fingers 303
Don't Cross Your Fingers, Cross Your Heart 451
Don't Cry 247
Don't Cry, Baby, Don't Cry 377
Don't Cry, Sweetheart 333
Don't Ever Be Afraid to Go Home 199
Don't Ever Change 170, 175, 203
Don't Ever Leave Me 173
Don't Forget to Remember 133
Don't Gamble with Romance 494
Don't Get Around Much Any More 116, 426
Don't Go to Strangers 122, 296
Don't Let It Bother You 154, 396
Don't Let Julia Fool Ya 239
Don't Let Me Be Misunderstood 299
Don't Let That Moon Get Away 45, 331

Don't Let This Waltz Mean Goodbye 319
Don't Let Your Love Go Wrong 47, 225, 541
Don't Make Me Laugh 462
Don't Mention Love to Me 127, 263
Don't Play That Song 356
Don't Rain on My Parade 484
Don't Save Your Love 471
Don't Say Aloha When I Go 77
Don't Say You're Sorry Again 537
Don't Sit Under the Apple Tree 473, 497
Don't Smoke in Bed 412
Don't Sweetheart Me 137
Don't Take Your Love From Me 345
Don't Tell Her What Happened to Me 189
Don't Tempt Me 471
Don't Think It Ain't Been Charming 316
Don't Throw Cold Water on the Flame of Love 222, 348
Don't Try Your Jive on Me 430
Don't Wait for the Hearse to Take You to Church 394
Don't Wait Too Long 466
Don't Wake Me Up, Let Me Dream 527
Don't Wake Up My Heart 266, 322
Don't Worry 'Bout Me 33, 250
Don't You Know I Care? 80
Don't You Know or Don't You Care? 123, 233
Don't You Love Me Anymore? 80, 207, 274
Doo Dah Blues 418
Doo Wacka Doo 143
Doodle Doo Doo 239, 476
A Doolin' Song 259
The Door of My Dreams 139, 479
Dorsey Dervish 99
Dorsey Stomp 99
Double Shuffle 384
Double Trouble 385, 405
Down a Carolina Lane 365, 367
Down Among the Sheltering Palms 36
Down Among the Sugar Cane 287, 466
Down at the Old Bull and Bush 516
Down by the River 76
Down, Down, Down 392
Down Georgia Way 354
Down in Honky Tonk Town 466
Down in Jungle Town 287
Down in Sleepy Hollow Lane 400
Down in the Old Meadow Lane 547
Down on the Farm 516
Down South 96
Down South Camp Meetin' 187
Down t' Uncle Bill's 55
Down the Old Church Aisle 368
Down the Old Ox Road 73, 227
Down the River of Golden Dreams 246, 455
Down the Road A-Piece 388
Down Where the Cotton Blossoms Grow 474, 516
Down Where the Trade Winds Blow 362
Down Where the Wurzburger Flows 515
Down with Love 181
Downhearted 296
Downstream Drifter 114
Dream 316
Dream a Little Dream of Me 235
Dream Along With Me (I'm On My Way To a Star) 459
Dream Awhile 316
Dream, Dream, Dream 366
A Dream Is a Wish Your Heart Makes 80, 206, 273
Dream Kisses 222
Dream Lover 165, 434
Dream of Me 195

Dream Train 347
Dream Valley 44, 240, 241
The Dreamer 278, 440
Dreamer With a Penny 402
Dreamer's Cloth 427
Dreamer's Holiday 142, 528
Dreams Are a Dime a Dozen 59, 339
Dreams of Old Hawaii 477
Dreamsville 272
Dreamy Blues 116
Dreamy Lullaby 52
Dreamy Melody 341
Dreamy Monterey 372
Drifting and Dreaming 147, 509
Driftwood on the River 247
Drink It Down 406
Drinking Again 491
Drop Me Off in Harlem 241
Drums in My Heart 192, 565
Dry Bones 361, 414
Dry Martini 370
Dry Your Tears 195
Duerme 425
Dumbell 68
Dusk 116
Dusk in Upper Sandusky 63, 99
Dusky Dudes 441
Dusky Stevedore 224, 390
Dust Off That Old Pianna 302
Dusty Road 395

Eadie Was a Lady 40
An Earful of Music 97, 235
Early Autumn 191, 316
Early Bird 327, 378
Early in the Mornin' 357
Early Morning Blues 374
Early to Bed 468
East of the Sun 35
East Side of Heaven 45, 331
East St. Louis Toodle-Oo 115
Easter Sunday With You Brother 499
Easy Come, Easy Go 161, 193
Easy Living 386
Easy Melody 69
Easy to Say 450
Ebb Tide 406, 459
The Echo of a Song 310, 313
Eeny Meeny Miney Mo 292, 316
The Egg and I 228, 423
Egyptian Barn Dance 443
Egyptian Ella 102, 103
Eight Bars in Search of a Melody 213
Either It's Love or It Isn't 402
Elder Eatmore Sermons 402
Eleanor 306
Elenita 327
Eleven More Months and Ten More Days 124
Elmer's Tune 141, 231
Emaline 365, 367
Emily 295
The Emperior Waltz 45
Emperor Jones 559
An Empty Ballroom 64
Empty Bed Blues 225
An Empty Glass 540
Empty Saddles 197
Enchanted Forest 443
Endie 11
Ending with a Kiss 492
Endless Love 338
Endlessly 242
Englewood 424
Enjoy Yourself (It's Later Than You Think) 290, 458
Ennui 317
Erratique 317
Escape to Yesterday 312, 313
Evangeline 228
Evelina 14, 181
Evenin' 365
An Evening in June 255, 445
Evening Star 7
Every Day's a Holiday 73
Every Little Bit Helps 132
Every Little Moment 127
Every Little Movement 180, 210

Every Little Thing You Do 179
Every Minute of the Hour 240, 241, 473
Every Now and Then 453, 461
Every Once in Awhile 94, 188
Every Single Little Tingle of My Heart 462
Every Tub 23
Everybody Calls It Swing 524
Everybody Loves My Baby 363, 548
Everybody Loves My Gal 1
Everybody Rag with Me 234
Everybody Shimmies Now 537
Everybody Shuffle 57, 209
Everybody Step 436
Everybody Wants a Key to My Cellar 24
Everybody's Gone Crazy Bout the Doggone Blues 76
Everybody's Laughing 356
Everyone Says "I Love You" 422
Everyone's a Child at Christmas 303
Everything Depends On You 202
Everything Happens to Me 2, 87
Everything I Have Is Yours 3, 253
Everything Is Different Nowadays 472
Everything Is Hotsy Totsy Now 306
Everything is Okey Doakey 275
Everything Is Peaches Down in Georgia 4, 322
Everything Stops for Tea 206, 457
Everything Will Be All Right 501
Everything You Said Came True 134, 136
Everything's Been Done Before 3, 243
Everything's Coming Up Roses 484
Everything's Gonna Be All Right 8
Everything's in Rhythm with My Heart 149, 206, 456
Everything's Made for Love 452, 497
Everything's Movin' Too Fast 20, 258
Everytime I Meet You, Baby 338
Everywhere You Go 132, 152, 451
Ev'ry Day 123, 233
Ev'ry Night About This Time 331
Ev'ry Time 32, 304
Ev'rybody Loves You 269
Ev'rybody's Laughing 260
Exactly Like You 127, 307
Except with You 407
Experience 45
The Eyes of Love 427
The Eyes of the World Are on You 260

The Fable of the Rose 337, 394
A Face in the Crowd 571
Face to Face 370
A Faded Summer Love 25
Fair Thee Well, Annabelle 560
Faithful Forever 407
Faithfully Yours 283
Falling 125
Falling in Love Again 208, 260
Falling Leaves 52, 79
Falling Star 562
Far Away 352
Far Away Island 449
Far Away Places 251
The Far Green Hills of Home 69
Fare Thee Well to Harlem 177, 316
Fare-Thee-Well Dear Alma Mater 338
Farewell Blues 299, 435
Farewell, My Lovely 440
Farewell to Arms 461, 559
Farewell to Ebb 99
The Farmer Took Another Load Away, Hay Hay 356
Fascinating You 497, 499
Fatal Fascination 492
The Fatha Jumps 202
Fatha Steps In 202
Feather Your Nest 36, 223, 239
Feelin' High and Happy 33

Feelin' No Pain 270
Feeling the Spirit 424
Femininity 272
Feudin' and Fightin' 107
Fidgety Feet, Original Dixieland One Step 359
Fiesta 48, 430, 539
Fiesta in Blue 334
Fiesta in Brass 334
Fifty Million Frenchmen Can't Be Wrong 131
Fight On Michigan State 31
Fill Your Glasses with Kisses 175
Find Me 402
Fine and Dandy 488
A Fine Romance 127
The Finger of Suspicion 297
Fire Down Below 526
Firefly 259
First, Last, and Always 83
The First Time I Saw You 455, 560
Fishin' for the Moon 299, 444
Fit as a Fiddle 135, 149, 205
Five Foot Two, Eyes of Blue 188, 265, 566
Five Minutes More 50, 485
The Five O'Clock Whistle 141, 337
Five Piece Band 25
Flamenco Love 517
Flamin' Mamie 419
Flamingo 170
Flany Doodle Swing 201
Flashes 26
The Flat Foot Floogie 161, 393
A Flat in Montmartre 378
Flea on a Spree 381
The Flight of the Jitterbug 392
Flip 511
The Flippity Flop 406
Flirtation Walk 559
Flop 511
A Flower Is a Lovesome Thing 481
Flower of Dawn 84, 332
Flower of Love 423
Flowers for Madame 310, 347, 497
The Fly Flew Faster Than the Flea 451
Flyin' Home 150
Flying Down to Rio 115, 235, 564
Foggy Bottom 547
Follow Me 238
Follow the Band 338
Follow the Swallow to Hide-away Hollow 94, 188, 416, 531
Follow Your Heart 435
Following the Sun Around 493
Fond of You 144
Fool That I Am 316, 460
Fooled 491
Foolin' Myself 256, 494
Foolish Heart 341
Fools Rush In 33
For All We Know 72, 265
For Me and My Gal 261, 319
For Old Time's Sake 183
For Sale 211
For Sentimental Reasons 461
For the First Time (I've Fallen in Love) 497
For Tonight 142
For What? 510
For Whom the Bell Tolls 242
Forever Amber 316
Forever and a Day 304, 489
Forever and Ever 484, 562
Forgive Me 562
Forsaken Again 192, 336
Forty-Second Street 523
Four Months, Three Weeks, Two Days, One Hour Blues 502
Four Once More 151
The Four Rivers 115
Four Walls 105, 227, 417
Four Winds and the Seven Seas 79
Fractious Fingering 520
Frantic Atlantic 392
Freckle Face, You're Beautiful 280
Freckles 5

Freddy the Freshman 358
Free 486
Free for All 2
Free Wheeling 449
Frenesi 425
Freshman Hop 370, 371
Friday Night at the Hartys 352
Friendless Blues 176
The Friendly Mountains 45
Friends 432
Frim Fram Sauce 122
Frog-i-More Rag 334
From Monday On 21
From Now On 135
From One 'Til Two 506
From the Top of Your Head 154
From the Vine Came the Grape 540
From Your Heart to Mine 179
Fuddle Dee Duddle 497
The Fuddy Daddy Watchmaker 278
A Full Moon and Empty Heart 163
Fun to be Fooled 14
Funny Melody 117
The Funny Old Hills 386, 407
The Funny Thing Called Love 494
Futile Frustration 334
Futuristic Rhythm 307
Fuzzy Wuzzy 103, 207, 274

Gabriel Is Blowing His Horn 157
The Gaby Glide 202
A Gal in Calico 440
Gandy Dancer 119
Gandy Dancer's Ball 538
Garden of the Moon 107
Gary, Indiana 549
Gather Lip Rouge While You May 406
The Gaucho Serenade 58, 462
G'Bye now 121, 271
Gee, Baby, Ain't I Good to You 390, 392
Gee! But I Hate to Go Home Alone 151, 179
Gee, But I'd Like to Make You Happy 451
Gee, But It's Great to Meet a Friend From Your Home Town 502
Gee, But You're Swell 20, 497
The Gentle Grifter 450
Georgette 39
Georgia 223
Georgia Jubilee 150
Georgia on My Mind 54, 55
Georgia Rockin' Chair 132
Georgianna 52
Get Happy 13, 248
Get Me to the Church on Time 279
Get Out and Get Under the Moon 222, 451, 496
Get Out of Town 393
Get Out Those Old Records 275
Get the Money 407
Gettin' My Boots 183
Getting Some Fun Out of Life 44, 261
Getting the Beautiful Girls 524
Getting to Know You 174
A Ghost of a Chance 525, 570
The Ghost of Smokey Joe 33
Ghost of the Freaks 424
The Ghost That Never Walked 441
GI Jive 316
Gigi 259, 279
Gimme a Little Kiss, Will Ya, Huh? 376, 504
Ginger Brown 287
Girl Friend of the Whirling Dervish 316
The Girl from Jones Beach 299, 444
The Girl I Left Behind Me 261, 321
The Girl in My Dreams Tries to Look Like You 117
The Girl in the Little Green Hat 398
A Girl in Your Arms 157, 536
A Girl Like You 13
A Girl Like You, a Boy Like Me 217
The Girl Next Door 156, 338

Girl Talk 185
The Girl Without a Name 486
Give a Broken Heart a Break 133
Give a Little Credit to Your Dad 502, 513
Give Me a Heart to Sing To 525, 526, 570
Give Me a Kiss for Tomorrow 129
Give Me a Moment Please 406
Give Me a Night in June 136
Give Me a Smile and a Kiss 175
Give Me Just a Little Bit of Your Love 364
Give Me Liberty or Give Me Love 387, 406
Give Me My Saddle 389
Give Me the Moonlight, Give Me the Girl 515
Give Me the Simple Life 33, 422
Give Me Time 544
Give Me Your Affection, Honey 42
Give My Regards to Broadway 65
Give Trouble the Air 406
Glad Rag Doll 5, 101, 562
Glad to Be Me 183
Gloomy Sunday 265
The Glory of Love 197
Glow Worm 316
Go Fly a Kite 331
Go Slow 75
Go South 336
Gobs of Love 122
God's Rain 357
Goin' Back to Brooklyn 221
Goin' Nowhere Fast 461
Goin' Places 511
Going, Going, Gone 25
Going Harlem in Havana 372
Going My Way 45, 510
Going Out the Back Way 204
The Gold Digger's Song 106, 107
The Golden Dawn 69
Golden Day 341
Golden Earrings 121, 570
Golden Gate 105, 227, 324
The Golden Touch 52
Golden Wedding Day 239
Golden Wedding Waltz 356
The Golden Years 63
Gone 235, 267
Gone Fishin' 241
Gone For Ever 313
Gone With the Dawn 486
Gone With the Wind 289, 560
Gone with the Wind, Tara's Theme 80
Gonna Get a Girl 263
The Good Earth 185
Good Enough to Keep 151
Good Evenin' 356, 444, 445
Good Evening, Caroline 515
Good for Nothin' 544
Good for Nothin' But Love 510
Good for Nothing, Joe 33
Good, Good, Good 130, 402
Good Little Bad Little You 161, 473
Good Morning Blues 23
Good Morning, Carrie 287, 466, 515
Good Morning Glory 154, 396
Good Night Germany 322
Goodbye 220
Goodbye Blues 307, 317
Goodbye Boys 474
Goodbye Broadway, Hello France 24, 80
Goodbye Girls, I'm Through 148
Goodbye, John 544
Goodbye, Little Girl, Goodbye 64, 111, 356
Goodbye, My Dreams, Goodbye 531
Goodbye, My Lady Love 212
Goodnight 154
Goodnight, Angeline 464
Goodnight Kisses 422
Goodnight Ladies 509, 546
Goodnight, Little Angel 333
Goodnight Little Girl of My Dreams 496

Goodnight, Lovely Little Lady 396
Goodnight, My Love 154, 310, 397
Goodnight, My Someone 549
Goodnight Sweetheart 234, 351, 546
Goodnight, Vienna 379
Goodnight Wherever You Are 403, 533
Goody Goodbye 58, 462
Goody-Goody 292, 316
Goofus 235, 244
The Goona Goo 569
Gorgeous 83
Got a Bran' New Suit 94, 440
Got a Date with An Angel 164
Got Me Doin' Things 154, 396
Got My Mind on Music 155
Got No Time 33
Got the Bench, Got the Park (But I Haven't Got You) 263, 453
Got the Gate on the Golden Gate 502
Got the Jitters 274, 418, 529
Got the Moon in My Pocket 45
Got the South in My Soul 570
Gotta Be This or That 465
Gotta Feelin' for You 503
Gotta Get a Girl 229, 235
Gotta Get Some Shut-eye 97
Gotta Great Big Date with a Little Bitta Girl 432, 497, 499
Grand Canyon Suite 167
Grand Central Gateway 99
Grand Central Stations 533
Grandfather's Clock 68
Grandpa's Spells 334
Great Day 114, 564
A Grecian Melody 352
Green Eyes 147
The Green Leaves of Summer 531
Green Pastures 390
Green-up Time 533
Grievin' 480
Guess I'll Hang My Tears Out to Dry 484, 485
Guess There's an End to Everything 69
Guess Who? 136, 253
Guess Who's in Town 224
Guessing 529
Guilty 8, 9, 235, 542
Gulf Coast Blues 545
Gunfight at the OK Corral 526
Gypsy 290, 460
Gypsy Blues 464
Gypsy Fiddles 559
The Gypsy in My Soul 34, 219
Gypsy Love Song 189, 190, 467
A Gypsy Without a Song 153, 495

Hair of Gold, Eyes of Blue 466
Half a Mile Away from Home 369
Half a Mile to Honeysuckle Lane 468
Half Moon on the Hudson 471
Half-Caste Woman 74
Half-Way to Heaven 106, 360
Hallelujah 165, 404, 563
Hallelujah, Things Look Rosy Now 537
Hamlet Was a Melancholy Dane 441
A Handful of Keys 520
A Handful of Stars 257, 449
Hands Across the Table 365
Hang On to Love 315
Hang Out the Stars in Indiana 329, 555
Hang Your Head in Shame 344
Hang Your Heart on a Hickory Limb 331
The Hanging Tree 80
Hannah, Won't You Open That Door? 474
Happiness 356
Happiness Ahead 559
Happiness Bound 531
Happiness Is Just a Thing Called Joe 14
Happy and Contented 351
Happy and Satisfied 430

Happy as a Lark 531
Happy as the Day is Long 249
Happy Birthday to Love 134
Happy Days Are Here Again 5, 357, 398, 562
The Happy Farmer 443
Happy Feet 5, 562
Happy Go Lucky 422
Happy Go Lucky Lane 324
Happy Little Farmer 369
Happy New Year, Darling 303
Happy Nothing to You 357
Happy-Go-Lucky Local 117
Happy-Go-Lucky You 206
Harbor Lights 169
Harbor of My Heart 406, 565
Hard-Hearted Hannah (the Vamp of Savannah) 5, 561
Harlem Blues 176, 413
Harlem Butterfly 316
Harlem Fuss 520
Harlem Mood 57
Harlem Sandman 484
Harlem Twist 270
Harmonica Harry 25
Harrigan 65
Hasegawa General Store 538
Hassan the Man 184
Hasta Manana 494
Hat Check Girl 172
The Hat My Father Wore on St. Patrick's Day 442
Hats Off, Here Comes a Lady 369
Hats Off to MacArthur 437
Haunted Heart 94
Haunting Blues 48
Haunting Me 84, 337
Havana 35
Have a Heart 42, 253, 550
Have a Little Dream on Me 25, 335
Have a Little Faith in Me 265, 522, 567
Have You Ever Been in Heaven 256, 494
Have You Ever Been Lonely 89
Have You Ever Seen a Dream Walking 396
Have You Forgotten (the Thrill)? 405, 485
Have You Forgotten So Soon 191
Have You Got Any Castles, Baby? 316
Have Yourself a Merry Little Christmas 32, 304
Haven't Got a Worry 272
Havin' a Wonderful Wish 272
Havin' Myself a Time 407
Hawaii 80
Hawaii Calls 362
Hawaii My Island 362
Hawaiian Butterfly 432
Hawaiian Heat Wave 372
Hawaiian Paradise 361
Hawaiian War Chant 136, 349
Hawaiian Wedding Song 206
Hay Hay (Farmer Gray Took Another Load Away) 356
He Fought for a Cause He Thought Was Right 104
He Never Looked Better in His Life 427
Head over Heels in Love 155
Headin' for Louisville 323
Heading for Harlem 179
Heads You Do (And Tails You Don't) 370
Hear My Song, Violetta 119
Heard a Mocking Bird Sing (In California) 413
Heart and Soul 55, 277, 393
Heart Breaker 133
Heart of Love 532
Heart of Paris 366
Heart of Wetona 433
Heart to Heart 394
Heartaches 205, 246
Hearts Without Flowers 517
Heartsease 78

The Heather on the Hill 259
Heaven Can Wait 84, 510
Heaven Drops Her Curtain Down 339
Heaven Help This Heart of Mine 381, 431, 540
Heaven Only Knows 104, 481
Heavenly, Isn't It? 163
A Heavenly Party 128
He'd Have to Get Under—Get Out and Get Under 1, 62, 261
Heigh Ho, Everybody, Heigh Ho 555
Heigh Ho! The Gang's All Here 253
Hello, Aloha, How Are You? 19
Hello, Baby 524
Hello, Beautiful 97
Hello Bluebird 137
Hello Central, Give Me Heaven 183
Hello, Central, Give Me No Man's Land 265, 441, 565
Hello, Frisco, Hello 42, 202
Hello, Hawaii 442
Hello, I've Been Looking for You 212
Hello Ma Baby 212
Hello, Ma! I Done It Again 407
Hello, My Dearie 472
Hello, My Lover, Goodbye 161
Hello, Sunshine, Hello 335
Hello, Sweetheart, Hello 409, 464
Hello, Young Lovers 174
Hell's Bells 239
Help Yourself to Happiness 153, 400
Helter Skelter 402
Hep Cat's Ball 364
Hep Te Hootie 99
Her Bathing Suit Never Got Wet 462
Her Beaus Are Only Rainbows 322
Her Name Is Rose 516
Here and Now 75
Here Come the British 177, 316
Here Comes Cookie 396
Here Comes Emily Brown 318
Here Comes My Ball and Chain 72
Here Comes the Showboat 376, 417
Here Comes the Springtime and There Goes My Heart 549
Here Comes Your Pappy (With the Wrong Kind of Load) 172
Here I'll Stay 532
Here Is My Heart 385, 406
Here It Is Monday and I Still Have a Dollar 62, 456
Here Lies Love 385, 406
Here We Are 235
Here You Are 407
Here You Come With Love 78, 503
Hereafter 275
Here's Hoping 72
Here's Love 550
Here's Love in Your Eye 386, 406
Here's That Rainy Day 45, 510
Here's to My Lady 33
Here's to Romance 71, 289
Here's to Us 259
Herman at the Sherman 191
He's a Carousel Cowboy 537
He's a Cousin of Mine 287, 466
He's A-1 in the Army 122
He's Had No Lovin' for a Long, Long Time 502
He's Home for a Little While 449
He's My Friend 550
He's My Guy 88, 388
He's Not Worth Your Tears 94, 522
He's So Unusual 452
He's the Last Word 96, 235
He's the Man I Adore 486
Hesitation Blues 176
Hey, Good Looking 293
Hey Look Me Over 259
Hey, Young Fella 127, 307
Hi Lili, Hi Lo 238
Hiawatha 77
Hick Stomp 374
Hide and Seek 374
Higgenbotham Blues 424
High and Low 94, 439

The High and the Mighty 526
High Fever 432
High, High Up in the Hills 1
High Hopes 50, 51, 510
High on a Windy Hill 250
High on the List 45
High School 219
High Society 309
High Society Blues 179, 306
Highways Are Happy Ways 450
Hi-Lee Hi-Lo 433, 536
Hills of Old Wyomin' 387, 406
Hilo Hattie 349
Hindustan 518
Hines Rhythm 202
Hip Hip Hooray 345
Hip Hop 99
His Feet Too Big for de Bed 339
His Majesty the Baby 529
His Own Little Island 272
His Servant 454
Hitchy-Koo 146, 147
Hittin' the Bottle 13, 250
Hittin' the Ceiling 70, 326
H'lo, Baby 290, 524
(Ho Ho, Ha Ha) Me Too 452, 496, 553
Hocus Pocus 424
Hodge Podge 204
Ho-Hum 192, 486
Hold Me 195, 269, 358, 437
Hold Me Closer 398
Hold Me in Your Arms 186
Hold My Hand 105, 188, 336, 562
Hold That Bulldog 327
Holding My Honey's Hand 29, 370, 372
Holiday 35
Holiday for Strings 141
A Holly Jolly Christmas 303
Hollywood at Vine 166
Home Again Blues 9
Home Cookin' 272
Home Sweet Heaven 304
Homesick—That's All 221
Homespun 333
Honest and Truly 418
Honestly 161, 230, 269, 347
Honey 463, 542
Honey Babe 105
Honey Boy 515
Honey Gal 38
Honey in the Honeycomb 254
Honey-Love 322
Honeysuckle Rose 390, 520
Hong Kong Blues 55
Honolulu 235
Honolulu Blues 62
Honolulu Rag 547
Hoop-De-Doo 85
Hoopdee Whodee 430
Hoops 440
Hooray for Captain Spaulding 421
Hooray for Hollywood 316
Hooray for Love 127, 307
Hoot Mon 510
Hop Scotch Polka 459
Hop, Skip and Jump 450
Hopkins' Scream 209
Horn Tootin' Blues 48
Hors D'oeuvres 374
A Horse That Knows His Way Home 510
The Horse With the Lavender Eyes 339
Horses Don't Bet on People 275
Horseshoes Are Lucky 95
Hot Aire 436
Hot Diggity 206
Hot Heels 370, 371
Hot Lips 48
Hot Moonlight 157
Hot Toddy 57
Hotter Than 'Ell 187
The Hour of Parting 235
The House Is Haunted (By the Echo of Your Last Goodbye) 4, 193, 418

The House Jack Built for Jill 209, 406
The House of Blue Lights 389
House of David Blues 436
House of Joy 178
House of Morgan 522
Houseboat 10
How About You? 136, 254
How Am I to Know? 242
How Are Things in Glocca Morra 181, 254
How Bitter, My Sweet 145
How Can I? 520
How Can I Be Anything but Blue 126
How Can I Hi De Hi? 392
How Can I Thank You? 471
How Can You Face Me? 391, 520
How Come You Do Me Like You Do 17
How Do I Know It's Sunday 233
How Do I Look? 406
How Do You Speak to an Angel? 199
How I'd Like to be with You in Bermuda 34
How I'll Miss You (When the Summer Is Gone) 101
How It Lies, How It Lies, How It Lies! 531
How Little We Know 55, 259, 316
How Long Has This Been Going On 290, 551, 560
How Long Is Forever? 303
How Long Is the Journey 225
How Long Will It Last 324
How Many Hearts Have You Broken? 490
How Much I Love You 533
How Strange 235
How the Irish Beat the Band 521
How Will I Remember You? 168
How Ya, Baby 520
How Ya Gonna Keep 'Em Down on the Farm? 96, 265, 565, 566
Howd'ja Like to Love Me 253
How'm I Doin' 392
Huckleberry Duck 443
Huckleberry Finn 265, 565
Hud 80
Huggable Kissable You 31
Huggin' and Chalkin' 184
Huggin' and Kissin' You 372
Huggin' and Muggin' 287
Hugs and Kisses 10
Huguette Waltz 138
Hula Blues 349
Hula Breeze 362
Hullabaloo 95
Hummin' to Myself 123, 289
Humorestless 68
Humpty Dumpty 324, 406
A Hundred Years From Today 525, 570
Hunkadola 324, 325
Hurrah for Today 407
Hurricane 317
Hurry Home 30, 119, 324
Hurt 375
Hush, Hush, Sweet Charlotte 80
Hustlin' and Bustlin' for Baby 556
Hypnotized 453, 461

I Adore You 406
I Ain't Down Yet 549
I Ain't Gonna Give Nobody None o' My Jelly Roll 545, 548
I Ain't Got Nobody 548
I Ain't Got Nothin' but the Blues 145
I Ain't Lazy—I'm Just Dreamin' 133
I Am an American 437, 540
I Apologize 149, 205, 344
I Ask the Stars 17, 450
I Beg Your Pardon, Mademoiselle 290
I Begged Her 484
I Behold You 398
I Believe in Miracles 265, 321, 534
I Bought a Wooden Whistle 99
I Built a Dream One Day 416

I Came Here to Talk to Joe 473, 497
I Came, I Saw, I Conga'd 533
I Can Dance With Everybody but My Wife 148
I Can Dream, Can't I? 123, 233
I Can Never Think of the Words 118
I Can Wiggle My Ears 149, 456, 457
I Can't Afford to Dream 497
I Can't Begin to Tell You 331
I Can't Believe It's True 29, 230, 346
I Can't Believe That You're in Love With Me 143, 306
I Can't Break the Habit of You 391
I Can't Escape from You 406, 542
I Can't Face the Music (Without Singing the Blues) 33, 250
I Can't Forget That You Forgot about Me 29
I Can't Get Mississippi off My Mind 9, 567
I Can't Get Started 59, 108
I Can't Get the One I Want 175
I Can't Get You Out of My Mind 328
I Can't Give You Anything but Love 127, 307
I Can't Lose That Longing for You 94, 164
I Can't Resist You 539
I Can't Tell You Why I Love You, But I Do 112
I Can't Waltz Alone 127
I Could Have Danced All Night 259, 279
I Could Make You Care 60
I Couldn't Be Mean to You 2
I Couldn't Believe My Eyes 380, 431, 540
I Couldn't Sleep a Wink Last Night 308
I Couldn't Tell Them What to Do 255
I Cover the Waterfront 161, 162, 191, 192
I Cried For You 16, 135, 282
I Did It and I'm Glad 501
I Didn't Go Home at All 261
I Didn't Know 52
I Didn't Know About You 116, 426
I Didn't Mean a Word I Said 308
I Didn't Raise My Boy to Be a Soldier 41
I Didn't Want to Love You 427
I Do, Do You? 384
(I Don't Believe It But) Say It Again 399
I Don't Care 101
I Don't Care If It Rains All Night 485
I Don't Care if the Sun Don't Shine 80
I Don't Care Who Knows It 3, 308
I Don't Get It 491
I Don't Know Enough About You 20, 258
I Don't Know If I'm Comin' or Goin' 102
I Don't Know Why 7, 505
I Don't Know Your Name (But You're Beautiful) 260, 302
I Don't Like Music 356
I Don't Mind Walkin' in the Rain (When I'm Walkin' in the Rain with You) 204, 398
I Don't See Me in Your Eyes Anymore 27
I Don't Wanna Be Kissed by Anyone but You 117
I Don't Wanna See You Cryin' 477
I Don't Want to Be Loved 274, 490
I Don't Want to Cry Anymore 435
I Don't Want to Get Well 223
I Don't Want to Make History 387, 406
I Don't Want to Set the World on Fire 27, 298, 443
I Don't Want to Take a Chance 364
I Don't Want to Walk Without You 277, 482
I Don't Want You to Cry Over Me 283

I Don't Want Your Kisses (If I Can't Have Your Love) 131
I Double Dare You 447
I Dream Too Much 127
I Dreamt I Dwelt in Harlem 159, 160
I Dreamt I Dwelt in Marble Halls 63
I Fall in Love Too Easily 50, 483
I Fall in Love With You Every Day 12, 276, 453, 473
I Fear Nothing 427
I Feel a Song Coming On 127, 307
I Feel Like a Feather in the Breeze 154, 397
I Feel Sorry for the Poor People 172
I Found a Dream 157
I Found a Million Dollar Baby In a Five-and-Ten Cent Store 94, 417, 523
I Found a Rose in the Snow 432
I Found a Roundabout Way to Heaven 399
I Found the End of the Rainbow 493
I Found You 351
I Gave You Up Just Before You Threw Me Down 7, 422
I Get Along without You Very Well 55
I Get the Neck of the Chicken 278
I Go for That 277, 292
I Got a Dode Id by Dose 124
I Got 'Em Again 423
I Got It Bad (And That Ain't Good) 116, 530
I Got Plenty O' Nuttin' 193
I Got Ya 392
I Gotta Have You 431
I Gotta Ride 11
I Gotta Right to Sing the Blues 14, 248
I Gotta Take Off My Hat to You 489
I Guess I'll Be on My Way 231
I Guess I'll Go Back Home Next Summer 412, 413
I Guess I'll Have to Change My Plan 94, 438
I Guess It Had to Be That Way 73
I Had a Little Talk With the Lord 328
I Had the Craziest Dream 523
I Had Too Much to Dream Last Night 159
I Hadn't Anyone Till You 352, 393
I Happen to Love You 427
I Hate Myself (For Being So Mean to You) 6, 83, 461, 568
I Hate to Lose You (I'm So Used to You Now) 157
I Have But One Heart 490
I Have Eyes 386, 407
I Have No Words to Say I Love You 438
I Have One Gift 427
I Have to Have You 406
I Haven't Been Home in Three Whole Nights 384
I Haven't Changed a Thing 344
I Haven't Got a Hat 119
I Haven't Time to Be a Millionaire 331
I Hear a Dream 407
I Hear Music 254, 277
I Heard the Bells on Christmas Day 303
I Heard the Birdies Sing 407
I Heard You Cried Last Night 170
I Hope Gabriel Likes My Music 133
I Hope to Die (If I Told a Lie) 269
I Idolize My Baby's Eyes 221
I Just Can't Make My Eyes Behave 65, 112
I Just Couldn't Take It, Baby 207, 348
I Just Roll Along (Havin' My Ups and Downs) 88, 503
I Keep Remembering 229, 346
I Kiss Your Hand, Madame 265, 566
I Knew You When 72, 290
I Know, I Know, I Know 427

I Know That You Know 563
I Know What He'll Look Like 338
I Know What It Means to Be Lonesome 513
I Left My Sugar Standing in the Rain 123, 233
I Let a Song Go Out of My Heart 116, 325, 344
I Like a Big Town Happy Ending 422
I Like It Here 35, 407
I Like Mountain Music 58, 533
I Like You As You Are 565
I Live for Love 94, 560
I Live the Life I Love 34
I Lost My Gal Again 164, 265
I Lost My Sugar in Salt Lake City 395
I Love a Man in Uniform 331
I Love a Parade 248
I Love an Old Fashioned Song 485
I Love Being Here with You 258
I Love Louisa 94, 439
I Love Love in New York 221
I Love My Baby (My Baby Loves Me) 160, 522
I Love to Ride the Horses on the Merry-Go-Round 379
I Love to Walk in the Rain 471
I Love to Watch the Moonlight 337
I Love You (And You Love Me) 12, 471, 492
I Love You and I Like You 440
I Love You, I Hate You 322
I Love You More Than Yesterday 324
I Love You Much Too Much 388
I Love You So Much 237, 421
I Loves You, Porgy 193
I May Be Dancing with Somebody Else 71, 269
I May Be Gone for a Long, Long Time 515
I May Hate Myself in the Morning 267
I Met Her on Monday 348
I Miss a Little Miss 444
I Miss My Swiss (My Swiss Miss Misses Me) 19
I Miss You Most of All 329
I Must Be Dreaming 106, 453
I Must Have That Man 127, 307
I Must See Annie Tonight 134, 137
I Nearly Let Love Go Slipping through My Fingers 73, 557
I Need Lovin' 224
I Need You So 440
I Need Your Love Tonight 393
I Never Had a Dream 395
I Never Knew (I Could Love Anybody) 113, 235
I Never Knew Heaven Could Speak 155, 156
I Never Saw a Better Night 144
I Only Found You for Somebody Else 230
I Only Have Eyes for You 107, 523
I Only Saw Him Once 251
I Picked a Flower the Color of Your Eyes 541
I Played Fiddle for the Czar 153
I Promise You 260, 269, 316
I Remember 527
I Remember It Well 279
I Remember Mama 499
I Remember You 316, 435
I Remember You From Somewhere 261, 522
I Said No 278
I Saw Esau 524
I Saw Stars 149, 205, 456
I Scream, You Scream, We All Scream for Ice Cream 223, 328
I See God 310
I See the Moon 549
I See Two Lovers 560
I See Your Face before Me 94, 440
I Sent a Letter to Santa 319
I Should Care 50, 477, 537